Harmony of Colours
Harmonie der Farben

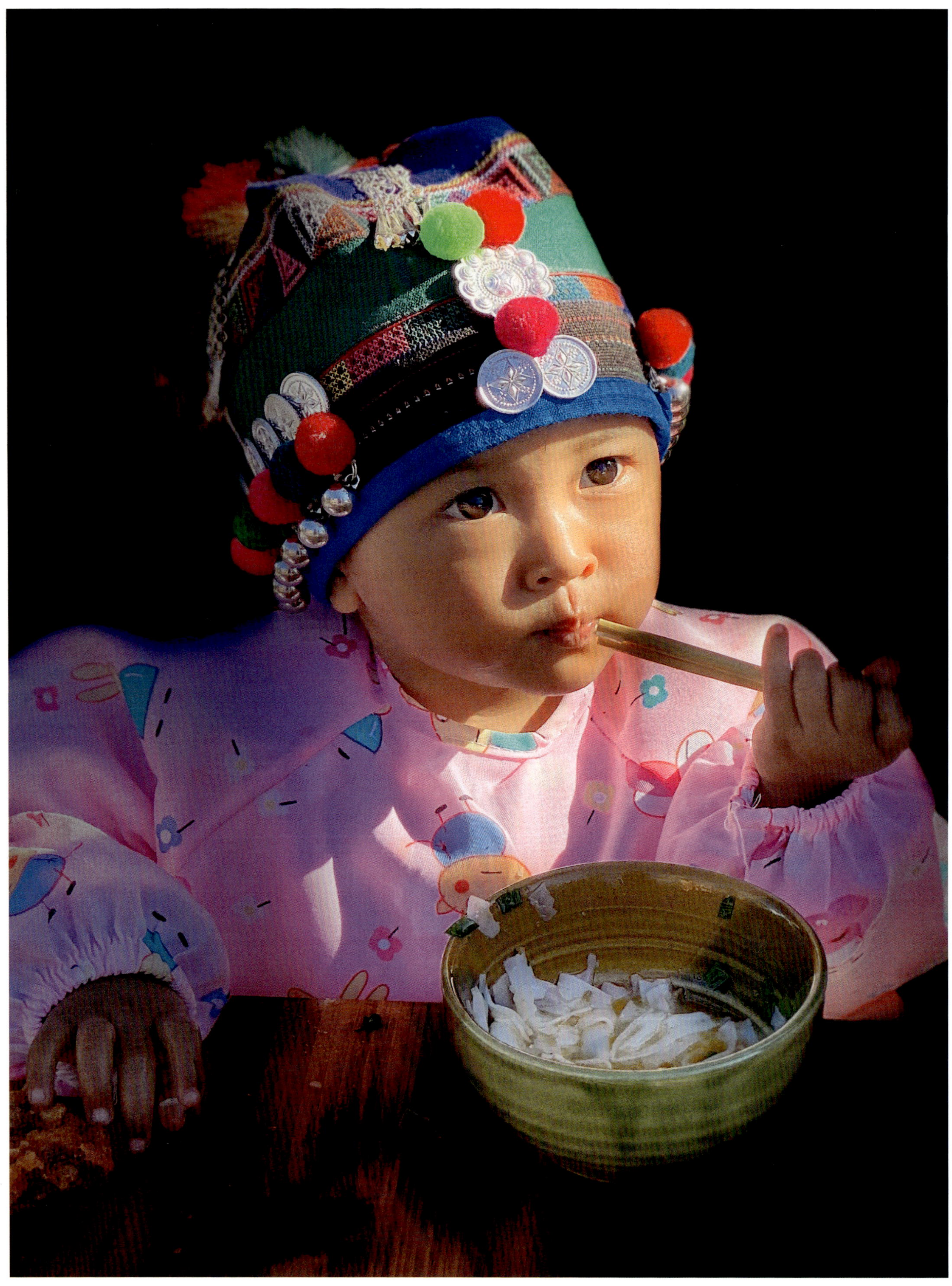

Annette Morheng
Edited by Peter Feierabend

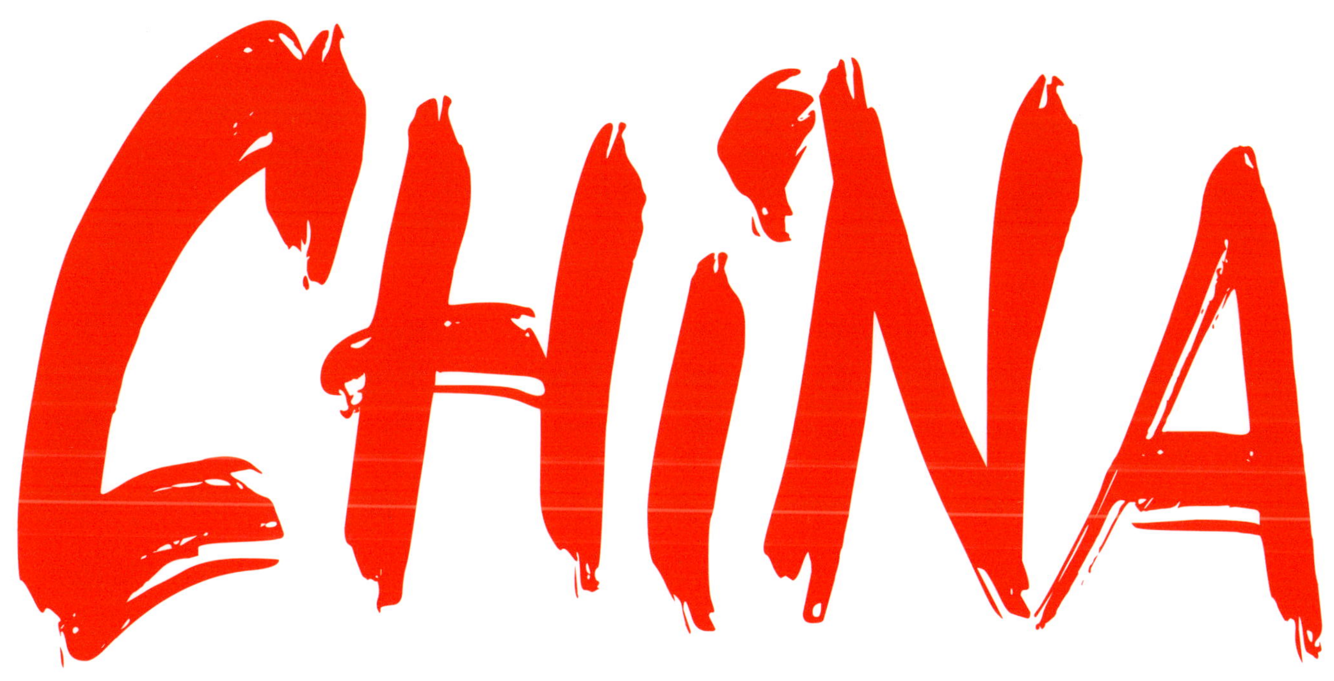

Harmony of Colours
Harmonie der Farben

teNeues

Dedication

With loving gratitude, I dedicate this book to my parents. I owe them my unprejudiced, cheerful open-mindedness, my thirst for knowledge, fun doing photography and bold delight in discovery.

Widmung

In liebevoller Dankbarkeit widme ich dieses Buch meinen Eltern. Ihnen verdanke ich unvoreingenommene fröhliche Aufgeschlossenheit, wissensdurstige Neugier, Spaß am Fotografieren und mutige Freude am Entdecken.

Page 2: The Akha, an ethnic subgroup of the Hani minority in mountainous southern Yunnan, wear their caps, elaborately embroidered by their mothers, until they are about twelve years old. The traditional costume of the women is very colourful, they wear black caps with silver coins. Akha women identify their age or marital status by the style of their headdress. Men wear black pants with a short jacket loosely held together with a few buttons. The clothing is made of homespun cotton.
It is generally believed that the Akha originated in the Tibetan highlands and moved from there through Yunnan to northern Burma and Laos, reaching Thailand from the mid-19th century.

Seite 2: Die Akha, eine ethnische Teilgruppe der Hani-Minderheit im gebirgigen Süden Yunnans, tragen ihre von den Müttern kunstvoll bestickten Mützen bis zum Alter von ca. zwölf Jahren. Die traditionelle Tracht der Frauen ist sehr farbig, sie tragen dazu schwarze Mützen mit Silbermünzen. Akha-Frauen definieren ihr Alter oder ihren Familienstand anhand des Kopfschmuckstils. Die Männer tragen schwarze Hosen mit einer kurzen Jacke, die mit wenigen Knöpfen lose zusammengehalten werden. Die Kleidung besteht aus selbstgesponnener Baumwolle. Nach allgemeiner Auffassung stammen die Akha aus dem tibetischen Hochland und sind von dort über Yunnan in das nördliche Burma und Laos gezogen, Mitte des 19. Jahrhunderts erreichten sie auch Thailand.

Content | Inhalt

Preface
Vorwort

"Why are most people smiling in your colourful photos?" This is the most-asked question in response to my China photos. I usually answer with a counter question, "What does smiling at the sight of a complete stranger stand for?"

After nine years of working, travelling and photographing in the Chinese Empire, I still feel the unprejudiced, natural cordiality in new encounters between "white and yellow". The fundamentally harmony-oriented open-mindedness of my counterpart, even though I am unmistakably the white stranger. Long before I enter a new village street, I can hear the children openly shouting *waiguoren, waiguoren*, "foreigner, foreigner", cheerfully through the village.

I can still recall the horrified expression on the face of my elderly Chinese neighbour in the grey Beijing *hutong* when, defying tradition, I attached a white lantern to our wooden double door. Her comforting condolences immediately made me realize that this had to be a colour misunderstanding. Yellow and red are considered happy colours, while white represents mourning. My curiosity was aroused, as was the need to avoid such colour faux pas in the future. The potpourri of colours in modern China is overwhelming, and yet the traditional colour concepts still run through everyday life in the 21st century like unwritten laws. Rarely does a colourful brushstroke occur arbitrarily or according to purely aesthetic consideration.

A look at the philosophical concepts behind Beijing's exclusively yellow, green or blue glazed roof tiles, for example, will shed light on the meaning behind China's array of colours. Above all, however, it will be an attempt to explain people's smiles and the happiness that one senses behind them.

Unobtrusive harmony stands above demanding confrontation, an essential trait of the Asian life tradition and philosophy. Neither the other person nor oneself wants to "lose face". Perhaps, however, the fundamentally Taoist and Confucian Chinese society is also based on a core concept of Tibetan Buddhist thought that has been lived for thousands of years, the internalised notion of interdependence.

"The need to receive and give love and tenderness proves interdependence. If our happiness did not depend on one

„Warum lachen die meisten Menschen auf deinen bunten Fotos?" ist die mir am häufigsten gestellte Frage zu meinen China-Bildern. Ich antworte meist mit einer Gegenfrage: „Wofür steht das Lächeln beim Anblick eines völlig fremden Menschen?"

Nach neun Jahren Arbeiten, Reisen und Fotografieren im Reich der Mitte spüre ich noch immer die unvoreingenommene, natürliche Herzlichkeit bei neuen Begegnungen von Weiß und Gelb. Die grundsätzlich auf Harmonie ausgerichtete Aufgeschlossenheit meines Gegenübers, obwohl ich unverkennbar die weiße Fremde bin. Schon lange bevor ich eine neue Dorfstraße betrete, höre ich die Kinder unverhohlen fröhlich die Botschaft *Waiguoren, Waiguoren*, „Ausländerin, Ausländerin", durch den Ort rufen.

Tief hat sich bei mir der entsetzte Gesichtsausdruck meiner älteren chinesischen Nachbarin im grauen Pekinger *Hutong* eingebrannt, als ich, den Traditionen trotzend, eine weiße Laterne an unserer hölzernen Doppeltür anbringen wollte. Ihre tröstenden Kondolenzbezeugungen machten mir umgehend klar, dass es sich hier um ein farbliches Missverständnis handeln musste. Gelb und Rot gelten als glückliche Farben, Weiß steht für Trauer. Meine Neugier war geweckt, ebenso das Bedürfnis, solche Farbfettnäpfchen in Zukunft zu vermeiden. Das Potpourri der Farben im modernen China ist überwältigend, und dennoch ziehen sich die traditionellen Farbkonzepte wie ungeschriebene Gesetze auch noch durch den Alltag des 21. Jahrhunderts. Selten erfolgt ein bunter Pinselstrich willkürlich oder nach rein ästhetischen Gesichtspunkten.

Der Blick auf die philosophischen Konzepte, die sich beispielsweise hinter den ausschließlich gelb, grün oder blau glasierten Dachziegeln Pekings verbergen, wird Licht ins bunte Farbenallerlei bringen. Vor allem aber wird er ein Versuch sein, das Lächeln der Menschen zu erklären und das Glück, das man dahinter spürt.

Zurückhaltende Harmonie steht über fordernder Auseinandersetzung, ein wesentlicher Grundzug der asiatischen Lebenstradition und Philosophie. Weder soll das Gegenüber, noch möchte man selbst „das Gesicht verlieren". Vielleicht liegt der grundsätzlich daoistisch und konfuzianistisch

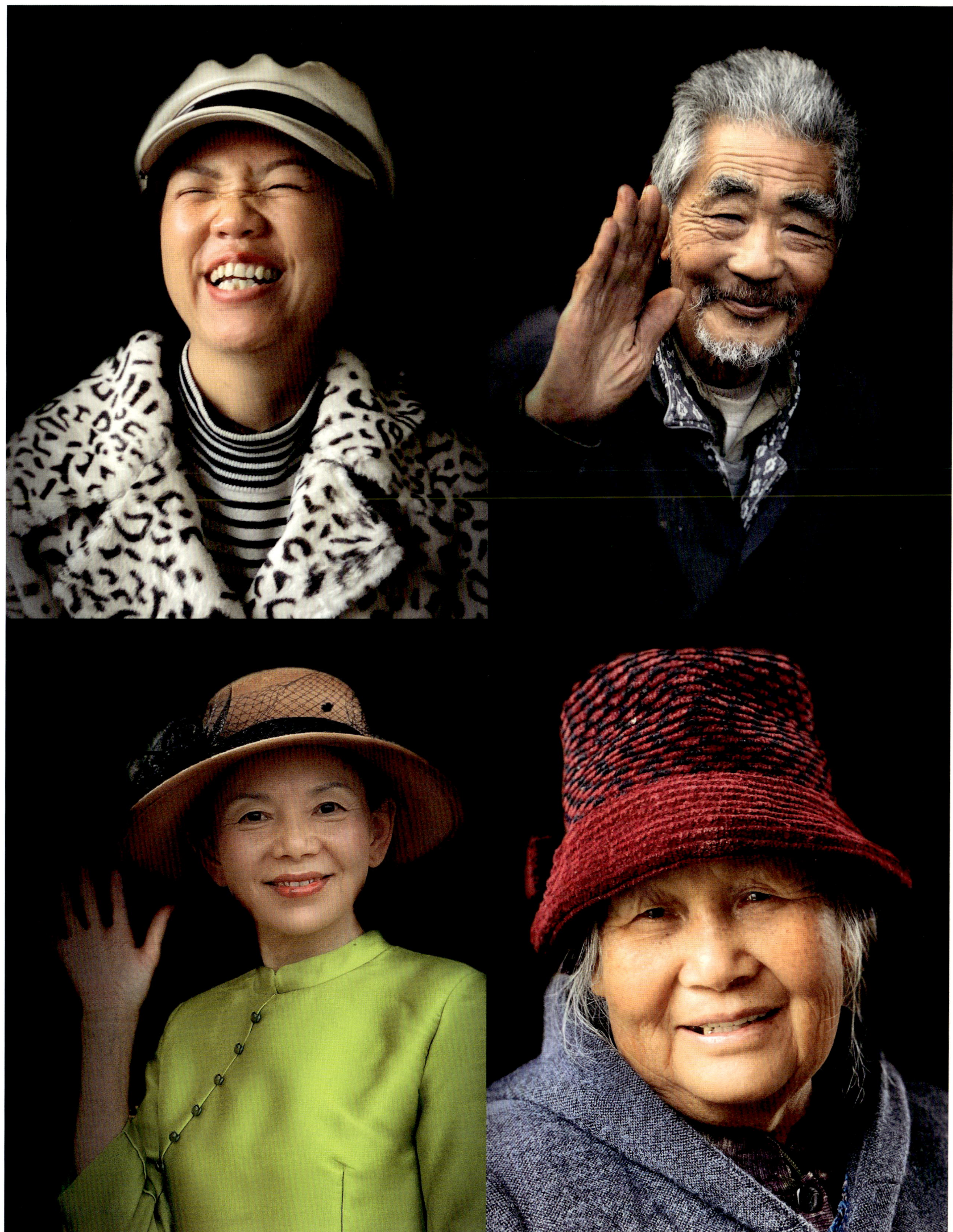

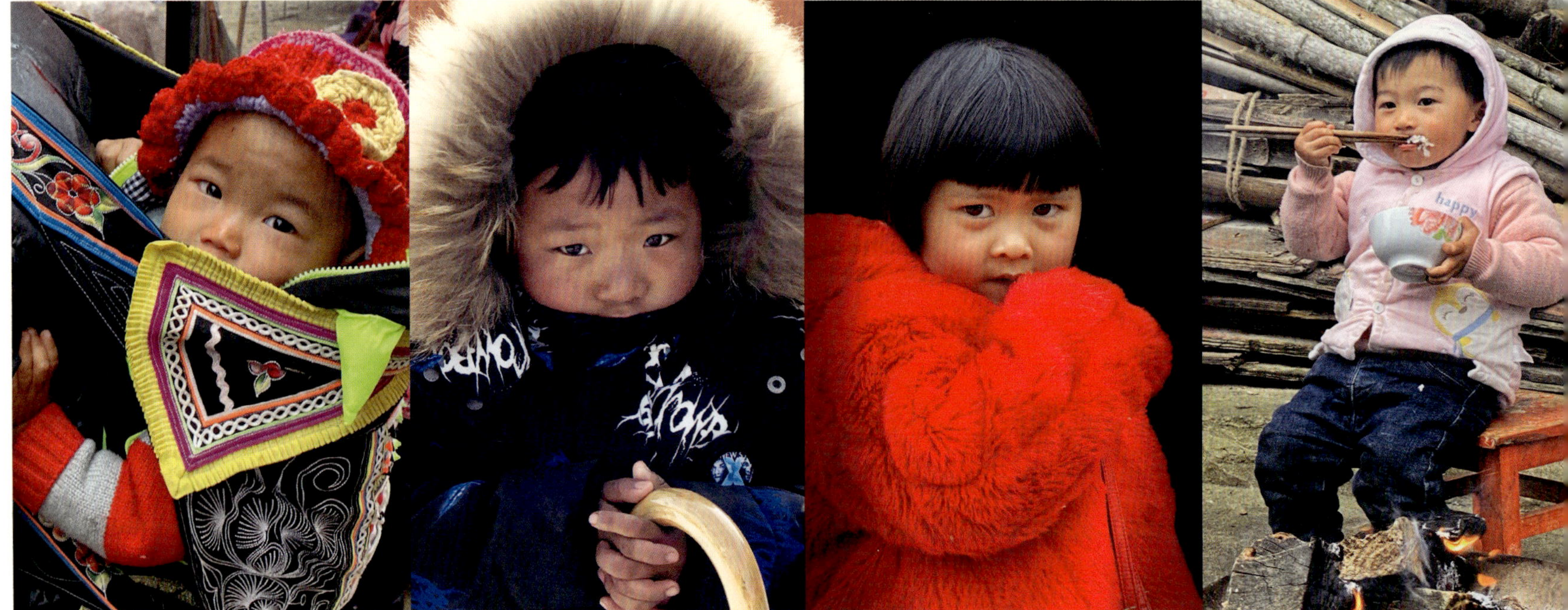

another, if it existed in and of itself, love would have no meaning at all."

Our happiness is necessarily contingent on that of others. This basic attitude leads to positive, smiling openness, benevolent reciprocity and happiness on both sides.

This made a lasting impression on a young German missionary named Richard Wilhelm, who is regarded as a cultural mediator between Asia and Europe like no other. In 1901, his ship docked in Qingdao, a large port city on the northeast coast of China. Wilhelm set foot ashore with the goal of converting as many inhabitants as possible to Christianity. He was increasingly impressed by "cheerful China" and by the "great harmony of life".

So he decided to explore the secrets of Chinese civilisation in its sacred scriptures and philosophical teachings. After 25 years of living in China, he returned to Europe as a Confucian. With his translations of Chinese classics, he is said to have had a significant influence on the worldview of Hermann Hesse, which was influenced by Asian philosophy, and thus on his poetic work. Hesse explained that what fascinated him about Wilhelm was his attainment of harmony in life and the perfection of his personality through the internalisation of Far Eastern philosophy and wisdom. This was the goal to which both Hesse himself and the protagonists of his works aspired.

It is the totality, the permanence, the existence beyond historical changes, which this great people has deeply internalised. Customs, culture, habits and ideas as a lived and supporting basis, indestructible! These are the elements

geprägten chinesischen Gesellschaft aber auch ein seit Tausenden von Jahren vorgelebter Kernbegriff tibetisch-buddhistischen Denkens zu Grunde, die verinnerlichte Erkenntnis der „wechselseitigen Abhängigkeit".

„Das Bedürfnis, Liebe und Zärtlichkeit zu empfangen und zu geben, beweist die gegenseitige Abhängigkeit. Wenn das Glück nicht von einem anderen abhängen würde, wenn es aus sich selbst existieren würde, hätte die Liebe überhaupt keinen Sinn."

Unser Glück ist notwendigerweise durch dasjenige der anderen bedingt. Diese Grundeinstellung führt zu positiver, lächelnder Offenheit, wohlwollendem Entgegenkommen und Glück auf beiden Seiten.

Genau dies beeindruckte nachhaltig einen jungen deutschen Missionar namens Richard Wilhelm, der wie kein anderer als Kulturvermittler zwischen Asien und Europa gilt. Sein Schiff legte 1901 in Qingdao an, einer großen Hafenstadt an der Nordostküste Chinas. Wilhelm setzte seinen Fuß an Land mit dem Ziel, möglichst viele Einwohner zum Christentum zu bekehren. Er war zunehmend beeindruckt von dem „heiteren China" und von der „großen Harmonie des Lebens". So entschied er sich, die Geheimnisse der chinesischen Zivilisation in deren heiligen Schriften und philosophischen Lehren zu erkunden. Nach 25 Jahren Aufenthalt in China kehrte er als Konfuzianer nach Europa zurück. Er soll mit seinen Übersetzungen chinesischer Klassiker die von asiatischer Philosophie geprägte Weltanschauung Hermann Hesses und somit dessen dichterisches Schaffen wesentlich mitbestimmt haben. Hesse erklärte, dass das, was ihn an Wilhelm faszinierte, das Erreichen der Lebens-

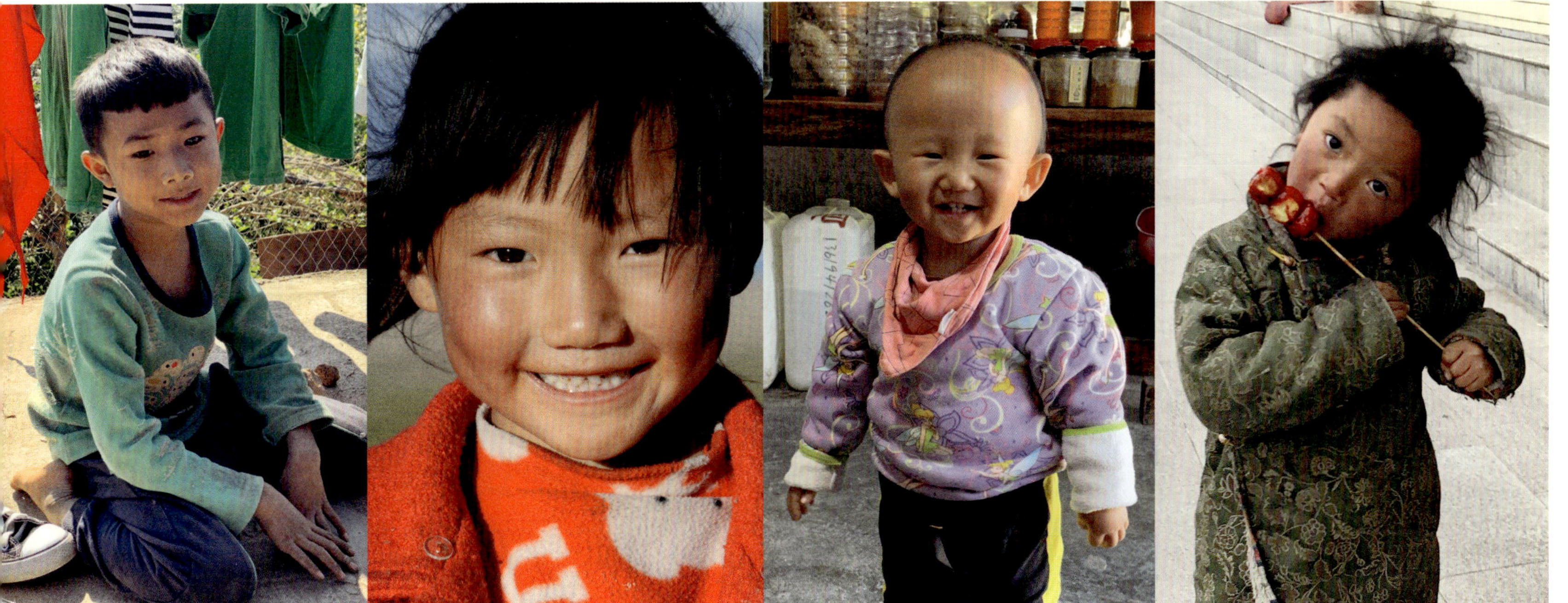

Of China's 56 recognised nationalities, the Han represent the largest group with more than 1.2 billion people. The 55 remaining ethnic groups are spread over 60 percent of the country's territory with about 110 million people, only 8 percent of the total population.

Von den 56 anerkannten Nationalitäten Chinas stellen die Han mit mehr als 1,2 Milliarden Menschen die größte Gruppierung. Die 55 verbleibenden Ethnien verteilen sich mit rund 110 Millionen Menschen, nur 8 Prozent der Gesamtbevölkerung, auf über 60 Prozent des Staatsgebietes.

which connect the people and whose symbolism can open a gate to a better understanding. As mediators, the colours run vividly through all spheres of life in China.

They are also a part of feng shui, the concept of holistic harmony in design that has also become renowned in the West. In China, even in the age of artificial intelligence and autonomous driving, no ground is broken in the construction of large new projects without taking feng shui, translated as "wind-water", into consideration. feng shui aims to create balance in our living environment as a basis for a happy, successful and healthy life.

In this book, colours lead to unusual places and people whose lives are closely connected with certain hues. If you understand the colours, you understand a little more of the overall picture of China, which is not only difficult to grasp in terms of language. Perhaps I can make a small contribution to cultural mediation, to the understanding between East and West, by opening China's paint box a little with my photographs and bringing the colourful palette of artists to light.

harmonie und die Vollendung der eigenen Persönlichkeit durch die Verinnerlichung fernöstlicher Philosophie und Lebensweisheit sei. Nach diesem Ziel strebten sowohl Hesse selbst als auch die Protagonisten seiner Werke.

Es ist das Gesamtheitliche, das Beständige, das über historische Veränderungen hinaus Bestehende, was dieses große Volk ganz tief verinnerlicht hat. Brauchtum, Kultur, Gewohnheiten und Gedankengut als gelebte und tragende Basis, unzerstörbar! Es sind dies die Elemente, welche die Menschen verbinden und deren Symbolik uns eine Pforte zum besseren Verständnis öffnen kann. Die Farben als Vermittler ziehen sich anschaulich durch alle chinesischen Lebensbereiche.

Sie sind auch ein Teilbereich der Feng-Shui-Lehre, jenes auf gestalterische ganzheitliche Harmonie ausgerichteten Konzeptes, das auch im Westen bekannt geworden ist. Ohne Berücksichtigung von Feng-Shui, übersetzt „Wind-Wasser", erfolgt in China auch im Zeitalter von künstlicher Intelligenz und autonomem Fahren kein Spatenstich beim Neubau großer Projekte. Feng-Shui möchte im Lebensumfeld des Menschen ein Gleichgewicht schaffen als Basis für ein glückliches, erfolgreiches und gesundes Leben.

Die Farben führen in diesem Buch an außergewöhnliche Orte und zu Menschen, deren Leben eng mit bestimmten Farben verbunden ist. Versteht man die Farben, versteht man ein wenig mehr vom nicht nur sprachlich so schwer erschließbaren Gesamtbild „China". Vielleicht kann ich einen kleinen Beitrag zur Kulturvermittlung leisten, zur Verständigung zwischen Ost und West, indem ich mit meinen Fotografien den Farbkasten Chinas etwas öffne und die bunte Künstlerpalette ans Licht hole.

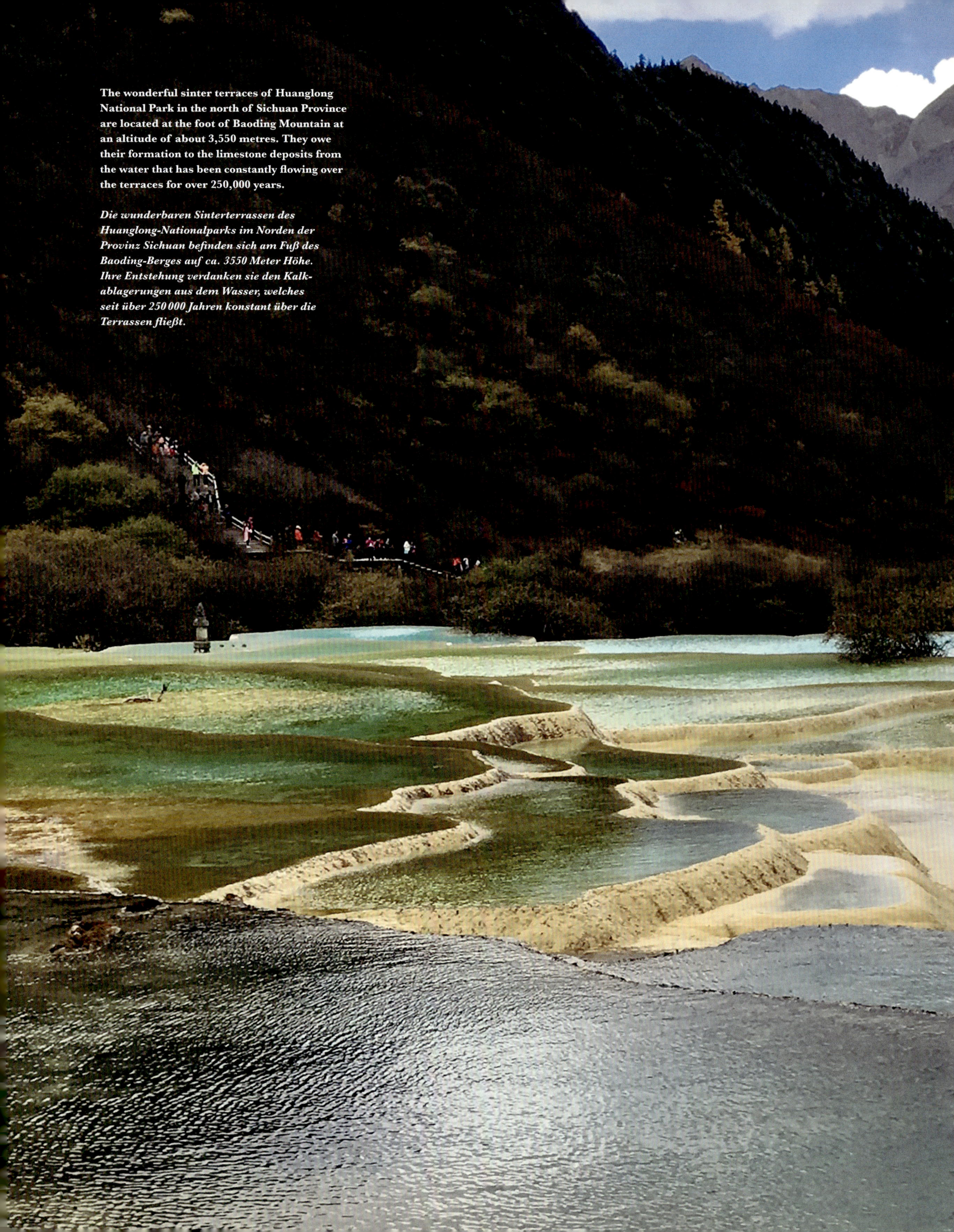

The wonderful sinter terraces of Huanglong National Park in the north of Sichuan Province are located at the foot of Baoding Mountain at an altitude of about 3,550 metres. They owe their formation to the limestone deposits from the water that has been constantly flowing over the terraces for over 250,000 years.

Die wunderbaren Sinterterrassen des Huanglong-Nationalparks im Norden der Provinz Sichuan befinden sich am Fuß des Baoding-Berges auf ca. 3550 Meter Höhe. Ihre Entstehung verdanken sie den Kalkablagerungen aus dem Wasser, welches seit über 250 000 Jahren konstant über die Terrassen fließt.

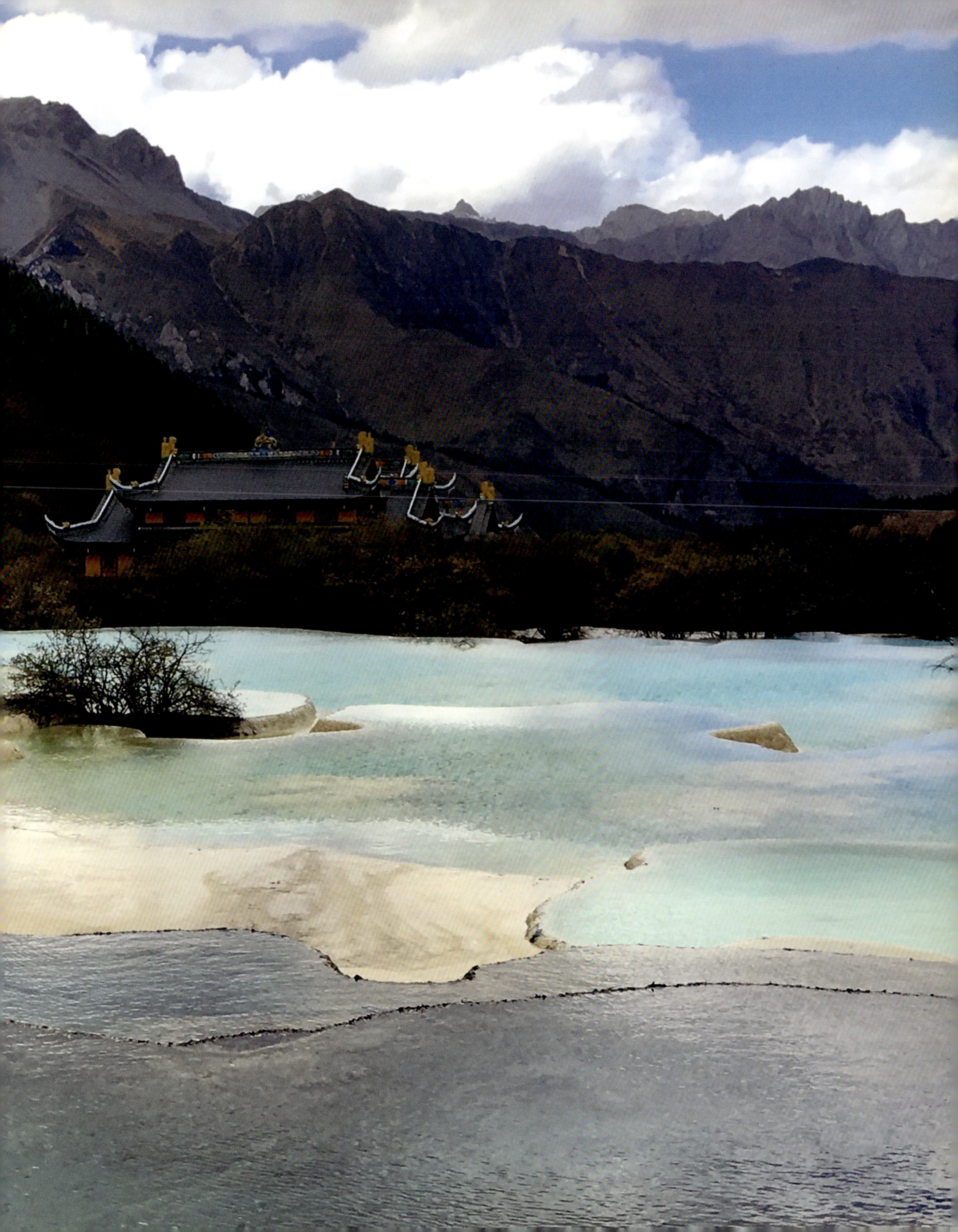

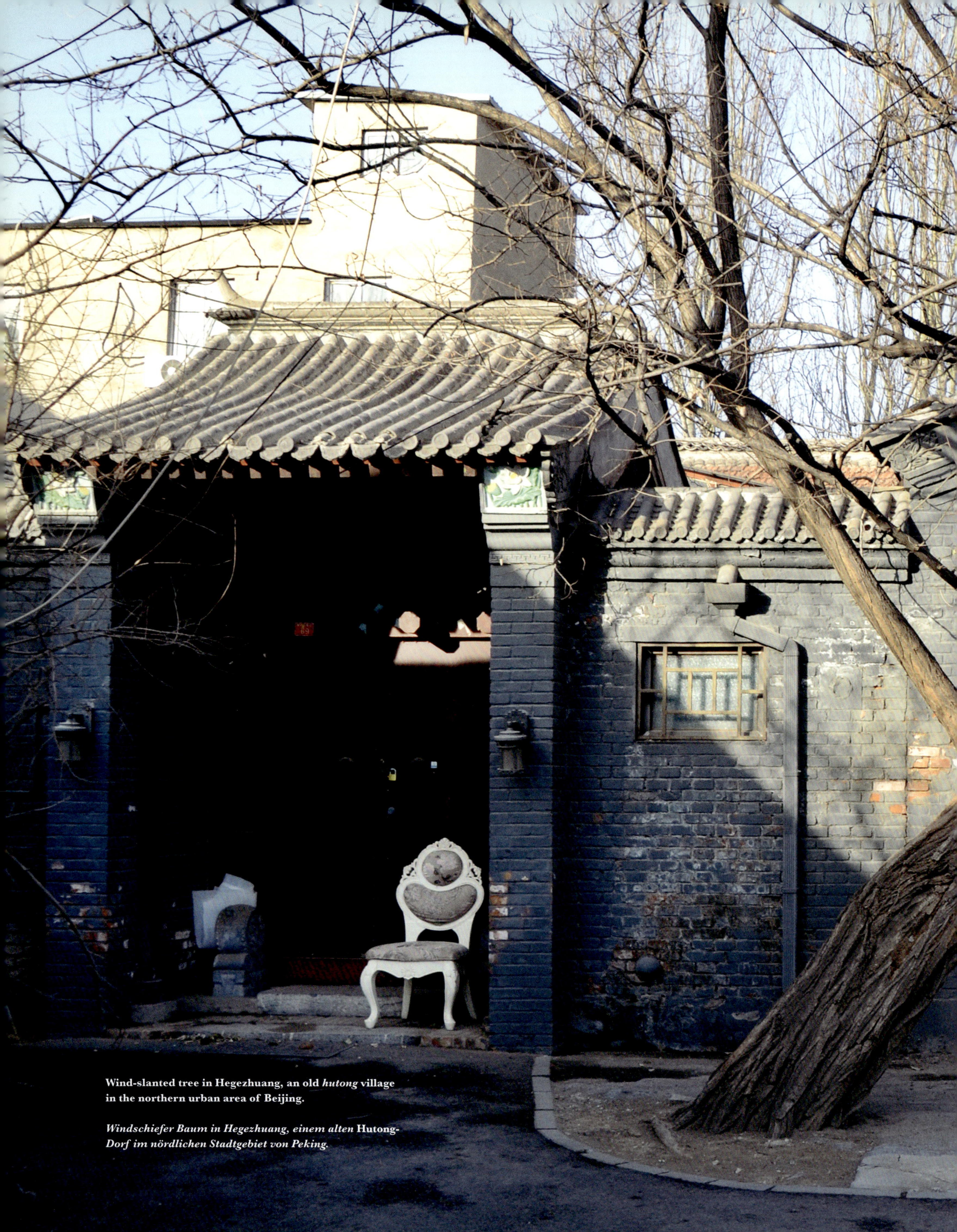

Wind-slanted tree in Hegezhuang, an old *hutong* village in the northern urban area of Beijing.

Windschiefer Baum in Hegezhuang, einem alten* Hutong*-Dorf im nördlichen Stadtgebiet von Peking.

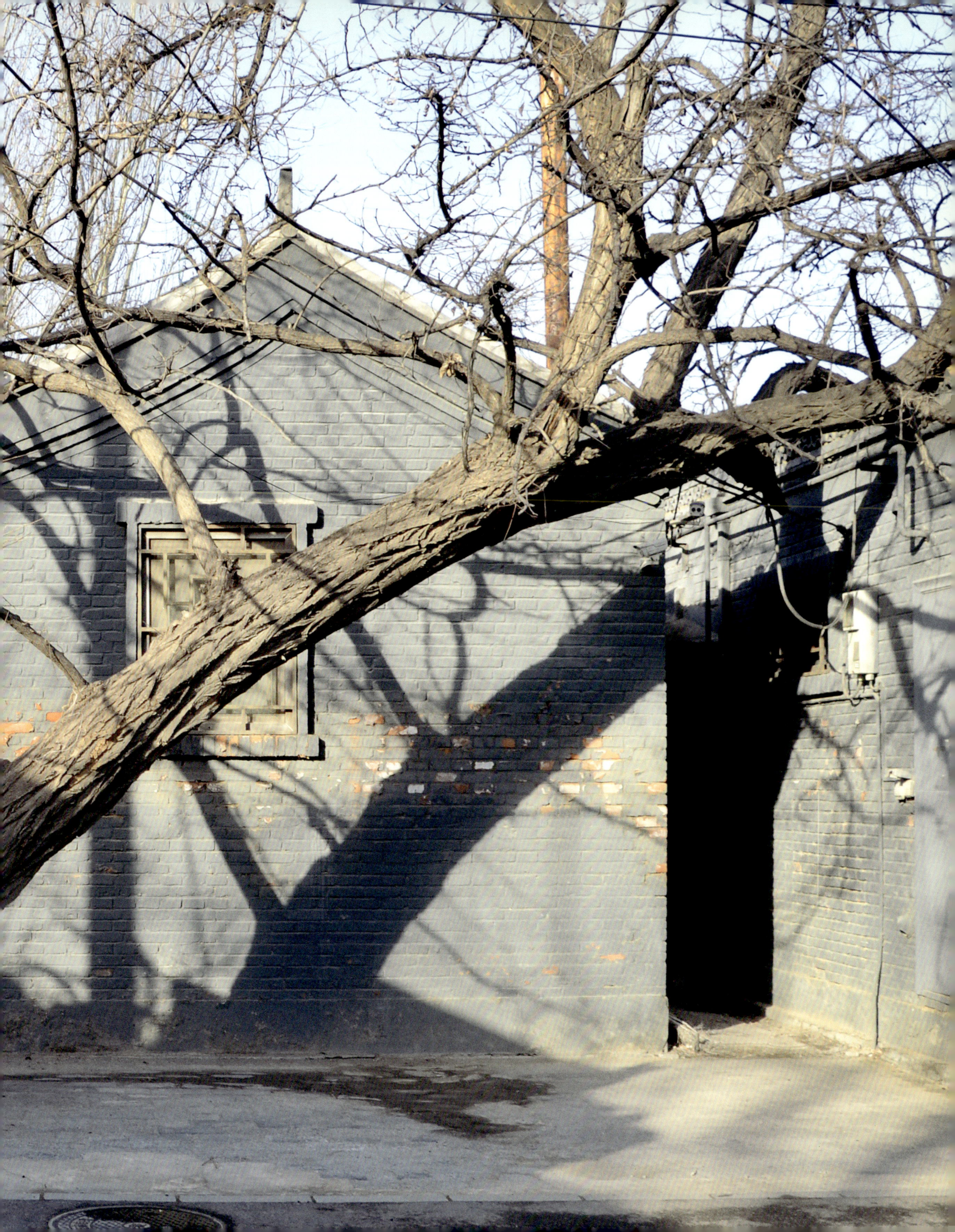

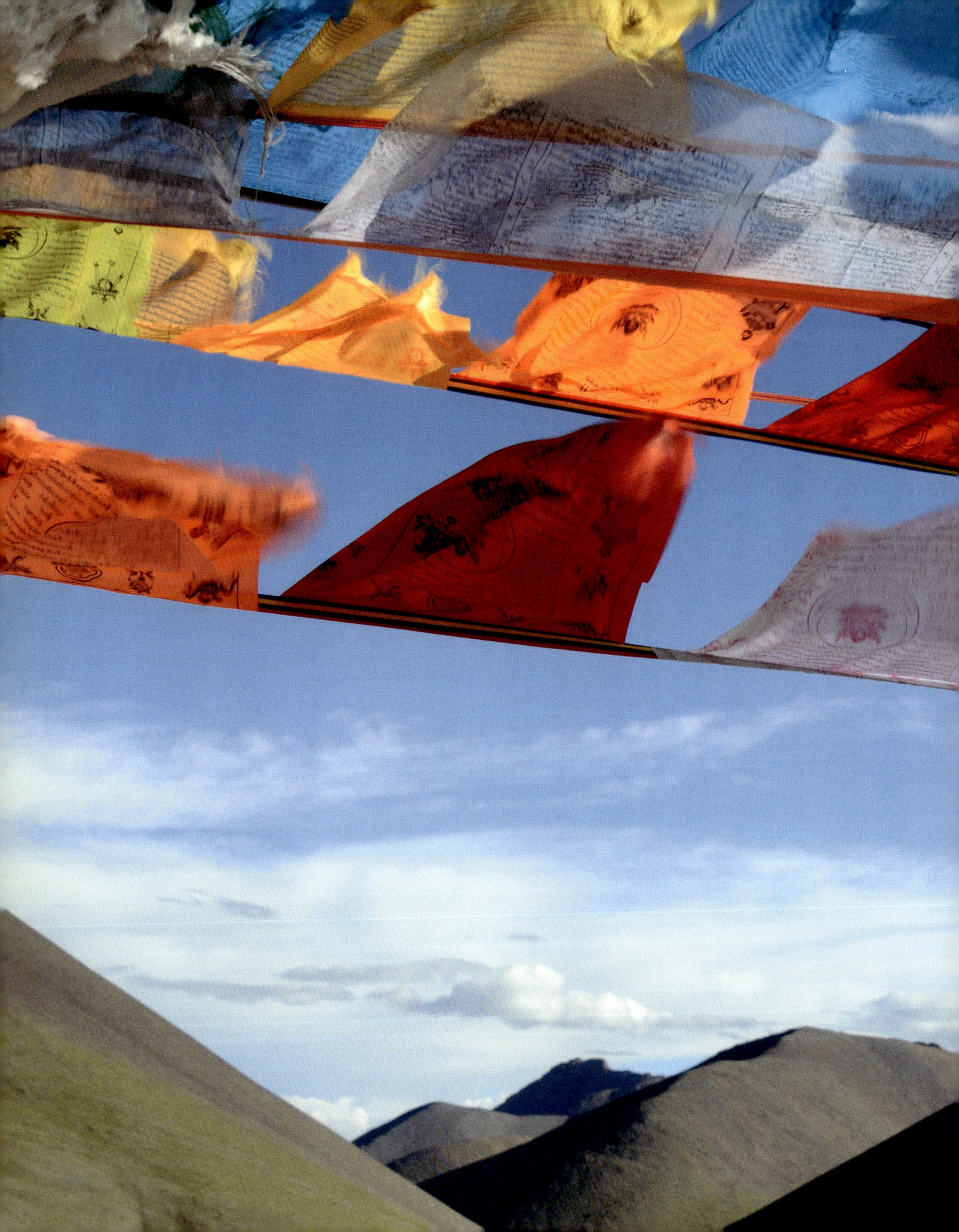

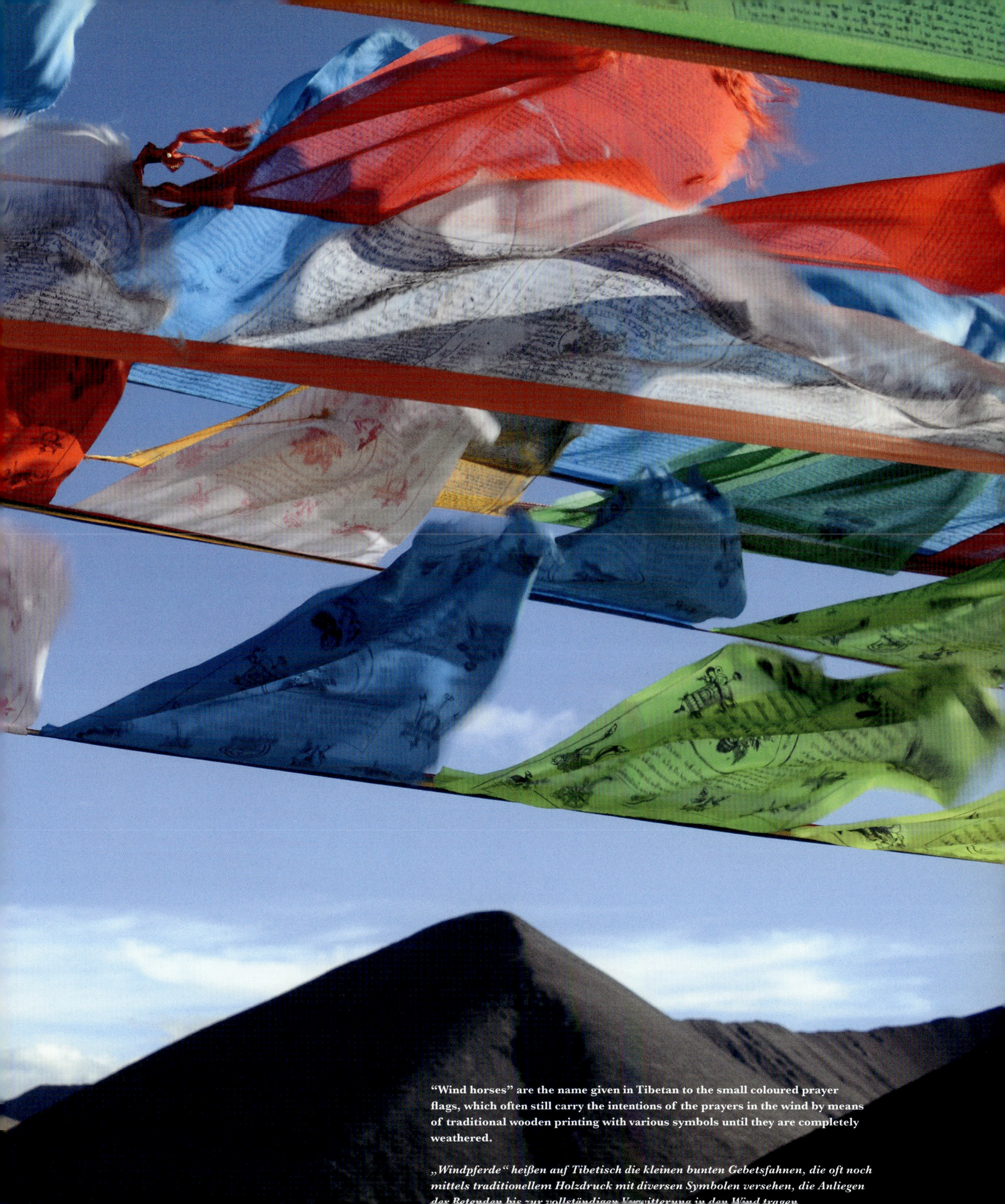

"Wind horses" are the name given in Tibetan to the small coloured prayer flags, which often still carry the intentions of the prayers in the wind by means of traditional wooden printing with various symbols until they are completely weathered.

„Windpferde" heißen auf Tibetisch die kleinen bunten Gebetsfahnen, die oft noch mittels traditionellem Holzdruck mit diversen Symbolen versehen, die Anliegen der Betenden bis zur vollständigen Verwitterung in den Wind tragen.

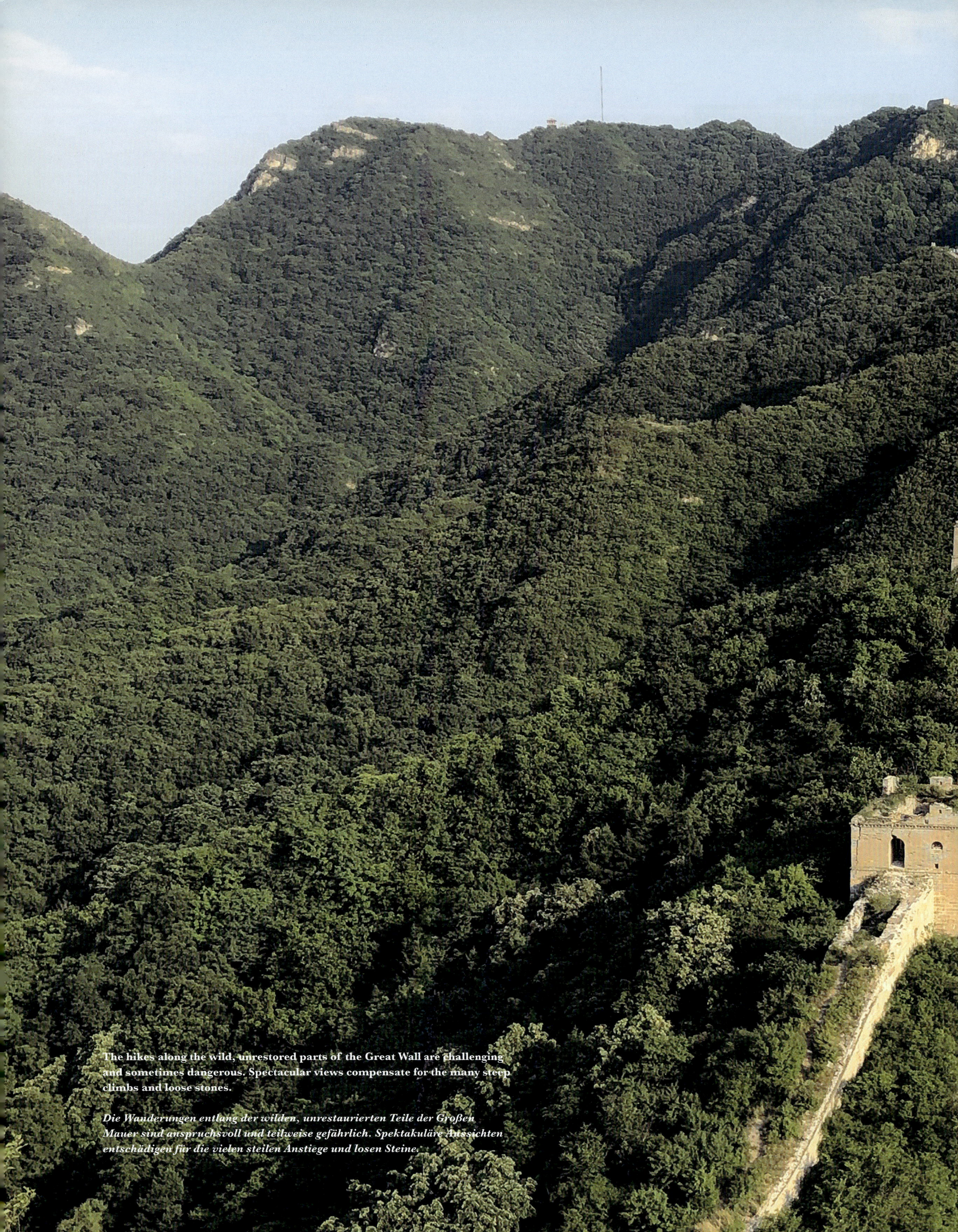

The hikes along the wild, unrestored parts of the Great Wall are challenging and sometimes dangerous. Spectacular views compensate for the many steep climbs and loose stones.

Die Wanderungen entlang der wilden, unrestaurierten Teile der Großen Mauer sind anspruchsvoll und teilweise gefährlich. Spektakuläre Aussichten entschädigen für die vielen steilen Anstiege und losen Steine.

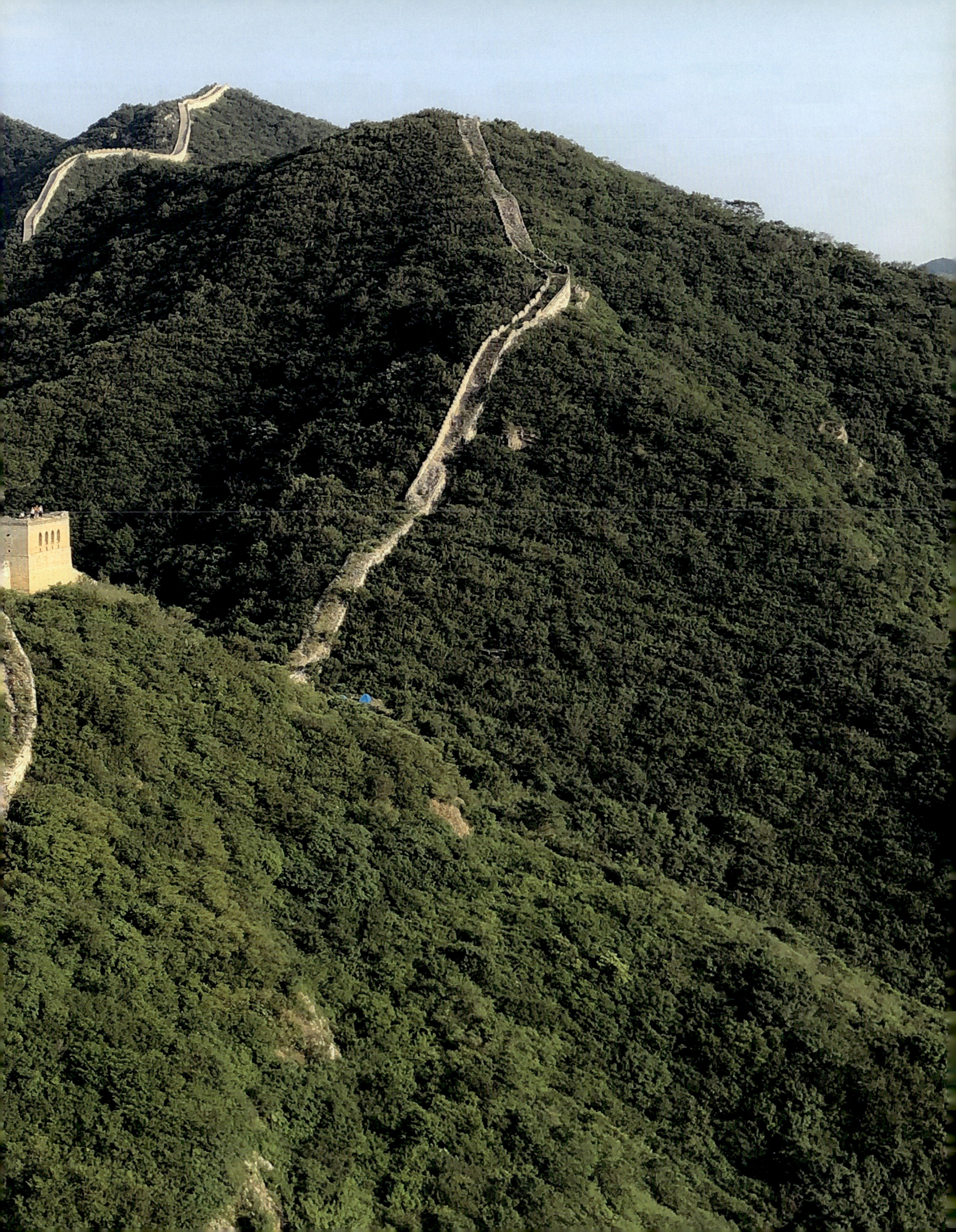

The luminosity of colourlessness
Von der Leuchtkraft der Farblosigkeit

The finest rice paper, a brush made of goat's whiskers, clear water and a drop of black ink rubbed from the ink stone – that's all it takes to make a bamboo stalk in moist, lush green bend in the steady breeze before the viewer's inner eye.

"In the eyes of the Taoists, a great artist is able to make a peacock look brightly coloured and a peach appear pink, in order to gain a deeper understanding of nature."

Even in 21st-century China, many things remain colourless and unclear. Not because people are incapable of expressing or depicting something clearly and colourfully, but because the tradition of quiet, restrained, leeway-giving communication is still practiced, whether consciously or unconsciously. It is always a matter of maintaining a calm mind and using one's energy and powers as effectively as possible. Water served the Taoists as a model for this.

Feinstes Reispapier, einen Pinsel aus Ziegenbarthaaren, klares Wasser und einen Tropfen schwarzer Tusche, vom Tintenstein gerieben – mehr bedarf es nicht, um einen Bambusstängel in feucht sattem Grün vor dem inneren Auge des Betrachters sich im steten Winde beugen zu lassen.

„In den Augen der Daoisten ist ein großer Künstler fähig, ohne farbige Pigmente einen Pfau leuchtend bunt und einen Pfirsich rosa erscheinen zu lassen, um auf diese Weise ein tieferes Verständnis der Natur zu gewinnen."

Auch im China des 21. Jahrhunderts bleibt vieles im Farblosen, im Unklaren. Nicht weil man nicht fähig wäre, es klar und bunt auszudrücken oder darzustellen, sondern weil nach wie vor bewusst oder unbewusst die Tradition der leisen, zurückhaltenden, spielraumgebenden Kommunikation gelebt wird. Es geht immer darum, einen ruhigen Geist zu bewahren und möglichst wirkungsvoll mit seiner Energie und seinen Kräften umzugehen. Als Vorbild dafür diente den Daoisten das Wasser.

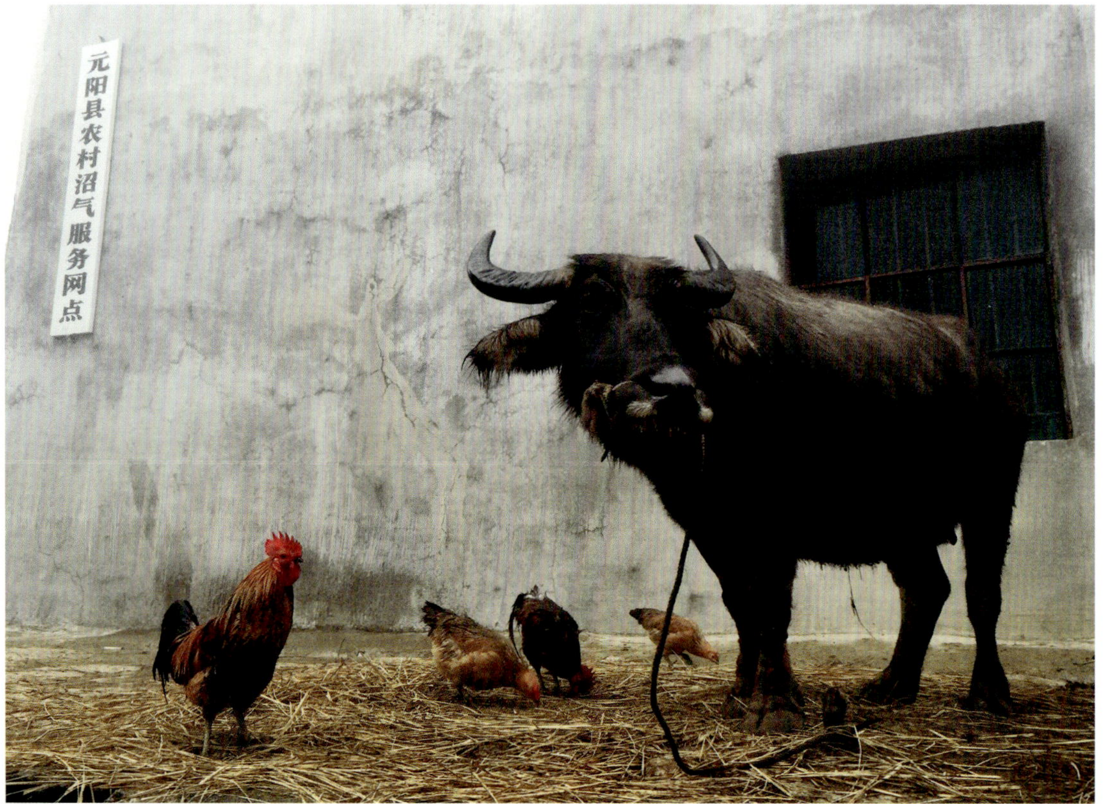

Water buffalo in the middle of a Hani village in the province of Yunnan

Wasserbüffel inmitten eines Hani-Dorfes in der Provinz Yunnan

Right page:
In the historic old town of Beihai, located directly on the South China Sea, the well-preserved Portuguese colonial houses take you back to the trading days when one of the Silk Road's main sea ports of departure was in use here.

Rechte Seite:
In der historischen Altstadt von Beihai, direkt am südchinesischen Meer gelegen, versetzen einen die gut erhaltenen portugiesischen Kolonialhäuser zurück in die Handelszeiten, als hier noch einer der wichtigsten Ausgangshäfen der Seidenstraße genutzt wurde.

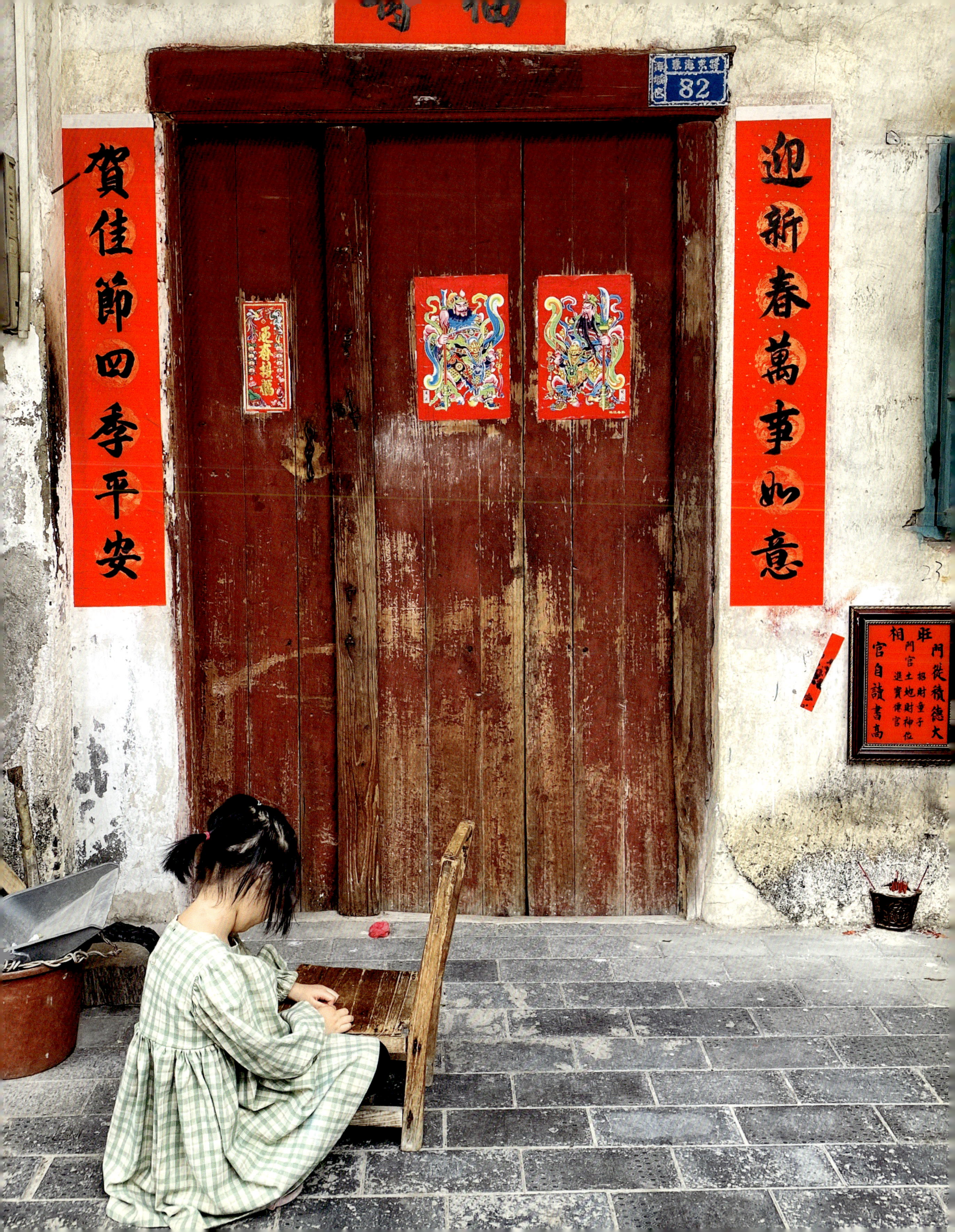

82
賀佳節四季平安
迎新春萬事如意

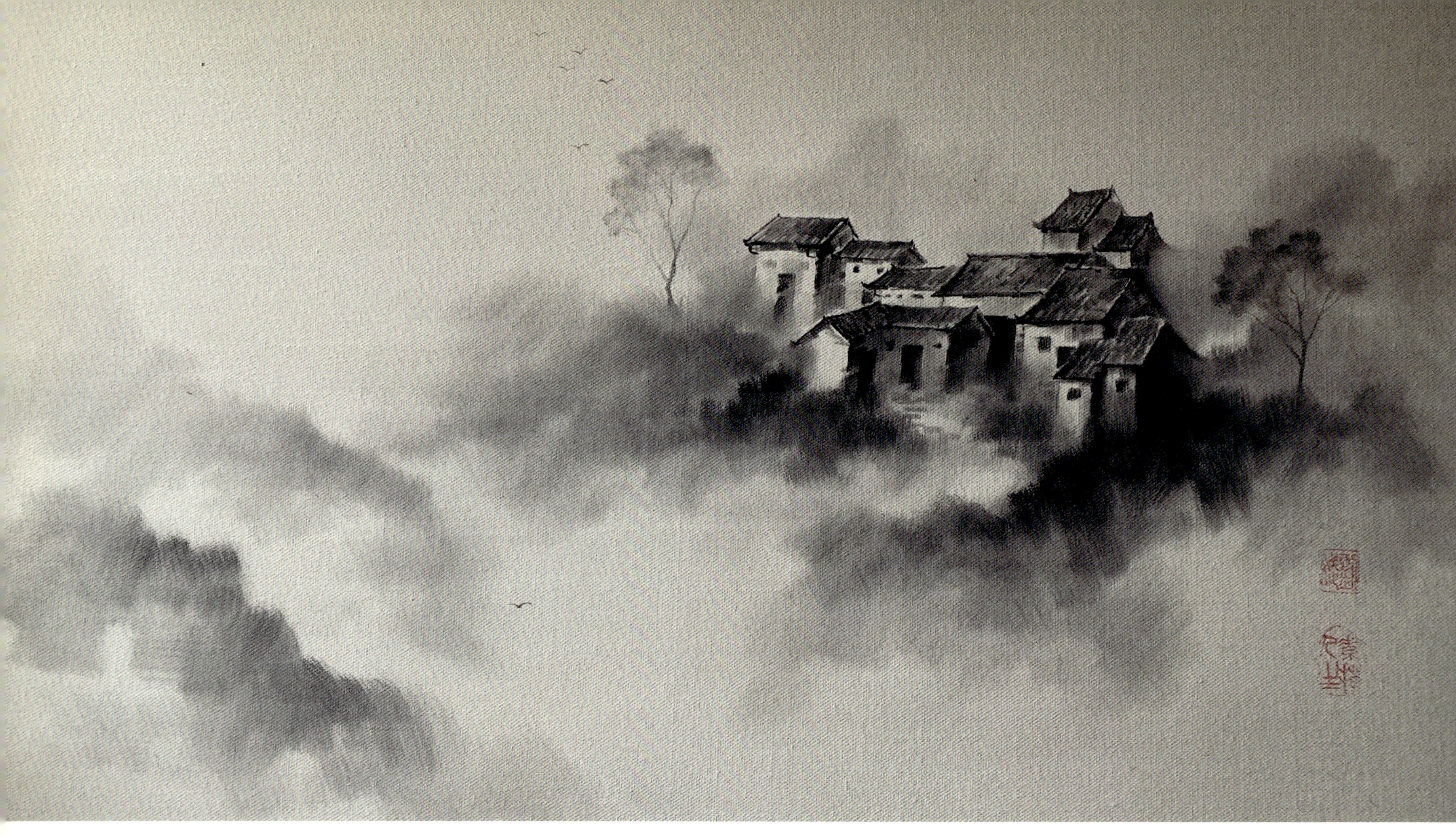

In all the world there is nothing softer and weaker than water, but because it always flows in harmony with nature, nothing equals it in the way it conquers the hard. The soft triumphs over the hard, the weak over the strong.

LAOZI

Auf der ganzen Welt gibt es nichts Weicheres und Schwächeres als das Wasser, aber weil es stets im Einklang mit der Natur fließe, kommt ihm in der Art, wie es dem Harten zusetzt, nichts gleich. Das Weiche siegt über das Harte, das Schwache über das Starke.

LAO-TSE

This applies to all areas of life and is considered desirable, cultivated and exemplary by the Chinese across all classes. A good master is the one who puts his considerations and decisions into calm, not rambling, pleasant words. A disciple worthy of the master is one who recognises, understands and correctly implements these statements.

Recognising this art of interaction that strives for harmony with the acceptance of ambiguities, tolerates uncertainties and the much longer negotiation processes requires from the untrained Westerner a reflective knowledge of the history of this way of expression which may seem confusing at first sight.

In other words, this means no clear instructions, but room for imagination and interpretation. Also, great works of the Chinese philosophers are no embellishing tomes. The

Dies trifft auf alle Lebensbereiche zu und wird von den Chinesen quer durch alle Schichten als erstrebenswert, gebildet und vorbildlich betrachtet. Ein guter Meister ist, wer seine Überlegungen und Entscheidungen in ruhige, nicht ausschweifende, angenehme Worte verpackt. Ein dem Meister würdiger Schüler ist, wer diese Aussagen erkennt, versteht und richtig umsetzt. Die Anerkennung dieser nach Harmonie strebenden Kunst der Interaktion mit der Inkaufnahme von Unklarheiten, dem Aushalten von Unsicherheiten und den wesentlich längeren Verhandlungsprozessen erfordert vom ungeübten Westler reflektiertes Wissen um die Historie dieser auf den ersten Blick verwirrenden Art des Ausdrucks.

Übersetzt bedeutet dies keine klaren Anweisungen, dafür Raum für Fantasie und Interpretation. Auch große Werke der chinesischen Philosophen sind keine ausschmückenden

Tao Te Ching of the legendary Laozi – the *Book of Meaning and Life* – written about 3,000 years ago is an inexhaustible source of wisdom. Its central figure, the Called One, lives in harmony with the Tao, the "meaning" of the universe, by "not acting" and staying away from worldly activity. The book has influenced Chinese thought far beyond Taoism.

The value and appreciation of the seemingly inaccurate, of what does not impose itself, up to the appreciation of that which is inactive, that which is accepting, is learned by the Chinese not only in literature, in poetry and in oral tradition. For thousands of years, Asian artists have tirelessly depicted philosophical thought in the landscape scenes of mountains, rivers and isolated pagodas or pine trees in gentle, blurred brushstrokes, which are very popular in China.

Immersed in the big picture, the person is shaped by his or her environment. When travelling in China, it is a surprisingly common occurrence to encounter poems or paintings that have become reality, landscape scenes that look like traditional ink paintings in grey and white, with a splash of red if you are lucky.

The true red corresponds to the red stamp seals of the artists in the grey and white paintings.

It was deemed honourable for the painter if another artist considered the work so great that he asked to be allowed to continue painting it. This explains why numerous paintings have multiple stamp signatures. This is unthinkable in Western culture: imagine the signatures of several artists on

Left page:
Typical cloudy view of a grey and white mountain farming village in Anhui province

Linke Seite:
Typische wolkenverhangene Sicht auf ein grau-weißes Bergbauerndorf in der Provinz Anhui

Schinken. Das vor rund 3000 Jahren entstandene *Tao-Tê-King* des legendären Lao-Tse – das *Buch vom Sinn und Leben* – ist gerade in seiner epigrammatischen Kürze ein unerschöpflicher Weisheitsquell. Seine zentrale Figur, der Berufene, lebt im Einklang mit dem Dao, dem „Sinn" des Universums, indem er „nicht handelt" und sich vom weltlichen Wirken fernhält. Das Buch hat weit über den Daoismus hinaus das chinesische Denken geprägt.

Die Wertigkeit und Würdigung des oberflächlich Ungenauen, des sich nicht Aufdrängenden, bis hin zur Würdigung des Inaktiven, des Annehmenden, erlernen die Chinesen aber nicht nur in der Literatur, in der Poesie und in der mündlichen Überlieferung. Asiatische Künstler stellen

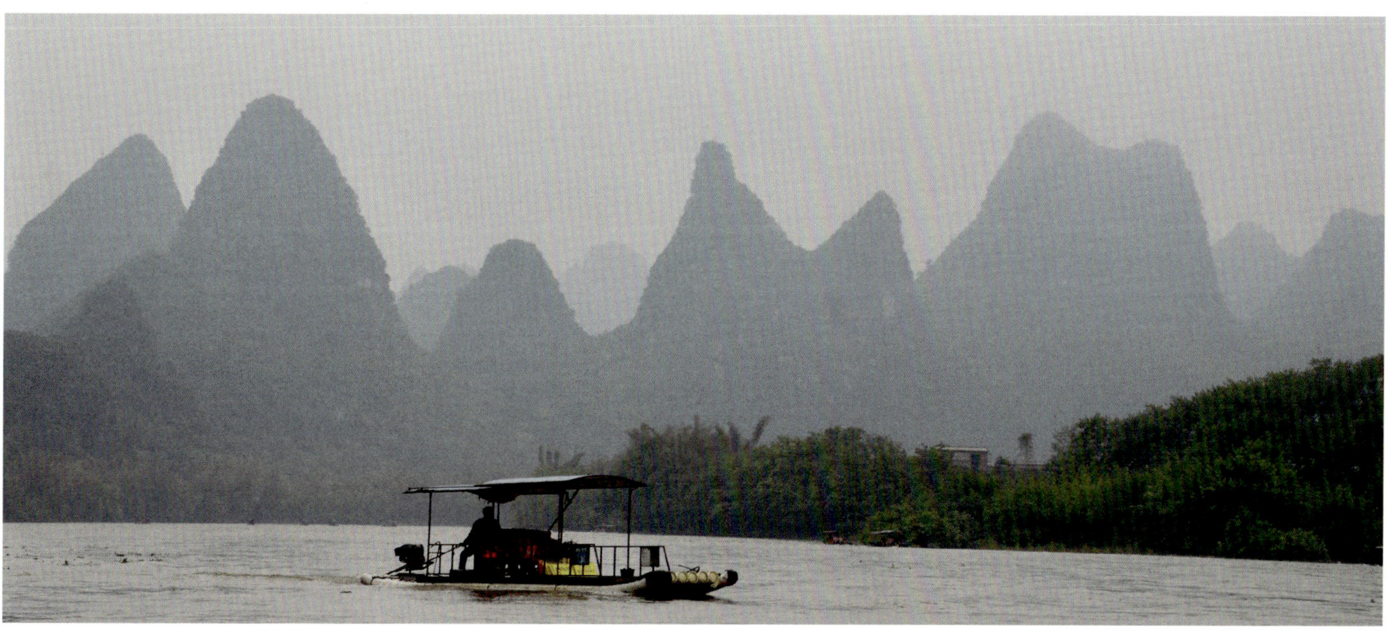

A thoughtful bamboo raft on the famous Li River near Yangshuo in Guangxi Province. The prominent karst mountains were depicted on the Chinese 20 Renminbi bank bill.

Ein bedachtes Bambusfloß auf dem bekannten Li-Fluß bei Yangshuo in der Provinz Guangxi. Die prominenten Karstberge wurden auf der chinesischen 20 Renminbi-Banknote abgebildet.

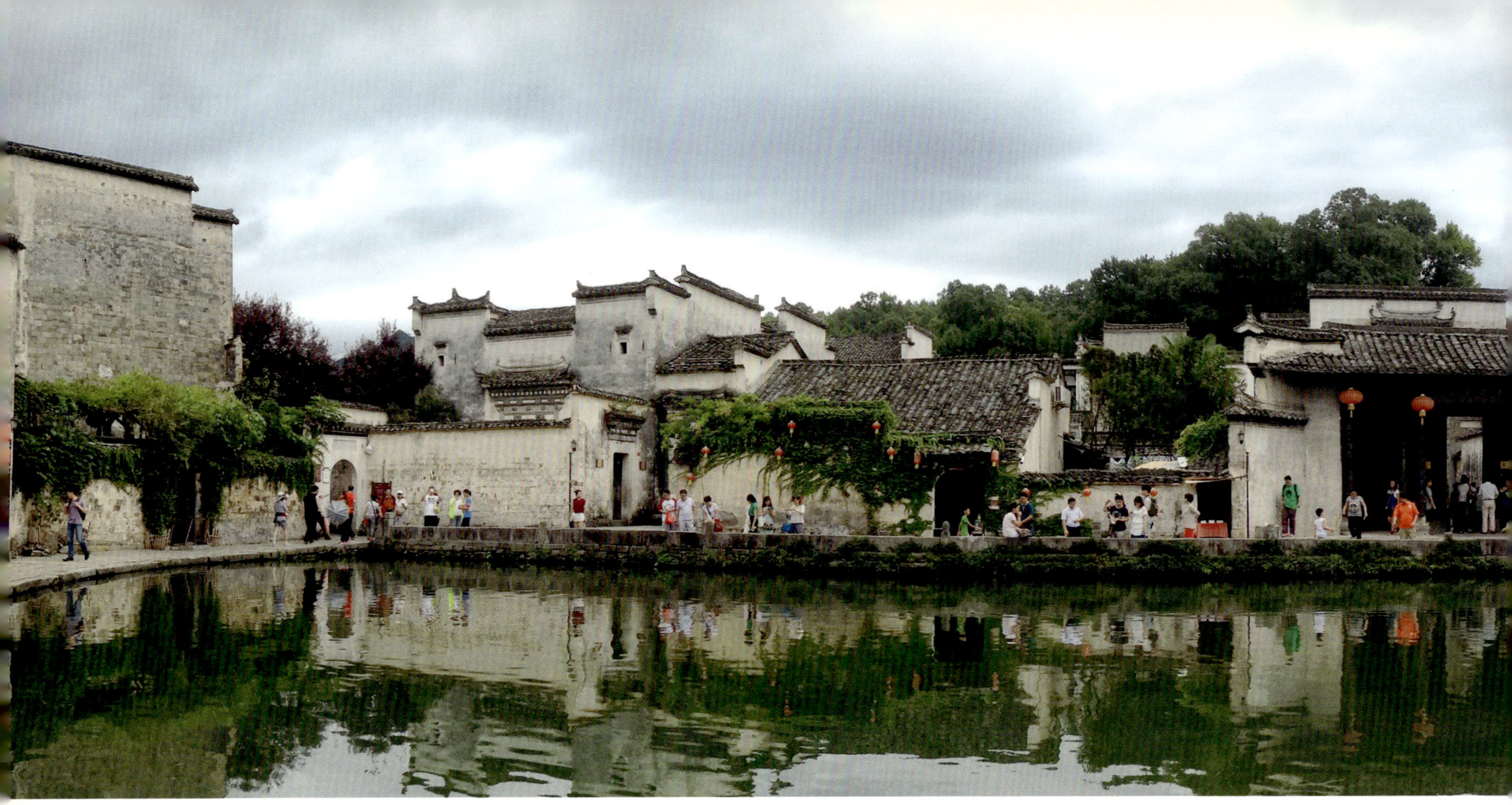

The Hongcun village with the picturesque Moon Pond is well over 860 years old. It is probably the most famous village near the city of Huangshan, as it served as a backdrop in the Oscar-winning film *Crouching Tiger, Hidden Dragon*.

Schon über 860 Jahre alt ist das Dorf Hongcun mit dem malerischen Mondsee. Es ist das wohl bekannteste Dorf nahe der Stadt Huang Shan, da es dem mehrfach oscarprämierten Film *Tiger & Dragon* als Kulisse diente.

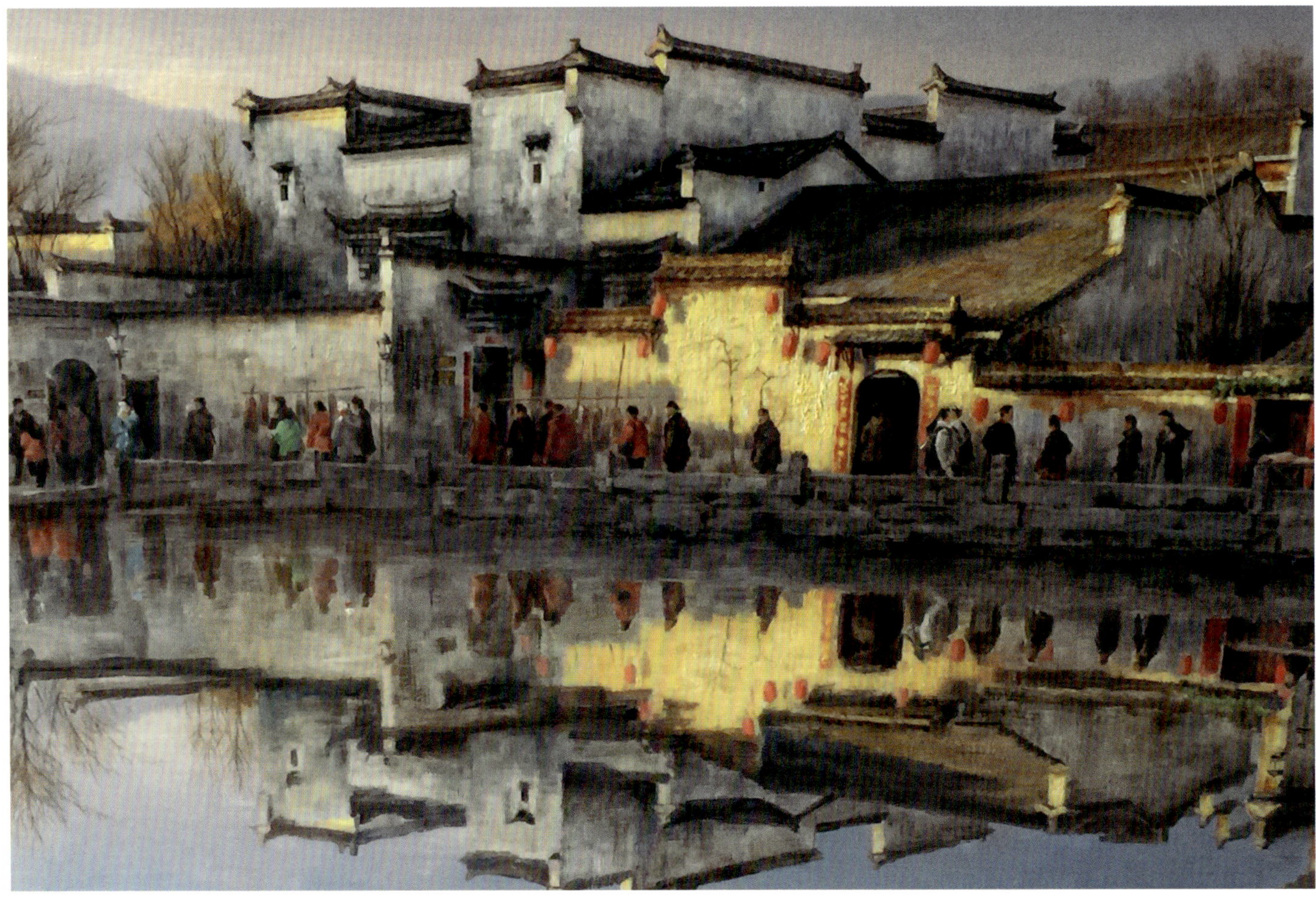

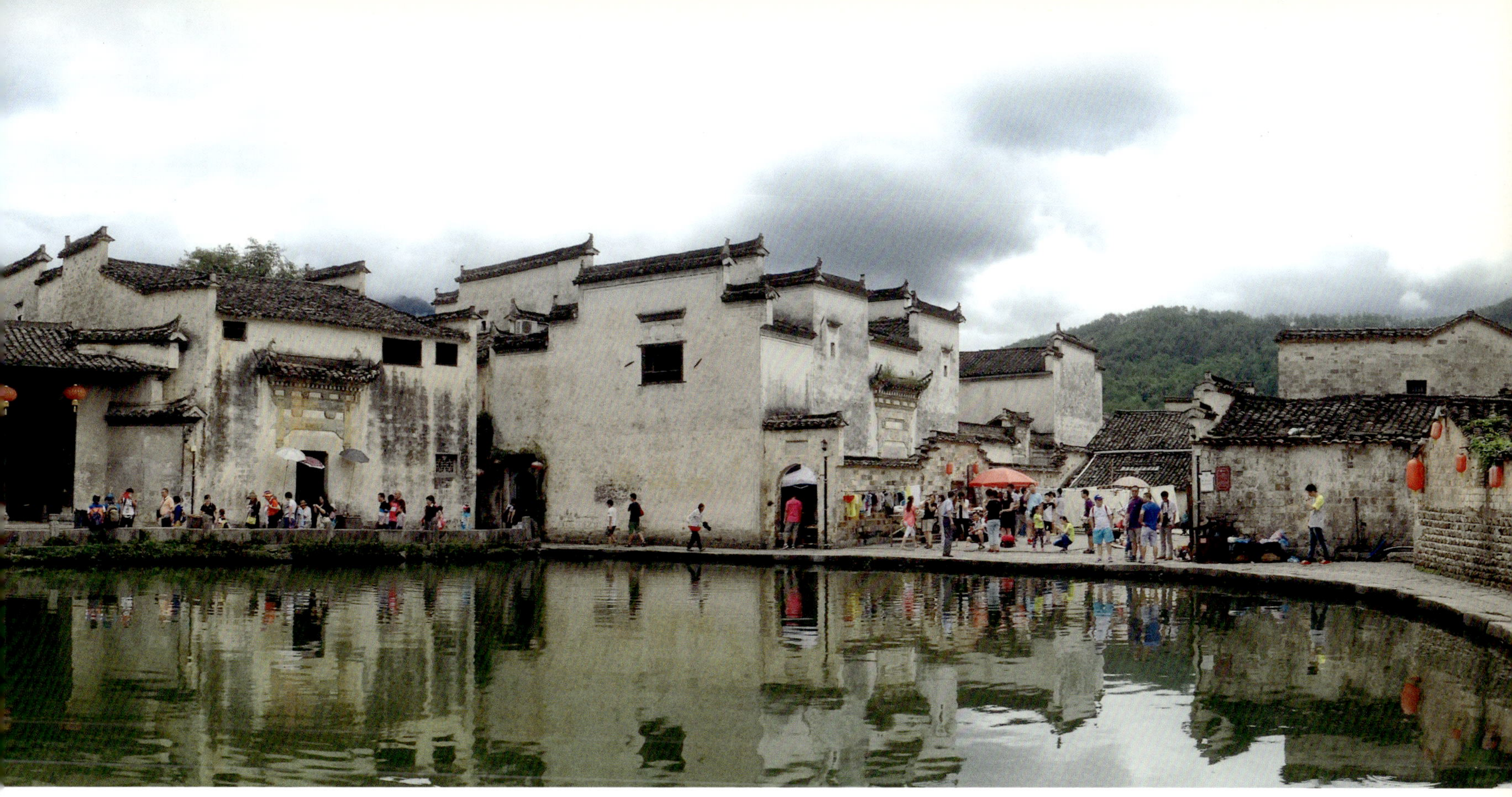

Leonardo da Vinci's *Mona Lisa*! In China, it is considered exemplary diligence to copy the master until, after many years, one reaches the maturity to produce one's own work.

In Anhui Province, this choice of colour also presents itself in architecture. The rich merchants of Huishang from the Ming and Qing periods built large, ornately decorated houses in grey, white and black.

Walking around the Moon Pond in the middle of the picturesque village of Hongcun in the evening, when the crowds of visitors have died down, you can still feel transported back to the China of about 900 years ago in the light of the red lanterns.

Presumably, the builders of these picturesque villages were inspired by the grey-white sea of clouds enveloping Huangshan, which literally means "yellow mountains", located just a few kilometres to the north. There, Lotus Blossom, Radiant Light and Heavenly Capital, as the three highest peaks are poetically called, rarely rise above the grey haze. The fascinating area of uniquely shaped granite peaks and pine trees has always served Chinese painters as a model and inspiration.

What appears cloudy and dreary to the Western observer at first glance, immediately surprises with imaginative, constantly changing individual discovery and wonderful

unermüdlich seit Jahrtausenden das philosophische Gedankengut in den in China sehr beliebten Landschaftsszenen von Bergen, Flüssen und vereinzelten Pagoden oder Kiefern in sanften verschwommenen Pinselstrichen dar.

Eingebettet in das große Ganze, prägt die Umgebung den Menschen. Beim Reisen in China trifft man überraschend häufig auf Realität gewordene Gedichte oder Gemälde, auf Landschaftsszenen, die aussehen wie traditionelle Tuschemalerei in Grau-Weiß, mit etwas Glück mit einem Farbtupfer Rot.

Das wahrhaftige Rot entspricht den roten Stempelsiegeln der Künstler in den grau-weißen Gemälden.

Es galt als ehrenhaft für den Maler, wenn ein anderer Künstler das Werk als so großartig betrachtete, dass er darum bat, daran weitermalen zu dürfen. Dies erklärt, warum zahlreiche Gemälde mehrere Stempelsignaturen aufweisen. Undenkbar im westlichen Kulturbereich: Man stelle sich die Signaturen mehrerer Künstler auf Leonardo da Vincis *Mona Lisa* vor! In China gilt es als vorbildlich fleißig, den Meister zu kopieren, bis man nach vielen Jahren die Reife erlangt, ein eigenes Werk zu fertigen.

In der Provinz Anhui stellt sich diese Farbauswahl auch architektonisch dar. Die reichen Kaufleute von Huishang aus der Ming- und Qing-Zeit erbauten große, kunstvoll dekorierte Häuser in Grau-Weiß und Schwarz.

tranquillity in the otherwise vibrant, noisy country. In Chinese mythology, mountains have a special meaning as a connection between heaven and earth. This is where the emperors offered sacrifices, where the hermits retreated. Painting and poetry have always been closely linked in the Chinese tradition. The nature-loving Taoists mainly painted landscapes. Similarly unique in terms of colour and scenery is Zhangjiajie National Park in Hunan Province. It is China's first national park and UNESCO Geopark, a breath-taking natural scene of more than 3,000 columnar quartz sandstone formations. Clear ponds, enchanting waterfalls, deep gorges, strange karst caves, lush jungle, bizarre rocks and fascinating wildlife make this national park one of the most beautiful in China.

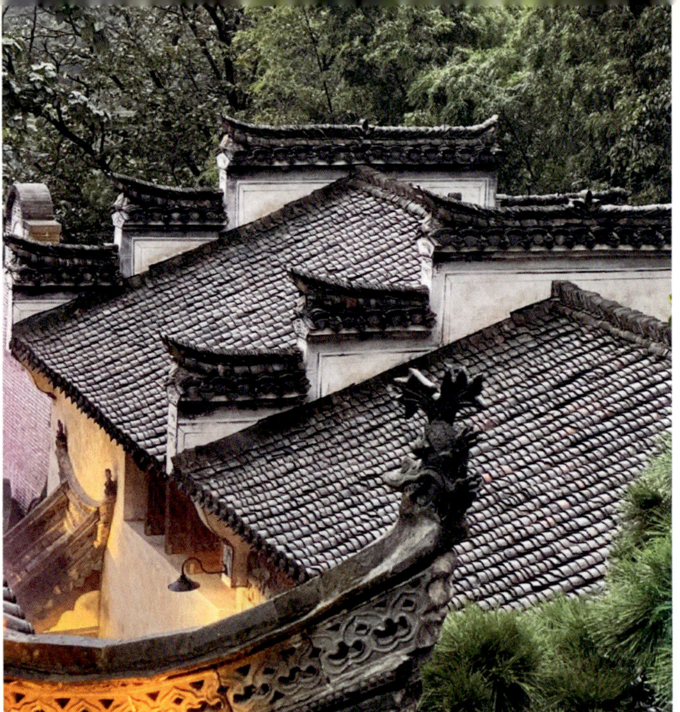

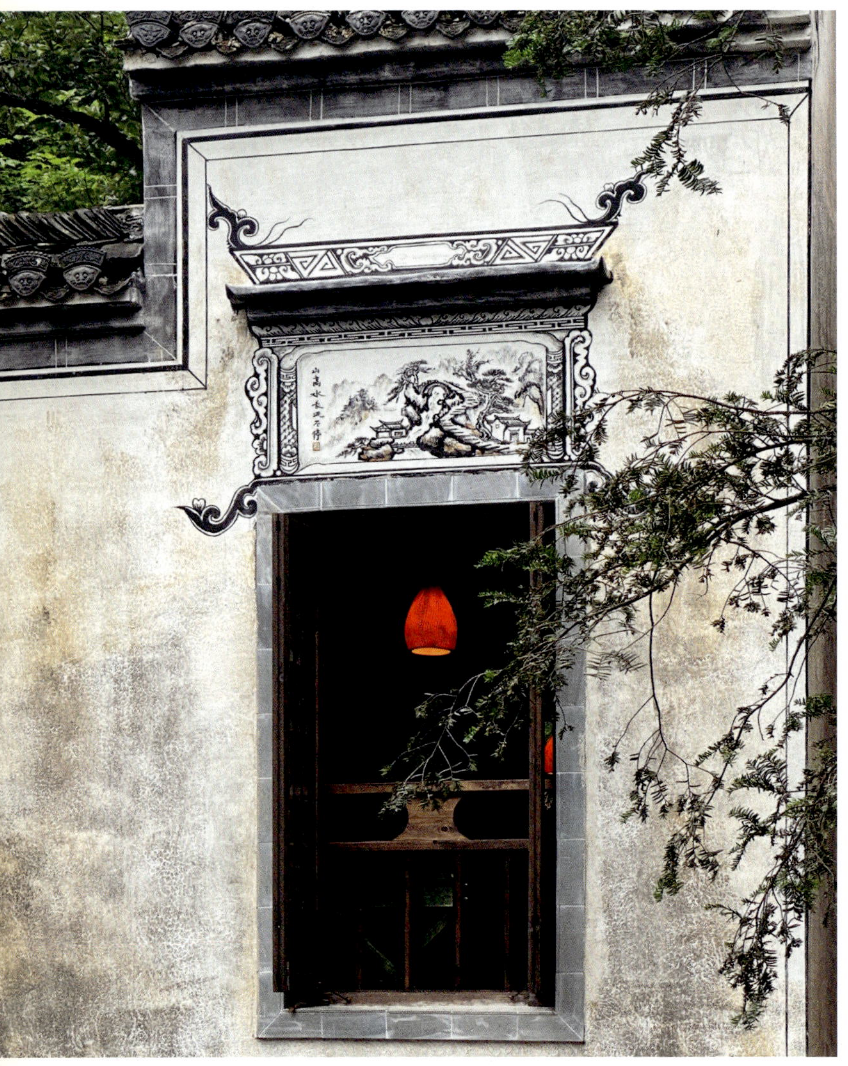

Above:
Artfully decorated houses, belonging to the wealthy merchants of Huishang or Hui, lend this part of China a unique style.

Oben:
Die kunstvoll dekorierten Häuser der reichen Kaufleute von Huishang oder Hui verleihen diesem Teil Chinas einen einzigartigen Stil.

Bei einem Spaziergang um den Mondteich mitten im malerischen Dorf Hongcun kann man sich abends, wenn die Besuchermassen verebbt sind, auch heute noch im roten Laternenlicht in das China von vor etwa 900 Jahren zurückversetzt fühlen.

Vermutlich inspirierten sich die Erbauer dieser pittoresken Dörfer am grau-weiß einhüllenden Wolkenmeer des sich nur wenige Kilometer nördlich befindenden Huangshan, wörtlich übersetzt „gelbes Gebirge". Dort ragen Lotusblüte Strahlendes Licht und Himmlische Hauptstadt, wie die drei höchsten Gipfel poetisch heißen, nur selten aus dem grauen Dunst hervor. Das faszinierende Areal aus einzigartig geformten Granitgipfeln und Kiefernbäumen dient chinesischen Malern seit jeher als Vorlage und Inspiration. Was dem westlichen Betrachter auf den ersten Blick wolkenverhangen und trist erscheint, überrascht umgehend mit fantasievollem, sich stetig wandelndem individuellem Entdecken und wunderbarer Ruhe in dem sonst so sinnesreichen, lauten Land. Berge als Verbindung zwischen Himmel und Erde haben in der chinesischen Mythologie eine besondere Bedeutung. Hier brachten die Kaiser Opfer dar, hierher zogen sich die Eremiten zurück. Malerei und Poesie waren schon immer eng verknüpft in der chinesischen Tradition. Die naturliebenden Daoisten malten überwiegend Landschaften.

Farblich und landschaftlich ähnlich einzigartig ist der Zhangjiajie-Nationalpark in der Provinz Hunan. Er ist Chinas erster Naturpark und UNESCO-Geopark, ein atemberaubendes Naturbild aus mehr als 3000 säulenartigen Quarzsandsteinformationen. Klare Teiche, bezaubernde Wasserfälle, tiefe Schluchten, seltsame Karsthöhlen, üppiger Urwald, bizarre Felsen und eine faszinierende Tierwelt machen diesen Nationalpark zu einem der schönsten Chinas.

Here, too, the grey-white and various shades of green capture the hiker's imagination. Only the sun is able to dispel the clouds now and then and make the lush greenery shine in a refreshing way. It is difficult to decide at the fork in the road between the path to the Pillar of Southern Heaven, Nantian Yizhu, the one to the Magic Needle for Calming the Sea, Dinghai Shenzhen, and the one to the Platform for Picking Stars, Zhaixingtai.

The 150-metre-high Pillar of Southern Heaven is said to have inspired the floating Hallelujah Mountains in the movie *Avatar*. Hikers tie red ribbons on trees, rocks and bridges so that their prayers and wishes will be carried by the wind through the nearby Heaven's Gate in Tianmen Mountain up to the Heaven's Gate Mountain. Not infrequently accompanied by the death-defying wingsuit flyers, who glide through the otherwise visually tranquil landscape like long, colourful brushstrokes. In 2013, the American Jeb Corliss was the first to fly through the Gate of Heaven in the approximately 1,580-metre-high Tianmen Mountain by wingsuit.

Only the howling of the cheeky monkeys startles the wanderer, both today and then. Li Bai, one of the most important lyrical poets of the Tang Dynasty, immortalised this in the poem *Leaving Baidi in the Morning*, which is famous in China.

Auch hier beflügeln das Grau-Weiß und diverse Grünschattierungen die Fantasie des Wanderers. Nur die Sonne kann ab und zu die Wolken vertreiben und das feuchte Grün erfrischend leuchten lassen. Es fällt schwer, sich an der Weggabelung zwischen dem Pfad zur Säule des südlichen Himmels, Nantian Yizhu, dem zur Zaubernadel zur Beruhigung des Meeres, Dinghai Shenzhen, und dem zur Plattform für das Pflücken von Sternen, Zhaixingtai zu entscheiden.

Die 150 Meter hohe Säule des südlichen Himmels soll zu den schwebenden Hallelujah-Bergen im Film *Avatar* inspiriert haben. Wanderer knüpfen rote Bänder an Bäume, Felsen und Brücken, damit ihre Gebete und Wünsche vom Wind durch das nahegelegene Himmelstor im Tianmenshan, dem Himmelstorberg, getragen werden. Nicht selten gemeinsam mit den todesmutigen Wingsuit-Fliegern, die wie lange, bunte Pinselstriche das ansonsten optisch so ruhige Landschaftsbild durchstreifen. 2013 flog der Amerikaner Jeb Corliss als Erster per Wingsuit durch das Himmelstor im rund 1580 Meter hohen Tianmenshan.

Einzig das Brüllen der vorwitzigen Affen lässt den Wanderer heute wie damals aufschrecken. Li Bai, einer der bedeutendsten lyrischen Dichter der Tang-Dynastie, hat dies in dem in China bekannten Gedicht *Am Morgen Baidi verlassen* verewigt.

早發白帝城，李白

Leaving Baidi in the Morning by (Tang) Li Bai
Am Morgen Baidi verlassen von Li Bai

朝辞白帝彩云间

We set off in the morning by river from the city Baidi to Jiangling surrounded by colourful clouds.
Baidi verließ ich am frühen Morgen, in farbige Wolken gerückt.

千里江陵一日还

We arrive at Jiangling in one day travelling thousands of miles.
Den langen Weg hinab nach Jiangling, in einem Tag war ich zurück.

两岸猿声啼不住

The echoes of the apes keep reverberating in the mountains.
Von beiden Ufern tönten die Affen in ständigem Jubelgeschrei.

轻舟已过万重山

While the light boat we are in has passed range upon range of mountains.
So kam das Boot auf seiner Fahrt an unzähl'gen Bergen vorbei.

…

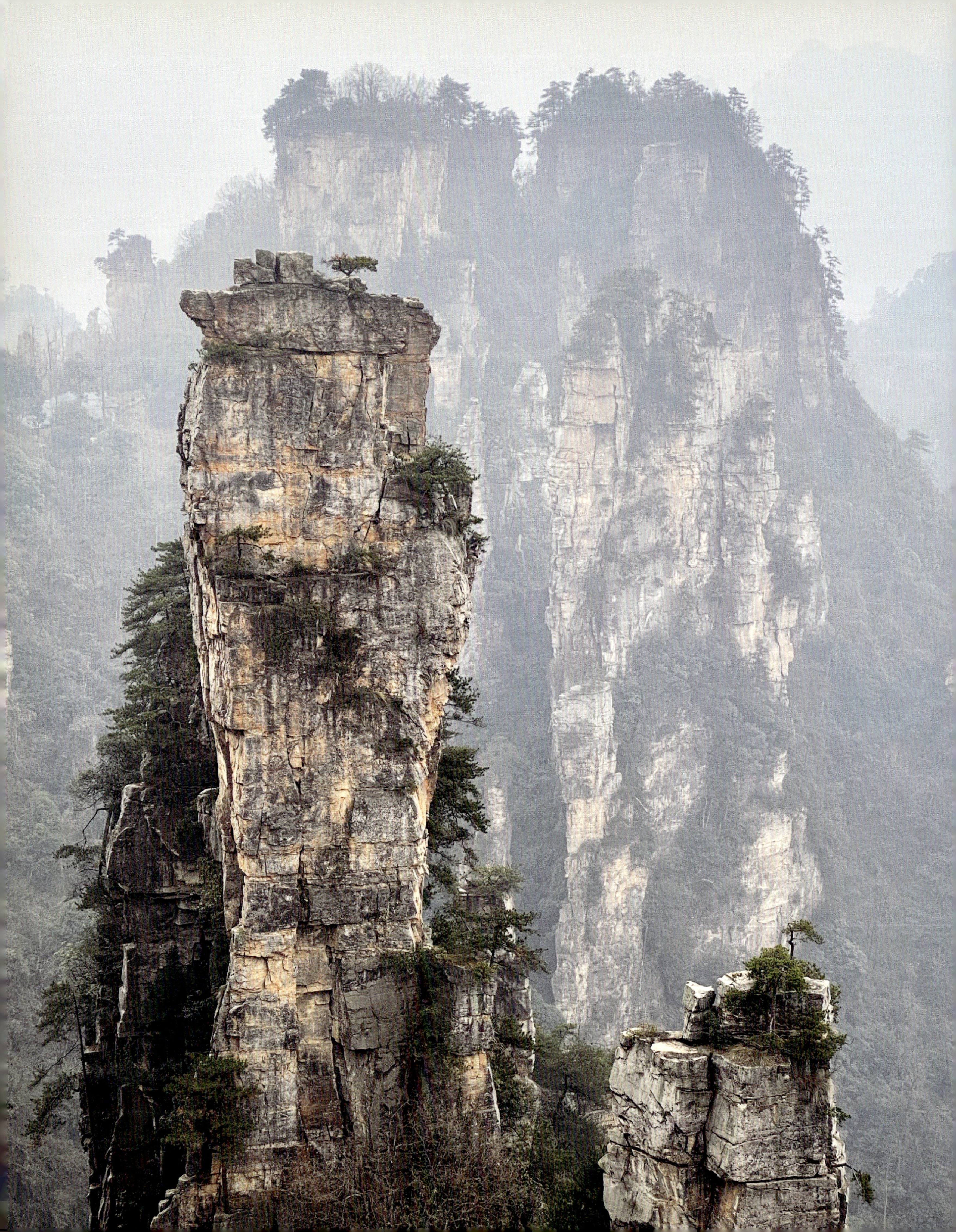

Deep in Zhangjiajie National Park, the natural rock bridge Tiansheng Qiao impresses with a height of 358 metres, a span of 50 metres and a width of only 2 metres. Intrepid hikers leave red ribbons inscribed with prayers and wishes.

Tief im Zhangjiajie-Nationalpark beeindruckt die natürliche Felsenbrücke Tiansheng Qiao mit 358 Metern Höhe, einer Spannweite von 50 Metern und nur 2 Metern Breite. Unerschrockene Wanderer hinterlassenen rote Bänder, die mit Gebeten und Wünschen beschriftet sind.

Page 28:
The mountain farmers of Huangling in Jiangxi Province decorate their village with a very special spicy "red chili flag" every autumn.

Seite 28:
Mit einer ganz besonders scharfen „Rote-Chili-Flagge" schmücken die Bergbauern von Huangling in der Provinz Jiangxi jährlich im Herbst ihr Dorf.

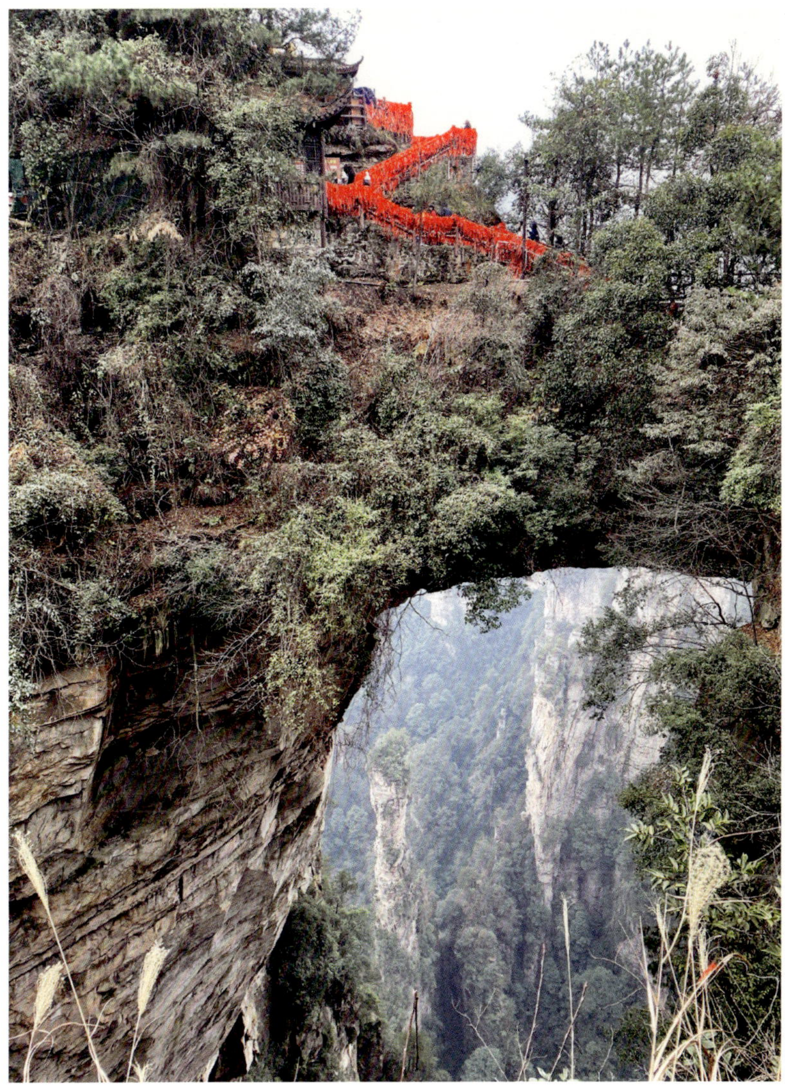

The Tang poems have a special place in the hearts of Chinese people. They are a treasure of Chinese culture. Many of the noteworthy Tang poems not only reach a very high literary standard, they also use concise and easy-to-understand words. They are loved by the people and passed down from generation to generation. The meaning of the Tang poems in Chinese culture and their influence on the Chinese nation is another significant, colourful piece of the puzzle for those who want to understand China. There is a saying that "Tang poems are to Chinese culture what DNA is to humanity." They are a key to understanding Chinese culture.

Concise and vague in their statements, giving the reader mere food for thought, they resemble the sentences of the legendary Laozi. In the *Tao Te Ching*, he warns artists against dividing the world into the five colours black, white, yellow, red and green, because this blinds perception. His message is: "If we looked at the world as a whole, our thoughts would be much clearer."

Die Tang-Gedichte haben im Herzen der Chinesen einen ganz besonderen Platz. Sie sind ein Schatz der chinesischen Kultur. Viele herausragende Tang-Gedichte erreichen nicht nur ein sehr hohes literarisches Niveau, sondern verwenden auch prägnante und leicht verständliche Wörter. Sie werden vom Volk geliebt und von Generation zu Generation weitergegeben. Die Bedeutung der Tang-Gedichte in der chinesischen Kultur und ihr Einfluss auf die chinesische Nation ist für diejenigen, die China verstehen wollen, ein weiterer bedeutender, bunter Mosaikstein. Ein Sprichwort besagt: „Tang-Gedichte sind für die chinesische Kultur das, was die DNA für die Menschheit ist." Sie sind ein Schlüssel zum Verständnis der chinesischen Kultur.

In ihren Aussagen knapp und vage, dem Leser lediglich Denkanstöße gebend, ähneln sie den Sätzen des legendären Lao-Tse. Er warnt im *Tao-Tê-King* die Künstler davor, die Welt in die fünf Farben Schwarz, Weiß, Gelb, Rot und Grün einzuteilen, weil dies für die Wahrnehmung blind mache. Seine Botschaft lautet: „Würden wir die Welt als Ganzes betrachten, wären unsere Gedanken um vieles klarer."

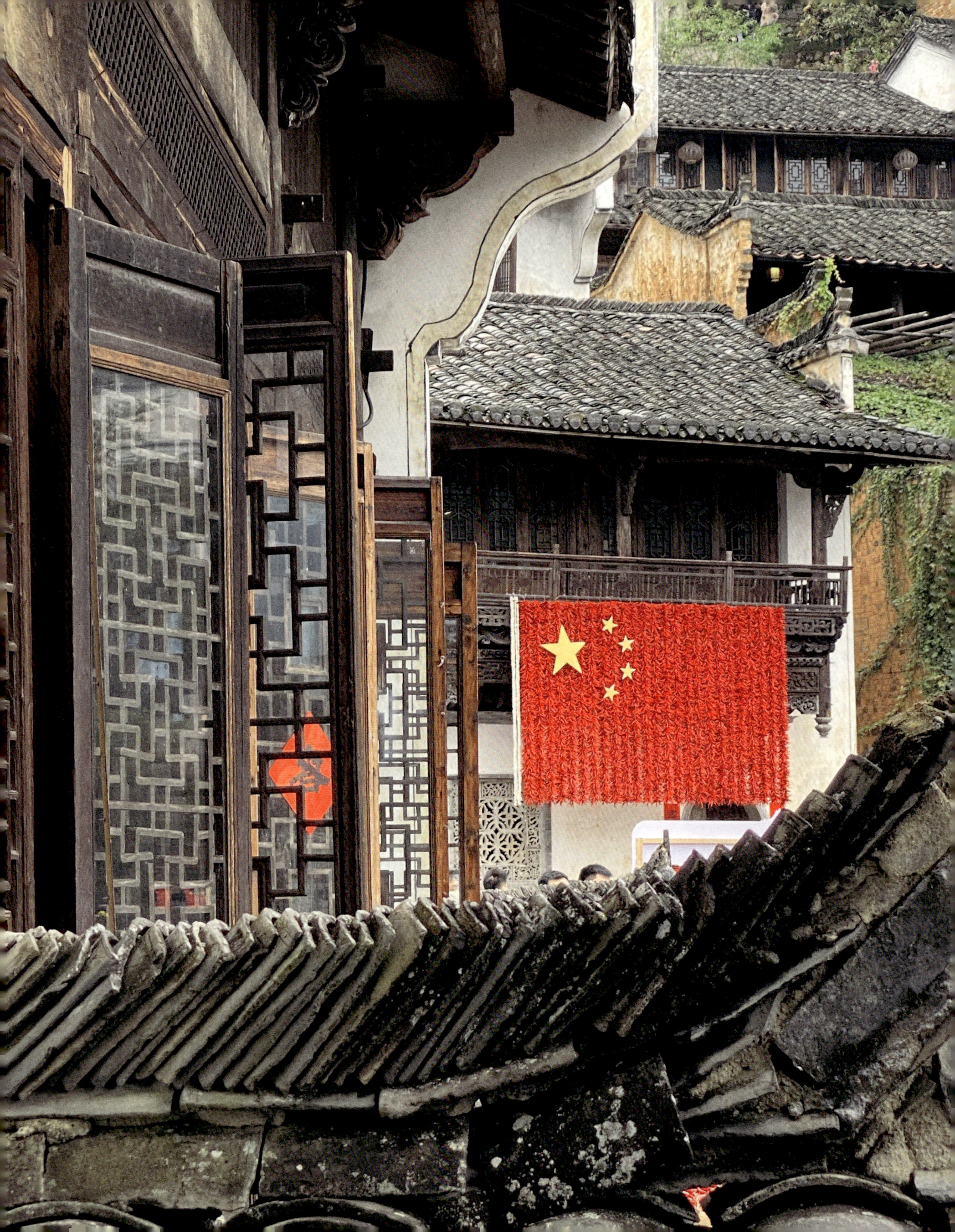

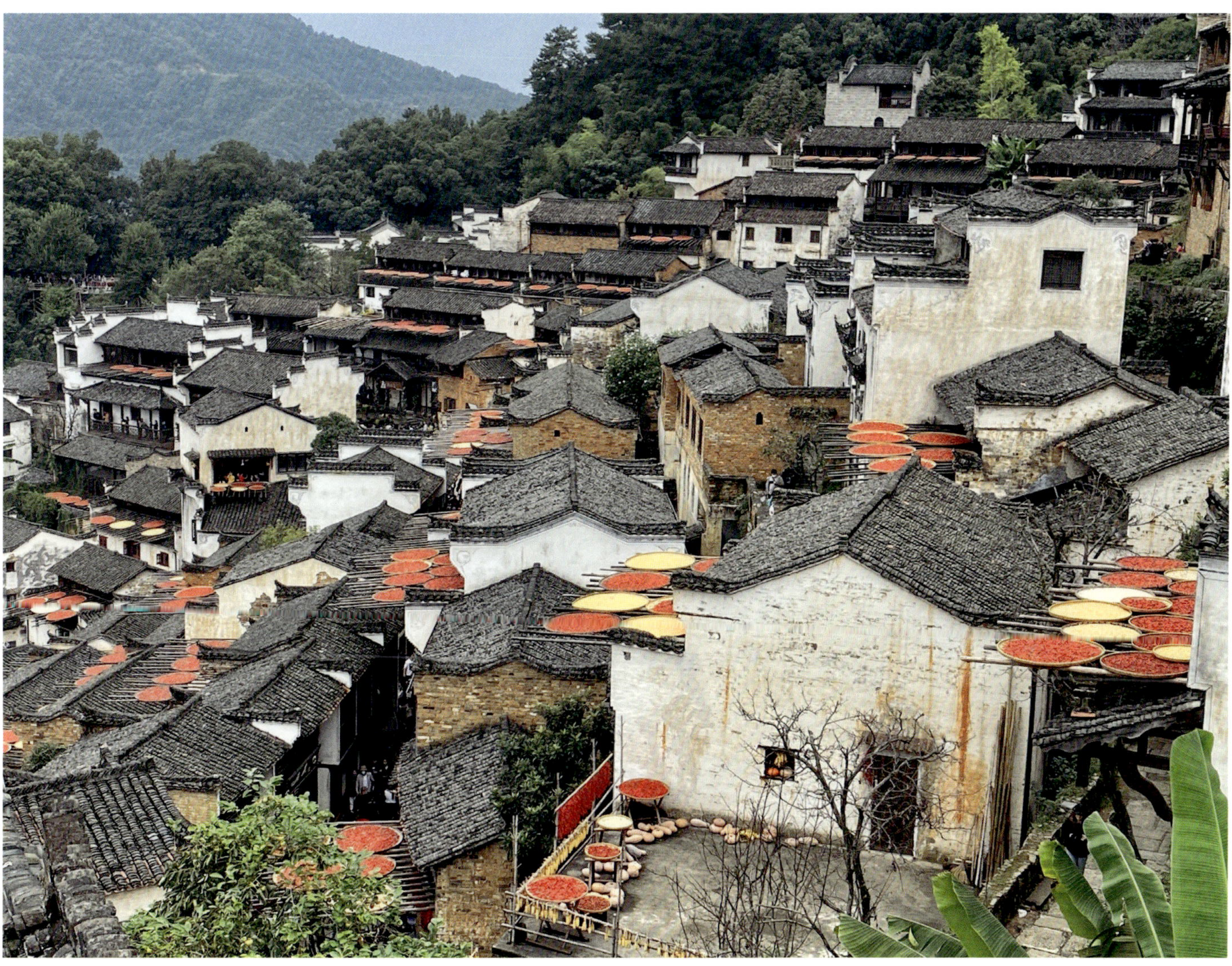

THE SENSUOUS – A WAY TO SENSE

Colour's five hues from the eyes their sight will take;
Music's five notes the ears as deaf can make;
The flavours five deprive the mouth of taste;
The chariot course, and the wild hunting waste
Make mad the mind; And objects rare and strange,
Sought for, Men's conduct will to evil change.
Therefore the sage seeks to satisfy the craving of the belly,
and not the insatiable longing of the eyes.
He puts from him the latter, and prefers to seek the former.
Translated by James Legge, 1891, Chapter 12

In the mountain villages of Jiangxi Province, visitors can quench their longing for splashes of colour all year round. But the scenery gets especially colourful in early fall, when villagers dry their harvest – fiery red chilies, yellow corn kernels, white beans and sand-coloured pumpkin slices – in flat bamboo baskets on village rooftops in the sun.

DAS SINNLICHE – EIN WEG ZUM SINN

Der Farben Vielfalt blendet die Augen.
Der Töne Fülle betäubt das Gehör.
Der Gewürze Reichtum verdirbt den Geschmack.
Der Leidenschaften Drang verwirrt das Herz.
Die Gier nach schwer Erreichbarem zerstört die Sitten.
Der Weise, von seinem Inneren geleitet,
bestimmt seiner Sinne Grenzen.
Alles Sinnliche ist ihm auch nur ein Weg zum Sinn.

In den Bergdörfern der Provinz Jiangxi können Besucher ihre Sehnsucht nach bunten Farbtupfern ganzjährig stillen. Ganz besonders bunt wird es aber im Frühherbst, wenn die Dorfbewohner ihre Ernte – feuerrote Chilis, gelbe Maiskörner, weiße Bohnen und sandfarbene Kürbisscheiben – in flachen Bambuskörben auf den Dächern des Dorfes in der Sonne trocknen.

The cycle of Chinese life and its colours

Der Kreislauf des chinesischen Lebens und seine Farben

The Taijitu is the world-famous black and white symbol of wholeness and the complement of opposites. Anchored in both Taoism and Neo-Confucianism, this symbol represents the unity of the complementary polarities of yin (black) and yang (white). This natural philosophy of opposites forms the basis for all Chinese-Japanese spiritual traditions. The female yin includes the moon, darkness, silence and earth. The male yang stands for sun, light, movement and sky.

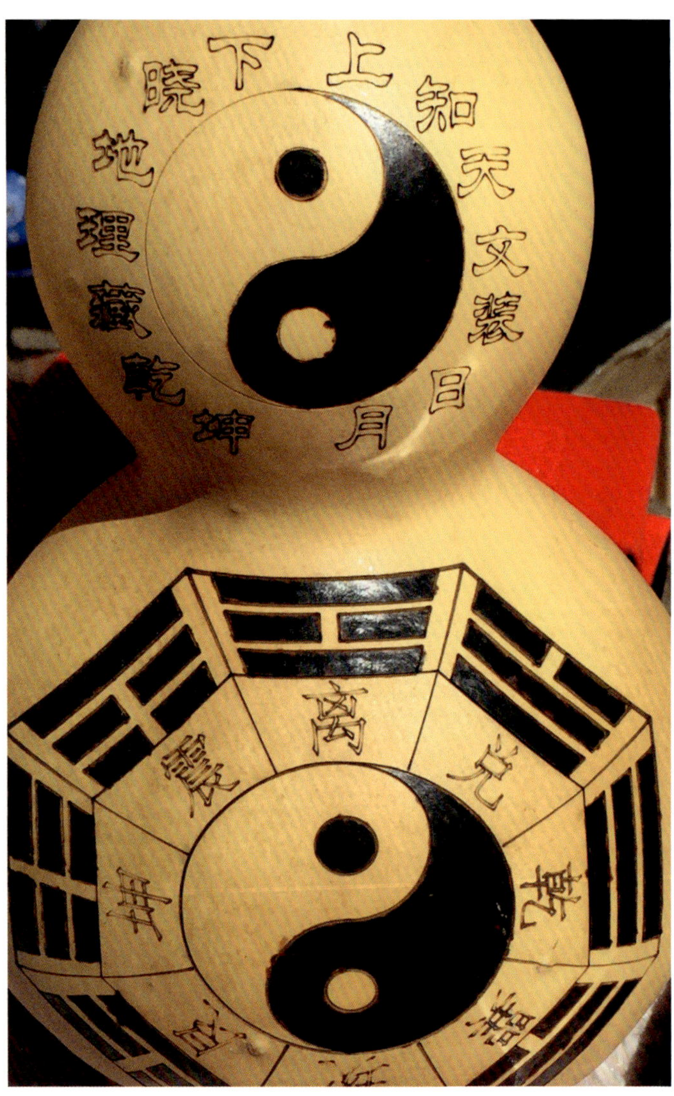

Decorating gourds is prized in China and tying them artfully in the shape of a figure eight is said to bring good luck. On this one, the well-known yin and yang symbol is depicted. The dried vessels were used to transport water, wine, medicine and magic lotions.

Das weltweit bekannte schwarz-weiße Symbol für das Ganzheitliche und die Ergänzung der Gegensätze ist das Taijitu. Sowohl im Daoismus als auch im Neokonfuzianismus verankert, verbildlicht dieses Symbol die Einheit der komplementären Polaritäten Yin (schwarz) und Yang (weiß). Diese beiden, also die Naturphilosophie, bildeten das Fundament für sämtliche geistige chinesisch-japanische Traditionen. Zum weiblichen Yin gehören Mond, Dunkelheit, Stille und Erde. Das männliche Yang steht für Sonne, Licht, Bewegung und Himmel.

Neben den beiden Urkräften Yin und Yang bestimmt seit Jahrtausenden Wuxing, die Fünf-Elemente-Lehre, den Kreislauf des chinesischen Lebens. Demnach besteht der Kosmos aus Holz, Feuer, Erde, Metall und Wasser, und dies fünf Elemente stehen in komplexen Beziehungen zueinander. Jedes Element wird durch eine bestimmte Farbe, Himmelsrichtung, Jahreszeit, einen Planeten, eine Symboltier und weitere Dinge repräsentiert. Alle Elemente interagieren innerhalb vier gleichzeitig stattfindender Zyklen miteinander, deshalb sind die fünf Grundfarben Schwarz, Weiß, Grün/Blau, Rot und Gelb auch Symbole für den ständigen Wandel der Welt.

Und mit den fünf Elementen haben diese fünf chinesischen Grundfarben in nahezu alle Lebensbereiche Einzug gehalten. Von der Lehre des Feng-Shui bis zu Tai-Chi-Chuan und Qigong, von der Traditionellen Chinesischen Medizin bis zum Buddhismus. Es gibt aber neben den fünf Farben auch noch die fünf Töne, die fünf Organe, die fünf Geschmäcker, die fünf Richtungen, und einige mehr. Auch die Sternzeichenlehre entstammt der Naturphilosophie Yin und Yang. In Kombination mit den zwölf Tierkreiszeichen ergeben die fünf Wandlungsphasen den sogenannten Sechzigerzyklus, eine der elementaren Kategorien der traditionellen Zeitmessung und der Kalenderkunde. Das Jahr der Ratte im Element Metall, zuletzt 2020, hat als unglücksbringendes Jahr alle sechzig Jahre schon Tradition.

Das Verzieren der Flaschenkürbisse ist in China geschätzt, und das kunstvolle Abbinden in Form einer Acht soll Glück bringen. Auf diesem ist das bekannte Yin-und-Yang-Symbol abgebildet. Gebraucht wurden die getrockneten Gefäße zum Transport von Wasser, Wein, Medizin und Zauberlotionen.

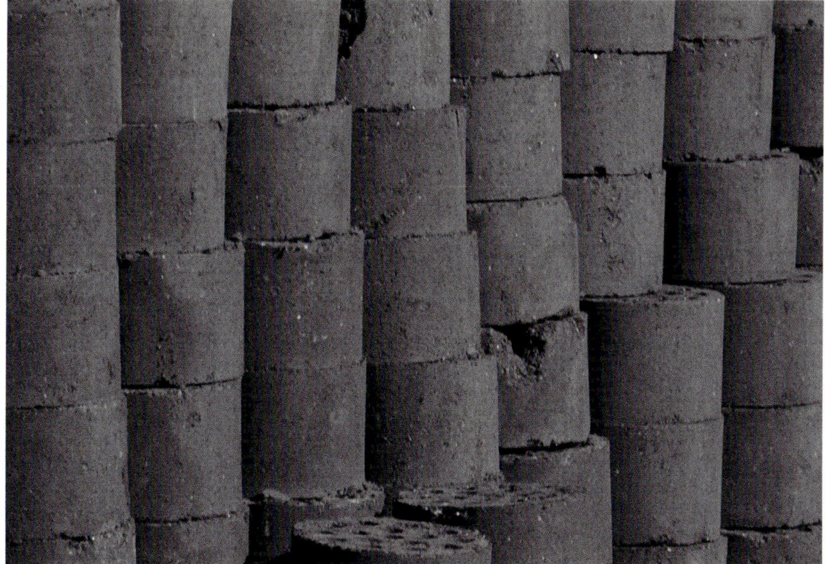

Oily black charcoal / Ölig schwarze Holzkohle

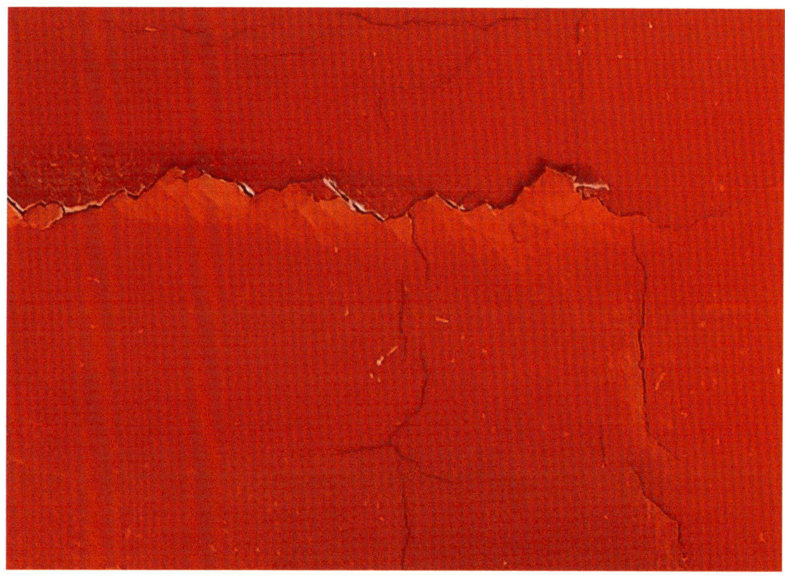

The red national colour of China / Die rote Nationalfarbe Chinas

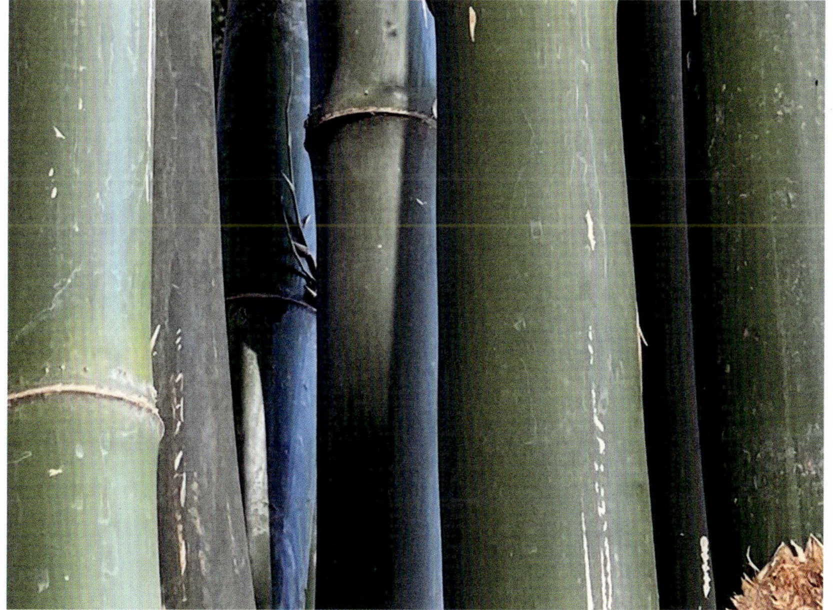

Green bamboo canes / Grüne Bambusrohre

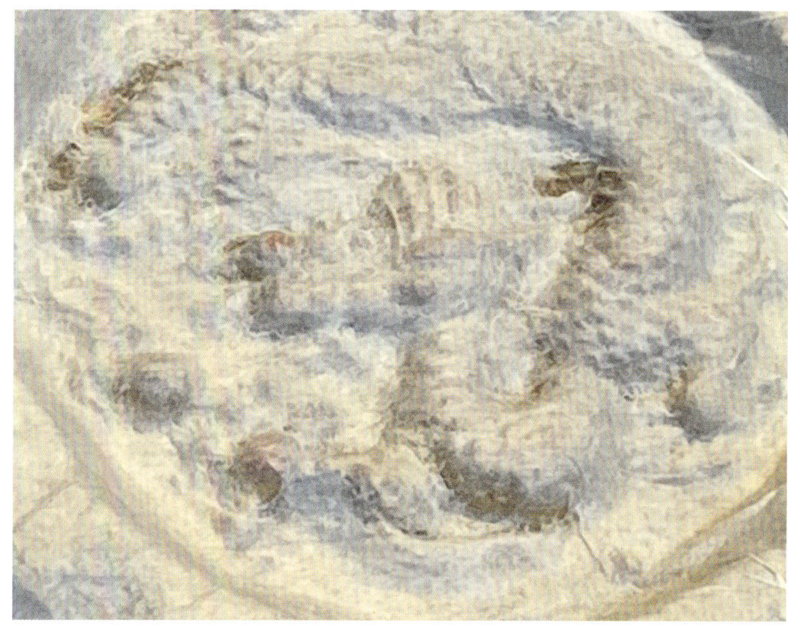

White dragon-decorated cap of a roof tile / Weiße drachenverzierte Kappe eines Dachziegels

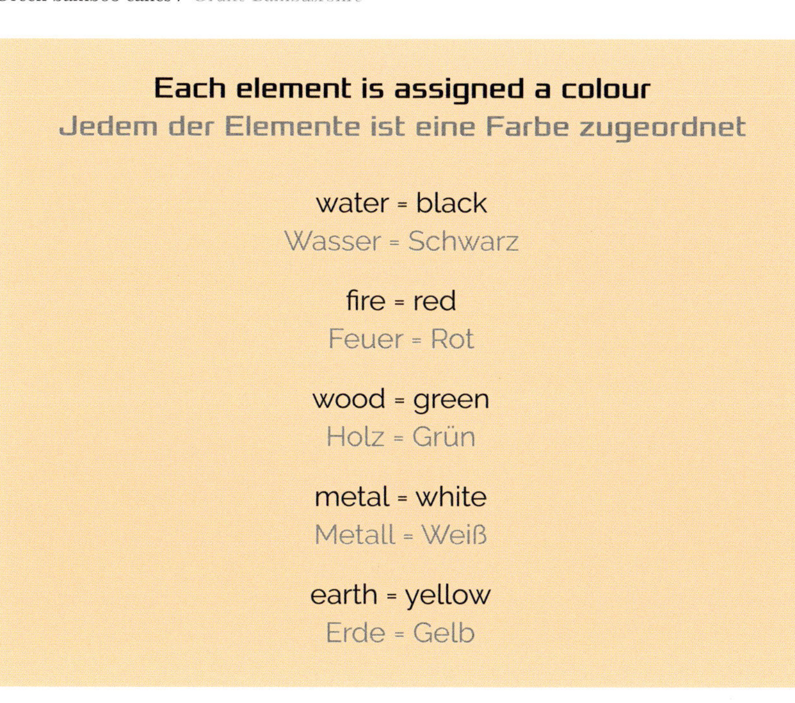

Each element is assigned a colour

Jedem der Elemente ist eine Farbe zugeordnet

water = black
Wasser = Schwarz

fire = red
Feuer = Rot

wood = green
Holz = Grün

metal = white
Metall = Weiß

earth = yellow
Erde = Gelb

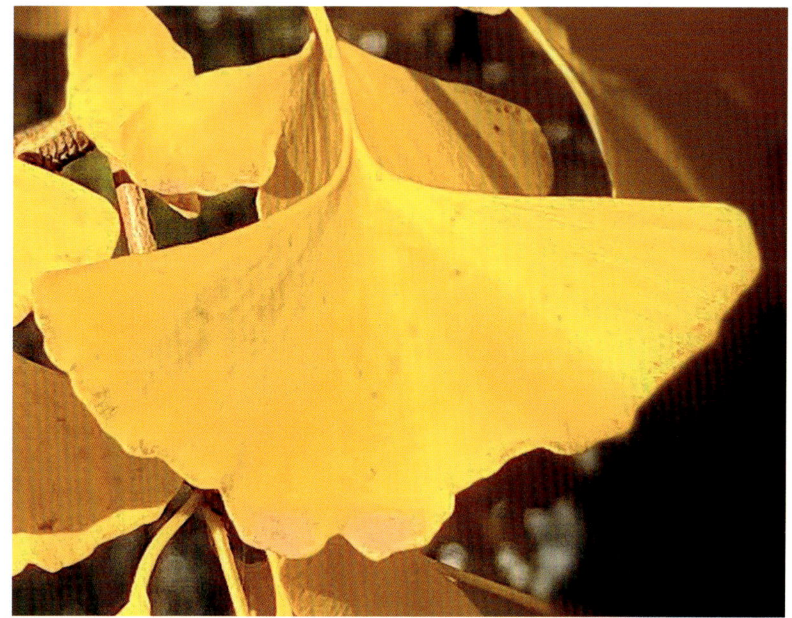

Gold-yellow ginkgo leaf / Goldgelbes Ginkgo-Blatt

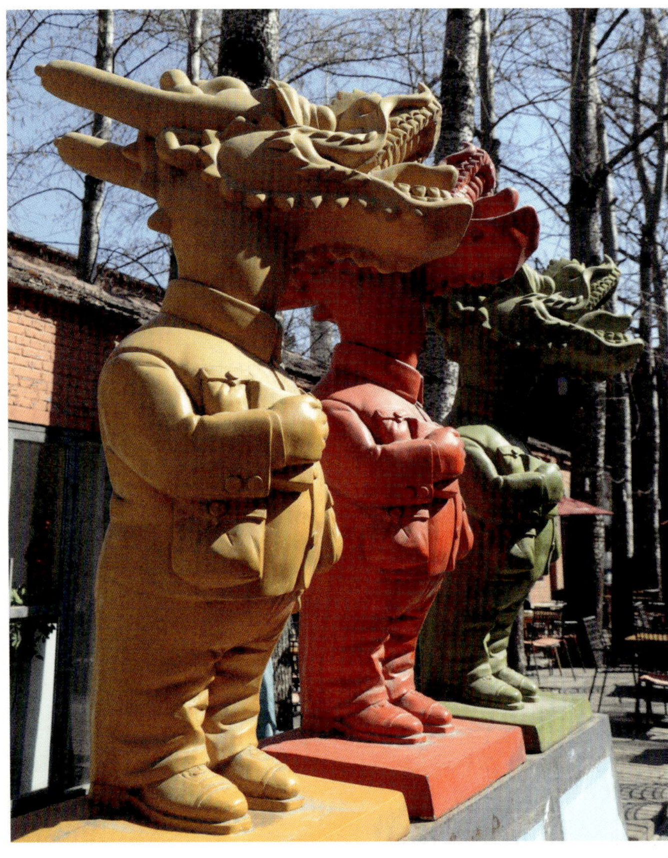

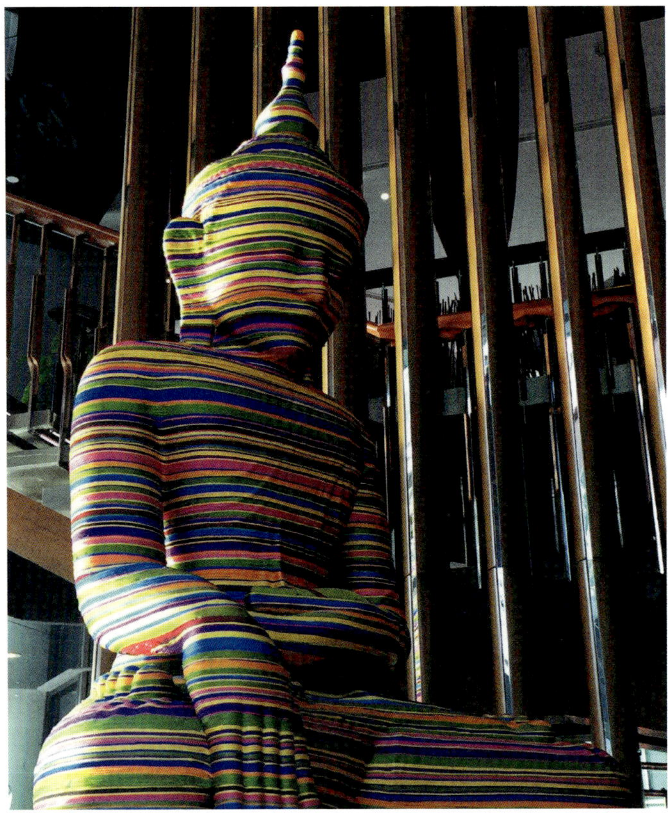

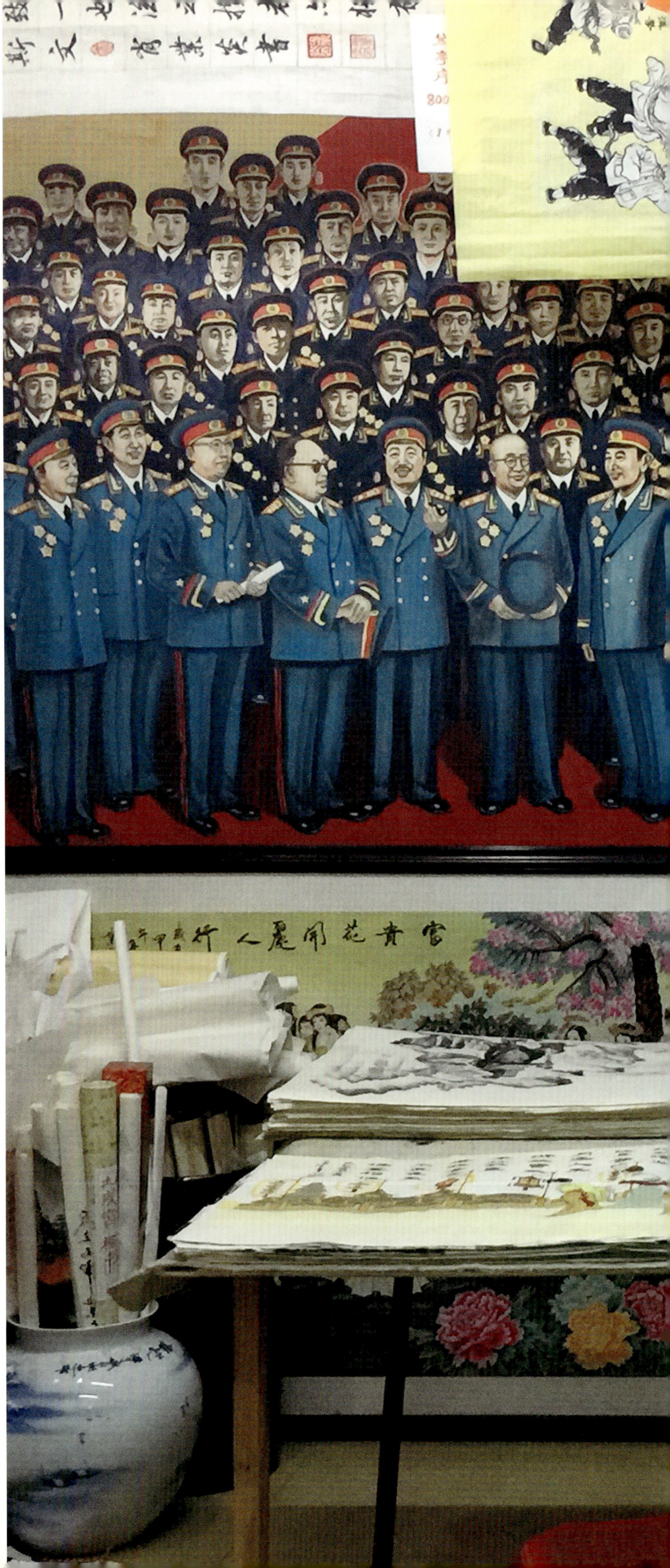

Above all, art reflects the historical development of a country, a social or cultural area. And thus contemporary Chinese art is also a reflection of China's history.

In der Kunst spiegelt sich vor allen Dingen die geschichtliche Entwicklung eines Landes, eines Sozial- oder Kulturraums. Und so ist auch die zeitgenössische chinesische Kunst ein Abbild der Geschichte Chinas.

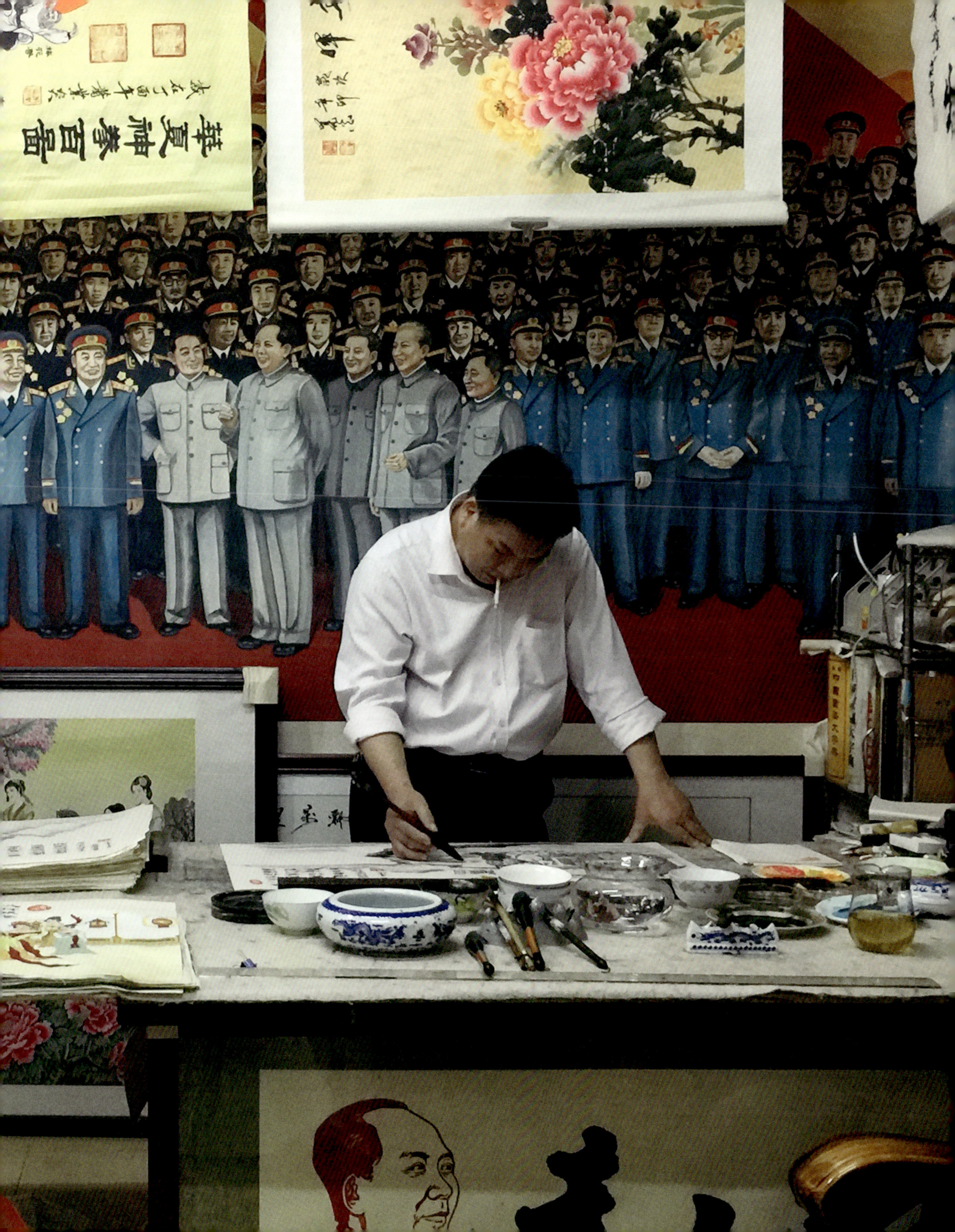

Alongside the elemental forces of yin and yang, Wuxing, the five elements doctrine, has determined the cycle of Chinese life for thousands of years. According to it, the cosmos consists of wood, fire, earth, metal and water, and these five elements are in complex relationships with each other. Each element is represented by a particular colour, cardinal direction, season, planet, symbolic animal and other things. All elements interact with each other within four simultaneous cycles, therefore the five primary colours black, white, green/blue, red and yellow are also symbols of constant change in the world.

And with the five elements, these five basic Chinese colours have found their way into almost all areas of life. From the teachings of feng shui to t'ai chi chuan and qigong, from traditional Chinese medicine to Buddhism. But besides the five colours, there are also the five tones, the five organs, the five tastes, the five directions, and some more. The zodiac signs also derive from the natural philosophy of yin and yang.

In combination with the twelve signs of the zodiac, the five transformation phases result in the so-called sixties cycle, one of the elementary categories of traditional timekeeping and calendar lore. The year of the rat in the element metal, most recently in 2020, already has a tradition as an unlucky year every sixty years.

Wherever possible, Chinese natural philosophy either looks for dual opposites, which can be interpreted as the interaction of yin or yang, or groups of five, which are related to each other according to the above schemes. In traditional Chinese medicine, both forces are in balance in a healthy person. If this balance gets out of sync, diseases can occur. Therefore, according to the understanding of traditional Chinese medicine, every illness is due to an imbalance of the dynamic interplay between black and white, yin and yang.

For the Taoists, black was the colour of true artists, because black ink contained all colours, and a true master was able to represent what was thought, not what was seen. The freedom-loving Taoists thus reacted to the strict Confucian world, which divided everything into categories (colours) and hierarchies.

The monochrome paintings of the Tang Dynasty were unfortunately lost in the checkered history of the vast country, but some specimens from the 13th century, the time of the Southern Song Dynasty, can still be seen in the National Palace Museum in Taipei. One of the most valuable,

The Chinese Huang Jiang succeeded in making money from brightly coloured oil paints when he founded the first workshop for copying well-known works of art in 1989 in the "artists' village" Dafen, just a few kilometres from Hong Kong. Today over 50 percent of the world's oil painting production is made here. In order to be able to produce large quantities in a short time, these are produced as if on an assembly line. Every painter has a colour and goes from one painting to the next once he's done his part. Every year around five million paintings are exported all over the world. Many graduates from the best art schools in China also come to Dafen, the payment is based on the number of copies made.

Aus bunten Ölfarben Geld zu machen, gelang dem Chinesen Huang Jiang, als er 1989 im „Künstlerdorf" Dafen, nur wenige Kilometer von Hongkong entfernt, die erste Werkstatt zum Kopieren bekannter Kunstwerke gründete. Heute entstehen hier über 50 Prozent der weltweiten Produktion an Ölgemälden. Um in kurzer Zeit große Stückzahlen herstellen zu können, werden diese wie am Fließband produziert. Jeder Maler hat eine Farbe und geht von einem Bild zum nächsten, sobald er seinen Teil erledigt hat. Jährlich werden ca. fünf Millionen Gemälde in alle Welt exportiert. Auch viele Absolventen der besten Kunsthochschulen Chinas kommen nach Dafen, bezahlt wird nach der Anzahl der erstellten Kopien.

Wo immer es möglich ist, sucht die chinesische Naturphilosophie entweder nach dualen Gegensätzen, die sich als Wechselwirkung von Yin oder Yang interpretieren lassen, oder nach Fünfergruppen, die nach den oben genannten Schemata miteinander in Beziehung gebracht werden. In der Traditionellen Chinesischen Medizin befinden sich bei einem gesunden Menschen beide Kräfte im Gleichgewicht. Gerät dieses Gleichgewicht aus dem Takt, kann es zu Krankheiten kommen. Nach dem Verständnis der Traditionellen Chinesischen Medizin ist daher jede Krankheit auf ein Ungleichgewicht des dynamischen Zusammenspiels zwischen Schwarz und Weiß, Yin und Yang zurückzuführen.

Für die Daoisten war Schwarz die Farbe der wahren Künstler, denn schwarze Tinte enthielt alle Farben, und ein wahrer Meister vermochte das Gedachte, nicht das Gesehene darzustellen. Die freiheitsliebenden Daoisten reagierten damit auf die streng konfuzianische Welt, die alles in Kategorien (Farben) und Hierarchien einteilte.

Die monochromen Gemälde der Tang-Dynastie gingen leider verloren in der wechselhaften Geschichte des riesigen Landes, doch einige Exemplare aus dem 13. Jahrhundert, der Zeit der südlichen Song-Dynastie, sind noch heute im Nationalen Palastmuseum in Taipeh zu sehen. Eines der wertvollsten, ein 8 Meter langes Rollbild, trägt den Titel *Flüsse und Berge von weitem betrachtet* und stammt von Xia Gui.

Man trifft in China auch heute immer noch auf Künstler, die in zeitgenössischer chinesischer Tuschemalerei die traditionelle Maltechnik mit moderner Abstraktion verbinden. Die bunte Szene jedoch überwiegt.

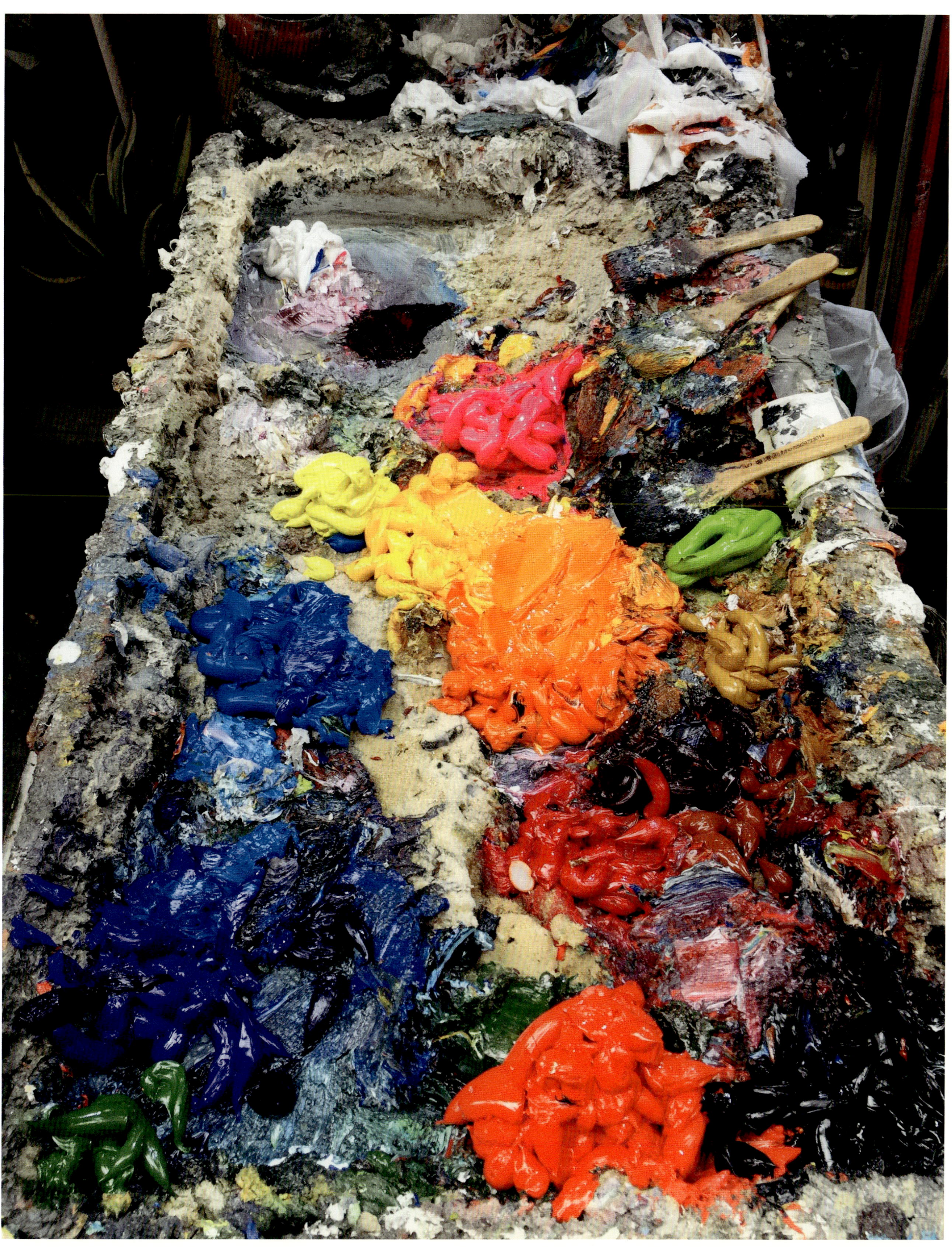

an 8-metre-long scroll painting, is titled *Rivers and Mountains Seen from a Distance* and is by Xia Gui.

In China today, one still encounters artists who combine the traditional painting technique with modern abstraction in contemporary Chinese ink painting. The colourful scene, however, predominates.

The Chinese art scene of the 21st century is incredibly creative, diverse and surprisingly expressive. There are no limits to the interpretations. Confucian and Taoist ideas also meet there in a figurative sense.

For thousands of years, colours in China have been much more than visual ornaments: they carry symbolic meaning. Even in modern China, the right choice of colour is crucial for a happy family life or success at work. The customs and rules to be observed are extensive and linked in a network that inevitably determines the fate of every Chinese child from birth. So it is not surprising that even in modern China the employer expects not only the best certificates from the prestigious elite universities of China, but also checks the date of birth of the job candidates and the resulting

Die chinesische Kunstszene des 21. Jahrhunderts ist äußerst kreativ, vielfältig und überraschend ausdrucksstark. Den Interpretationen sind keine Grenzen gesetzt. Konfuzianisches und taoistisches Gedankengut treffen im übertragenen Sinne auch dort aufeinander.

Farben sind in China seit Jahrtausenden weit mehr als optisches Schmuckwerk: Sie besitzen symbolische Bedeutung. Die richtige Farbwahl ist auch im modernen China entscheidend für ein glückliches Familienleben oder Erfolg in der Arbeit. Die Bräuche und Regeln, die es zu beachten gibt, sind umfangreich und in einem Netzwerk verknüpft, welches für jedes chinesische Kind ab Geburt unweigerlich schicksalsbestimmend ist. So ist es nicht verwunderlich, dass selbst im modernen China der Arbeitgeber nicht nur beste Zeugnisse der renommierten Elite-Universitäten Chinas erwartet, sondern auch das Geburtsdatum der Bewerbungskandidaten und das sich daraus ergebende astrologische Zeichen auf Tauglichkeit und Harmonie in der Zusammenarbeit überprüft. So kann der Ochse nicht mit der Schlange neue Wolkenkratzer planen und bauen. Dafür würden sie ein wunderbares Ehepaar abgeben, wenn beide im gleichen Jahr geboren wären. Diese Aufteilung macht vor nichts halt,

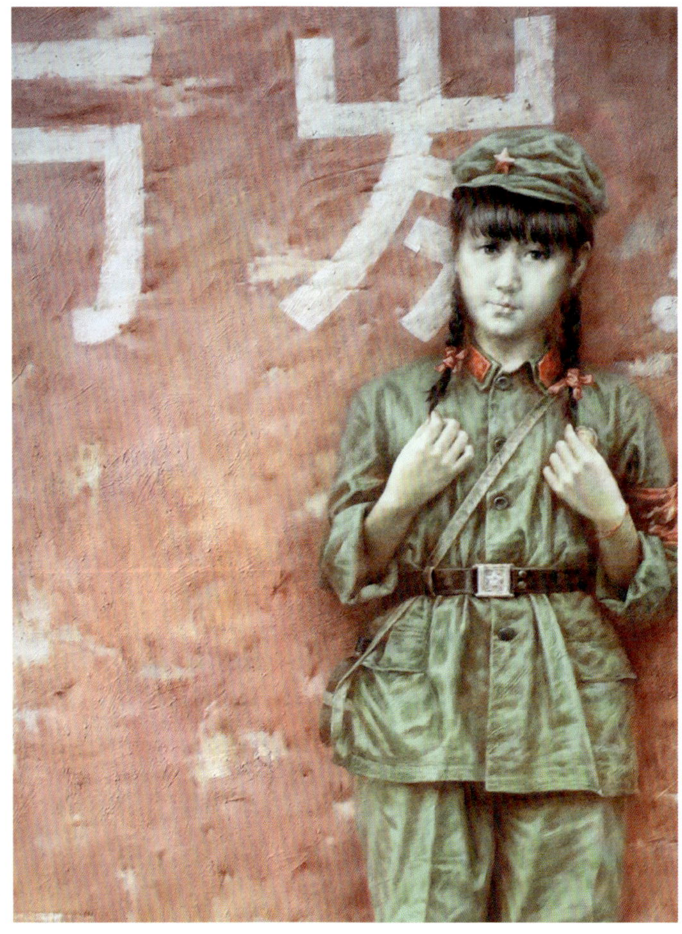

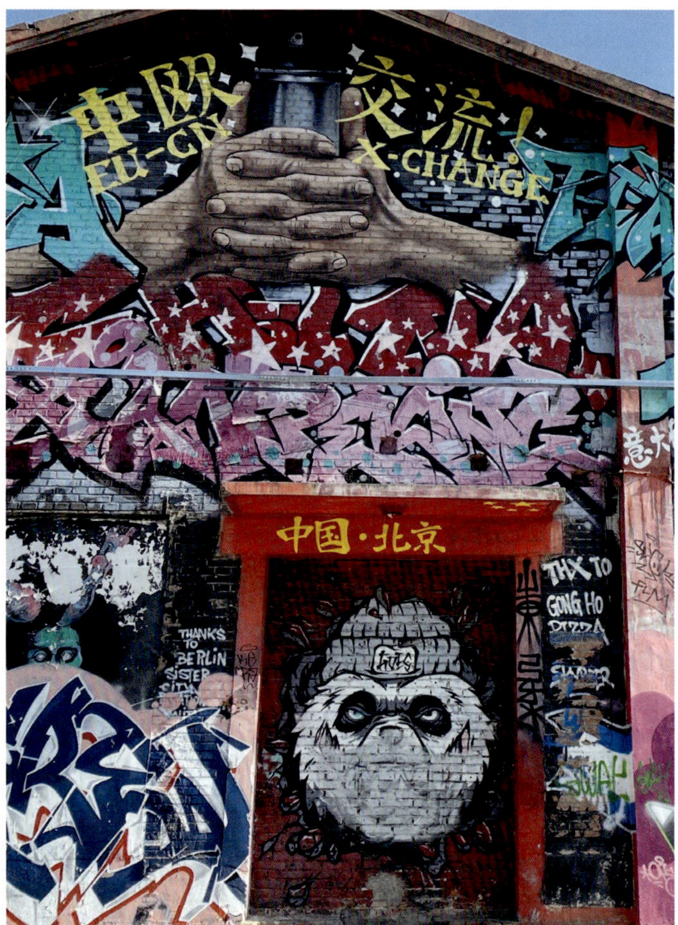

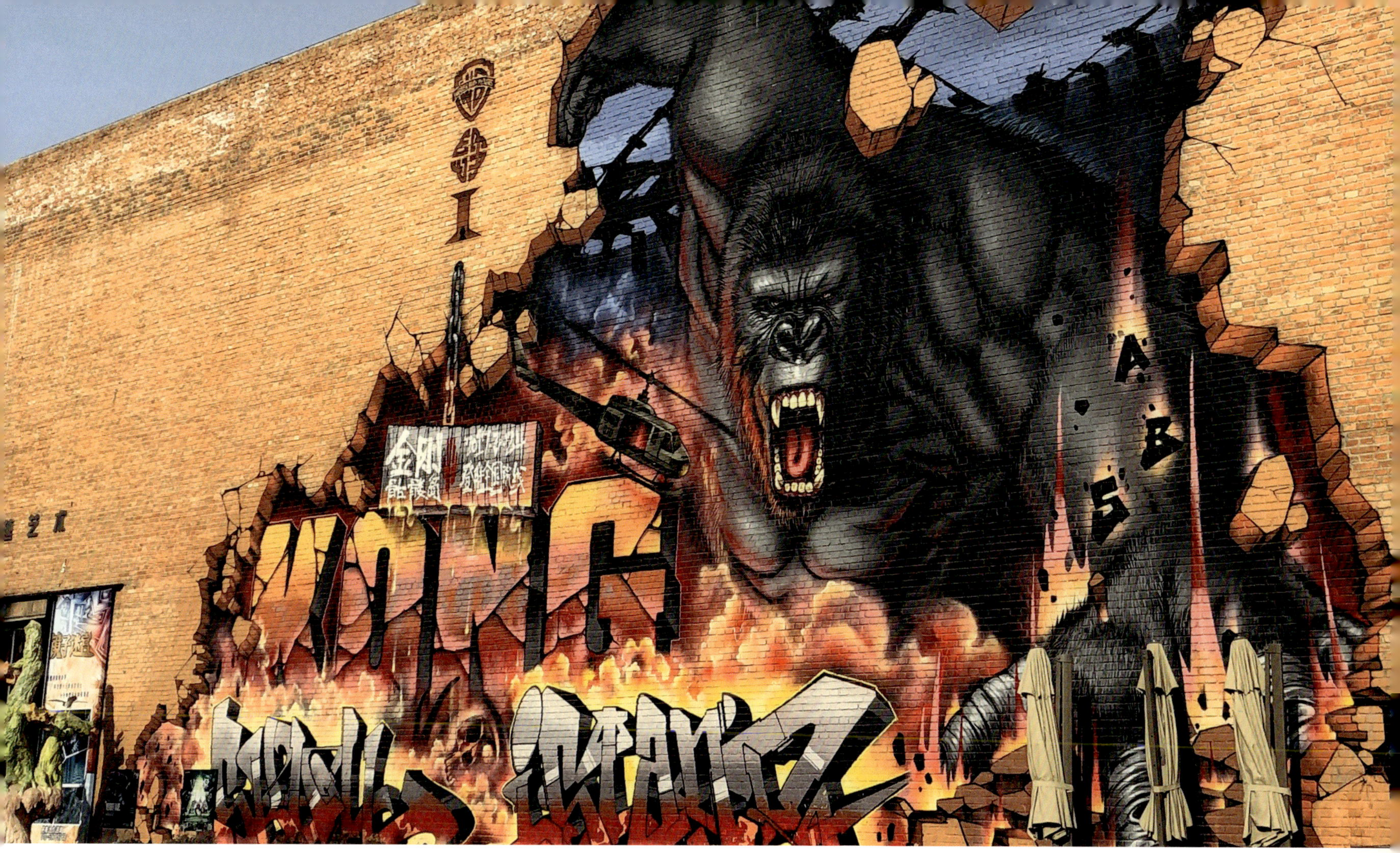

Left page and above:
Beijing is repeatedly and rightly declared to be an exciting art metropolis. However, the colourful street art murals are polarising. Modern art, Bauhaus architecture and many young people can be found in the so-called district 798.

Linke Seite und oben:
Peking wird zu Recht immer wieder als aufregende Kunstmetropole deklariert. Die bunten Street-Art-Murals polarisieren jedoch. Moderne Kunst, Bauhaus-Architektur und viele junge Leute trifft man im sogenannten Stadtteil 798.

astrological sign for suitability and harmony in the professional relationship. Thus, the ox cannot plan and build new skyscrapers with the snake. However, they would make a wonderful couple if both were born in the same year.

This division does not stop at anything, it includes all spheres of life. For example, it is advisable, if the year begins in the zodiac sign you embody yourself, to always protect yourself with red clothes, preferably red underwear. For this reason, in 2021 all-female or male oxen wear red knickers or red socks: This is supposed to avert misfortune and bring good luck.

sie umfasst alle Lebensbereiche. Beispielsweise ist anzuraten, falls das Jahr beginnt, dessen Tierkreiszeichen man selber verkörpert, sich immer mit roter Kleidung, bevorzugt roter Unterwäsche, zu schützen. Aus diesem Grund tragen 2021 alle weiblichen oder männlichen Ochsen rote Schlüpfer oder rote Socken: Das soll Unheil abwenden und Glück bringen.

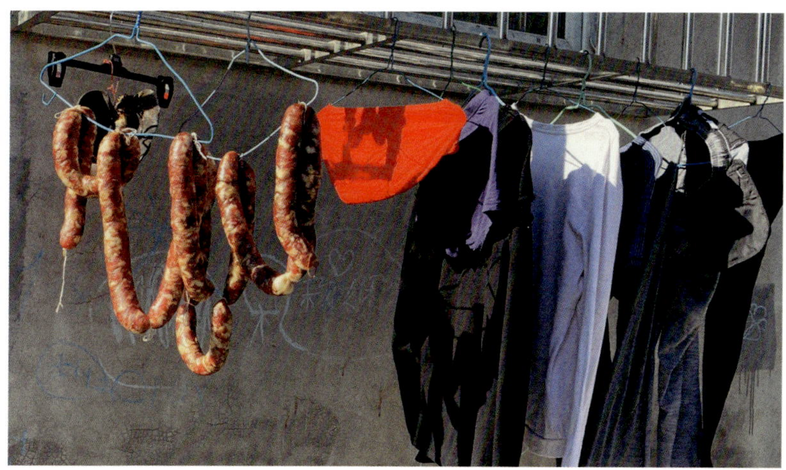

As soon as the late autumn temperatures no longer exceed the freezing point, the longtime residents of the *hutongs* hang up their homemade sausages to dry with the clothes on the clotheslines.

Sobald die Temperaturen im Spätherbst tagsüber nicht mehr über den Gefrierpunkt steigen, hängen die alteingesessenen Bewohner der *Hutongs* die selbstgemachten Würste zum Trocknen mit der Kleidung an die Wäscheleinen.

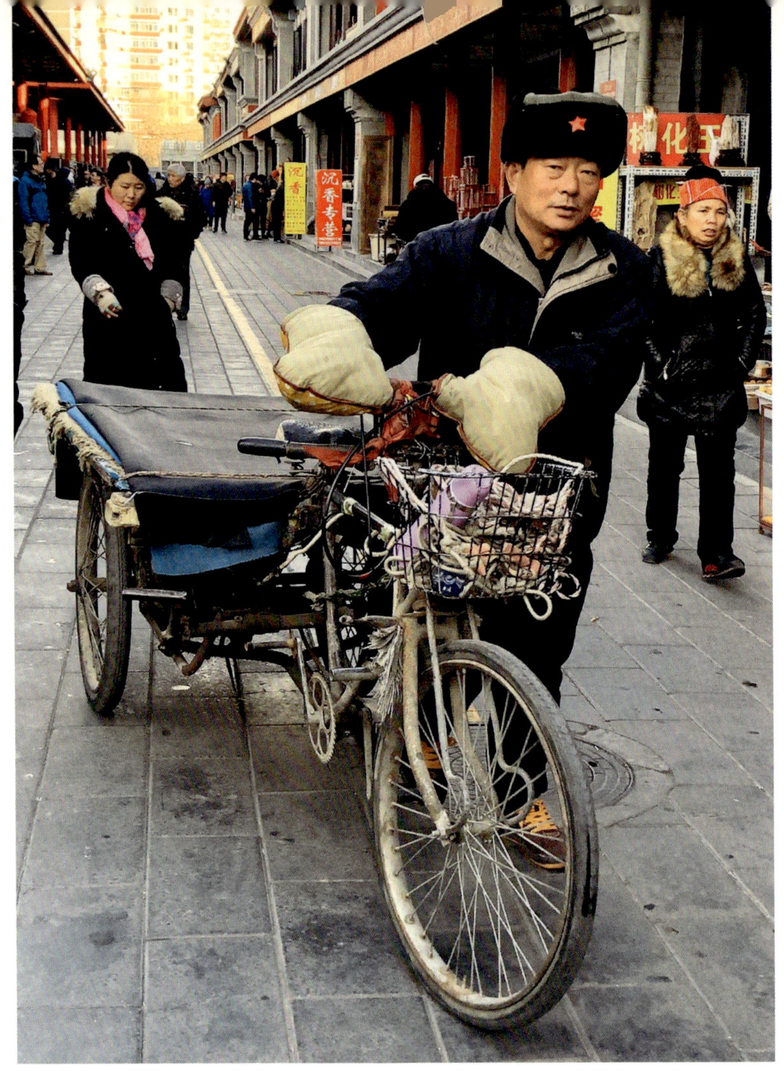

Despite the large ethnic diversity and economic inequality within the giant empire, the urban and rural population of China is a strong social and familiar network of customs and health-conscious behavior. Thus, people in the big city meet to play mah-jongg every evening just as the rice farmers meet in the village square and the *ayis*, literally meaning "aunties", dance in the light of the billboards or in traditional dress next to the tea fields. The colourful traditional costumes are worn with pride and handicrafts are still passed down from grandparents to the young every day.

Trotz der großen ethnischen Diversität und des wirtschaftlichen Ungleichgewichts innerhalb des Riesenreichs verbindet die urbane und ländliche Bevölkerung Chinas ein starkes soziales und familiäres Netz aus Gepflogenheiten und gesundheitsbewusstem Verhalten. So treffen sich die Menschen in der Großstadt zum allabendlichen Mah-Jongg-Spiel genauso wie die Reisbauern auf dem Dorfplatz und die *Ayis*, wortwörtlich „Tanten", tanzen im Licht der Werbetafeln oder in traditioneller Kleidung neben den Teefeldern. Die bunten Trachten werden mit Stolz getragen und Handwerkskunst noch tagtäglich von den Großeltern an die Jungen weitergegeben.

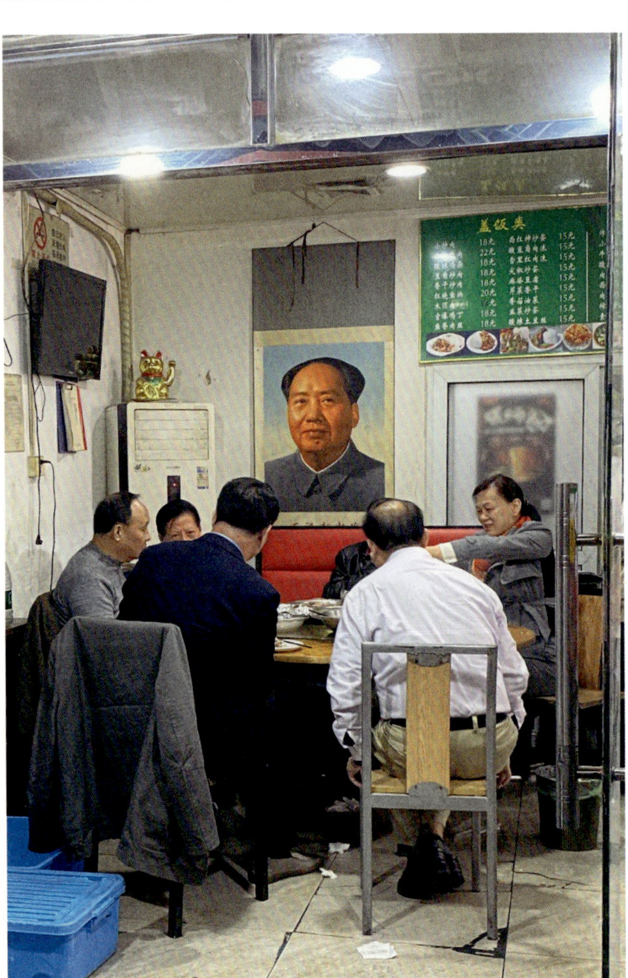

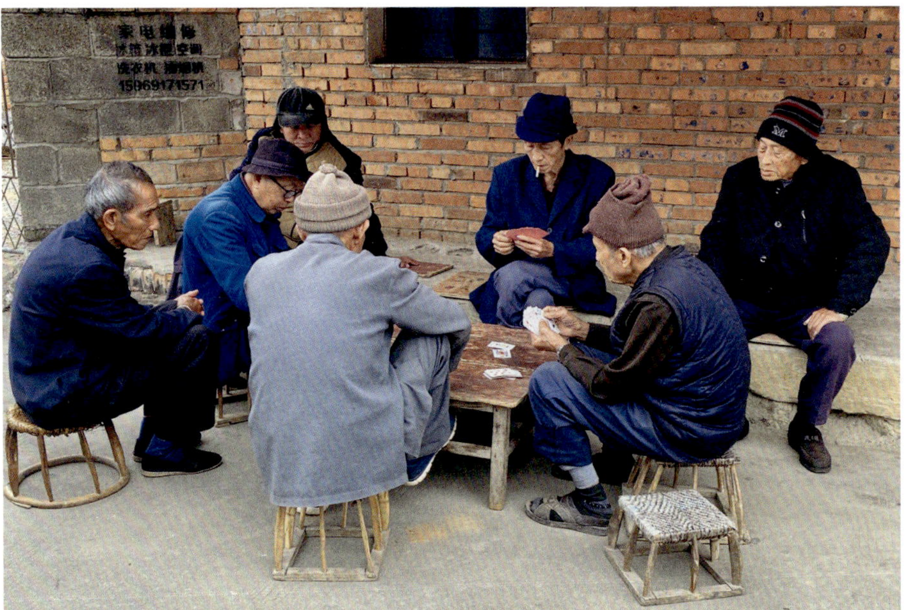

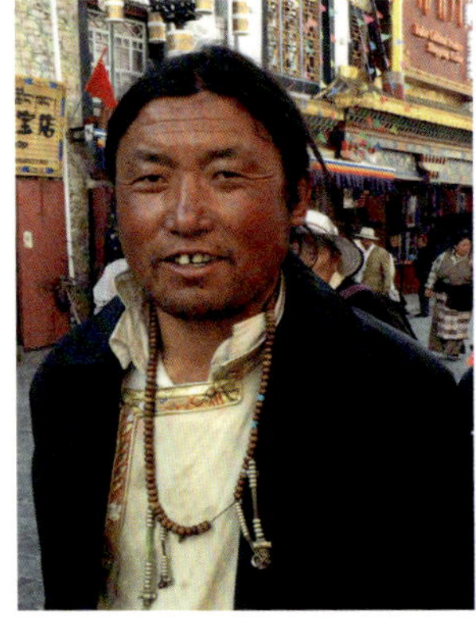

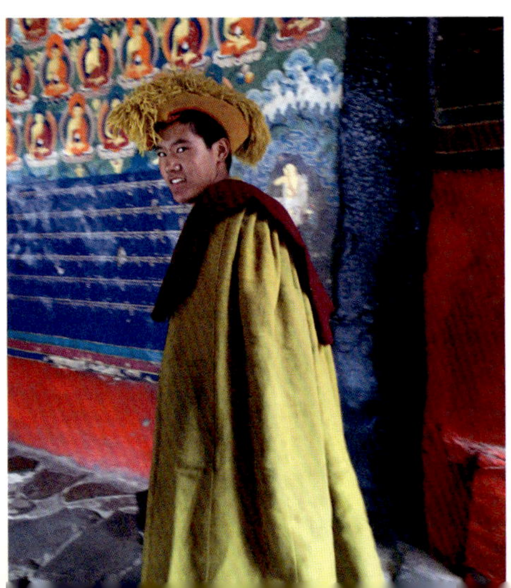

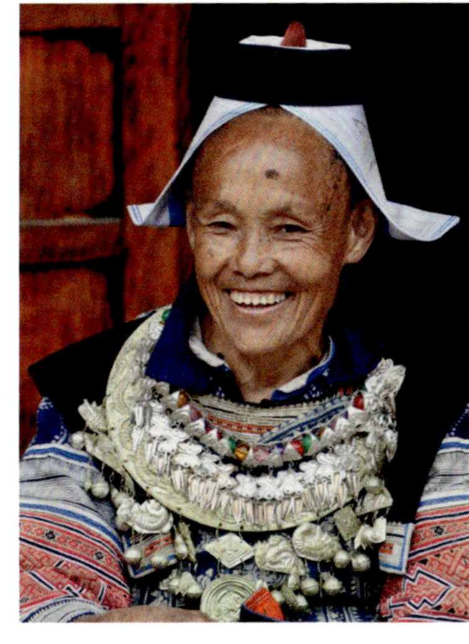

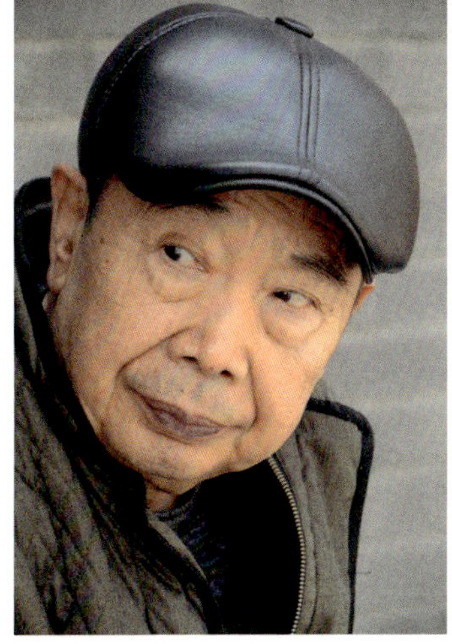

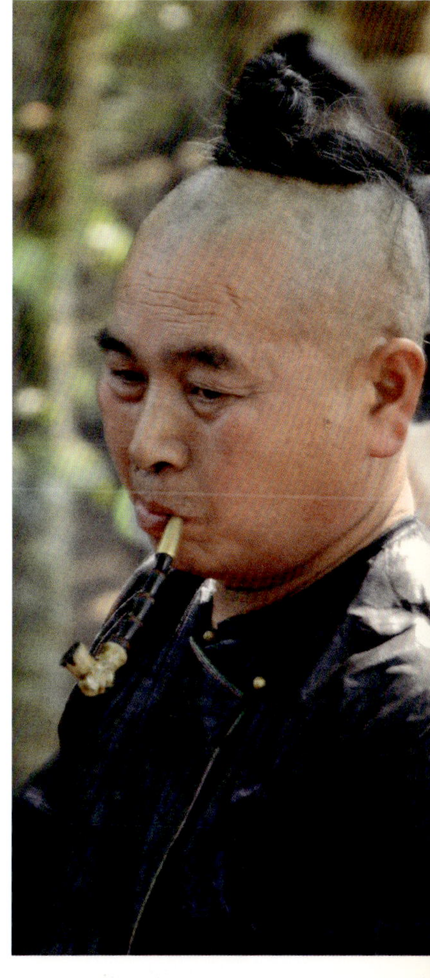

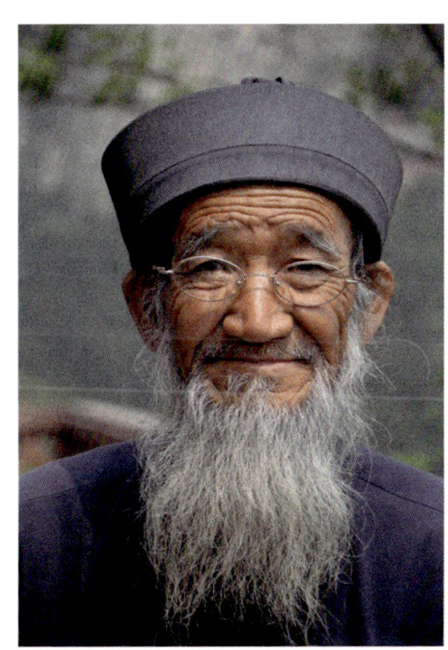

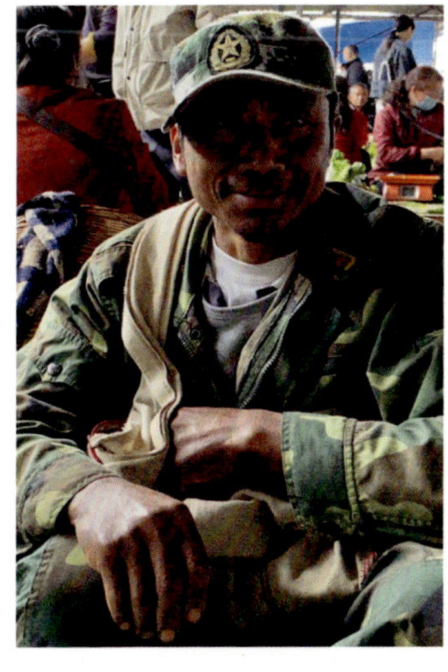

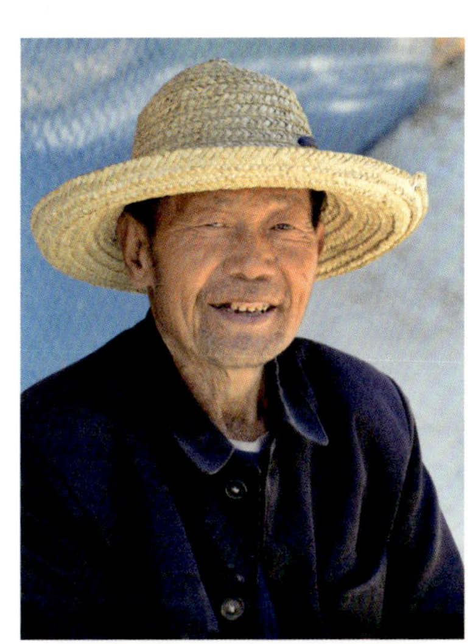

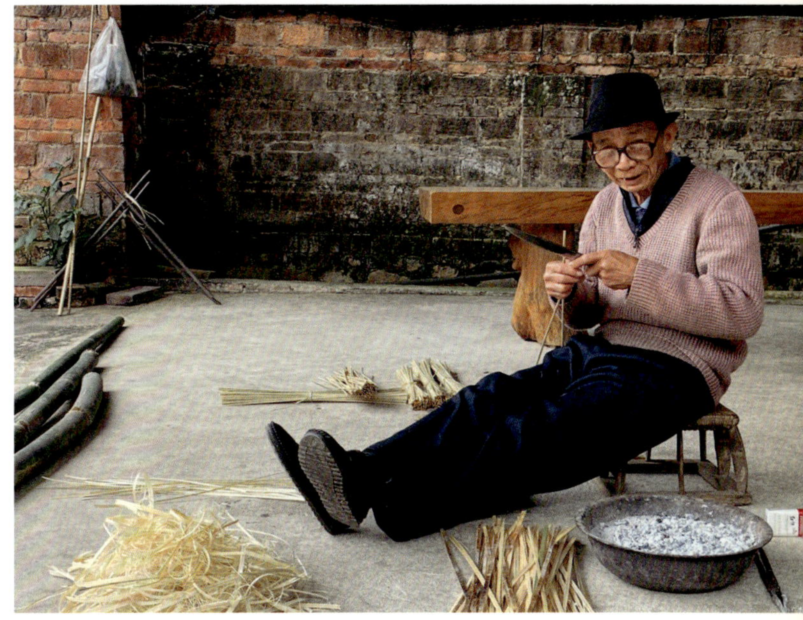

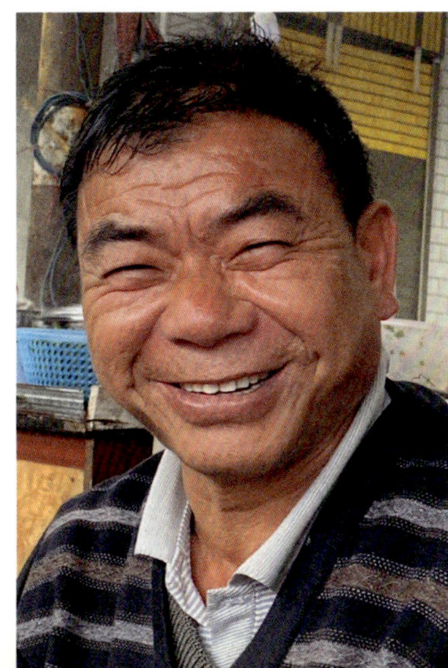

Symbolism and the force of colours
Symbolik und Macht der Farben

According to the Chinese, colours represent energies, cosmic cycles, dynasties, deities or planets. For this reason, colour glazes on ancient Chinese ceramics or on roof tiles often have deeper meanings. They may indicate the function of an object, limit its range of users, or represent a philosophical idea.

The evocative colour messages were directed at the human observer, but often they were also intended for the gods. Each Chinese imperial dynasty chose one of the five elements and thus also a colour as its dynastic symbol. Many official porcelains from the Yuan (white), Ming and Qing (yellow) dynasties were therefore glazed in their dynastic colours. The ceremonial robe also always corresponded to the colour of the porcelain used.

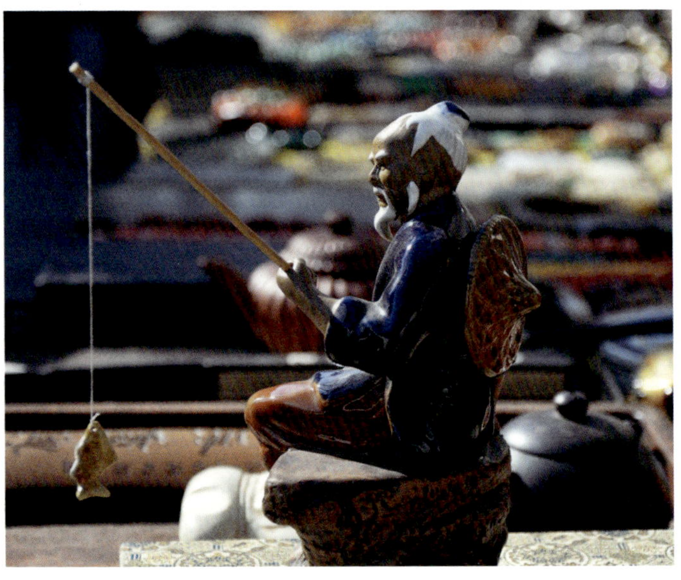

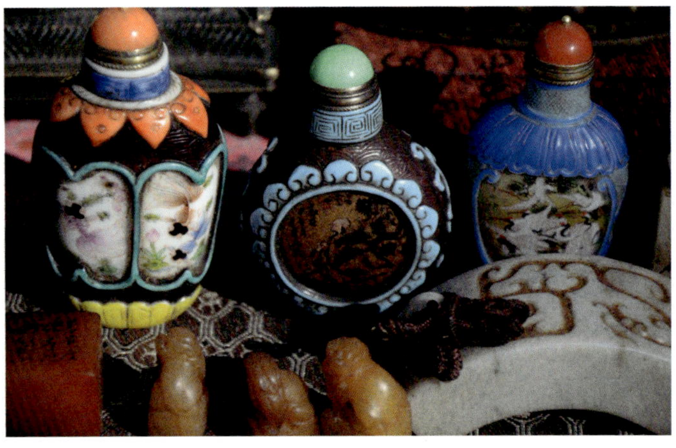

Since the Zhou Dynasty (ca. 1100–256 BC) or the Qin Dynasty (221–207 BC), there is still disagreement in scientific circles about the existence of strict official guidelines for the use of colours. Colours were divided into five main and five intermediate colours. Besides the five main colours green, white, red, black and yellow, as described in the *Yellow*

Above and left page:
The antique markets of the villages and cities are colourful treasure troves for collectors – they are filled with little particularities that tell about the country and its people. For example, the old snuff tobacco bottles, which are painted from the inside, or old badges, witnesses of younger periods of China's history.

Oben und linke Seite:
Die Antikmärkte der Dörfer und Städte sind bunte Fundgruben für Sammler kleiner Besonderheiten, die von Land und Leute erzählen. So zum Beispiel die meist kunstfertig von innen bemalten Schnupftabakfläschchen oder alte Anstecknadeln, Zeitzeugen der jüngeren Geschichte Chinas.

Die Farben repräsentieren nach dem Verständnis der Chinesen Energien, kosmische Zyklen, Dynastien, Gottheiten oder Planeten. Aus diesem Grunde besitzen auch Farbglasuren auf alter chinesischer Keramik oder auf Dachziegeln oft tiefere Bedeutungsinhalte. Sie konnten die Funktion eines Objekts anzeigen, seinen Benutzerkreis einschränken oder eine philosophische Vorstellung repräsentieren. Die suggestiven Farbbotschaften richteten sich an den menschlichen Betrachter, oft waren sie aber auch für die Götter bestimmt. Jede chinesische Kaiserdynastie wählte eines der fünf Elemente und damit auch eine Farbe als ihr dynastisches Symbol. Viele offizielle Porzellane aus der Yuan- (Weiß), Ming- und Qing-Dynastien (Gelb) wurden daher in deren dynastischen Farben glasiert. Auch das Zeremonialgewand entsprach stets der Farbe des verwendeten Porzellans.

Seit der Zhou-Dynastie (ca. 1100–256 v. Chr.) oder der Qin-Dynastie (221–207 v. Chr.), darüber ist man sich in wissenschaftlichen Kreisen noch nicht einig, bestehen für den Umgang mit Farben strenge offizielle Richtlinien. Die Farben wurden in fünf Haupt- und fünf Zwischenfarben eingeteilt. Neben denen im *Klassiker des Gelben Kaisers zur Inneren Medizin* beschriebenen fünf Hauptfarben Grün, Weiß, Rot, Schwarz und Gelb liegen Zwischenfarben wie Rosa oder Blauviolett. Der *Klassiker des Gelben Kaisers zur Inneren Medizin* ist eines der ältesten Standardwerke der chinesischen Medizin und bis heute grundlegend und richtungsweisend für die

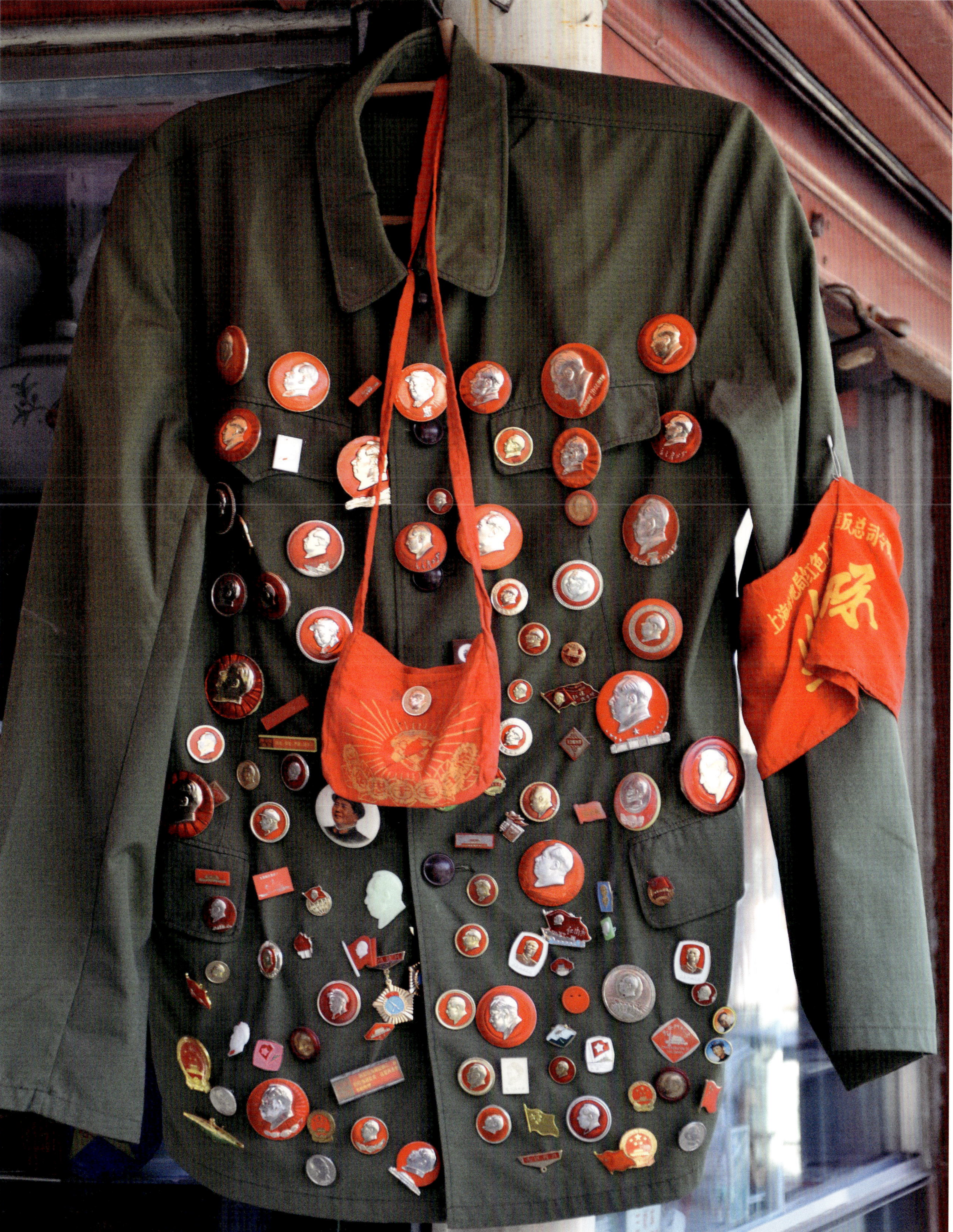

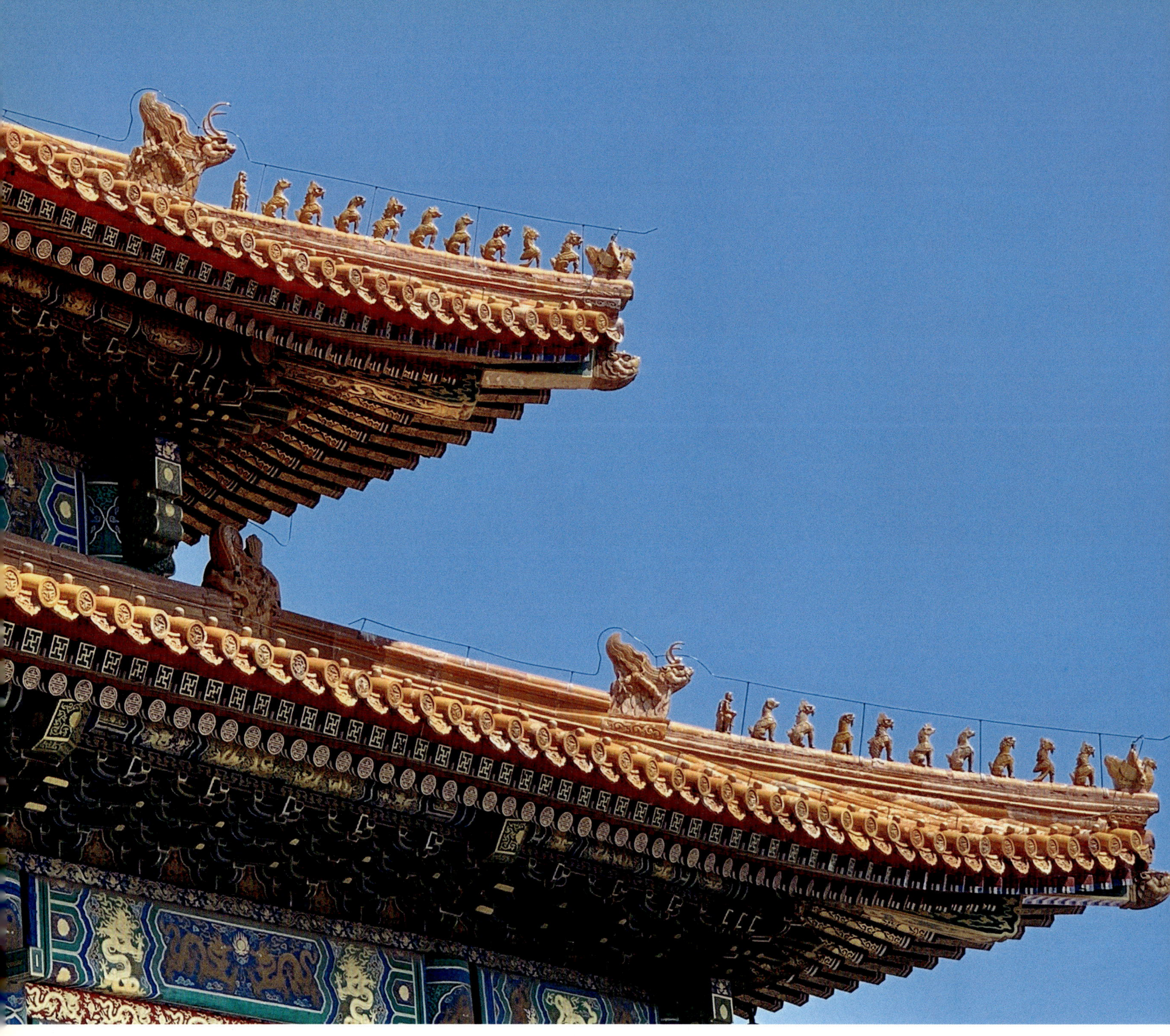

Many of the ridges and arched roofs bear figurative decorations, usually made of glazed ceramics. Often the ends of the ridge are occupied by dragons. This has been taken to mean protection from lightning. However, the most trusted were the rows of small figures running on the ridge of the rafters, made of fired and glazed clay to represent mythical creatures or real animals.

The higher a building is estimated in its spiritual value, the greater the number of figures. On the Hall of Supreme Harmony in the Forbidden City in Beijing, the number of twelve is the highest possible. However, the furthest figure is modeled after a historical model: Prince Min Qi (479–502) who was notorious for cowardice, riding a hen. When his subjects were threatened in a war, he abandoned them and fled.

Viele der Firste und geschwungenen Dächer tragen figuralen Schmuck, der meist aus glasierter Keramik besteht. Oft werden die Enden des Firstes von Drachen eingenommen. Das ist als Schutz vor Blitzen gedeutet worden. Am meisten vertraute man aber den Reihen von kleinen, aus Ton gebrannten oder glasierten mythischen Wesen oder Tierfiguren, die auf dem Dachfirst sitzen.

Je höher ein Gebäude in seinem spirituellen Wert eingeschätzt wird, desto größer ist die Zahl der Figuren. Auf der Halle der Höchsten Harmonie in der Verbotenen Stadt in Peking ist mit zwölf an der Zahl die höchstmögliche erreicht. Ganz außen findet sich eine historische Figur: Prinz Min Qi (479–502). Weil er seine Untertanen im Krieg im Stich gelassen hatte, wurde er als Feigling dargestellt, der auf einer Henne reitet.

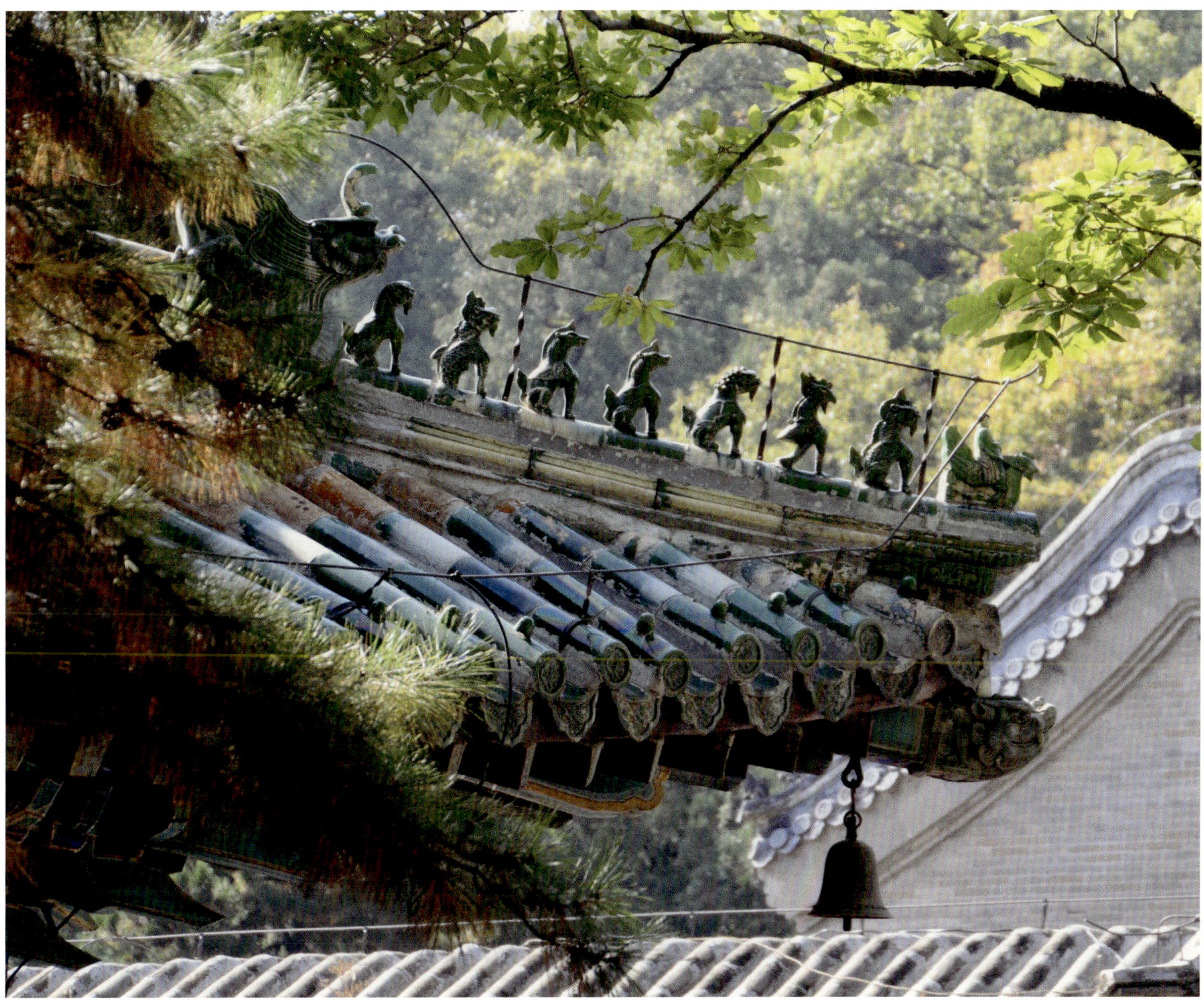

Emperor's Classic Work on Internal Medicine, there are intermediate hues such as pink or blue-violet. The *Yellow Emperor's Classic Work on Internal Medicine* is one of the oldest standard works of Chinese medicine and is still fundamental, shaping the direction of education within this discipline. The Yellow Emperor himself, Huangdi, and his master, Qibo, are known as the authors.

The bible of Confucianism, the *Book of Rites*, prescribes main colours for the upper garment and intermediate colours for the skirt with regard to clothing. Thus, the general perception of colours was strongly influenced. The *Book of Rites* is one of the five classics attributed to Confucius. In it, social behaviours and court ceremonies are described.

During the Sui (581–618) and Tang (618–907) dynasties, red and purple robes were reserved for high officials, and

Ausbildung innerhalb dieser Disziplin. Der Gelbe Kaiser selbst, Huangdi, und sein Meister Qi Bo sind als Verfasser bekannt.

Die konfuzianische „Bibel", das *Buch der Riten*, schreibt bezüglich der Bekleidung Hauptfarben für das Oberteil und Zwischenfarben für den Rock vor. So wurde das allgemeine Farbempfinden stark beeinflusst. Das *Buch der Riten* ist einer der fünf Klassiker, die Konfuzius zugeschrieben werden. Darin werden soziale Verhaltensweisen und Hofzeremonien beschrieben.

Während der Sui-Dynastie (581–618) und der Tang-Dynastie (618–907) waren rote und violette Gewänder hohen Beamten vorbehalten, und in rötliches Gelb durfte sich allein der Kaiser kleiden. Gewöhnliche Menschen hatten sich mit Weiß oder Ocker zu begnügen. Rot als Symbol von Feuer

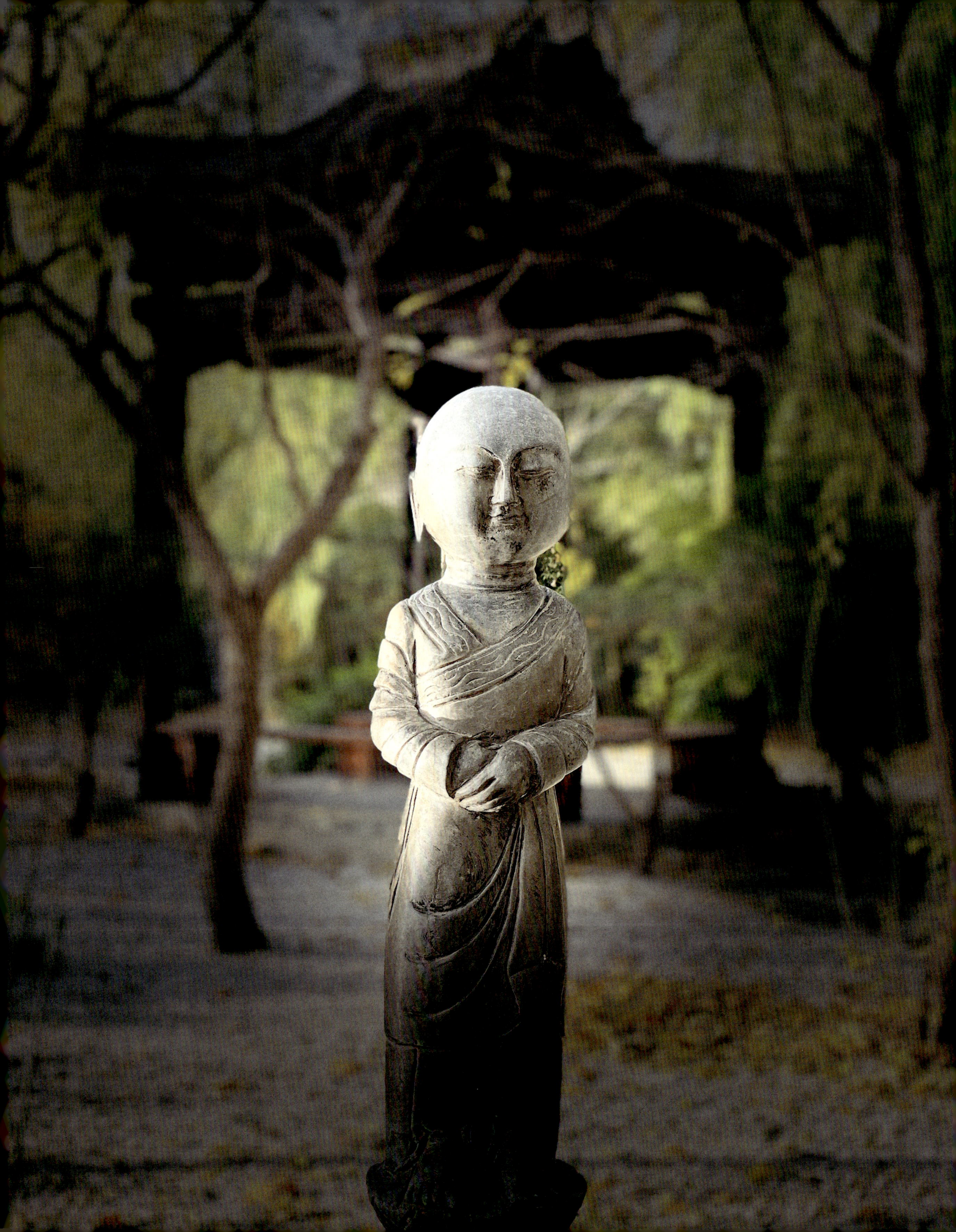

only the emperor was allowed to dress in reddish yellow. Ordinary people had to make do with white or ochre. Red, as a symbol of fire and colour to drive away baleful influences, was only allowed to be used at weddings and festivities. That is why it is said that the typical China red is still so popular throughout the country today.

In contrast, Chinese writers cultivated an aesthetics of simplicity. At the latest in the Song Dynasty (960–1279) the literati practiced modest restraint apart from the official offices and especially appreciated the unedited and simple. These inclinations, combined with a dismissal of the colourful cheerfulness of the lower classes, also had to do with the constant reinforcement of the imperial exercise of power and the ensuing, ever stricter regulation of the use of colours.

In 1759, Emperor Qianlong had the colour and shape of the ritual porcelains for the state stamps specified in an official set of rules. Thus, a concubine could rise in the emperor's favour by bearing a son and thus also rise in the harem hierarchy. From then on, and thus for all to see, she was allowed to eat her rice from bowls colour-coded as "higher-ranking".

Only the emperor, the empress and the empress widow (his mother) were allowed to dine from completely yellow-glazed bowls. The higher the rank of a wife, the closer the dishes were to the elevated throne where the emperor dined alone under the plaque reading "The Great Righteous Shine Bright!", *Zhen da guang ming*.

It was not until the fall of the Qing Dynasty (1644–1911) that colour regulations were completely abolished. Colour was no longer associated with hierarchy of rank, but became an object of personal preference. It was only since this time that the popular use of colour and colour combinations could develop independently and enrich itself anew. After the proclamation of the People's Republic, the revolutionaries made use of the old culture of colour assignment to visibly attract broad masses.

In the magical, park-like garden of the Green T. House in Beijing, the smiling stone statue welcomes visitors right in front of the inviting, historic wooden pavilion.

Die lächelnde Steinstatue empfängt im bezaubernden parkähnlichen Garten des Green T. House in Peking die Gäste direkt vor dem einladenden historischen Holzpavillon.

und Farbe zum Vertreiben unheilvoller Einflüsse durfte nur zu Hochzeiten und Festlichkeiten verwendet werden. Deshalb, sagt man, ist das typische China-Rot auch heute noch landesweit so beliebt.

Im Gegensatz dazu pflegten die chinesischen Literaten eine Ästhetik der Schlichtheit. Spätestens ab der Song-Dynastie (960–1279) übten sich die Literaten im Abseits der offiziellen Ämter in bescheidener Zurückhaltung und schätzten besonders das Unbearbeitete und Schlichte. Diese Neigungen, verbunden mit einer Ablehnung der buntfröhlichen Farbigkeit niederer Volksschichten, hatte auch mit der stetigen Verstärkung der kaiserlichen Machtausübung und der damit einhergehenden, immer strenger werdenden Regulierung im Umgang mit Farben zu tun.

Kaiser Qianlong ließ 1759 die Farb- und Formgebungen der Ritualporzellane für die Staatstempel in einem offiziellen Regelwerk festhalten. So konnte eine Konkubine durch die Geburt eines Sohnes in der Gunst des Kaisers aufsteigen und somit auch in der Haremshierarchie. Sie durfte von nun an, und damit für alle sichtbar, ihren Reis aus farblich als „höherrangig" gekennzeichneten Schälchen essen.

Nur der Kaiser, die Kaiserin und die Kaiserinwitwe (seine Mutter) durften von vollständig gelbglasierten Schalen speisen. Je höher der Rang einer Gemahlin, desto näher standen die Speisen am erhöhten Thron, wo der Kaiser alleine unter der Plakette mit der Aufschrift „Der große Rechtschaffene erstrahle hell!", *Zhen da guang ming*, speiste.

Erst mit dem Sturz der Qing-Dynastie (1644–1911) wurden die farblichen Vorschriften gänzlich aufgehoben. Farbe war nicht länger mit Ranghierarchie verbunden, sondern wurde zum Gegenstand persönlicher Vorliebe. Erst seit diesem Zeitpunkt konnte sich der volkstümliche Umgang mit Farbe und Farbkombinationen selbstständig entwickeln und neu bereichern.

Nach der Ausrufung der Volksrepublik bedienten sich die Revolutionäre der alten Kultur der Farbzuweisung, um breite Massen sichtbar an sich zu binden.

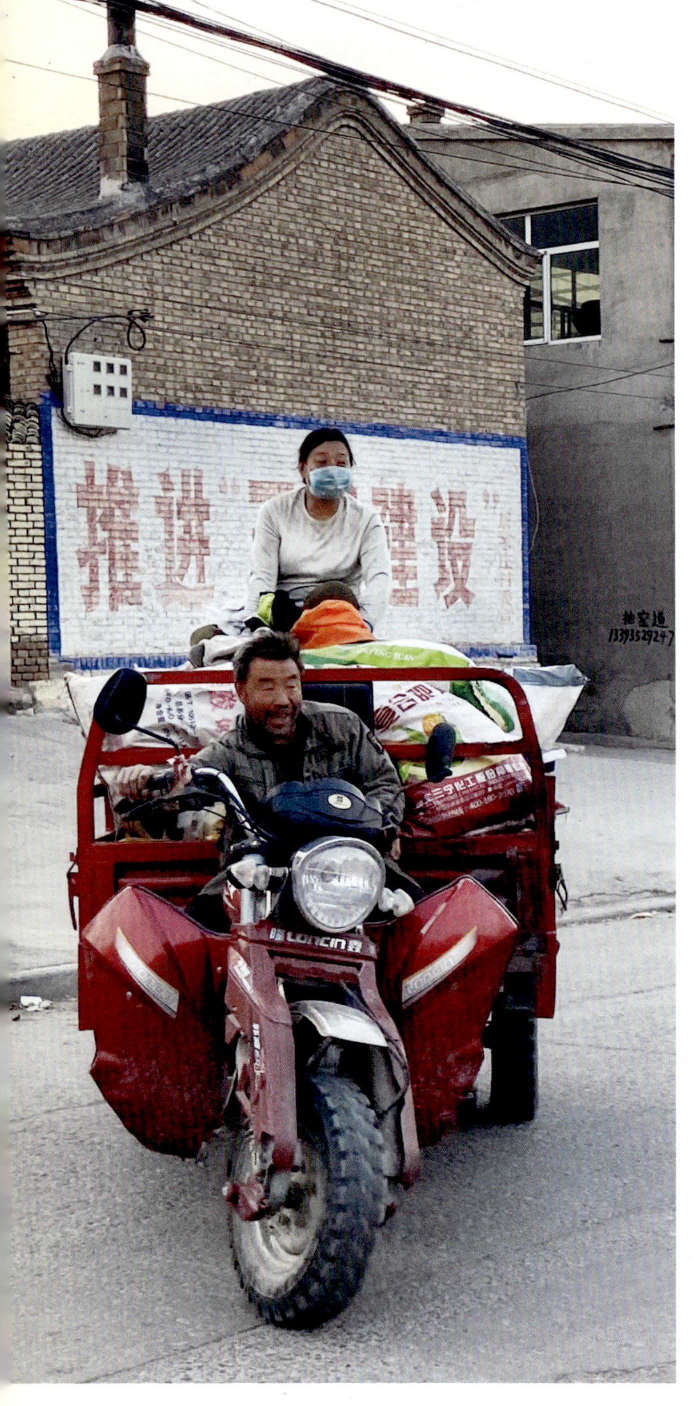

推进
建设
13393529247
LONCIN

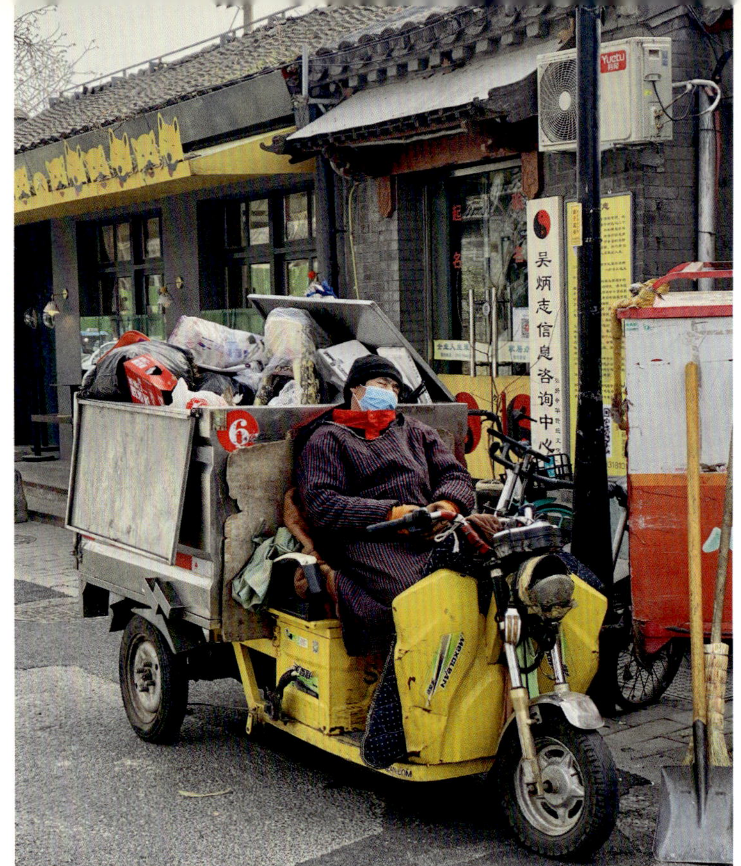

吴炳志信息咨询中心

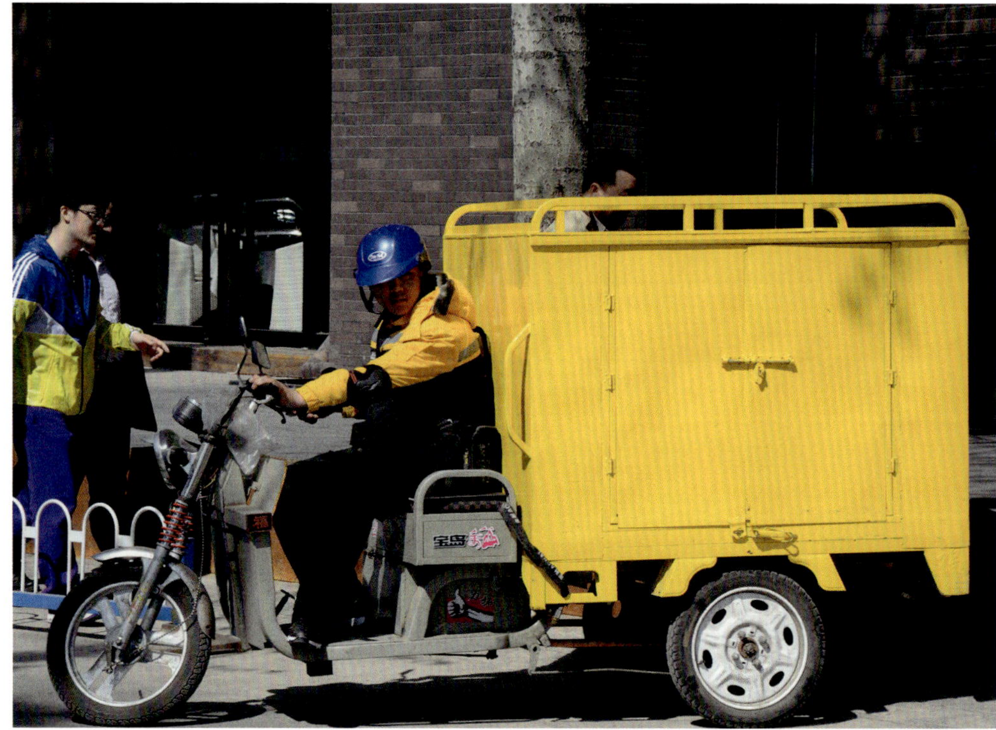

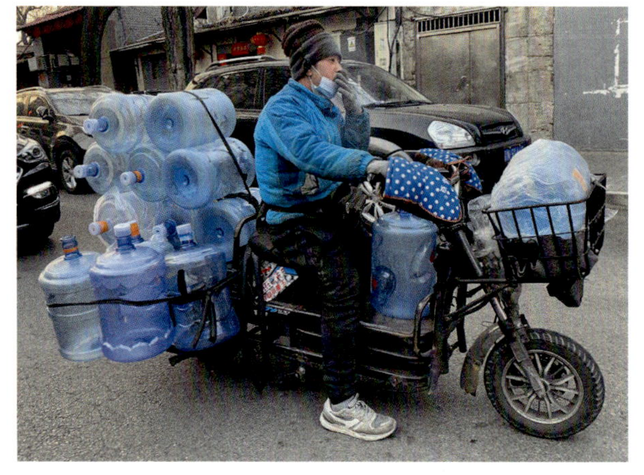

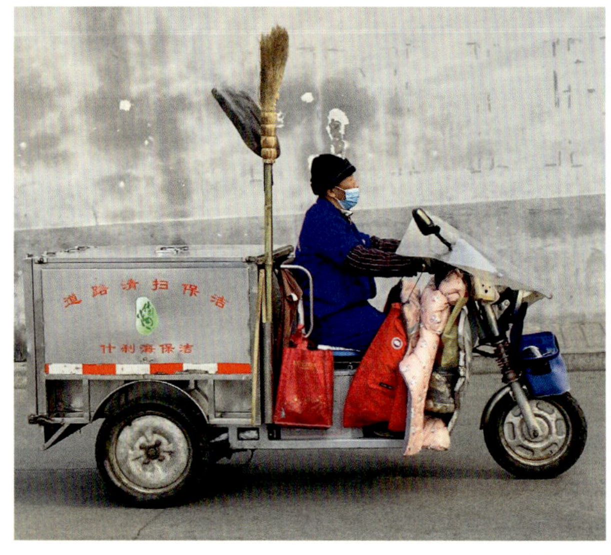

道路清扫保洁
什刹海保洁

The creative variety of three-wheeled, mostly electric vehicles for transporting people and goods is abundant. Officially, these means of transportation, which are ideally suited for the narrow alleys of the *hutongs*, are only permitted in the city for professional purposes.

Die kreative Vielfalt an dreirädrigen, meist elektrischen Fahrzeugen zum Transport von Menschen und Waren ist überbordend. Offiziell zugelassen sind diese für die schmalen Gassen der *Hutongs* bestens geeigneten Fortbewegungsmittel in der Großstadt nur noch zum Ausüben einer beruflichen Tätigkeit.

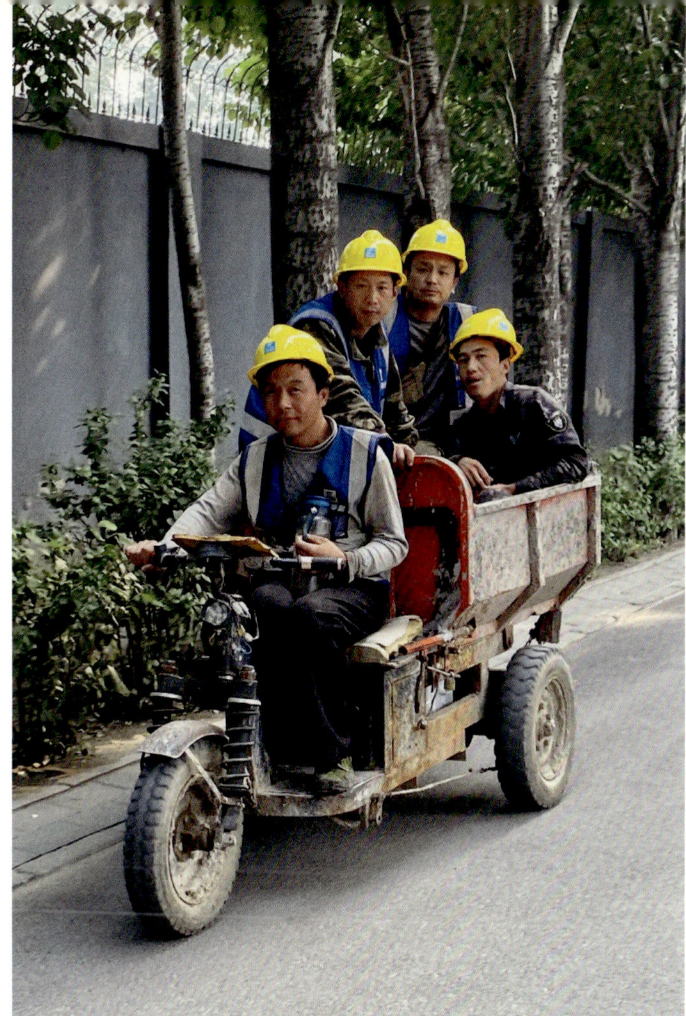

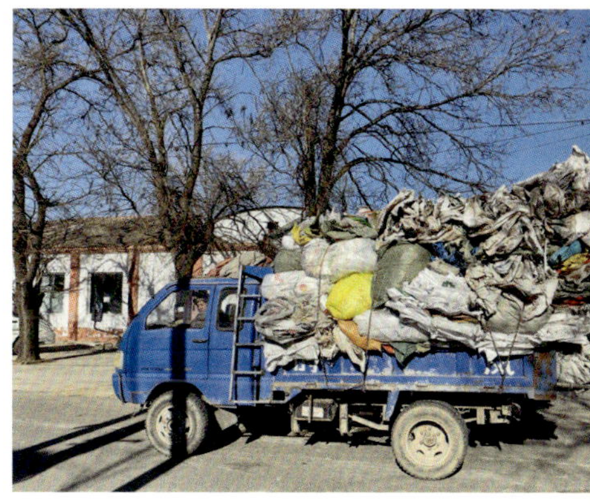

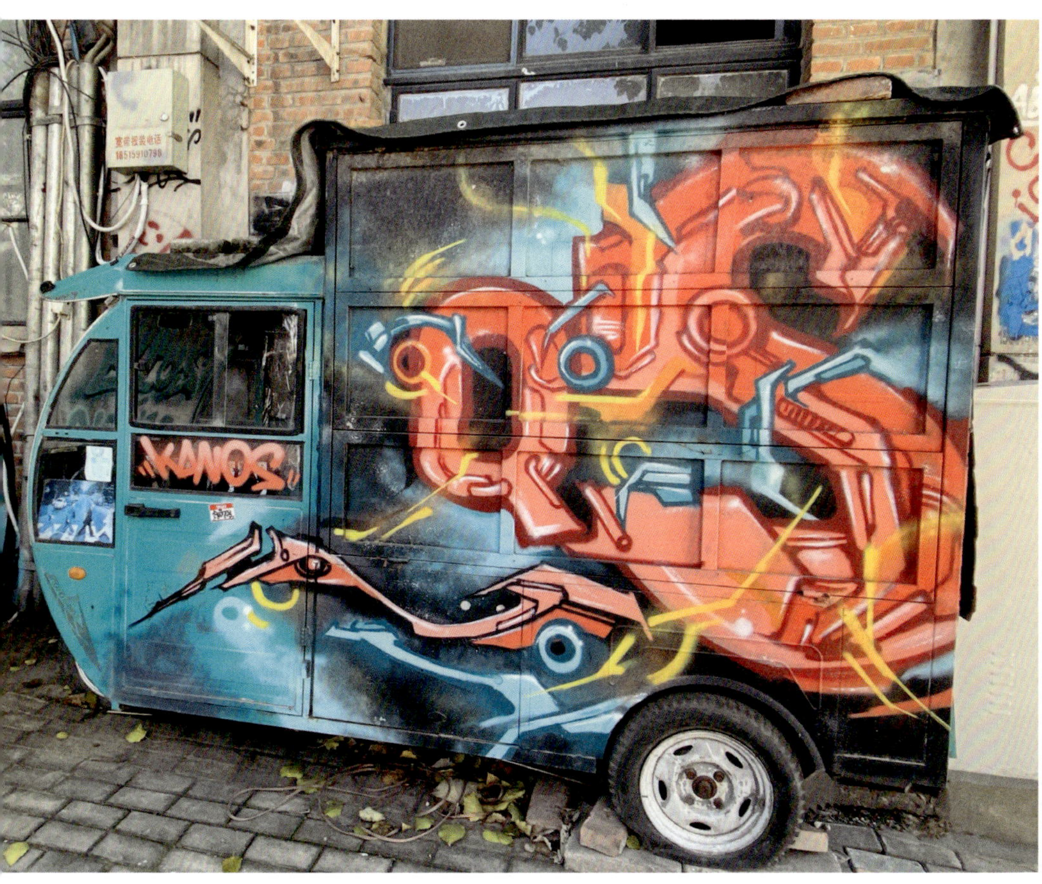

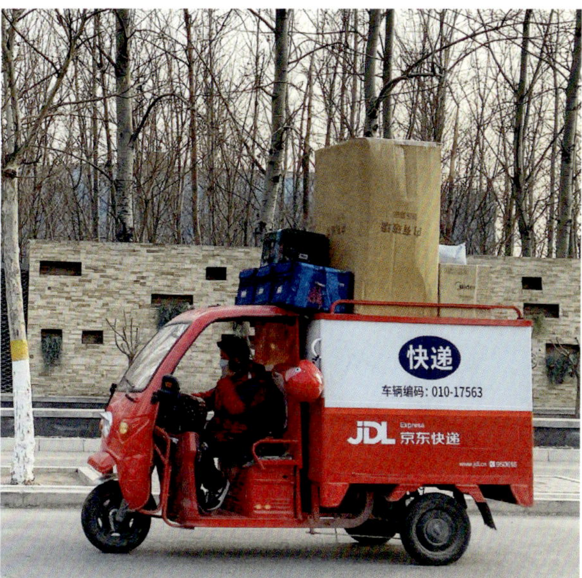

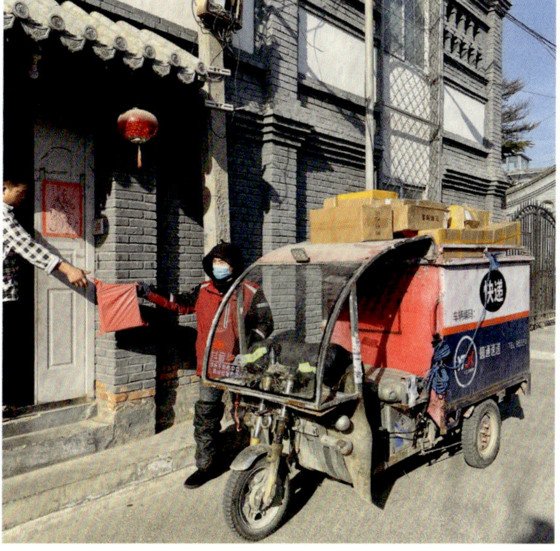

The grey masses
Von grauen Massen

Colour as an accompanying means of ideological leadership did not only exist in China, however. In England, King Richard I passed a law in 1197 forbidding ordinary people under penalty of law to wear any colour other than grey. In 2008, shortly before the Olympic Games in China, all residents of *hutongs* (traditional old city residential districts with single-story houses in central Beijing) were given a bucket of grey wall paint so that they could spruce up their houses in a uniform manner befitting their status.

The sand-coloured grey of the roof tiles, carried by the anthracite concrete of the house's walls, and occasionally shade-giving, rich green treetops, still characterises the bird's eye view of the city in Beijing's summertime.

In autumn, the grey cityscape is crowned by the vibrant, imperial yellow of the towering, old ginkgo trees in the narrow alleys, courtyards or parks.

Farbe als begleitendes oder unterstützendes Mittel ideologischer Führung gab es aber nicht nur in China. In England erließ König Richard I. im Jahre 1197 ein Gesetz, das einfachen Leuten bei Strafe verbot, irgendeine andere Farbe als Grau zu tragen. 2008, kurz vor den Olympischen Spielen in China, erhielten alle Einwohner der *Hutongs* (traditionelle Altstadtwohnviertel mit einstöckigen Häusern im Zentrum Pekings) einen Eimer grauer Wandfarbe, damit sie ihre Häuser einheitlich und standesgerecht herausputzen konnten.

Das sandige Grau der Dachziegel, getragen vom Anthrazitton der Hauswände, und zwischendurch vereinzelt schattenspendende, satt-grüne Baumkronen, das war und ist im Sommer die Vogelperspektive in Pekings Altstadtkern.

Gekrönt wird das Grau in Grau im Herbst vom leuchtenden kaiserlichen Gelb der großen alten Ginkgo-Bäume in den schmalen Gassen, Innenhöfen oder Parkanlagen.

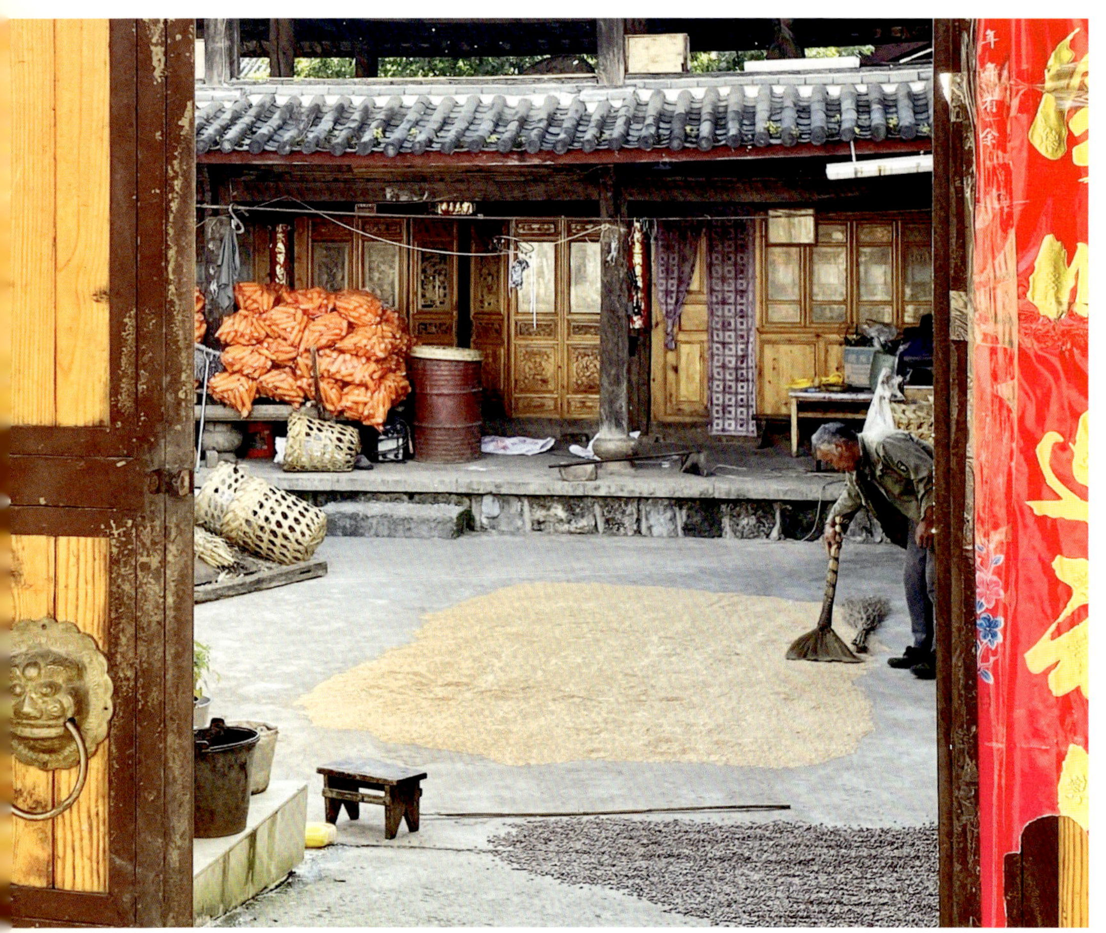

Inside his courtyard in Lijiang, an old man carefully spreads the yellow corn grains with a broom to dry in the warming autumn sunshine. The carrots are already stacked close to the house under the canopy, in front of them the large self-woven harvest baskets. The red-brown beans are spread out directly at the entrance, also for winter stocking.

Im Inneren seines Hofes in Lijiang verteilt ein alter Mann in der wärmenden Herbstsonne sorgfältig mit dem Reisigbesen die gelben Maiskörner zum Trocknen. Die Möhren liegen dicht am Haus unter dem Vordach gestapelt, davor große selbstgeflochtene Erntekörbe. Direkt am Hauseingang sind rot-braune Bohnen ausgebreitet, ebenfalls zur Winterbevorratung.

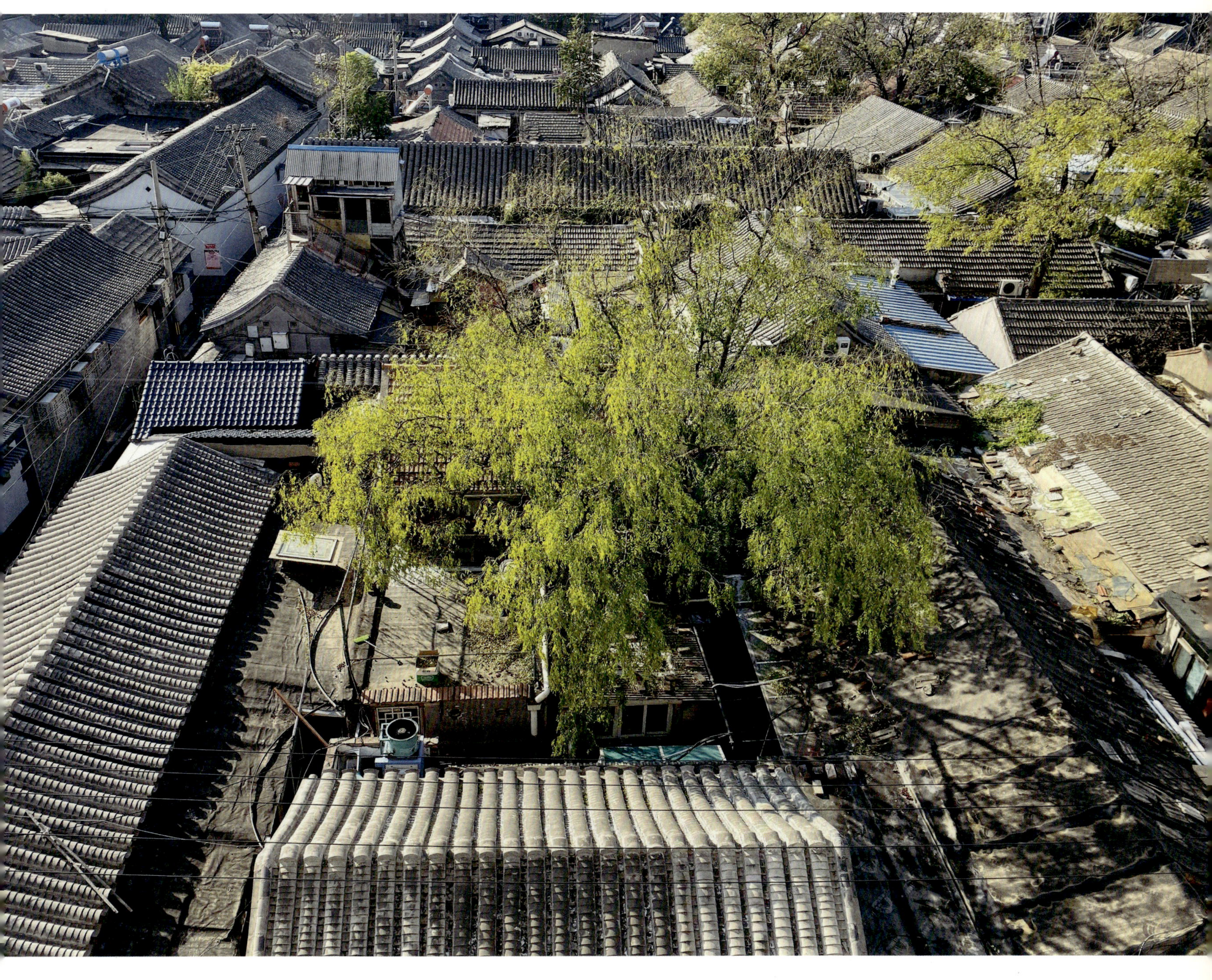

A bird's eye view of the *hutongs* reveals that the once airy courtyards of the traditional *siheyuan* four-sided courtyard houses generally still have the usual tree but have unfortunately been built over due to the housing shortage.

Die Vogelperspektive auf die *Hutongs* lässt erkennen, dass die ehemals luftigen Innenhöfe der traditionellen *Siheyuan*-Vierseithofhäuser meist noch den üblichen Baum aufweisen aber bedauerlicherweise aufgrund der Wohnungsnot zugebaut wurden.

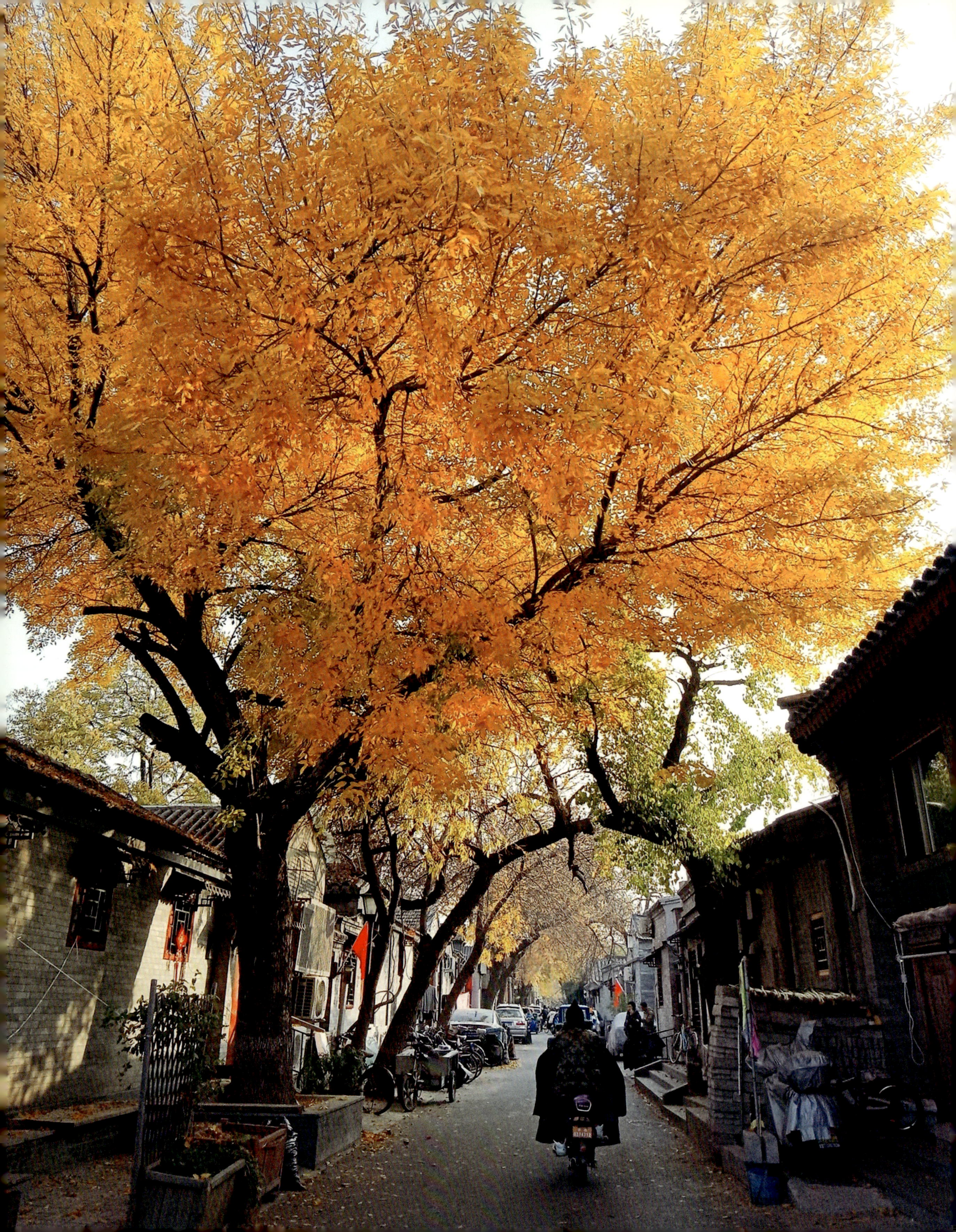

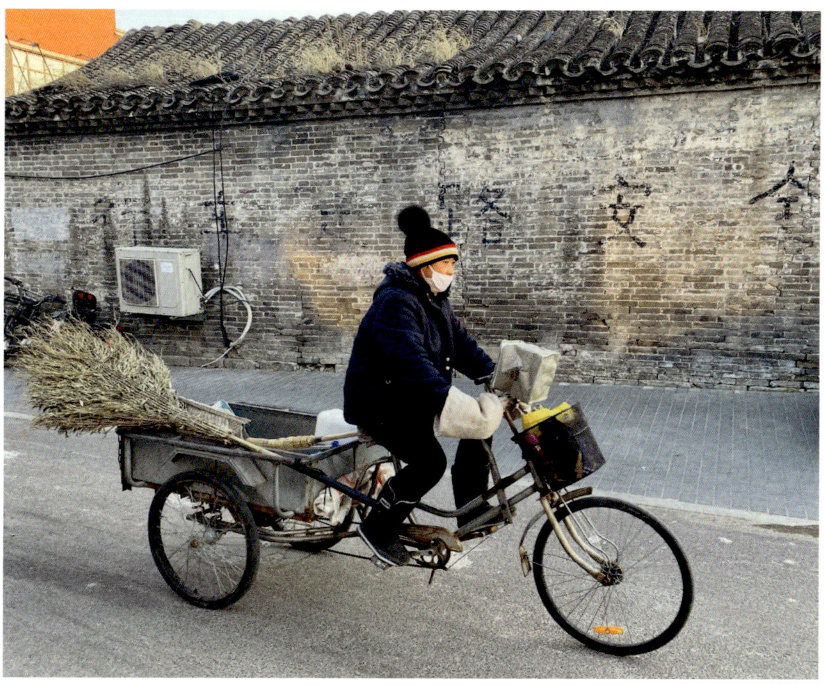

Female street sweeper on a tricycle with brushwood broom

Straßenkehrerin auf Dreirad mit Reisigbesen

In the centre of the historic district, amidst the *hutongs*, is Beijing's only notable elevation, the Coal Hill, also known as the Longevity Hill. It was created by piling up excavated material when the protective moat of the imperial city was constructed in 1421. It is said that the grey bricks for the imperial palace were also stored here. From its highest point, the Pavilion of Ten Thousand Springs, you can look to the south over a very large collection of gleaming yellow roof tiles covering an area of about 960 × 960 metres and bordered by a crimson, 10-metre-high wall and a 52-metre-wide blue-black moat. The colour scheme and number symbolism highlight the uniqueness and grandeur of this special complex, called the Purple Palace or the Forbidden City.

The naming and colour symbolism of this huge architectural complex, today called the Palace Museum, in which more than 25 emperors ruled over a period of 500 years (1420–1924) and which was abandoned by the last emperor only about 100 years ago, could not be more unambiguous and enigmatic at the same time.

Im Zentrum der Altstadt, inmitten der *Hutongs*, befindet sich die einzige nennenswerte Erhebung Pekings, der Kohlehügel, auch als Hügel der Langlebigkeit bekannt. Er entstand durch die Aufschüttung mit Aushubmaterial, als man 1421 den Schutzgraben der Kaiserstadt anlegte. Angeblich lagerte man hier auch die grauen Brennklötze für die kaiserliche Palastanlage. Vom höchsten Punkt, dem Pavillon des Zehntausendfachen Frühlings, blickt man in Richtung Süden auf eine sehr große Ansammlung gelb glänzender Dachziegel, die eine Fläche von ca. 960 × 960 Meter bedecken und eingefasst wird von einer purpurfarbenen 10 Meter hohen Wand und einem 52 Meter breiten, blau-schwarzen Wassergraben. Farbgebung und Zahlensymbolik verdeutlichen die Einzigartigkeit und Erhabenheit dieser besonderen Anlage, die Purpurner Palast oder auch Verbotene Stadt genannt wird.

Die Namensgebung und Farbsymbolik dieses riesigen Gebäudeareals, heute Palastmuseum genannt, in welchem über 25 Kaiser in 500 Jahren (1420–1924) herrschten und welches erst vor rund 100 Jahren vom letzten Kaiser verlassen wurde, könnte nicht zugleich eindeutiger und rätselhafter sein.

Left page:
In autumn, the yellow of the ginkgo trees makes the streets and parks glow.

Linke Seite:
Im Herbst bringt das Gelb der Ginkgo-Bäume die Straßen und Parks zum Leuchten.

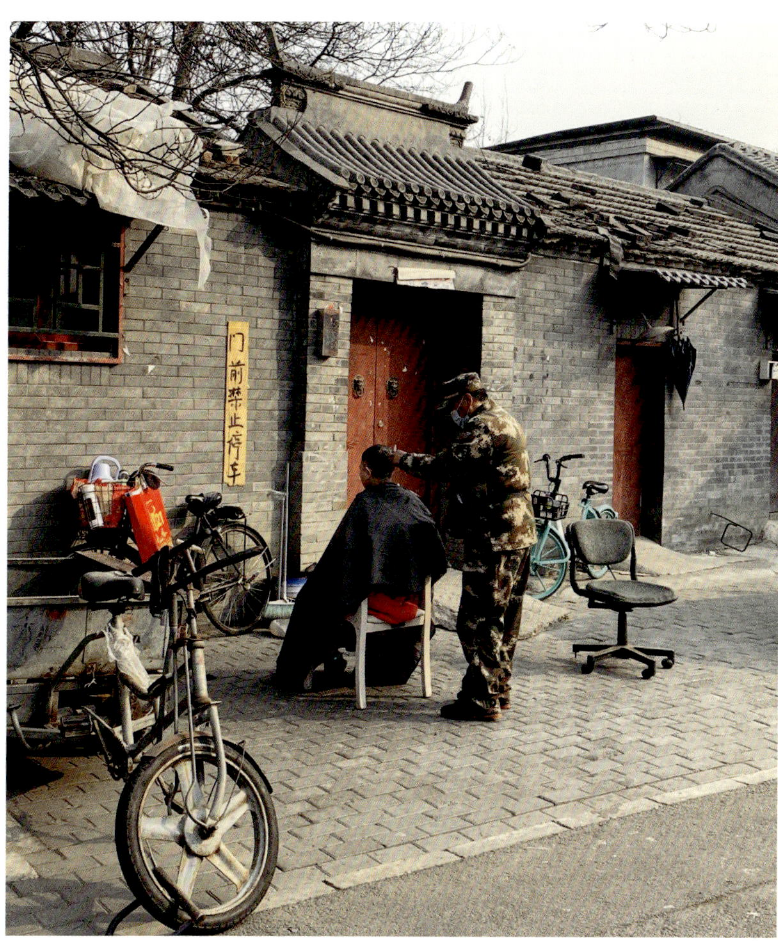

Outdoor hairdressers in China are still mostly found in the old town districts.

Freiluftfrisöre trifft man in China noch überwiegend in Altstadtvierteln.

At the east entrance to the Forbidden City, the purple-coloured wall measures a proud 10 metres in height.

Am Osteingang zur Verbotenen Stadt misst die purpurfarbene Wand stolze 10 Meter Höhe.

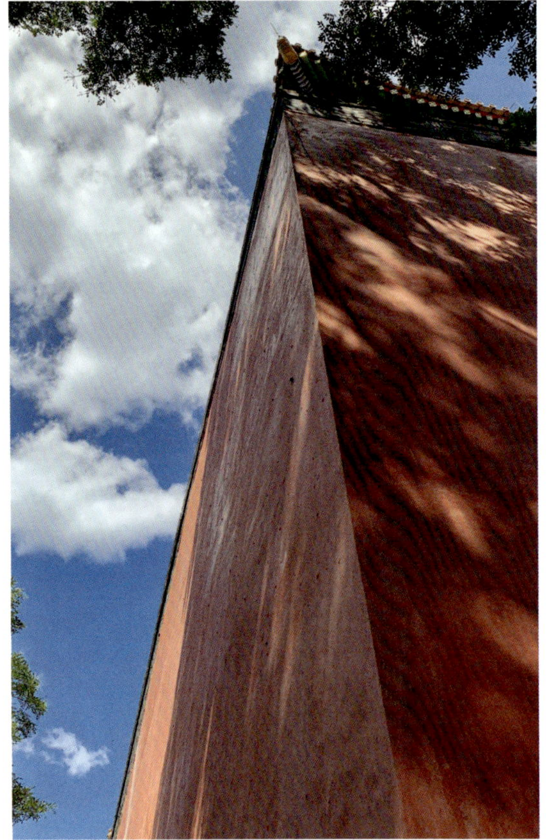

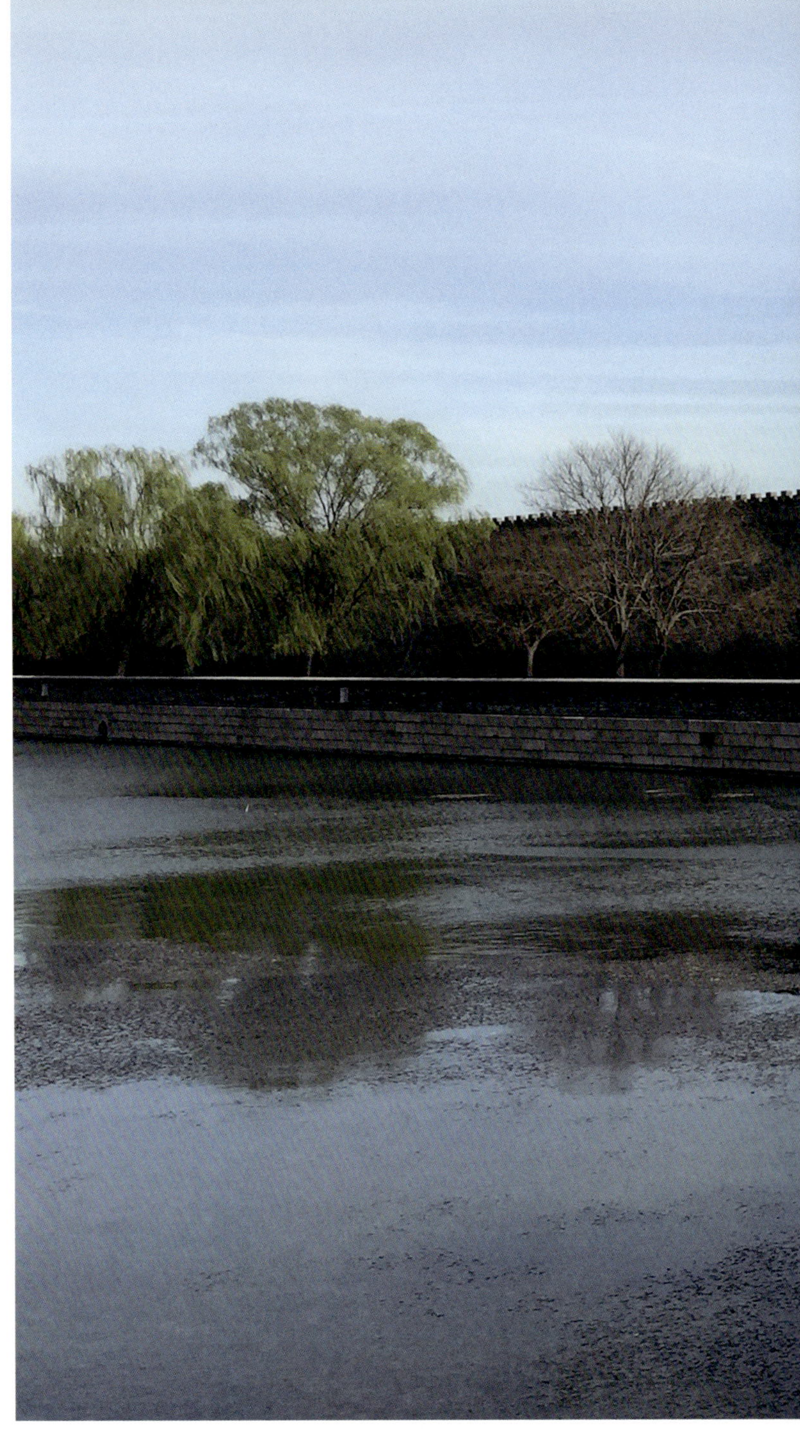

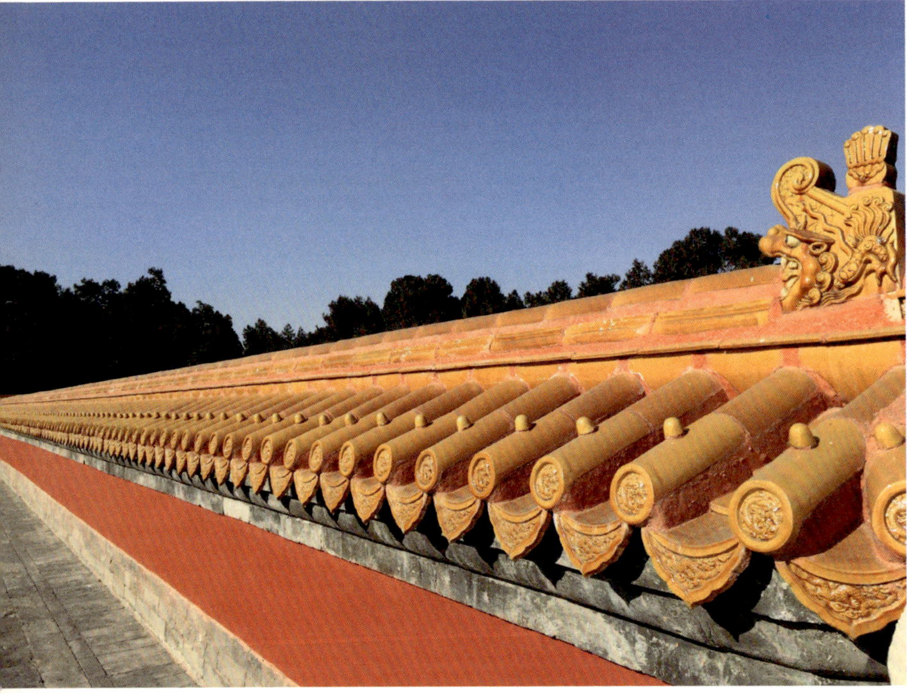

The yellow for the emperor and supported by purple walls. The contrasting colours are surprising in their luminosity and especially beautiful to look at in the Ditan Temple, the Temple of the Earth in the west of Beijing, after one of the rare rainy days in the capital.

Das Gelb für den Kaiser wird von purpurfarbenen Wänden getragen. Die kontrastierenden Farben überraschen in ihrer Leuchtkraft und sind besonders schön anzusehen im Ditan-Tempel, dem Erdaltar im Westen Pekings, nach einem der seltenen Regentage in der Hauptstadt.

Above:
View across the 52-metre-wide moat to the west wall of the Forbidden City

Oben:
Blick über den 52 Meter breiten Wassergraben auf die Westmauer der Verbotenen Stadt

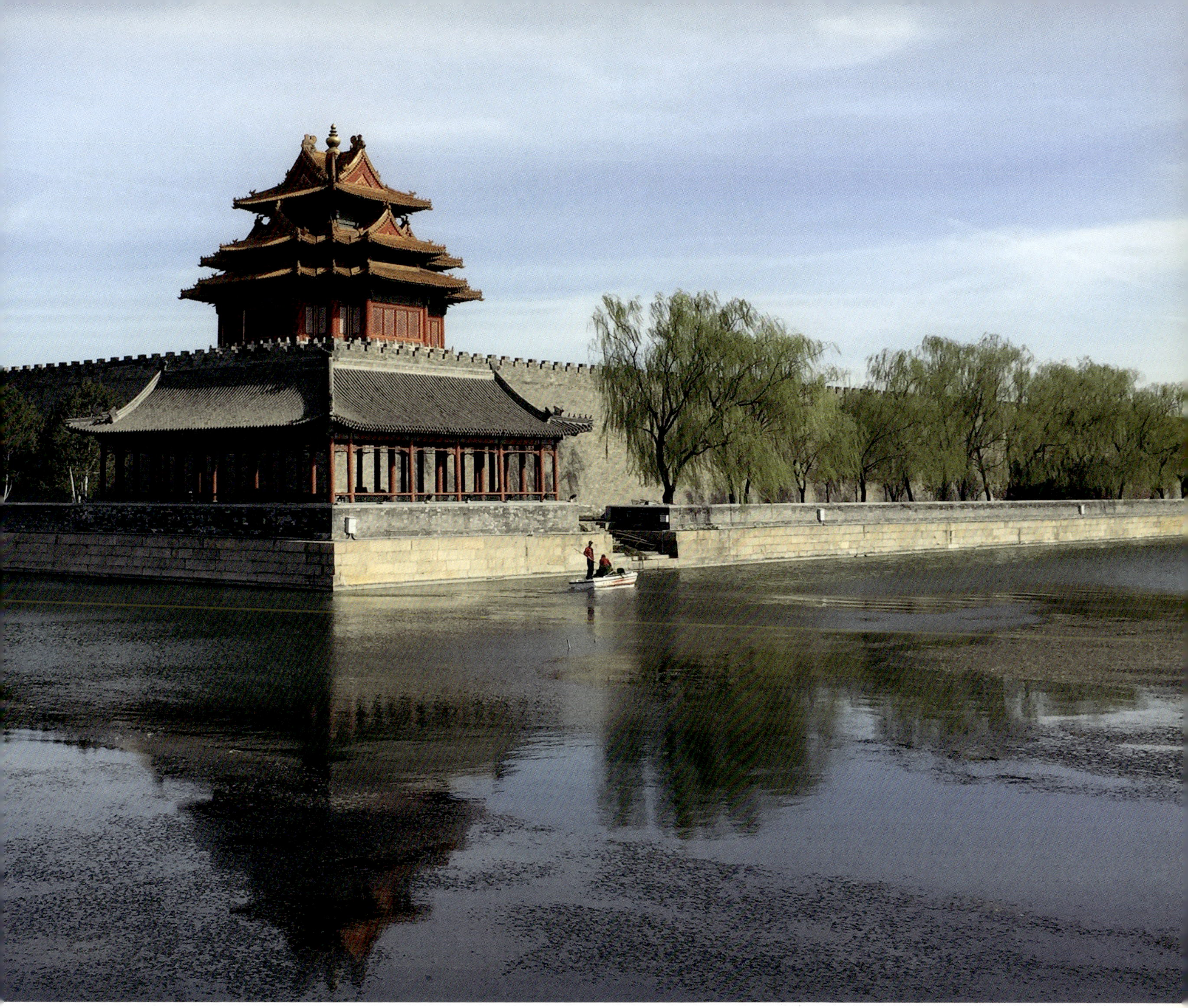

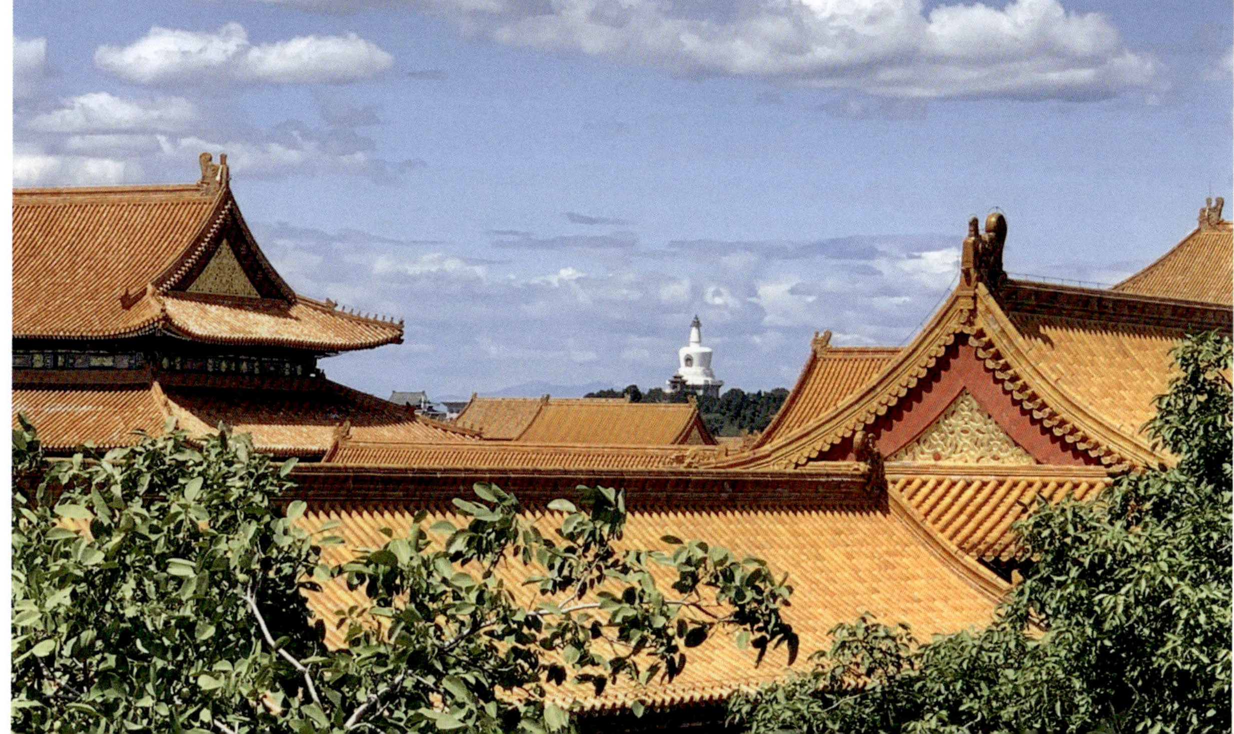

In the northwest of the Forbidden City, the white Dagoba in Beihai Park commemorates the fifth Dalai Lama, Ngawang Lobsang Gyatso. It was erected in his memory in 1651 when he visited the city.

Im Nordwesten der Verbotenen Stadt erinnert die weiße Dagoba im Beihai-Park an den fünften Dalai Lama, Ngawang Lobsang Gyatso. Sie wurde 1651, als er die Stadt besuchte, zu seinem Gedenken errichtet.

Imperial purple and star cult
Kaiserliches Purpur und Sternenkult

The name and choice of the colour purple can be traced back to the star cult that prevailed in China even before Taoism. The god Hokushin represents the deification of the North Star and is closely related to its religious counterparts, Taiitsu in Taoism and Myoken Bosatsu in Buddhism.

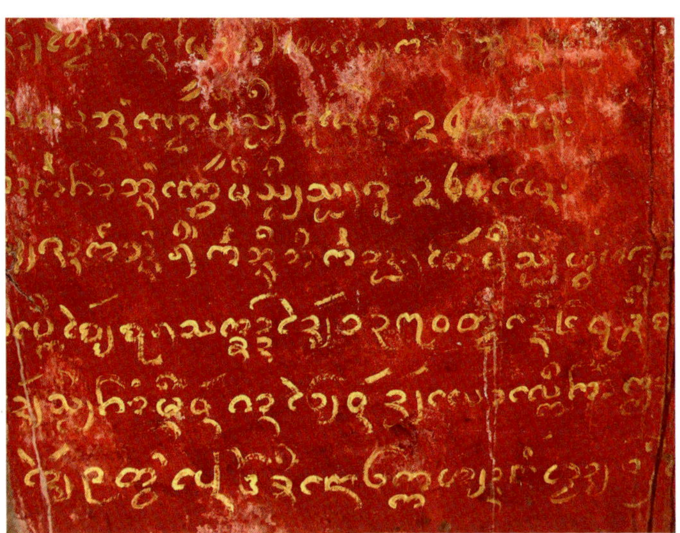

Right:
With the unification of the Chinese empire under the first emperor Qin Shihuangdi in 221 BC, a great standardisation of writing took place. Nevertheless, old scripts for local use can still be found in remote parts of the country, mostly close to the border. The Chinese script is the oldest writing system in continuous use in the world.

Rechts:
Mit der chinesischen Reichseinigung unter dem ersten Kaiser Qin Shihuangdi 221 v. Chr. fand eine große Schriftvereinheitlichung statt. Trotzdem findet man noch in abgelegenen, überwiegend grenznahen Landesteilen alte Schriftweisen für den lokalen Gebrauch. Die chinesische Schrift ist das älteste Schriftsystem der Welt, das heute noch in Gebrauch ist.

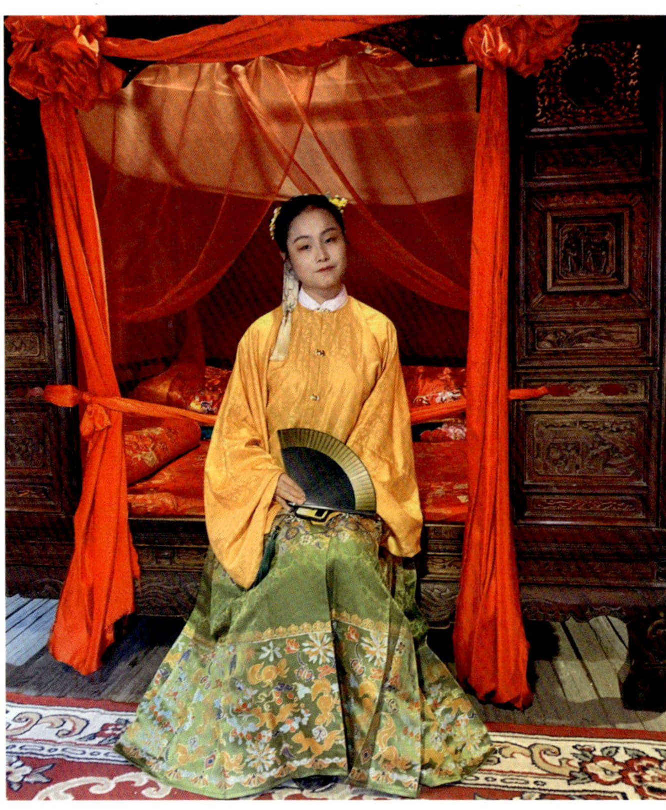

A government-backed revival of Chinese culture has given a boost to the wearing of *hanfu* or "Han clothing" by young people. Since taking office in 2012, President Xi Jinping has supported the idea of promoting a Han-centric version of Chinese heritage.

Eine von der Regierung unterstützte Erweckung der chinesischen Kultur hat dem Tragen der *Hanfu* oder „Han-Kleidung" von jungen Menschen einen Schub gegeben. Seit seinem Amtsantritt 2012 unterstützt Präsident Xi Jinping die Idee, eine Han-zentrierte Version des chinesischen Erbes zu fördern.

Zurückzuführen ist die Bezeichnung und Farbwahl Purpur auf den Sternenkult, der in China noch vor dem Daoismus herrschte. Der Gott Hokushin stellt die Vergöttlichung des Polarsterns dar und ist eng verbunden mit seinen religiösen Gegenstücken, dem Taiitsu im Daoismus und dem Myoken Bosatsu im Buddhismus.

Der Polarstern spielte ebenfalls in der Astronomie und Mythologie Chinas eine wichtige Rolle. Laut dem *Shiji – Aufzeichnungen des Chronisten*, geschrieben 109–91 v. Chr. von Sima Qian, wurde der Himmel in der chinesischen Astronomie in fünf Regionen aufgeteilt: die vier Kardinalrichtungen und das Zentrum, in dessen Mitte der Polarstern liegt. Die Region des Nordsterns wird auch als „Purpurne Verbotene Einfriedung" bezeichnet, jener Ring aus 15 Sternen, der den Polarstern umgibt. Der Nordstern wird aufgrund der Tatsache, dass sämtliche andere Sternkonstellation um ihn rotieren, gesehen als oberste Gottheit, die über das Universum herrscht. Dieses Himmelszentrum wird auf Erden vom Kaiser dargestellt.

Chinesische Sternenkarten weisen die Bezeichnung *Tianhuang*, übersetzt „Kaiser", für den Polarstern auf. In den *Analekten* des Konfuzius wird er als Ideal des politischen Handelns erwähnt: Ein Herrscher, der die Regierung durch seine Rechtschaffenheit ausübt, wird mit dem Polarstern verglichen, der „seinen Platz hält, während alle anderen Sterne ihm Ehre erweisen". Der Polarsternglaube in China wurde später überlagert vom daoistischen Konzept des *Taiitsu*, des „Großen Einen", das zugleich das ursprüngliche monistische Prinzip war.

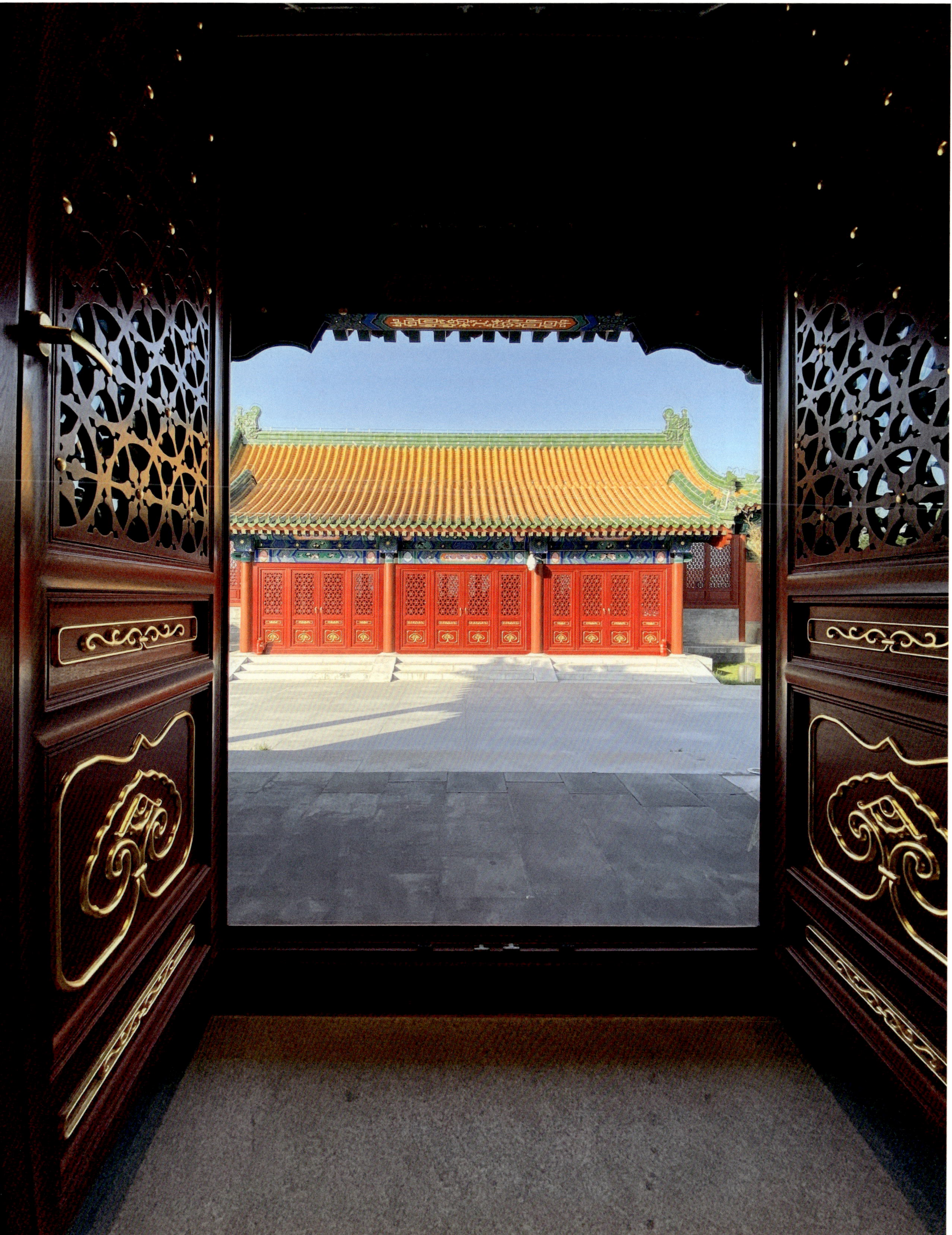

Page 55:
On the roof terrace of a ten-storey modern office building in Beijing's hip Longfusi district, one is surprised to encounter historic buildings and grounds that serve as a provocative backdrop for modern art exhibitions.

Seite 55:
Auf der Dachterrasse eines zehnstöckigen modernen Bürogebäudes im hippen Pekinger Longfusi-Viertel trifft man überraschend auf historische Gebäude und Anlagen, die als provozierende Kulisse für moderne Kunstaustellungen dienen.

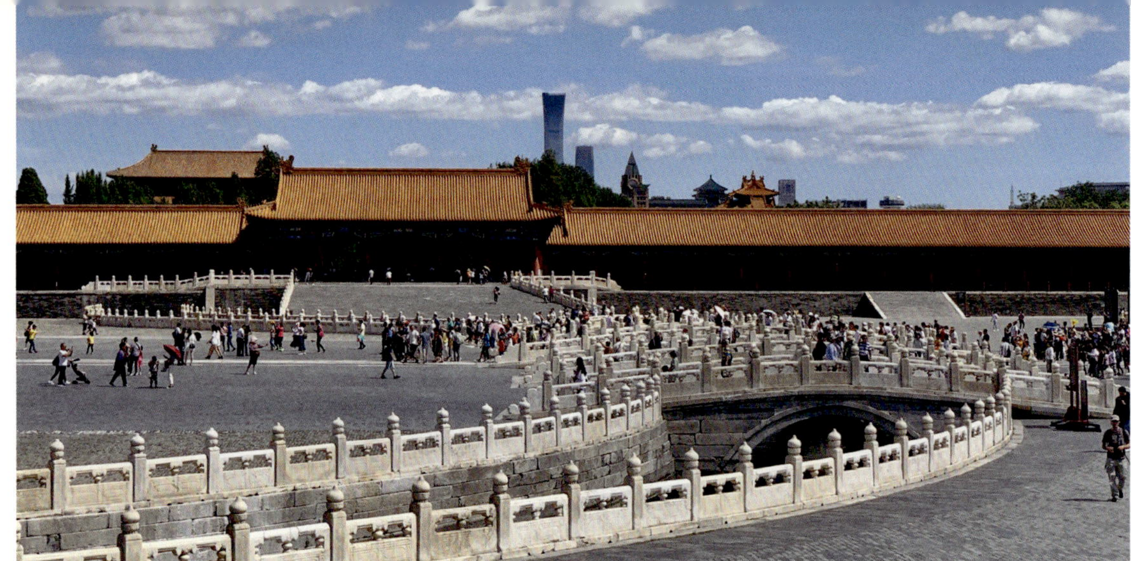

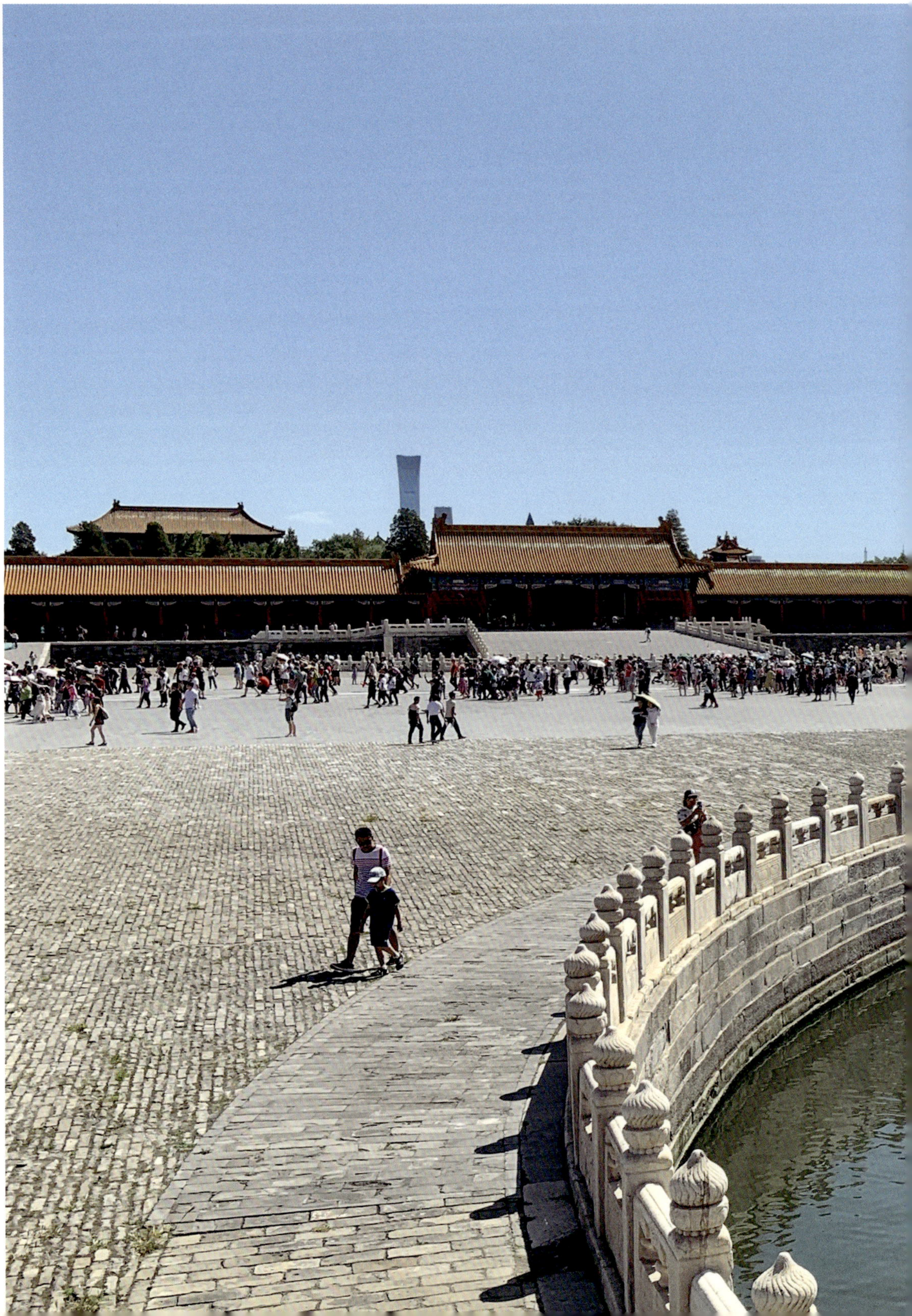

One enters the Forbidden City from the south through the Noon Gate, the most magnificent gate building in China. Of its five passages, the middle one was reserved for the emperor. In the adjoining first courtyard, five white bridges lead across the Gold Water Stream to the Gate of Supreme Harmony.

Man betritt die Verbotene Stadt von Süden durch das Mittagstor, das mächtigste Torgebäude Chinas. Von seinen fünf Durchgängen war der mittlere dem Kaiser vorbehalten. Im anschließenden ersten Hof führen fünf weiße Brücken über den Goldwasserbach zum Tor der höchsten Harmonie.

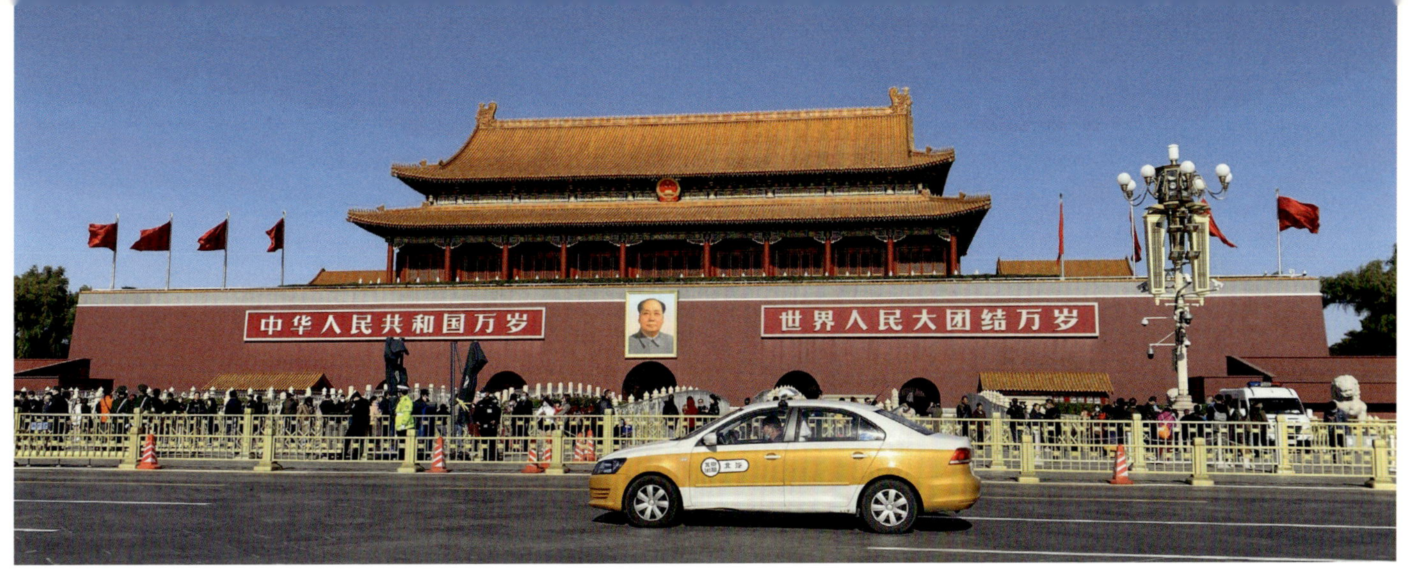
中华人民共和国万岁
世界人民大团结万岁

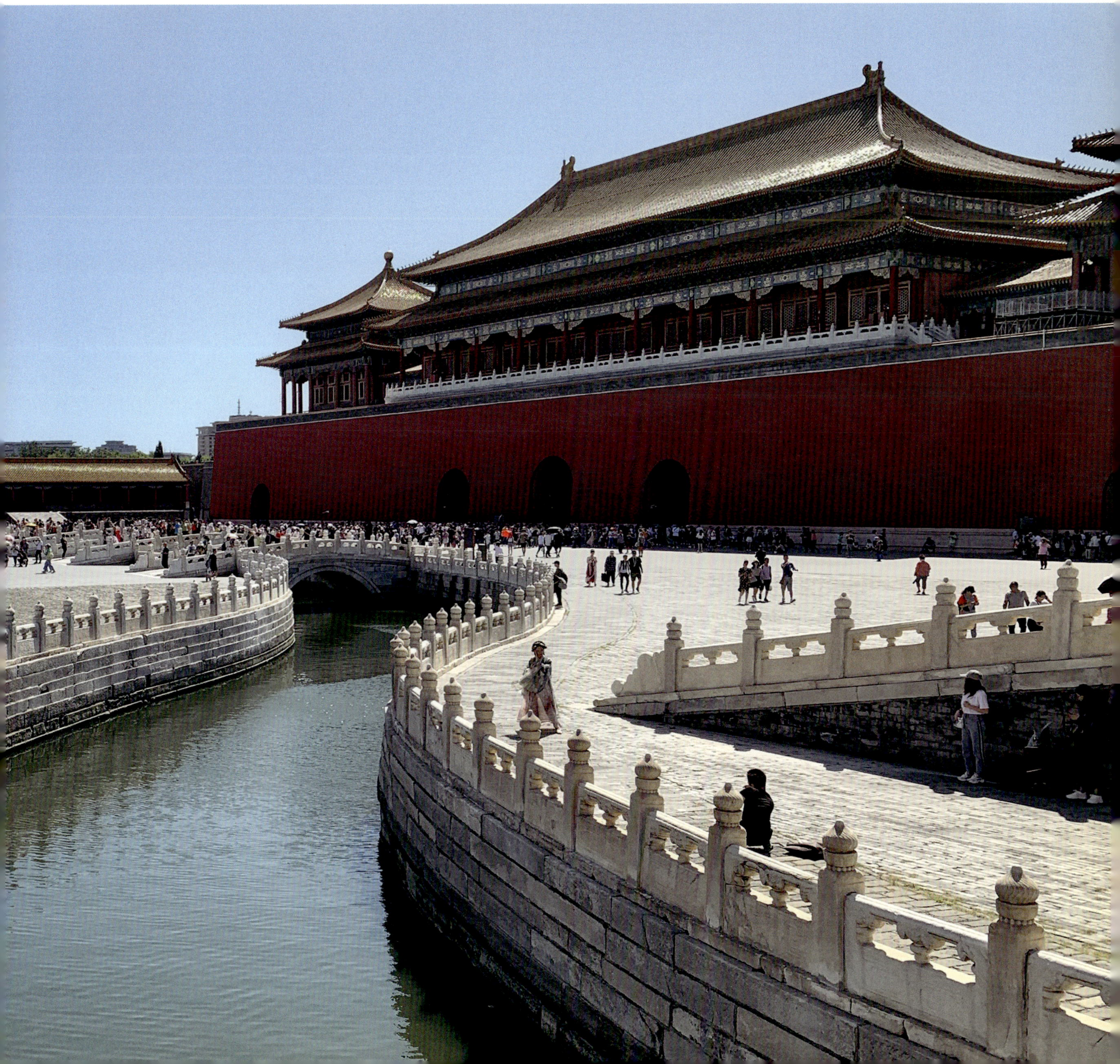

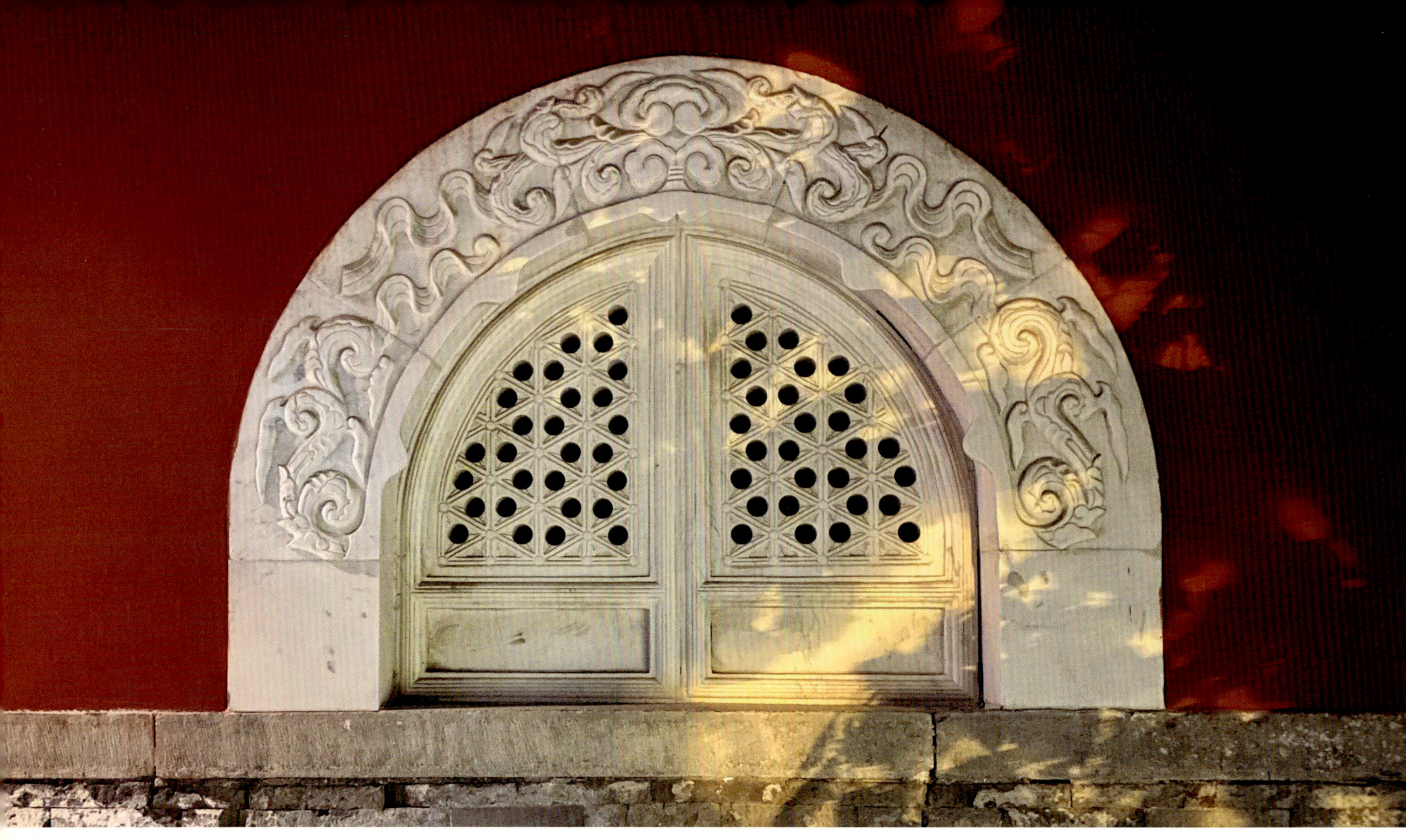

A particularly successful example of renovation in Beijing is the 600-year-old Songzhu Temple in the *Shatan Hutong* with its famous temple restaurant.

Als besonders gelungenes Beispiel einer Renovierung in Peking gilt der 600-jährige Songzhu-Tempel im *Shatan-Hutong* mit dem berühmten Tempelrestaurant.

The North Star likewise played a key role in the astronomy and mythology of China. According to the *Shiji – Records of the Chronicler*, written 109–91 BC by Sima Qian, in Chinese astronomy the sky is divided into five regions: the four cardinal directions and the centre, in the middle of which is the North Star. The region of the North Star is also known as the Purple Forbidden Enclosure, a ring of 15 stars which surround the North Star. Due to the fact that all other constellations rotate around it, the Pole Star is seen as the supreme deity that rules over the universe. This celestial centre is represented by the emperor on earth.

Chinese star charts display the name *tianhuang*, which means "emperor", for the North Star. In the Confucius' *Analects*, he is mentioned as the ideal of political action: a ruler who exercises government through his righteousness is compared to the Pole Star, which "holds its place while all the other stars pay homage to it". The North Star belief in China is later superimposed by the Taoist concept of *taiitsu*, the "Great One", which was also the original monastic principle.

In the sense of an earthly reflection of the prevailing order in the universe, the emperor symbolises the North Star and his palace symbolises the Purple Forbidden

Im Sinne einer irdischen Spiegelung der im Universum herrschenden Ordnung symbolisiert der Kaiser den Polarstern und sein Palast den Verborgenen Purpurnen Bereich. Im Chinesischen wurde die Palastanlage mit dem Begriff *Zijincheng*, übersetzt „Purpurne Verbotene Stadt", bezeichnet; heute nennt man sie *Gugong*, Alter Palast.

Auch bei den Römern galt Purpur als ein Symbol der Macht. Nur der Kaiser durfte ein mit echtem Purpur gefärbtes Gewand tragen. Die Senatoren mussten sich mit einem purpurnen Band an der Toga begnügen. Wie bei den römischen Kaisern war auch bei den deutschen Kaisern das Tragen von purpurnen Gewändern ein Statussymbol der Macht.

Auch in der weitläufigen grünen Parkanlage des in Lapislazuli-Farben gedeckten Himmelstempels, des architektonischen Symbols für die Beziehung zwischen Erde und Himmel und für die vom Kaiser gespielte Rolle, sind klare Hinweise auf den Sternenkult in China zu finden. Auf der Altarterrasse brachte der Kaiser aufwendige Tieropfer dar, und am kreisrunden, dreifach gestuften Himmelsaltar bat er um eine gute Ernte. Steinnachbauten in Form von Meteoriten liegen auf der grünen Wiese, umgeben von alten Pinien und Kiefern. Man spricht von heiligen Ster-

Enclosure. In Chinese the palace complex was called *Zijincheng*, translated Purple Forbidden City; today it is called *Gugong*, Old Palace.

Purple was also considered a symbol of power by the Romans. Only the emperor was allowed to wear a robe dyed with real Tyrian purple. The senators had to make do with a purple ribbon on their toga. As with the Roman emperors, the wearing of purple robes was a status symbol of power among the German emperors.

There are also clear references to star worship in China in the expansive green park of the Temple of Heaven, which is covered in the hues of lapis lazuli and is the architectural symbol of the relationship between earth and sky and of the role played by the emperor. On the altar terrace, the emperor made elaborate animal sacrifices, and at the circular, three-tiered sky altar, he asked for a good harvest. Stone replicas in the form of meteorites are lying on the green meadow, surrounded by old pine trees. They are called sacred star stones, and the place of impact is honoured appropriately with dignity. Right next to it, you can also see the daily morning shadow boxing, the multicoloured fan or ribbon dance, and enjoy musical singing performances by talents of the famous Beijing Opera. And certainly the weekly marriage market takes place in the shadow of the purple walls, because this place is considered particularly lucky and pioneering.

In keeping with the old tradition, which is still common throughout the country, marriage brokers or the parents themselves search for the most suitable daughter-in-law. Anyone who is female, unmarried and older than 27 is considered a "leftover woman" and difficult to place. This is likely to change significantly at present with the shortage of girls resulting from the one-child policy. The social status, occupation and possession of a partner all play an important role in arranging marriage, but nothing works even in the 21st century if the zodiac signs do not match.

In the cityscapes of modern China, the crimson red hue explicitly refers to historically significant buildings and stands out from the neighbouring uniform grey of historic, one-story residential areas.

nensteinen, und der Ort des Einschlags wird entsprechend würdevoll verehrt. Gleich daneben kann man zudem das allmorgendliche Schattenboxen, den vielfarbigen Fächer- oder Bändertanz sehen und sich an musikalischen Gesangseinlagen von Talenten der berühmten Pekingoper erfreuen. Und sicher findet der wöchentliche Heiratsmarkt im Schatten der purpurnen Mauern statt, weil dieser Ort als besonders glücksbringend und wegweisend gilt.

Der alten und durchaus noch landesweit üblichen Tradition entsprechend, suchen hier plakativ Heiratsvermittler oder die Eltern selbst nach der am besten geeigneten Schwiegertochter. Wer weiblich, unverheiratet und älter als 27 Jahre ist, gilt als „übriggebliebene Frau", als schwer vermittelbar. Dies dürfte sich aktuell mit dem aufgrund der bisherigen Ein-Kind-Politik entstandenen Mangel an Mädchen deutlich verändern. Der soziale Status, Beruf und Besitz eines Partners spielen beim Arrangieren der Ehe eine wichtige Rolle, aber nichts geht auch im 21. Jahrhundert, wenn die Sternkreiszeichen nicht zueinander passen.

Im modernen Stadtbild Chinas weist das purpurfarbene Rot ausdrücklich auf historisch bedeutsame Gebäude hin und grenzt sich klar ab von dem angrenzenden Einheitsgrau der historischen, einstöckigen Wohnviertel.

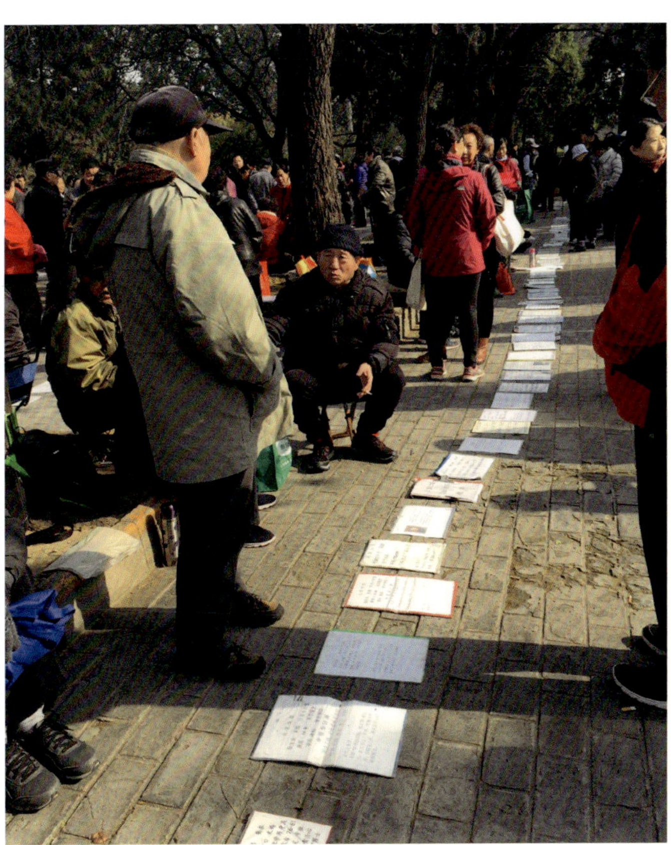

One of the weekly marriage markets in the parks of Beijing

Einer der wöchentlichen Heiratsmärkte in den Parkanlagen von Peking

Secretive black
Geheimnisvolles Schwarz

The Chinese proverb "Heaven and earth of mysterious black" was rooted in the observation that the northern sky was black. Perhaps this explains why this is the colour worn by Qin Shi Huang Di, the first emperor of China, when he assumed the throne. He was called the Yellow Emperor, but he chose black as the colour of his flags and pennants: the colour of the element water, the symbol of winter, the north, and at the same time of honour and high dignity. But water also stands for peace, strength and new beginnings.

In Maoism, black represented counterrevolution, in contrast to the red inherent in the system. In many Asian martial arts, the black belt is awarded after passing the master's examination.

Das chinesische Sprichwort „Himmel und Erde von geheimnisvollem Schwarz" wurzelte in der Beobachtung, dass der nördliche Himmel schwarz war. Vielleicht erklärt dies, warum dies die Farbe ist, die Qin Shi Huang Di, der erste Kaiser Chinas, bei seiner Thronbesteigung trug. Er wurde Gelber Kaiser genannt, doch er wählte Schwarz als Farbe seiner Fahnen und Wimpel: die Farbe des Elements Wasser, das Symbol für den Winter, den Norden und gleichzeitig für Ehre und hohe Würden. Wasser steht aber auch für Ruhe, Kraft und Neubeginn.

Im Maoismus repräsentierte Schwarz im Gegensatz zum systemimmanenten Rot die Konterrevolution. In vielen asiatischen Kampfkünsten wird nach dem Bestehen der Meisterprüfung der schwarze Gurt verliehen, und auch im Westen treffen Bogenschützen gern ins Schwarze.

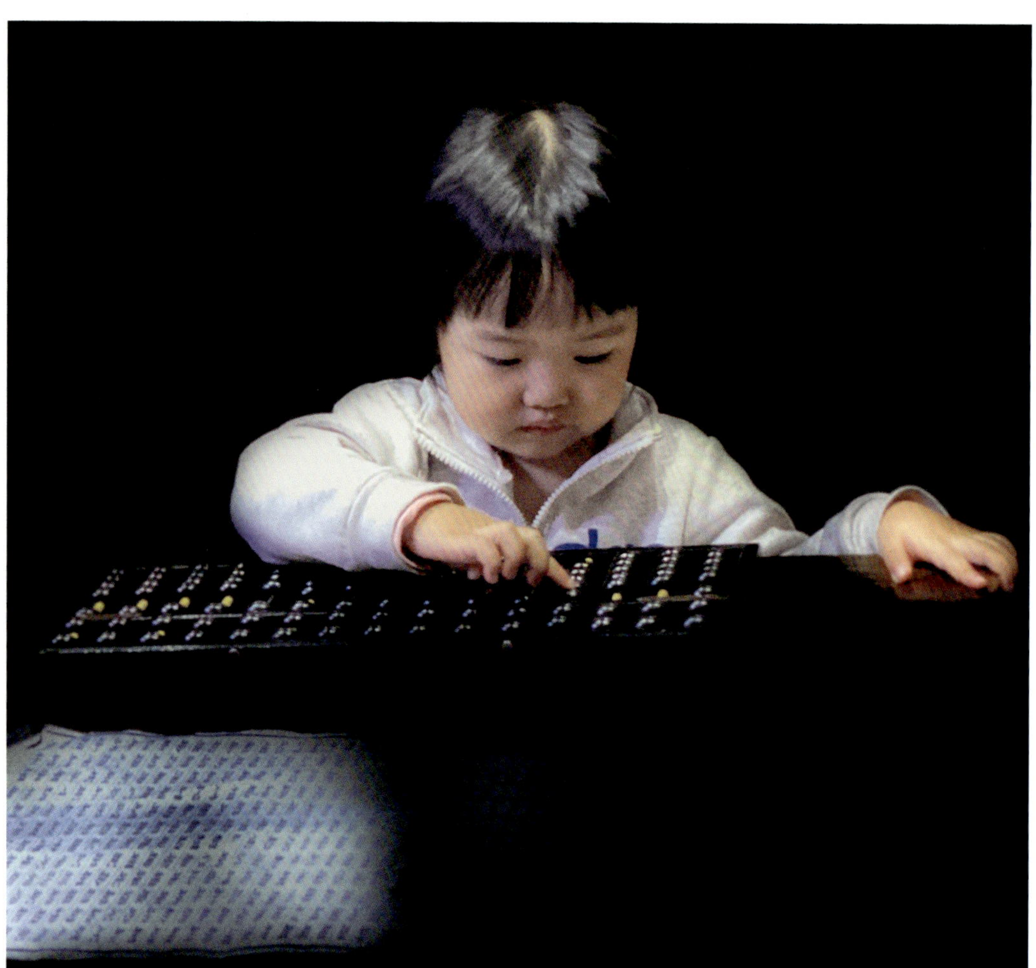

The abacus was first mentioned in China in the sixth century as a "bead calculator". Today it is a museum instrument replaced by the pocket calculator. The traditional calculation method, however, was added to UNESCO's Intangible Cultural Heritage List in 2013.

Als „Perlenrechnung" fand der Abakus erstmals im sechsten Jahrhundert in China Erwähnung. Heute ist er ein museales Instrument, abgelöst vom Taschenrechner. Die traditionelle Rechenmethode jedoch wurde 2013 in die Liste des immateriellen Kulturerbes der Menschheit der UNESCO aufgenommen.

Right page:
Column with gold inscription "loyalty" at the residence of a former imperial civil servant.

Rechte Seite:
Säule mit goldener Inschrift „Loyalität" an der Wohnresidenz eines ehemaligen kaiserlichen Staatsbeamten.

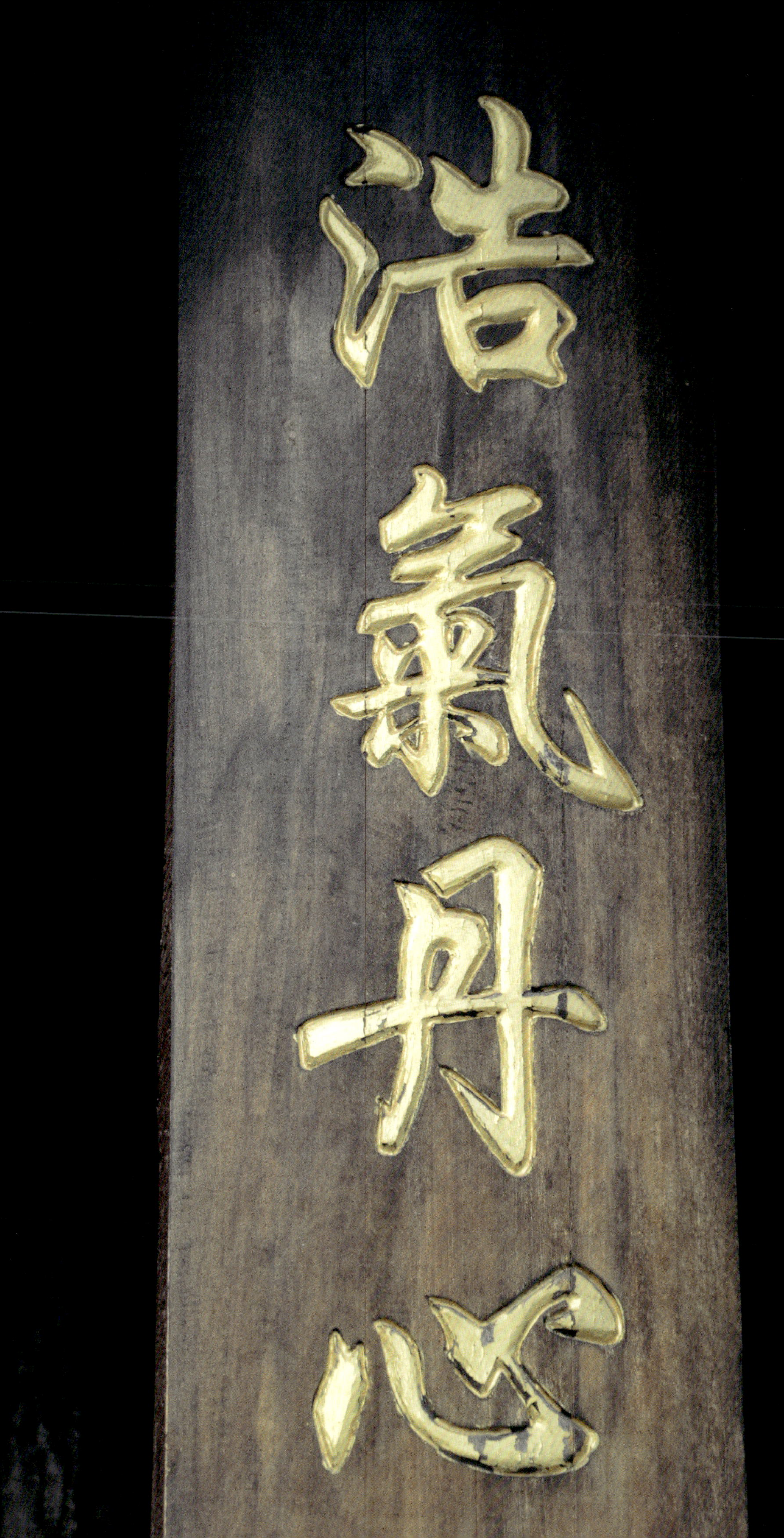
浩氣丹心

Yellow creates yin and yang
Gelb erzeugt Yin und Yang

During the Qing Dynasty (1644–1911), a certain shade of yellow was reserved solely for the emperor and his family. Anyone who nevertheless dared to take a Sunday stroll in a bright yellow summer coat was threatened with the death penalty. The yellow earth is the fertile soil of Chinese life. With good irrigation, fruitful arable soil developed from it. The Huang He, the Yellow River, and the highlands along its middle reaches are considered the source region of ancient Chinese culture. The river owes its colour to the sediments of the loess soil and is the second longest river in China after the Yangtze with an estimated 5,464 kilometres. The Huang He has its source in western Qinghai and flows through nine provinces before it joins the Bohai Sea in Shandong Province.

Even today, the Chinese refer to themselves as those with the yellow skin and speak of Westerners as the whites. As early as the 4th century AD, eastern China had problems with overpopulation because of the many immigrants. The rulers then decided to register them on "white lists". The long-established inhabitants, on the other hand, were registered on "yellow lists", with which privileges of settlement and land use were associated vis-à-vis the newcomers, the whites. The whites, *baixing*, who had lived in the region for a long time, thus received a kind of "yellow citizenship" and were called *huangji*.

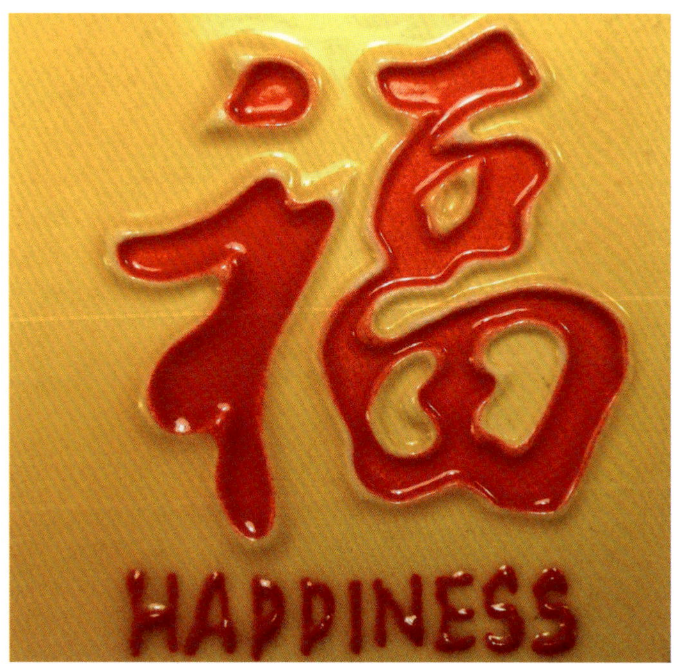

Während der Qing-Dynastie (1644–1911) war ein bestimmter Gelbton einzig dem Kaiser und seiner Familie vorbehalten. Wer seinen Sonntagsspaziergang dennoch im zitronenfaltergelben Sommermantel wagte, dem drohte die Todesstrafe. Die gelbe Erde ist der Nährboden chinesischen Lebens. Aus ihr entstand bei guter Bewässerung fruchtbarer Ackerboden. Der Huang He, der Gelbe Fluss, und das Hochland an seinem Mittellauf gelten als Ursprungsregion der alten chinesischen Kultur. Der Fluss verdankt seine Farbe den Sedimenten der Lösserde und ist nach dem Yangtze mit geschätzten 5464 Kilometern der zweitlängste Fluss Chinas. Der Huang He entspringt im westlichen Qinghai, fließt durch neun Provinzen und mündet in das Bohai-Meer in der Provinz Shandong.

Auch heute bezeichnen Chinesen sich selbst als die mit der gelben Hautfarbe und sprechen von den Westlern als den Weißen. Schon im 4. Jahrhundert n. Chr. gab es im östlichen China Probleme mit der Überbevölkerung wegen der vielen Einwanderer. Die Herrscher entschlossen sich daraufhin, diese auf weißen Listen zu erfassen. Die alteingesessenen Bewohner registrierte man hingegen auf gelben Listen, womit Privilegien der Siedlung und Bodennutzung gegenüber den Neuankömmlingen, den Weißen, verbunden waren. Die Weißen, *Baixing*, die schon lange in der Region lebten, erhielten damit eine Art gelbe Staatsbürgerschaft und wurden *Huangji* genannt.

Gelb wird in neuerer Zeit mit Prostitution und Pornografie in Verbindung gebracht. Pornografische Filme und Zeitschriften werden als „gelbe Filme oder Heftchen" bezeichnet. Auch werden Damen, die wegen Prostitution verhaftet werden, in gelbe Kleider gesteckt und so zur Schau gestellt. Traditionell ist Gelb die Farbe des Elements Erde und des sechsten Monats. Sie ist ein Zeichen für Ausgeglichenheit und Neutralität. Aufgrund ihrer Ähnlichkeit mit der Farbe des Goldes wurde Gelb außerdem ein Symbol für Wohlstand und Fortschritt. Gelb gilt als die schönste und prestigeträchtigste Farbe in China.

White marble bridges are a popular feature in Chinese landscape gardens. Here in Ritan Park, Beijing's Sun Temple Park.

Die weißen Marmorbrücken sind ein beliebtes Element in chinesischen Landschaftsgärten. Hier im Ritan-Park, dem Sonnentempelpark Pekings.

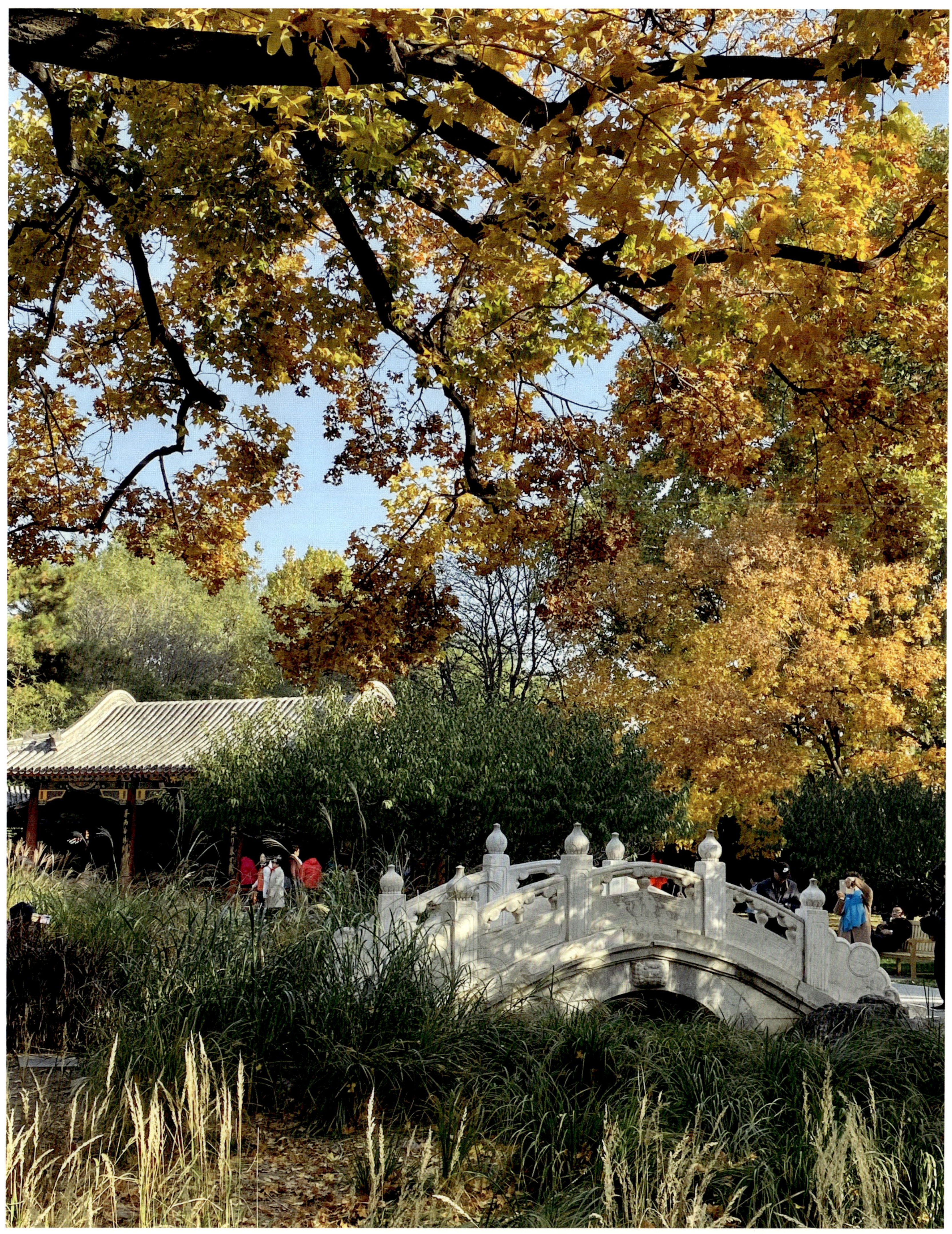

Yellow has more recently been associated with prostitution and pornography. Pornographic films and magazines are called "yellow films or booklets". Also, ladies arrested for prostitution are put on display in yellow dresses. Yellow is traditionally the colour of the element of earth and the sixth month. It is a sign of balance and neutrality. Due to its similarity with the colour gold, yellow also became a symbol of prosperity and progress. Yellow is considered the most beautiful and prestigious colour in China. It was the symbolic colour of the five legendary emperors of ancient China. Yellow often decorates royal palaces, altars and temples and was used in the robes and clothing of the emperor.

The Chinese proverb "yellow creates yin and yang" implies that yellow is the centre of everything. Moreover, because it was considered a sign of freedom from worldly worries and needs, yellow is also given a special role in Buddhism – the robes of Buddhist monks are yellow, and entire temple complexes are often designed in shades of yellow.

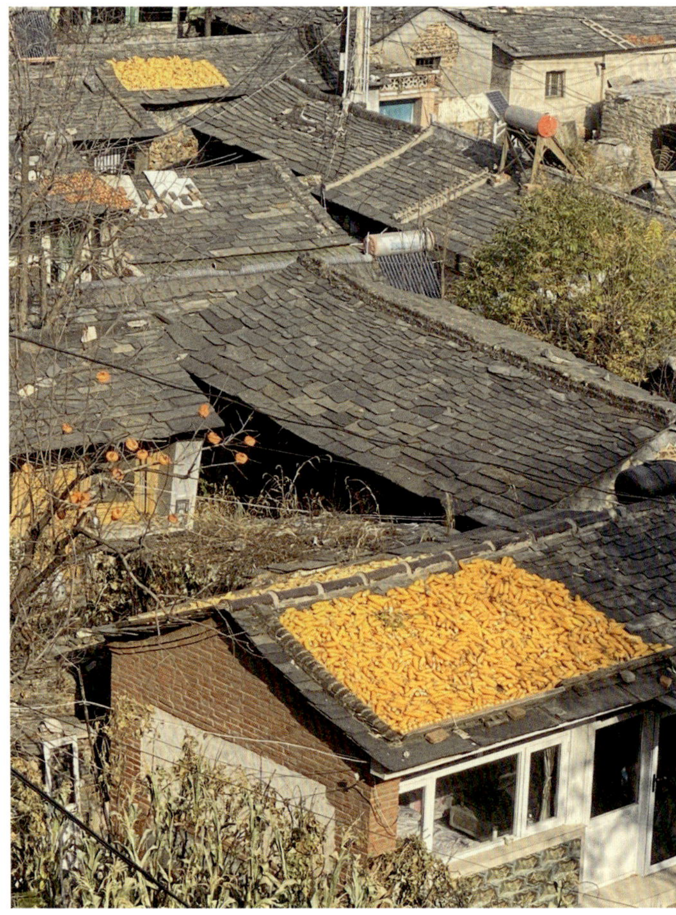

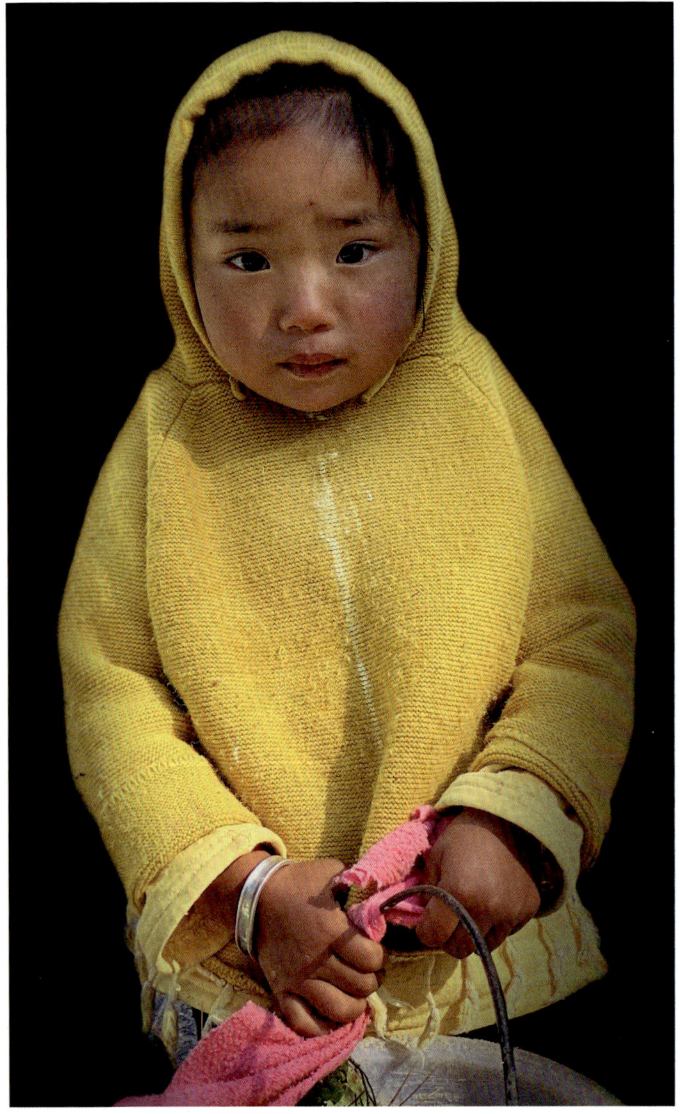

Es war die symbolische Farbe der fünf legendären Kaiser des alten China. Gelb schmückt oft königliche Paläste, Altäre und Tempel und wurde in den Gewändern und Kleidern der Kaiser verwendet.

Das chinesische Sprichwort „Gelb erzeugt Yin und Yang" impliziert, dass Gelb das Zentrum von allem ist. Weil es zudem als Zeichen für die Freiheit von weltlichen Sorgen und Nöten galt, wird Gelb auch im Buddhismus eine besondere Rolle zugemessen – die Gewänder buddhistischer Mönche sind gelb, und sogar ganze Tempelanlagen sind oft in Gelbtönen gestaltet.

Little herb-picking girl from the mystical city of Shangri-La in the northwestern Yunnan Province, mostly inhabited by Tibetans and Naxi. The native Tibetan name of the city is Gyelthang. In 2001, the Chinese name Zhongdian was changed to Shangri-La in reference to the novel *The Lost Horizon* by British author James Hilton. The name change was accompanied by a drastic increase in visitor numbers.

Kleines Kräuter pflückendes Mädchen aus der überwiegend von Tibetern und Naxi bewohnten mystischen Stadt Shangri-La im Nordwesten der Provinz Yunnan. Der einheimische tibetische Name der Stadt ist Gyelthang. Erst 2001 änderte man den chinesischen Namen Zhongdian in Shangri-La in Anspielung auf den Roman *Der verlorene Horizont* des britischen Schriftstellers James Hilton. Mit der Namensänderung einher ging ein drastischer Anstieg der Besucherzahlen.

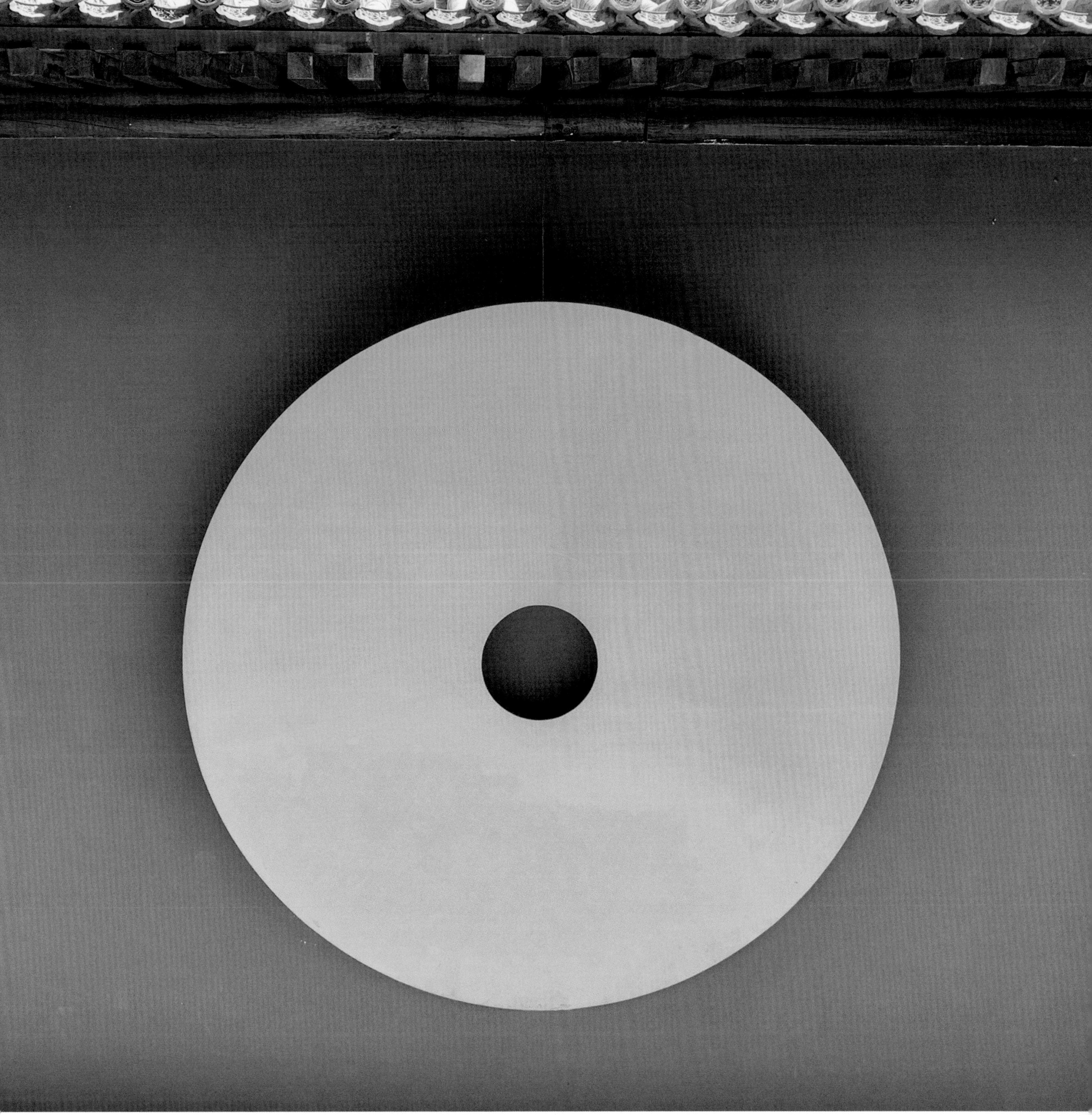

Left page, above:
Corn is dried on the flat roofs of farmhouses in late summer.

Linke Seite, oben:
Im Spätsommer wird der Mais auf den flachen Dächern der Bauernhäuser getrocknet.

Circular and golden yellow, both extremely popular and promising attributes in China. The revolving round table, set in red and gold, is traditional and omnipresent even in modern China.

Kreisrund und goldgelb, beides äußerst beliebte und vielversprechende Attribute in China. Die drehende runde Tafel, eingedeckt in rot und gold, ist Tradition und auch im modernen China omnipräsent.

Saffron and vermilion
Safran und Zinnober

For Buddhists, orange represents the highest level of human enlightenment. In Confucianism, it was the colour of transformation. In China and India, the colour got its name not from the orange fruit but from saffron, the finest and most expensive dye in Asia. Yellow was the colour of perfection and nobility; red the colour of luck and power. Yellow and red were compared to light and fire, spirituality and sensuality, seemingly opposites but actually complementary. Orange, the colour of transformation, was born from the interaction between the two.

A great diversity of colours, from a light orange-yellow to a deep orange-red, all of which are simply called saffron, is closely connected to Hinduism and Buddhism and is commonly worn by monks and holy men throughout Asia. The robe and its colours symbolise the rejection of the outside world and the commitment to an order.

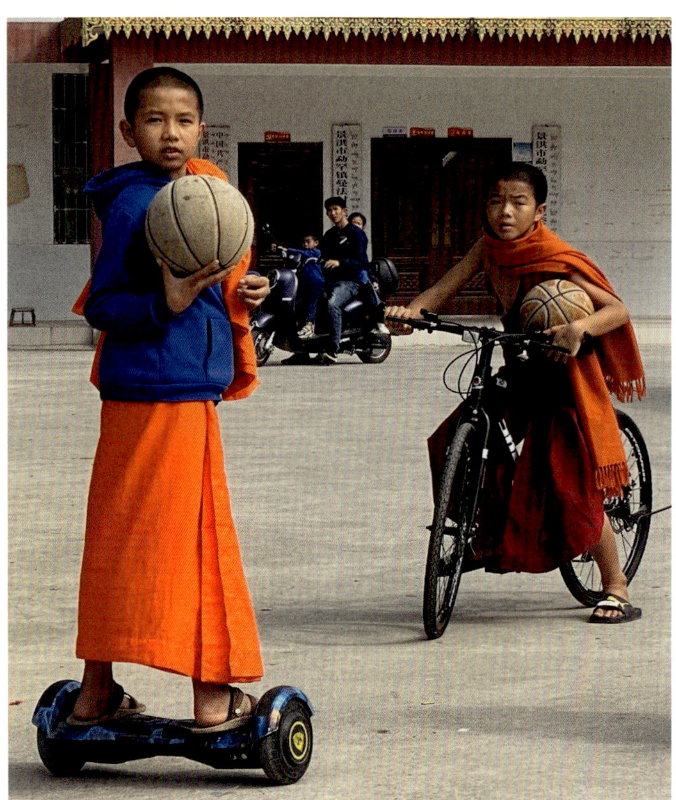

For children in poorer areas, living in a monastery is often the best way to get a good education. Here in Xishuangbanna in southern Yunnan.

Für die Kinder in den ärmeren Gegenden ist das Leben im Kloster oft die beste Möglichkeit eine gute Schulausbildung zu bekommen. Wie hier in Xishuangbanna im Süden von Yunnan.

Für Buddhisten steht Orange für die höchste Stufe der menschlichen Erleuchtung. Im Konfuzianismus war es die Farbe der Transformation. In China und Indien erhielt die Farbe ihren Namen nicht von der Orangenfrucht, sondern von Safran, dem feinsten und teuersten Farbstoff Asiens. Gelb war die Farbe der Vollkommenheit und des Adels; Rot die Farbe von Glück und Macht. Gelb und Rot wurden mit

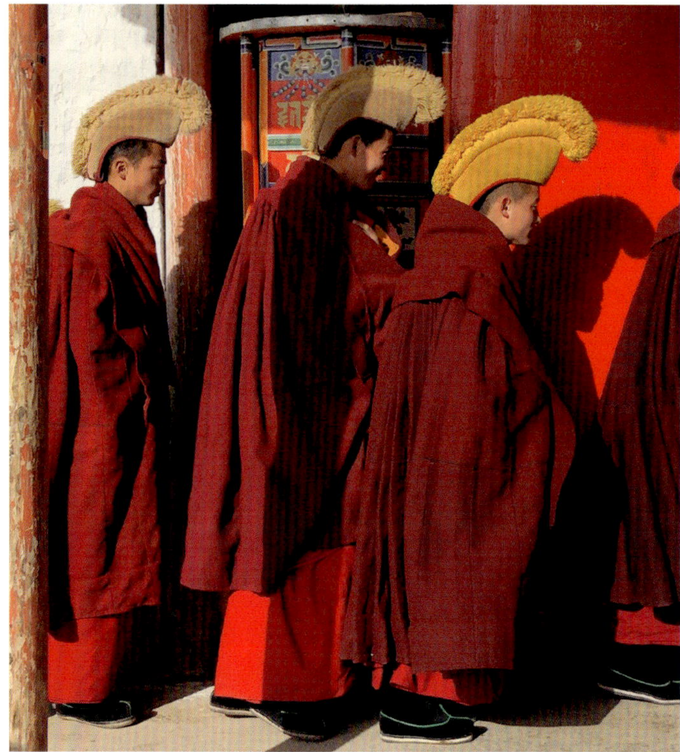

In 1578, Tibetan Buddhist Sonam Gyatso, then leader of the Gelugpa "Yellow Hat" school, travelled to the powerful Mongol prince Altan Khan. During this visit, the Khan bestowed upon him the title of "Dalai Lama" (Ocean of Knowledge). The other three Lamaist schools are also commonly referred to as the "Red Hat" schools.

Im Jahr 1578 reiste der tibetische Buddhist Sonam Gyatso, der damalige Führer der Gelugpa „Gelbmützen"-Schule, zum mächtigen Mongolenfürsten Altan Khan. Bei diesem Besuch verlieh ihm der Khan den Titel des „Dalai Lama" (Ozean des Wissens). Die drei anderen lamaistischen Schulen werden allgemein auch als „Rotmützen"-Schulen bezeichnet.

Right page:
The characters of this Tang poem are written from top to bottom and are read from right to left. This style was followed in China until 1955.

Rechte Seite:
Die Schriftzeichen dieses Tang-Gedichtes wurden von oben nach unten geschrieben und werden von rechts nach links gelesen. Bis zum Jahre 1955 folgte man in China ausschließlich dieser Schreibweise.

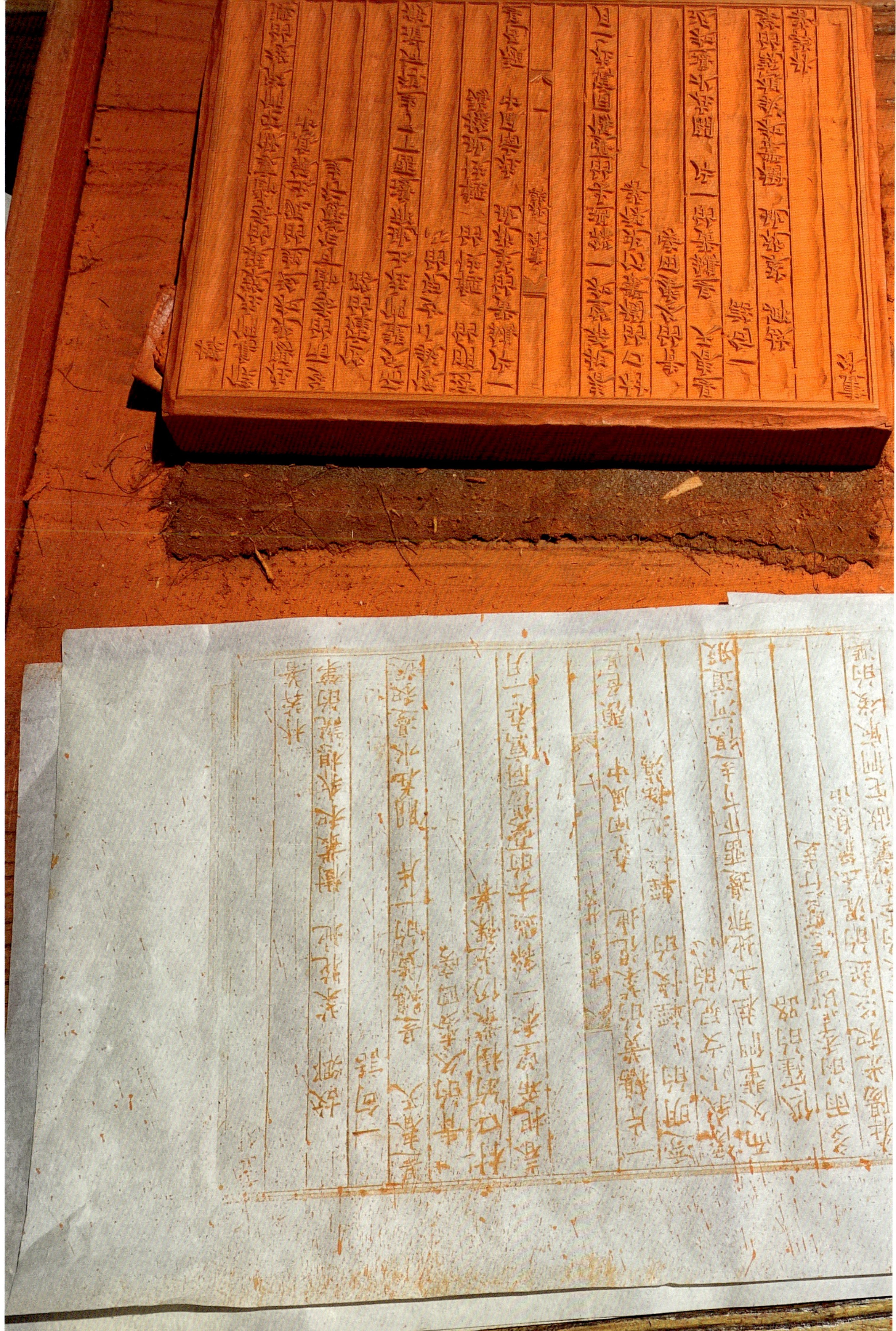

The candidate monk first appears with his master before the monks of the monastery in his own clothes. He holds his new robe under his arm and asks for the appointment. Then he takes the vow, puts on the robe and goes out into the world with his begging bowl. Thereafter, he spends his mornings begging and his afternoons in contemplation and with studying, either in the forest, in the garden or the monastery.

In the scientific depth psychology of the West, orange stands for communication and the wish for unity. It is considered to be mood-lifting and stimulating, and is associated with desire. In the West and the East, orange is also considered a warning colour, which is used in street traffic and in the transport of dangerous goods.

The persimmon can be eaten with its peel, like an apple. In autumn, the trees are heavy with persimmons, which radiate orange in the landscape. Picking the sweet plump fruit requires delicate skill.

Die Persimone, eine Zuchtform der Kaki, kann wie ein Apfel mitsamt Schale verspeist werden. Im Herbst leuchten auf dem Land die schwer behängten Bäume orangefarben. Das Pflücken der süßen prallen Früchte verlangt feinfühliges Geschick.

Licht und Feuer, Spiritualität und Sinnlichkeit verglichen, scheinbar entgegengesetzt, aber wirklich komplementär. Aus der Interaktion zwischen den beiden entstand Orange, die Farbe der Transformation.

Eine große Vielfalt an Farben, von einem leicht orangegelben bis zu einem tief orangen Rot, die alle einfach Safran genannt werden, sind eng mit Hinduismus und Buddhismus verbunden und werden üblicherweise von Mönchen und heiligen Männern in ganz Asien getragen. Die Robe und ihre Farbe ist ein Zeichen der Entsagung von der Außenwelt und des Engagements für die Ordnung. Der Kandidatenmönch erscheint mit seinem Meister zuerst in seinen eigenen Kleidern vor den Mönchen des Klosters. Er hält seine neue Robe unter dem Arm und fragt nach der Bestellung. Dann nimmt er seine Gelübde, zieht die Robe an und geht mit seiner Bettelschale in die Welt hinaus. Danach verbringt er seine Morgen bettelnd und seine Nachmittage in Kontemplation und Studium, entweder in einem Wald, in einem Garten oder im Kloster.

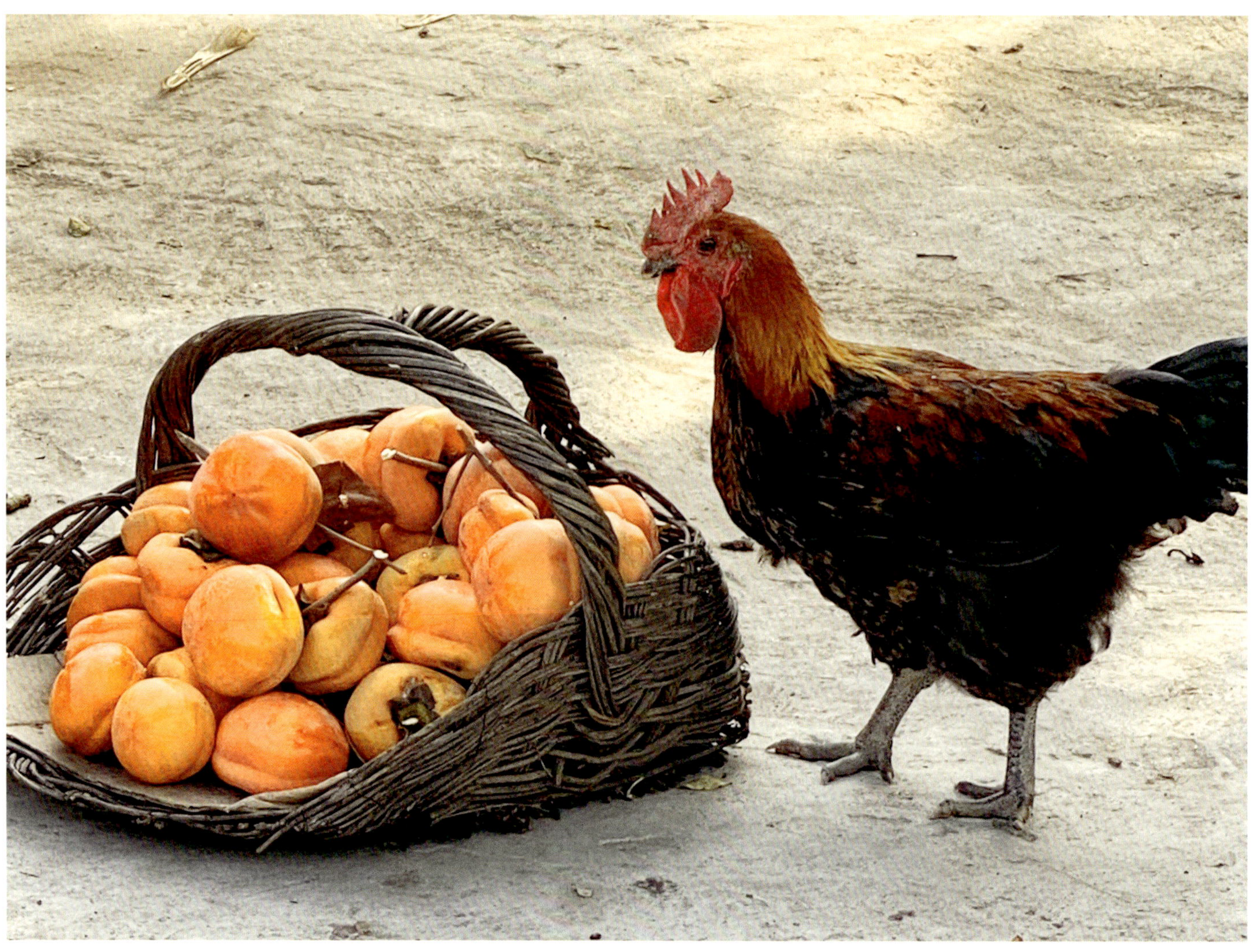

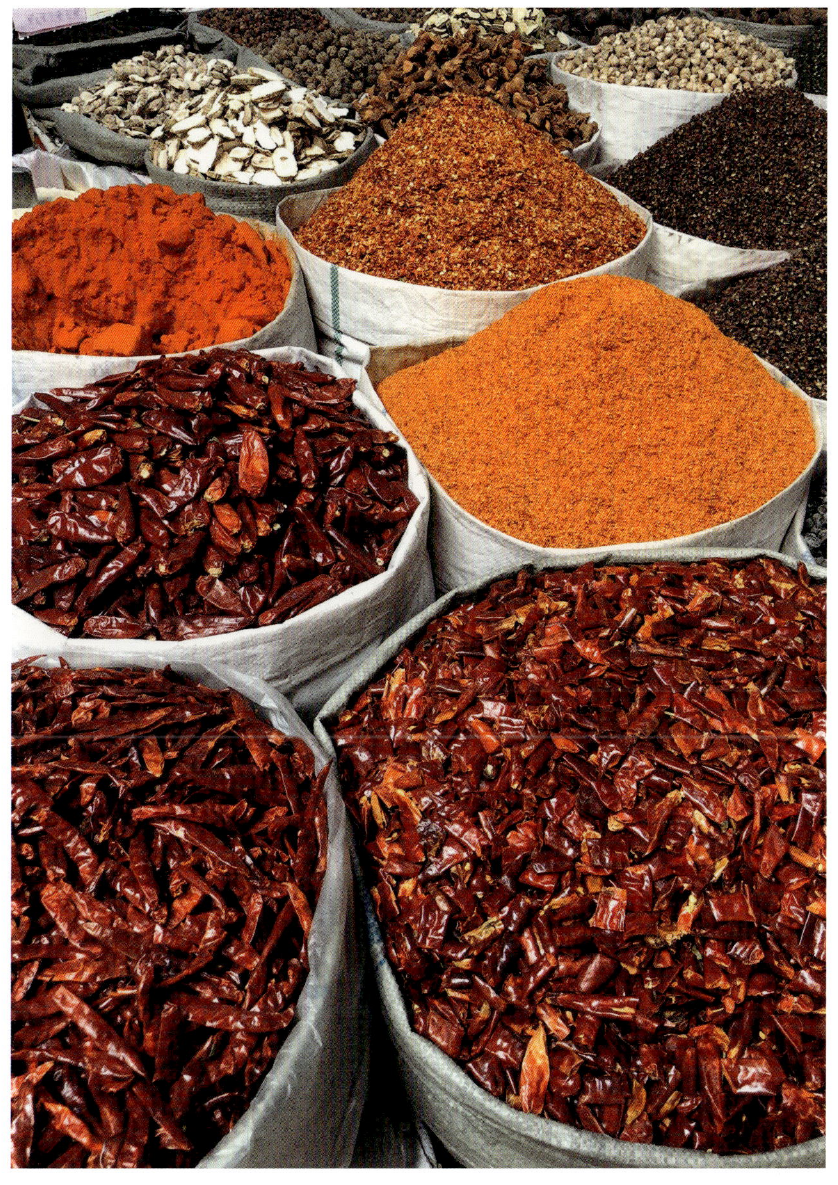

In der wissenschaftlichen Tiefenpsychologie des Westens steht Orange für Kommunikation und den Wunsch nach Einheit. Es gilt als stimmungsaufhellend und stimulierend und wird mit Lust verbunden. Im Westen und Osten ist Orange aber auch eine Warnfarbe, die im Straßenverkehr und in der Gefahrgutkennzeichnung eingesetzt wird.

Ein zu Rot tendierender Orangeton wird als Zinnober oder in einer pastellenen Variante als Koralle bezeichnet. In Peking bietet sich die besondere Gelegenheit, den wunderschönen, warmen Zinnoberfarbton „gefährlich" hautnah zu erleben. Jiang Xun (preisgekrönter Dichter, Maler, Designer und Art Director) renovierte kunstvoll und einfühlsam eine alte anglikanische Kirche und machte daraus einen ungewöhnlich poetischen und stimmungsvollen Bücherladen, den Mofan Bookstore. Mit etwas Glück kann man dort, wenn der Meister selber anwesend ist, unter fachkundiger Anweisung in wahrer Handwerkskunst erlernen, ein Gedicht der Tang-Dynastie in Zinnoberrot auf handgefertigtes Bambuspapier zu übertragen.

Ein Sprichwort aus dem chinesischen Sprachraum lautet: „Man kann den Zinnober nicht anfassen, ohne dass er abfärbt." Es vergleicht die geringe Festigkeit des Minerals mit der Natur der sozialen Wechselwirkungen.

Dried chillies are available in the markets in all degrees of heat and grind, from soft orange to deep red.

Auf den Märkten gibt es getrocknete Chilis in allen Schärfen, Mahlgraden und Farbtönen, von sanftem Orange bis sattem Rot.

A reddish orange tone is called vermilion, whereas the pastel variation is called coral. In Beijing, there is a special opportunity to experience the wonderful, warm shade of vermilion up close. The award-winning poet, painter, designer and art director Jiang Xun tastefully renovated an old Anglican church and made it into an unusually poetic, atmospheric bookstore, the Mofan Bookstore. With a little luck, when the master himself is there, you can expertly learn the true handcraft how to transfer a poem from the Tang Dynasty in vermilion red onto handmade bamboo paper.

One Chinese proverb is: "You cannot touch vermilion without getting stained." It compares the mineral's rather limited firmness with the nature of social interactions.

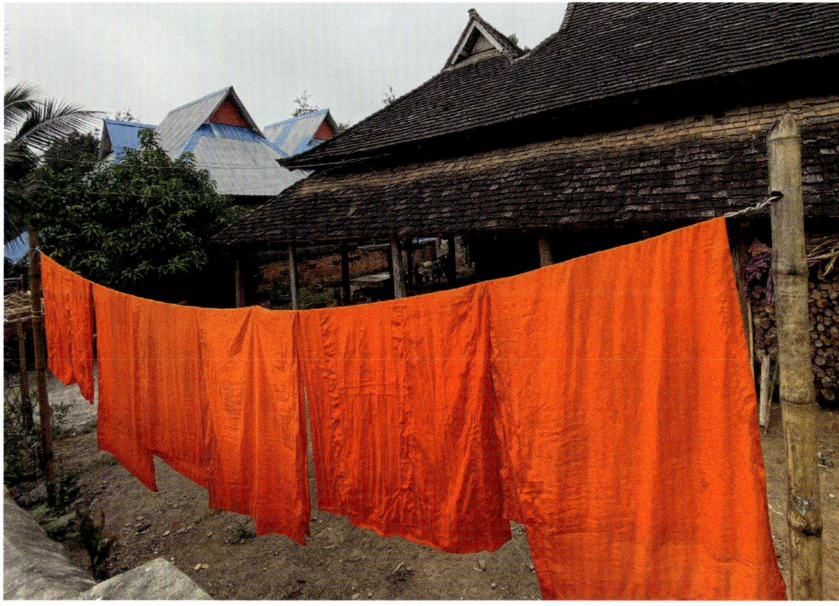

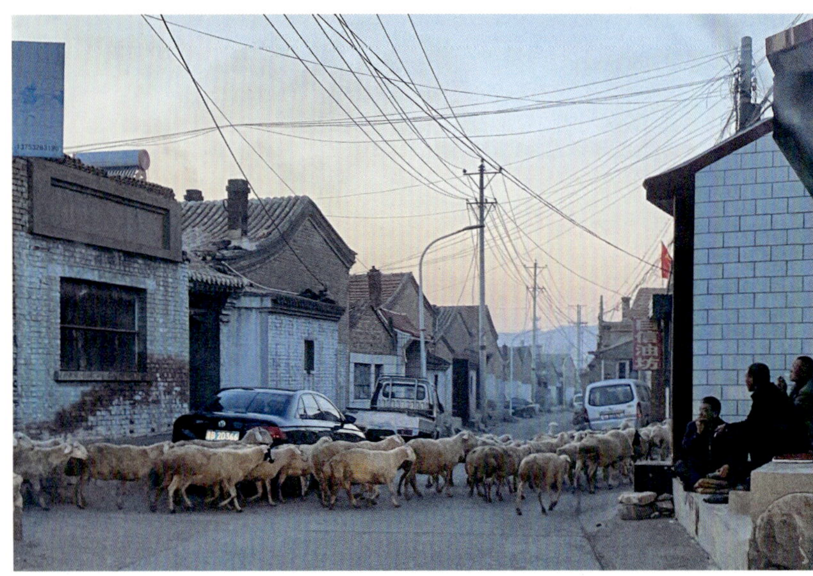

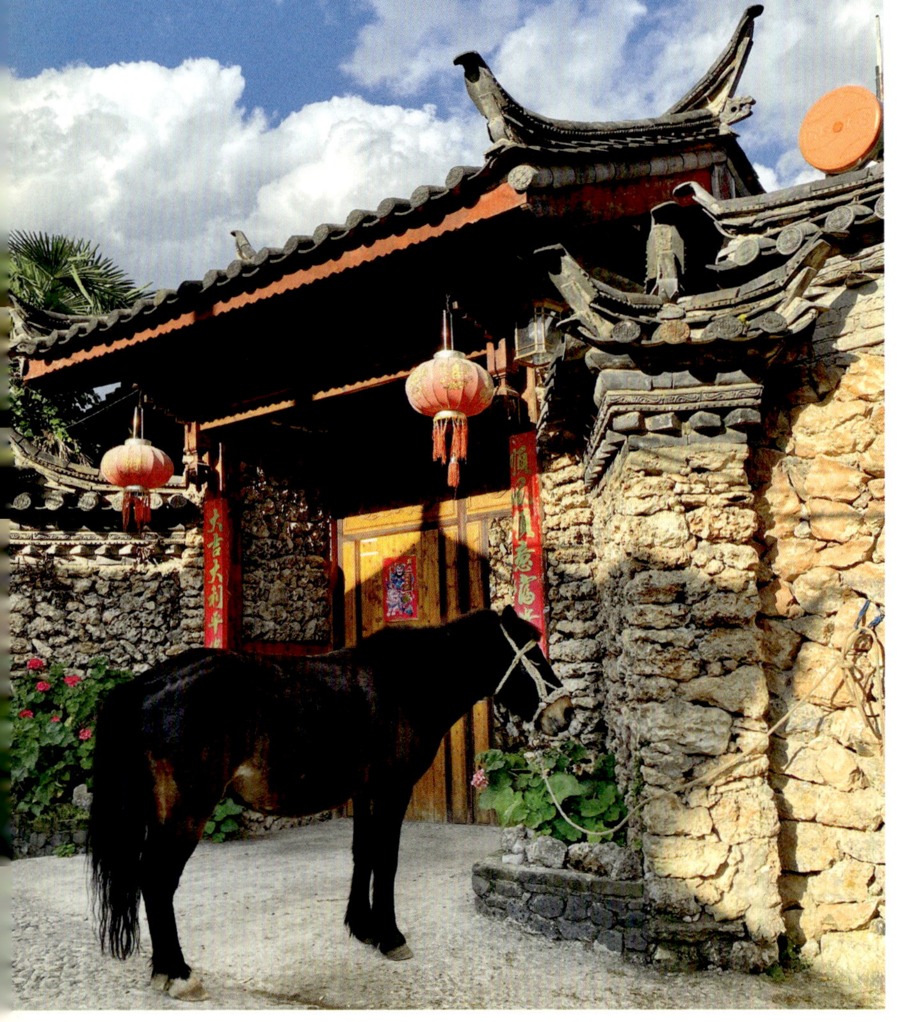

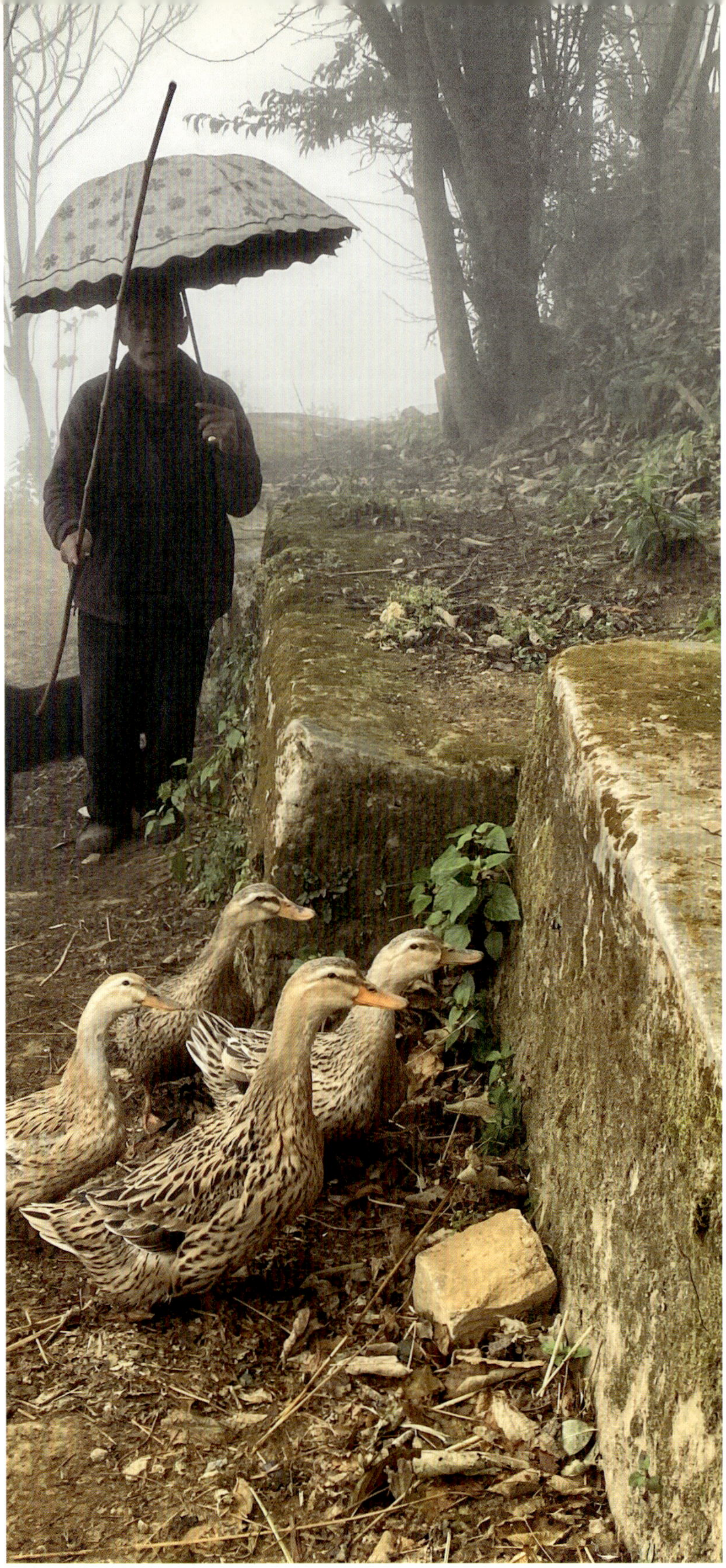

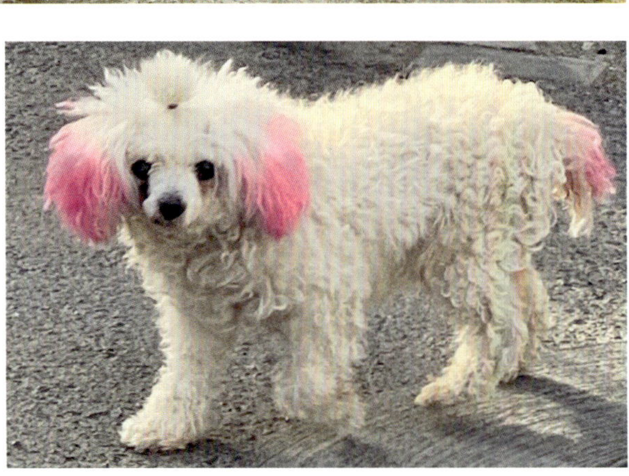

The pig is revered across cultures as a good luck charm. In China, it is also a sign of prosperity. Less highly regarded is the sheep. A Chinese saying goes, "nine out of ten sheep will lead an unhappy life". Keeping dogs and cats was considered bourgeois decadence in the Mao era. Only in 2021 did China's Ministry of Agriculture classify the dog as a pet, rather than a farm animal. China is the country with the most yaks in the world. Only the male grunt ox is called a yak in Tibet. The female animal is called *bri*.

Das Schwein wird über die Kulturen hinweg als Glücksbringer verehrt. In China ist es auch ein Zeichen für Wohlstand. Weniger hoch angesehen ist das Schaf. Eine chinesische Redensart besagt: „Neun von zehn Schafe werden ein unglückliches Leben führen." Hunde und Katzen zu halten, galt in der Mao-Zeit als bourgeoise Dekadenz. Erst 2021 klassifizierte das chinesische Landwirtschaftsministerium den Hund als Haustier, nicht mehr als Nutztier. China ist das yakreichste Land der Welt. Nur der männliche Grunzochse wird in Tibet als Yak bezeichnet. Das weibliche Tier heißt *Bri*.

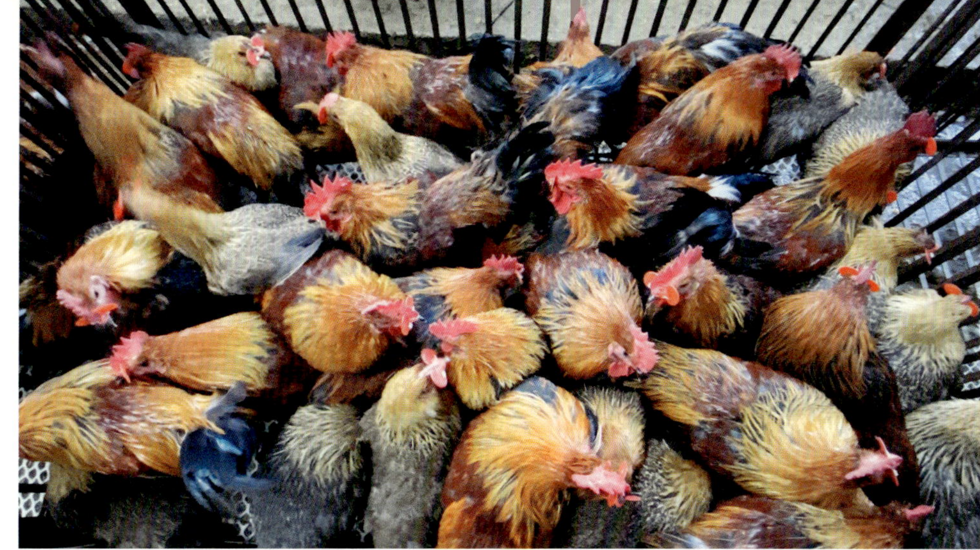

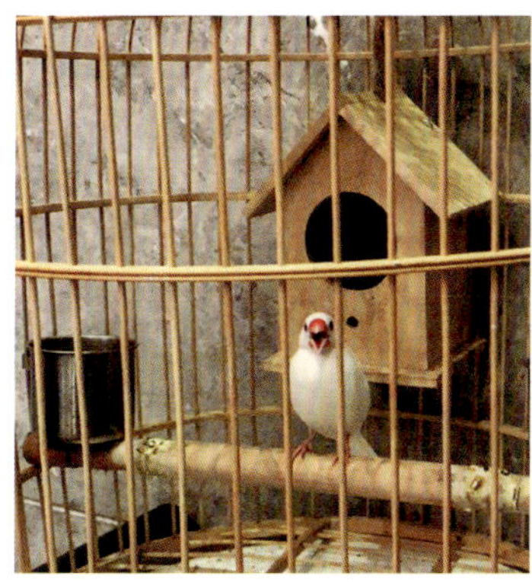

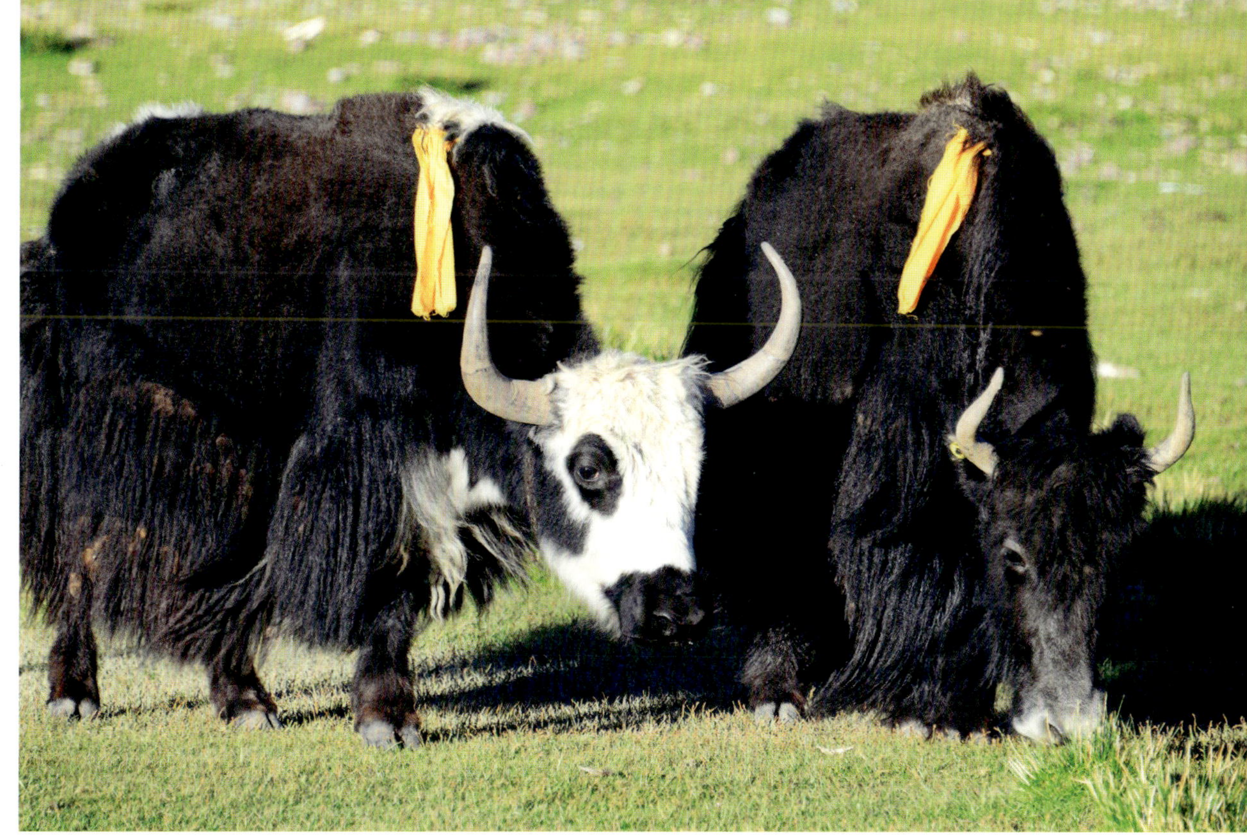

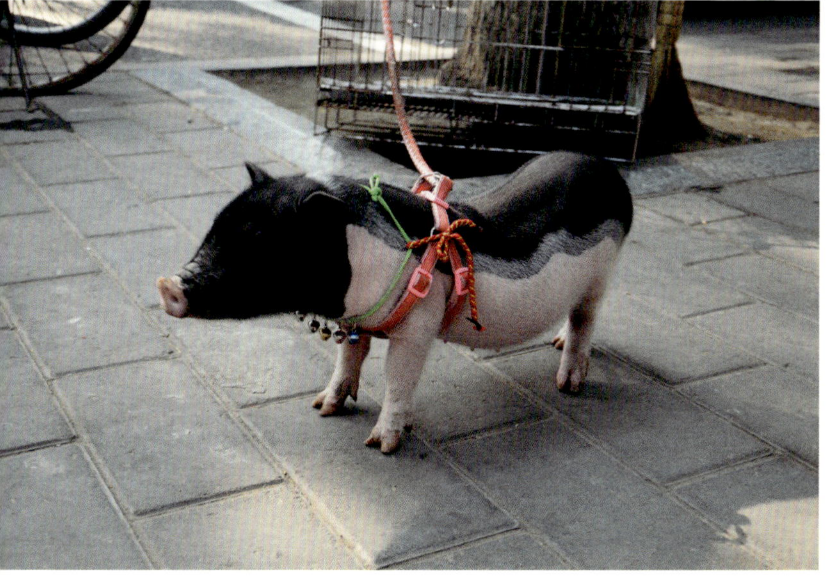

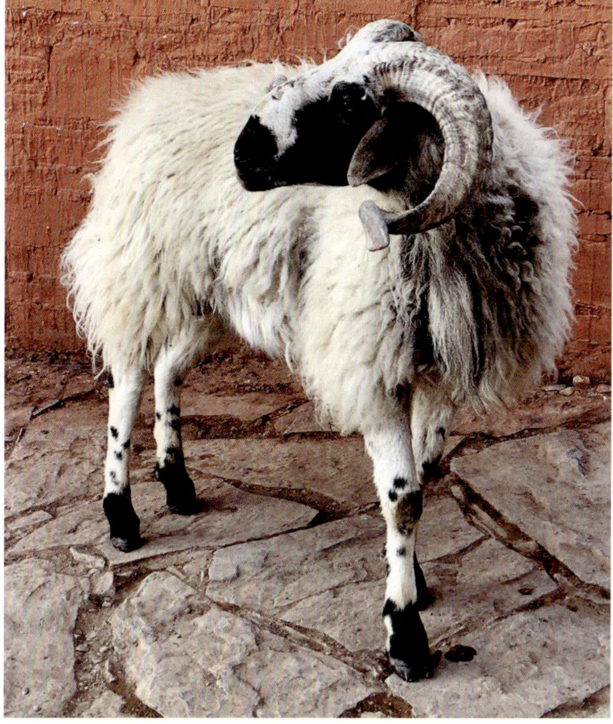

The red cloth

Das rote Tuch

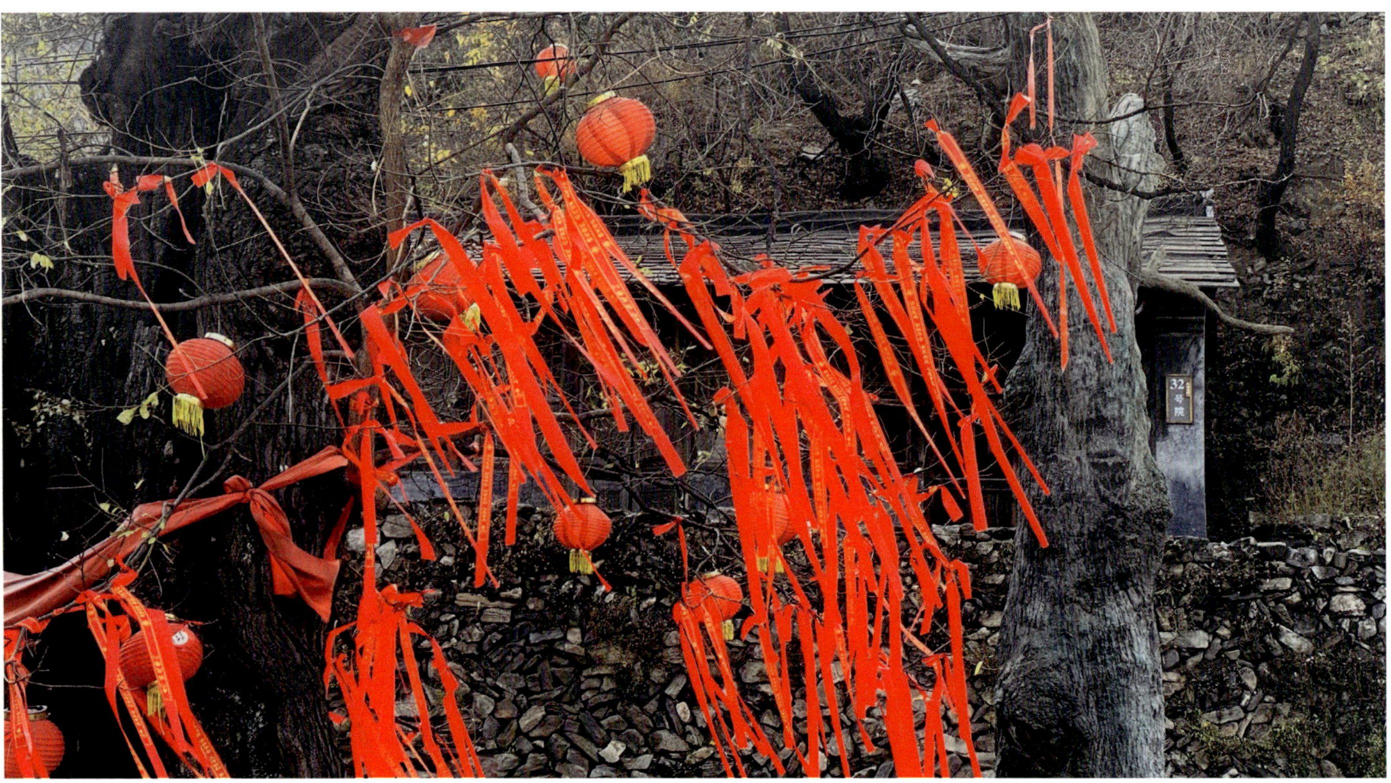

Red ribbons with prayers and wishes / Rote Bänder mit Gebeten und Wünschen

Red is *the* colour in China, since it symbolises luck, happiness and wealth. It stands for the element fire, for summer and the south. No New Year's festival, no birthday would be complete without the red ornaments, red decorations and red clothing. In the *hongbao*, the red envelope, money is given as a present. Relatives, friends and neighbours congratulate each other on the birth of a child with red eggs.

Wearing red ribbons or cloths was part of the wedding customs of many peoples. Long ago, Roman brides were shrouded with a fire-red cloth, the *flammeum*, which was supposed to guarantee fertility and love. Even today, Greek, Albanian and Armenian brides wear red bridal veils. In the west of the Sichuan province, married childless women are given a pair of homemade red pants sewn by their mother. It is said that wearing these red pants will help women conceive as soon as possible.

However, the Chinese dragon Nian is scared of the colour red. In order to scare him away on the Chinese New Year, fireworks are set off, and red lanterns and banners decorate houses and streets. Red underwear should be worn in order to ward off calamity.

Rot ist *die* Farbe in China, denn sie symbolisiert Glück, Freude und Wohlstand. Sie steht für das Element Feuer, für den Sommer und für den Süden. Kein Neujahrsfest, keine Hochzeit und keine Geburtstagsfeier wäre denkbar ohne rote Ornamente, rote Dekoration und rote Kleidung. Im *Hongbao*, dem roten Umschlag, werden Geldgeschenke übergeben. Verwandte, Freunde und Nachbarn überbringen ihre Glückwünsche zur Geburt eines Kindes in Form roter Eier.

Das Tragen roter Bänder oder Tücher gehörte bei vielen Völkern zu den Hochzeitsbräuchen. Schon die römischen Bräute wurden mit einem feuerroten Tuch umhüllt, dem *Flammeum*, welches Fruchtbarkeit und Liebe garantieren sollte. Noch heute tragen griechische,

With a particularly spicy "red chilli flag", the mountain farmers from Huangling in the province of Jiangxi decorate their village in autumn every year.

Mit einer ganz besonders scharfen „Rote-Chili-Flagge" schmücken die Bergbauern von Huangling in der Provinz Jiangxi jährlich im Herbst ihr Dorf. Stolz salutierend, posieren die Dorfkinder für ihre Familien und Besucher.

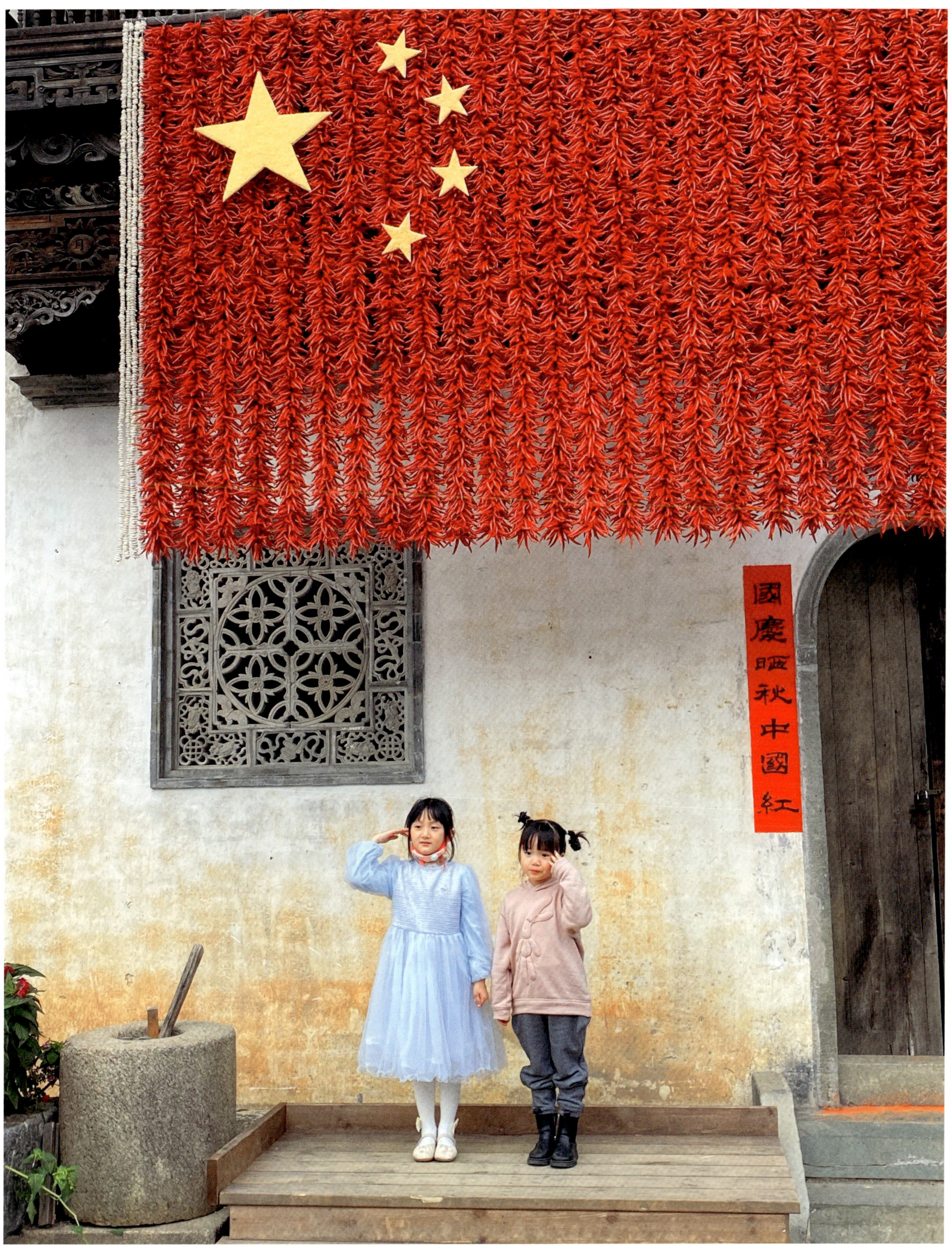
國慶晒秋中國紅

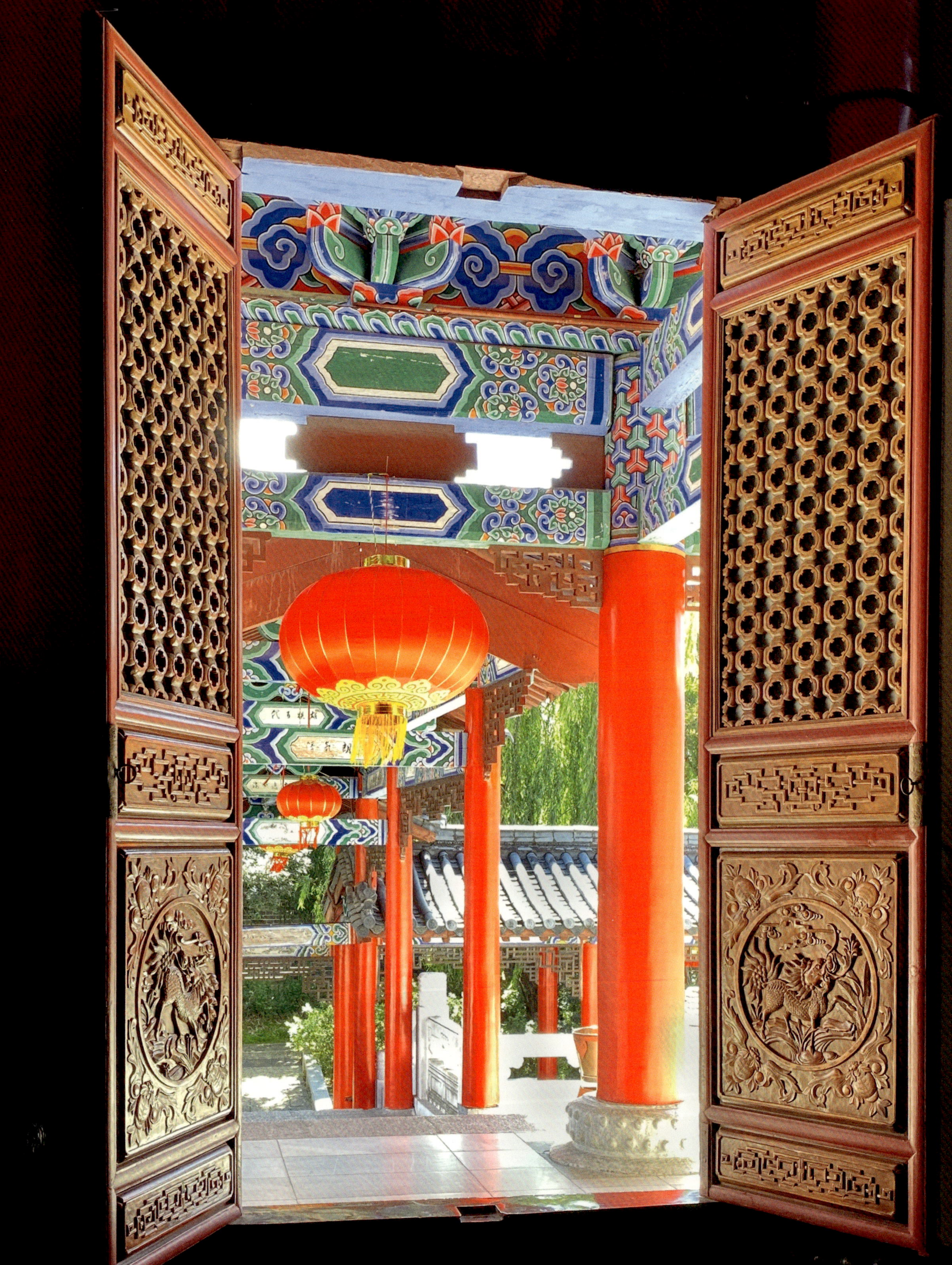

Red is omnipresent in China, not only at funerals. However, the names of the dead are written in red ink in the books of the dead and on funeral banners. That is why it can be considered offensive to sign something with a red pen. One's own name should not appear in red, but in black ink on one's business card.

Since 1949, the red cloth with one large and four smaller yellow stars in the upper left corner has been the flag of the People's Republic of China. Red symbolises both the Communist revolution and the colour of the historical Han Dynasty (206 BC–220 AD). The large star represents the Chinese Communist Party, while the four smaller stars represent the four social classes: Workers, peasants, petit bourgeois and so-called patriotic capitalists.

Until 1912, a triangular yellow cloth with a blue Chinese dragon, the *long*, was the flag of the Qing Dynasty. Its more modern rectangular variant was the national flag of China until then.

Subsequently, the five-colour flag with its vibrant horizontal stripes represented the peoples of China (1912–1949).

Red: Han Chinese
Yellow: Manchu
Blue: Mongolian
White: Hui and Uyghur
Black: Tibetans

The ornate and colourfully painted wooden construction of the roofs is relatively earthquake-proof, but extremely susceptible to fire. The various wooden lattice patterns in doors and windows are a special feature.

Die kunstvolle und farbenfroh bemalte Holzbauweise der Dächer erwies sich als relativ erdbebensicher, dafür aber als extrem brandanfällig. Eine Besonderheit sind die diversen Holzgittermuster in Türen und Fenstern.

albanische und armenische Bräute rote Brautschleier. Im Westen der Provinz Sichuan bekommen verheiratete kinderlose Frauen von ihrer Mutter eine selbstgenähte rote Hose geschenkt. Man sagt, dass das Tragen dieser roten Hose den Frauen helfen wird, so schnell wie möglich schwanger zu werden.

Aber der chinesische Drache Nian fürchtet sich vor der Farbe Rot. Um ihn an Neujahr abzuschrecken, wird kräftig geböllert, und rote Laternen und Schriftbänder zieren Häuser und Straßen. Rote Unterwäsche soll getragen werden, um Unheil abzuwenden.

Rot ist omnipräsent in China, nur nicht bei Beerdigungen. Jedoch werden die Namen der Toten in roter Schrift in Totenbücher und auf Beerdigungsbanner geschrieben. Deshalb kann es als anstößig empfunden werden, wenn ein roter Stift zum Unterschreiben verwendet wird. Auch sollte der eigene Name nicht in roter, sondern in schwarzer Schrift auf der Visitenkarte stehen.

Erst seit 1949 ist das rote Tuch mit einem großen und vier kleineren gelben Sternen in der oberen linken Ecke die Flagge der Volksrepublik China. Rot symbolisiert sowohl die kommunistische Revolution wie auch die Farbe der historischen Han-Dynastie (206 v. Chr.–220 n Chr.). Der große Stern steht für die kommunistische Partei Chinas, während die vier kleineren Sterne die vier sozialen Klassen repräsentieren: Arbeiter, Bauern, Kleinbürger und sogenannte patriotische Kapitalisten.

Bis 1912 war ein dreieckiges gelbes Tuch mit einem blauen chinesischen Drachen, dem *Long*, die Flagge der Qing-Dynastie. Ihre modernere rechteckige Variante war bis dahin die Nationalflagge Chinas.

Im Anschluss repräsentierte die Fünf-Farben-Flagge mit ihren bunten horizontalen Streifen die Völker Chinas (1912–1949).

Rot: Han-Chinesen
Gelb: Mandschu
Blau: Mongolen
Weiß: Hui und Uiguren
Schwarz: Tibeter

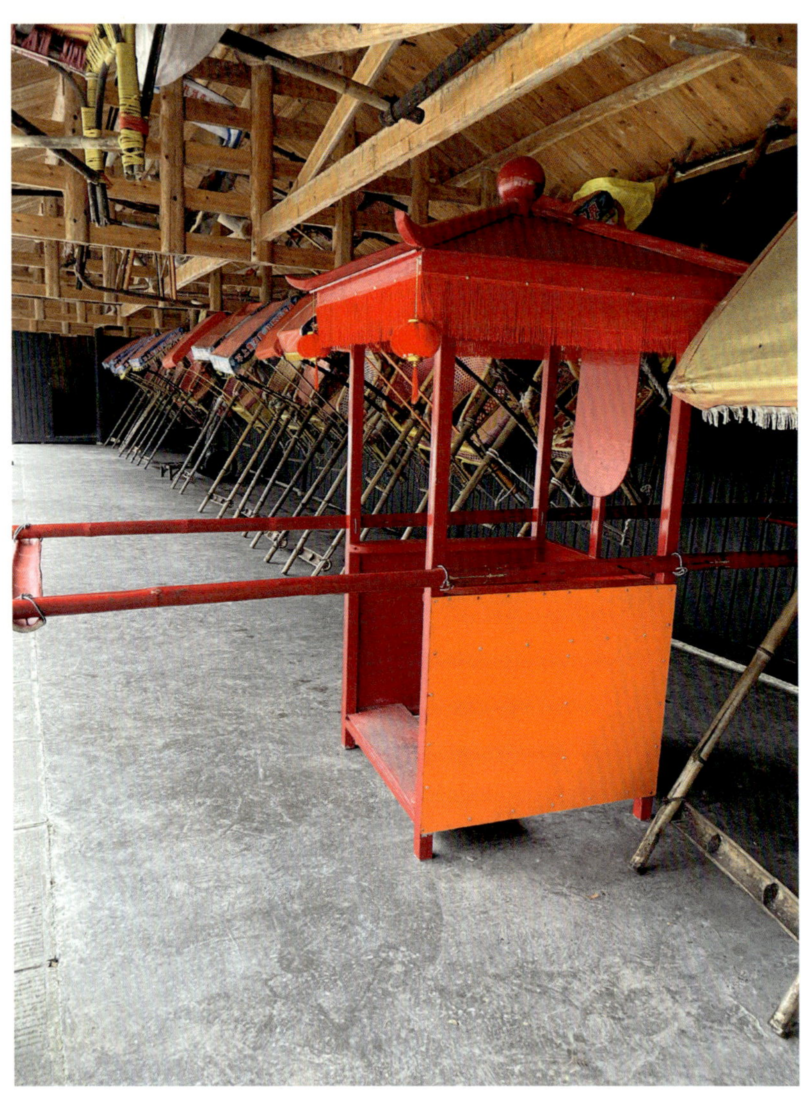

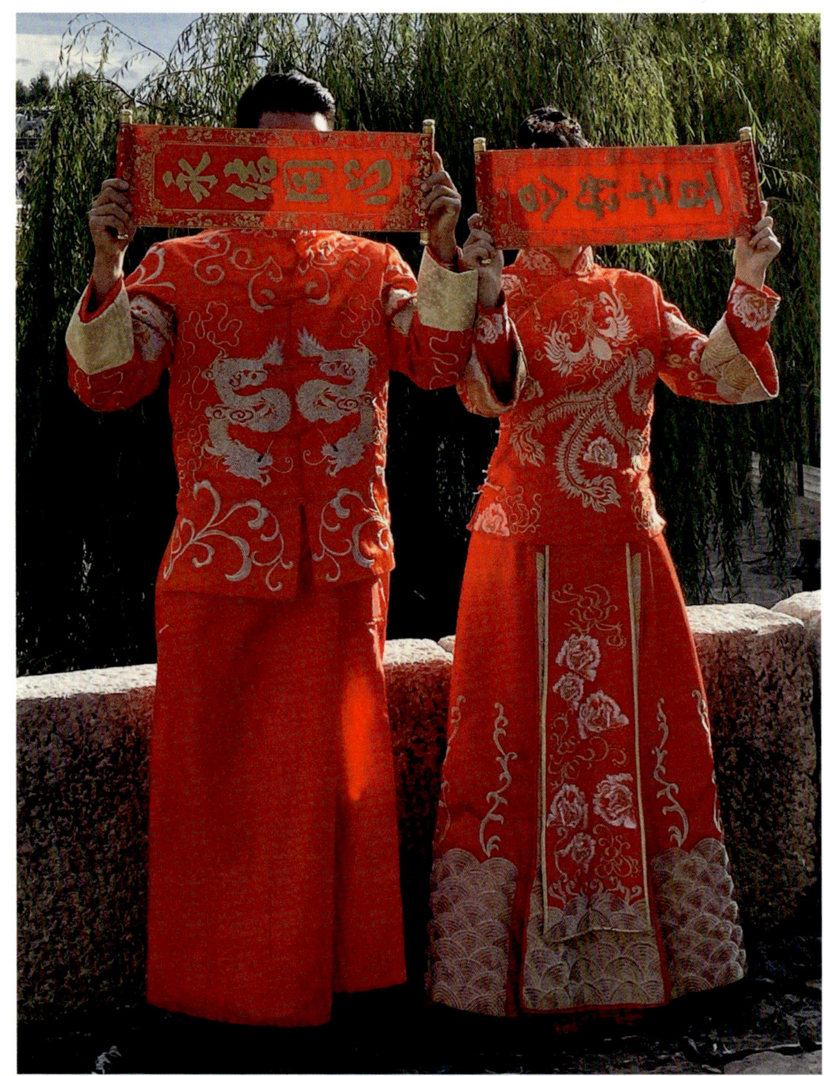

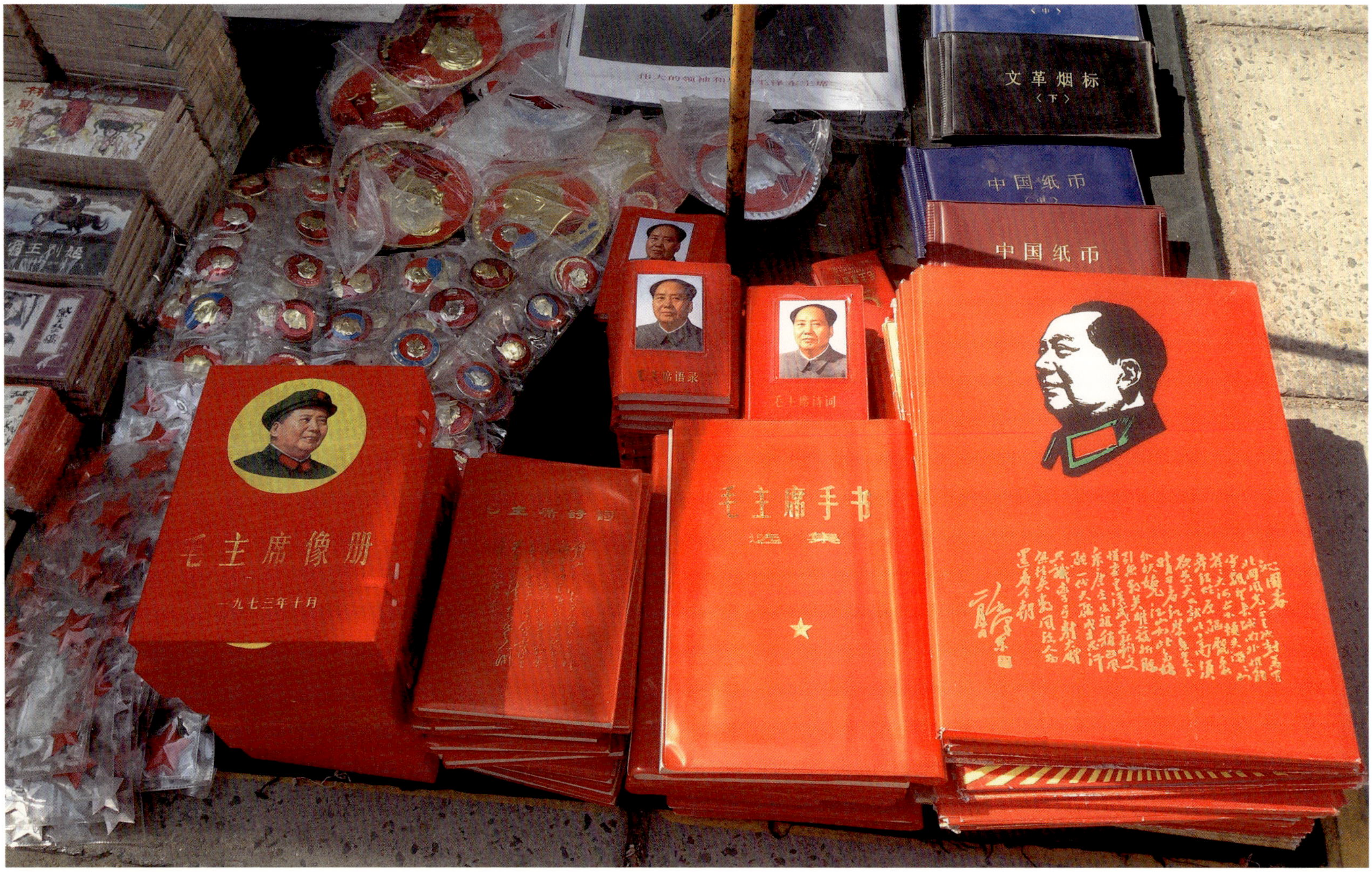

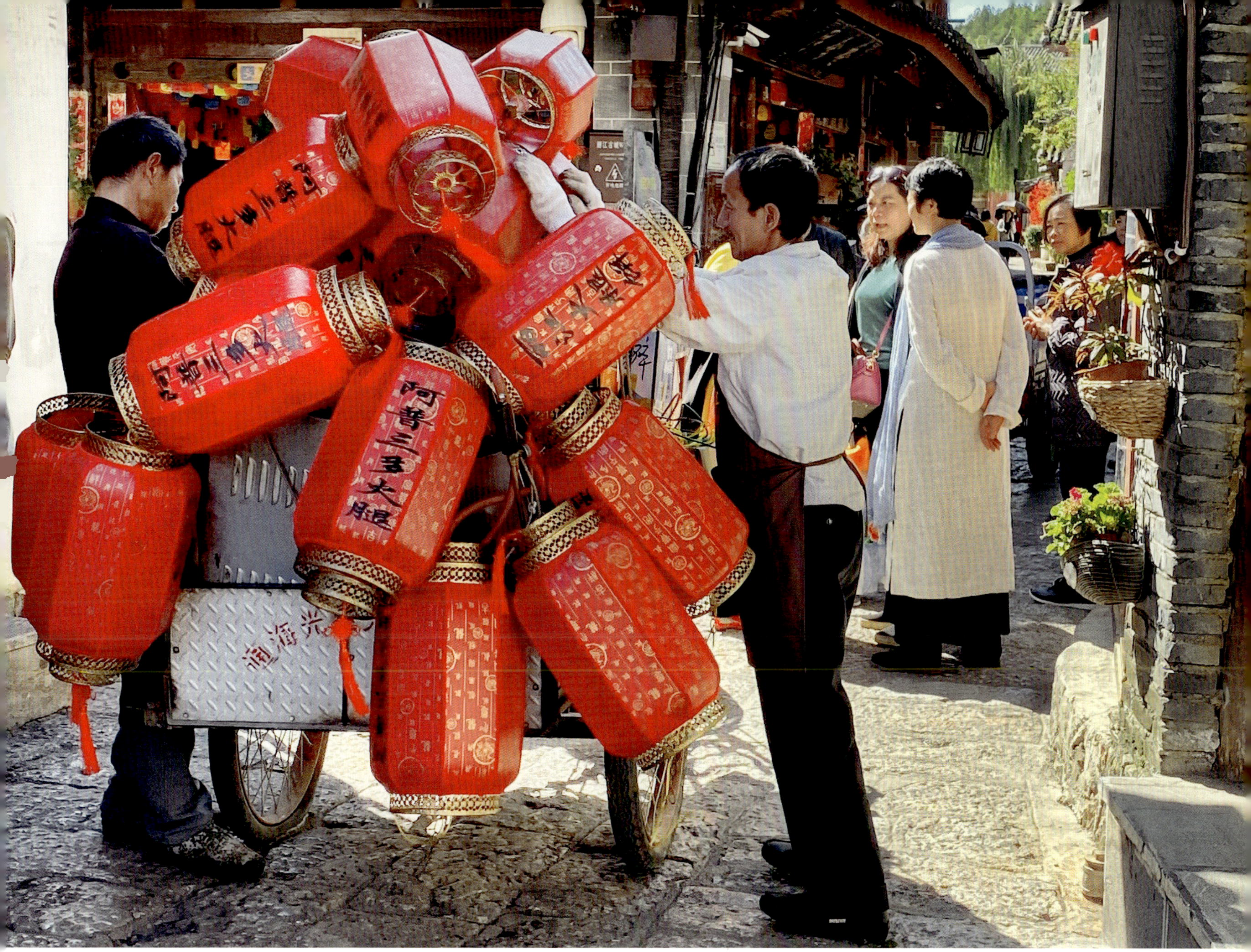

Clockwise from top left:
The Chinese litter had to be red for the wedding, when the bride was carried to the groom. Even today, young married couples like to be photographed in traditional red wedding attire. Red lanterns for the new tea store or on junks promise good luck. Millions of Chinese learned Mao's *Little Red Book* by heart. The small format was chosen so that the collection of sayings could fit into the breast pocket of the army uniform. Only the Bible has a higher circulation worldwide.

Von oben links, im Uhrzeigersinn:
Die chinesische Sänfte musste rot sein für die Hochzeit, wenn die Braut zum Bräutigam getragen wurde. Auch heute noch lassen sich junge Ehepaare gerne in roter traditioneller Hochzeitskleidung fotografieren. Rote Laternen für den neuen Teeladen oder an Dschunken verheißen Glück. Millionen Chinesen lernten das als Mao-Bibel bekannte rote Büchlein auswendig. Das kleine Format wurde gewählt, damit die Sprüchesammlung in die Brusttasche der Armeeuniform passt. Nur die echte Bibel hat weltweit eine höhere Auflage.

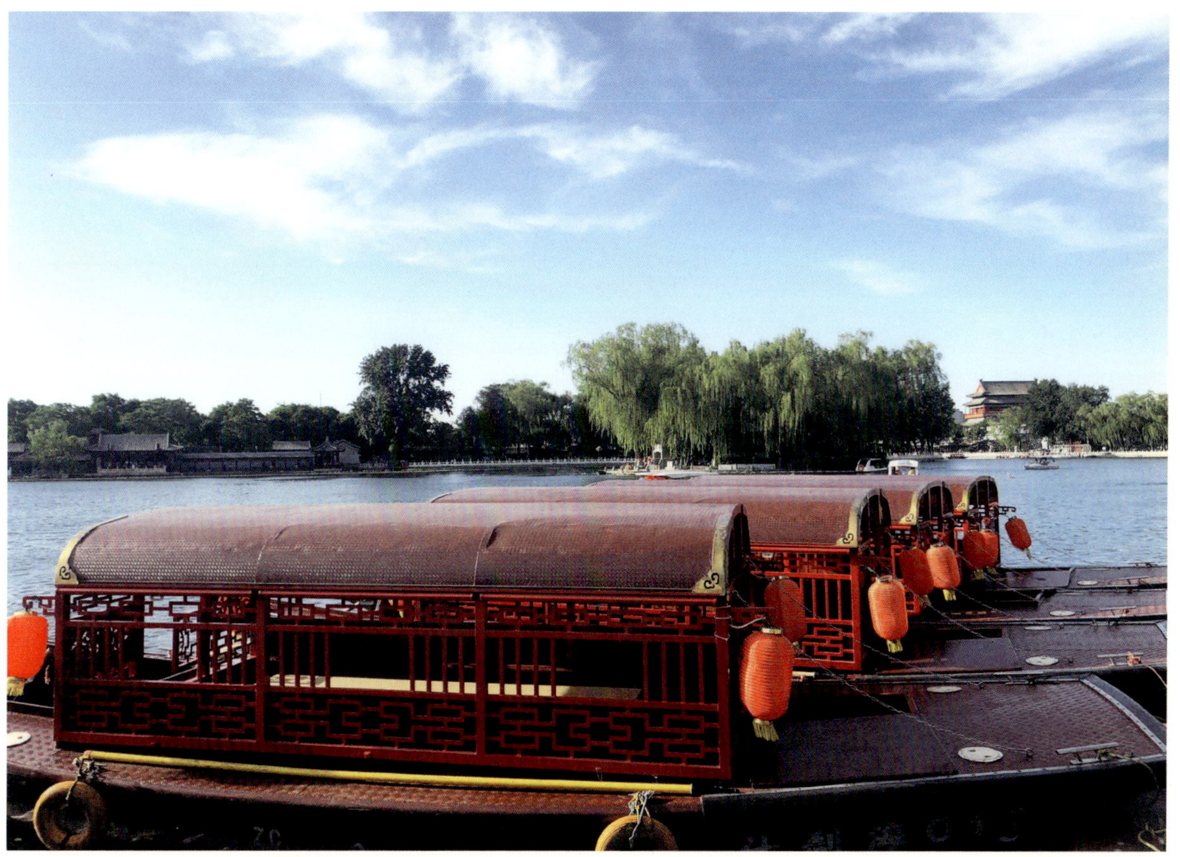

Immortal white
Unsterbliches Weiß

For wrapping gifts, it is best to use red or gold wrapping paper. Never use white, because white is the colour of mourning, it is associated with death. Deaths are announced by white lanterns, and white clothes and hats are reserved exclusively for attending mourning ceremonies, even in modern China. However, white is also the colour of metal, an image of autumn, harvest, the West, and it represents brightness, purity and fulfilment. Before the spread of blue and white porcelain, monochrome, mostly white ceramics were the most popular, and they remained so in elite circles until the end of the imperial period.

Zum Einpacken von Geschenken eignet sich am besten rotes oder goldenes Geschenkpapier. Niemals weißes, denn Weiß ist die Farbe der Trauer, sie wird mit dem Tod assoziiert. Todesfälle werden von weißen Laternen verkündet, und weiße Kleidung und Hüte sind auch im modernen China ausschließlich dem Besuch von Trauerzeremonien vorbehalten. Weiß ist aber auch die Farbe des Metalls, ein Bild für den Herbst, die Ernte, den Westen, und es steht für Helligkeit, Reinheit und Erfüllung. Vor der Verbreitung des Blauweißporzellans war die monochrome, meist weiße Keramik am beliebtesten, und sie blieb es in elitären Kreisen noch bis zum Ende der Kaiserzeit.

Weiße Tauben über den Dächern der Innenstadt sind ein vertrautes Bild in Peking. In den *Hutongs* hört man das Gurren und kann den Taubenverschlag oben auf den Häusern sehen. In China hat die Brieftaubenzucht eine lange Tradition. Nachrichten können über Hunderte Kilometer transportiert werden. In Flugwettbewerben gibt es Preisgelder in schwindelerregenden Höhen zu gewinnen. Dem aufmerksamen Spaziergänger in Peking mag das musikalisch pfeifende Geräusch beim Vorbeifliegen der weißen Vögel aufgefallen sein. Tatsächlich rührt es von der sogenannten Taubenflöte, einer kleinen Pfeife oder einem Set mehrerer Pfeifen, die einer Taube auf die mittleren Schwanzfedern gebunden werden und beim Flug, durch die Luftbewegung angeregt, pfeifende Geräusche erzeugt. Taubenflöten werden aus winzigen Schilf- oder Bambusröhrchen und aus Knochen geschnitzten Flötenköpfen hergestellt. Ursprünglich waren sie zur Abwehr von Greifvögeln gedacht. Mittlerweile hat sich ein Sport daraus entwickelt.

In Peking hat der Anzahl weißer Tauben, des Friedenssymbols schlechthin, nur die Vogelgrippe von 2003 bis 2004 etwas zugesetzt. 2019 rückten die Vögel nochmals in das Licht der Aufmerksamkeit, als ihnen Flugverbot über Peking erteilt wurde. Die Volksrepublik China feierte damals mit einer riesigen Militärparade ihr 70-jähriges Bestehen,

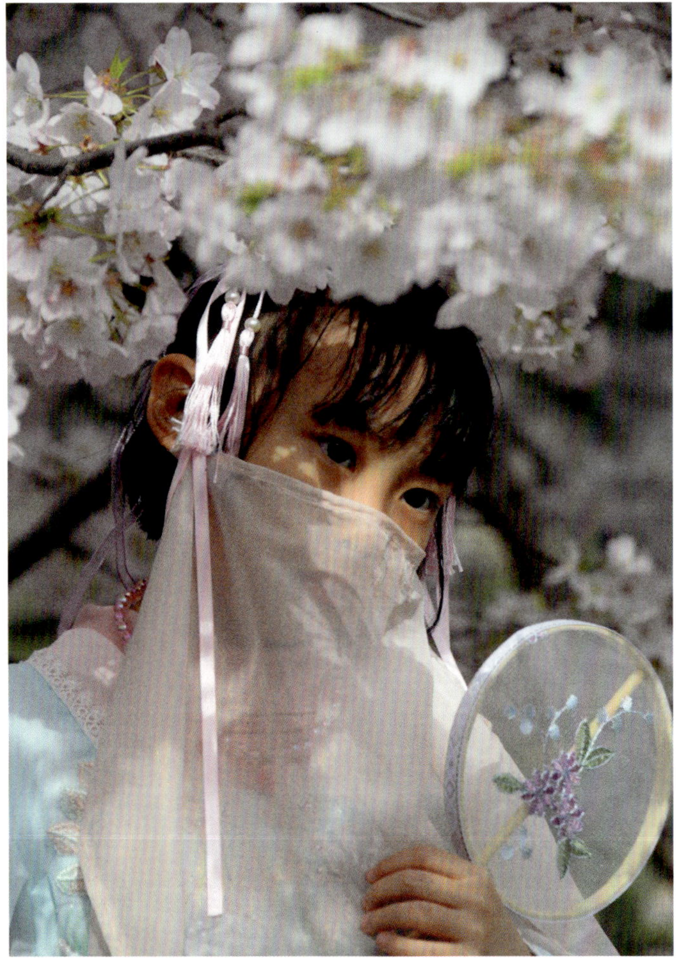

In Yuyuantan Park in Beijing alone, more than 20 different kinds of pink and white cherry trees bloom in April. From June, the large lotus blossoms on the lakes of the numerous green spaces are impressive.

Allein im Yuyuantan Park in Peking blühen im April mehr als 20 verschiedene Arten von Kirschbäumen in Rosa und Weiß. Ab Juni beeindrucken die großen Lotusblüten auf den Seen der zahlreichen Grünanlagen.

Right page:
The white Buddhist stupa in Jinghong's Manting Park in Xishuangbanna was built in 1203 in the shape of bamboo shoots. Unlike pagodas, stupas are not hollowed out.

Rechte Seite:
Die weiße buddhistische Stupa im Manting-Park von Jinghong in Xishuangbanna wurde 1203 in der Form von Bambussprossen erbaut. Im Unterschied zu Pagoden sind Stupas nicht ausgehöhlt.

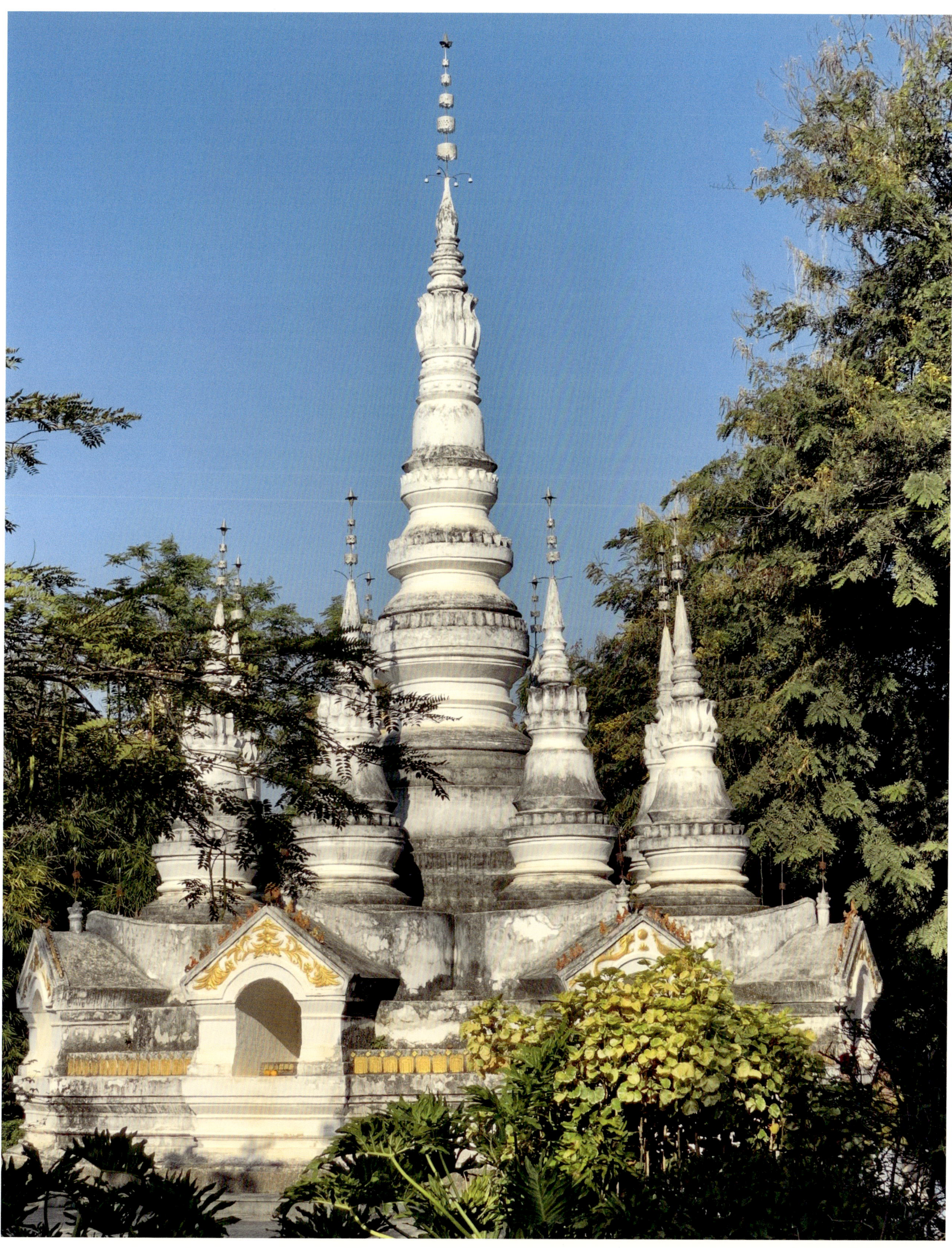

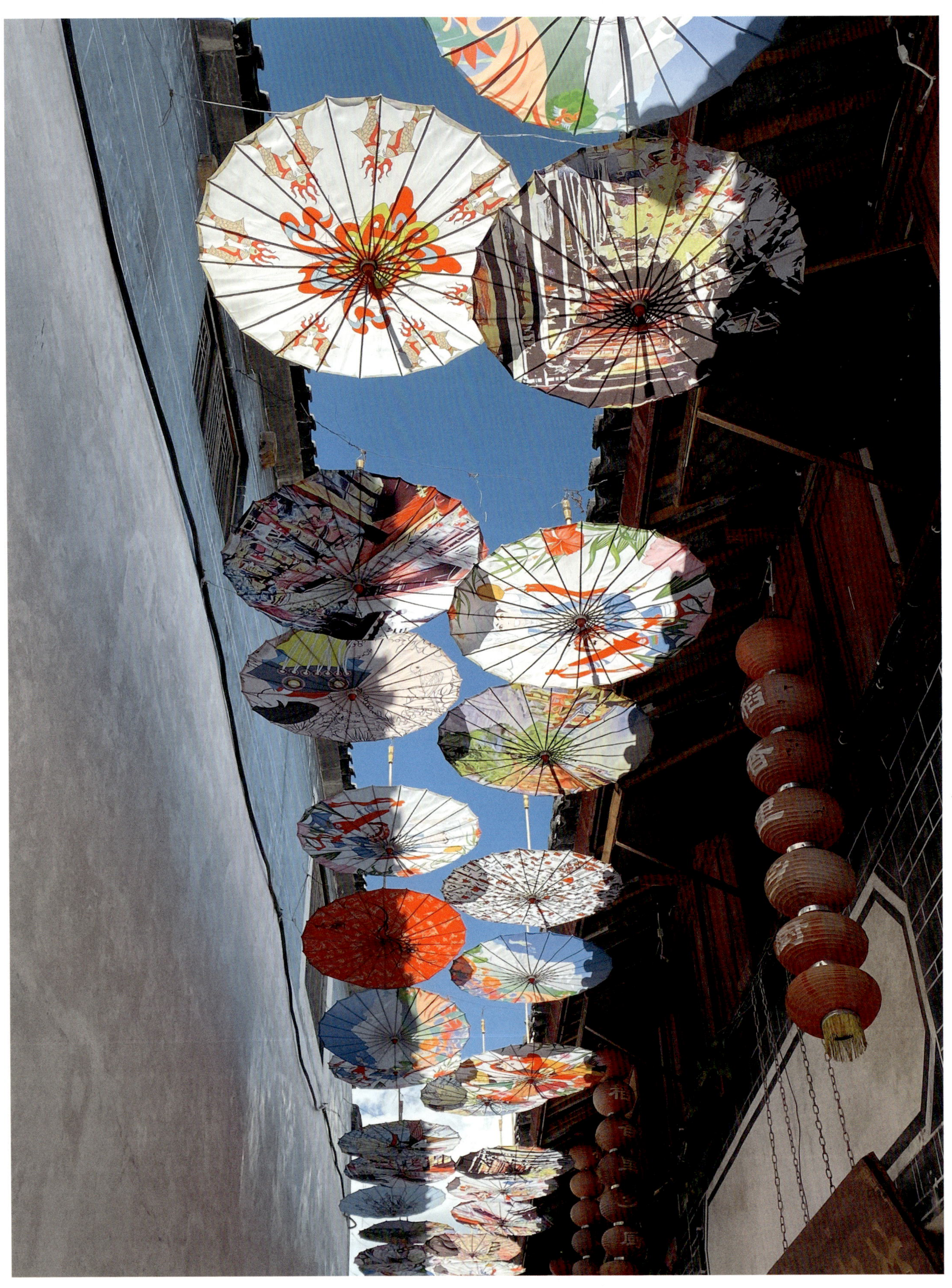

White pigeons above the rooftops of downtown are a familiar sight in Beijing. In the *hutongs* you can hear the cooing and see the pigeon coop on top of the houses. In China, the breeding of carrier pigeons has a long tradition. The birds can transport messages over hundreds of kilometres. In flying competitions, there are prizes to be won at dizzying heights. The attentive walker in Beijing may have noticed the musical whistling sound as the white birds fly by. In fact, it comes from the so-called pigeon flute, a small whistle or set of several whistles that are tied to a pigeon's middle tail feathers and produce whistling sounds as they fly, stimulated by air movement. Pigeon flutes are made from tiny reed or bamboo tubes and flute heads carved from bone. Originally, they were intended to repel birds of prey. In the meantime, a sport has developed out from it.

In Beijing, the number of white pigeons, the symbol of peace par excellence, has only been somewhat affected by the bird flu from 2003 to 2004. In 2019, the birds once again came into the spotlight when they were banned from flying over Beijing. At the time, the People's Republic of China was celebrating its 70th anniversary – the anniversary of the Communist Party's rule – with a huge military parade. Tanks and other military vehicles as well as airplanes and fighter jets were presented. The security precautions were correspondingly strict. No-fly zones were set up, curfews were imposed on hotel guests in Beijing, and flying carrier pigeons, drones and kites were taboo.

das Jubiläum der Herrschaft der kommunistischen Partei. Panzer und weitere militärische Fahrzeuge sowie Flugzeuge und Kampfjets wurden vorgestellt. Dementsprechend streng fielen auch die Sicherheitsvorkehrungen aus. Es wurden Flugverbotszonen eingerichtet, Ausgangssperren für Hotelgäste in Peking erlassen, und Brieftauben, Drohnen und Drachen fliegen zu lassen, war tabu.

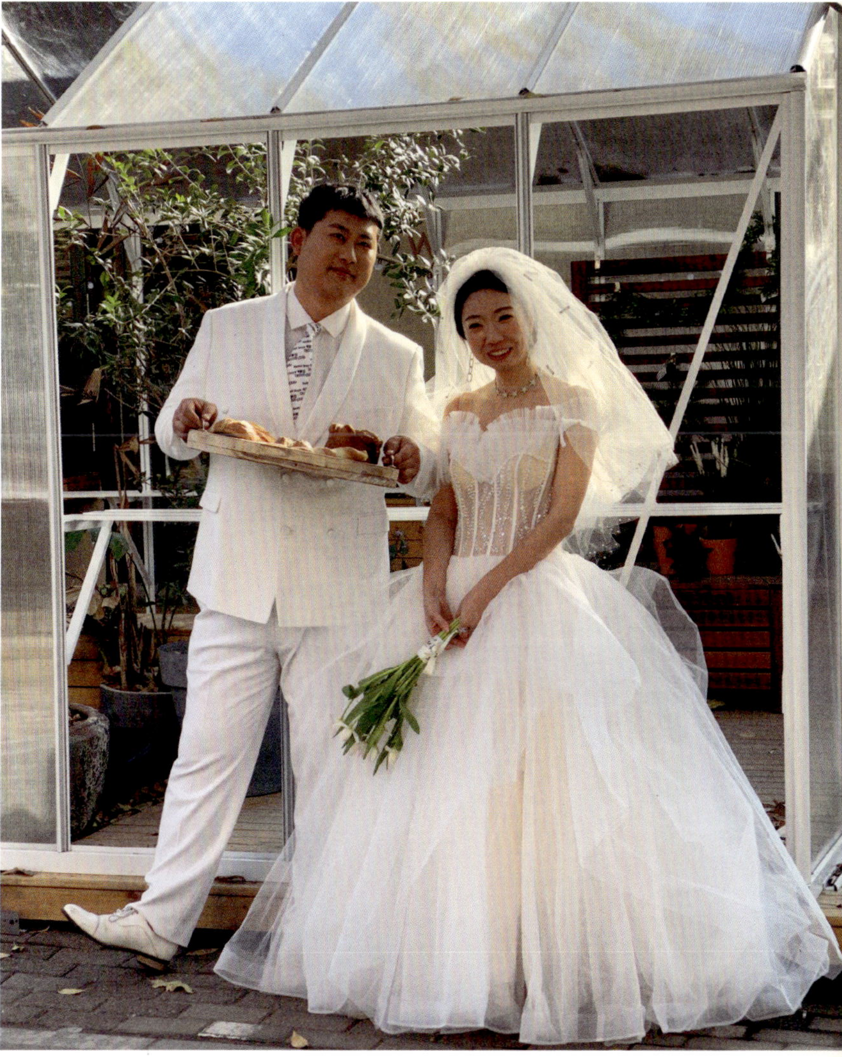

Young bridal couples increasingly like to follow western customs and marry all in white.

Junge Brautpaare folgen zunehmend westlichen Bräuchen und heiraten ganz in Weiß.

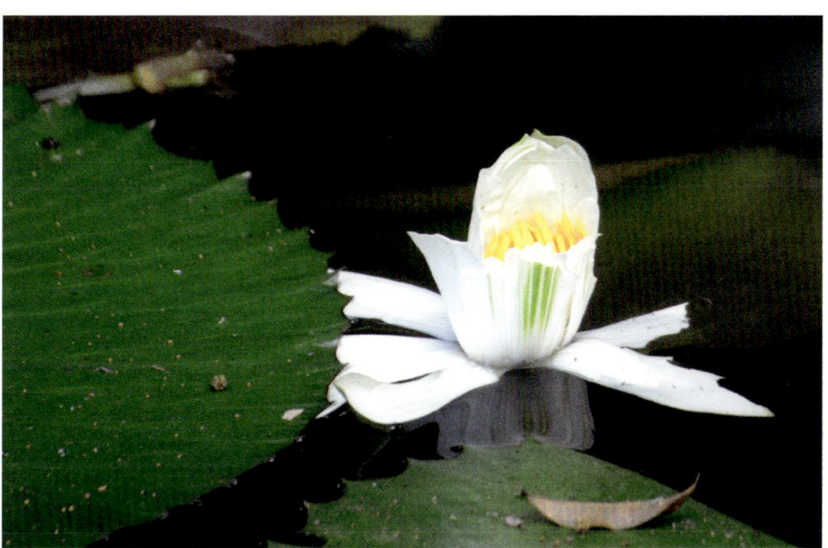

The white lotus flower stands for the purification of conscience and supernatural knowledge. She also represents the white Tara, a peaceful female *bodhisattva* who belongs to the deities of long life.

Die Weiße Lotusblume steht für die Reinigung des Gewissens und übersinnliches Wissen. Sie repräsentiert auch die weiße Tara, eine weibliche friedvolle *Bodhisattva*, die zu den Gottheiten des langen Lebens gehört.

Left page:
Hand-painted Chinese oil-paper umbrellas decorate the streets of Lijiang, Yunnan Province, while protecting them from the sun.

Linke Seite:
Handbemalte chinesische Ölpapierschirme schmücken die Straßen von Lijiang in der Provinz Yunnan und schützen gleichzeitig vor der Sonne.

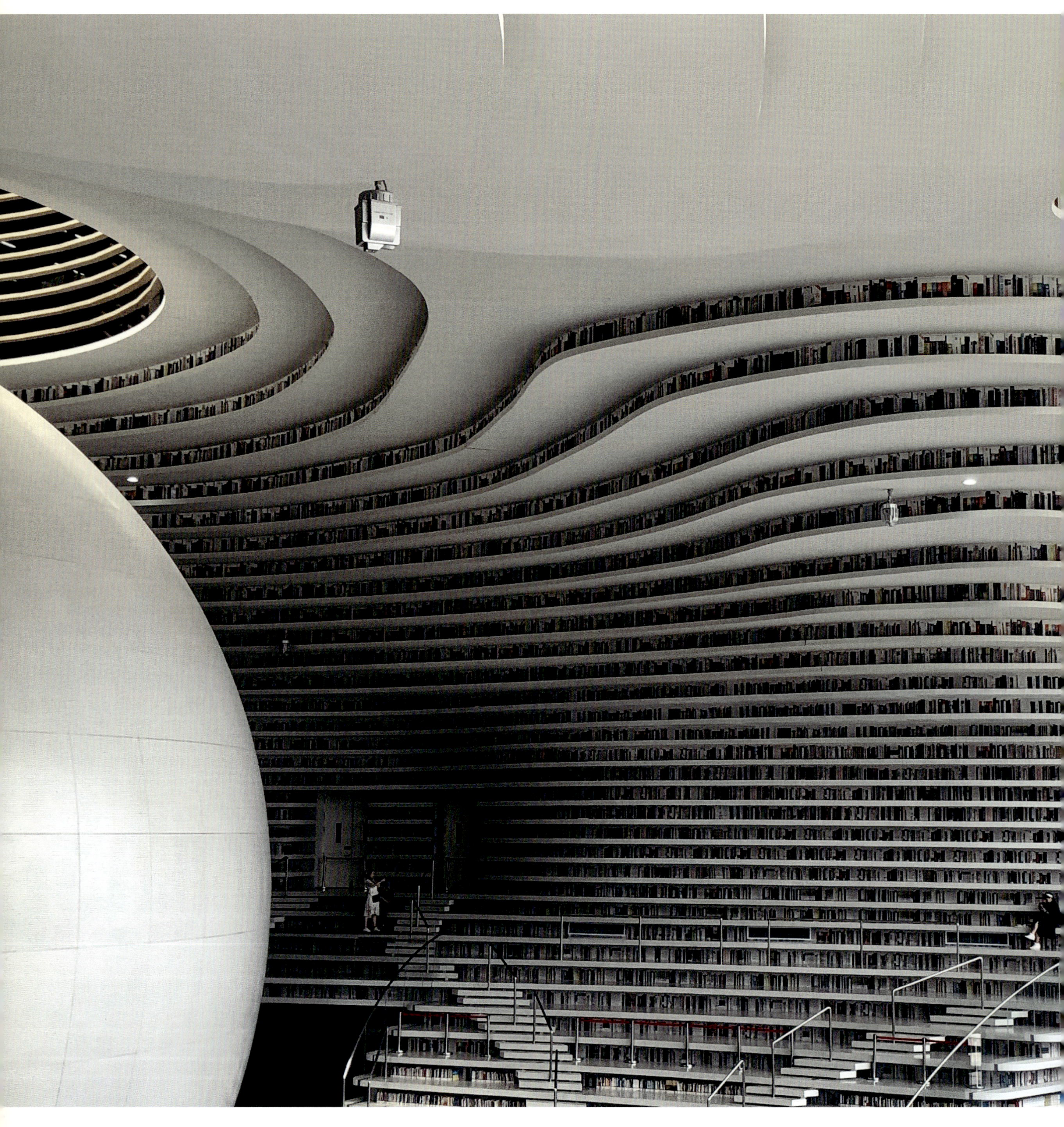

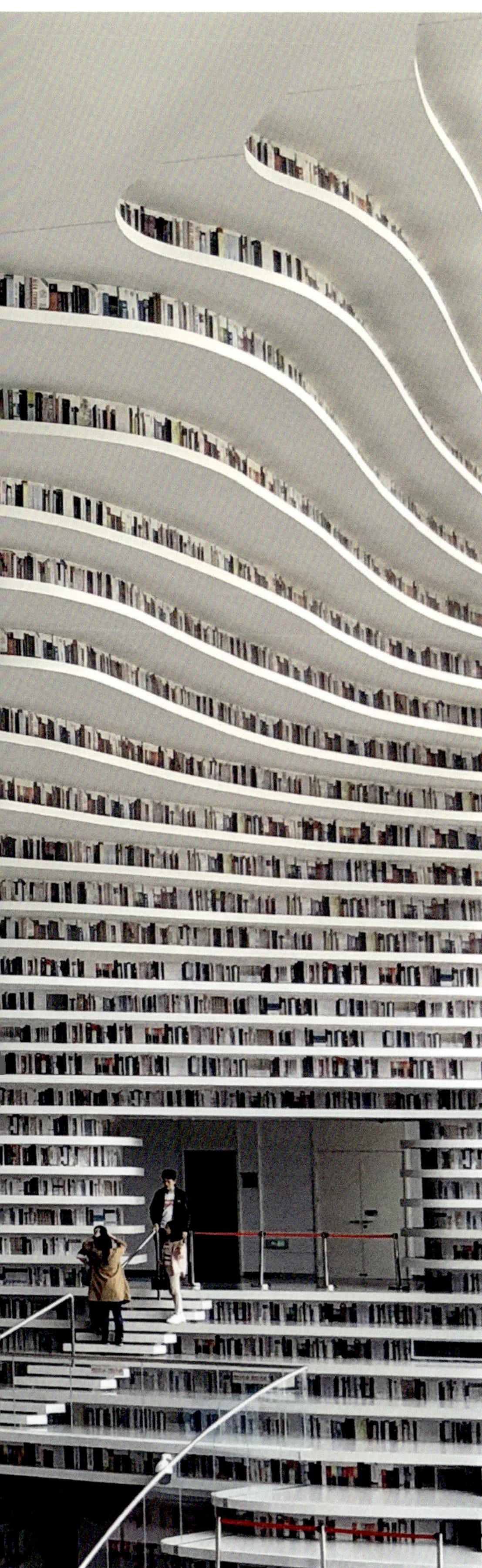

The futuristic Binhai Library in the coastal city of Tianjin, also called "The Eye", was opened in October 2017 and designed by the Dutch architecture firm MVRDV. Inside the five-story building, the white atrium is mesmerising with its undulating bookshelves from floor to ceiling. When necessary, the stairs serve as seating or as a space for discussions or lectures. 1.2 million books will occupy an area of 3,344 square metres! The design is meant to evoke the depths of the sea and the slopes of the Chinese countryside. The actual centre of the library is represented by the "eye" itself. Like an oyster pearl or the pupil of an eye, the large sphere housing the auditorium appears in the centre. A breath-taking reading atmosphere!

Die futuristische Binhai-Bibliothek in der Küstenstadt Tianjin, auch „Das Auge" genannt, wurde im Oktober 2017 eröffnet und von der niederländischen Architekturfirma MVRDV entworfen. Im Inneren des fünfstöckigen Gebäudes fasziniert das weiße Atrium mit seinen wellenförmig angeordneten Bücherregalen vom Boden bis zur Decke. Bei Bedarf dienen die Treppen als Sitzgelegenheiten oder als Raum für Diskussionen oder Vorträge. 1,2 Millionen Bücher werden auf einer Fläche von 3344 Quadratmetern stehen! Die Gestaltung soll an die Tiefen des Meeres und die Hänge der chinesischen Landschaft erinnern. Den eigentlichen Mittelpunkt der Bibliothek stellt das „Auge" selbst dar. Wie eine Austernperle oder die Pupille eines Auges wirkt die große, das Auditorium beherbergende Kugel in der Mitte. Atemberaubende Leseatmosphäre!

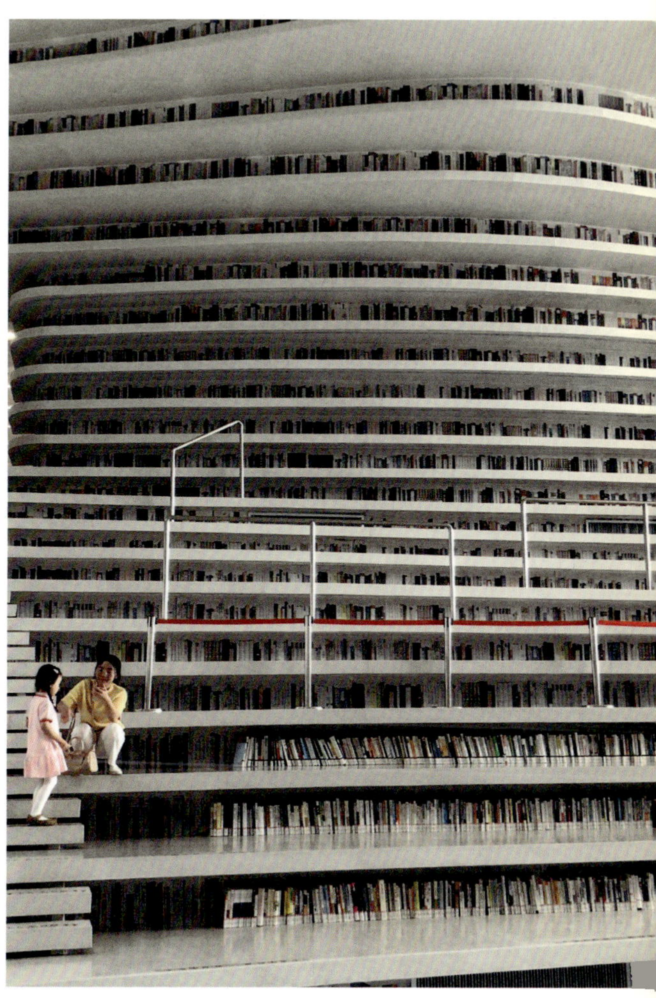

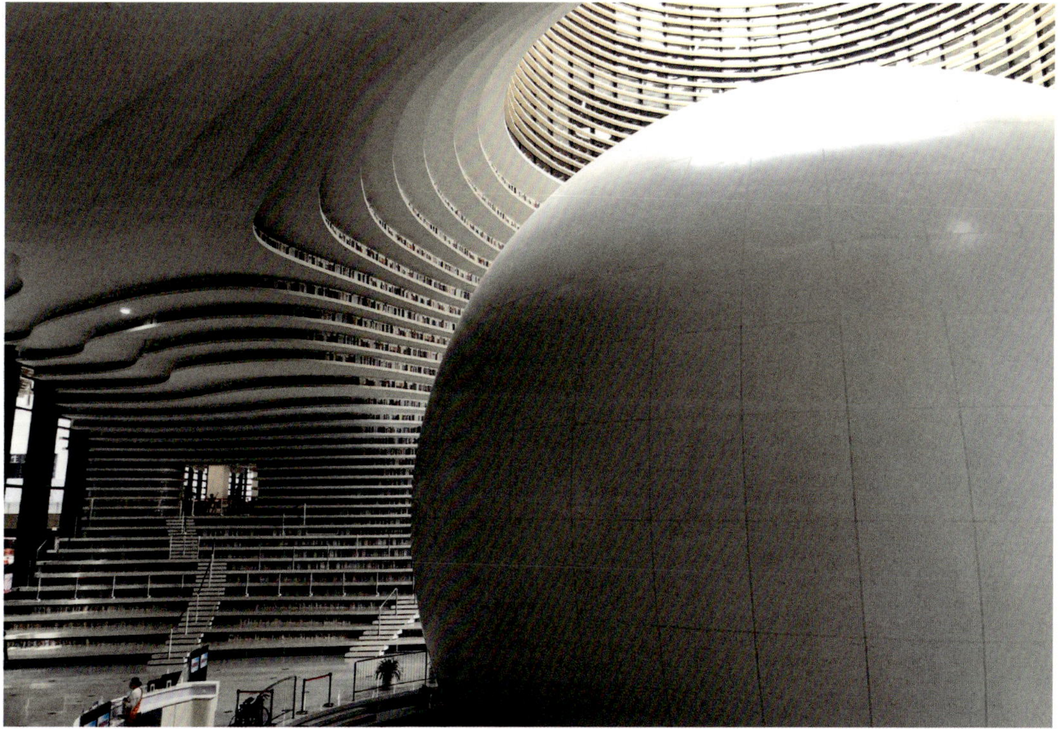

Jade white and jade green
Jadeweiß und Jadegrün

Green is traditionally the colour of the wood element and is a symbol of spring, the East, health and harmony in China. Green represents life and vitality. Jade green is a colour that is highly valued in China and has been used for at least 8,000 years. Over time, a real jade culture developed, and the value of jade temporarily exceeded even the value of pure gold. Meanwhile, the most popular colour of jade is white, and it also exists in green, orange, black or purple. The good quality stones coming from Burma shimmer blue-green and radiate an extraordinary transparency. Sometimes the jade is also a mottled green-black.

Jade as such does not exist, strictly speaking. It is the generic term for the two very similar minerals nephrite and jadeite, which were only distinguished towards the end of the 18th century. While nephrite had been deeply rooted in Asian culture for over seven millennia, interest then turned increasingly to jadeite. Jade is considered the stone of love and friendship, inner peace, balance as well as harmony. It was chosen as the protective stone for good.

However, in China a man never wears a green head covering. During the Yuan, Ming and Qing dynasties, green had a negative connotation. Members of the "inferior" professions, such as singers, actors and entertainers, were required by law to wear green head coverings as a sign of their shame. Later, this was also required of men whose families lived off prostitution. Green hats were and still are associated with infidelity and used as an idiom for a cheating husband. The green hat made even the Chinese Catholic bishops so uncomfortable that they compromised with the Vatican to be allowed to wear a purple miter – although in church heraldry a green miter

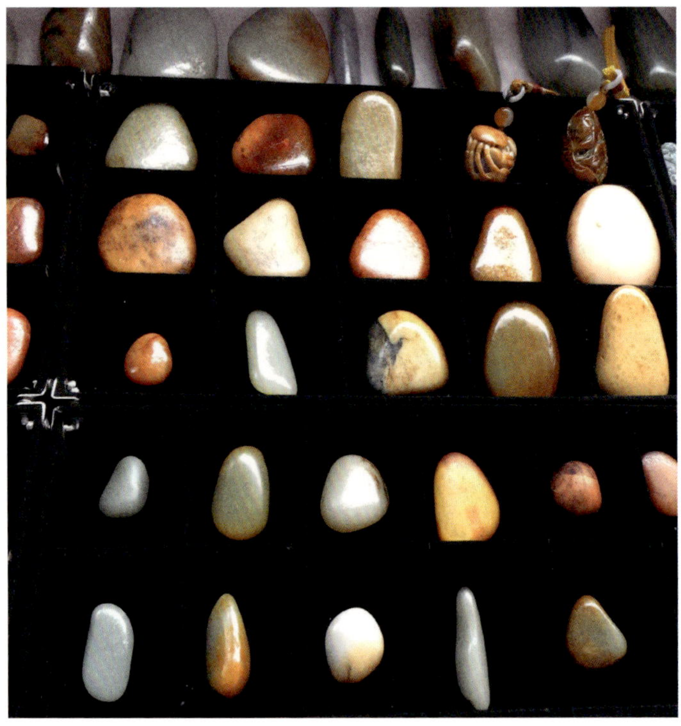

Various coloured jade stones / Verschiedenfarbige Jadesteine

Grün ist traditionell die Farbe des Holz-Elements und in China ein Symbol für den Frühling, den Osten, Gesundheit und Harmonie. Grün steht für Leben und Vitalität. Das Jadegrün ist eine Farbe, die in China sehr geschätzt und schon seit mindestens 8000 Jahren verwendet wird. Mit der Zeit entwickelte sich eine regelrechte Jadekultur, und der Jadewert überstieg temporär sogar den Wert puren Goldes. Die bekannteste Farbe von Jade ist derweil Weiß, und es gibt sie auch noch in Grün, Orange, Schwarz oder Violett. Die aus Burma stammenden Steine von guter Qualität schimmern blau-grün und strahlen eine außergewöhnliche Transparenz aus. Manchmal ist die Jade auch grün-schwarz-gefleckt.

Jade als solches gibt es genau betrachtet nicht. Es ist der Oberbegriff für die beiden sehr ähnlichen Minerale Nephrit und Jadeit, die erst gegen Ende des 18. Jahrhunderts unterschieden wurden. Während Nephrit schon seit über sieben Jahrtausenden in der asiatischen Kultur zutiefst verwurzelt war, wandte sich das Interesse dann vermehrt Jadeit zu. Jade gilt als Stein der Liebe und Freundschaft, des inneren Friedens, der Ausgeglichenheit sowie der Harmonie. Es wurde zum Schutzstein für das Gute auserkoren.

Right page:
A rare glimpse from the defensive wall of the Forbidden City, which has only been open to the public for about two years, across the moat and the roofs of the adjacent *hutongs* to the Central Business District.

Rechte Seite:
Ein seltener Blick von der erst seit rund zwei Jahren der Öffentlichkeit zugänglichen Wehrmauer der Verbotenen Stadt über den Wassergraben und die Dächer der angrenzenden *Hutongs* bis zum Central Business District.

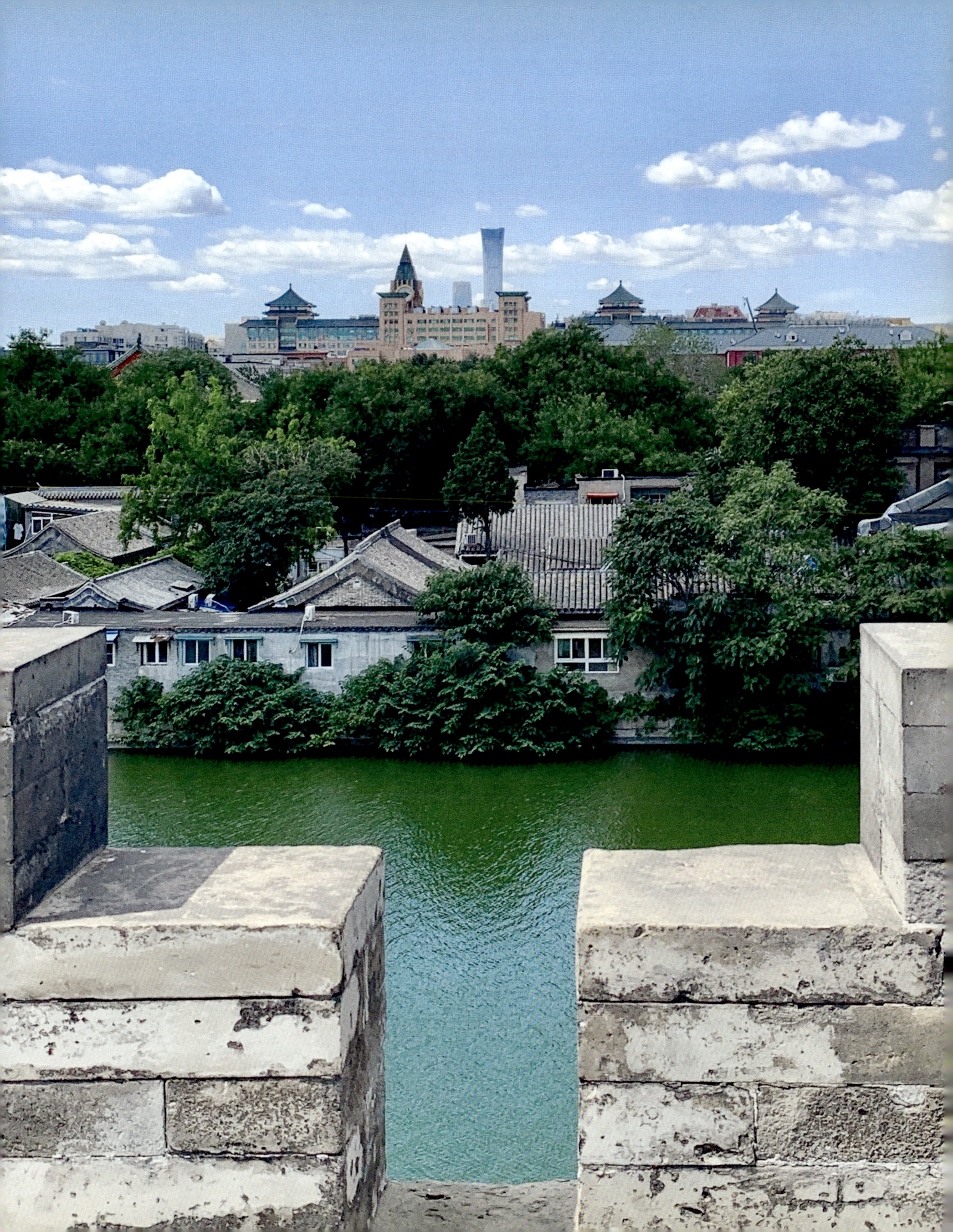

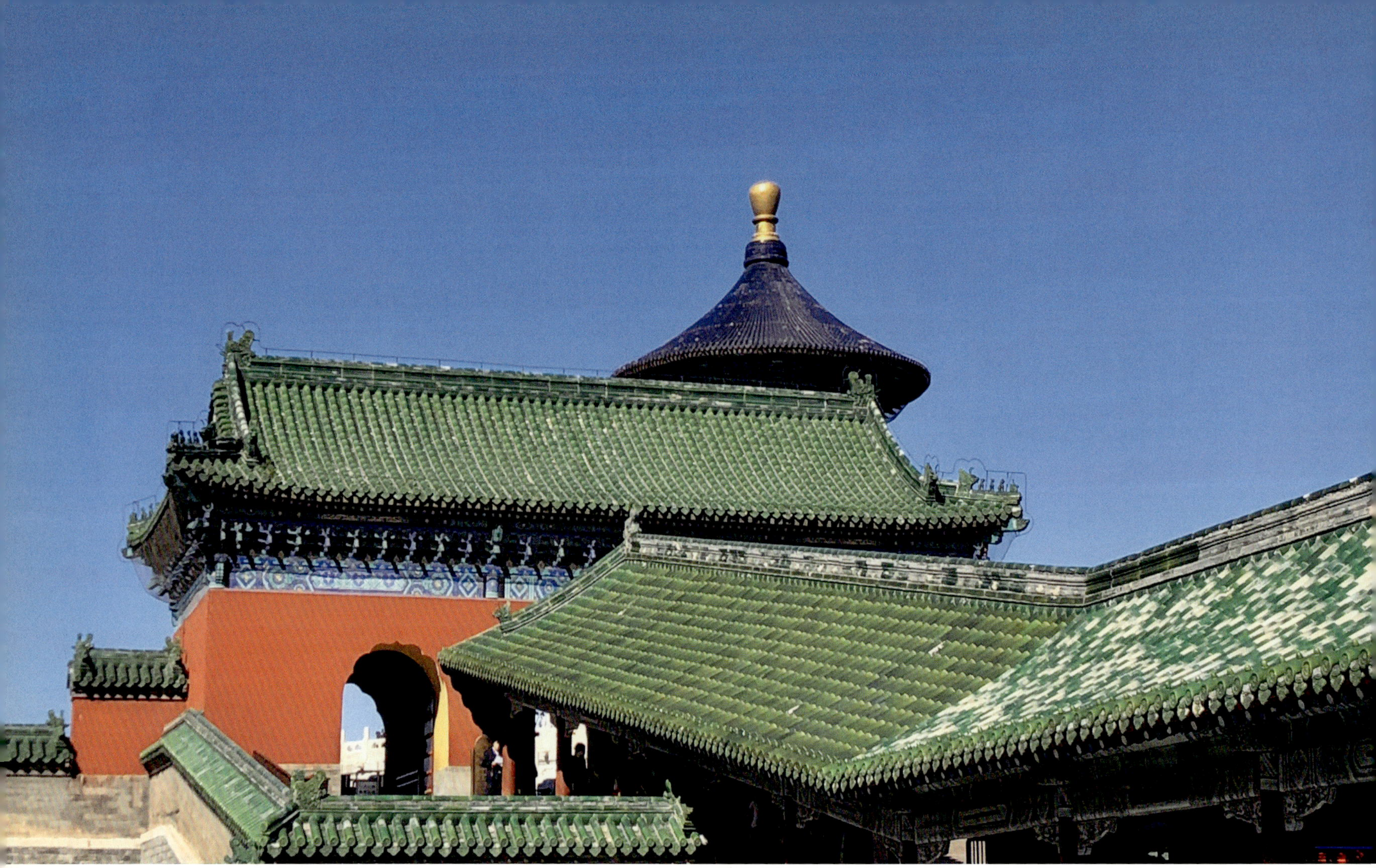

Above:
While we in the West live "on earth", the Chinese claim to live "under heaven". Nowhere in China is the worship of heaven more architecturally unique and colourful than in Beijing's Temple of Heaven.

Oben:
Während wir im Westen „auf der Erde" leben, postulieren die Chinesen „unter dem Himmel" zu leben. Nirgendwo in China ist die Verehrung des Himmels architektonisch so einzigartig und farblich so auffällig wie im Pekinger Himmelstempel.

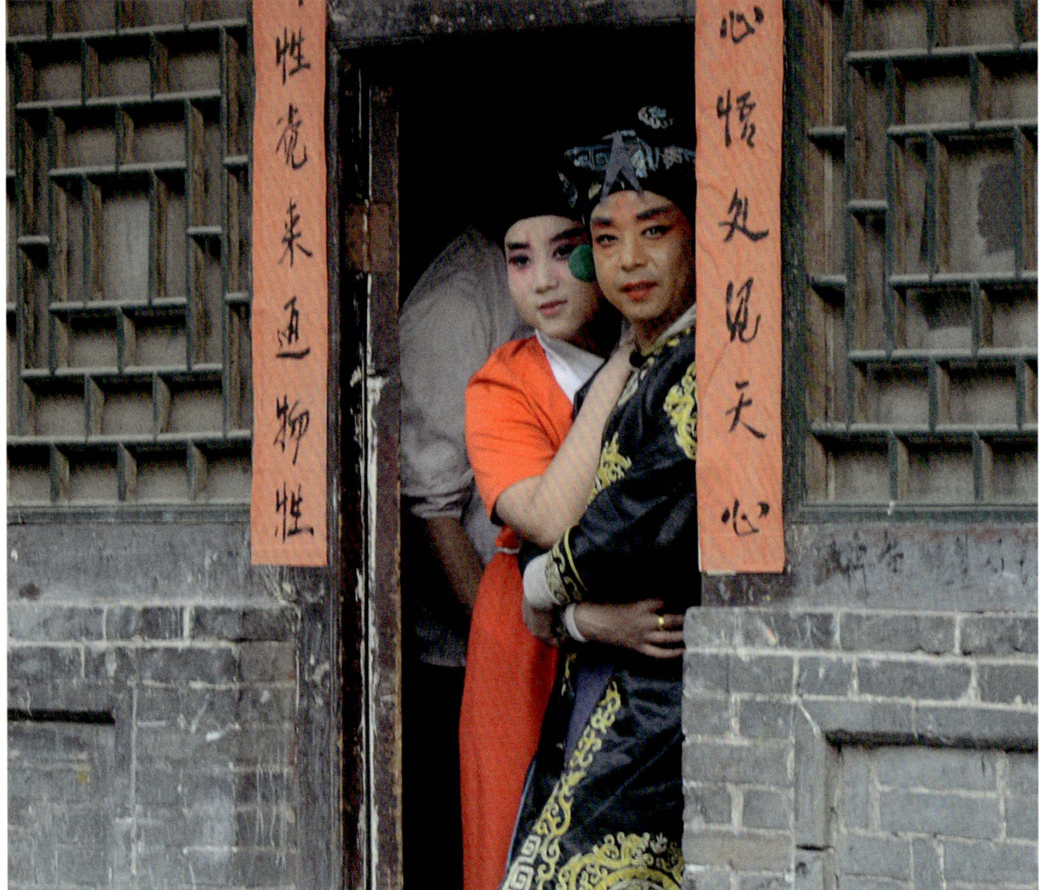

Actors in traditional costumes and makeup, watching the audience during breaks

Schauspieler in tradionellem Kostüm und Make-up, die während der Pausen das Publikum betrachten.

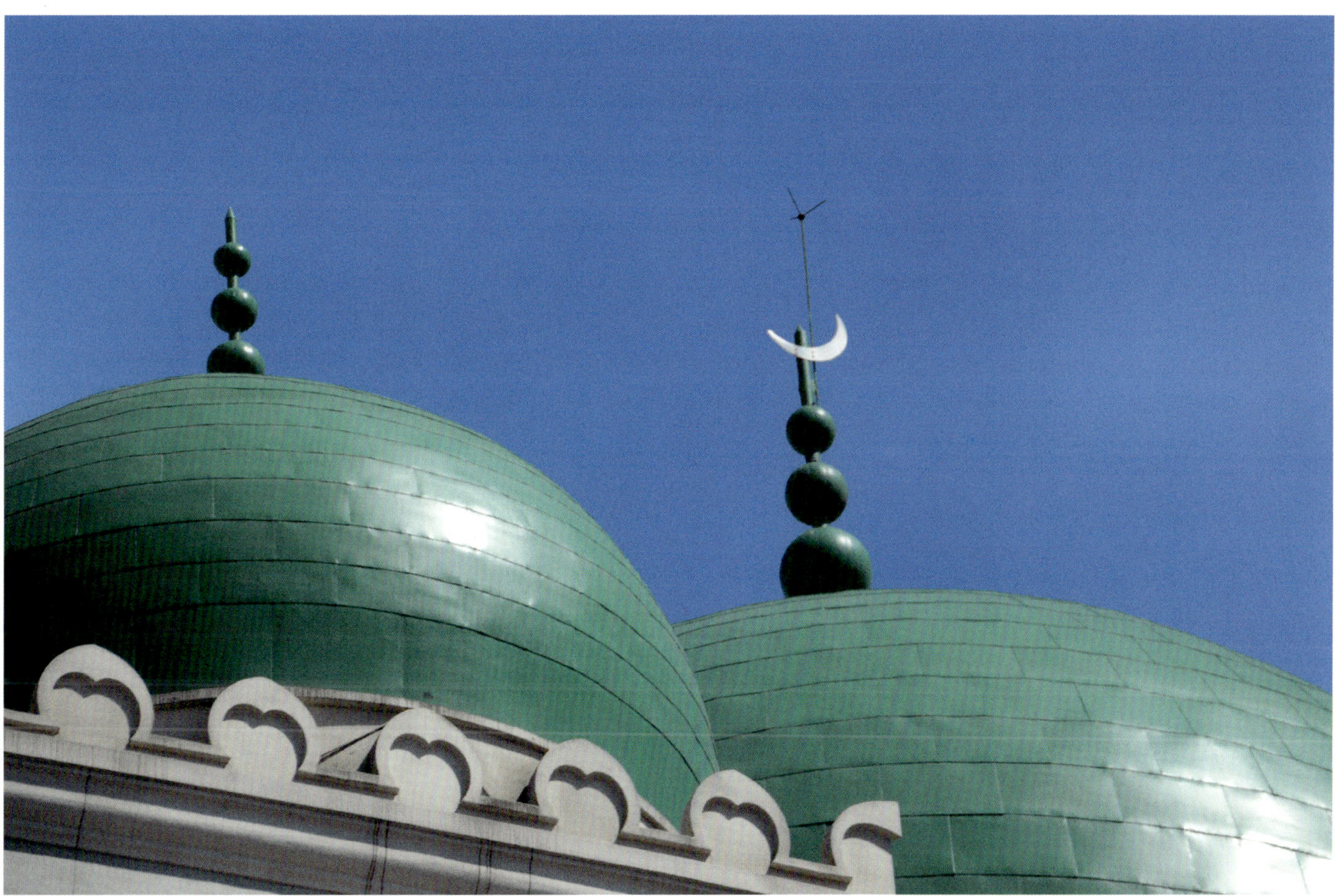

The Niujie Mosque, literally the "Cattle Alley Mosque", in the southern Beijing district of Xuanwu, is the oldest and largest mosque in the city. Its construction dates back to 996 AD. Today, the neighbourhood around the mosque is inhabited primarily by Muslim members of the Uyghur and Hui ethnic or religious minorities.

Die *Niujie* Moschee, wörtlich die „Moschee der Rindergasse", im südlichen Pekinger Stadtbezirk Xuanwu ist die älteste und größte Moschee der Stadt. Die Erbauung geht auf das Jahr 996 n. Chr. zurück. Das Viertel rund um die Moschee wird heute vorwiegend von muslimischen Angehörigen der ethnischen oder religiösen Minderheiten der Uiguren und Hui bewohnt.

would normally cover their head. In Christianity, green, with its reference to spring green, is the colour of the resurrection and of Easter. It is also known as the colour of hope.

The beautiful, spacious old mosque in the South of Beijing is covered in green and elaborately decorated with many green design elements. It is doubtlessly the colour of Islam – the prophet Mohammed is said to have preferred wearing green. His preference may have had to do with the fact that in a desert region like the area where Islam originated, as the colour of vegetation, green stands for life.

Niemals jedoch trägt ein Mann in China grüne Kopfbedeckung. Während der Yuan-, Ming- und Qing-Dynastien wurde Grün negativ besetzt. Angehörige der niederen Berufe, Sänger, Schauspieler und Entertainer, mussten als Zeichen ihrer Schande dem Gesetz nach grüne Kopfbedeckungen tragen. Später wurde dies auch von Männern verlangt, deren Familien von der Prostitution lebten. Grüne Hüte wurden und werden mit Untreue assoziiert und als Idiom für einen betrogenen Ehemann verwendet. Der grüne Hute bereitete selbst den chinesischen katholischen Bischöfen derart Unbehagen, dass sie mit dem Vatikan den Kompromiss schlossen, eine violette Mitra tragen zu dürfen – obwohl in der kirchlichen Heraldik normalerweise eine grüne Mitra ihr Haupt bedecken würde. Im Christentum ist Grün mit dem Bezug zum Frühlingsgrün die Farbe der Auferstehung und die Osterfarbe. Auch als die Farbe der Hoffnung ist es bekannt.

Die wunderschöne große alte Moschee im Süden Pekings ist grün gedeckt und mit vielen grünen Gestaltungselementen aufwendig dekoriert. Es ist zweifellos die Farbe des Islam – der Prophet Mohammed soll sich bevorzugt grün gekleidet haben. Seine Vorliebe hatte vielleicht damit zu tun, dass in einer Wüstenregion wie dem Ursprungsgebiet des Islam Grün als Farbe der Vegetation für das Leben steht.

Sky blue and blue ants

Himmelsblau und blaue Ameisen

The blue Mao suit gained wider recognition when millions of men and women in China were prescribed it as a uniform dress by Sun Yat-sen during the Chinese cultural revolution of 1965. Mao Zedong and his wife, Jiang Qing, likewise wore it. Indigo was chosen for the workers and peasants, khaki for the People's Liberation Army, and dove blue for the comrades in the party cadre. The *Little Red Boo*k stood out ubiquitously, but small, from the unified image of the Chinese workers, who were dubbed "blue ants" by the West. Today, this blue is still visible in China's daily street scene; however, it is no longer frequently worn by the younger generation.

Still common in everyday Chinese life today: the blue Mao suit

Auch heute noch im chinesischen Alltag üblich: der blaue Mao-Anzug

Das Blau des Mao-Anzugs erlangte weltweit Bekanntheit, als Millionen Männer und Frauen Chinas ihn zur Zeit der chinesischen Kulturrevolution 1965 von Sun Yat-sen nach der Gründung der Republik China als Einheitskleidung verordnet bekamen. Mao Zedong und seine Frau Jiang Qing trugen ihn ebenfalls. Indigo war dabei für die Arbeiter und Bauern festgelegt, Khaki für die Volksbefreiungsarmee und Taubengrau für die Genossen im Parteikader. Das rote Mao-Büchlein hob sich allgegenwärtig, aber klein ab vom Einheitsbild, das die vom Westen als „blaue Ameisen" titulierten chinesischen Arbeiter abgaben. Auch heute noch ist dieses Blau im täglichen Straßenbild Chinas sichtbar; von der jungen Generation wird es jedoch nicht mehr häufig getragen.

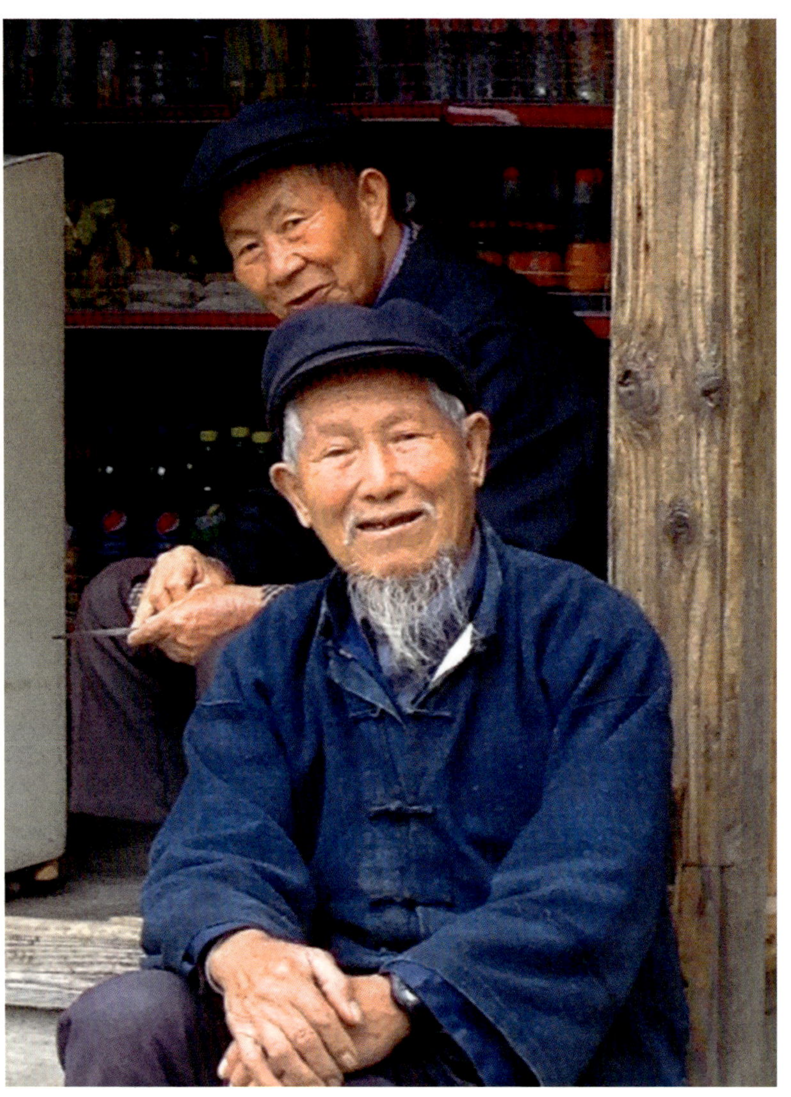

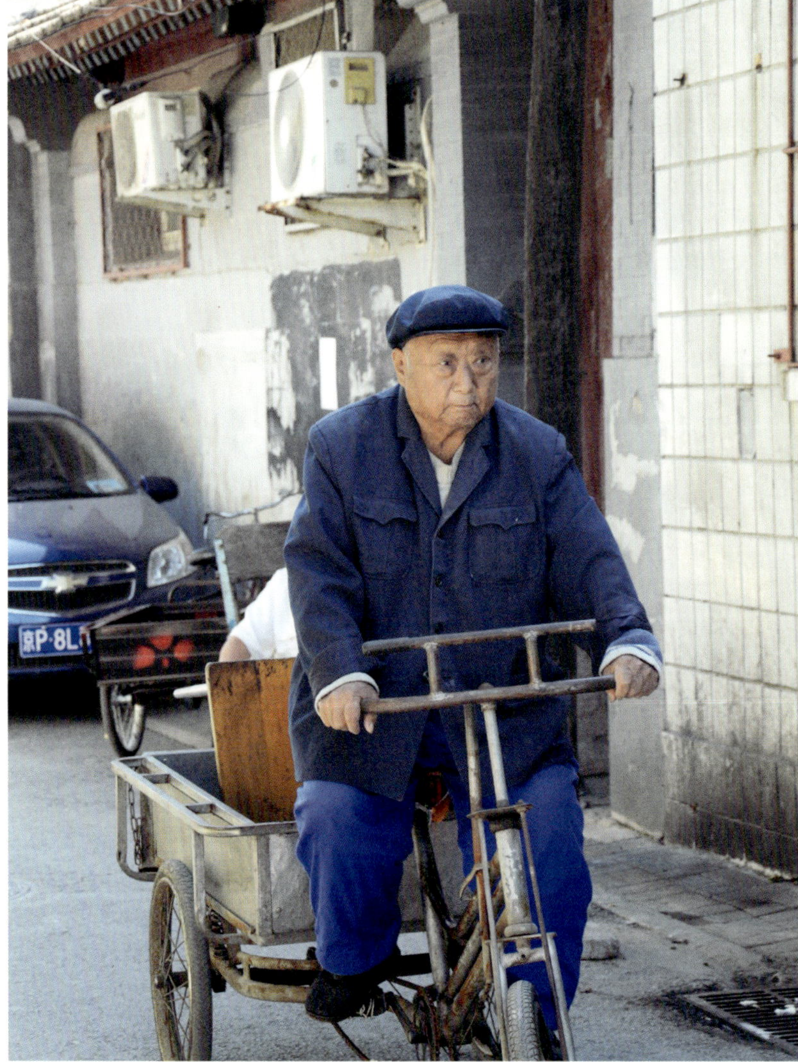

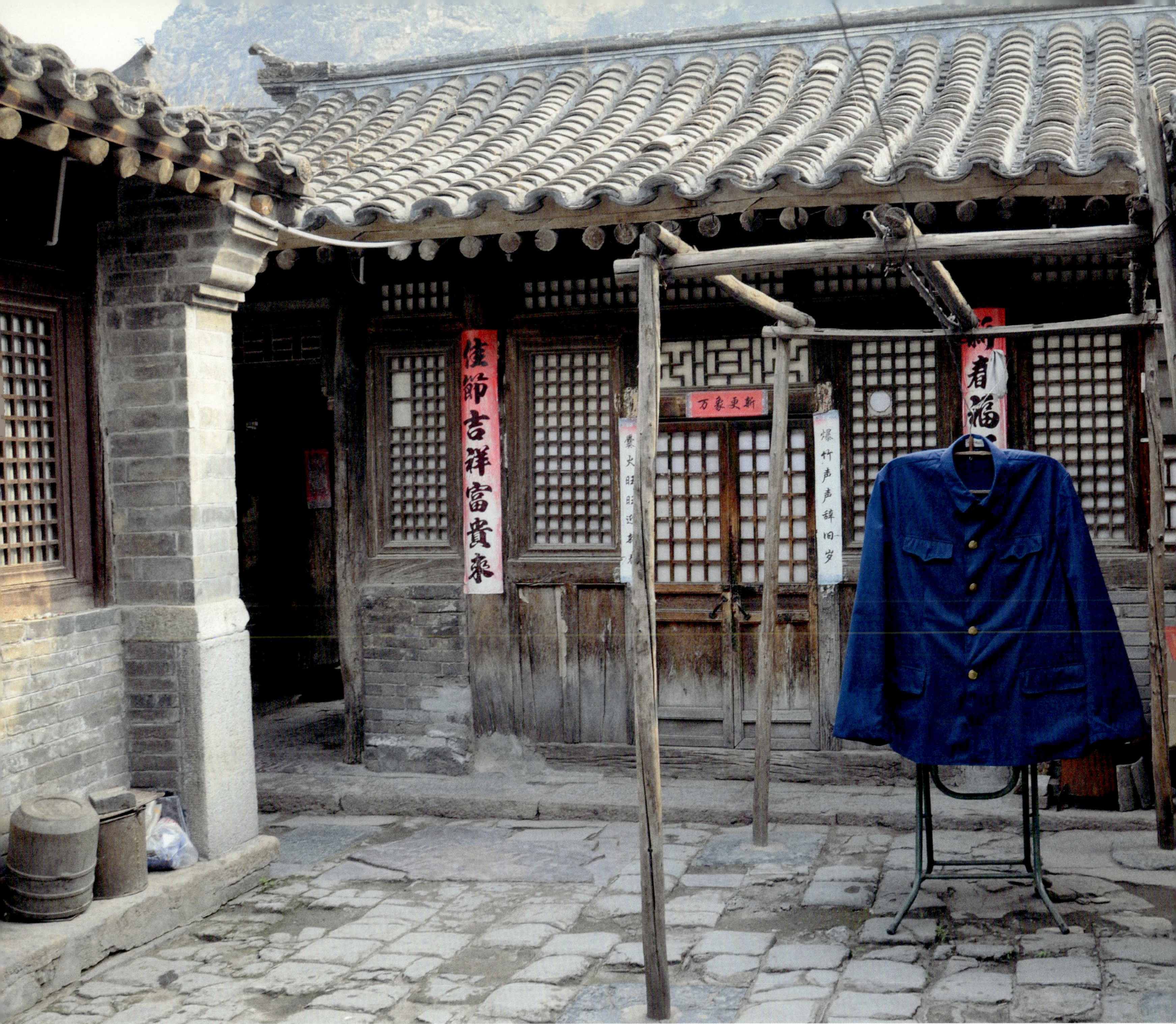

In Beijing there is no doubt that the most intense blue can be seen from the Heart of Heaven, the *Tiānxīn shí*. This is a round slate slab on the centre of the hill altar. This is also called the Highest Yang, *Tàiyáng shí*, because the emperor prayed for favourable weather there. Today, as a visitor you find yourself standing among Instagram freaks there, in order to suddenly get the feeling that you can communicate directly with the sky, or that you are standing where even the emperor of China could only go alone. At the winter solstice, the emperor stood in direct contact with the sky at this point, and the ceremony was even taboo for his closest followers.

Zweifellos das intensivste Blau kann man in Peking auf dem „Herz des Himmels", dem *Tiānxīn shí*, stehend erleben. Es handelt sich dabei um eine runde Schieferplatte auf der Mitte des Hügelaltars. Diese wird auch noch Höchste Yang, *Tàiyáng shí*, genannt, weil dort der Kaiser für günstiges Wetter betete. Heute findet man sich dort zwischen Instagram-Fotofreaks wieder, um einmal das Gefühl zu haben, direkt mit dem Himmel kommunizieren zu können oder dort zu stehen, wo selbst die Kaiser Chinas nur allein hingehen durften: Zur Wintersonnwende stand der Kaiser an diesem Ort in direktem Kontakt mit dem Himmel, und diese Zeremonie war sogar für sein engstes Gefolge tabu.

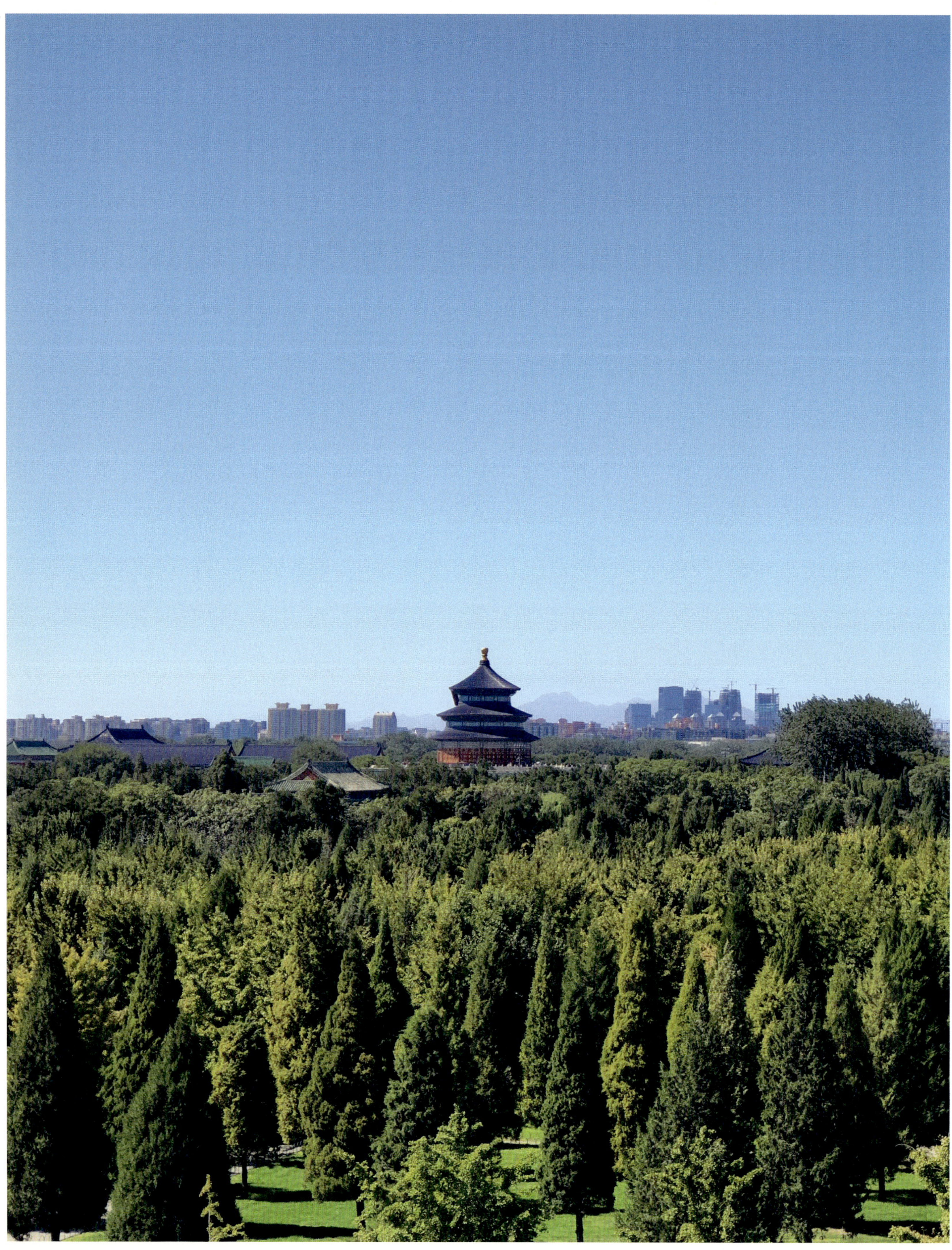

The temple premises are three times larger than those of the Forbidden City. This has a very special reason. As "Sons of Heaven", the Chinese emperors were forbidden to build facilities larger than the earthly residence of Heaven, the Temple of Heaven or *Tiāntán*.

The entire temple axis with terrace and galleries is 1,200 metres long and flanked by ancient trees. This makes the Temple of Heaven, according to its own information, the longest facility in the world for heavenly worship.

The northern part of the long wall surrounding the temple complex is semi-circular and symbolises the sky. The southern part, built as a square, symbolises the earth. According to traditional Chinese belief, the sky is round and the earth is square. Consequently, the northern part of the complex was built higher than the southern part.

Here in the Temple of Heaven, the brilliant blue and green glazed roof tiles are worthy representations of heaven and emblematic of the green trees, the wood, the earth. The whole complex is considered an architectural and design example of Chinese symbolism. Shapes, colours and numbers rival each other in their expressiveness.

The number 9, symbolizing the emperor, is especially found again and again. The central point of the hill altar is surrounded by nine plates, which in turn are enclosed by a ring of 18 plates, creating nine rings. The outermost ring comprises 9 × 9 = 81 plates.

The Hall of Prayer for Good Harvests has four inner, twelve middle and twelve outer pillars representing the four seasons, the twelve months and the twelve traditional Chinese hours. Taken together, the twelve middle pillars and the twelve outer pillars represent the traditional solar terms.

The Seven Star group of stones east of the Hall of Prayer for Good Harvests represents the seven peaks of Taishan Mountain. This mountain in eastern China, in Shandong Province, is one of the five sacred mountains of Taoism.

View over the mighty old trees of the Temple of Heaven in Beijing to the Hall of Prayer for Good Harvests. On the horizon, the western mountains.

Blick über die mächtigen alten Bäume des Himmelstempels in Peking auf die Halle der Ernteopfer. Am Horizont die Westberge.

Das Tempelareal ist dreimal größer als jenes der Verbotenen Stadt. Dies hat einen ganz besonderen Grund. Als „Söhne des Himmels" war es den chinesischen Kaisern verboten, Anlagen zu bauen, die größer waren als die irdische Residenz des Himmels, der „Himmelstempel" oder *Tiāntán*.

Die gesamte Tempelachse mit Terrasse und Hallen ist 1200 Meter lang und wird von alten Bäumen flankiert. Damit ist der Himmelstempel nach eigenen Angaben die längste Anlage der Welt für die Himmelsanbetung.

Die die Tempelanlage umgebende lange Mauer ist im nördlichen Teil halbkreisförmig angelegt und symbolisiert den Himmel. Der südliche Teil, quadratisch gebaut, symbolisiert die Erde. Nach traditioneller chinesischer Überzeugung sind der Himmel rund und die Erde quadratisch. Der nördliche Teil der Anlage ist folglich höher gebaut worden als der südliche Teil.

Hier im Himmelstempel repräsentieren die strahlend blau und grün glasierten Dachziegel würdig den Himmel und sinnbildlich die grünen Bäume, das Holz, die Erde. Die ganze Anlage gilt in ihrer Bauweise als architektonisches und gestalterisches Musterbeispiel für chinesische Symbolik. Formen, Farben und Zahlen wetteifern in ihrer Aussagekraft.

Besonders die Zahl 9, die den Kaiser symbolisiert, findet sich immer wieder. Der zentrale Punkt des Hügelaltars ist umgeben von neun Platten, die wiederum von einem Ring mit 18 Platten umschlossen sind, sodass neun Ringe entstehen. Der äußerste Ring umfasst 9 × 9 = 81 Platten.

Die Halle der Ernteopfer hat vier innere, zwölf mittlere und zwölf äußere Säulen, welche die vier Jahreszeiten, die zwölf Monate und die zwölf traditionellen chinesischen Stunden repräsentieren. Zusammengefasst stellen die zwölf mittleren und die zwölf äußeren Säulen die traditionellen Solarbegriffe dar.

Die Sieben-Stern-Steingruppe östlich der Halle der Ernteopfer repräsentiert die sieben Gipfel des Taishan-Berges. Dieser Berg im Osten Chinas, in der Shandong-Provinz, ist einer der fünf heiligen Berge des Daoismus.

Zweimal im Jahr mussten sich der Kaiser, der Sohn des blauen Himmels, und sein engstes Gefolge von der Verbotenen Stadt durch Peking zum Himmelstempel aufmachen. In diesem wurde ein zeremonielles Lager errichtet, es wurden

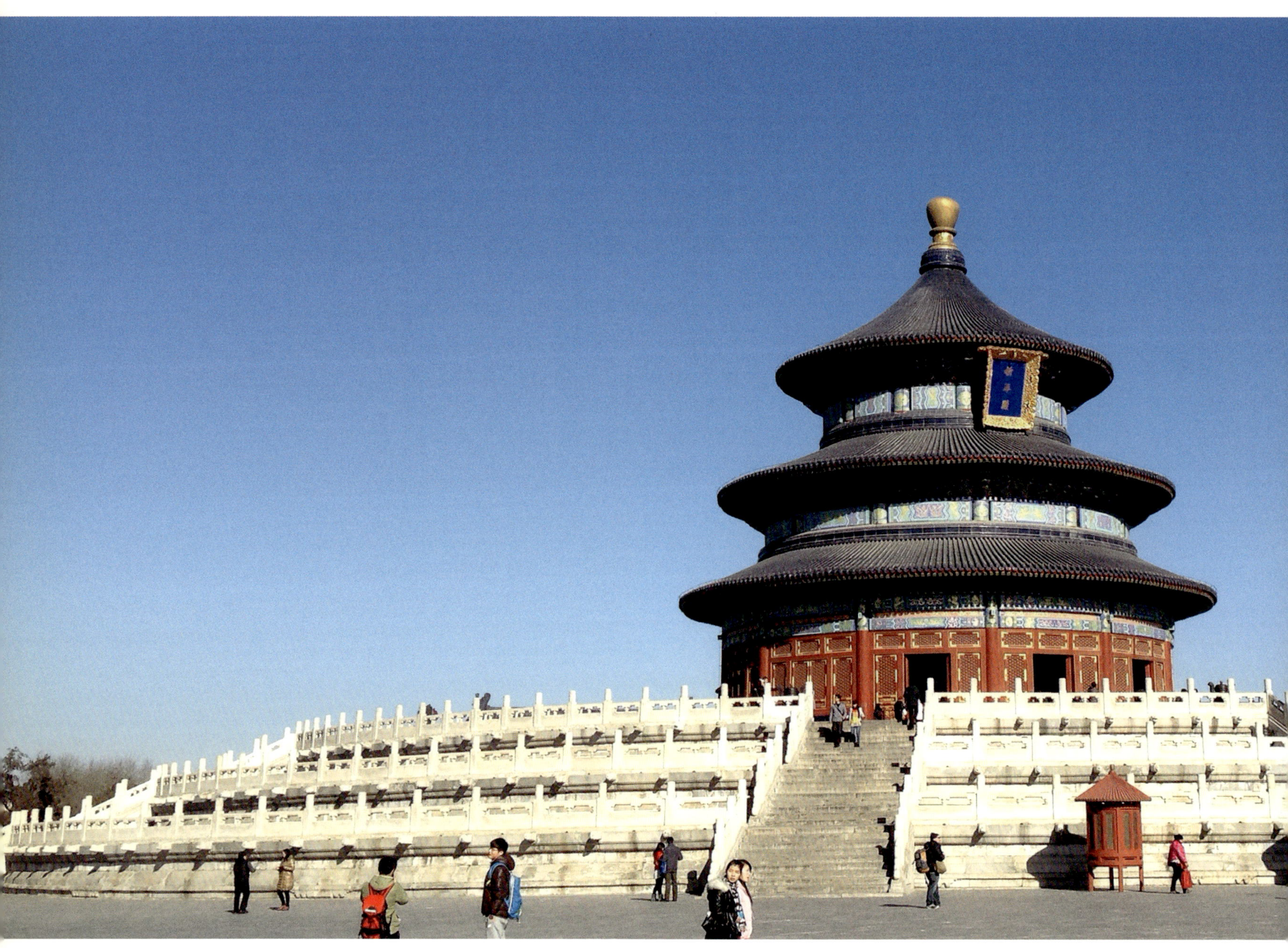

Two times each year, the emperor, the Son of the Blue Sky, and his closest followers make their way from the Forbidden City to the Temple of Heaven. Here a ceremonial camp was set up, particular robes were worn and strict protocols were kept. No common Chinese citizen was allowed to join the procession, let alone see the ceremony. The streets en route to the Forbidden City all the way to the Temple of Heaven were lined with reverent citizens, who were only allowed to stare at the ground.

The Hall of Prayer for Good Harvests, the circular blue-roofed building with triple gable roof, was where the imperial ceremonies were performed, such as offering sacrifices and lighting incense to pray for good weather and abundant harvests. This unique building, visually distinct from

besondere Roben getragen und strikte Protokolle eingehalten. Kein gewöhnlicher Chinese durfte die Prozession begleiten, geschweige denn die Zeremonien mitansehen. Die Straßen auf dem Weg von der Verbotenen Stadt bis zum Himmelstempel waren gesäumt von ehrerweisenden Bürgern, die aber alle nur zu Boden blicken durften.

In der Halle der Ernteopfer, dem kreisförmigen, blau gedeckten Gebäude mit Dreifach-Giebeldach, wurden die kaiserlichen Zeremonien durchgeführt, wie etwa Opfer dargebracht und Weihrauch angezündet, um für gutes Wetter und reiche Ernten zu beten. Dieses einzigartige, sich optisch von allen anderen Tempeln absetzende Gebäude ist zwischen 1406 und 1420 entstanden unter der Herrschaft des Yongle-Kaisers, der auch den Bau der

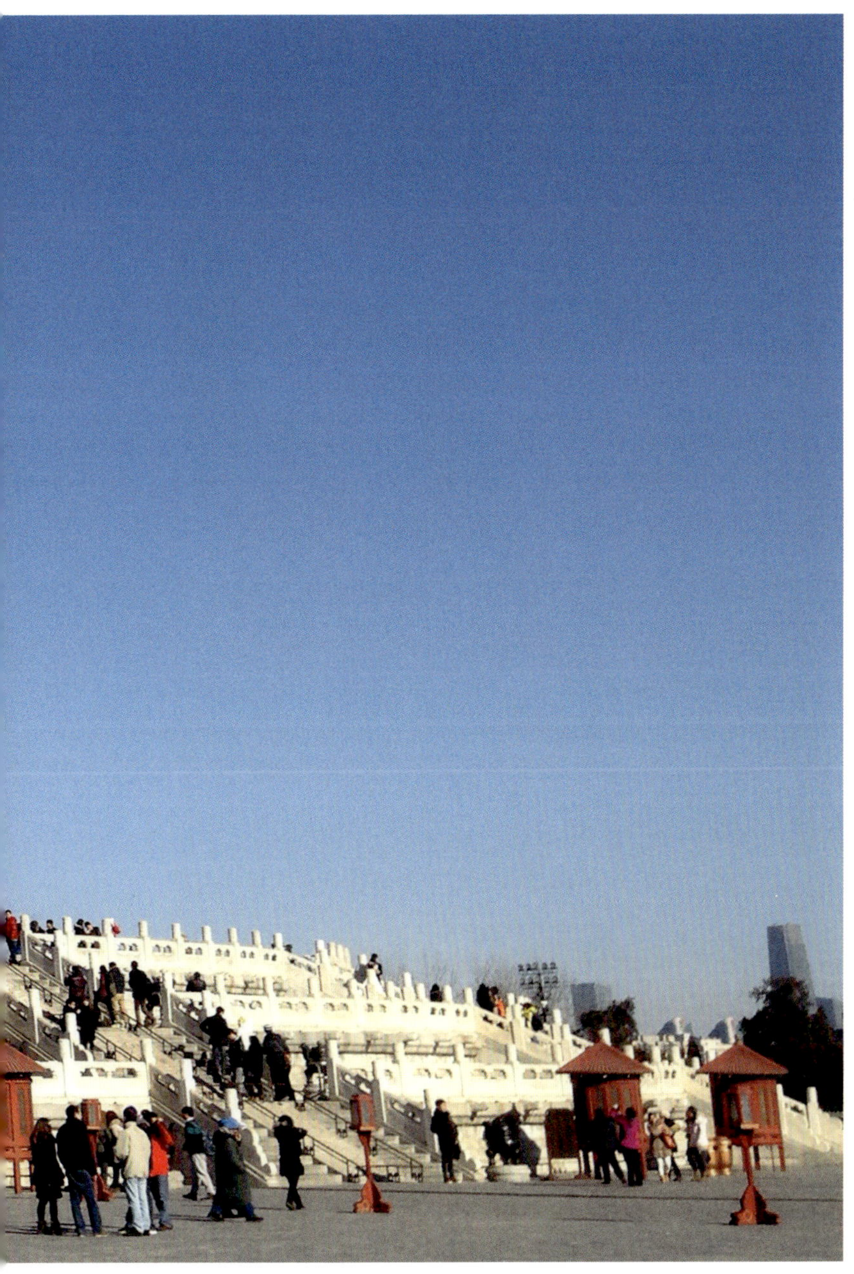

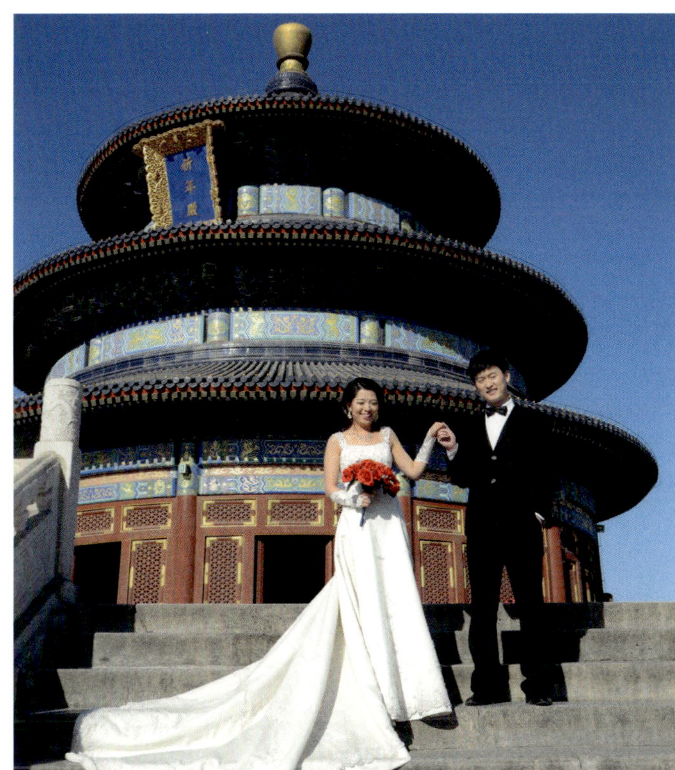

Popular motif for wedding couples: the symbolically meaningful Prayer Hall for Good Harvests

Beliebtes Fotomotiv für Hochzeitspaare: die symbolisch bedeutsame Halle der Ernteopfer

The three-tiered roof of the Hall of Prayer for Good Harvests is covered with 50,000 blue-glazed tiles and topped with a golden bead. Slender dragon heads on the balustrades drain rainwater when torrential downpours wash away the desert sand in the summer months of July and August.

Das dreistufige Dach der Halle der Ernteopfer ist mit 50 000 blau glasierten Ziegeln bedeckt und von einer goldenen Perle gekrönt. Schlanke Drachenköpfe an den Balustraden leiten das Regenwasser ab, wenn in den Sommermonaten Juli und August sinnflutartige Wassergüsse den Wüstensand hinwegwaschen.

all other temples, was built between 1406 and 1420 during the reign of the Yongle Emperor, who also ordered the construction of the Forbidden City. The building, made entirely of wood, measures a proud 36 metres in diameter and 38 metres in height.

The architectural masterpiece was built entirely without nails. In 1889, the original building burned down due to a fire caused by lightning, and the current building was rebuilt later.

Chinese wedding couples, but also school graduates prefer this temple, so close to the blue sky, to complete the moment of the souvenir photo with the dignified, colour-coordinated icing on the cake.

Verbotenen Stadt anordnete. Stolze 36 Meter Durchmesser und 38 Meter Höhe misst das komplett aus Holz errichtete Gebäude.

Das architektonische Meisterwerk kam völlig ohne Nägel aus. 1889 verbrannte das ursprüngliche Gebäude durch ein von einem Blitzschlag ausgelöstes Feuer, das heutige Gebäude wurde später neu aufgebaut.

Chinesische Hochzeitspaare, aber auch Schulabgänger wählen bevorzugt diesen dem blauen Himmel so nahen Tempel, um dem Augenblick des Erinnerungsfotos das würdevolle, farblich passende I-Tüpfelchen aufzusetzen.

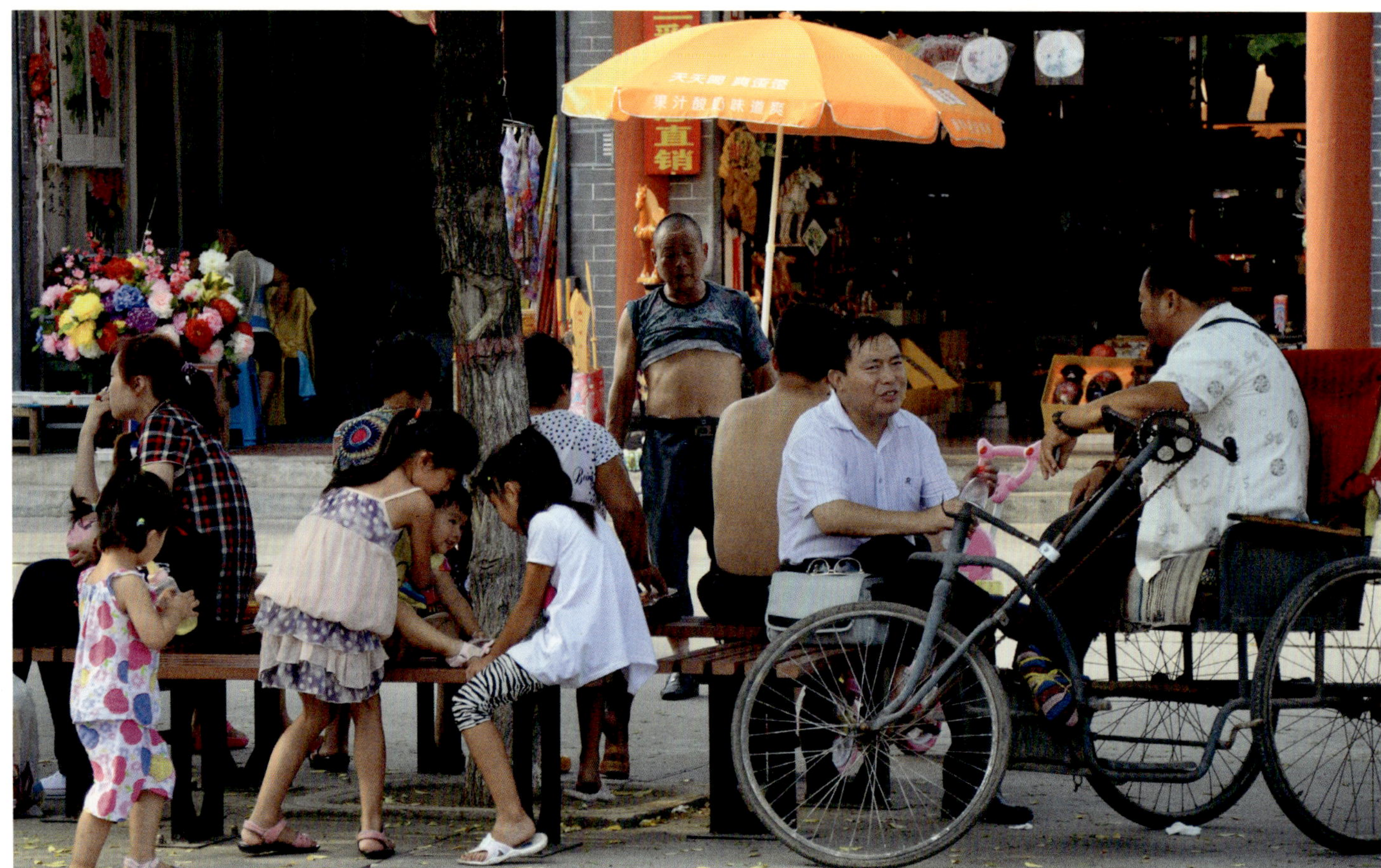

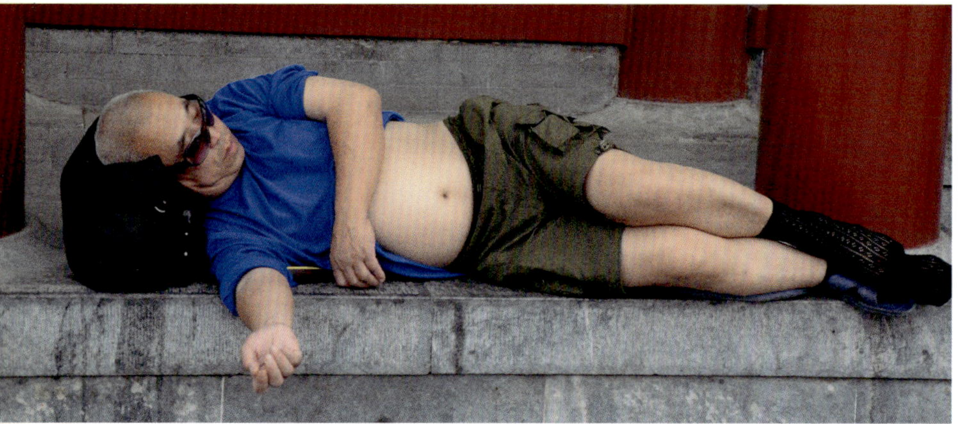

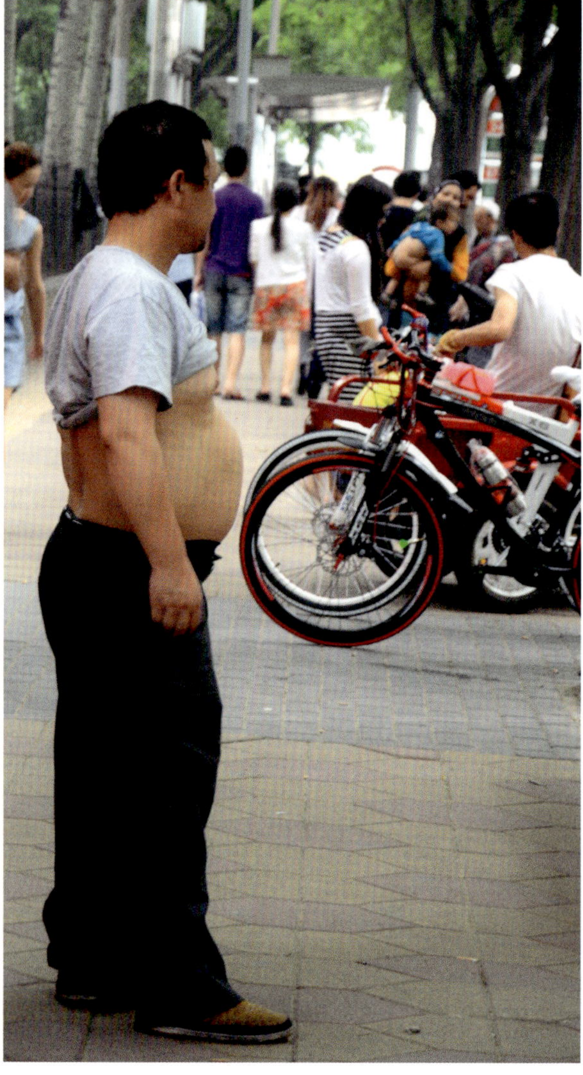

As soon as the shimmering summer heat melts the asphalt in the streets of Beijing in July and the singing cicadas lull all life into a dozing afternoon sleep with their loud chirping, the "Beijing bikini phenomenon" strikes in an aesthetically unpleasant way. These are men, mostly over 40, who roll their shirts up, exposing their bellies. In any case, the prerequisite for this is always the missing "six-pack". These exhibitionists, also called "Beikini babes", do this to cool off their "strong centre". Taking care of the energy of the middle is an essential factor in traditional Chinese medicine. A strong centre – translated into the terminology of Western medicine – corresponds to a well-functioning digestive tract. Recently, the display of the Beijing bikini has been officially banned.

Sobald im Juli die flirrende Sommerhitze in den Straßen Pekings den Asphalt zum Schmelzen bringt und die Singzikaden mit ihrem lauten Zirpen alles Leben in den dösenden Nachmittagsschlaf lullen, schlägt das „Beijing-Bikini-Phänomen" auf ästhetisch unsanfte Weise zu. Es handelt sich dabei um Männer, meist jenseits der 40, die ihre Oberkörperbekleidung bis über den Bauch hochrollen. Voraussetzung dafür ist jedenfalls immer der fehlende „Sixpack". Die auch noch „Beikini Babes" genannten Selbstdarsteller tun dies zum Kühlen ihrer „starken Mitte". Die Pflege der Energie der Mitte ist ein wesentlicher Faktor in der traditionellen chinesischen Medizin. Eine starke Mitte entspricht – übersetzt in die Terminologie der westlichen Medizin – einem gut funktionierenden Verdauungssystem. Seit kurzem ist das Zurschaustellen des Beijing-Bikini offiziell verboten worden.

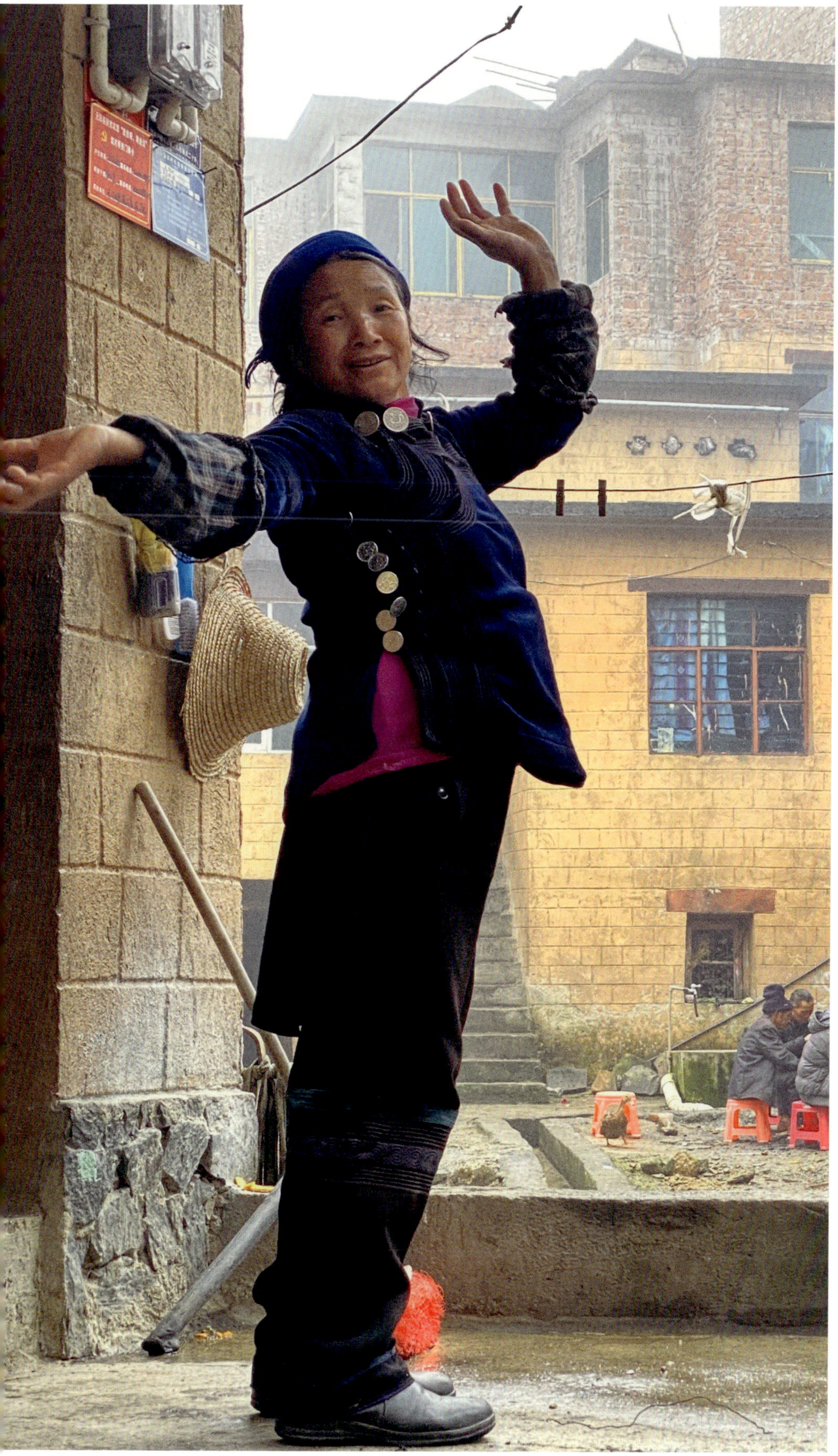

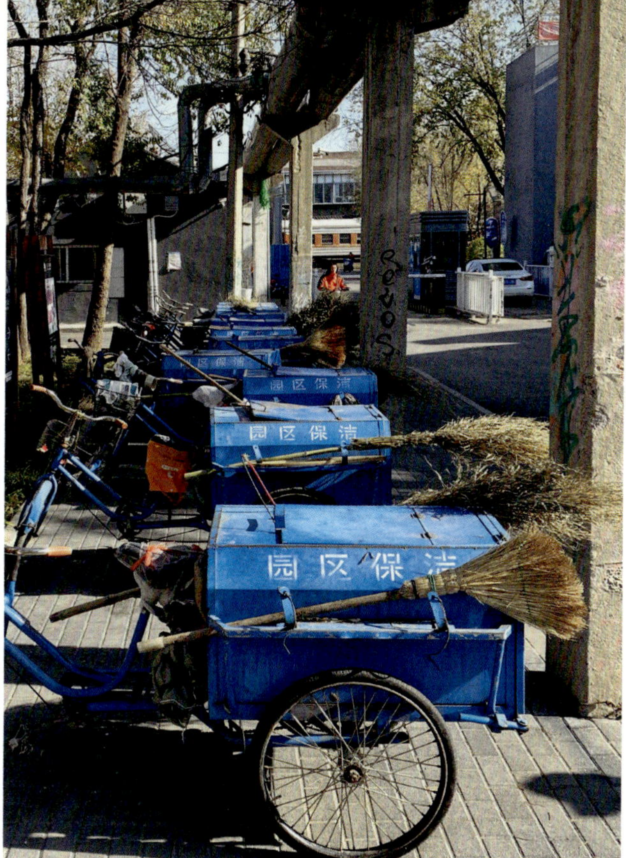

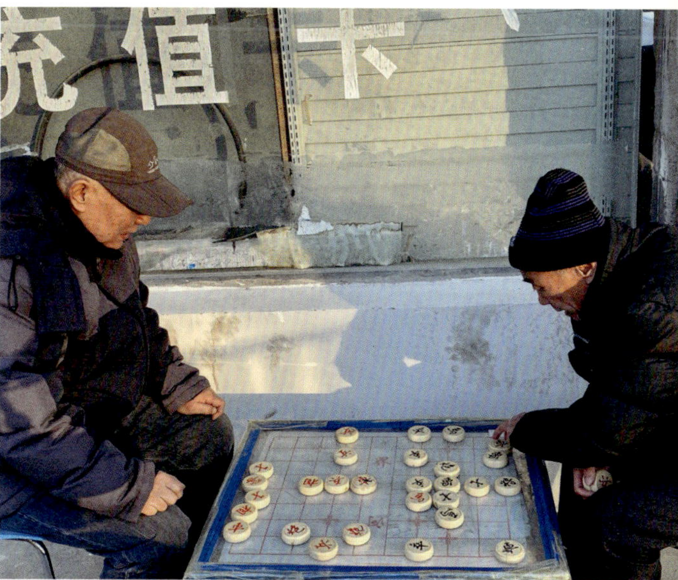

Throughout the year the Chinese play the traditional game of mah-jongg outside the houses and the blue street sweepers are an integral part of the cityscape.

Zu jeder Jahreszeit spielen die Chinesen draußen vor den Häusern das traditionelle Mah-Jongg-Steinspiel, und die blauen Straßenkehrfahrzeuge sind nicht aus dem Stadtbild wegzudenken.

Ethnic colour palette
Ethnischer Farbkasten

Modern China, with a population of 1.44 billion, is a giant country of colours, and its colour preferences differ not only by historical era, but clearly by geographic area or ethnic group.

It is 4,200 kilometres from Heilongjiang in the far north, bordering Siberia, to the tropical island of Hainan in the far south. And from the oriental trading city of Kashgar in western Xinjiang to the metropolis of Shanghai on the lower reaches of the Yangtze River, the distance is as much as 4,500 kilometres. Living conditions in the various places could hardly be more different.

The peoples of China include more than 90 ethnic groups, 56 of which are officially recognised as nationalities by the People's Republic of China. In addition to the Han, who make up the majority population in the whole of China (92 percent of the total population), there are thus another 55 nationalities with their own language, culture, cuisine and way of life. The traditional settlement areas of China's ethnic minorities cover a total of over 60 percent of the country's territory.

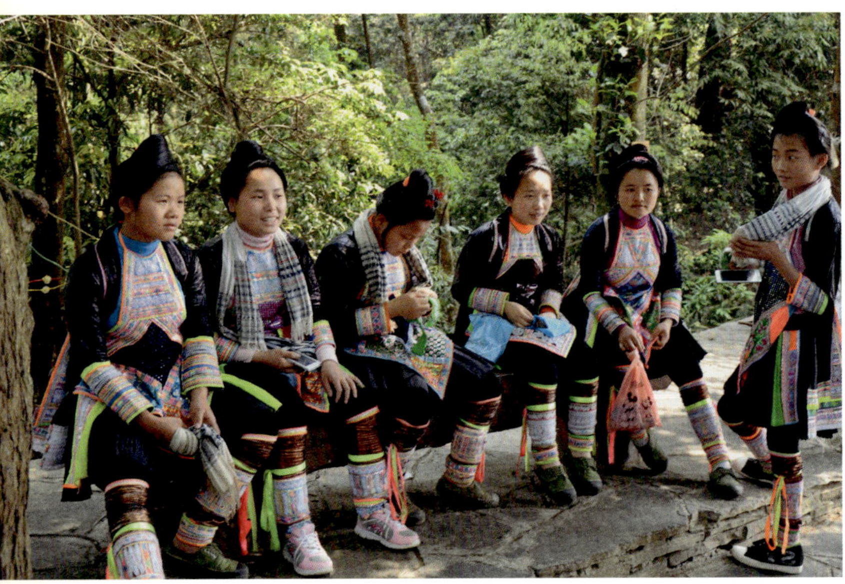

The offspring of the various minorities still proudly wear the colourful costumes every day. Here young women of the Dong minority and on the right page Tibetan girls.

Der Nachwuchs der diversen Minoritäten trägt mit Stolz noch täglich die bunte Tracht. Hier junge Frauen der Dong-Minderheit und auf der rechten Seite tibetische Mädchen.

Das moderne China mit 1,44 Milliarden Einwohnern ist ein buntes Riesenland, und seine farblichen Vorlieben unterscheiden sich nicht nur nach historischer Epoche, sondern ganz eindeutig auch nach geografischem Gebiet oder nach Volksgruppe.

Vom an Sibirien grenzenden Heilongjiang im hohen Norden bis zur tropischen Insel Hainan im äußersten Süden sind es 4200 Kilometer. Und von der orientalischen Handelsstadt Kashgar im Westen Xinjiangs bis zur Metropole Shanghai am Unterlauf des Yangtze muss man sogar 4500 Kilometer zurücklegen. Die Lebensbedingungen an den verschiedenen Orten könnten kaum unterschiedlicher sein.

Als Völker Chinas werden über 90 ethnische Gruppen bezeichnet, von denen 56 offiziell von der Volksrepublik China als Nationalitäten anerkannt sind. Neben den Han, welche die Mehrheitsbevölkerung in ganz China stellen (92 Prozent der Gesamtbevölkerung), sind das also weitere 55 Nationalitäten mit eigener Sprache, eigener Kultur, eigener Küche und eigener Lebensweise. Die traditionellen Siedlungsgebiete der ethnischen Minderheiten Chinas umfassen insgesamt über 60 Prozent der Fläche Chinas.

Die Vielfalt seiner Kulturen und Minderheiten verlangt nach differenzierteren Auslegungen der Farbsymbolik. So steht beispielsweise die Farbe Rot bei einigen Minderheiten für frisches Blut und wird nicht als glücksbringend angesehen. Sie findet daher auch in Architektur und Bekleidung kaum Verwendung. Unangenehm wird es für die einheimische Bevölkerung vor allem dann, wenn ganze Straßenzüge zwecks besserer touristischer Vermarktung mit roten Laternen dekoriert werden.

Chinas Landesoberfläche sieht aus wie eine Treppe, die von Westen nach Osten Stufe für Stufe abfällt. Die höchste Stufe ist das Qinghai-Tibet-Plateau, das im Durchschnitt mehr als 4000 Meter über dem Meeresspiegel liegt und als „Dach der Welt" bezeichnet wird. Der Mount Everest, tibetisch *Qomolangma*, übersetzt „Heilige Mutter", erhebt sich an der tibetisch-nepalesischen Grenze 8850 Meter über den Meeresspiegel. Gebirge, Hochplateaus und Hügellandschaften machen zwei Drittel der gesamten Landfläche Chinas aus.

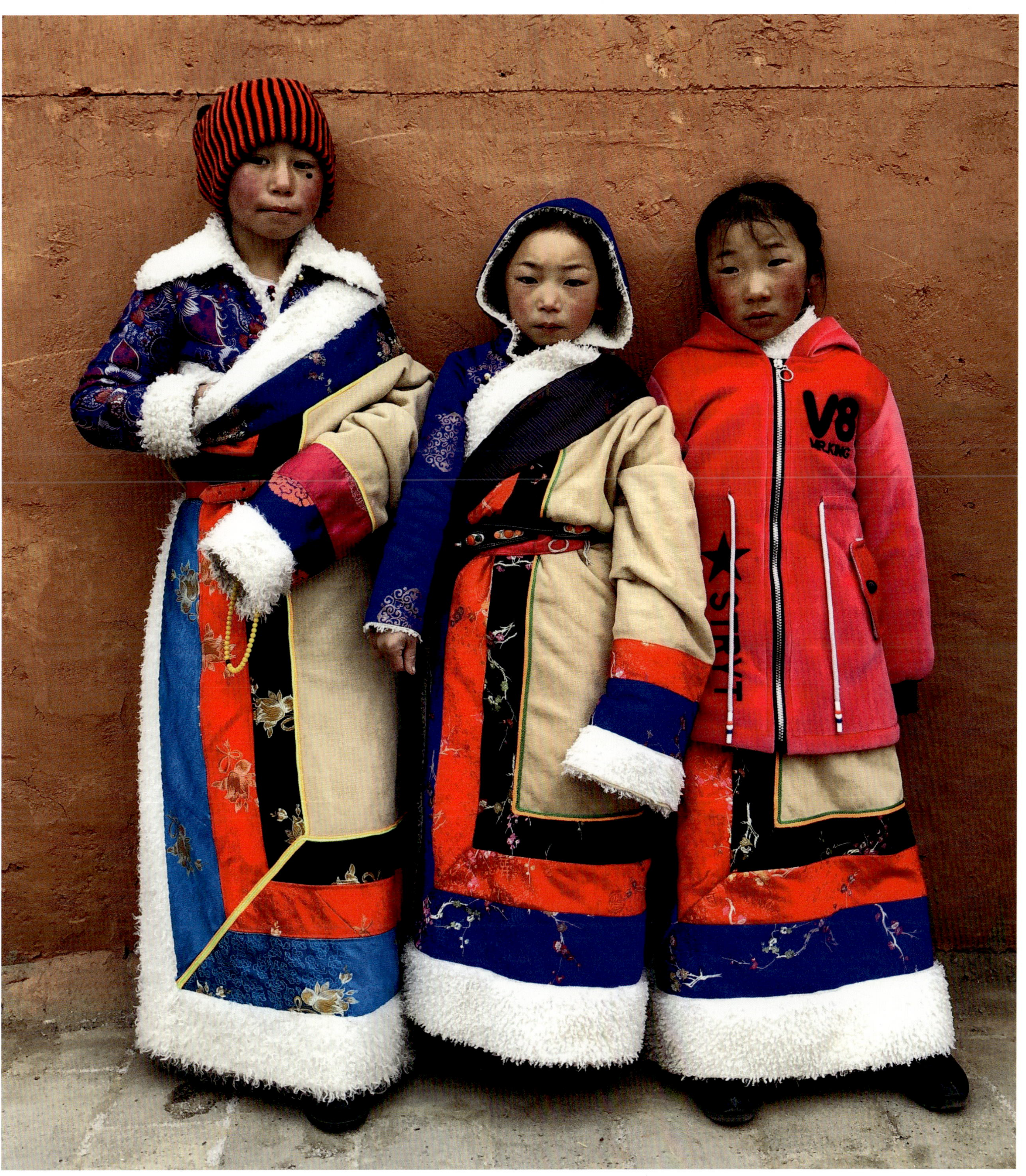
V8
MR.KING

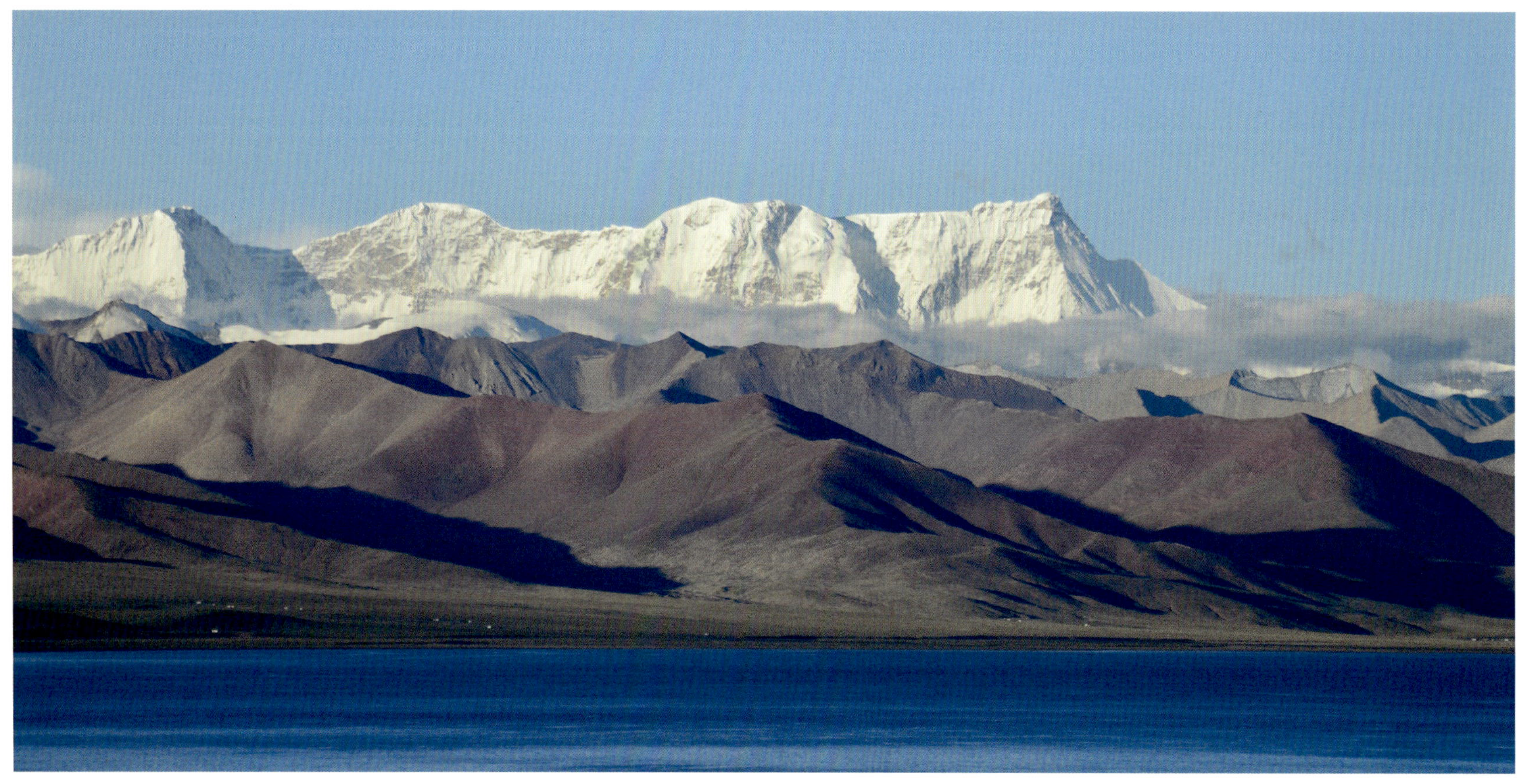

The diversity of its cultures and minorities calls for more differentiated interpretations of colour symbolism. For example, the colour red stands for fresh blood among some minorities and is not considered lucky. It is therefore hardly used in architecture and clothing. It is particularly unpleasant for the local population when entire streets are decorated with red lanterns for the purpose of better tourist marketing.

China's land surface looks like a stairway that descends from west to east step by step. The highest level is the Qinghai-Tibet Plateau, which averages more than 4,000 metres above sea level and is known as the "Roof of the World". Mount Everest, Tibetan *Qomolangma*, translated as "Holy Mother", rises 8,850 metres above sea level on the Tibet-Nepal border mountains, plateaus and hilly areas account for two-thirds of China's total land area.

Namtso Lake in the Tibet Autonomous Region, one of the three sacred lakes, is a salt lake and lies at an altitude of 4,718 metres. In Tibetan it is called "Heavenly Lake". Even in July, it is not unusual to see ice floes floating on it.

Der Namtso-See im autonomen Gebiet Tibet, einer der drei heiligen Seen, ist ein Salzsee und liegt auf einer Höhe von 4718 Metern. Im Tibetischen heißt er „Himmlischer See". Selbst im Juli ist es nicht ungewöhnlich, noch Eisschollen auf ihm treiben zu sehen.

Right page:
A mainstay of Tibetan jewellery is amber-coloured, petrified resin, which is believed to have healing properties. Because of its particular yellow hue, Baltic amber, which came to Tibet via Russia and Turkestan, is particularly sought after.

Rechte Seite:
Ein Protagonist des tibetischen Schmucks ist bernsteinfarbenes, versteinertes Harz, von dem angenommen wird, dass es heilende Wirkung hat. Wegen seines besonderen Gelbtones ist baltischer Bernstein, der über Russland und Turkestan nach Tibet kam, besonders begehrt.

The Tibetan Buddhist array of colours

In the high mountains of Tibet, white is considered a particularly welcoming colour. A white silk scarf is benevolently placed around the neck of foreign visitors as a greeting. The brightly coloured flags of Tibet, known worldwide, originate from the ancient Bon religion. It was the predominant religion of the Tibetans before Buddhism was established as the state religion in the 8th century.

Tibetisch-buddhistisches Bunt

Im Hochgebirge Tibets gilt Weiß als eine ganz besonders herzliche Farbe. Fremden Besuchern wird zur Begrüßung wohlwollend ein weißer Seidenschal um den Hals gelegt. Die weltweit bekannten bunten Flaggen Tibets stammen von der alten Bön-Religion. Sie war vor der Etablierung des Buddhismus als Staatsreligion im 8. Jahrhundert die vorherrschende Religion der Tibeter.

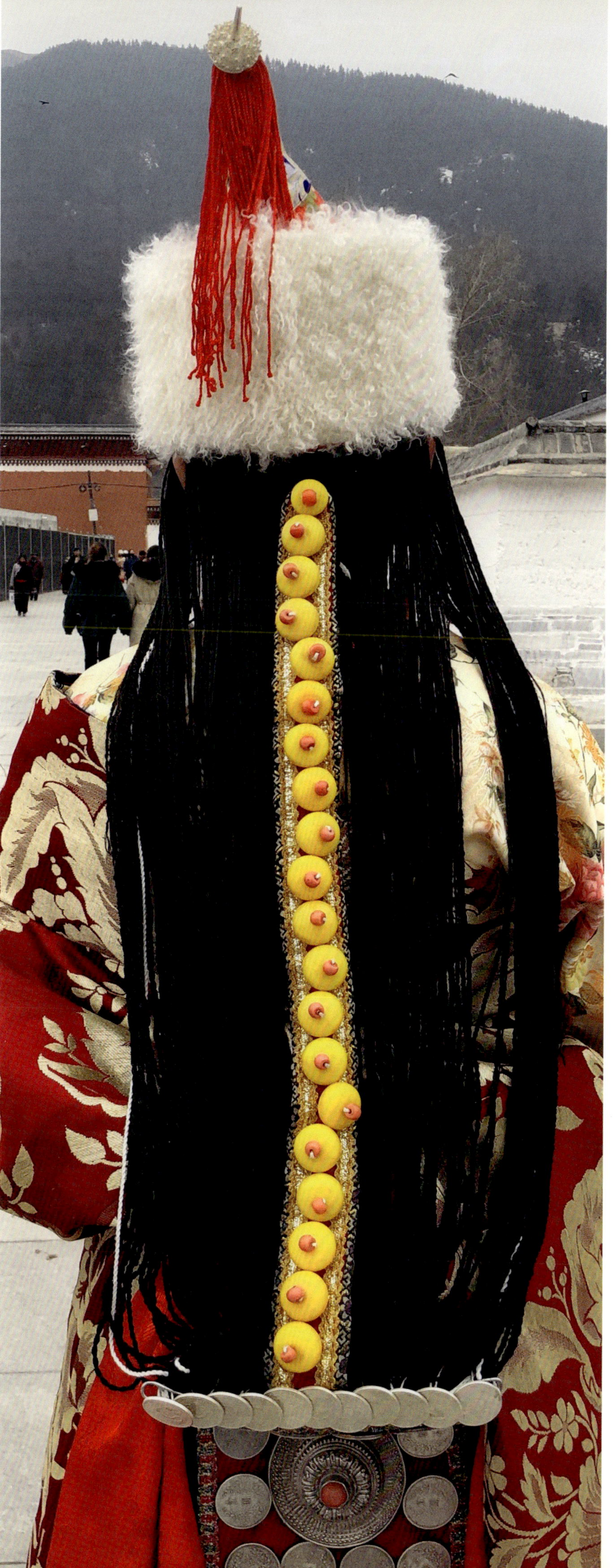

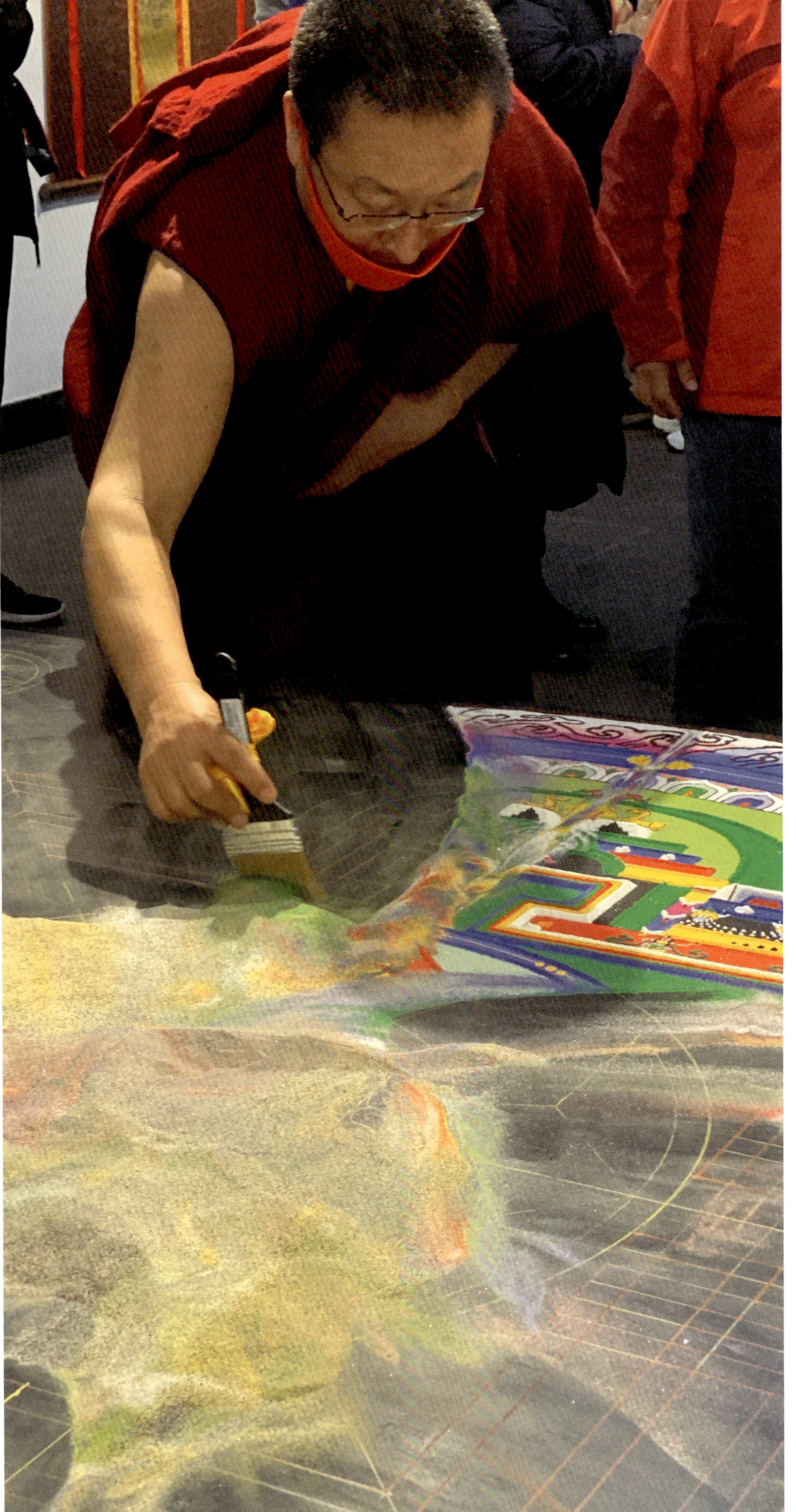

Right page:
Tibetan men in ceremonial garb with their striking red hats and colourfully decorated boots. The occasion is the annual, solemn unveiling ceremony of a huge thangka scroll painting, a Buddha image of about 50 × 30 metres, directly opposite the Labrang Monastery in Xiahe.

Rechte Seite:
Tibetische Männer im Zeremonialgewand mit den auffälligen roten Hüten und bunt verzierten Stiefeln. Anlass ist die jährliche, feierliche Enthüllungszeremonie eines riesigen Thangka-Rollgemäldes, eines Buddha-Bildnisses von ca. 50 × 30 Meter, direkt gegenüber des Labrang-Klosters in Xiahe.

The transience of all beauty as a basis for renewal is a ceremony of Buddhist monks. Here at the ritual dissolution of a wonderfully coloured sand mandala.

Die Vergänglichkeit alles Schönen als Basis für Erneuerung ist eine Zeremonie der buddhistischen Mönche. Hier beim rituellen Auflösen eines wunderbar farbigen Sandmandalas.

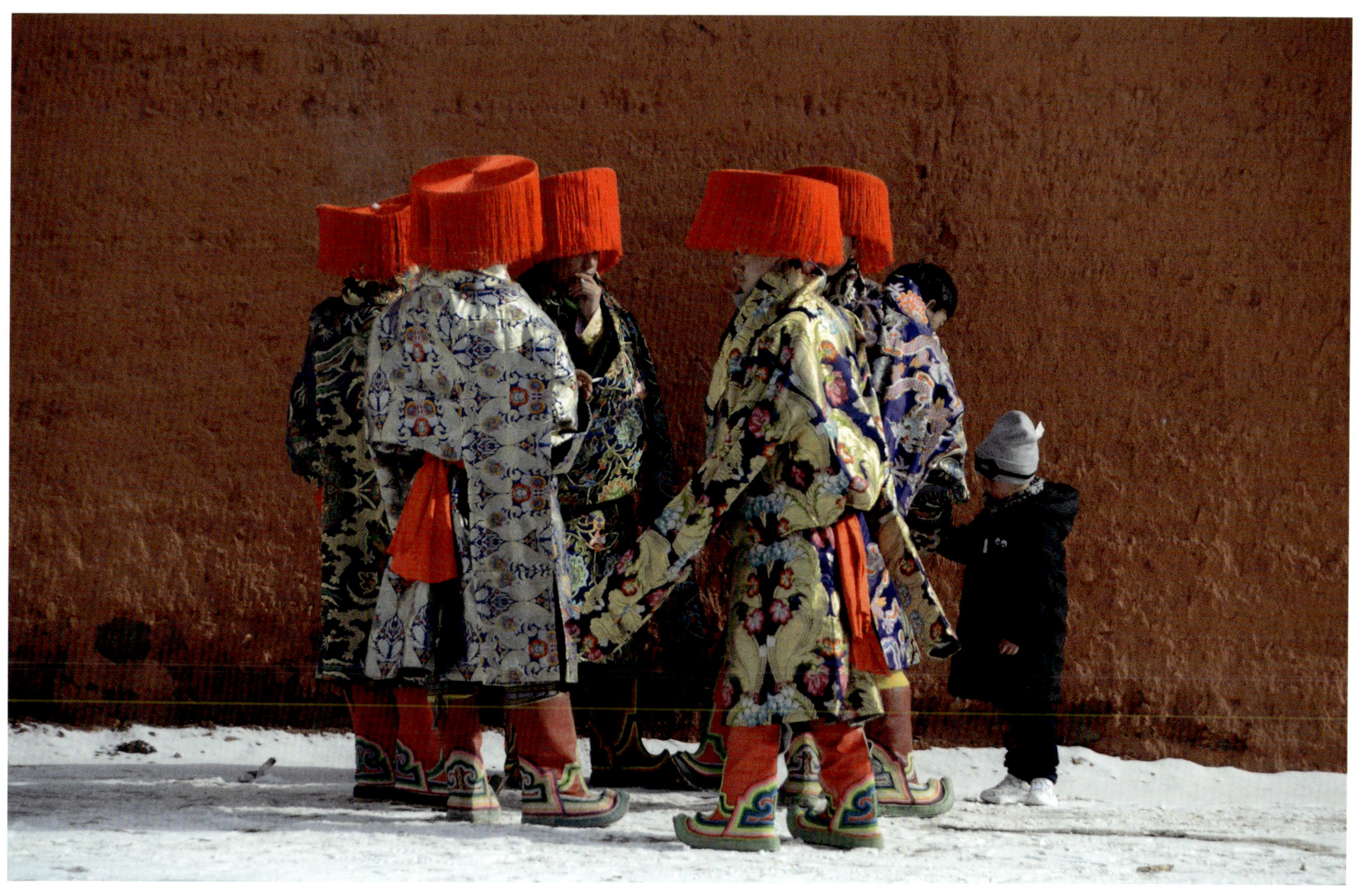

Bon is an animistic-polytheistic religion. In the vicinity of Lhasa, you can still watch shamanic priests performing their rites. They appease spirits through offerings, perform mask dances, and exorcise demons. The Bon religion is practiced not only in parts of China, but also in Nepal and Bhutan. One may pass under the coloured ropes, but never climb over or step on them. These colours differ in their symbolic meaning substantially from those presented so far in China. They are linked to the basic Tibetan Buddhist question of human happiness.

Every colour is assigned to a particular emotion, which is considered to be a fundamental hindrance in the search for happiness.

White = ignorance
Blue = anger
Yellow = pride, egotism
Red = desire
Green = stinginess, greed, envy

Der Bön ist eine animistisch-polytheistische Religion. In der Umgebung von Lhasa kann man heute noch Schamanenpriester bei der Ausübung ihrer Riten zuschauen. Sie besänftigen Geister durch Opfergaben, führen Maskentänze auf oder treiben Dämonen aus. Die Bön-Religion wird außer in Teilen Chinas heute auch noch in Nepal und in Bhutan praktiziert. Man darf unter den farbigen Strängen durchgehen, aber niemals drübersteigen oder drauftreten. Diese Farben unterscheiden sich in ihrer symbolischen Bedeutung wesentlich von den bislang in China vorgestellten. Sie sind verknüpft mit der tibetisch-buddhistischen Grundfrage nach dem Glück der Menschen.

Jeder Farbe wird eine bestimmte Emotion zugeordnet, die als grundlegend hinderlich angesehen wird auf der Suche nach dem Glück:

Weiß = Unwissenheit
Blau = Zorn
Gelb = Stolz, Ichsucht
Rot = Begierde
Grün = Geiz, Habgier, Neid

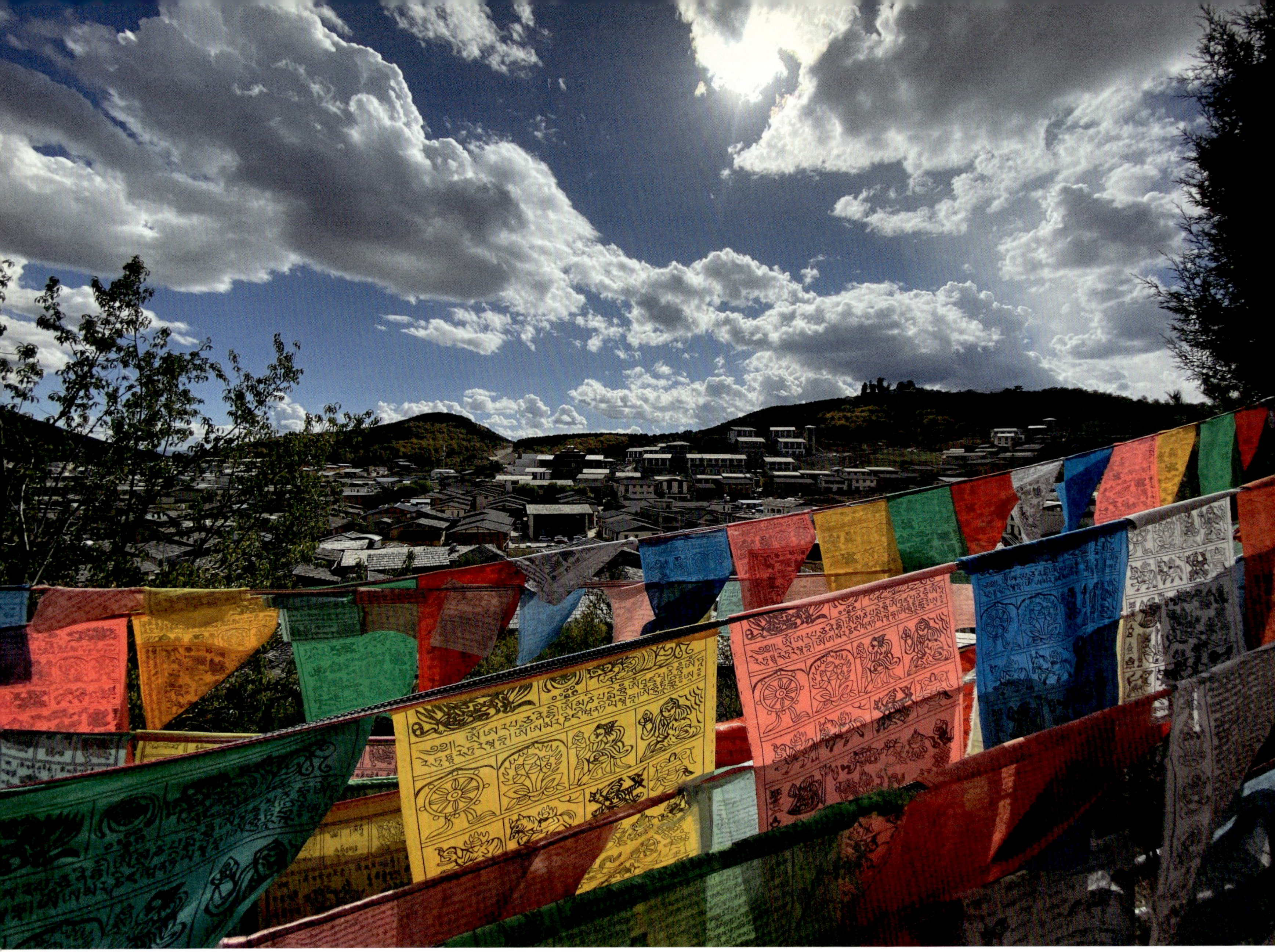

In the Tibetan cultural area, the colourful flags can be found on every mountain pass and peak.

Im tibetischen Kulturraum sind die bunten Fahnen an jedem Bergpass und auf jedem Gipfel zu finden.

According to this idea, in our ignorance and lack of wisdom, we chase after things that we hope will do us good and will distance us from our difficult mental states. So the idea of the prayer flags is to remind us that all the difficult emotions, everything that may ultimately harm us, are resolvable. If we harness these bringers of difficulty and combine them with a view that sees difficult emotions as potential, we can see that there is wisdom contained in the negative forces, as it were, as two sides of the same coin.

For example, the colour blue represents the transformation of anger into reflective wisdom. A wisdom that perceives and reflects outer and inner elements without shaking the "inside". One can rest in these elements. The colourful prayer flags thus serve as a reminder of our potential for happiness.

Laut dieser Vorstellung jagen wir in unserer Unwissenheit und mangelnden Weisheit Dingen nach, von denen wir hoffen, dass sie uns guttun und unsere schwierigen Geisteszustände nicht so spüren lassen. Die Idee der Gebetsfahnen ist es also, uns daran zu erinnern, dass alle schwierigen Emotionen, also alles, was uns letztendlich schadet, auflösbar sind. In den leidbringenden Emotionen ist unsere größte Energie gebunden. Wenn wir diese Schwierigkeitsbringer nutzen und mit einer Sichtweise kombinieren, die schwierige Emotionen als Potential versteht, so können wir erkennen, dass in den negativen Kräften, quasi als zwei Seiten einer Medaille, Weisheiten eingeschlossen sind.

Die Farbe Blau zum Beispiel steht für die Umwandlung von Zorn in spiegelgleiche Weisheit. Eine Weisheit, die äußere und innere Dinge wahrnimmt und abspiegelt, ohne dass das „Innere" geschüttelt wird. Man ruht in den Dingen. Die bunten Gebetsfahnen dienen also als Erinnerung an unser Potential zum Glücklichsein.

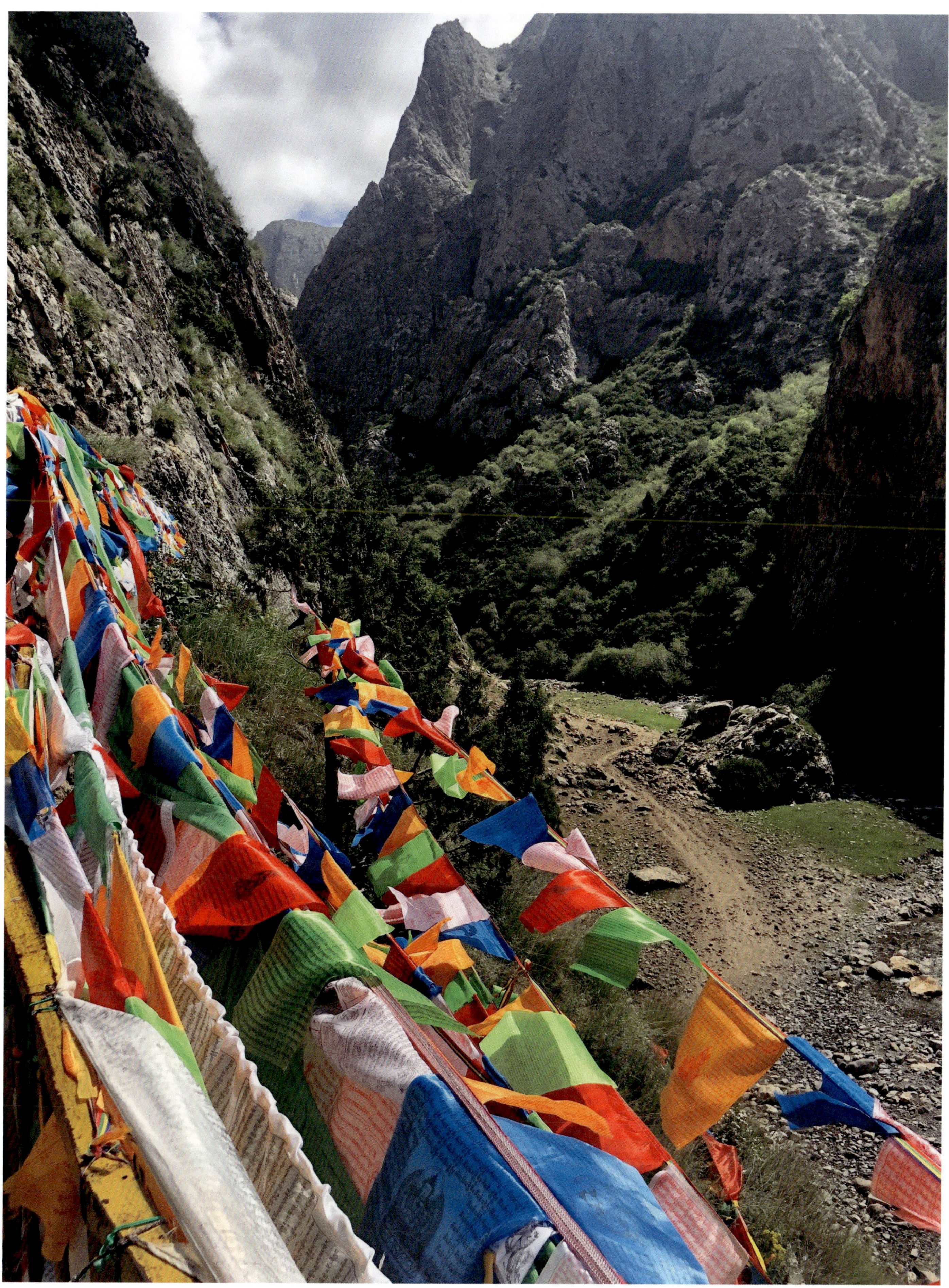

Warm white in the cold north

In northern China, Inner Mongolia, white is considered the colour of firelight and the sun, and thus warm and pure. The Mongols see themselves as descendants of a grey wolf and a white hind. Under the influence of Lamaist Buddhism, the Mongols' preference for the colour white has even increased. Thus, they refer to kind-hearted people as white people, a balmy breeze is called "white wind", charity enterprises are "white enterprises", and the first lunar month of the new year is considered a "white month", which is why the Spring Festival is also called "happiness of the white moon".

Also in white are the things that are indispensable in the nomadic life of the tundra, such as yurts or dairy products. Here, white is the colour of the homeland, so to speak. This is in interesting contrast to the view of the Han Chinese, who see white as a symbol of transience and in this sense describe a funeral as a "white affair".

Warmes Weiß im kalten Norden

Im Norden Chinas, der Inneren Mongolei, gilt Weiß als Farbe des Feuerscheins und der Sonne und damit als warm und rein. Die Mongolen verstehen sich als Abkömmlinge eines grauen Wolfes und einer weißen Hirschkuh. Unter dem Einfluss des lamaistischen Buddhismus hat sich die Vorliebe der Mongolen für die weiße Farbe sogar noch verstärkt. So bezeichnen sie gutherzige Menschen als weiße Menschen, eine laue Brise wird „weißer Wind" genannt, Wohltätigkeitsunternehmen sind „weiße Unternehmen", und der erste Mond-Monat des neuen Jahres gilt als „weißer Monat", weshalb das Frühlingsfest auch als „Glück des weißen Mondes" bezeichnet wird.

Ebenso in weißer Farbe gehalten sind die im nomadischen Leben der Tundra unentbehrlichen Dinge wie Jurten oder Milchprodukte. Weiß ist hier sozusagen die Farbe der Heimat. Dies steht in einem interessanten Kontrast zur Sichtweise der Han-Chinesen, welche Weiß als Symbol für Vergänglichkeit sehen und in diesem Sinne eine Beerdigung als „weiße Angelegenheit" bezeichnen.

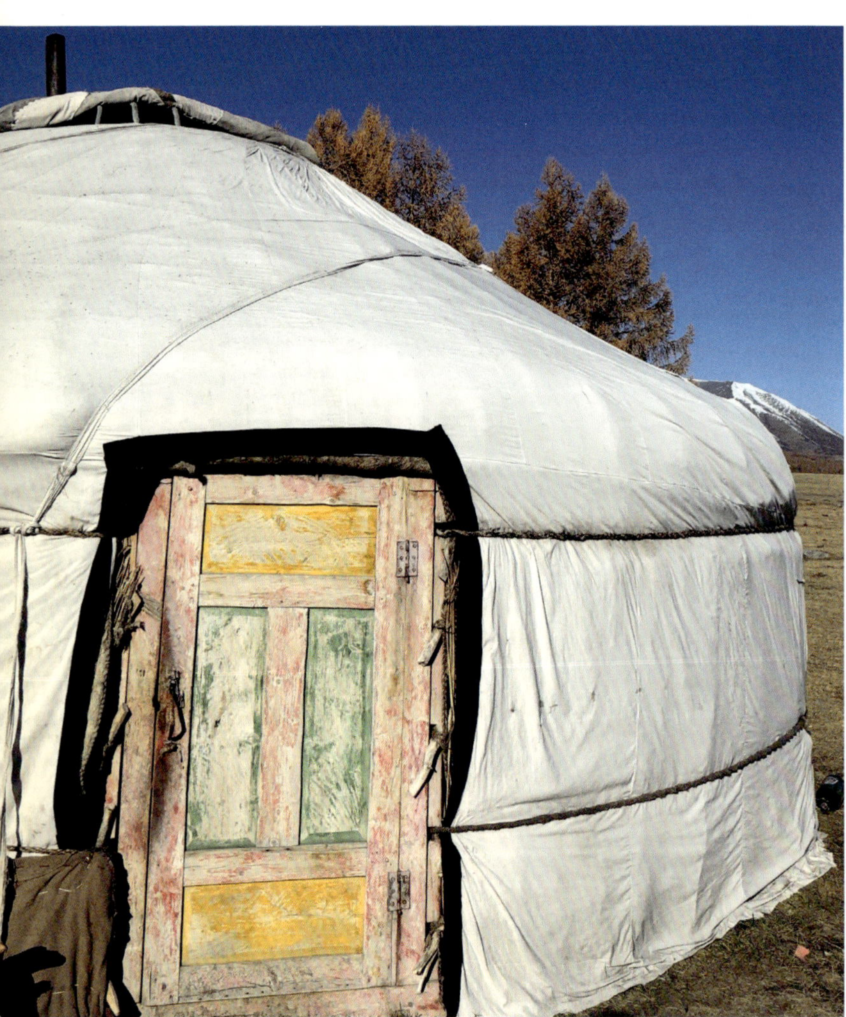

The framed wooden door of the yurt, which used to be a thick piece of felt, is always oriented to the south when setting up camp. The original Turkish word *jurt* means "tent, campsite, land, home or residence for the nomads". Similarly, the connection in usage between home and homeland. In Mongolian, yurt is called *ger*, which traditionally means "family". In some rural *gers*, up to twelve people live together. Often two *gers* stand close to each other and form a unit. The white exterior colour is common to all.

Die gerahmte Holztür der Jurte, früher nur ein dickes Stück Filz, wird beim Lagerplatzaufbau immer nach Süden ausgerichtet. Das ursprünglich türkische Wort *jurt* bedeutet für die Nomaden „Zelt, Lagerplatz, Land, Heimat oder Wohnort". Ähnlich auch die Verbundenheit im deutschen Sprachgebrauch von Heim und Heimat. Im Mongolischen heißt Jurte *Ger*, was traditionell soviel wie „Familie" bedeutet. In manchen *Gers* auf dem Land leben bis zu zwölf Personen. Häufig stehen auch zwei *Gers* nah beieinander und bilden eine Einheit. Allen gleich ist die weiße Außenfarbe.

Right page:
In southern Yunnan, the hilly, dense jungle-like border area with Myanmar, Laos and Vietnam, known as the Golden Triangle, one still encounters elderly opium-smoking members of various cross-border minorities.

Rechte Seite:
Im Süden Yunnans – dem hügeligen, dichten dschungelartigen Grenzgebiet zu Myanmar, Laos und Vietnam, und sogenannten Goldenen Dreieck – trifft man auch heute noch auf ältere opiumrauchende Angehörige diverser grenzübergreifender Minderheiten.

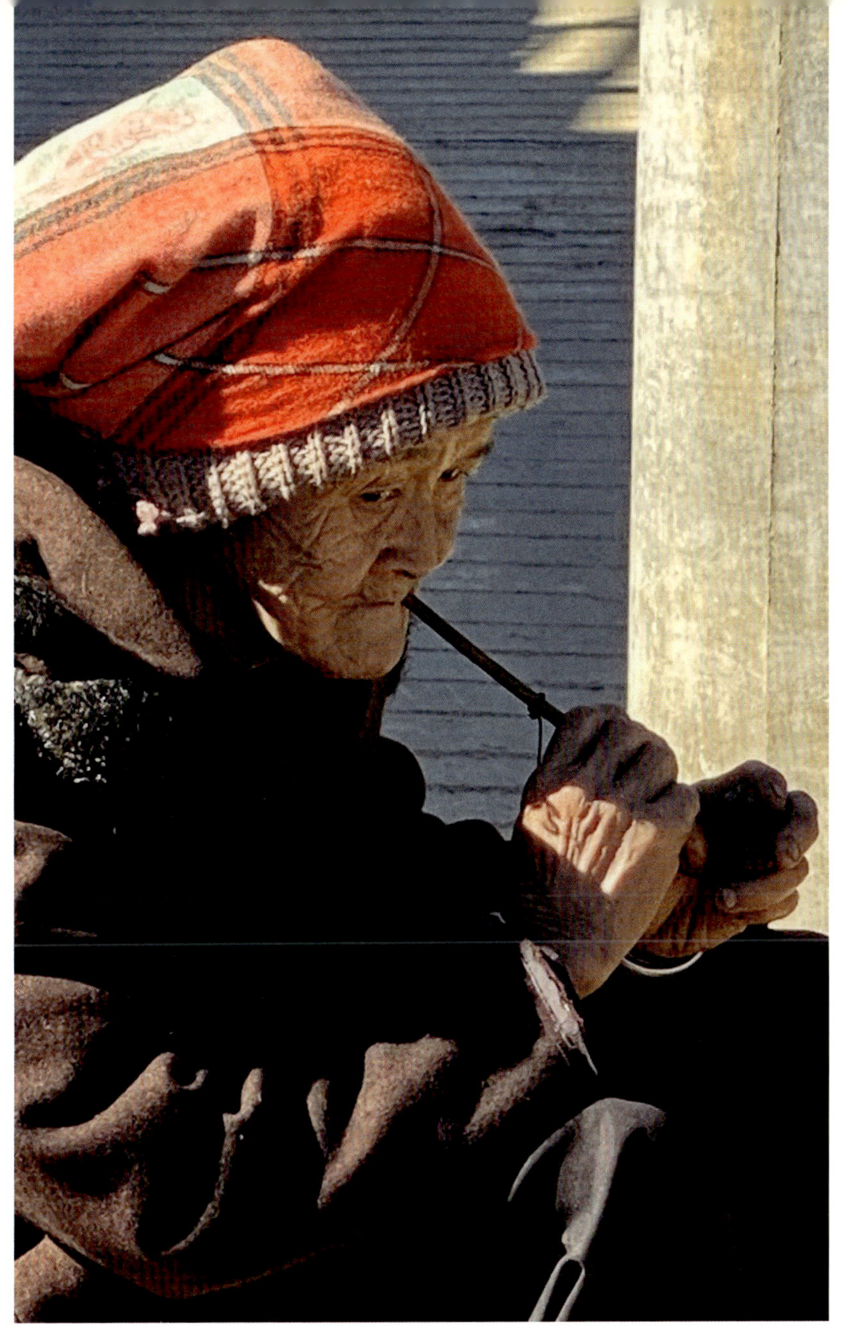

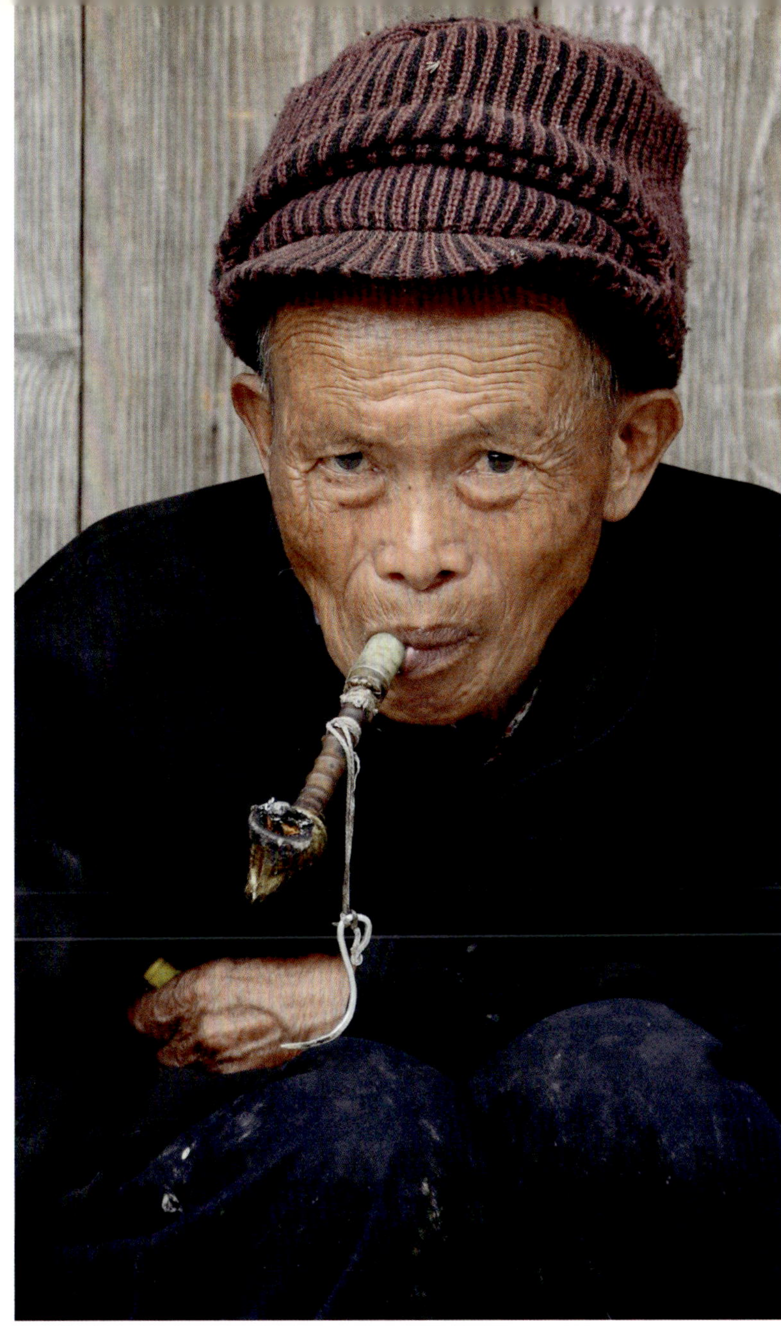

Of noble black and simple white

Even the colour black, which tends to be associated with mischief in Han Chinese culture, has a very different meaning for the Yi ethnic group, which resides in the mountainous area of Sichuan, Yunnan, Guizhou and Guangxi. The Yi divide themselves into "White Yi" and "Black Yi", with the blacks considered black-boned nobles, while the whites represent the common people. Marriage between the two groups is not possible. The appreciation for the colour black is also expressed in their clothing: Both men and women wear black turbans and black cloaks; for men there are blue and black pants, and for women there are patchwork skirts and black garments edged with coloured borders. Black is considered the colour of nobility and dignity here and is generally well-liked.

Von edlem Schwarz und einfachem Weiß

Auch die Farbe Schwarz, welche in der Han-chinesischen Kultur eher mit Unheil assoziiert wird, hat für die Volksgruppe der Yi, welche im gebirgigen Gebiet von Sichuan, Yunnan, Guizhou und Guangxi ansässig ist, eine ganz andere Bedeutung. Die Yi teilen sich selbst in „Weiße Yi" und „Schwarze Yi" ein, wobei die Schwarzen als Adelige mit schwarzen Knochen gelten, während die Weißen das gemeine Volk der Beherrschten darstellen. Eine Heirat zwischen den beiden Gruppen ist nicht möglich. Die Wertschätzung für die Farbe Schwarz drückt sich auch in ihrer Bekleidung aus: Männer wie Frauen tragen schwarze Turbane und schwarze Umhänge, für Männer gibt es blau-schwarze Hosen, für Frauen Patchwork-Röcke und mit farbigen Borden umrandete schwarze Kleidungsstücke. Schwarz gilt hier als Farbe des Adels und der Würde und findet allgemein Gefallen.

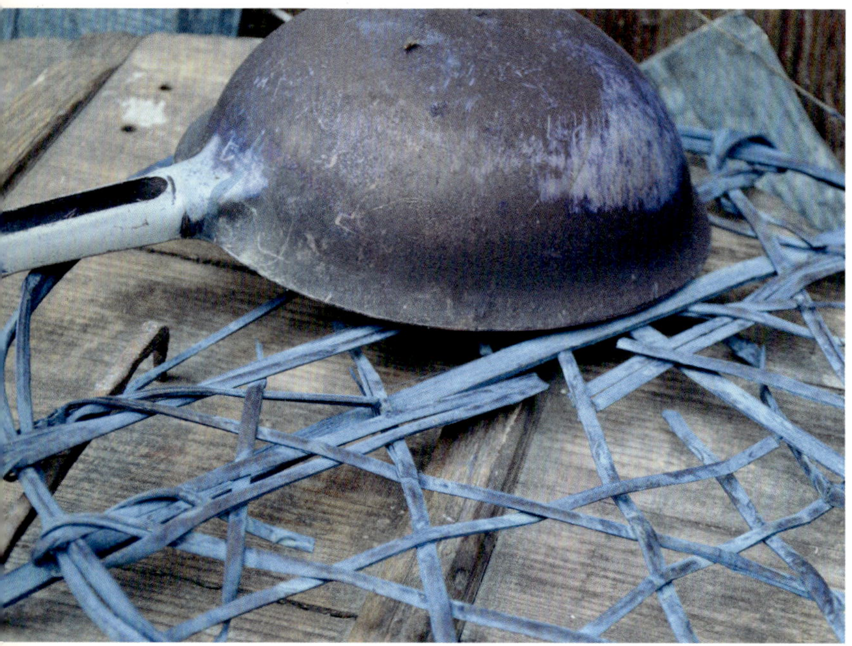

Indigoblau inmitten von sattem Dschungelgrün

Die Dong-Minderheit im Süden der Provinz Guizhou und im Norden der Provinz Guangxi ist bekannt für ihre indigogefärbte Bekleidung. Den besonderen Glanz erhalten die Stoffe durch konstantes Hämmern. Eine lautstarke Technik, die auch nachts daran erinnert, dass man hier noch Handwerk betreibt. Die Männer tragen einen kragenlosen, indigofarbenen Anzug und umwickeln sich den mit der Sichel rasierten Kopf mit einem Turbantuch. Nur oben bleibt ein Bündel langer Haare übrig, meist zu einem Knoten gedreht. Die Frauen tragen indigofarbene Röcke oder Hosen, blaue Blusen, silberne Halsringe und während der zahlreichen Singfestivals farbigen Kopfschmuck. Die Dong sind bekannt für Ihre Holzbauweise und zwar speziell für ihre Wind- und Regenbrücken sowie ihre Trommeltürme. Diese Brücken werden ohne Nägel konstruiert und sind reich mit buddhistischen Bildnissen verziert. Sie dienen meistens mehr als soziale Treffpunkte denn als Brücke. Die Dong gehören zum Volk der Miao und beten Bäume an. Sie glauben, dass die Geister ihrer Ahnen im Innern der Stämme leben. Wenn ein Baby geboren wird, pflanzt man einen Setzling. Ein Verstorbener erhält kein Grab, keinen Grabstein, sondern man legt ihn in die Erde, pflanzt auch dort einen Baum und kann beobachten, wie er wächst. Es ist streng verboten Bäume zu fällen. Nur eine Ausnahme gab es, als 1976 Mao Zedong starb. Um ihren Respekt zu zeigen, fällten die Miao einen großen Kampferbaum und bauten aus dem Holz eine Pagode zu Ehren des Großen Vorsitzenden. Doch die Wurzel des heiligen Baumes blieb erhalten und neue Zweige wuchsen.

Indigo blue in the midst of lush jungle green

The Dong minority in the south of Guizhou province and in the north of Guangxi province is known for its indigo-dyed clothing. The fabrics get their special sheen from constant hammering. A noisy technique that reminds us even at night that craftsmanship is still practiced here. The men wear a collarless, indigo-coloured suit and wrap their heads, shaved with a sickle, with a turban cloth. Only a bundle of long hair remains on top, usually twisted into a knot. The women wear indigo skirts or pants, blue blouses, silver neck rings, and during the numerous singing festivals, coloured headdresses. The Dong are known for their wooden construction, especially for their wind and rain bridges and their drum towers. These bridges are constructed without nails and are richly decorated with Buddhist images. They usually serve more as social meeting places than as bridges. The Dong belong to the Miao people and worship trees. They believe that the spirits of their ancestors live inside the trunks. When a baby is born, they plant a sapling. A deceased person is not given a grave, a tombstone, but is placed in the ground, a tree is planted there as well, and one can watch it grow. It is strictly forbidden to cut down trees. There was only one exception when Mao Zedong died in 1976. To show their respect, the Miao cut down a large camphor tree and used the wood to build a pagoda in honour of the Great Chairman. But the root of the sacred tree remained, and new branches grew.

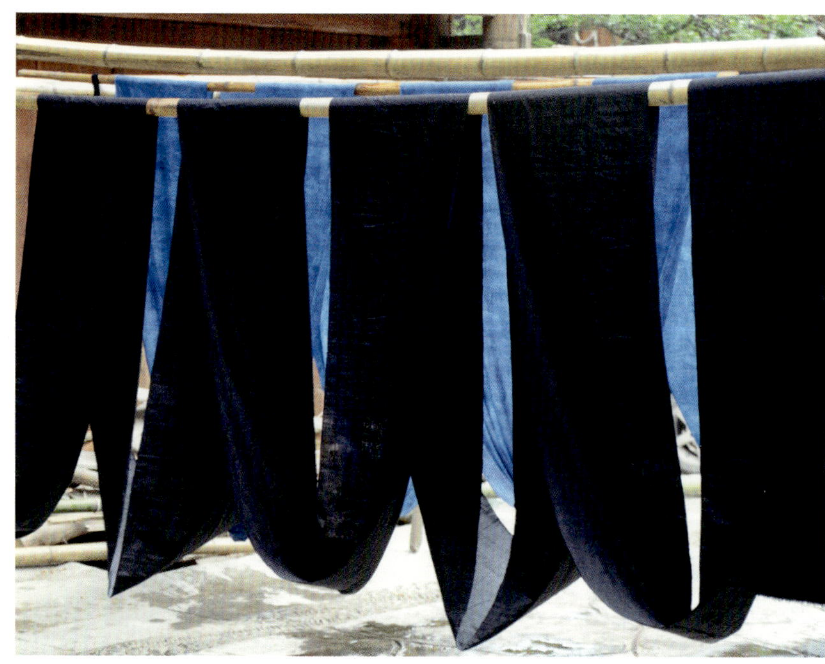

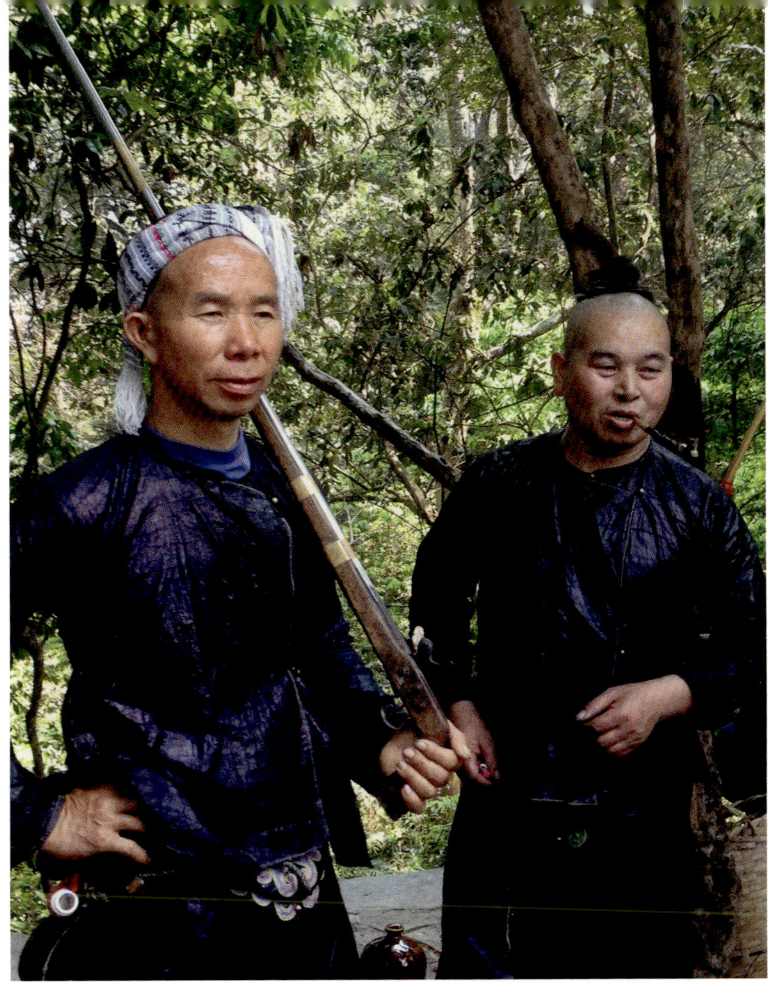

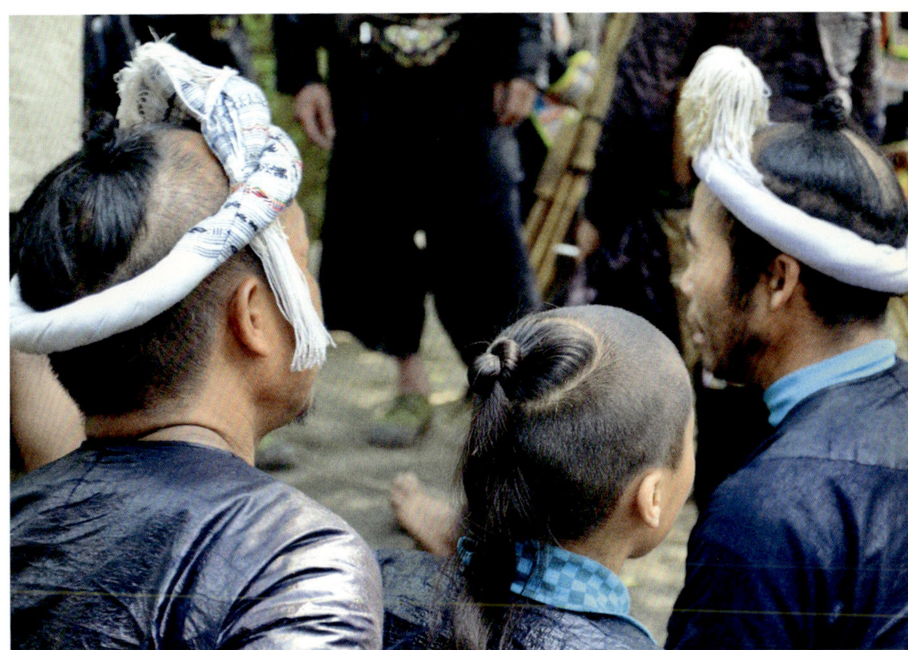

The Dong are known for their unique polyphonic choral singing. Traditional courtship takes place through the mutual exchange of colourfully embroidered garments and songs. Following the ancient rituals, the men carry their rifles and ammunition every day. Shots are fired into the air to greet guests.

Die Dong sind bekannt für ihren einzigartigen mehrstimmigen Chorgesang. Traditionelle Brautwerbung verläuft in wechselseitigem Austausch von bunt bestickten Kleidungsstücken und Liedern. Den alten Ritualen folgend, tragen die Männer täglich ihr Gewehr und ihre Munition mit sich. Zur Begrüßung von Gästen wird in die Luft geschossen.

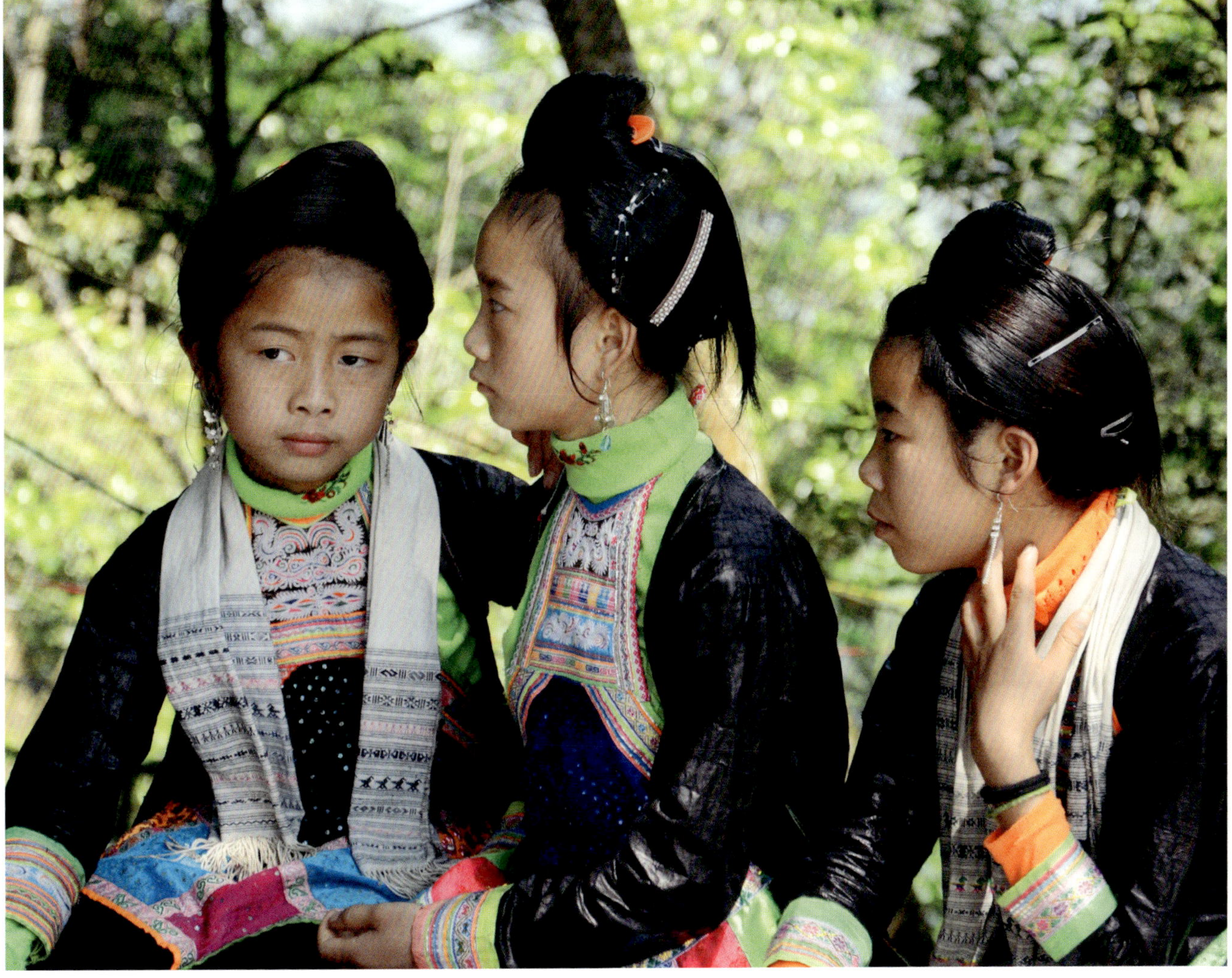

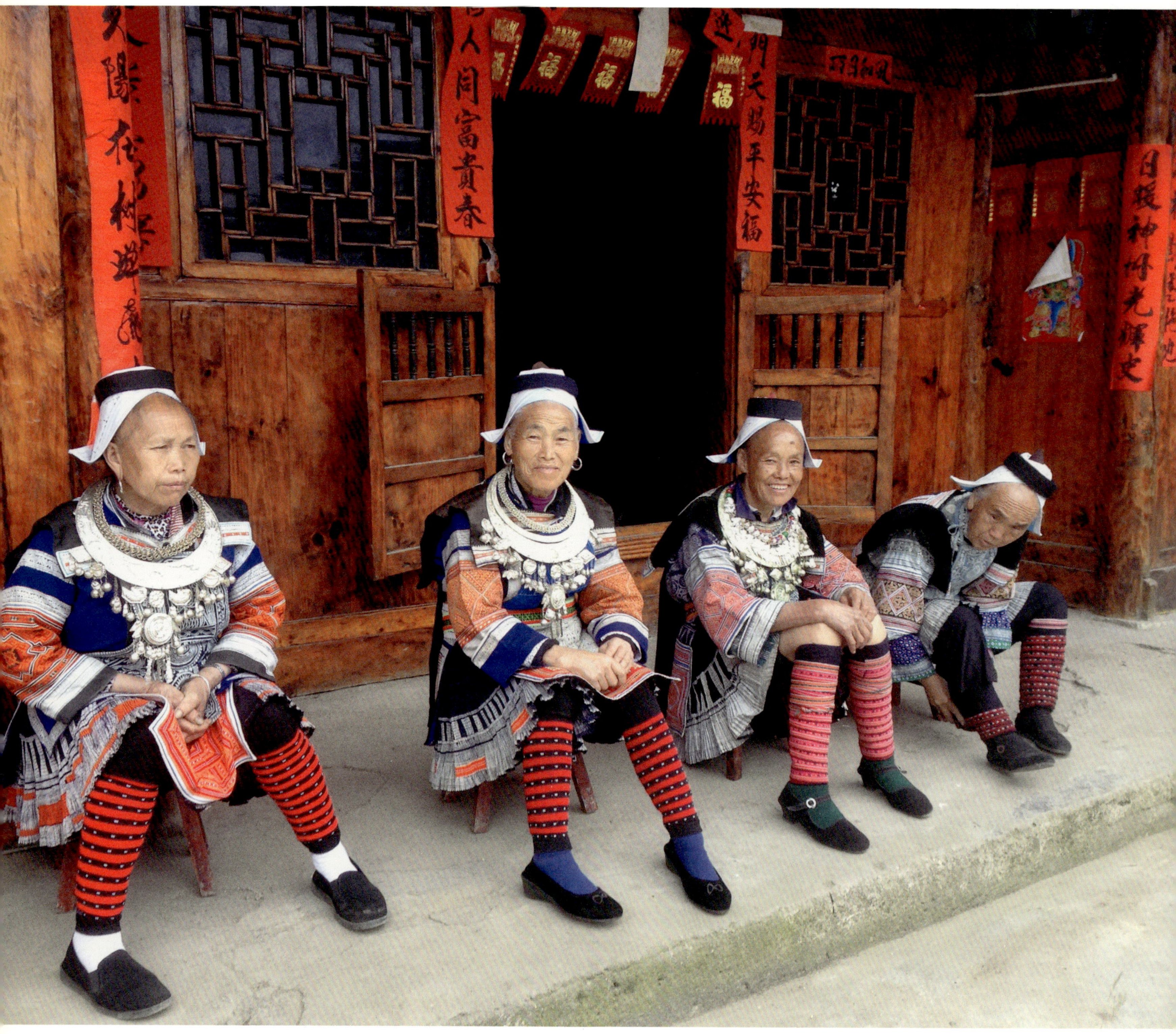

Protective silver

The indigenous Miao from the village of Xijiang in Guizhou, China's poorest province, believe that silver can drive away evil spirits. That's why they put all their artistry into silver-smithing. At the Panjayuan market in Beijing, which is called the "attic of China", you can see Miao women in colourful clothes and with magnificent silver jewellery on weekends.

Schützendes Silber

Die indigenen Miao aus dem Dorf Xijiang in Guizhou, der ärmsten Provinz Chinas, glauben, dass Silber böse Geister vertreiben könne. Deshalb legen sie ihre ganze Kunstfertigkeit in Silberschmiedearbeiten. Auf dem Panjayuan-Markt in Peking, dem „Dachboden Chinas", kann man an den Wochenenden Miao-Frauen in bunter Kleidung und mit prächtigem Silberschmuck sehen.

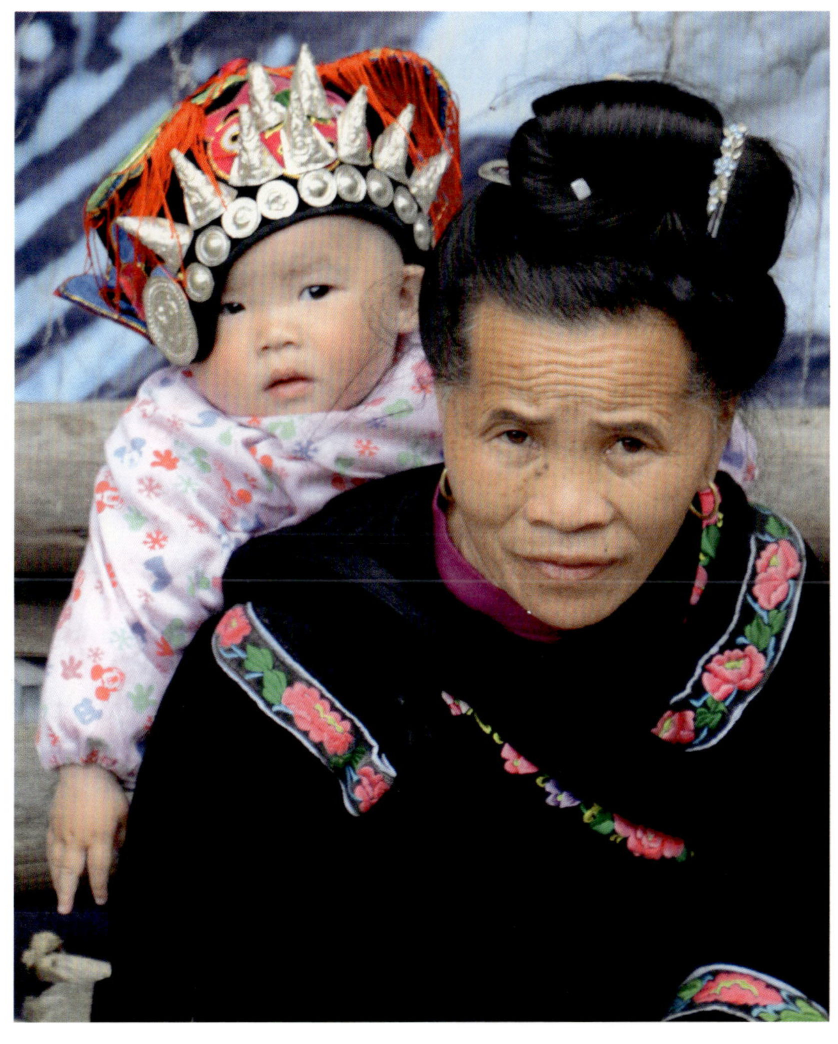

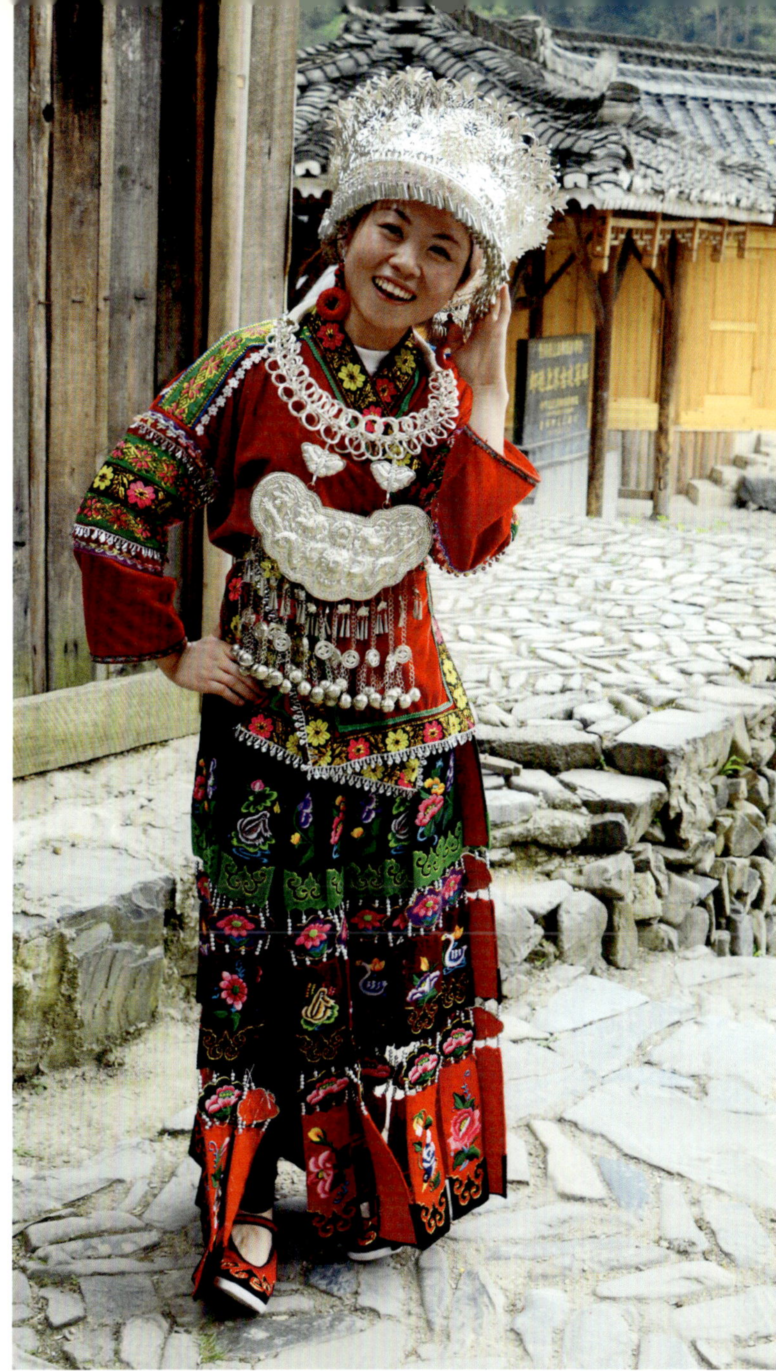

While both Dong grandparents still tend to the rice fields or pick and process the indigo leaves to dye cotton cloth, the younger village members are paid by the government to practice and perform the traditional songs and dances for tourists. In order to counteract the migration to the big cities, the state also supports the practice of silversmithing among the Miao and the display of silversmithing in the villages.

Während sich bei den Dong die Großeltern noch um die Reisfelder kümmern oder die Indigoblätter zum Färben der Baumwollstoffe pflücken und verarbeiten, werden die jüngeren Dorfmitglieder von der Regierung bezahlt, um für Touristen die traditionellen Gesänge und Tänze zu üben und aufzuführen. Um die Abwanderung in die Großstädte zu verringern, unterstützt der Staat bei den Miao auch die Ausübung der Silberschmiedekunst und das Zurschaustellen in den Dörfern.

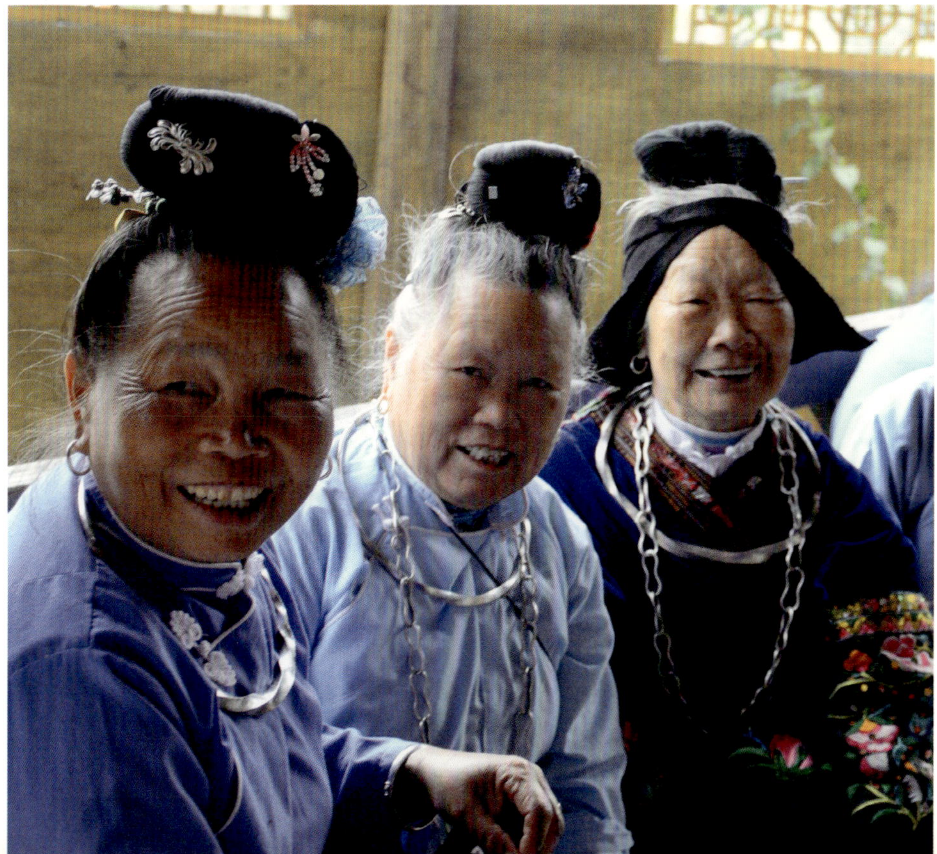

The most meaningful Buddhist shrine of the Tibetans is the Jokhang Temple, in the middle of the old town of Lhasa. It is surrounded by a colonnade with prayer wheels. For the Tibetans, one should make a pilgrimage there at least once in a lifetime. The roof is covered with gilded bronze tiles and decorated with a *dharma* wheel flanked by gazelles.

Das bedeutendste buddhistische Heiligtum der Tibeter, der Jokhang-Tempel, steht inmitten der Altstadt von Lhasa. Er wird von einem Wandelgang mit Gebetsmühlen umgeben. Jeder Tibeter sollte nach Möglichkeit mindestens einmal im Leben dorthin gepilgert sein. Das mit vergoldeten Bronzeziegeln gedeckte Dach ist mit einem von Gazellen flankierten *Dharma*-Rad geschmückt.

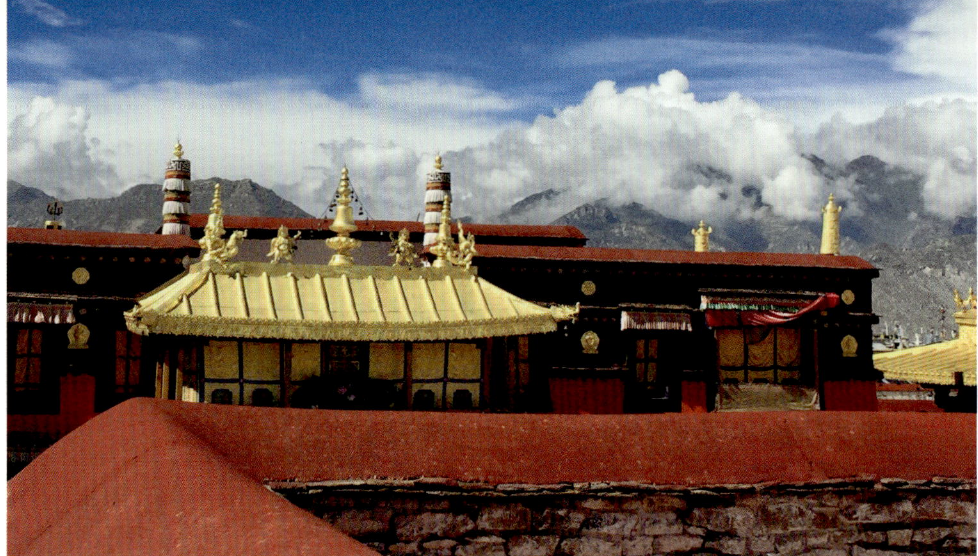

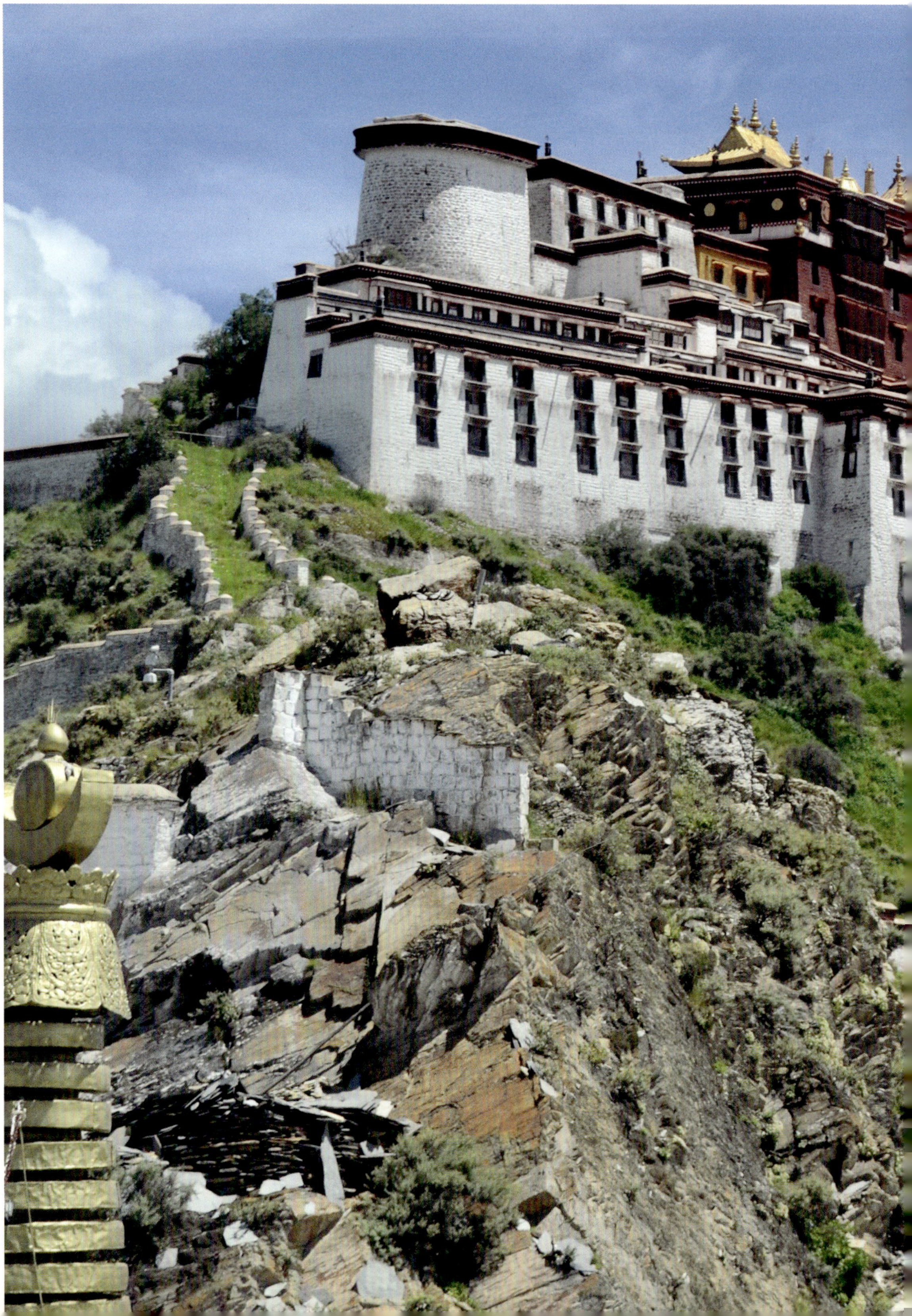

The giant Potola Palace is atop the Mar-po-ri mountain, which literally means "Red Mountain", and rises 130 metres over Lhasa.

Der riesige Potala-Palast liegt auf dem Berg Mar-po-ri, aus dem Tibetischen wörtlich übersetzt „Roter Berg", der sich 130 Meter über Lhasa erhebt.

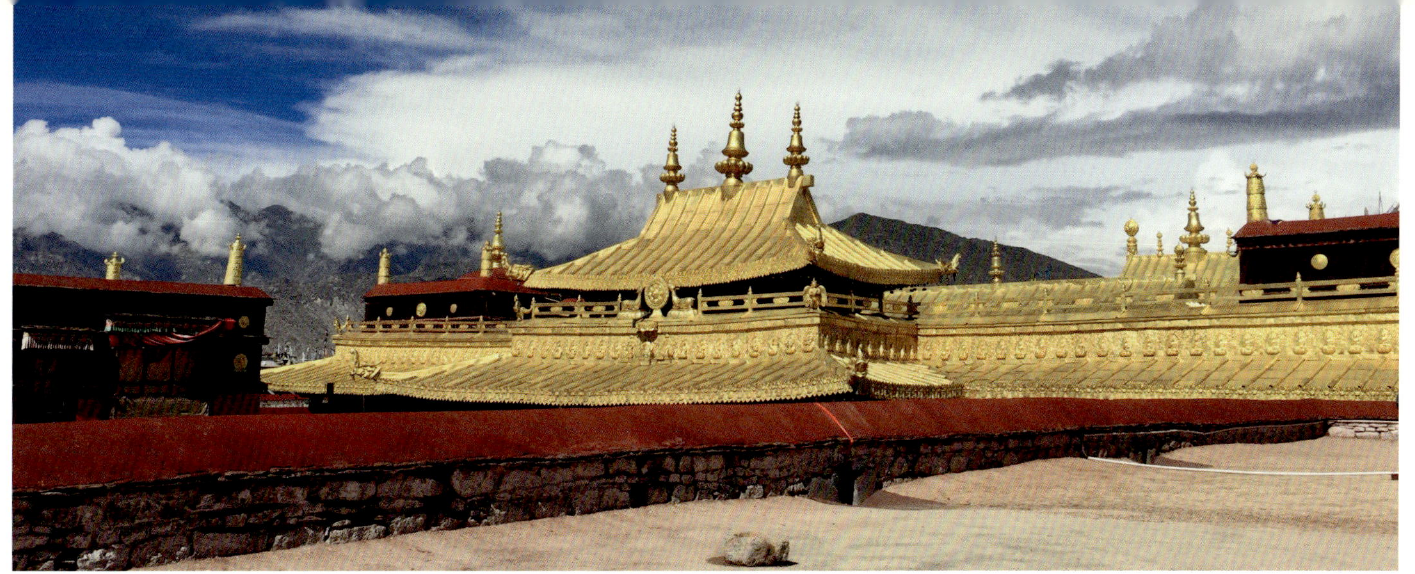

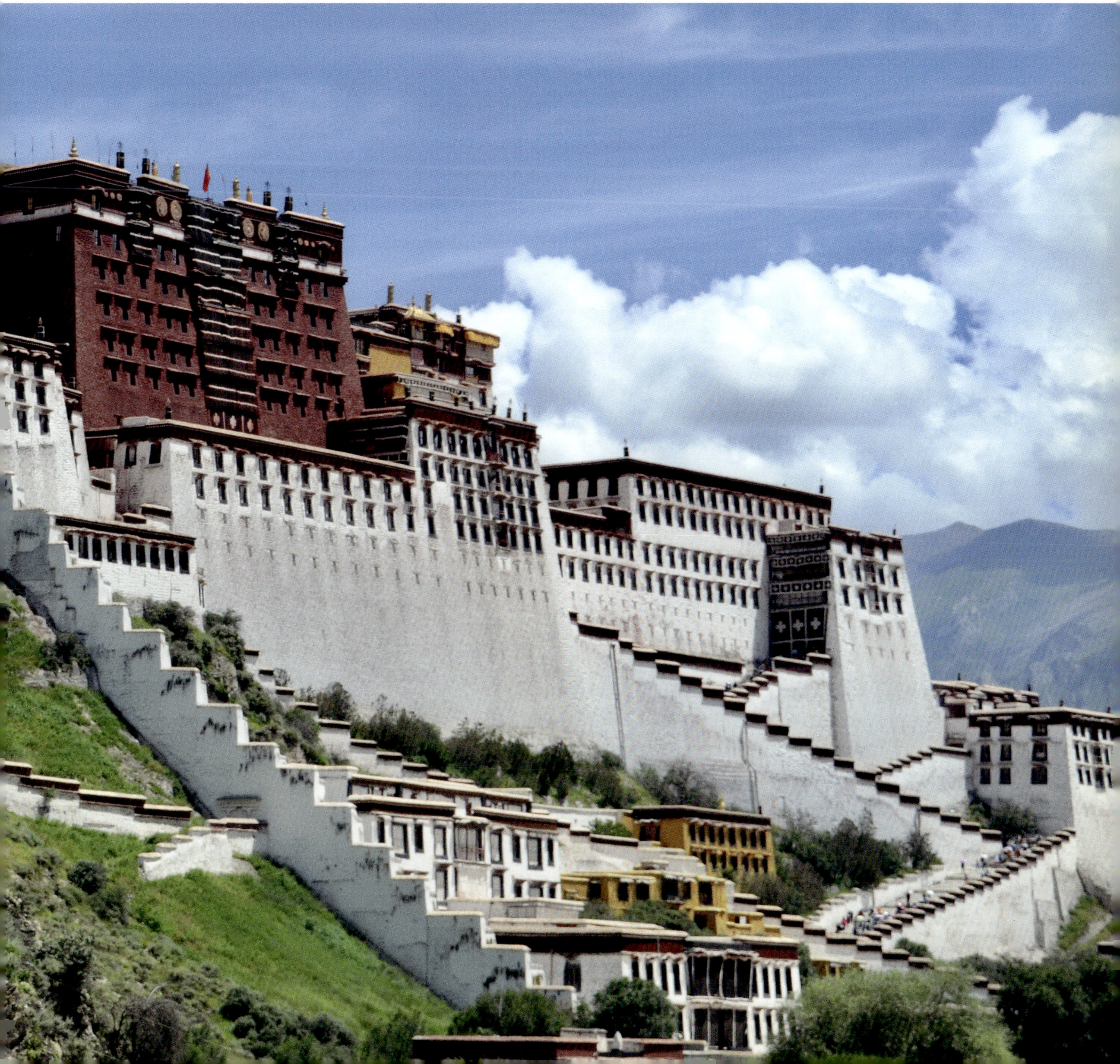

South of the white clouds
Südlich der weißen Wolke

A particularly large number of different languages can be heard in Yunnan Province, which translates as "southern cloud", the province with the highest ethnic diversity. In Kunming, the provincial capital, alongside the Han Chinese live many Yi, Bai, Zhuang, Miao, Sani, Dai, Naxi and also Hui, or Chinese of the Muslim faith. Their ancestors were Mongolian, Turkic or other Central Asian settlers who travelled to China along the Silk Road. The Hui on the southeast coast of China are mostly descended from Arab seafaring traders. This explains the surprising sight here in southern China of a Turkish building or Muslim-influenced towns with large mosques and kebab stands with delicious flatbreads.

The enchanting colours of autumn can be experienced in the unusual Shilin Stone Forest near Kunming. The unique karst landscape resembles a natural labyrinth of dense vegetation and rock spurs of various shapes and sizes that rise up to the sky. The creative formations feed folk superstitions and many Chinese legends. Poetic and meaningful names such as Moonstruck Rhino, Immortal Mushroom,

Ganz besonders viele verschiedene Sprachen kann man in der Provinz Yunnan, übersetzt „südliche Wolke", hören, der Provinz mit der höchsten ethnischen Diversität. In Kunming, der Provinzhauptstadt, leben neben Han-Chinesen noch viele Yi, Bai, Zhuang, Miao, Sani, Dai, Naxi und auch viele Hui, das sind Chinesen muslimischen Glaubens. Ihre Vorfahren waren mongolische, türkische oder andere zentralasiatische Siedler, die entlang der Seidenstraße nach China reisten. Die Hui an der Südostküste Chinas stammen meist von arabischen seefahrenden Händlern ab. So erklärt sich hier im Süden Chinas der überraschende Anblick eines türkischen Bauwerks und muslimisch geprägter Ortschaften mit großen Moscheen und Kebab-Ständen mit leckeren Fladenbroten.

Eine bezaubernd bunte Herbstfärbung kann man im ungewöhnlichen Steinwald Shilin in der Nähe von Kunming erleben. Die einzigartige Karstlandschaft ähnelt einem natürlichen Labyrinth aus dichter Vegetation und Felsspornen verschiedener Formen und Größen, die bis zum Himmel emporragen. Die kreativen Formationen nähren den volks-

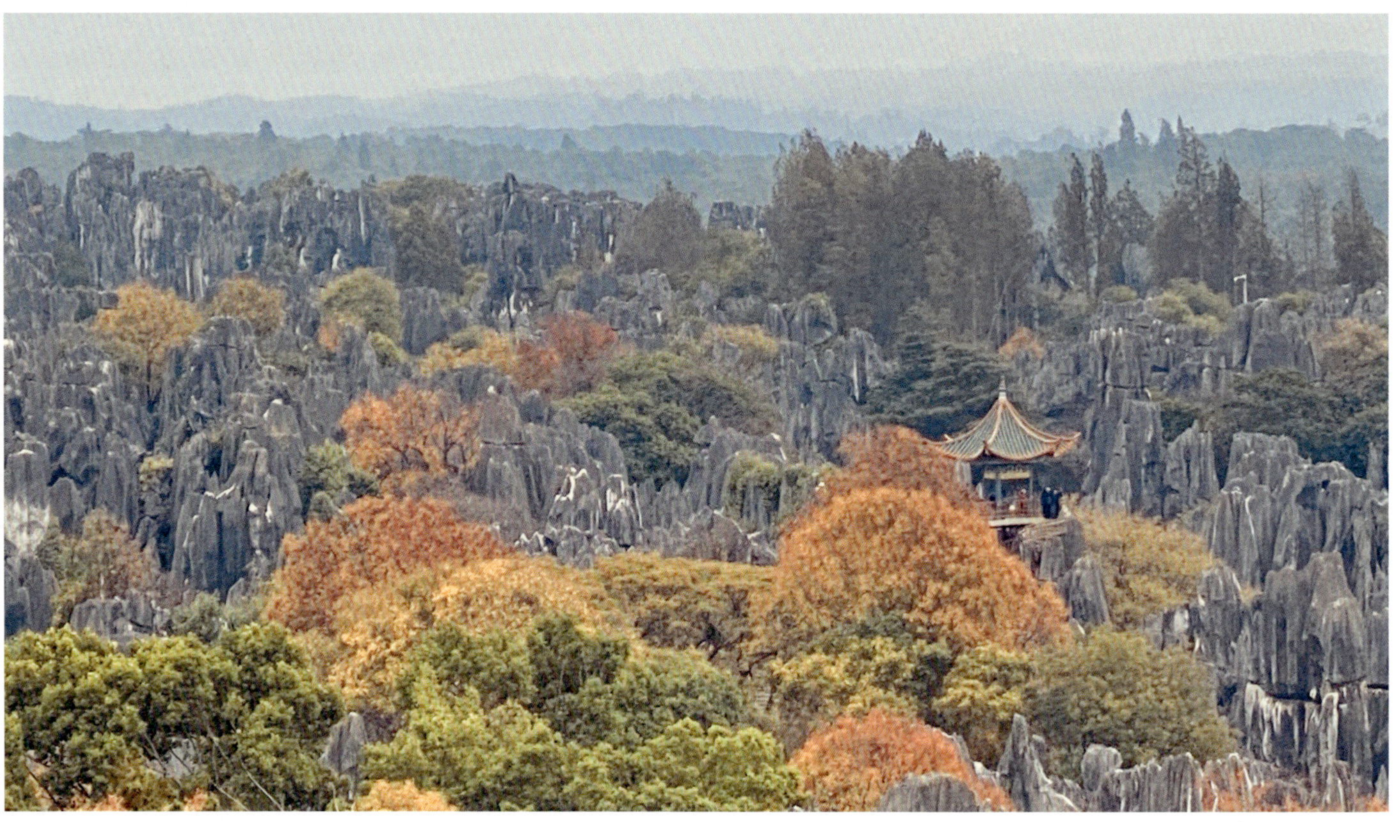

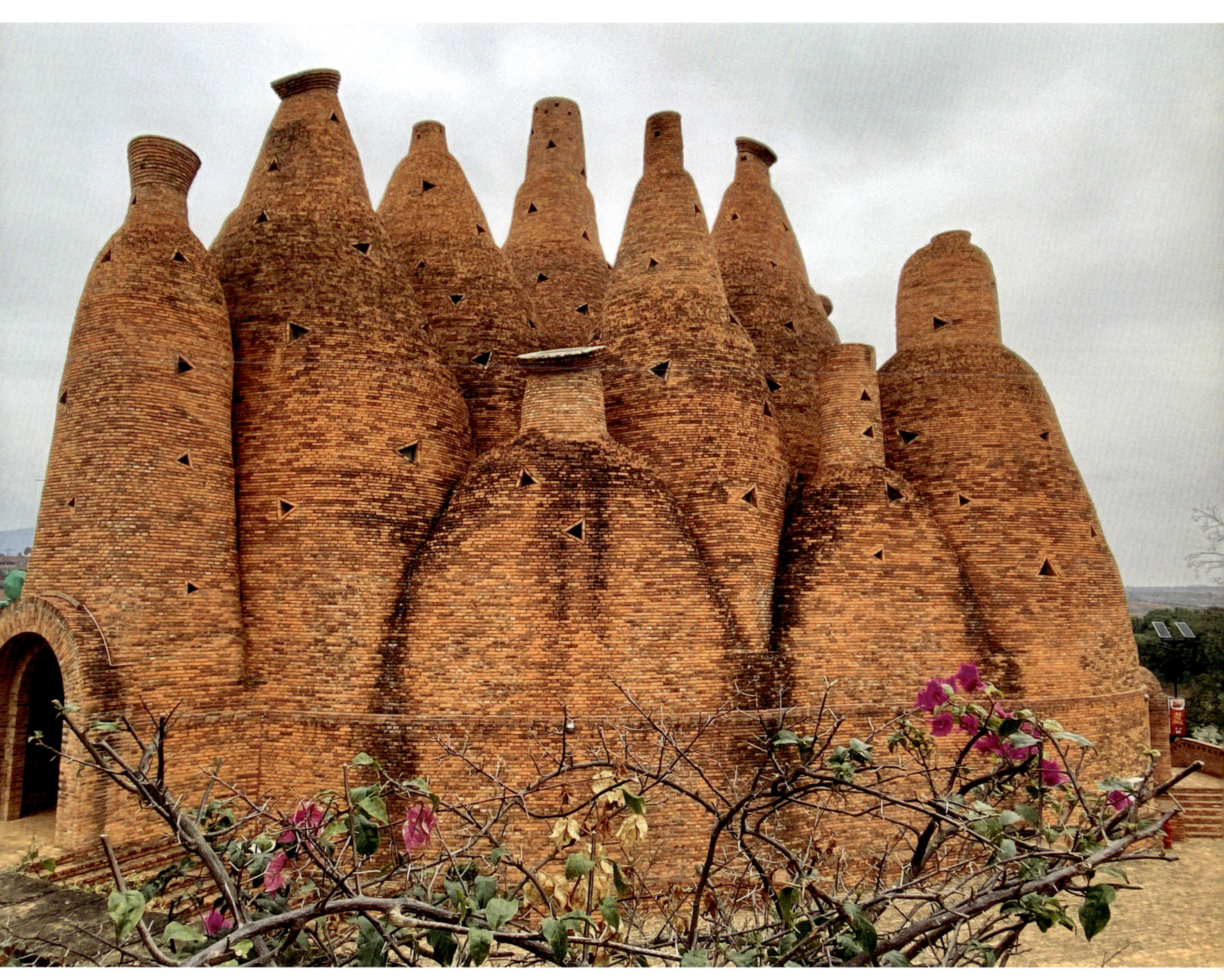

One would almost think that the creative forms of Kunming's famous stone forest inspired artist Luo Yi's postmodern red brick architectural complex in the city of Dongfengyun in Yunnan. Also called "turkish castle" or "kaleidoscope", the large work of art located on a beautiful lakeshore serves as a modern hotel.

Fast möchte man meinen, dass die kreativen Formen des berühmten Steinwaldes von Kunming den Künstler Luo Yi zu dem postmodernen architektonischen Komplex aus roten Backsteinen inspirierten. Auch „Turkish Castle" oder „Kaleidoscope" genannt, dient das große Kunstwerk an einem schönen Seeufer in der Stadt Dongfengyun in Yunnan als modernes Hotel.

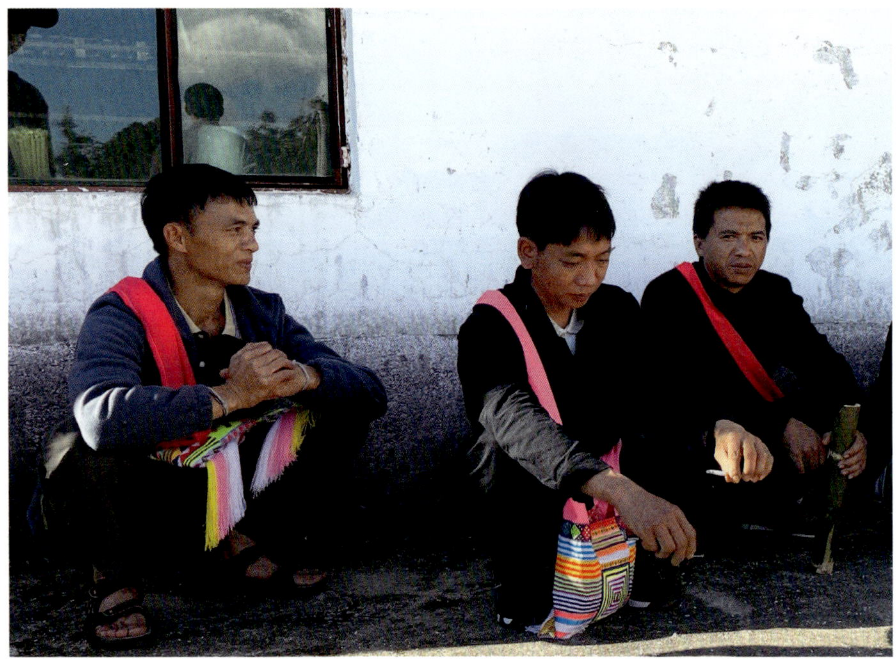

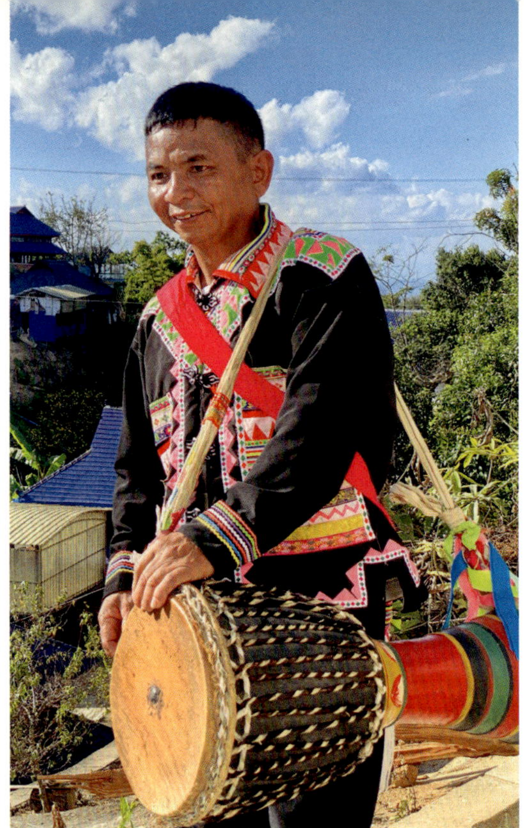

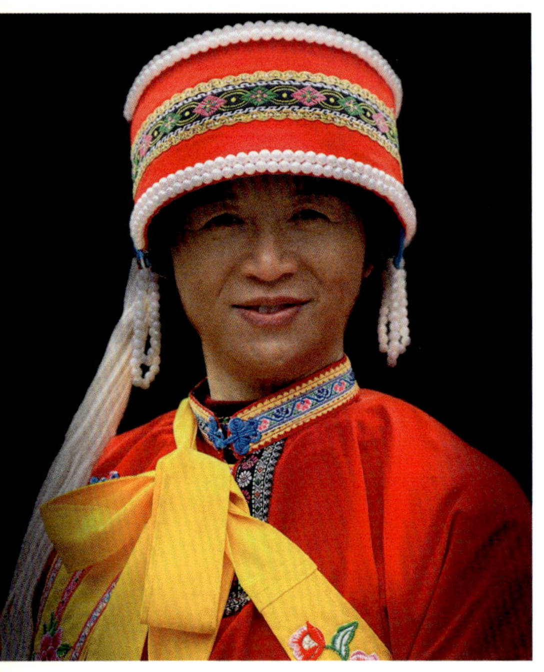

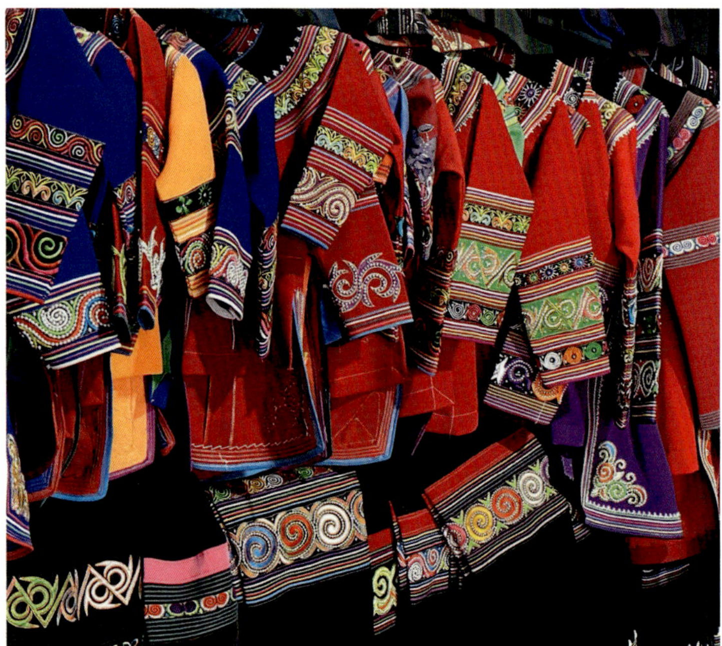

The colourful Lahu, one of the 56 officially recognised minorities, distinguish themselves by black, red, yellow or white Lahu and proudly wear the corresponding colour.

Die bunten Lahu, eine der 56 offiziell anerkannten Minderheiten, unterscheiden sich selbst nach schwarzen, roten, gelben oder weißen Lahu und tragen mit Stolz die entsprechende Farbe.

The smiling lady with the beaded headdress belongs to the Sani people, a word which literally means "happy", a subgroup of the Yi. She is wearing the costume of Ashima, the main character of the national poem of the Sani. The Yi live in matriarchal structures according to their own ten-month (36 days each) calendar.

Die lächelnde Dame mit der perlenverzierten Kopfbedeckung gehört zum Volk der Sani, übersetzt die „Fröhlichen", einer Untergruppe der Yi. Sie trägt das Kostüm der Ashima, der Hauptfigur des Nationalgedichtes der Sani. Die Yi leben in matriarchalischen Strukturen nach ihrem eigenen Kalender, der zehn Monate à 36 Tage ausweist.

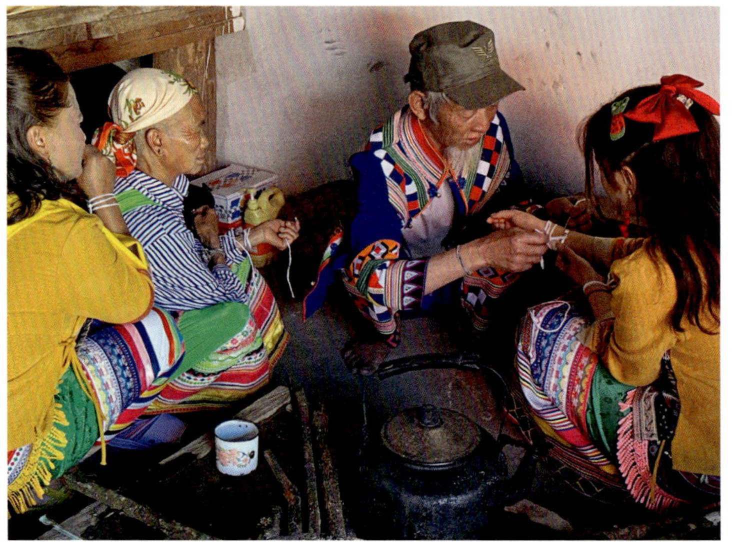

Right page:
The Great Buddha Temple in Manting Park in Jinghong is the most significant shrine of the Dai ethnic group. They originally come from Laos, Myanmar, Vietnam and Thailand.

Rechte Seite:
Der Große-Buddha-Tempel im Manting-Park in Jinghong ist das bedeutendste Heiligtum der ethnischen Gruppe der Dai. Sie stammen ursprünglich aus Laos, Burma, Vietnam und Thailand.

Woman Waiting for Her Husband or the Camel Riding the Elephant spur one's own creative word formations. Away from the especially laid-out circular paths, the fantasy-inspiring stone spectacle can be admired at leisure.

A panoply of colours in the tropical south

About an hour‘s flight further south, near the border with Laos and Myanmar, the autonomous district of Xishuangbanna, literally translated as "the twelve communities", impresses with garishly coloured temple markets and a chaotic street scene reminiscent of its proximity to Thailand. Large golden Buddha statues and richly decorated pagodas can be found in every village here.

On the wide, light-brown Mekong River, large barges transport colourfully packed goods day in and day out through the Golden Triangle between western China and Southeast Asia. All the Tai peoples living in Yunnan have been grouped together by the Chinese authorities as the Dai group. This explains the diversity and variety in their language, clothing, appearance and customs.

tümlichen Aberglauben und viele chinesische Legenden. Poetische und vielsagende Namen wie Mondsüchtiges Nashorn, Unsterblicher Pilz, Frau, die auf ihren Ehemann wartet oder das Kamel, das auf dem Elefanten reitet spornen zu eigenen kreativen Wortgestaltungen an. Abseits der eigens angelegten Rundwege lässt sich das fantasieanregende Steinspektakel in aller Ruhe bewundern.

Farbenvielfalt im tropischen Süden

Etwa eine Flugstunde weiter südlich, nahe der Grenze zu Laos und Myanmar, beeindruckt der autonome Bezirk Xishuangbanna, wörtlich übersetzt „die zwölf Gemeinden", mit grellbunten Tempelmärkten und einem chaotischen Straßenbild, das an die Nähe zu Thailand erinnert. Große goldene Buddhastatuen und reich verzierte Pagoden findet man hier in jedem Dorf. Auf dem breiten hellbraunen Mekong schippern tagein, tagaus große Lastkähne bunt verpackte Waren durch das Goldene Dreieck zwischen Westchina und Südostasien. Alle im Yunnan lebenden Tai-Völker wurden von den chinesischen Behörden als Dai-Gruppe zusammengefasst. Dies erklärt die Verschiedenartigkeit und Vielfalt in Sprache, Kleidung, Aussehen und Gebräuchen.

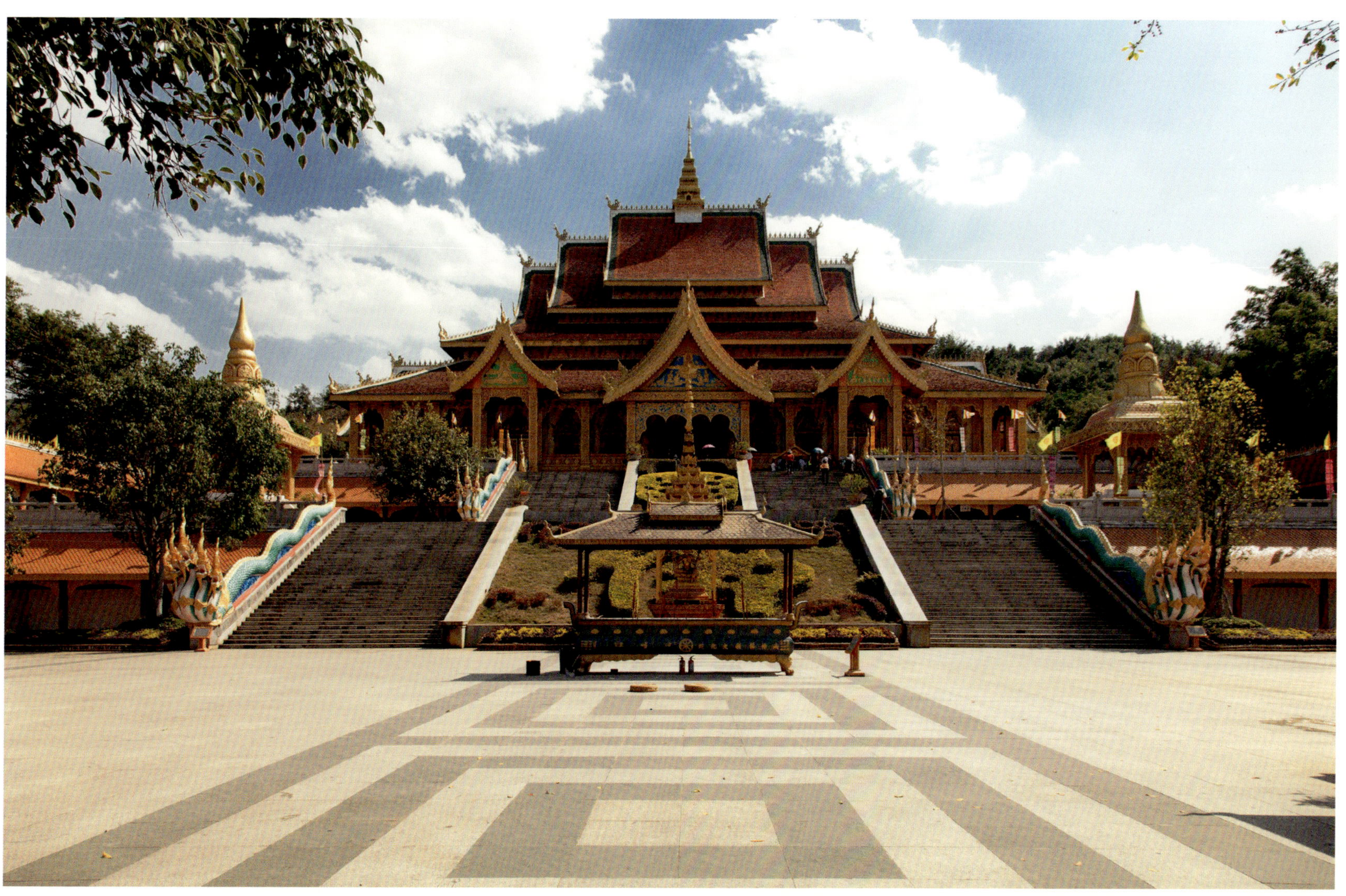

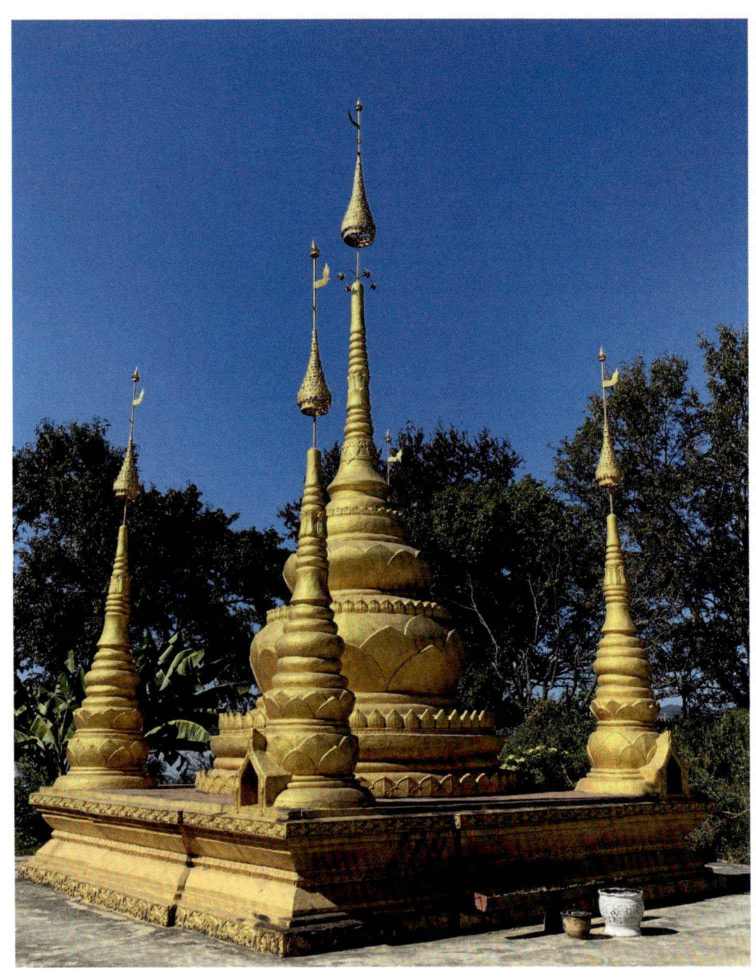

In every village along the Mekong River are small or larger gilded or whitewashed stupas, often in lotus flower or bamboo shoot form to commemorate the deceased or simply as Buddhist places of prayer. Inside the stupas, relics, sacred scriptures, or special prayers are often kept.

In jedem Ort entlang des Mekong-Flusses stehen kleine oder größere vergoldete oder weiß gekalkte Stupas, oft in Lotusblüten- oder Bambussprossenform zur Erinnerung an Verstorbene oder einfach als buddhistische Gebetsorte. Im Inneren der Stupas werden oft Reliquien, heilige Schriften oder besondere Gebete aufbewahrt.

Right page:
Situated directly on the Lancang River, called the Mekong River a little further downstream, the Buddhist Mange Temple of the Dai people in Jinghong, built in 1477 in Thai style, impresses visitors with its rich Southeast Asian decorations.

Rechte Seite:
Direkt am Lancang, etwas weiter flussabwärts Mekong genannt, gelegen, beindruckt der 1477 im thailändischen Stil gebaute buddhistische Mange-Tempel des Dai-Volkes in Jinghong mit seinen reichen südostasiatischen Verzierungen.

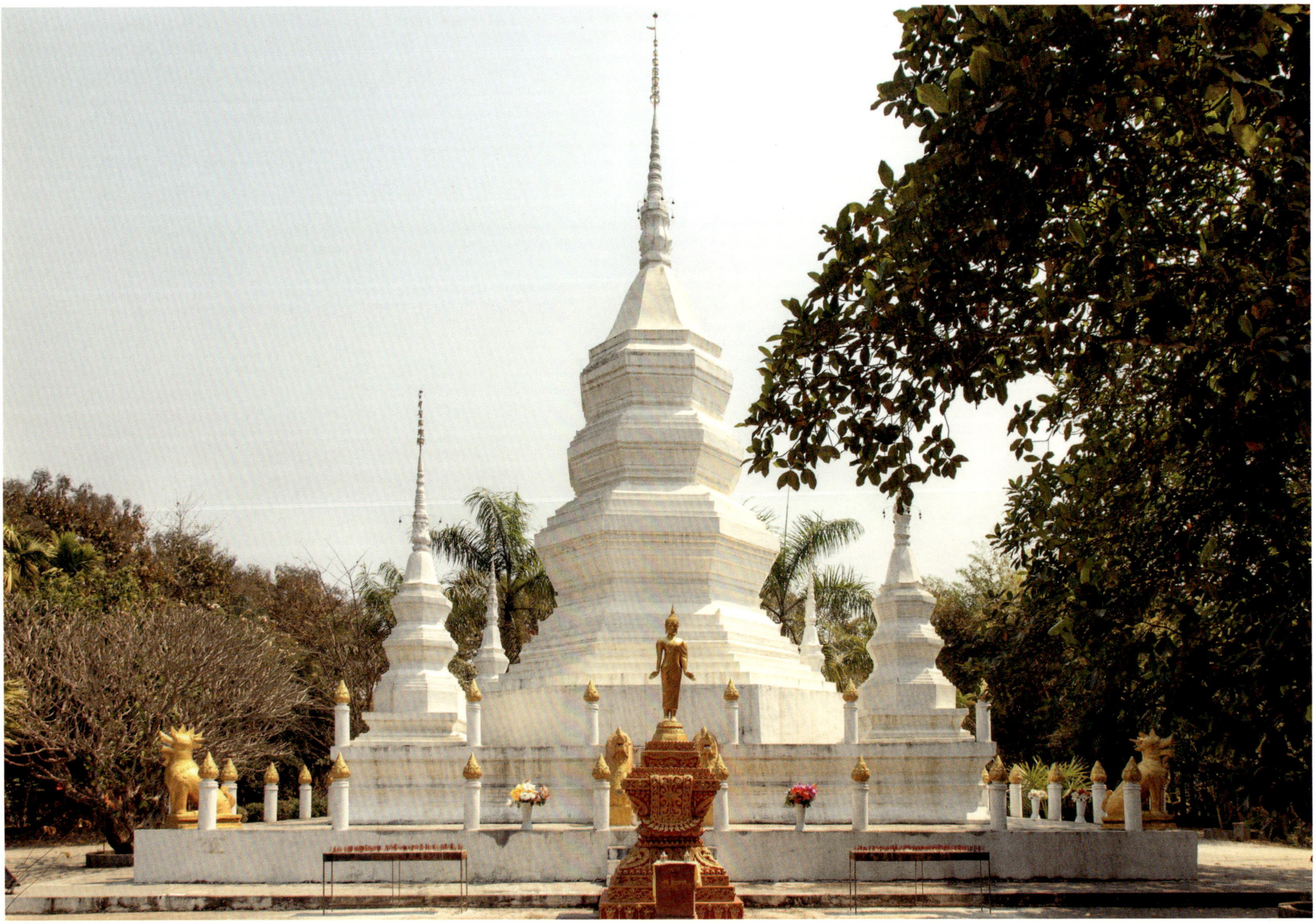

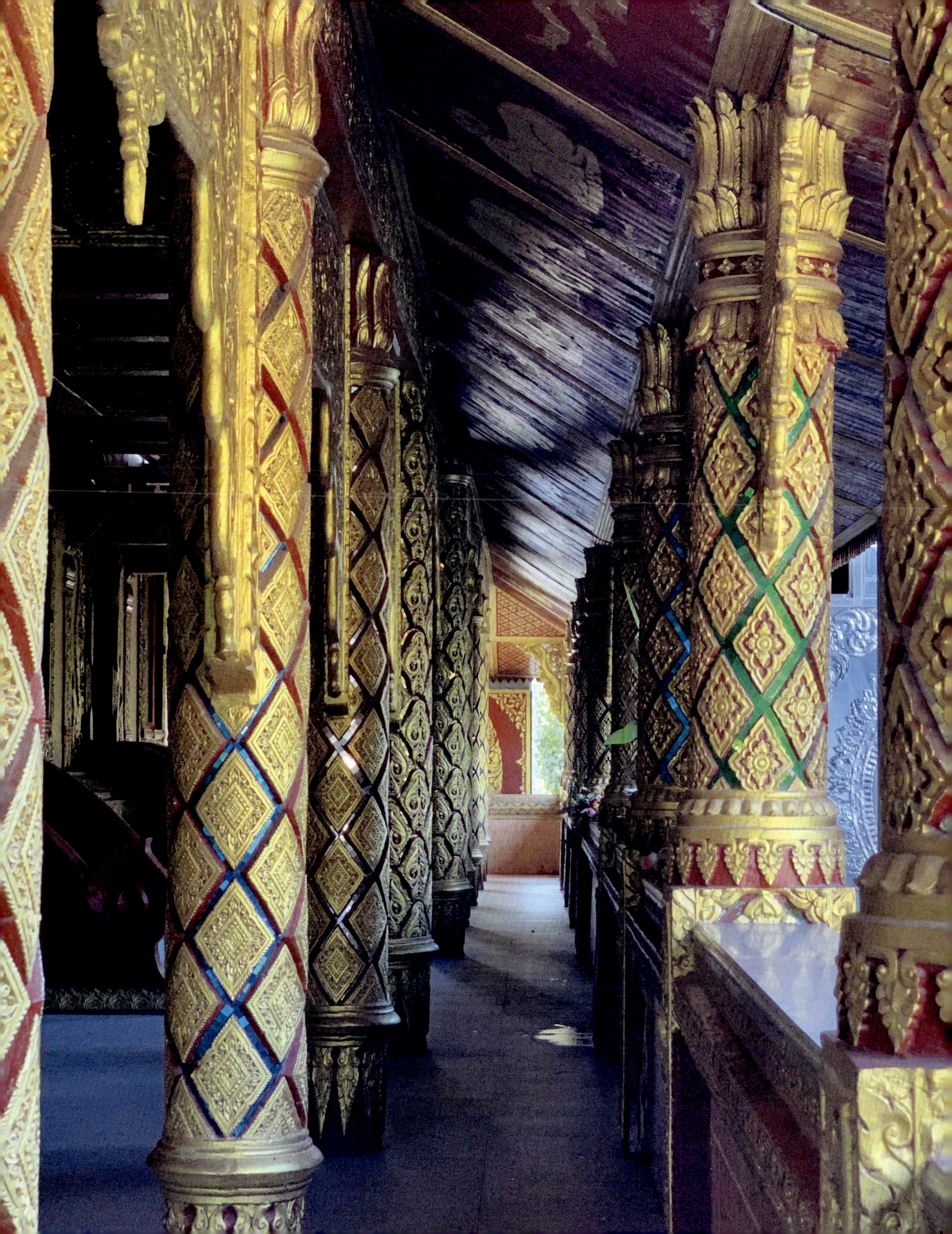

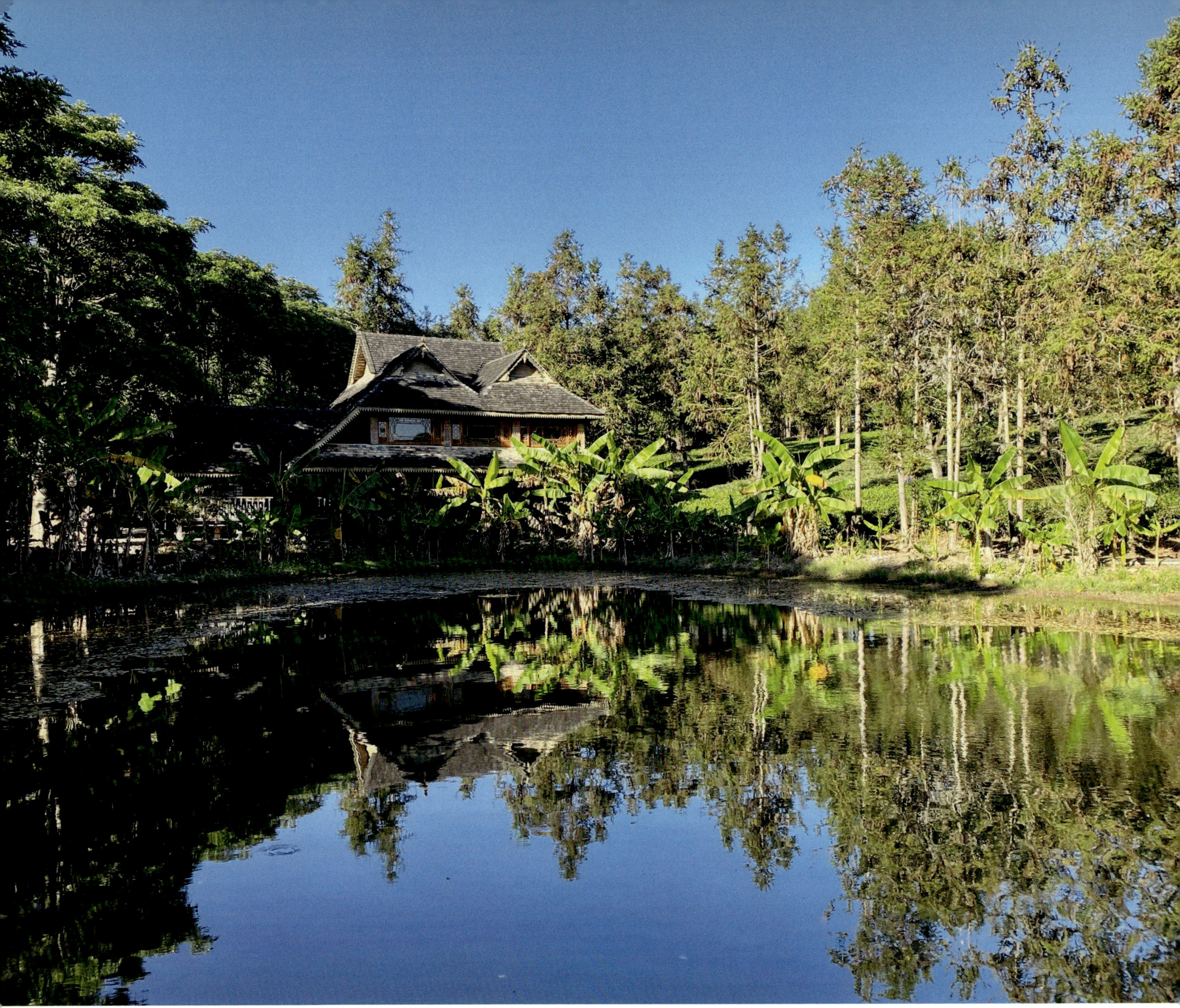

Jungle lake in the valley of the last wild elephants in Xishuangbanna

Urwaldsee im Tal der letzten wilden Elefanten in Xishuangbanna

Close to the city of Jinghong is the valley where the last free-roaming elephants live in China. A narrow wooden path leads through the dense, lush green treetops of tall jungle trees, and with a lot of luck you can supposedly observe the elephants at the brown river about 20 metres below in the early morning hours.

The birdsong and high humidity make it clear that southern Yunnan already belongs to the tropical climate belt. In Jinghong there is a research institute for tropical plants and a unique botanical garden, the largest in China.

Nahe der Stadt Jinghong liegt das Tal der letzten freilebenden Elefanten Chinas. Durch die dichten, sattgrünen Baumkronen hoher Urwaldbäume führt ein schmaler Holzpfad, und mit sehr viel Glück kann man angeblich in den frühen Morgenstunden ca. 20 Meter tiefer die Elefanten am braunen Fluss beobachten.

Das Vogelgezwitscher und die hohe Luftfeuchtigkeit machen eindeutig klar, dass der Süden Yunnans schon zum tropischen Klimagürtel zählt. In Jinghong befindet sich ein Forschungsinstitut für tropische Pflanzen und ein einzigartiger botanischer Garten, der größte Chinas.

The difference between red and black tea

Yunnan coffee is now recognised worldwide, but locals prefer to drink the no less famous pu'er tea. It is created from the delicate leaves of the Assam variety of tea plant, which is native to the border region between South China, Myanmar, Laos and Vietnam. You shouldn't miss a visit to the workshop, where the dried tea leaves are artfully pressed into decorative shapes. Pressed tea can be stored for years to decades while continuing to mature. The dark, reddish-brown tea with the earthy, spicy flavour is sold in China as black tea. Its method of production distinguishes pu'er from the tea known in the West as black tea. The Chinese refer to the latter as red tea.

Driving along the mountainous border towards Vietnam, you can still find isolated, traditional villages comprised completely of wooden huts. Green, semi-circular shapes grow on the hilly mountainsides, there where the natives disputed the land of the banana trees and the huge trees of the dense jungle: These are pu'er tea plantations, stretching as far as the eye can see.

Lush green banana plantations and tea plantations along Yunnan's mountain roads

Sattgrüne Tee- und Bananenstaudenplantagen entlang der Gebirgsstraßen Yunnans

Von rotem und schwarzem Tee

Yunnan-Kaffee ist mittlerweile weltweit anerkannt, doch vor Ort genießt man bevorzugt den nicht minder bekannten und beliebten Pu'er-Tee. Er wird aus den zarten Blättern der Assam-Variante der Teepflanze hergestellt, die hier in der Grenzregion zwischen Südchina, Myanmar, Laos und Vietnam heimisch ist. Nicht entgehen lassen sollte man sich den Besuch einer Werkstatt, in der die getrockneten Teeblätter kunstvoll in dekorative Formen gepresst werden. Gepresster Tee kann über Jahre bis Jahrzehnte hinweg aufbewahrt werden und dabei weiter reifen. Der dunkle, rotbraune Tee mit dem erdig-würzigen Geschmack wird in China als schwarzer Tee angeboten. Seine Herstellungsweise unterscheidet Pu'er von dem Tee, der im Westen als schwarzer Tee bekannt ist. Letzteren bezeichnen die Chinesen als roten Tee.

Entlang der gebirgigen Grenze Richtung Vietnam fahrend, kann man noch vereinzelt urtümliche, ganz aus Holzhütten bestehende Dörfer finden. Grüne, halbrunde Kugeln wachsen an den hügeligen Berghängen, dort wo die Eingeborenen den Bananenstauden und den riesigen Bäumen des dichten Dschungels das Land streitig machten: Das sind Pu'er-Teeplantagen, soweit das Auge reicht.

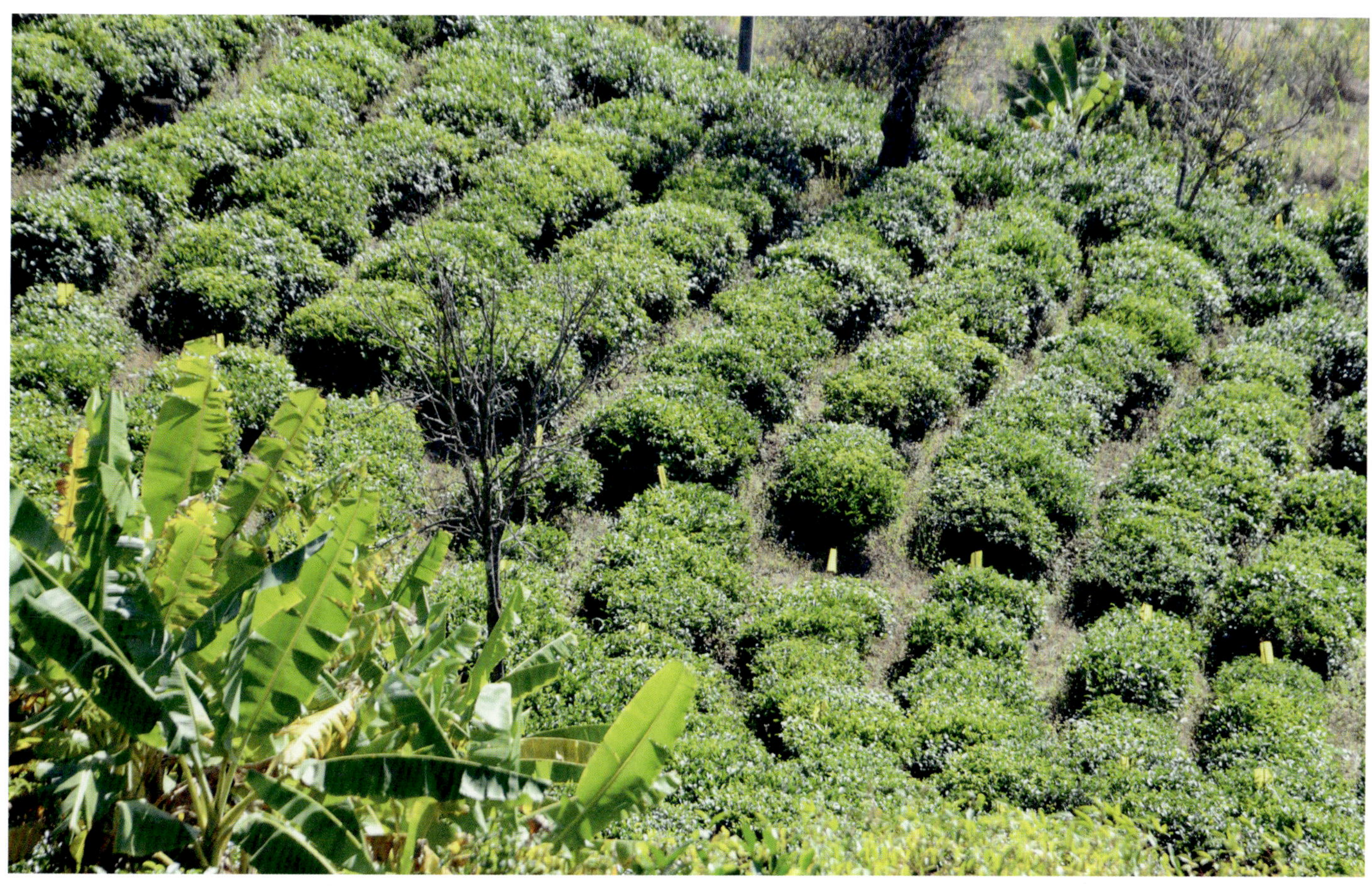

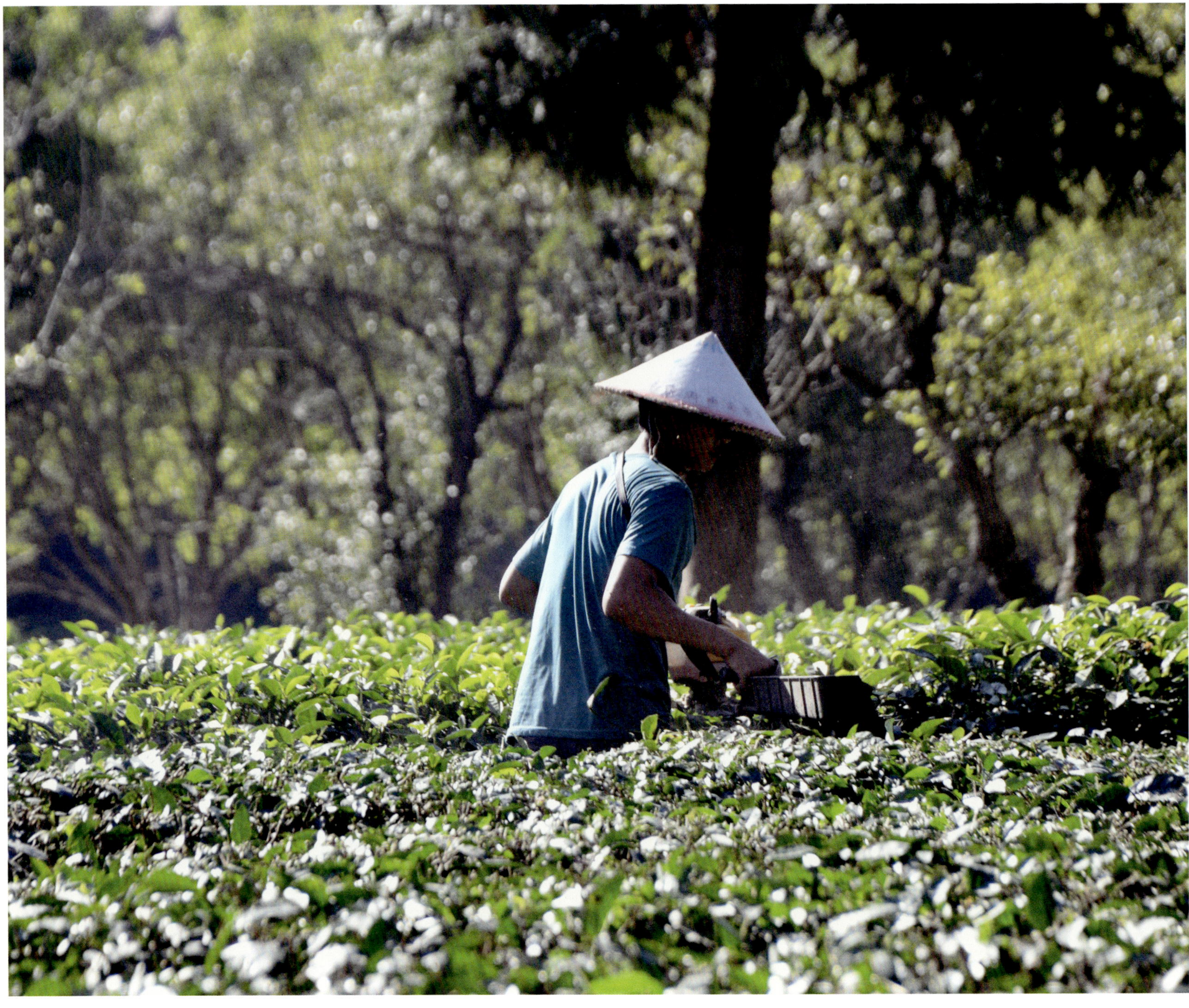

The metre-tall tea trees in Yunnan can become several hundred years old. A few specimens are even supposedly over 1,000 years old. The older the tree is, the better the quality of its leaves and the more expensive the pu'er tea is. The tea lover in China is in no way inferior to the wine connoisseur, when it comes to paying a pretty penny to enjoy a highly valued drink. And the environmentally and health-conscious connoisseur can also enjoy the trend that allegedly fewer and fewer pesticides are being used in tea cultivation.

Die meterhohen Teebäume im Yunnan können mehrere hundert Jahre alt werden. Einige wenige Exemplare sind angeblich sogar über 1000 Jahre alt. Je älter der Baum, desto besser die Blattqualität und desto teurer der Pu'er-Tee. Der Teeliebhaber in China steht dem Weinkenner in nichts nach, wenn es darum geht, tief in die Tasche zu greifen, um ein geschätztes Getränk zu genießen. Und auch der umwelt- und gesundheitsbewusste Genießer kann sich an dem Trend erfreuen, dass angeblich immer weniger Pestizide im Tee-Anbau eingesetzt werden.

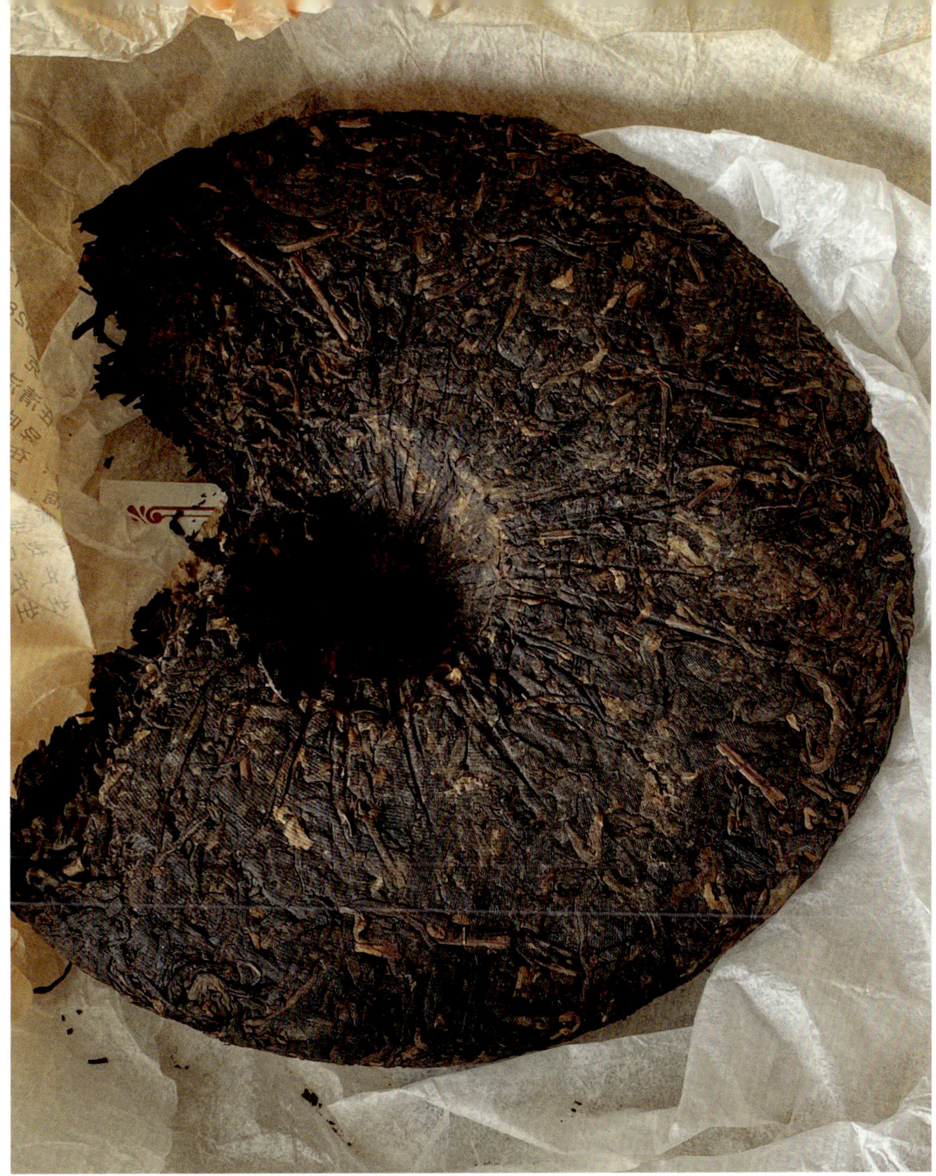

Dark reddish-brown pu'er tea, a protected trade name since 2008, with an earthy, spicy flavor is considered black tea in China. Its leaves are dried, pressed into molds and dried again.

Der dunkle rotbraune Pu'er-Tee, seit 2008 ein geschützter Handelsname, mit erdigem, würzigem Geschmack zählt in China zu den Schwarzteesorten. Seine Blätter werden getrocknet, in Formen gepresst und weiter getrocknet.

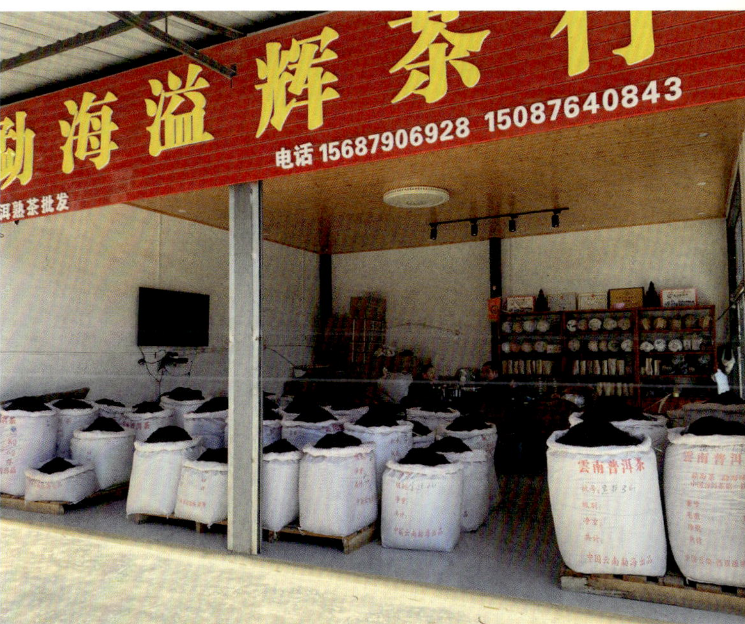

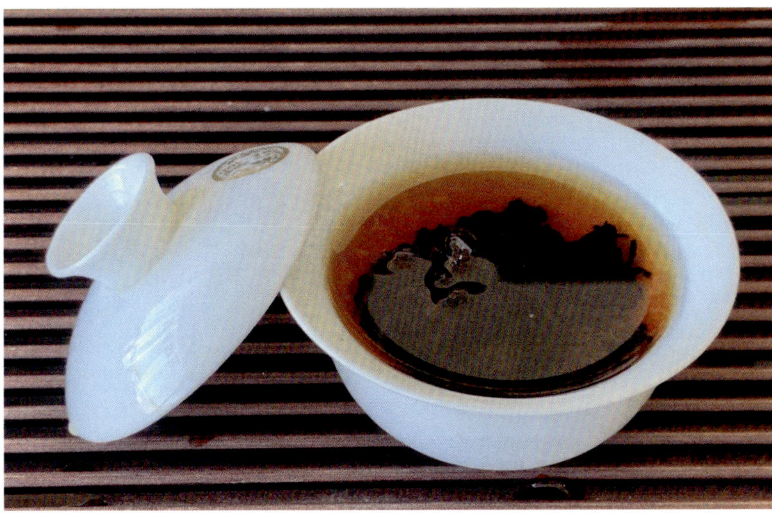

Mountain villages line the old tea trade routes and tea tastings invite you to linger at every turn.

Bergdörfer säumen die alten Teehandelsstraßen, und Teeverköstigungen laden auf Schritt und Tritt zum Verweilen ein.

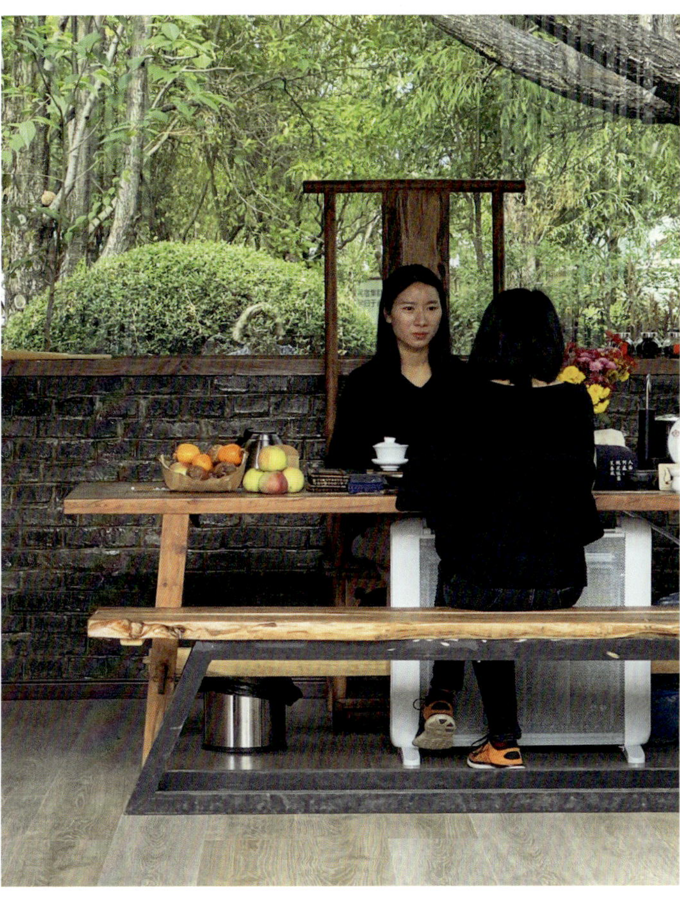

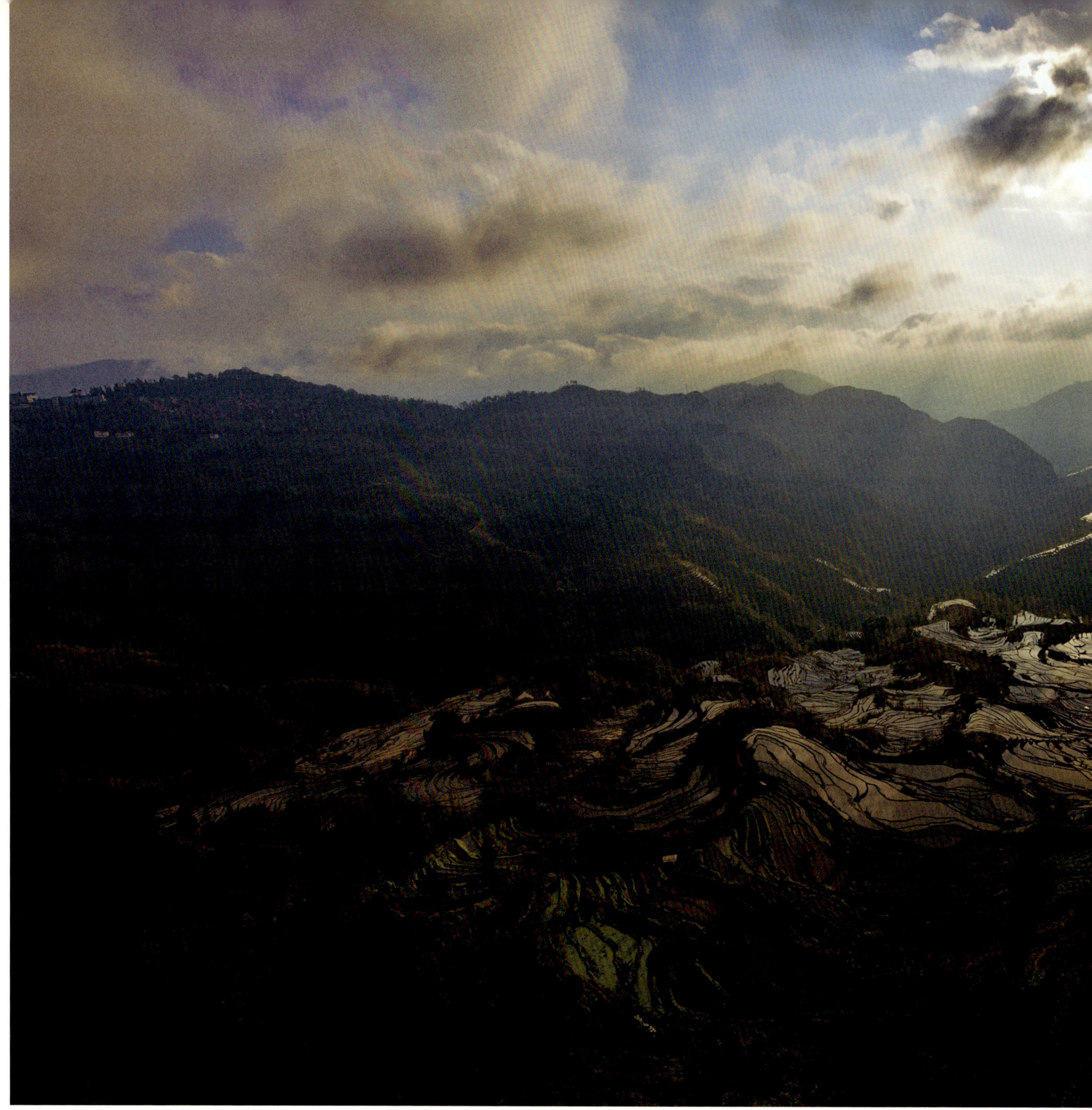

Gold-shimmering rice terraces

An entirely different kind of cultivation, though no less impressive, is practiced by the Hani people in the region of the Honghe Hani. Presumable these are the most beautiful rice terraces in all of China. Visitors must have a lot of patience on the way there, because the nearest airport is about seven hours away by car, in Kunming, and dense warm clouds obscure visibility 90 percent of the day. As if the clouds knew that this breath-taking scenery could only be enjoyed in small bites. It's an indescribable sight when the sun's rays

Goldglänzende Reisterrassen

Einen Anbau ganz anderer Art, aber nicht minder beeindruckend, betreibt das Volk der Hani im Honghe-Gebiet. Es sind dies wahrscheinlich die schönsten Reisterrassen Chinas. Viel Geduld muss der Besucher auf dem Weg dahin mitbringen, denn der nächste Flughafen liegt rund sieben Autostunden entfernt, in Kunming, und dichte warme Wolken verhängen zu 90 Prozent des Tages die Sicht. Als wüssten sie, dass dieses atemberaubende Szenario nur in kleinen Happen genossen werden kann. Unbeschreiblich,

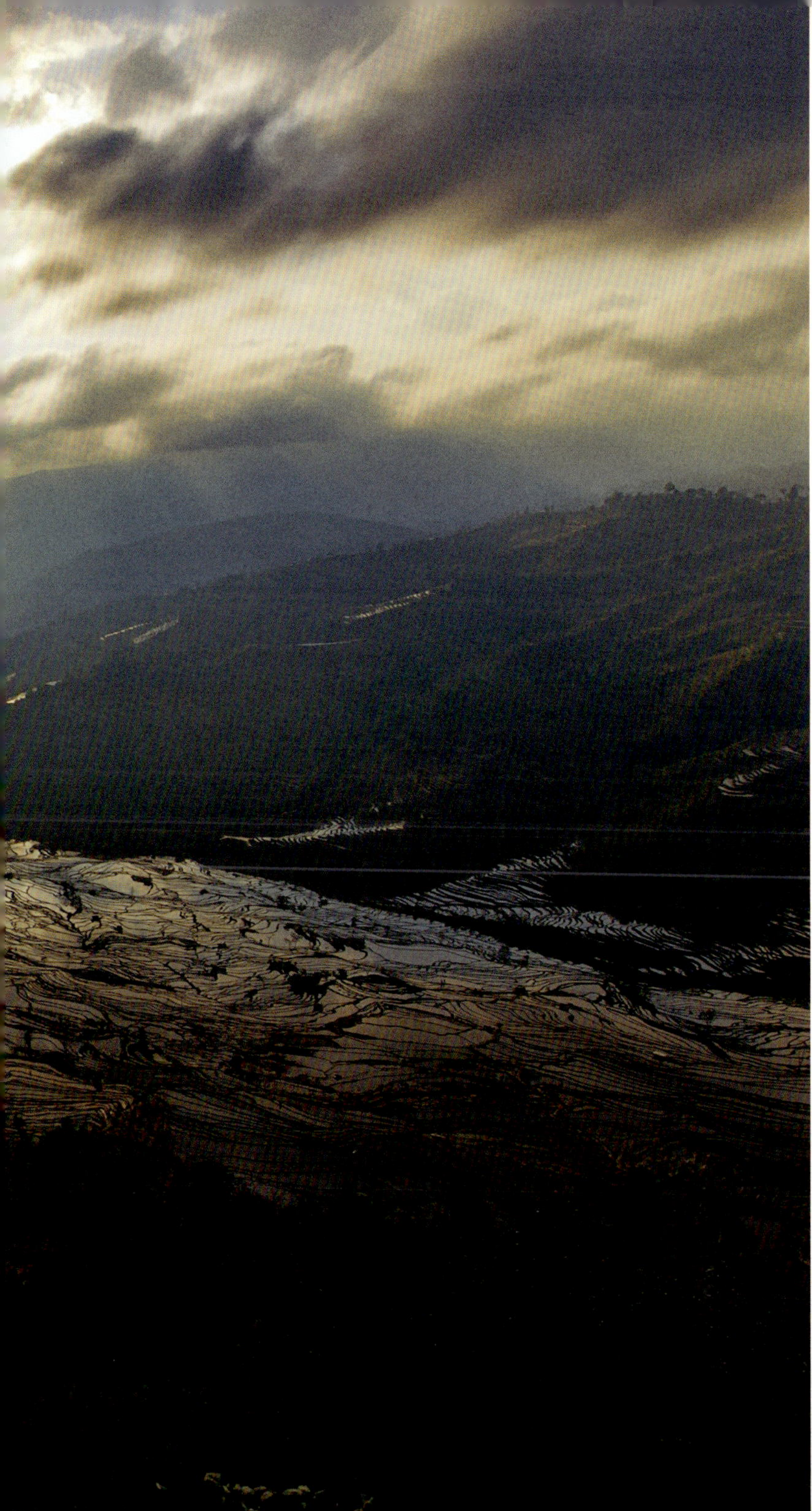

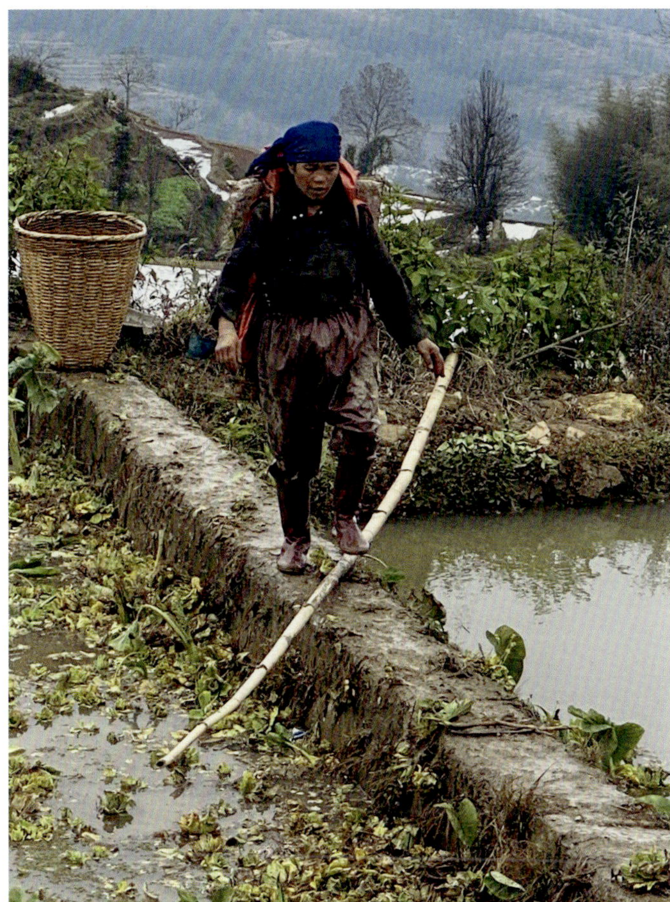

The Yuanyang rice terraces are located at an altitude of about 2,000 metre on steep mountain slopes. Especially in winter and spring there are beautiful moments when they are filled with water and reflect the sky.

Die Yuanyang-Reisterrassen liegen auf rund 2000 Metern Höhe an steilen Berghängen. Besonders im Winter und Frühling gibt es wunderschöne Momente, wenn sie mit Wasser gefüllt den Himmel reflektieren.

The indigenous Hani minority worship the sun, moon, mountains, rivers, forests and other natural phenomena and have shamans who take the role of priest, doctor and village chief. In addition to red rice, they also raise fish in the terraces.

Die einheimische Hani-Minderheit verehrt Sonne, Mond, Berge, Flüsse, Wälder und andere Naturereignisse und hat Schamanen, die die Rolle als Priester, Arzt und Dorfvorsteher einnehmen. Neben rotem Reis züchten sie auch noch Fische in den Terrassen.

in the morning or evening light make the countless terraces filled with water shine in pure golden yellow.

The rice terraces in Honghe Hani were recognised as a world heritage site by UNESCO in 2013. The area gets its name from the red Honghe River. The Hani have cultivated these rice terraces on the steep mountainsides in the southwest of the Yunnan Province for over 1,000 years. To this day, the families of the 82 small villages, each with fewer than 100 households, live by cultivating two irrigated

wenn die Sonnenstrahlen im Morgen- oder Abendlicht die unzähligen mit Wasser gefüllten Terrassen in Goldgelb zum Strahlen bringen.

Die Reisterrassen von Honghe-Hani wurden 2013 von der UNESCO als Welterbe anerkannt. Der Bezirk erhielt seinen Namen von dem roten Fluss Honghe. Die Hani haben die Terrassen an den steilen Berghängen im Südwesten der Provinz Yunnan vor mehr als 1000 Jahren angelegt. Bis heute leben die Familien der 82 kleinen Dörfer mit jeweils

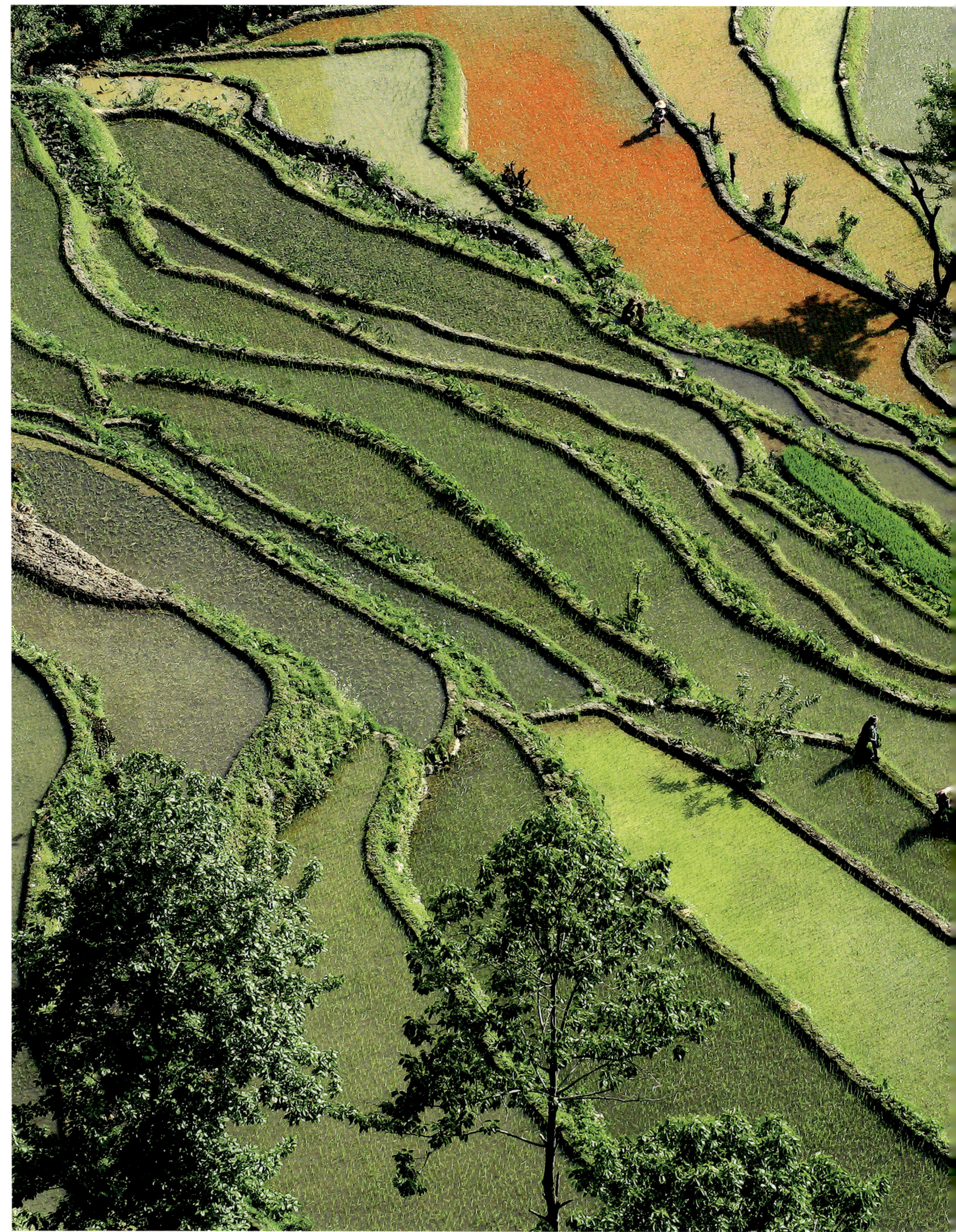

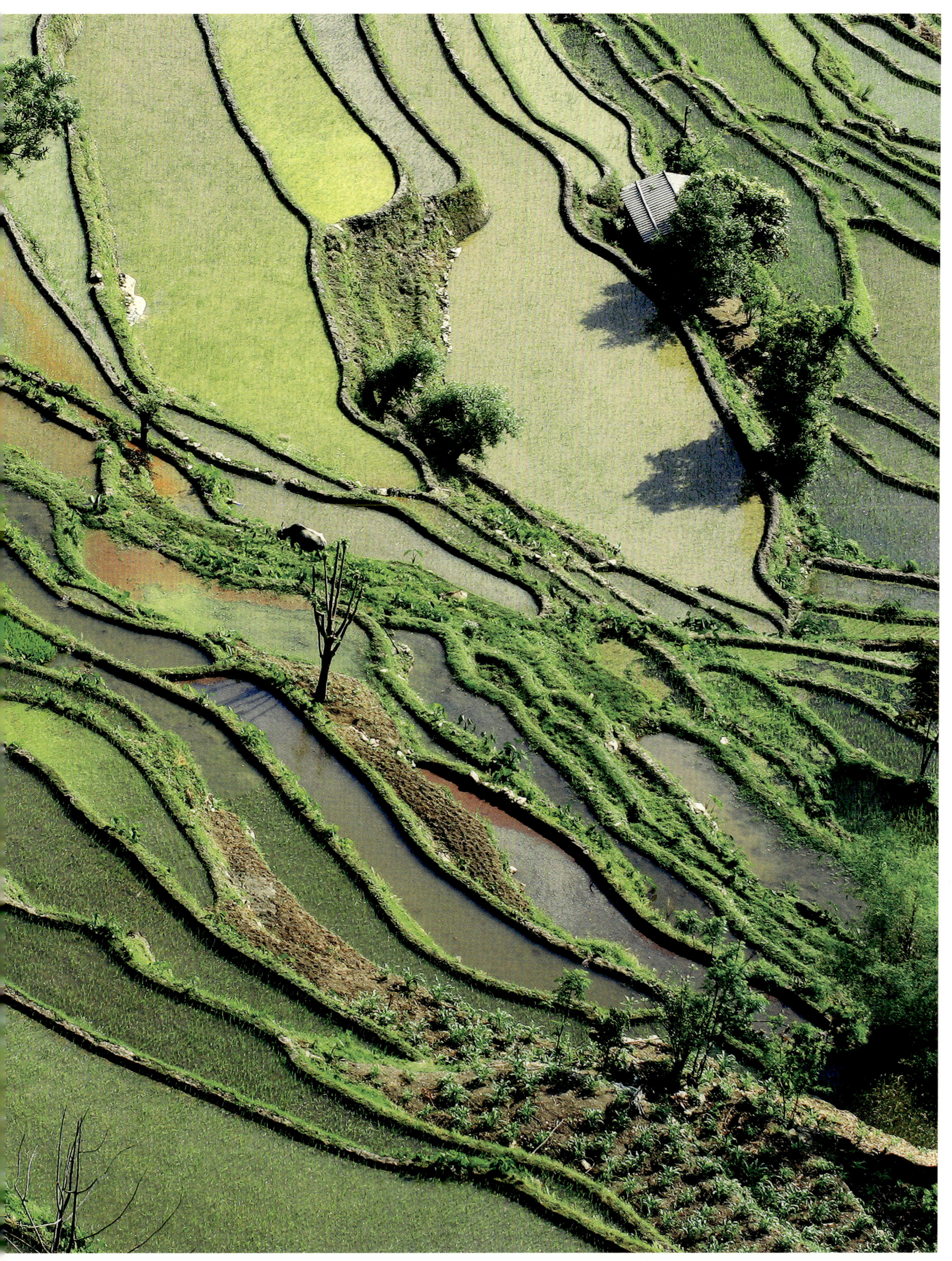

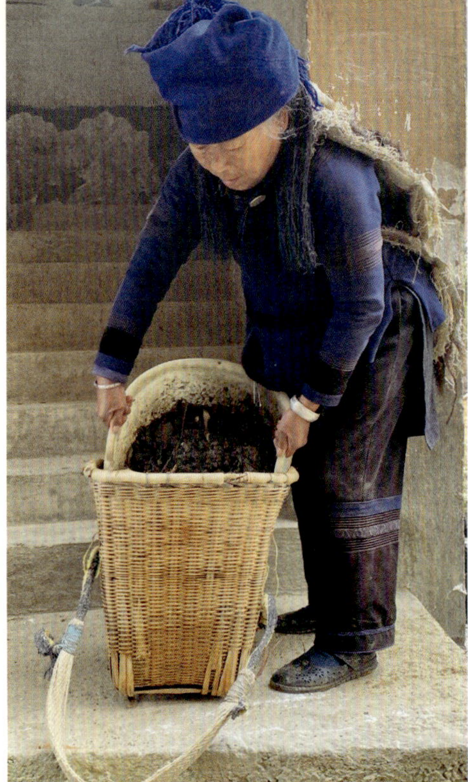

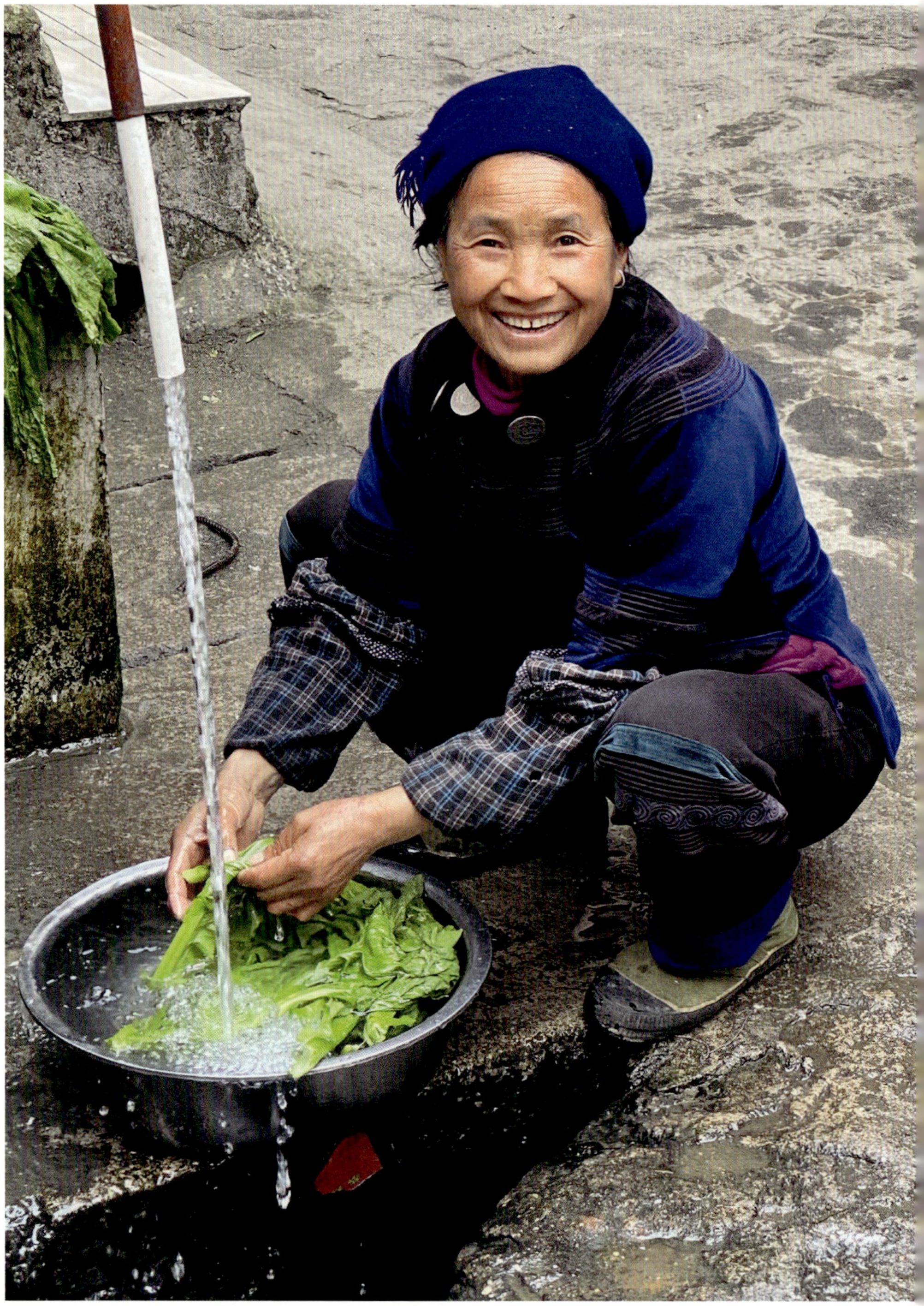

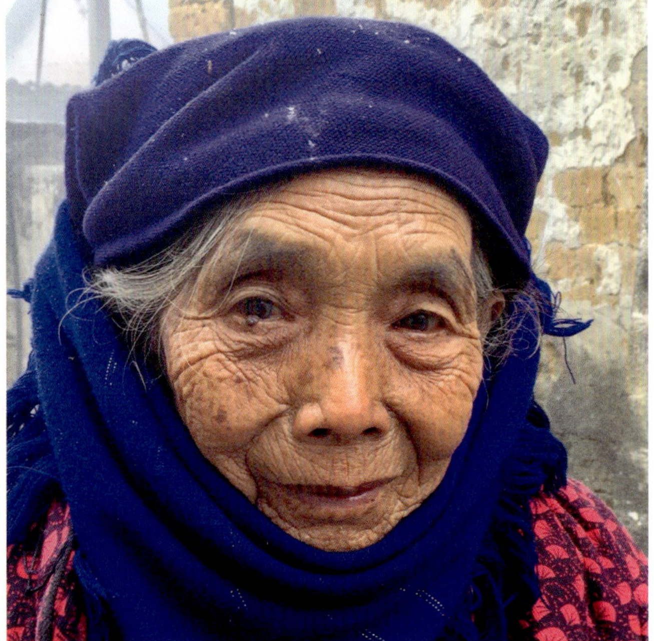

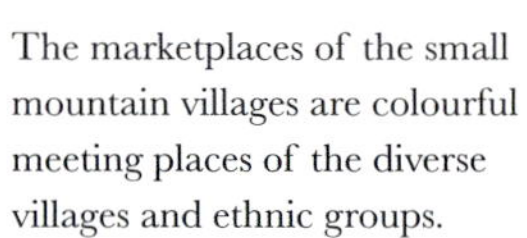

The marketplaces of the small mountain villages are colourful meeting places of the diverse villages and ethnic groups.

Die Marktplätze der kleinen Bergdörfer sind bunte Treffpunkte diverser Dörfer und Ethnien.

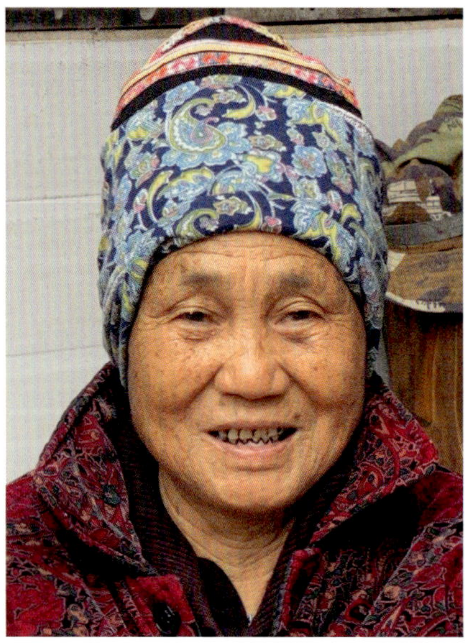

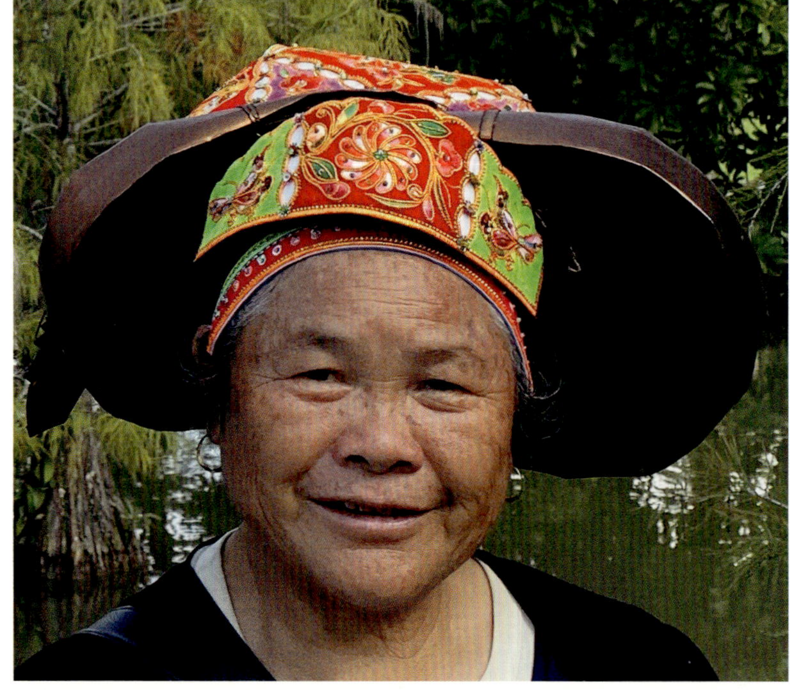

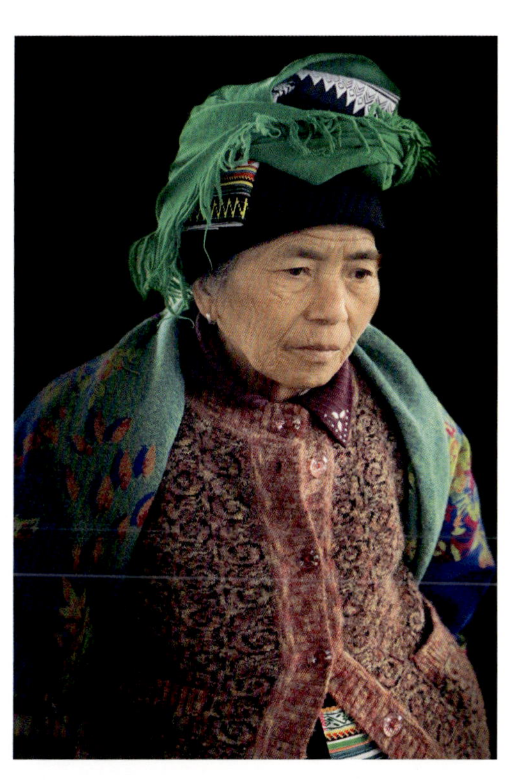

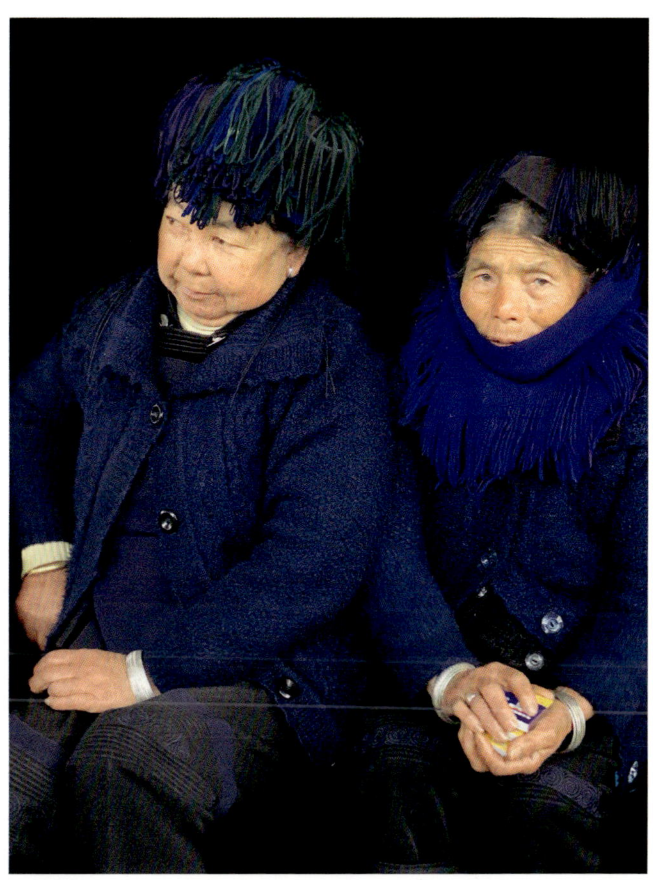

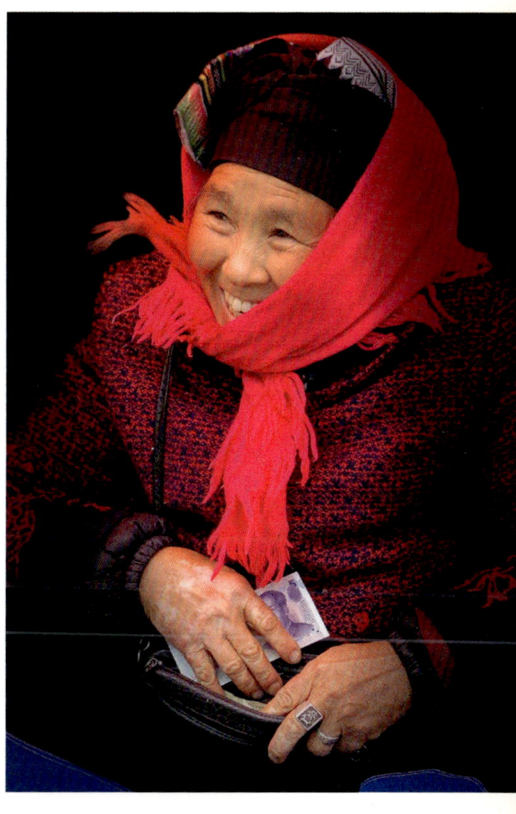

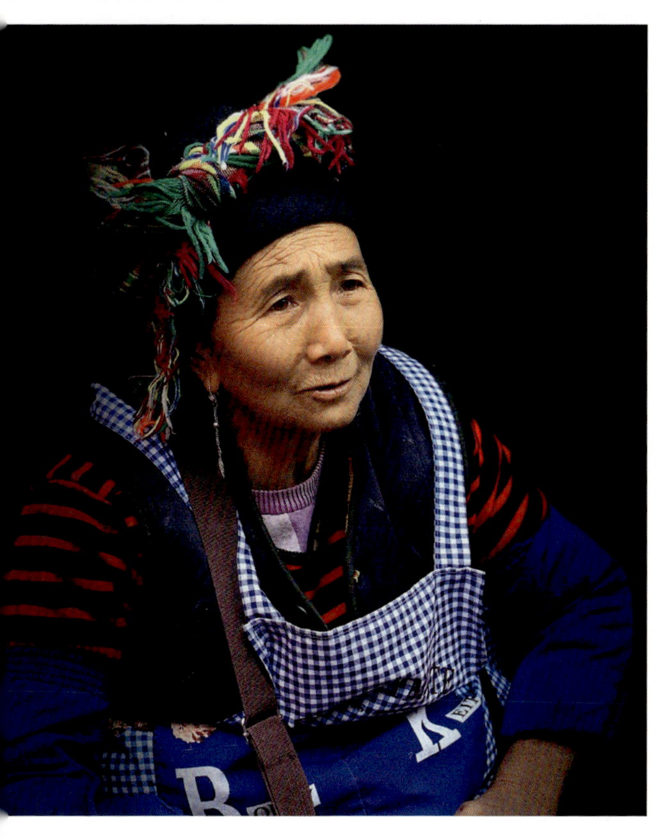

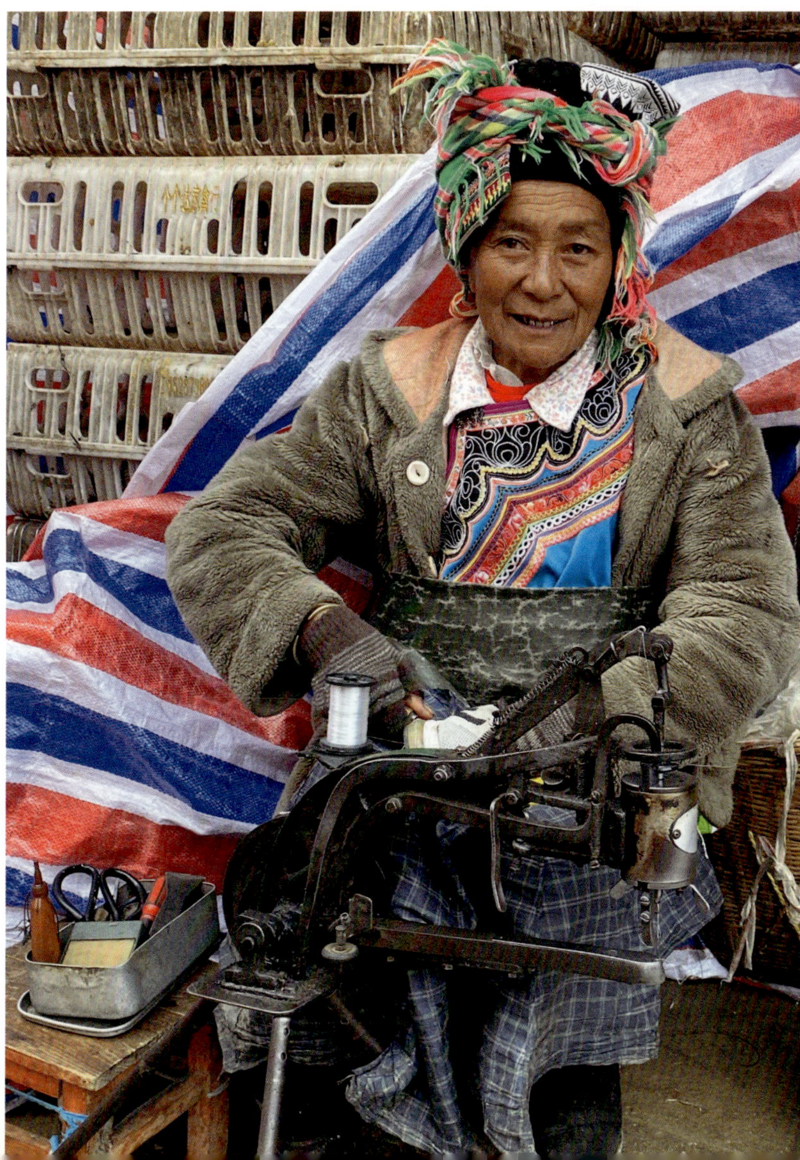

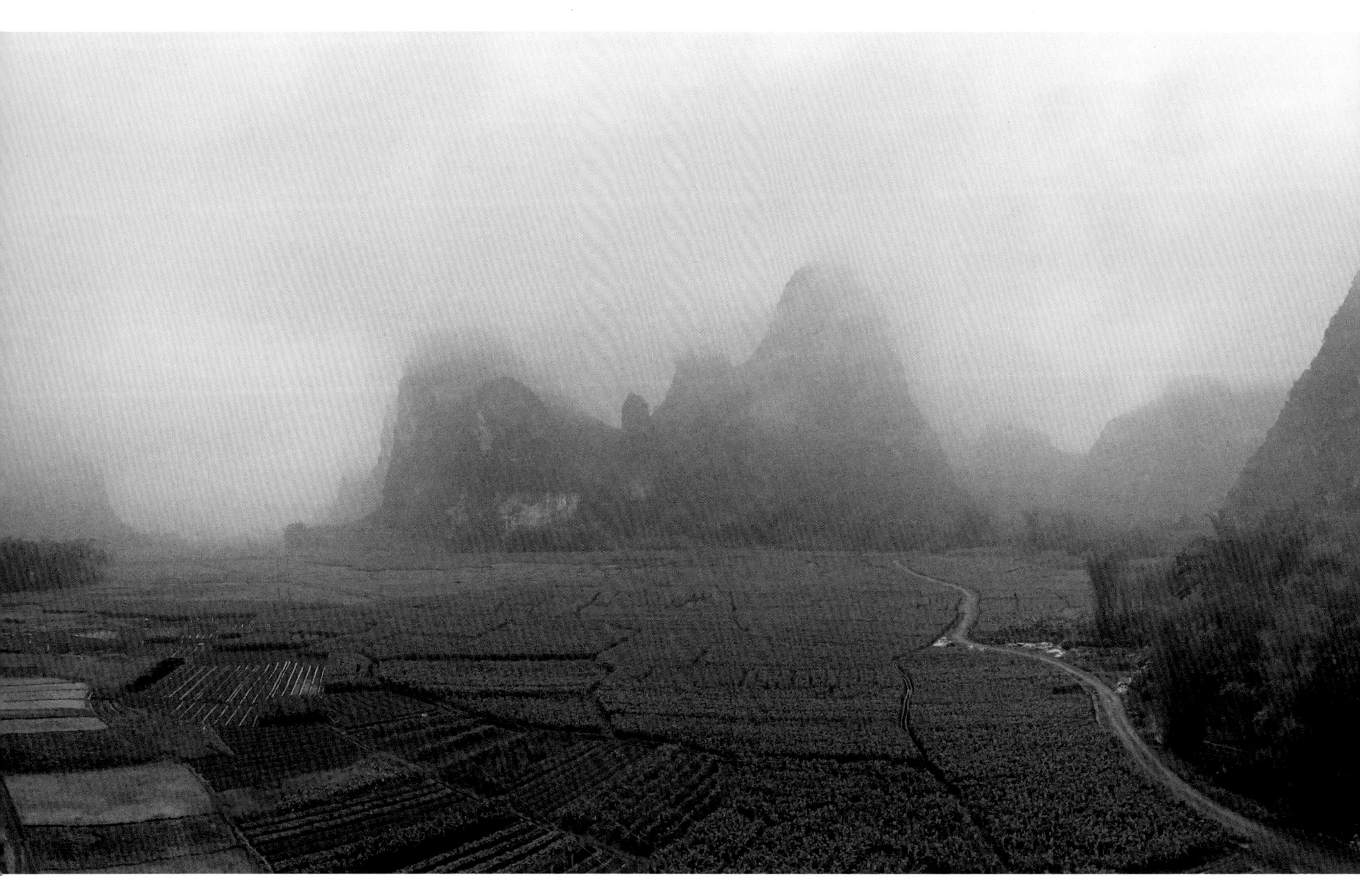

The spectacular karst mountains in the south of Guangxi province

Die spektakulären Karstberge im Süden der Provinz Guangxi

terraces. In addition to rice cultivation, the fields are also used for livestock and fish farming. Ducks fertilise the young rice plants, chickens and pigs contribute manure, water buffalo plough the fields and snails destroy pests. Among the Hani, childcare is a man's job. Meanwhile, the women do the heavy construction work on the impassable, steep mountain slopes.

The terrace agriculture system is based on the traditional religious and social structures of the Hani. The water and also the forest above the terraces, which provide the fields with water, are seen as holy. They are shared as a divine gift by humans and animals alike, who do not overuse and endanger them. This respect for nature, together with the individual's obligations to the community, has sustained the terraced

weniger als 100 Haushalten von der Bewirtschaftung von je zwei bewässerten Terrassen. Neben dem Reisanbau dienen die Felder auch der Vieh- und Fischzucht. Enten befruchten die jungen Reispflanzen, Hühner und Schweine tragen Dünger bei, Wasserbüffel pflügen die Felder und Schnecken vernichten Schädlinge. Bei den Hani ist die Kinderversorgung Männeraufgabe. Die Frauen erledigen derweil die schweren Bauarbeiten an den unwegsamen, steilen Berghängen.

Das System der Terrassenwirtschaft basiert auf den traditionellen religiösen und sozialen Strukturen der Hani. Das Wasser und auch der Wald oberhalb der Terrassen, welche die Felder mit Wasser versorgen, gelten als heilig. Sie werden als göttliches Geschenk von Menschen und Tieren gemeinsam genutzt, ohne sie dabei zu übernutzen und zu gefährden. Dieser Respekt vor der Natur, in Kombination mit den Verpflichtungen des Einzelnen der Gemeinschaft gegenüber, hat die Terrassenwirtschaft über alle Umbrüche hinweg bis heute erhalten. Die vier Hauptkanäle und 392 Seitengräben mit einer Gesamtlänge

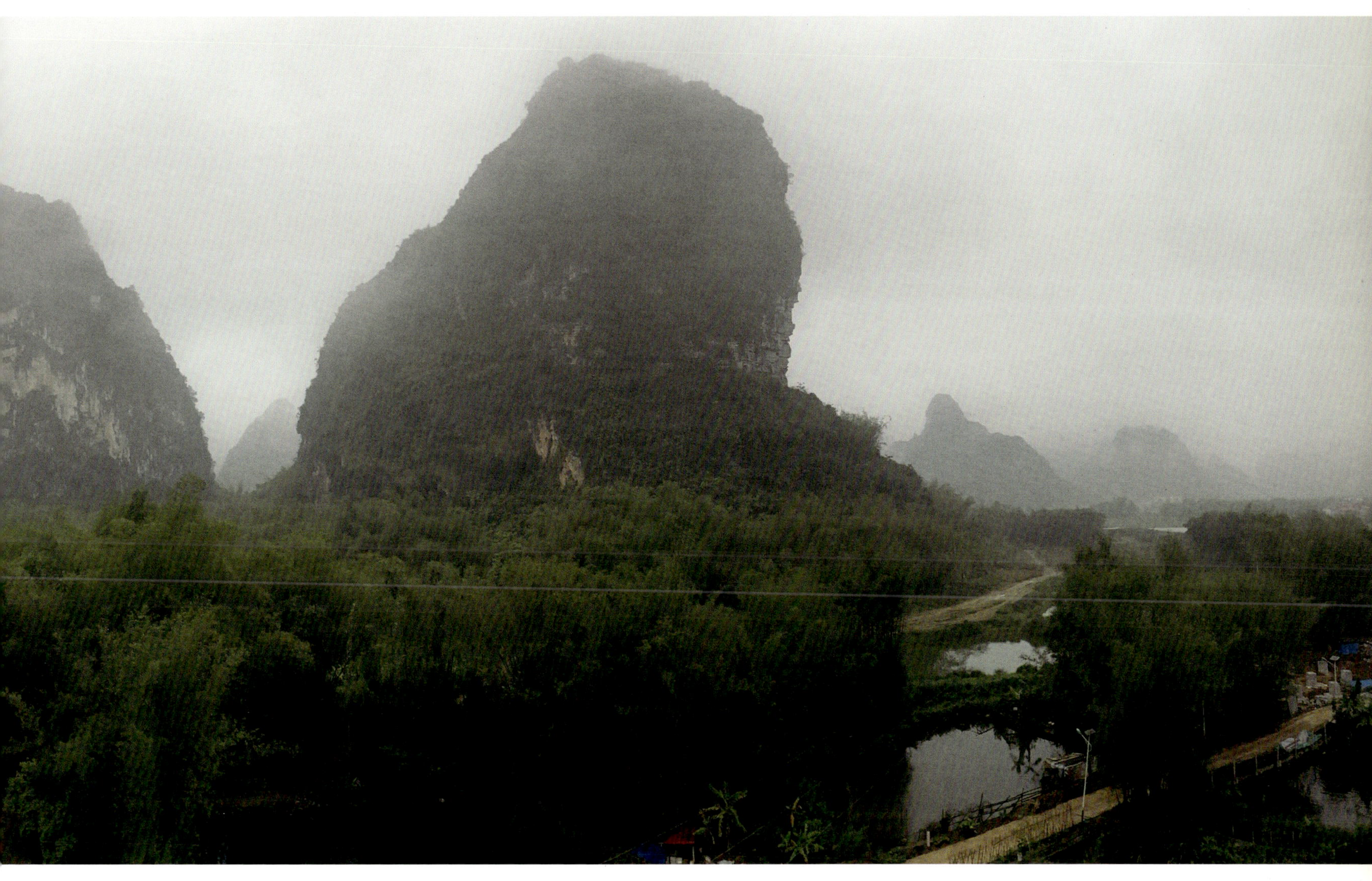

economy through all the upheavals to the present day. The four main channels and the 392 side channels, with a total length of 445 kilometres, are cared for in cooperation.

Unlike the Hani, the Zhuang farm their green-reflecting rice fields in the plains between surreal, often hollowed-out karst mountains and small brown rivers. Here in the south of Guangxi, in the border area with Vietnam is also the second widest waterfall in the world.

White matriarchy

Mosuo people live in western Yunnan, on the shores of Lake Lugu. Among them, women determine everything that is important: they are responsible for the family, choose their lovers, and pass on names and possessions to their daughters. The Mosuo's patron goddess is also female. The *ama* is the female head of the family. At the age of 13, the girls are dressed for the first time in the festive, long white Mosuo women's dresses, which are complemented with

von 445 Kilometern werden gemeinschaftlich gepflegt. Im Gegensatz zu den Hani bewirtschaften die Zhuang ihre grünreflektierenden Reisfelder in der Ebene zwischen surrealen, oft ausgehöhlten Karstbergen und kleinen braunen Flüssen. Hier im Süden von Guangxi, im Grenzgebiet zu Vietnam befindet sich auch der zweitbreiteste Wasserfall der Welt.

Weißes Matriarchat

Im westlichen Yunnan, am Lugu-See, lebt das Volk der Mosuo. Bei ihnen bestimmen die Frauen über alles, was wichtig ist: Sie tragen die Verantwortung für die Familie, wählen ihre Liebhaber, vererben Namen und Besitz an die Töchter. Auch die Schutzgöttin der Mosuo ist weiblich. Die *Ama* ist das weibliche Oberhaupt der Familie. Mit 13 Jahren werden den Mädchen zum ersten Mal die festlichen, langen weißen Mosuo-Frauenkleider angelegt, welche mit fröhlichbunten Westen und Schärpen ergänzt werden. Beim sogenannten Volljährigkeitsfest dann bekommen die 14-Jährigen die Verantwortung übertragen. Die Mosuo sind

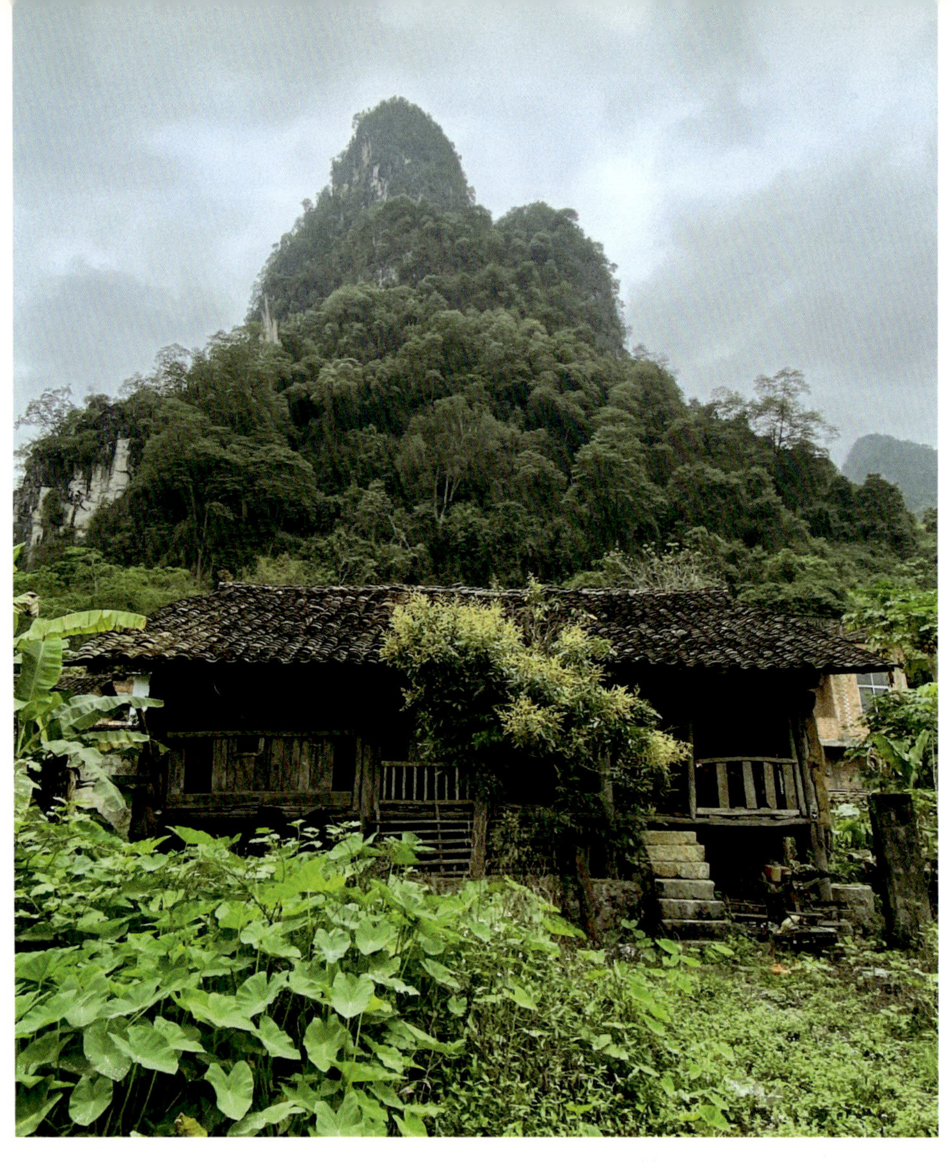

In the lesser-known southern Guangxi, one still encounters isolated old villages in wooden construction and can enjoy the landscape scenery while floating on a bamboo raft far from the tourist crowds. The area around Mingshi is particularly beautiful.

Im weniger bekannten südlichen Guangxi trifft man noch vereinzelt auf alte Dörfer in Holzbauweise und kann die Landschaftsszenerie fernab der Touristenströme auf dem Bambusfloß treibend genießen. Besonders schön ist das Gebiet um Mingshi.

Right page:
At the Detian waterfall, directly on the border river with Vietnam, some karst mountains have been made accessible with elevators and offer great views into the neighbouring country and daring circumnavigations of the mountain peaks on glass panorama paths.

Rechte Seite
Am Detian-Wasserfall, direkt am Grenzfluss zu Vietnam, wurden einige Karstberge mit Aufzügen zugänglich gemacht und bieten tolle Ausblicke ins Nachbarland und wagemutige Umrundungen der Bergspitzen auf Glaspanoramawegen.

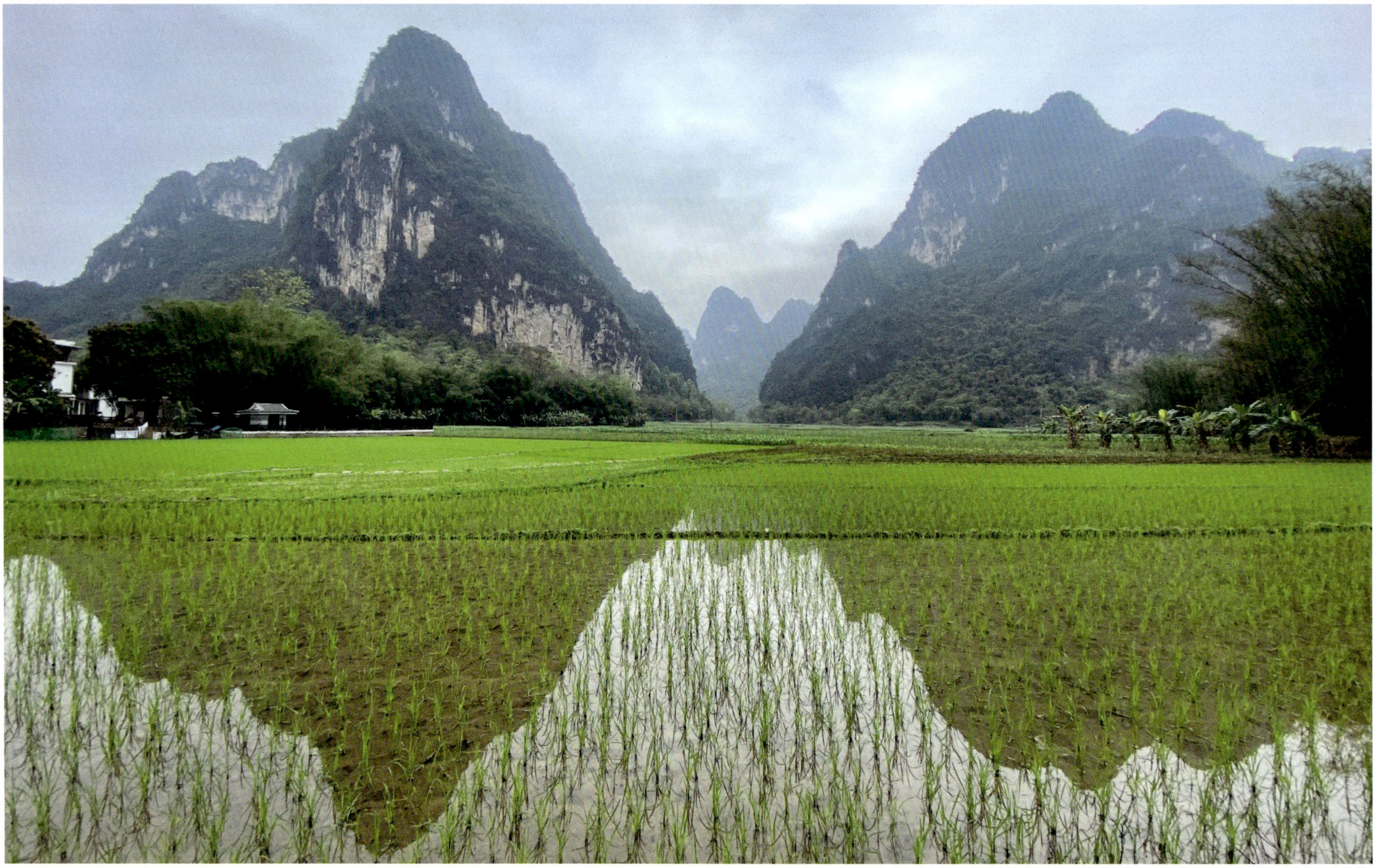

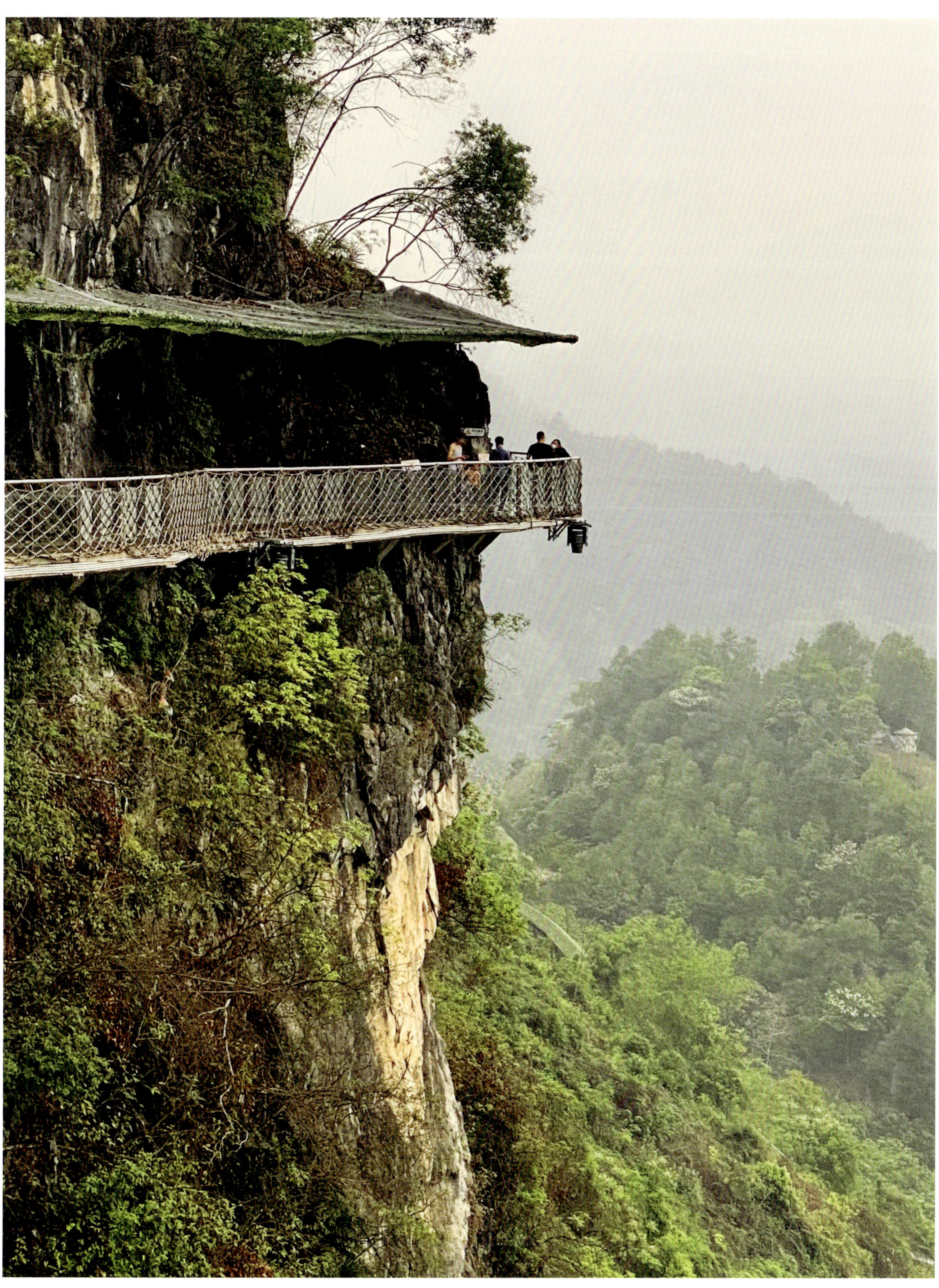

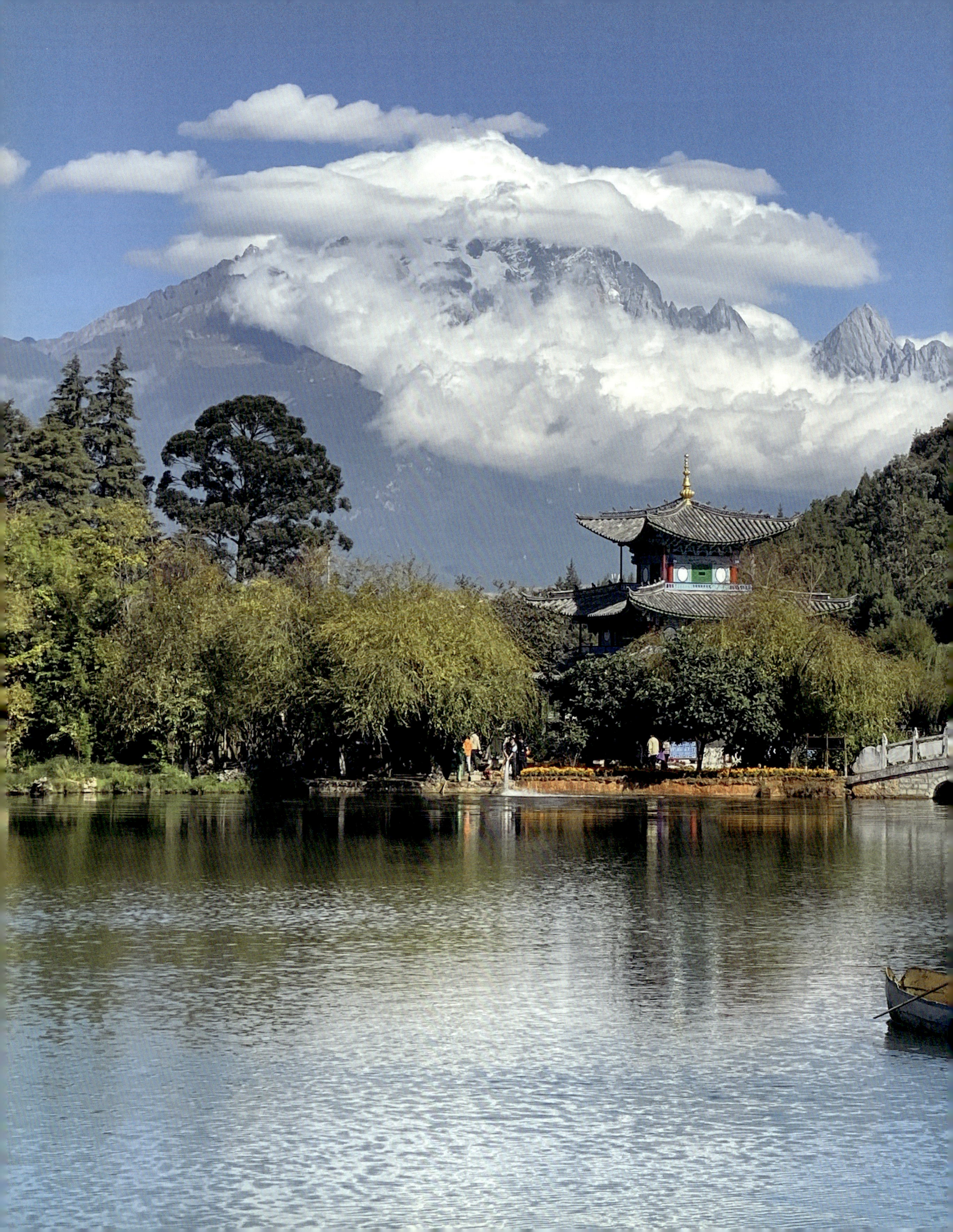

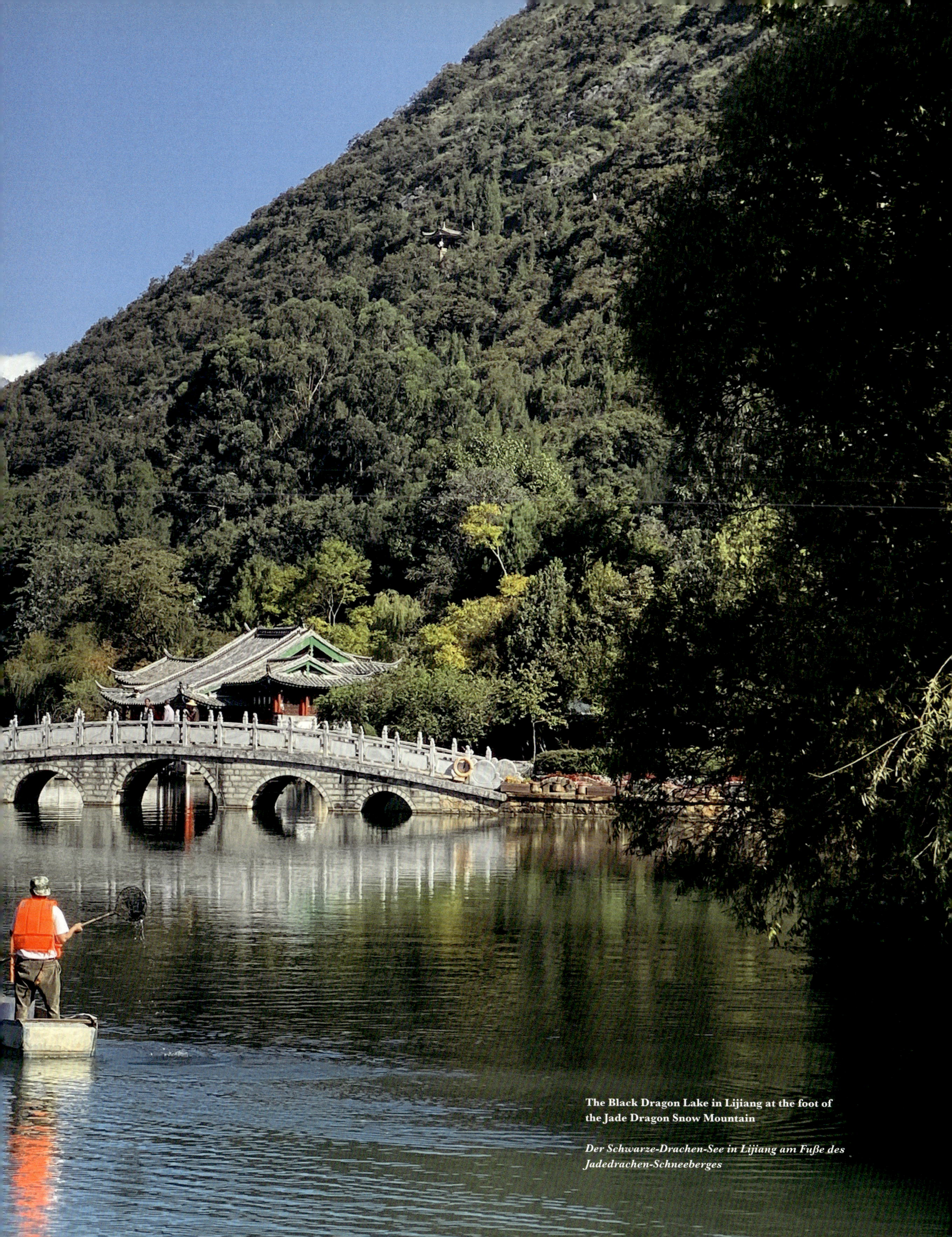

The Black Dragon Lake in Lijiang at the foot of the Jade Dragon Snow Mountain

Der Schwarze-Drachen-See in Lijiang am Fuße des Jadedrachen-Schneeberges

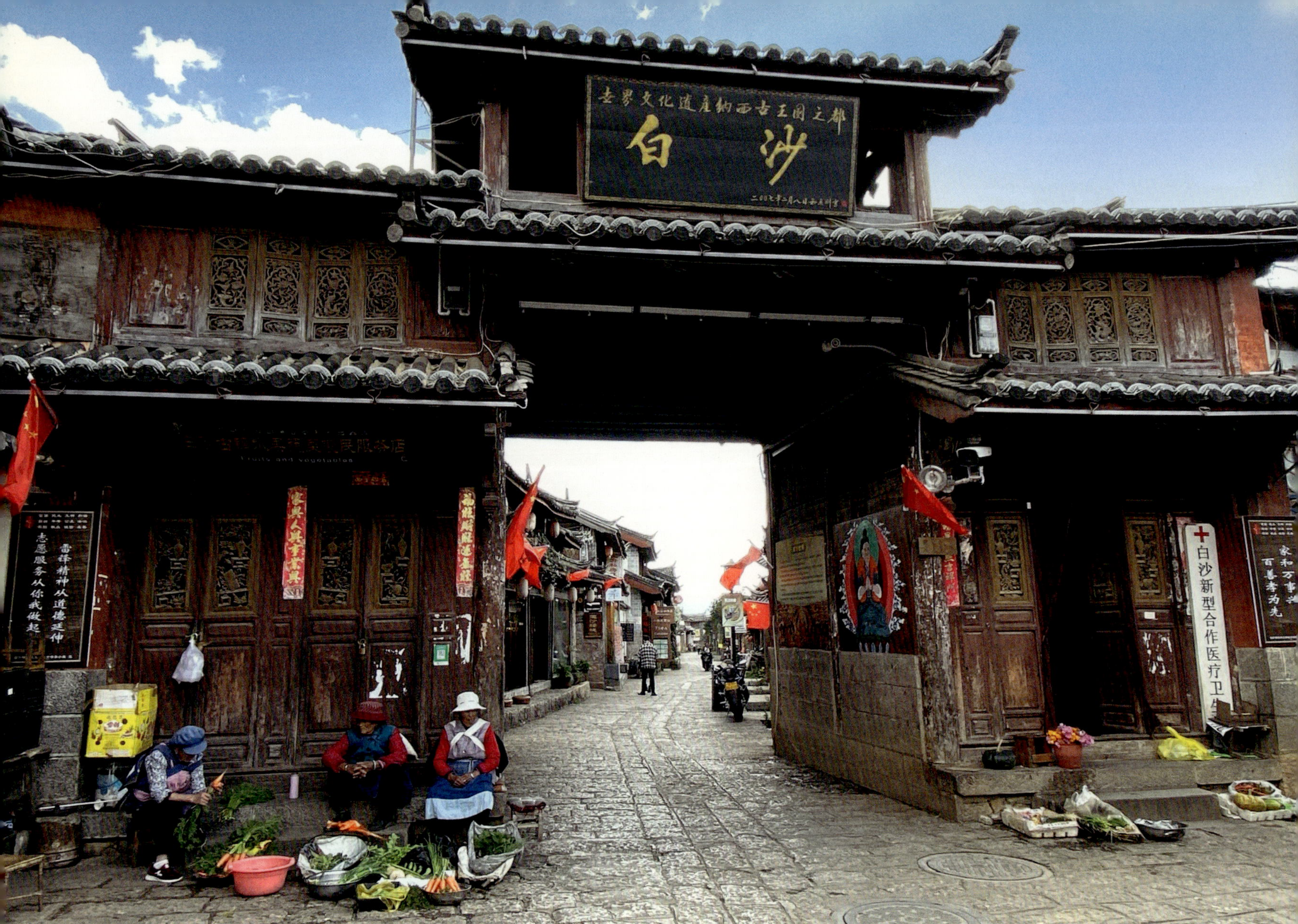

brightly coloured vests and sashes. At the so-called coming-of-age festival, responsibility is then handed over to the 14-year-olds. The Mosuo are one of the last matriarchies in modern-day China and are known for what is called "visiting marriage". This open marriage, in which different men are allowed to visit the women at night, is practiced far less often than is proclaimed. Today, the Mosuo people still number about 40,000 and traditionally live off agriculture in the Chinese foothills of the Himalayas.

White Sons and daughters

In the North of Yunnan, in the region bordering Tibet, there is a minority that names itself after the term for "white", *bai*. The members of the *bai* describe themselves as the "white sons and daughters" and call good people "the ones with white hearts and a white liver". They prefer to wear white clothing, live in whitewashed houses, and plant white orchids in the garden. The neighbouring ethnic group, the Naxi, traditionally hold the colour white in high esteem. The colour represents luck and blessings to them.

eines der letzten Matriarchate im heutigen China und bekannt für die sogenannte „Besuchsehe". Diese offene Ehe, bei der verschiedene Männer die Frauen nachts besuchen dürfen, wird weit weniger oft praktiziert als proklamiert. Zum Volk der Mosuo gehören heute noch etwa 40 000 Menschen, die in den chinesischen Ausläufern des Himalajas traditionell von der Landwirtschaft leben.

Weiße Söhne und Töchter

Im nördlichen Yunnan, im Grenzgebiet zu Tibet, gibt es eine Minderheit, die sich selbst nach dem Begriff für „Weiß", *Bai*, benennt. Die Angehörigen der *Bai* bezeichnen sich als „weiße Söhne und Töchter" und nennen gute Menschen solche mit „weißem Herzen und weißer Leber". Sie tragen mit Vorliebe weiße Kleider, wohnen in weiß getünchten Häusern und pflanzen im Garten weiße Orchideen an. Auch die benachbarte Volksgruppe der Naxi hält traditionellerweise die Farbe Weiß in Ehren. Für diese Bevölkerungsgruppe symbolisiert Weiß Glück und Segen.

Splash of colour in the white north of Yunnan

With its beautiful, postcard-pretty views over Lake Heilongtan, the Black Dragon Lake, along the Yulong mountain range, Lijiang is home to the Naxi and several ethnic minorities. The old town was a hub of trade in the 14th century. Today you can still find cobblestone streets, water canals and a lively, colourful marketplace where a wide variety of minorities offer goods in their traditional dress.

The view of Xueshan, the Jade Dragon Snow Mountains, with *De Yue Lou Pavilion*, the "Garden of the Recovered Moon", in the foreground, is beyond description. Located on the "Horse and Tea Trade Road", Lijiang is a good starting point to hike the infamous Tiger Leaping Gorge and explore the little-known, enchanting white and light blue sinter terraces. On the way to Shangri-La, yaks and wild horses can be seen grazing. Incense is burned in white lime kilns at the entrances to the village, and multi-coloured flag pennants now clearly indicate the area's proximity to Tibet.

Farbtupfer im weißen Norden Yunnans

Lijiang mit seiner wunderschönen Postkartenaussicht über den Heilongtan-See, dem Schwarzer-Drachen-See, auf die Bergkette des Yulong ist Heimat der Naxi und mehrerer anderer ethnischer Minderheiten. Die Altstadt war im 14. Jahrhundert ein Knotenpunkt des Handels. Noch heute findet man hier Kopfsteinpflasterstraßen, Wasserkanäle und einen quirligen, bunten Marktplatz, auf dem die verschiedensten Minderheiten in ihrer traditionellen Kleidung Waren anbieten.

Der Ausblick auf den Xueshan, das Jadedrachen-Schneegebirge, mit dem Pavillon De Yue Lou, dem „Garten des wiedergewonnenen Mondes", im Vordergrund, ist unbeschreiblich. An der „Pferde-und-Tee-Handelsstraße" gelegen, ist Lijiang ein guter Startpunkt, um die berühmt-berüchtigte Tigersprung-Schlucht zu erwandern und die wenig bekannten, bezaubernden, weiß-hellblauen Sinterterrassen zu erkunden. Auf dem Weg nach Shangri-La kann man Yaks beim Weiden und Wildpferde beim Grasen sehen. An den Ortseingängen wird in weißen Kalköfen Weihrauch verbrannt und vielfarbige Fahnenwimpel weisen jetzt eindeutig auf die Nähe zu Tibet hin.

Left page:
City gate to the old town of Baisha with market women near Lijiang

Linke Seite:
Stadttor zur Altstadt von Baisha mit Marktfrauen in der Nähe von Lijiang

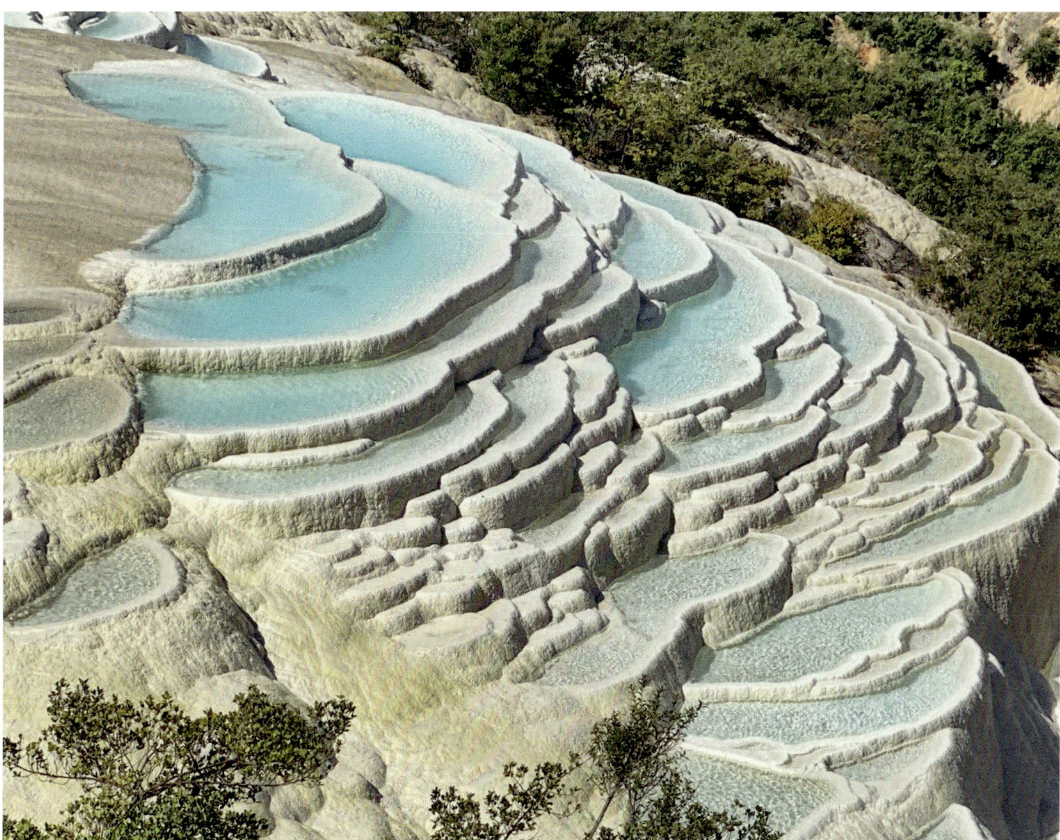

The beautiful Baishuitai, literally "white-water terraces" are located between Lijiang and Shangri-La.

Die wunderschönen Baishuitai, wörtlich „Weißwasser-Terrassen", liegen zwischen Lijiang und Shangri-La.

Along the ancient caravan routes
Entlang der alten Karawanenstraßen

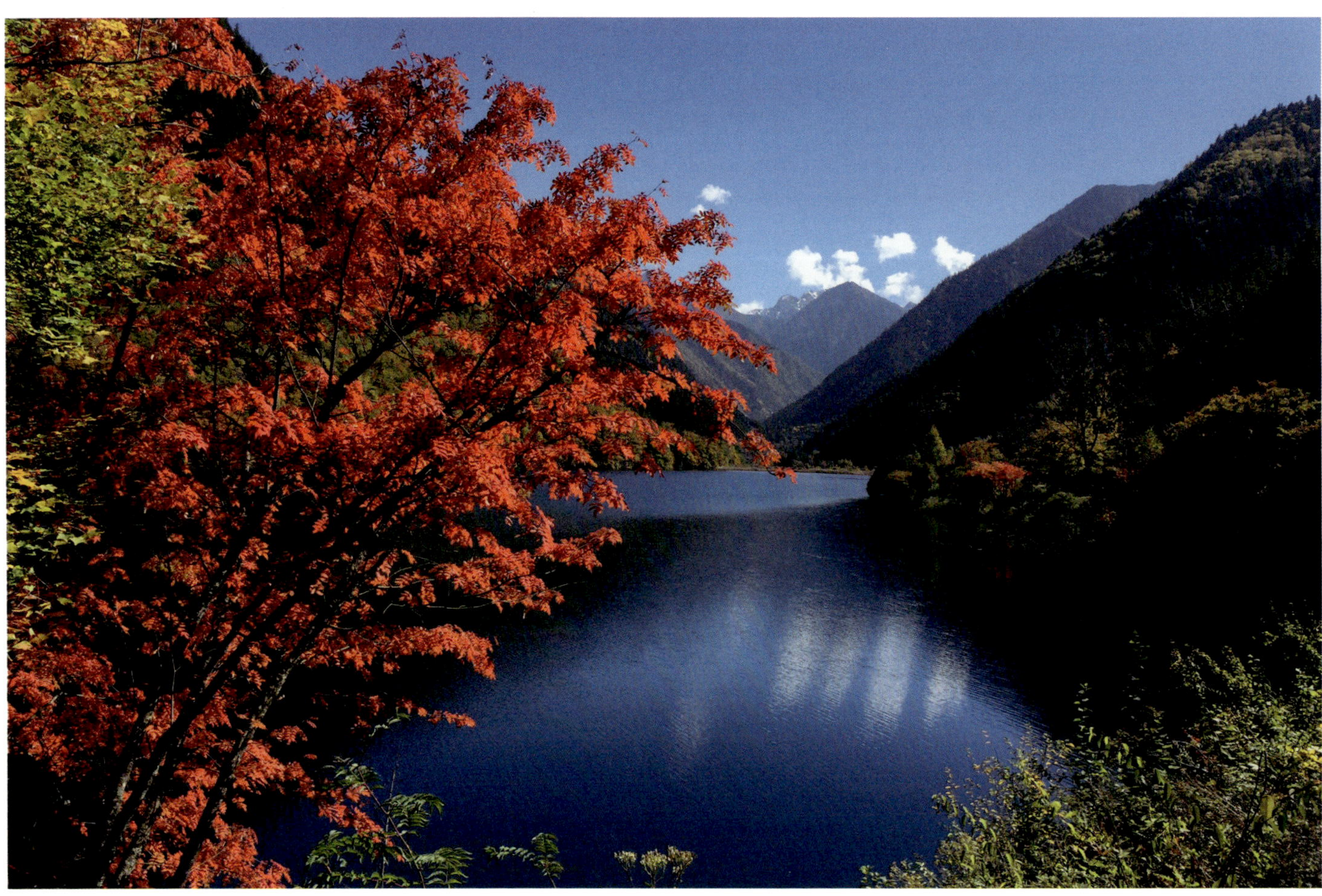

Northern Sichuan, home of the most famous bears of China, is unfortunately also a highly active earthquake area. Here, where the black and white panda bear munches on delicate green bamboo, nature made particularly good use of China's paint box. In Jiuzhaigou National Park, named after the "Valley of the Nine Tibetan Villages" which is located here, incredible crowds push their way along hard-surfaced wooden paths, past surreally beautiful scenery.

In the neighbouring Huanglong National Park, the "Yellow Dragon" meanders through the valleys for several kilometres. Here, the formation of the sinter dams and lakes can be observed in classic splendour. Depending on the depth of the water, the lake sediments, the sunlight and the environment, the lakes shine in different colours. The predominantly yellow tone of the limestone sinter here gave the valley its name. The protected area of these two national parks, which were included in the UNESCO World

Das nördliche Sichuan, die Heimat des wohl bekanntesten Bären Chinas, ist leider auch eine seismografisch hochaktive Gegend. Hier wo der schwarz-weiße Pandabär sich am frischen, zart-grünen Bambus labt, hat die Natur den Farbkasten Chinas ganz besonders weit aufgemacht. Im Jiuzhaigou-Nationalpark, nach dem „Tal der neun tibetischen Dörfer" benannt, die er beheimatet, schiebt man sich mit unglaublichen Menschenmassen über fest angelegte Holzpfade vorbei an surreal schönen Landschaftsszenerien. Im benachbarten Huanglong -Nationalpark schlängelt sich der „Gelbe Drache" auf mehreren Kilometern durch die Täler. Hier ist die Bildung der Sinterdämme und Seen in klassischer Schönheit zu beobachten. In Abhängigkeit von der Wassertiefe, den Seesedimenten, der Sonneneinstrahlung und der Umgebung leuchten die Seen in verschiedenen Farben. Die hier vorwiegend gelbe Farbe der Kalksinter gab dem Tal seinen Namen. Im Schutzgebiet dieser beiden von der UNESCO schon im Jahr 1992 in die Welterbeliste

Sichuan Province is also poetically known in China as the "Land of Abundance". The Jiuzhaigou Nature Reserve certainly lives up to its name. Picturesque mountain landscapes, thundering waterfalls and shimmering lakes make the national park one of the most beautiful places in China.

Die Provinz Sichuan ist in China poetisch auch als „Land des Überflusses" bekannt. Diesem Namen wird das Naturschutzgebiet Jiuzhaigou ganz sicher gerecht. Malerische Berglandschaften, tosende Wasserfälle und schimmernde Seen machen den Nationalpark zu einem der schönsten Orte Chinas.

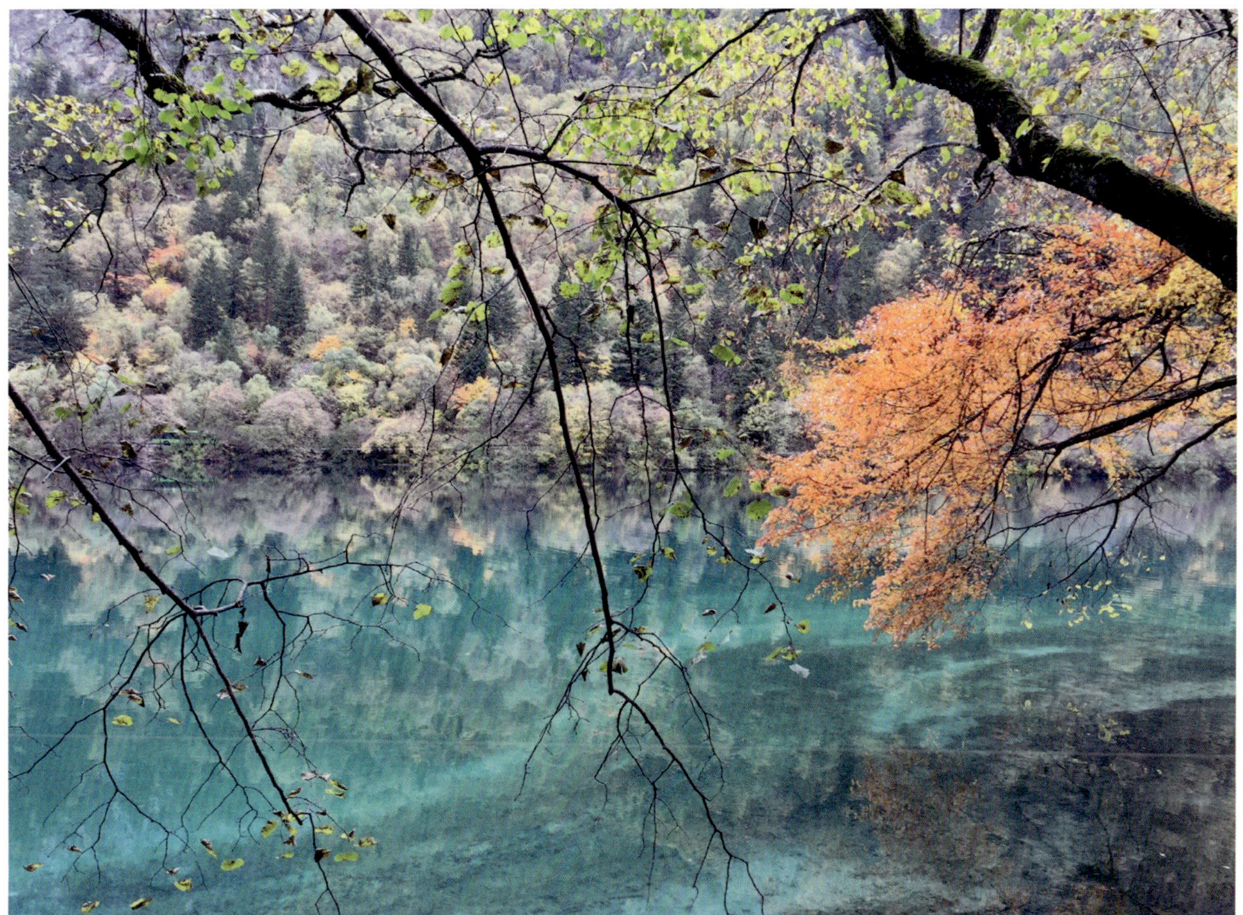

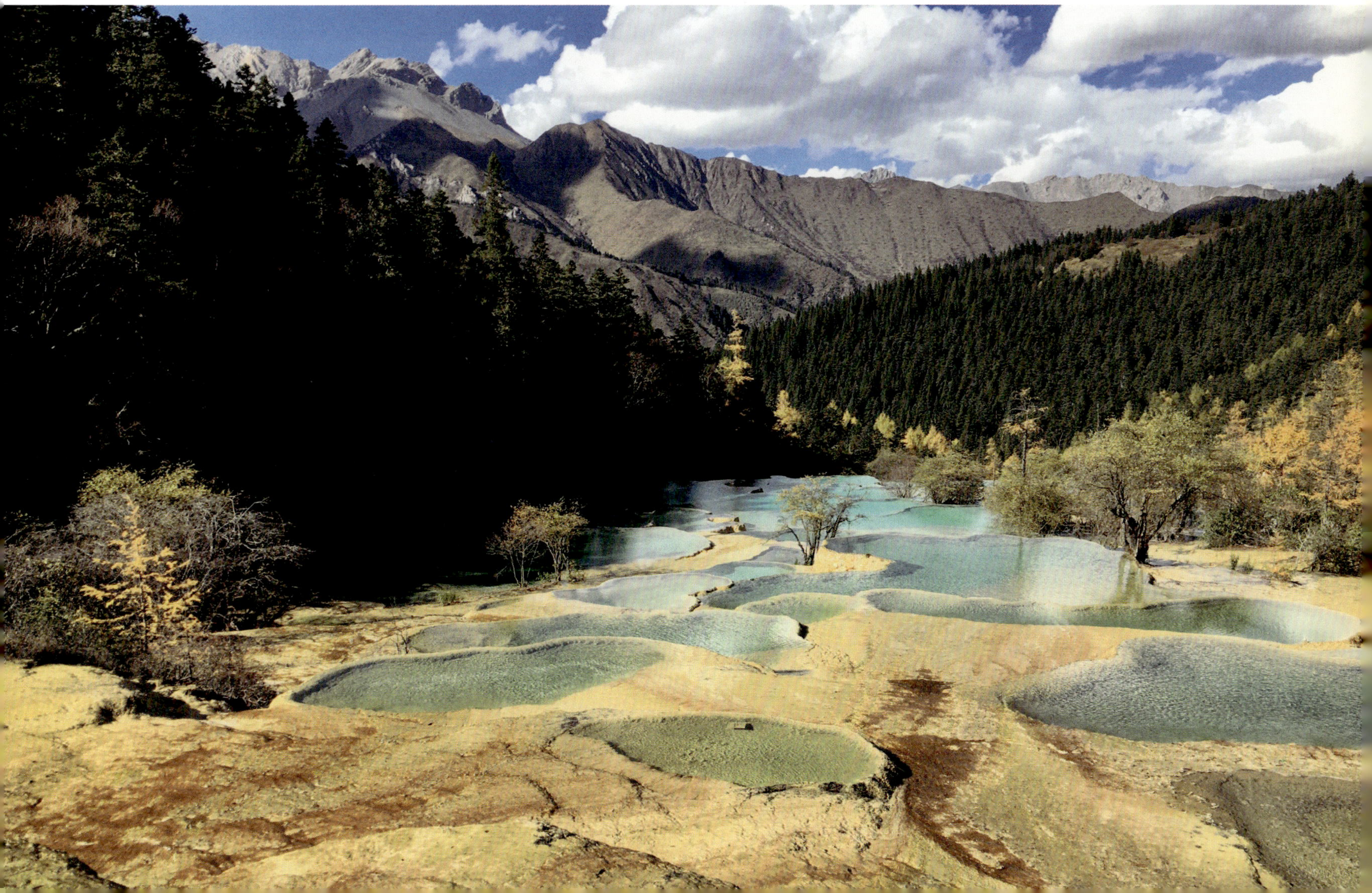

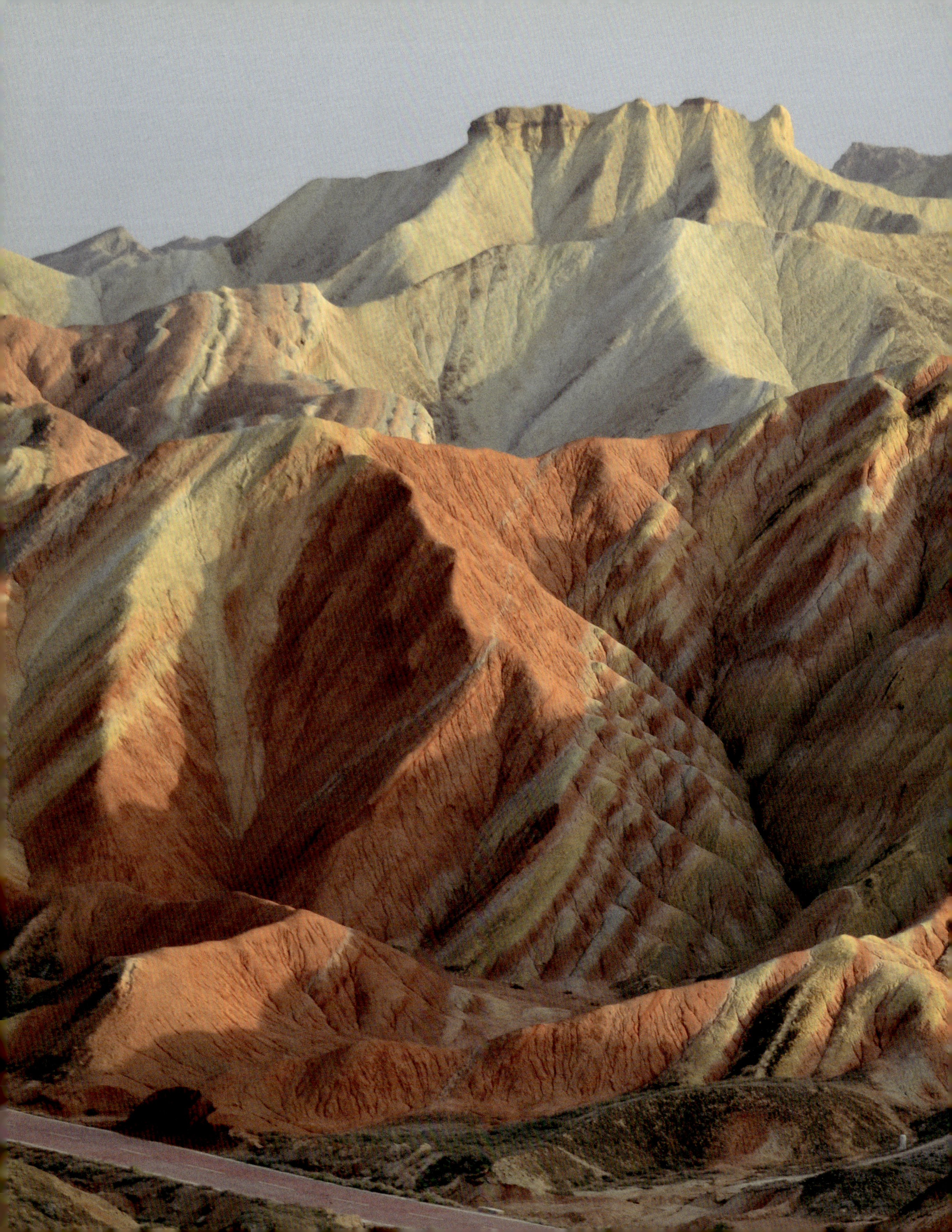

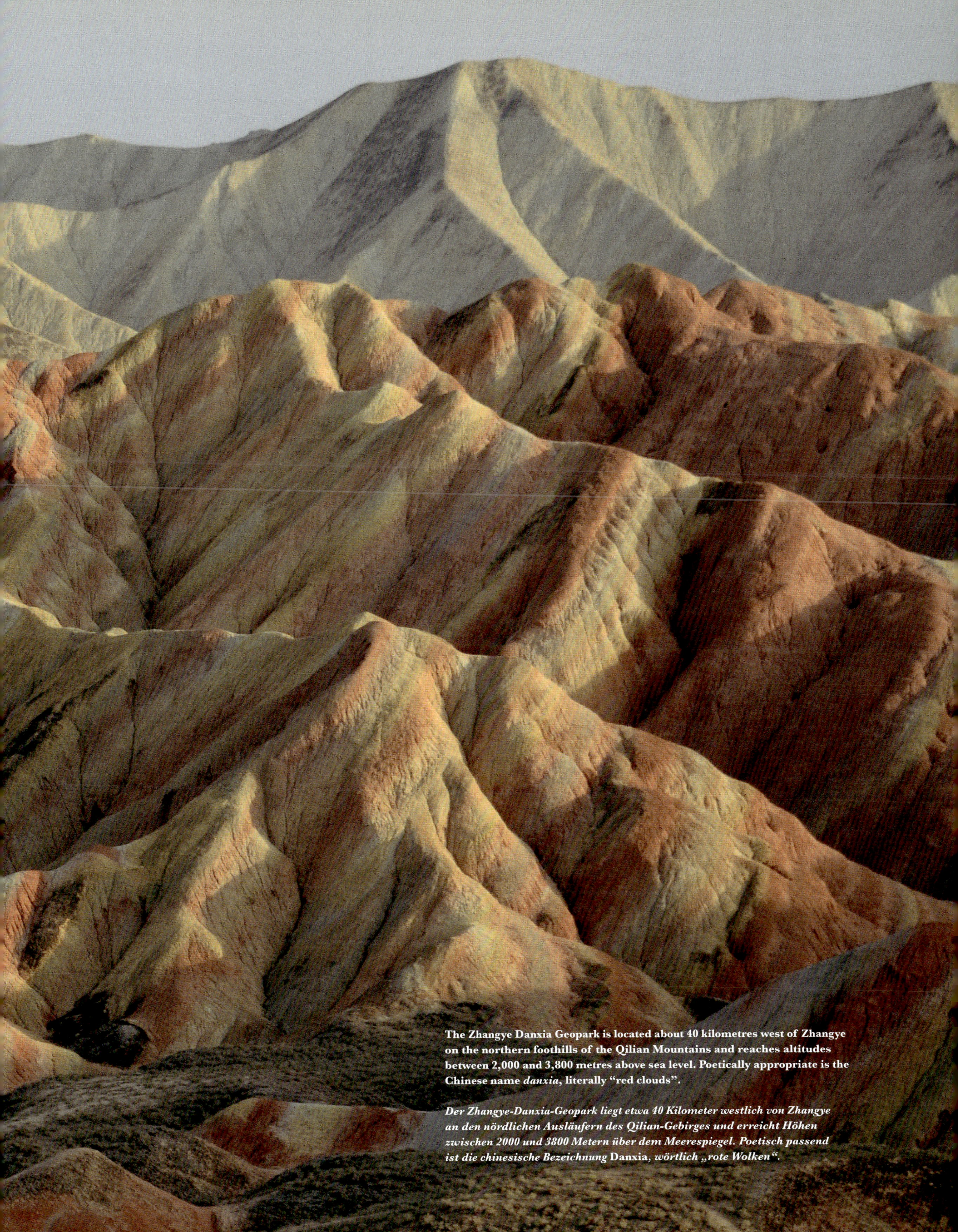

The Zhangye Danxia Geopark is located about 40 kilometres west of Zhangye on the northern foothills of the Qilian Mountains and reaches altitudes between 2,000 and 3,800 metres above sea level. Poetically appropriate is the Chinese name *danxia*, literally "red clouds".

Der Zhangye-Danxia-Geopark liegt etwa 40 Kilometer westlich von Zhangye an den nördlichen Ausläufern des Qilian-Gebirges und erreicht Höhen zwischen 2000 und 3800 Metern über dem Meerespiegel. Poetisch passend ist die chinesische Bezeichnung* Danxia*, wörtlich „rote Wolken".

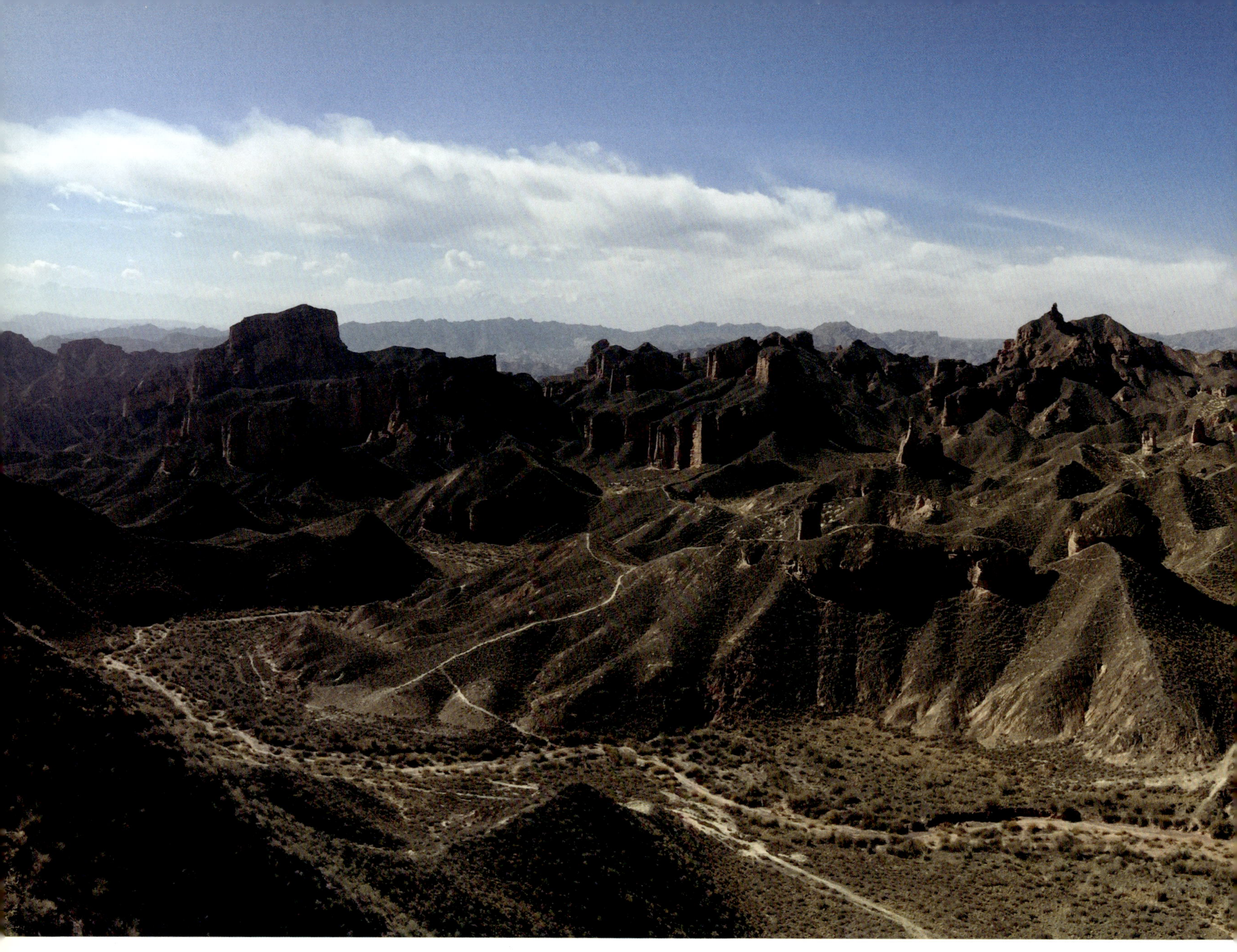

Heritage List in 1992, is home to rare plants, endangered animals such as the giant panda, the Sichuan takin, a type of cattle, the golden yellow blunt-nosed monkey and countless bird species. The inhabitants of the area are mainly Tibetans and Qiang, followers of the Bonpo religion and Tibetan Buddhism. They worship the snow-capped mountains as deities and consider the waters of the limestone sinter as sacred. However, Han and Hui people also live here.

Along the Silk Road through the Hexi Corridor between the Gobi Desert in the east and the Taklaman Desert in the west, the air becomes increasingly dusty and the landscape varies in all shades of sand – unless some unique minerals have become visible due to wind and erosion.

The colourful, rainbow-streaked mountains of the Zhangye Danxia Geopark in Gansu Province are consid-

aufgenommen Nationalparks leben neben seltenen Pflanzen, vom Aussterben bedrohte Tiere wie der Große Panda, der Sichuan Takin, eine Rinderart, der goldgelbe Stumpfnasenaffe sowie unzählige Vogelarten. Die Bewohner der Gegend sind vorwiegend Tibeter und Qiang, Anhänger der Bönpo-Religion und des tibetischen Buddhismus. Sie verehren die schneebedeckten Berge als Gottheiten und betrachten das Wasser der Kalksinter als heilig. Es leben hier aber auch Han und Hui. An der Seidenstraße entlang durch den Hexi-Korridor zwischen der Wüste Gobi im Osten und der Taklaman-Wüste im Westen wird die Luft immer staubiger und das Landschaftsbild variiert in allen Sandtönen – es sei denn, durch Wind und Erosion sind ein paar besondere Mineralien sichtbar geworden.

Die bunt gestreiften Regenbogenberge des Zhangye-Danxia-Geopark in der Provinz Gansu gelten als einer der schöns-

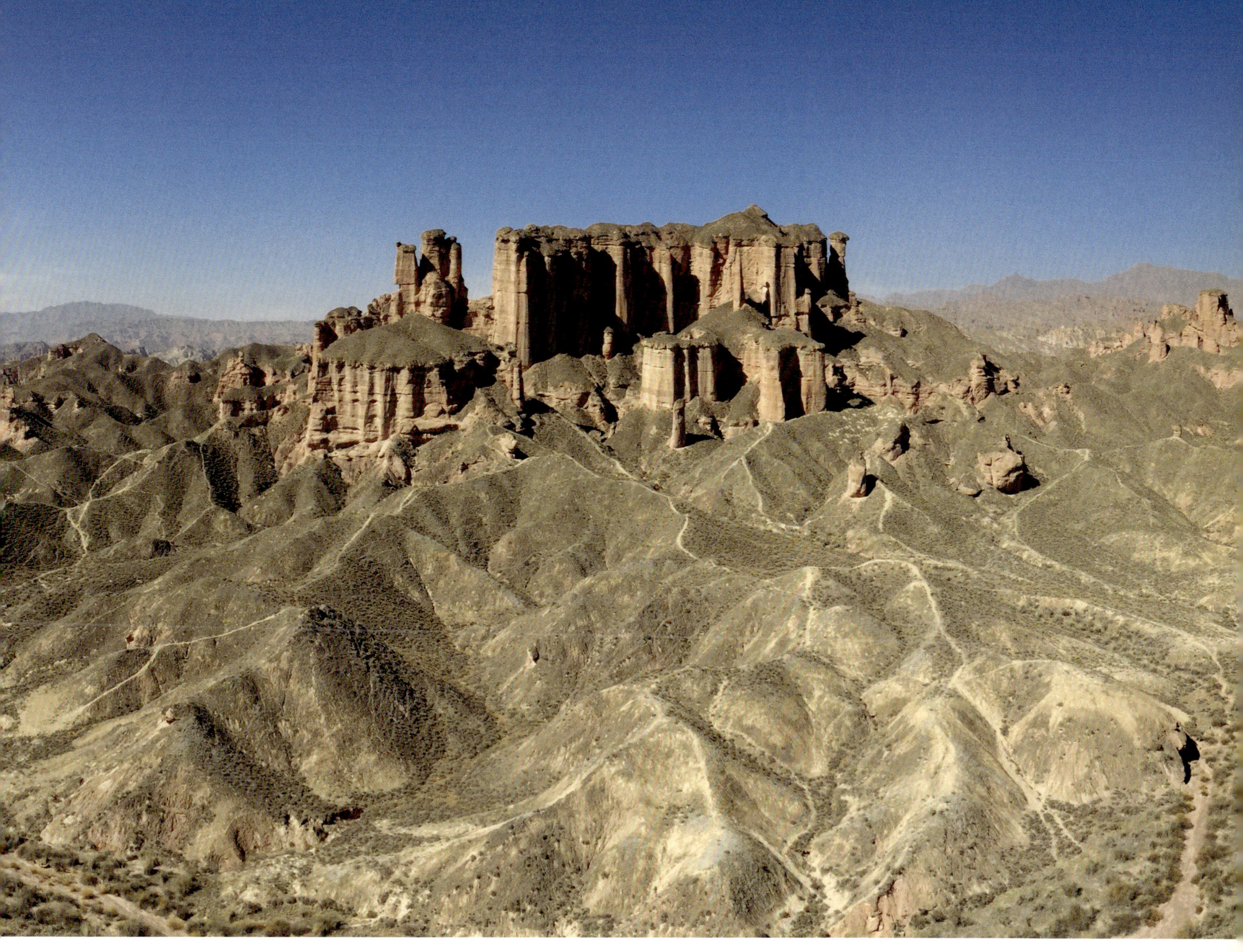

Binggou National Park, also called Ice Valley, is not quite as colourful as its well-known neighbour but no less spectacular. The numerous whimsical rock formations surprise and stimulate the imagination.

Der Binggou-Nationalpark, auch Eistal genannt, ist nicht ganz so farbenfroh wie sein bekannter Nachbar, dafür nicht minder spektakulär. Die zahlreichen skurrilen Gesteinsformationen überraschen und regen die Fantasie an.

ered one of the most beautiful and unusual places in all of China. This geological wonder was discovered just a few years ago by a travelling photojournalist. Allegedly, he showed a local farmer photos of the grey-green mountains in his native Europe during a dinner at the village tavern. In turn, the local man invited him to take a walk through his colourful mountains the following day. Shortly thereafter, the Chinese online network trembled with disbelieving excitement when some of the rainbow-streaked photographs became public. The geographical remoteness of this natural spectacle still protects it from mass tourism. The so-called Ice Valley, Binggou, with its fantastic huge rock formations of red sandstone, is also part of the spectacular Zhangye Danxia Geopark.

ten und ungewöhnlichsten Orte in ganz China. Dieses geologische Wunder wurde erst vor ein paar Jahren von einem durchreisenden Fotojournalisten entdeckt. Angeblich zeigte er einem dort ansässigen Bauern beim Abendessen in der Dorfschänke Fotos von den grau-grünen Bergen in seiner Heimat in Europa. Daraufhin lud ihn der Einheimische für den darauffolgenden Tag zu einem Spaziergang durch seine farbigen Berge ein. Das chinesische Online-Netz bebte kurz darauf vor ungläubiger Begeisterung, als einige der bunt-gestreiften Fotoaufnahmen bekannt wurden. Die geografische Abgelegenheit dieses Naturspektakels schützt es noch vor Massentourismus. Das sogenannte Eistal, Binggou, mit seinen fantastischen riesigen Felsformationen aus rotem Sandstein gehört ebenfalls zum spektakulären Zhangye-Danxia-Geopark.

It is only a few hours from there in a 4 × 4 to the mysterious black lakes of the Badain Jaran Desert in the western region of Inner Mongolia. It was named the most beautiful desert in China by *China National Geography* magazine. There you can find the "Everest of the desert", the Biluthu sand peak with a height of almost 500 metres. On guided camel tours lasting several days with overnight stays under the starry sky or in tents and yurts, you can experience the peace and solitude of this fascinating landscape up close.

It is alternatively accessible by four-wheel drive vehicle, but that requires abilities similar to sailing. Crossing the huge yellow sandpit with its towering, soft peaks, each of which is conquered diagonally to the right or left, is strongly reminiscent of a roller coaster ride. The reflections in the numerous crystal-clear desert lakes and the unexpected sight of the Tibetan Buddhist temple, where only a monk-father and his monk-son live, repeatedly bring the shaken interior to a grateful, almost meditative calm. With a total area of 49,000 square kilometres, the Badain Jaran Desert is the third largest sand desert in China, after the Taklamakan and Junggar Deserts and before the Tengger Desert. The fascinating, endlessly undulating, ochre-yellow landscape is best explored on foot in the golden light of dusk.

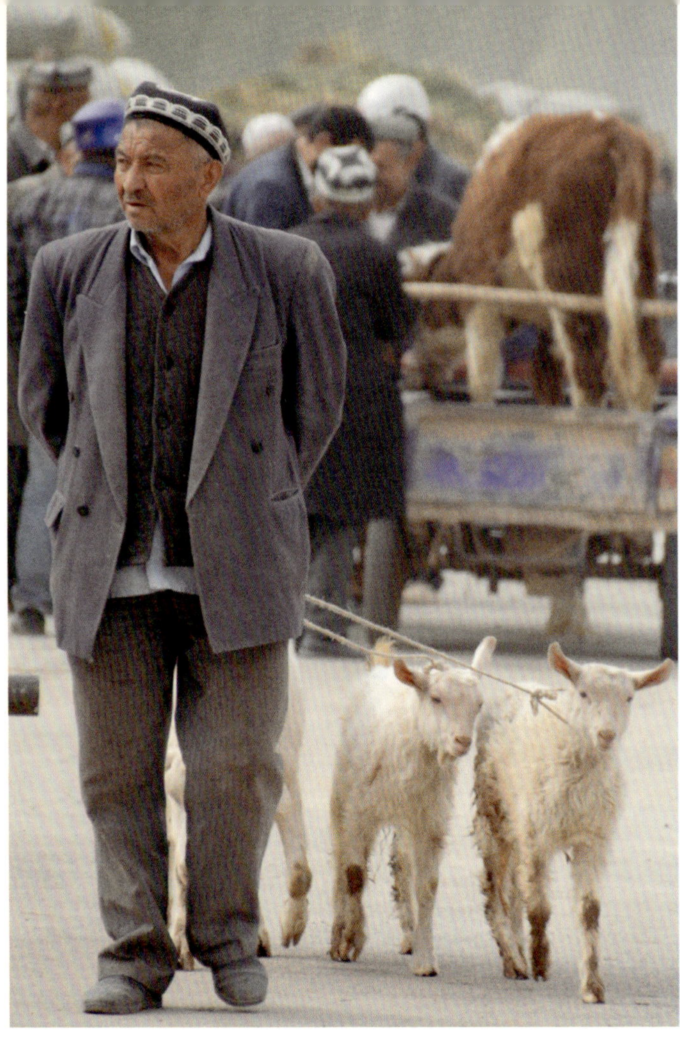

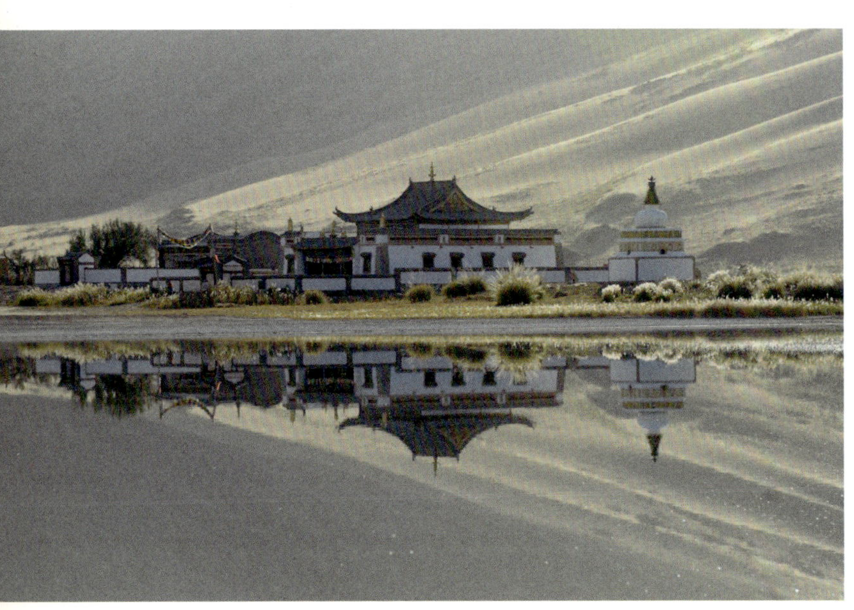

Lake Nouerto is the largest lake in the Badai Jaran Desert. On its shore is a Lamaist monastery. The building materials were brought from hundreds, even over a thousand kilometres away by camels.

Der Nouerto-See ist der größte See der Badai-Jaran-Wüste. An seinem Ufer befindet sich ein lamaistisches Kloster. Das Baumaterialien wurden aus hunderten, sogar über tausend Kilometern Entfernung mit Kamelen herangeschafft.

Nur ein paar Stunden sind es von dort im Geländewagen zu den geheimnisvollen schwarzen Seen der Badain-Jaran-Wüste im Westgebiet der Inneren Mongolei. Sie wurde von der Zeitschrift *China National Geography* als schönste Wüste Chinas bezeichnet. Man findet dort den „Everest der Wüste", den Biluthu-Sandgipfel mit einer Höhe von fast 500 Metern. Auf mehrtägigen geführten Kameltouren mit Übernachtungen unterm Sternenhimmel oder in Zelten und Jurten kann man die Ruhe und Einsamkeit dieser faszinierenden Landschaft ganz intensiv erleben. Alternativ per Vierradantrieb, aber das setzt Seefahrerqualitäten voraus. Das Durchkreuzen des riesigen gelben Sandkastens mit seinen hoch aufragenden, weichen Gipfeln, die jeweils rechts oder links diagonal bezwungen werden, erinnert stark an eine Achterbahnfahrt. Die Spiegelungen in den zahlreichen kristallklaren Wüstenseen und der unerwartete Anblick des tibetisch-buddhistischen Tempels, in dem nur ein Mönch-Vater und sein Mönch-Sohn leben, bringen das durchgeschüttelte Innere immer wieder zu einer dankbaren, fast meditativen Ruhe. Mit einer Gesamtfläche von 49.000 Quadratkilometern ist die Badain-Jaran-Wüste die drittgrößte Sandwüste Chinas, nach der Taklamakan- und der Junggar-Wüste und vor der Tengger-Wüste. Das faszinierende, endlos wellige, ockergelbe Landschaftsbild lässt sich am Schönsten zu Fuß bei orangem Abendlicht erkunden.

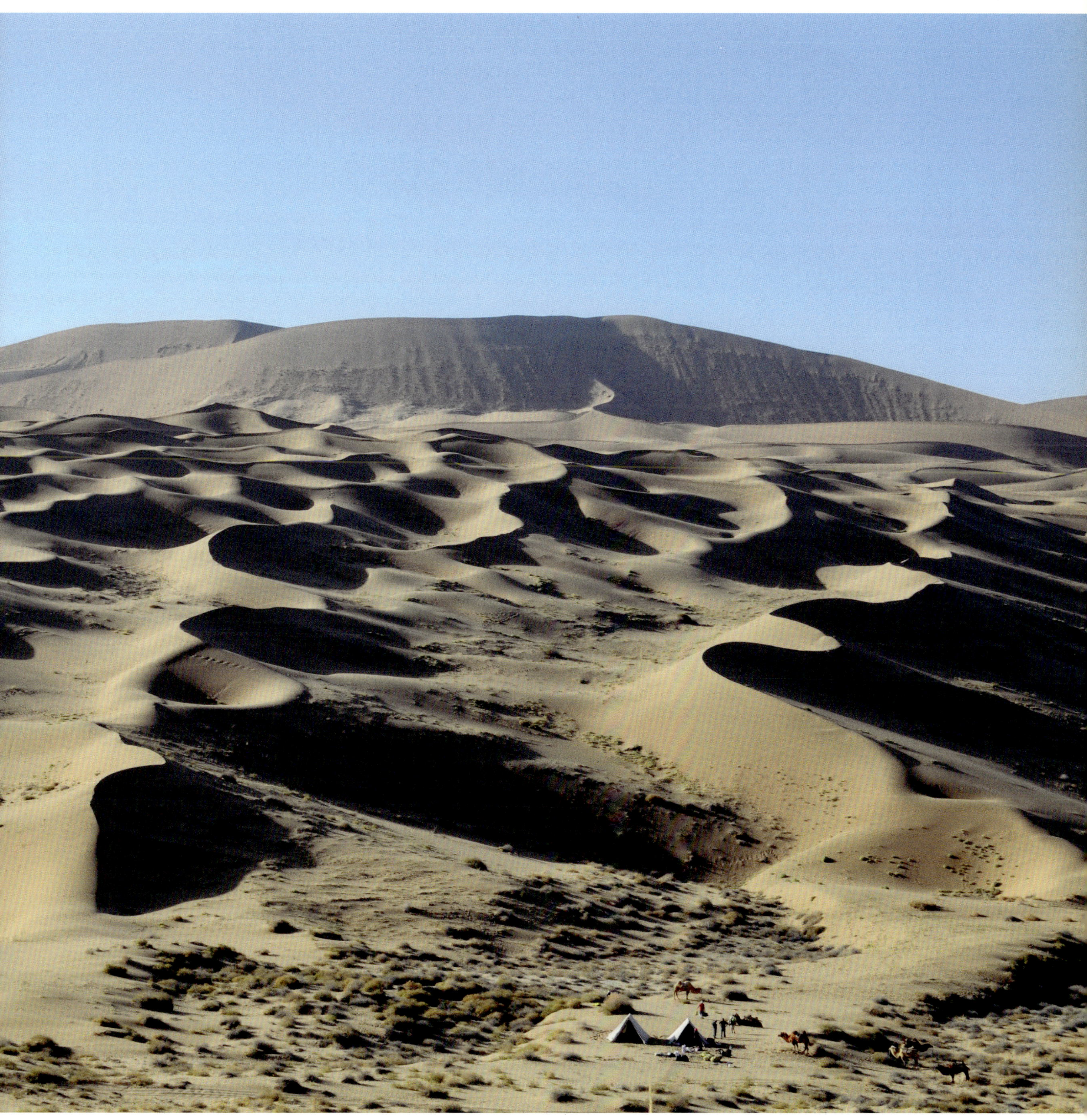

The sand sea of the Badain Jaran Desert with its mega dunes and more than 142 drainless lakes

Das Sandmeer der Badain-Jaran-Wüste mit seinen Megadünen und mehr als 142 abflusslosen Seen

From the tip of the dragon's tail to his head

Von der Schwanzspitze bis zum Kopf des Drachen

Still in Gansu Province, but further north, at Jiayuguan Pass, located at the narrowest point of the Hexi Corridor, begins the western end of the Great Wall. In the eyes of the Chinese emperor, it is also the end of the "civilised world": "And beyond it existed only the demons and the barbarians from the desert and Central Asia."

Jiayuguan Pass, built in 1372, borders the Gobi Desert. It was considered one of the most important checkpoints on the Silk Road. The construction of the over 6,000-kilometre long wall, this symbol of the Chinese nation, began in 210 BC and lasted until the end of the Ming Dynasty in the 17th century. According to legend, the mythical winged horse of the first Chinese emperor Qin Shi Huang covered exactly this distance in one day. Where its hooves touched the ground, watchtowers were built. In fact, the distance between the towers was strictly measured – two flights of arrows – so that any part of the wall could be shot through by the defenders. The eastern end of the wall, Shanhaiguan, literally "Mountain-and-Sea Pass", lies about 300 kilometres east of Beijing. The end of the wall that juts into the sea is affectionately known as the "Old Dragon's Head".

Immer noch in der Provinz Gansu, aber weiter nördlich an der engsten Stelle des Hexi-Korridors, am Jiayuguan-Pass, beginnt das westliche Ende der Großen Mauer. In den Augen des chinesischen Kaisers auch das Ende der „zivilisierten Welt". „Und jenseits davon existierten nur die Dämonen und die Barbaren aus der Wüste und Zentralasiens."

Der Jiayuguan-Pass, erbaut 1372, grenzt an die Wüste Gobi. Er galt als einer der wichtigsten Kontrollposten auf der Seidenstraße. Der Bau der mehr als 6000 km langen Mauer, dieses Symbols der chinesischen Nation, begann 210 v. Chr. und dauerte bis zum Ende der Ming-Dynastie im 17. Jahrhundert. Eben genau diese Entfernung ritt der Legende nach das mythische geflügelte Pferd des ersten chinesischen Kaisers Qin Shi Huang an einem Tag. Wo die Hufe den Boden berührten, entstanden Wachtürme. Tatsächlich wurde der Abstand zwischen den Türmen streng gemessen – zwei Pfeilflüge –, so dass jeder Teil der Mauer von den Verteidigern durchgeschossen werden konnte. Das östliche Ende, der Shanhaiguan, wörtlich „Berg-und-Meer-Pass", liegt rund 300 km östlich von Peking. Das ins Meer hineinragende Ende der Mauer wird liebevoll „Alter Drachenkopf" genannt.

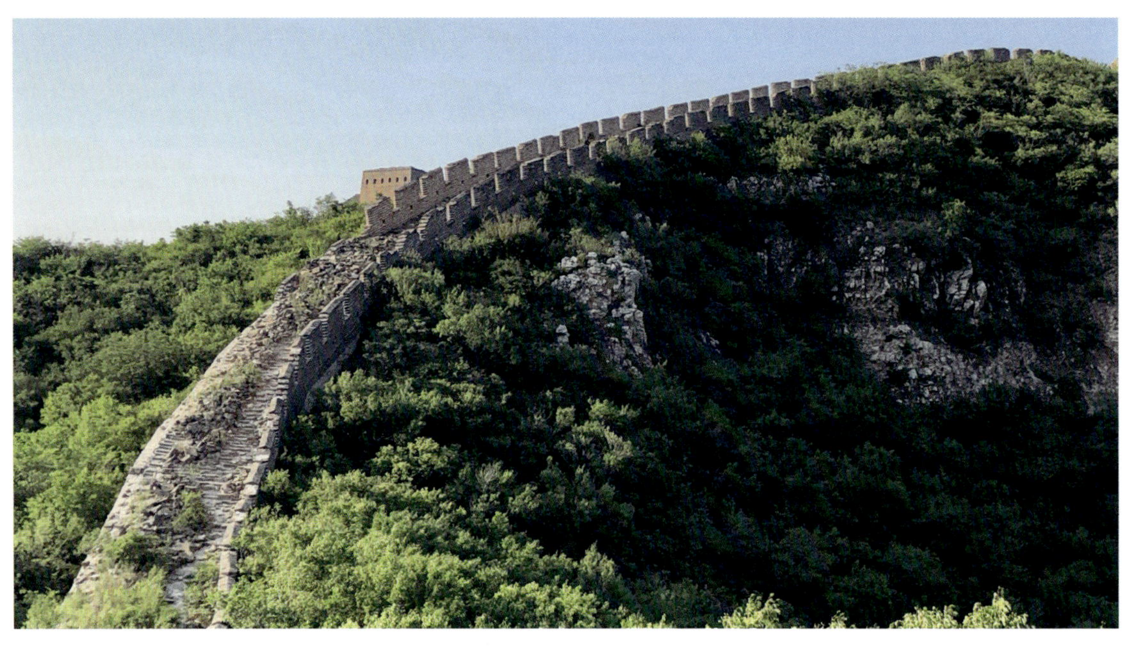

The Great Wall at sunset near Jinshanling, about two hours north of the capital

Die Große Mauer im Sonnenuntergang in der Nähe von Jinshanling, ca. zwei Stunden nördlich der Hauptstadt.

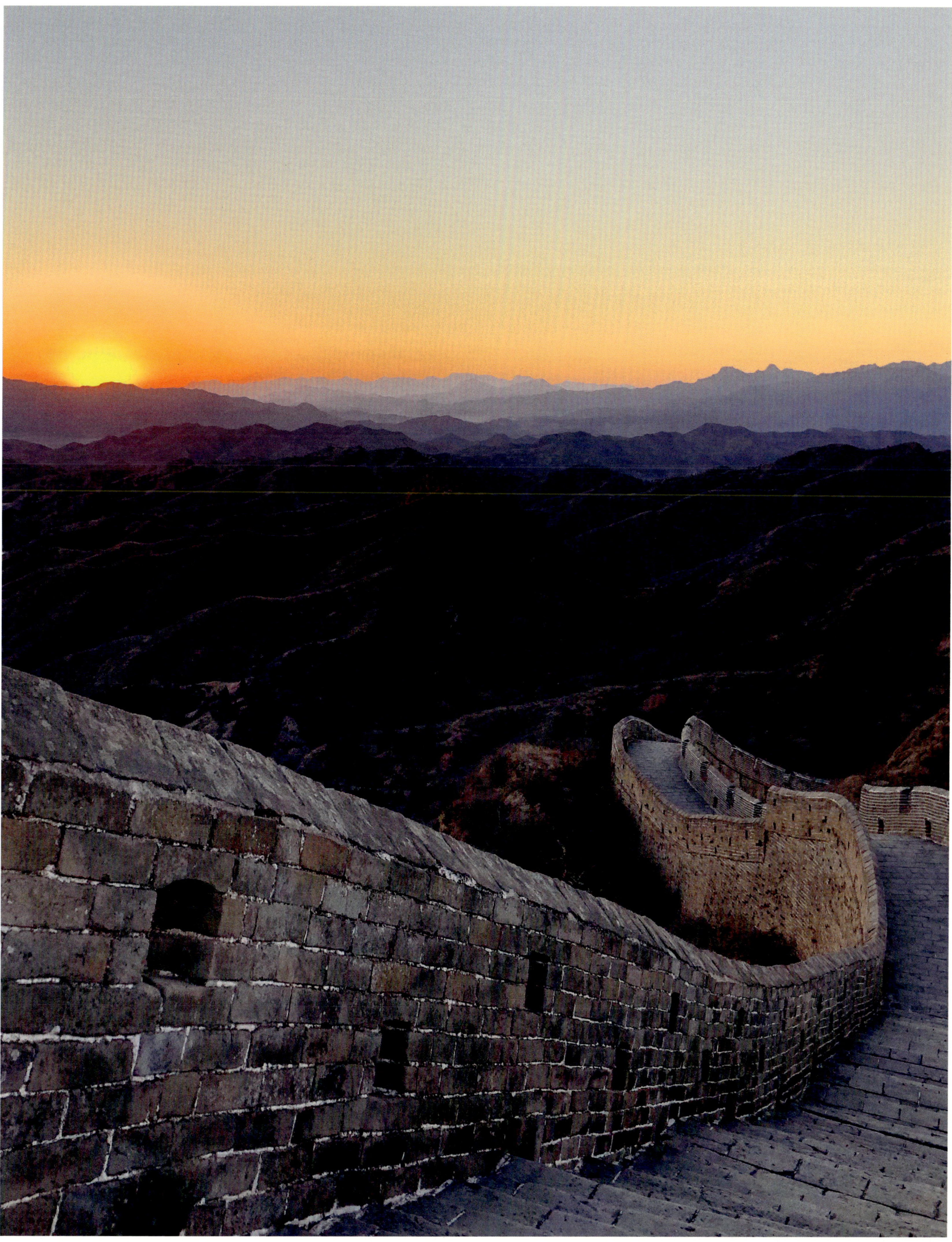

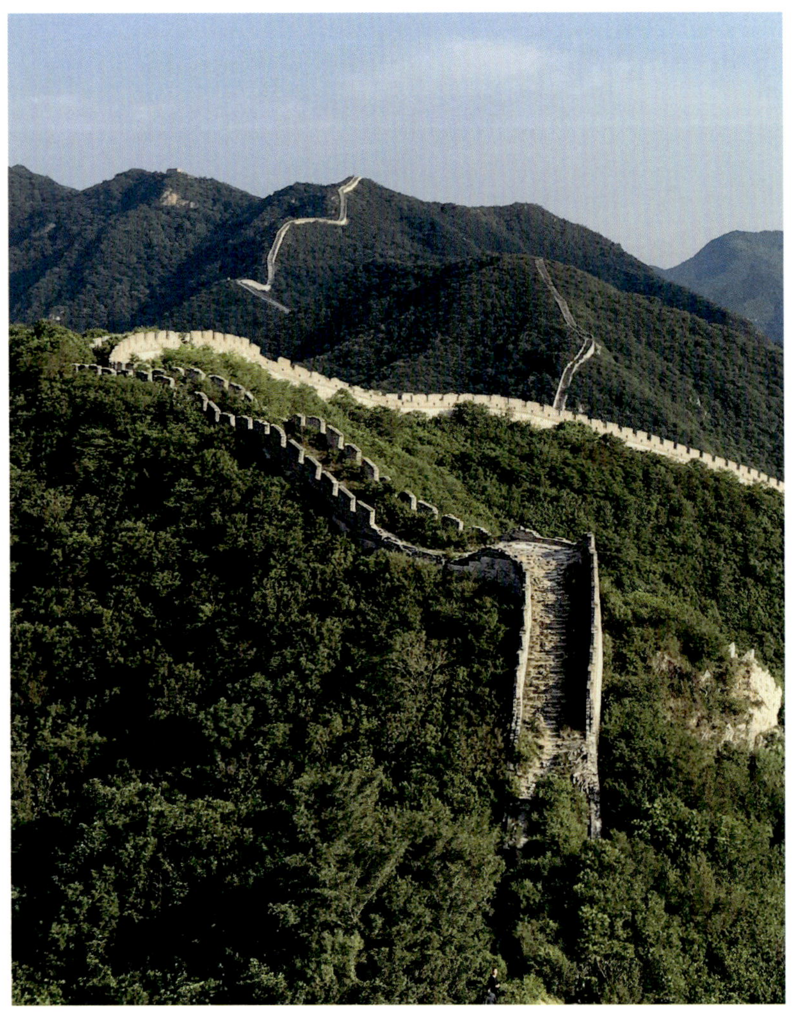

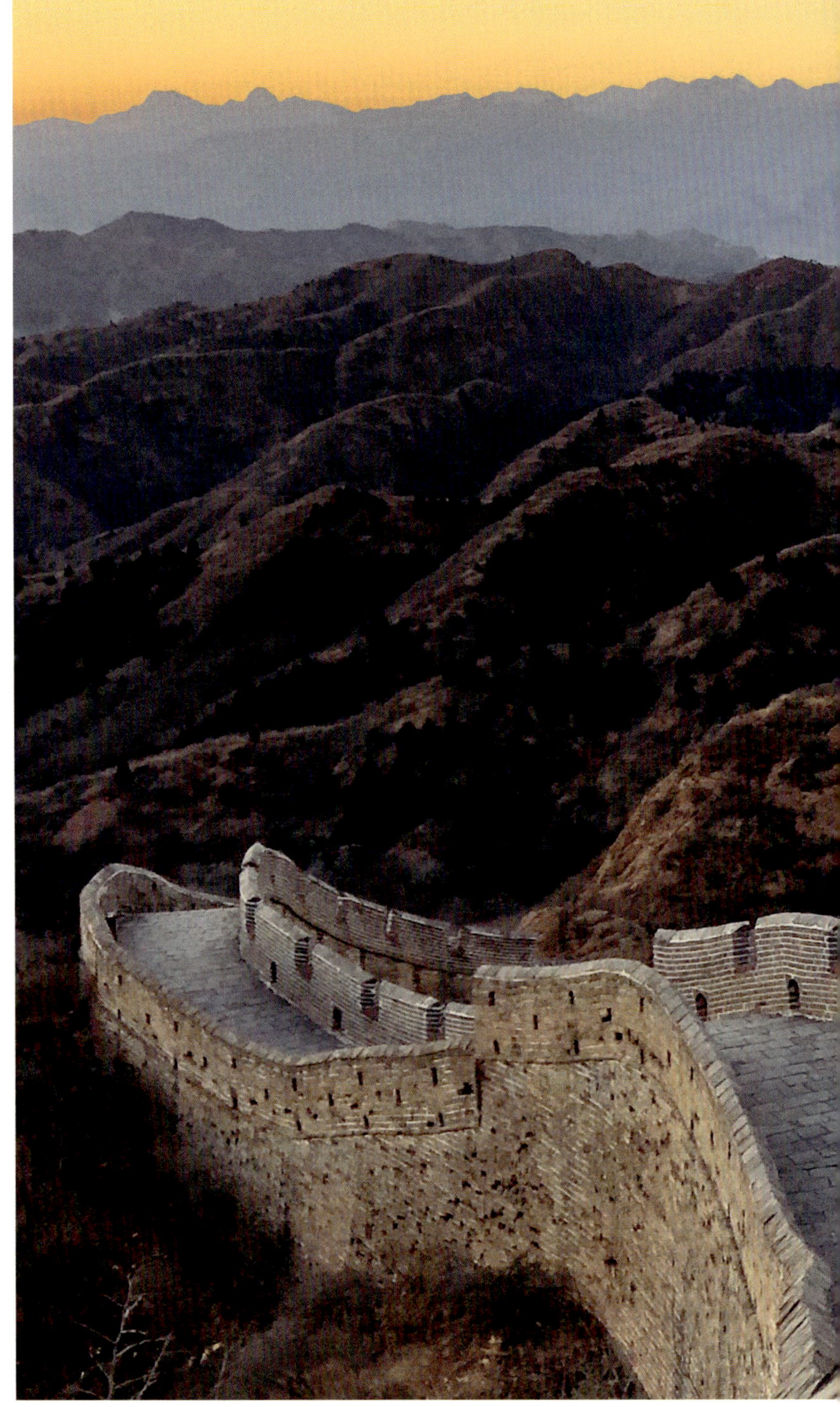

The Great Wall, the longest man-made structure and one of the Seven Wonders of the World, always runs high above the ridges of the curving hill ranges because of its favourable defensive position and distant visibility. The wild, unrestored parts are difficult to access.

Die Große Mauer, das längste menschengemachte Bauwerk und eines der sieben Weltwunder, führt wegen der besseren Verteidigungsposition und Fernsicht immer hoch oben über die Bergrücken der geschwungenen Hügelketten. Die „wilden", nicht restaurierten Teile sind nur schwer zugänglich.

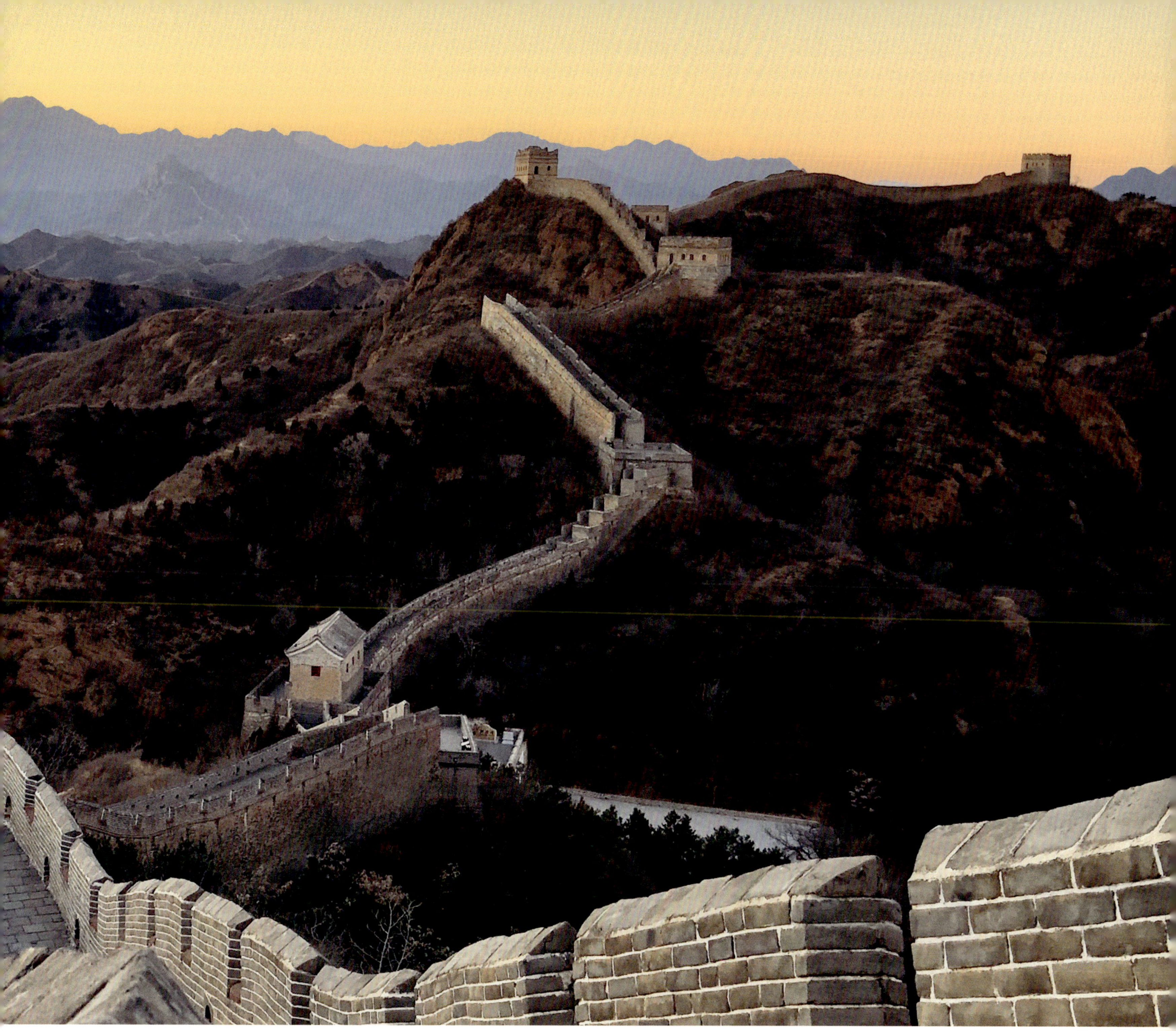

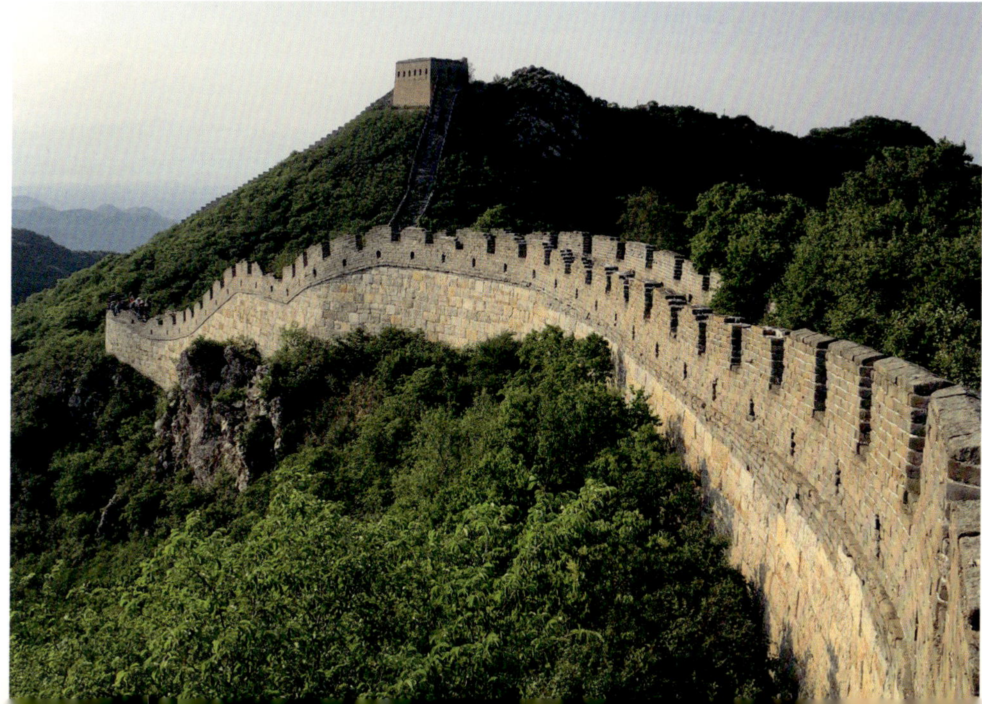

The yellow cradle
Die gelbe Wiege

The cradle of Chinese culture is located deep inland, south of Inner Mongolia around the present-day cities of Xian and Luoyang, in the provinces of Shaanxi and Shanxi, where the so-called Middle Kingdom found its origin at least 5,000 years ago on the loess plateau in the headwaters of the Yellow River. There lived the Yellow Emperor, Huangdi, from whom all Han derive, who make up over 90 percent of China's population today. The northern Chinese plateau was agricultural land and shaped the Chinese society through its rural and paternalistic family structure. The families had to stick together to survive, and the high value placed on the family in Confucian philosophy and Chinese thought is explained as a result of this agricultural order to this day.

Despite its more than 5,000 kilometres of coast, China's gaze has always been strongly inward-looking. The Chinese were not seafarers and only came into contact with foreign peoples when Western colonialists invaded in the 19th century. This shaped their character and mentality.

Tief im Landesinnen, südlich der inneren Mongolei um die heutigen Städte Xian und Luoyang, in den Provinzen Shaanxi und Shanxi, wo vor mindestens 5000 Jahr auf dem Lössplateau im Quellgebiet des Gelben Flusses das sogenannte Reich der Mitte seinen Ursprung nahm, steht die Wiege der chinesischen Kultur. Dort lebte Huangdi, der Gelbe Kaiser, von dem sich alle Han herleiten und die heute über 90 Prozent der Bevölkerung Chinas ausmachen. Diese nordchinesische Ebene war Agrarland und prägte nachhaltig die chinesische Gesellschaft durch ländliche und paternalistische Familienstruktur. Aus existentiellen Gründen mussten die Familien zusammenhalten, und man erklärt sich den hohen Stellenwert, den die Familie in der konfuzianischen Philosophie und im chinesischen Denken bis heute einnimmt, als Ergebnis dieser landwirtschaftlichen Ordnung.

Trotz seiner über 5000 km langen Meeresküste war Chinas Blick immer stark nach innen gerichtet. Die Chinesen waren keine Seefahrer und kamen erst im 19. Jahrhundert, als die westlichen Kolonialisten einfielen, mit fremden Völkern in Kontakt. Dies prägte ihren Charakter und ihre Mentalität.

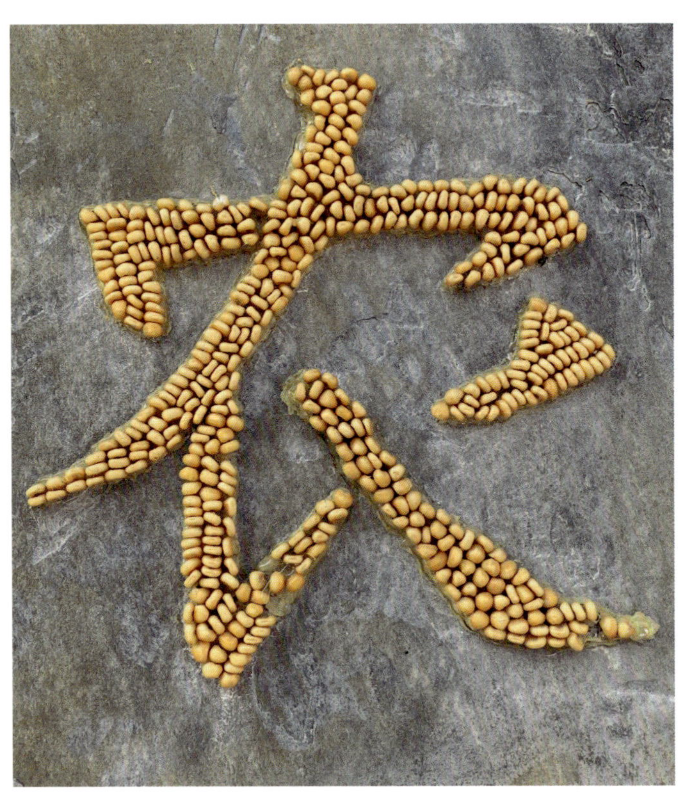

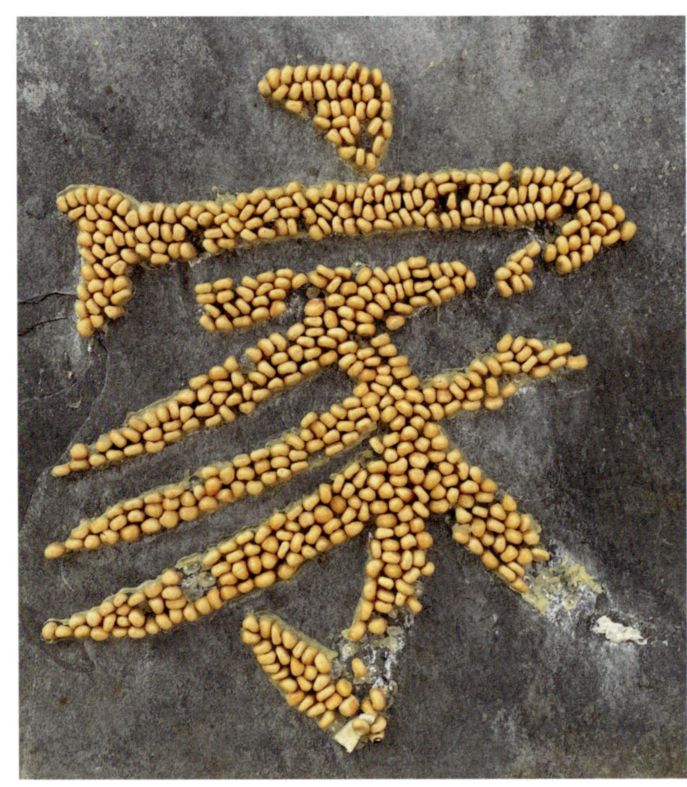

Left page:
The Chinese characters formed from yellow corn kernels mean "farmer". They are located at the entrance to the village square of an old mill town.

Linke Seite:
Die aus gelben Maiskörnern geformten chinesischen Schriftzeichen bedeuten „Landwirt". Sie befinden sich am Eingang zum Dorfplatz eines alten Mühlenortes.

Below:
The famous terracotta warriors are used throughout the country in a variety of creative ways to commemorate but also to provoke.

Unten:
Die berühmten Terrakotta-Krieger werden landesweit vielfältig und kreativ zur Erinnerung, aber auch zur Provokation genutzt.

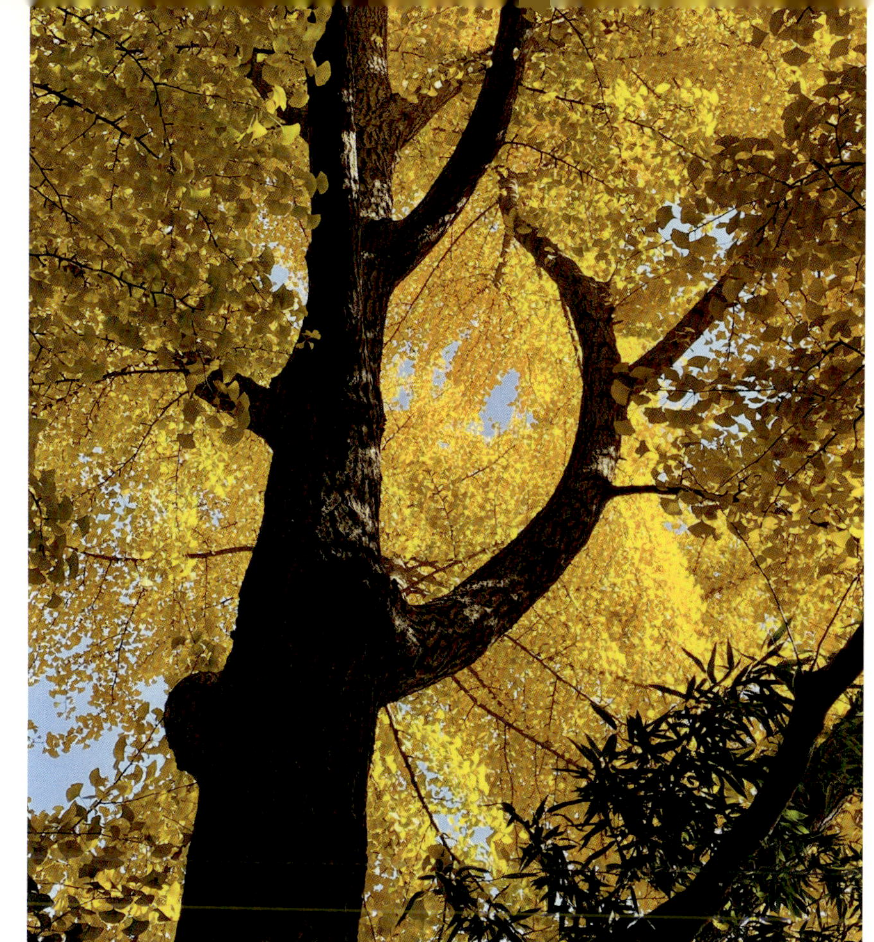

The Ginkgo Biloba tree, a living fossil, can live to be 1,000 years old. No tree can make the yellow of China shine more splendidly in autumn. It already impressed Goethe and Darwin. At the turn of the century, the ginkgo was named "Tree of the Millennium". In Chinese philosophy, the two-part leaf shape stands for yin (gentleness) and yang (vitality).

Der Ginko-Biloba, ein lebendes Fossil, kann 1000 Jahre alt werden. Kein Baum bringt das Gelb Chinas im Herbst prächtiger zum Strahlen. Er beeindruckte schon Goethe und Darwin. Zur Jahrhundertwende wurde der Ginkgo zum Baum des Jahrtausends gekürt. In der chinesischen Philosophie steht die zweiteilige Blattform für Yin (Sanftheit) und Yang (Lebenskraft).

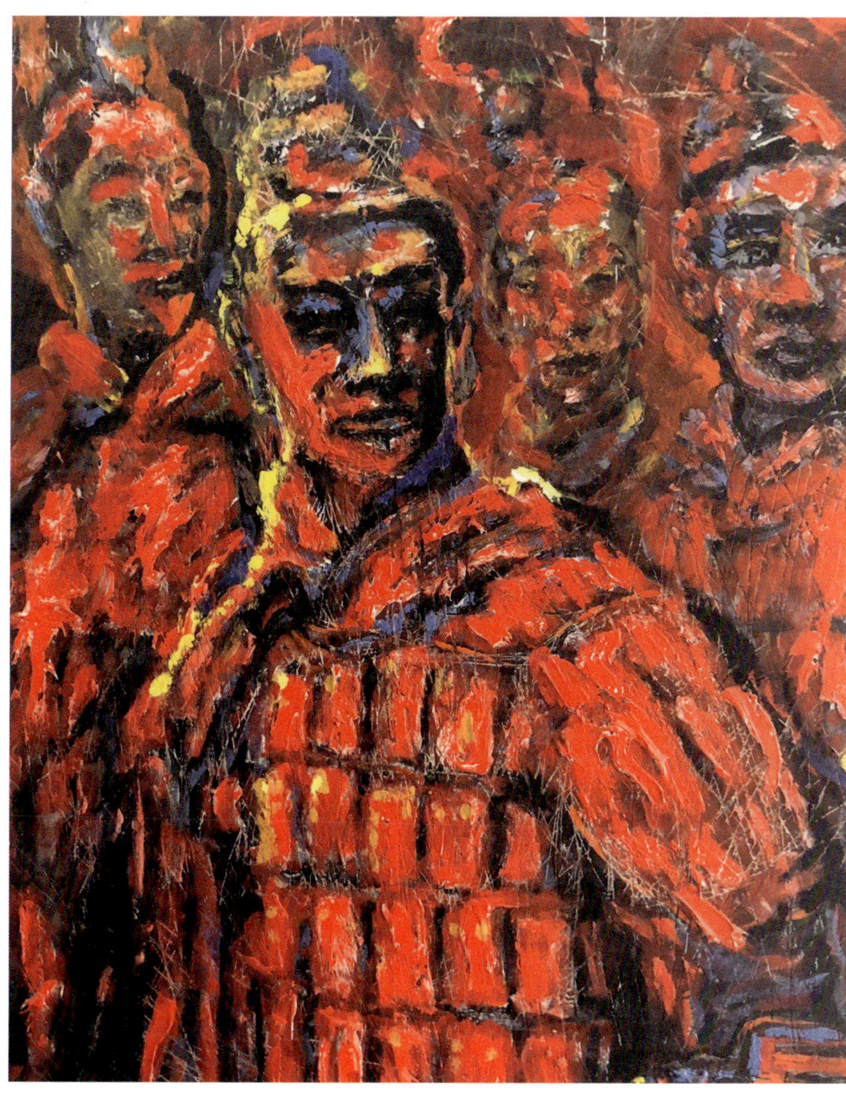

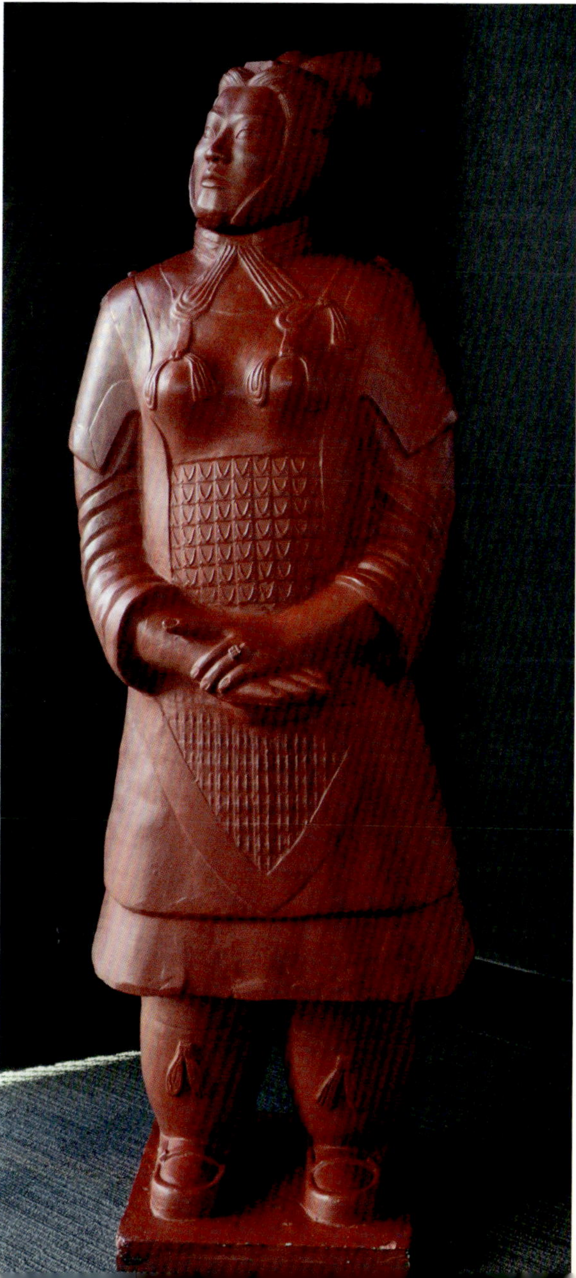

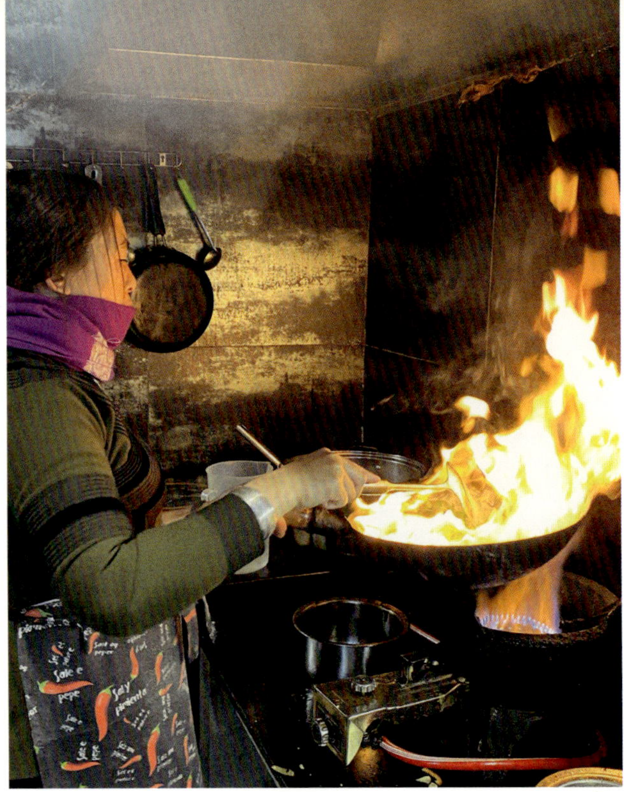

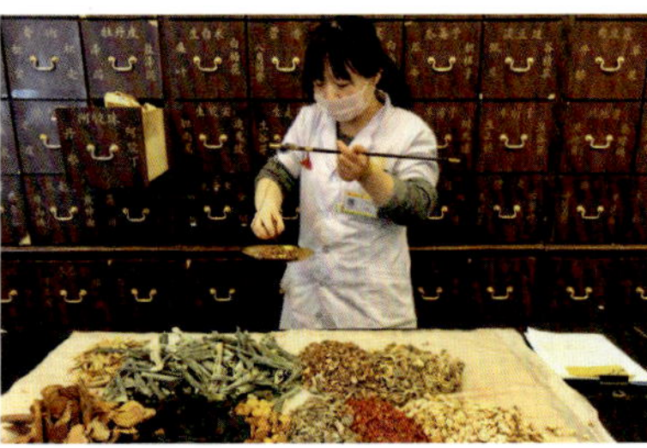

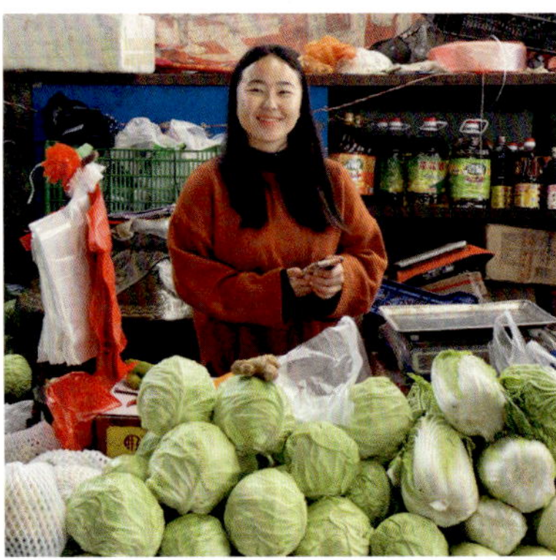

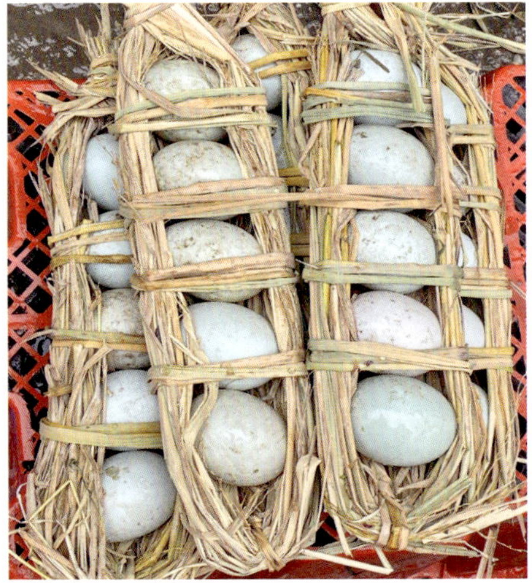

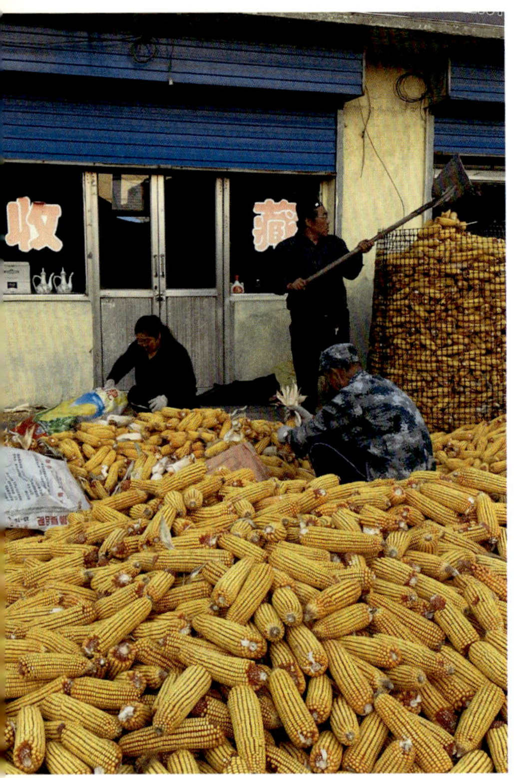
收

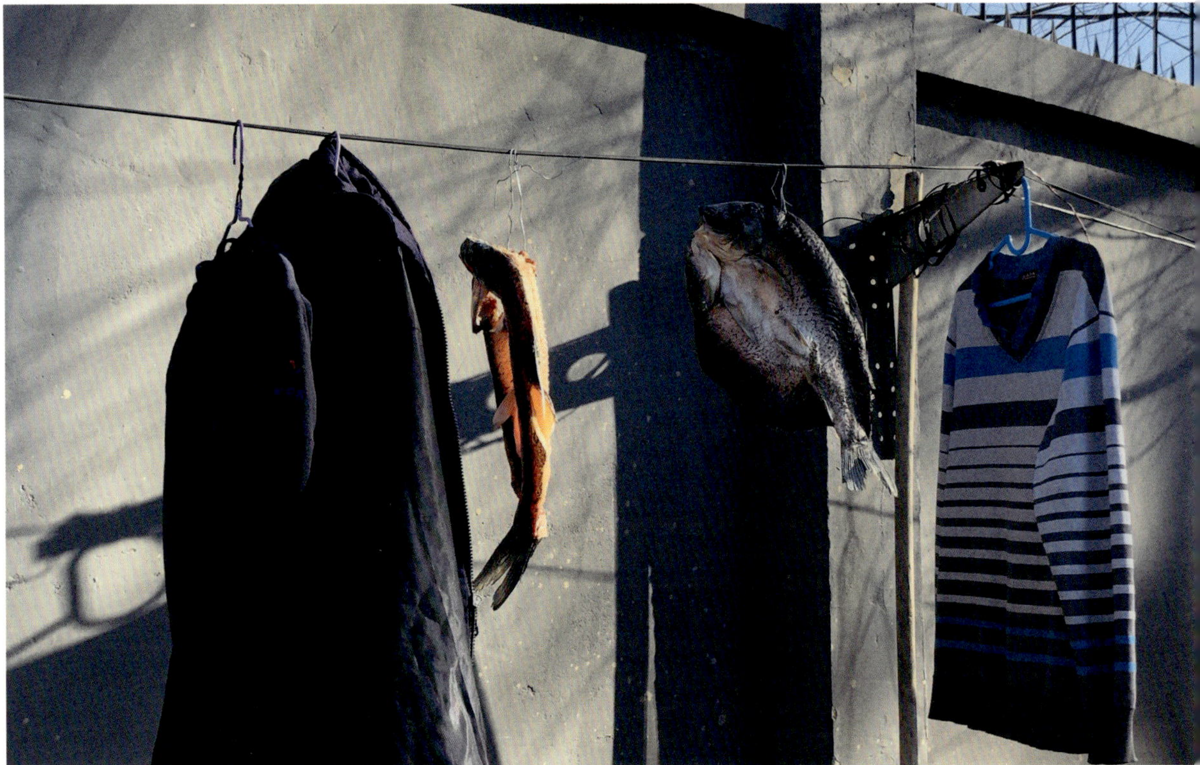

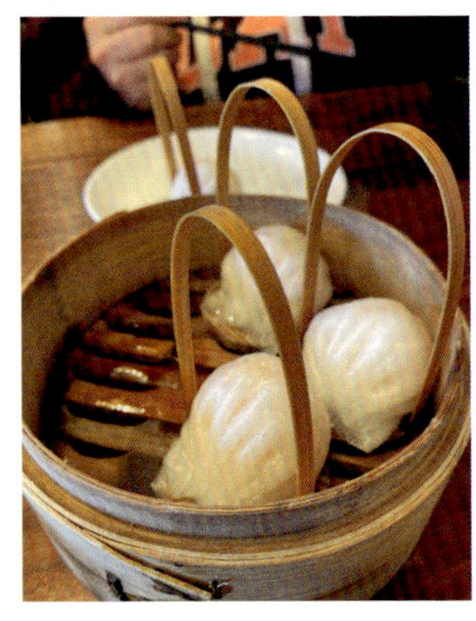

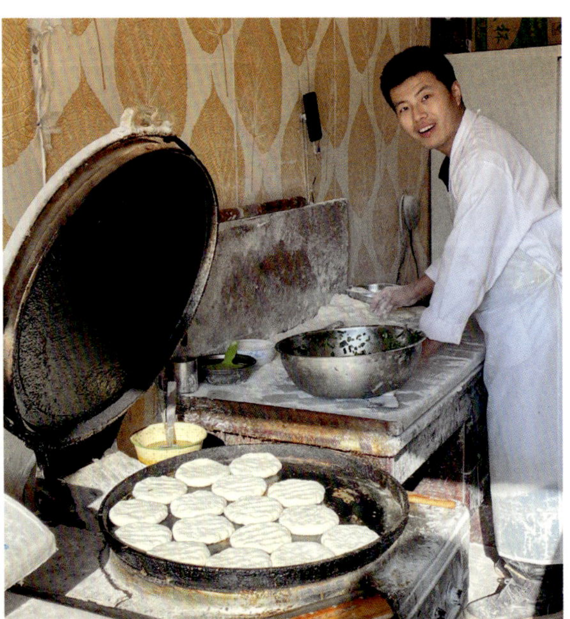

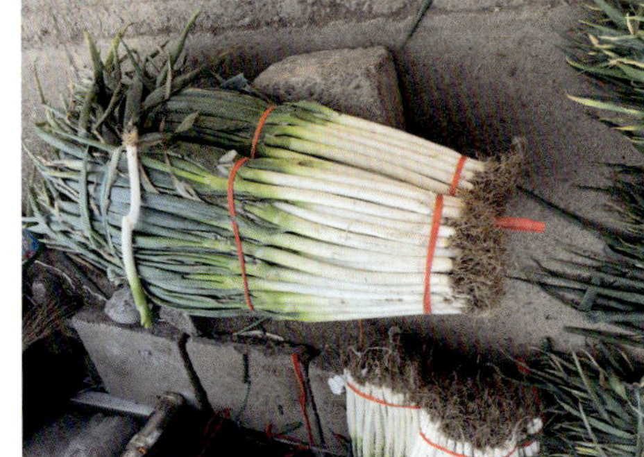

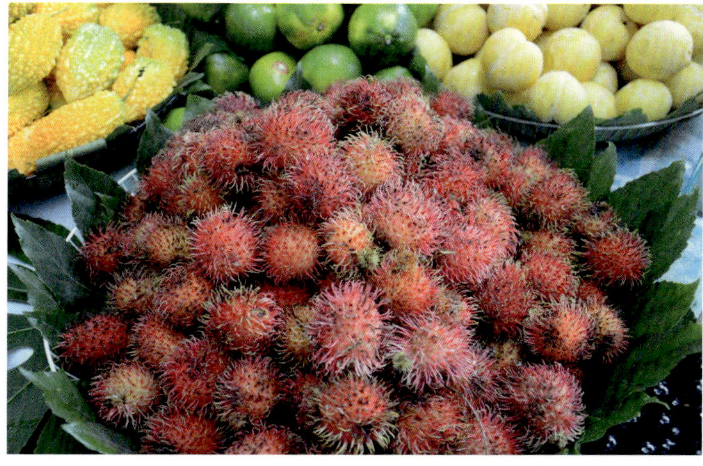

What distinguishes Chinese cuisine is its diversity. Vegetables, herbs, fish and meat usually come fresh from the market. In China, food is more than nutrition: It is the art of balancing soul and body with nourishing "means of life". Roughly speaking, food is eaten salty in the north, sour in the east, sweet in the south and spicy in the west. Whether mushrooms, dates, bamboo shoots or cilantro, chili and tea leaves, fish and seafood or classic Peking duck, tofu, soybeans, hand-pulled fresh noodles, *dim sum*, *jiaozi*, *jianbing* or Chinese cabbage, two ingredients cannot be missing: garlic and ginger.

Was die chinesische Küche auszeichnet, ist ihre Vielfalt. Gemüse, Kräuter, Fisch und Fleisch stammen meistens frisch vom Markt. Essen ist in China mehr als Ernährung: Es ist die Kunst, Seele und Körper mit „Lebens-Mitteln" auszubalancieren. Grob eingeordnet lässt sich sagen, dass im Norden Chinas salzig, im Osten sauer, im Süden süß und im Westen scharf gegessen wird. Ob Pilze, Datteln, Bambussprossen oder Koriander, Chili und Teeblätter, Fisch und Meeresfrüchte oder klassische Peking-Ente, Tofu, Sojabohnen, handgezogene frische Nudeln, *Dim Sum*, *Jiaozi*, *Jianbing* oder Chinakohl, zwei Zutaten dürfen nicht fehlen: Knoblauch und Ingwer.

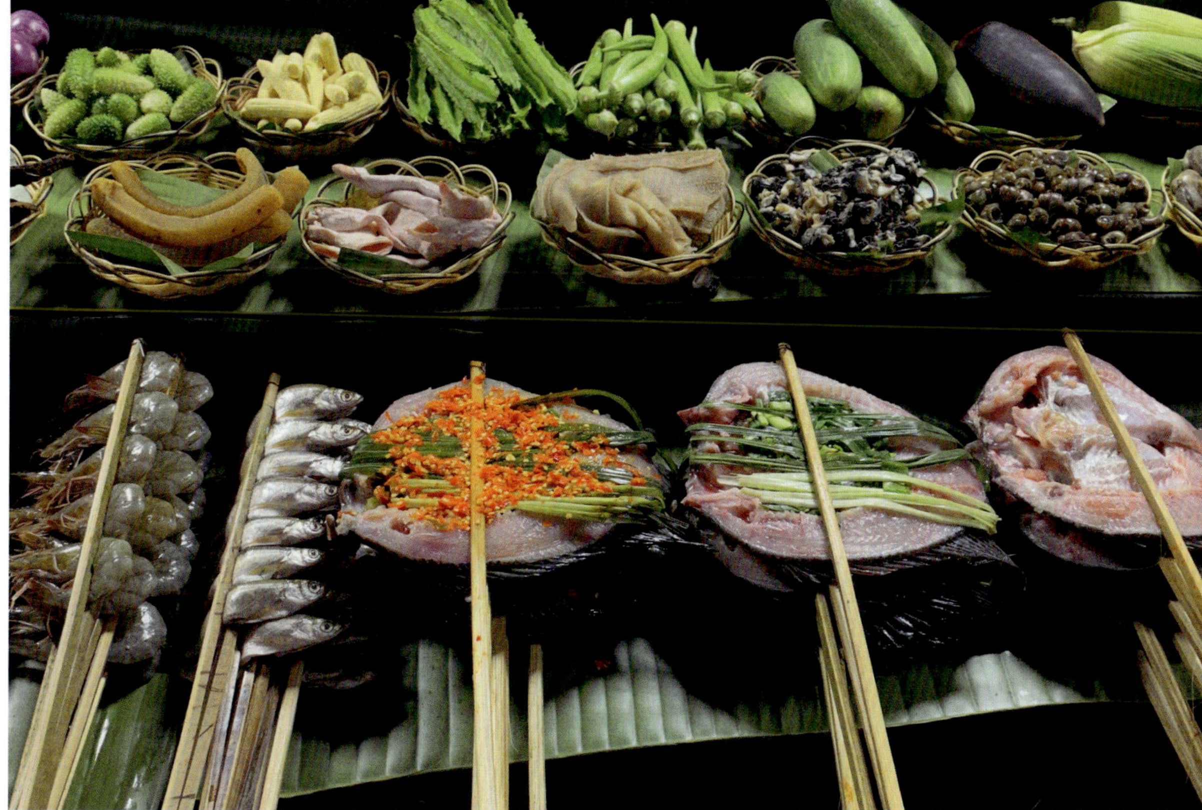

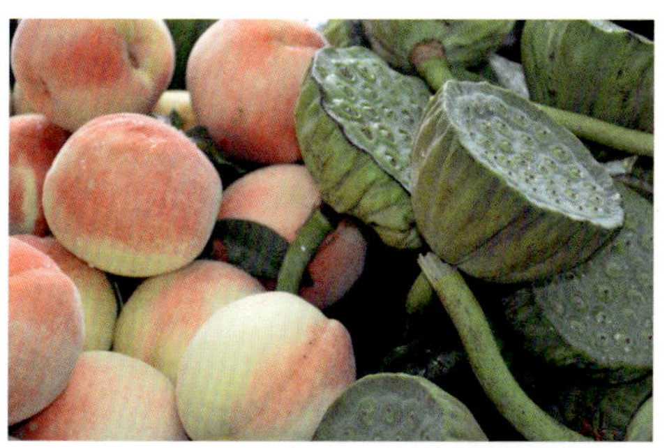

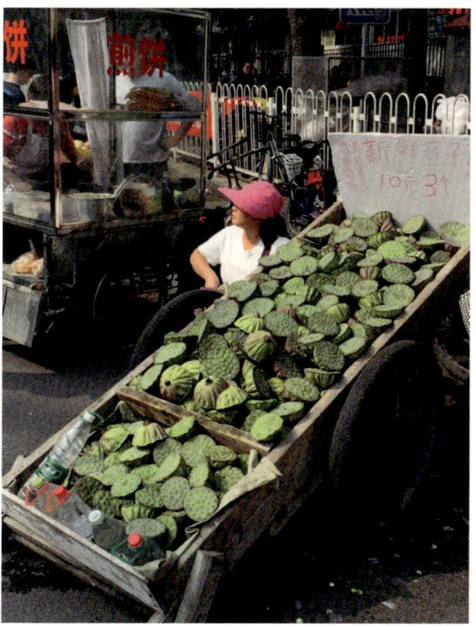

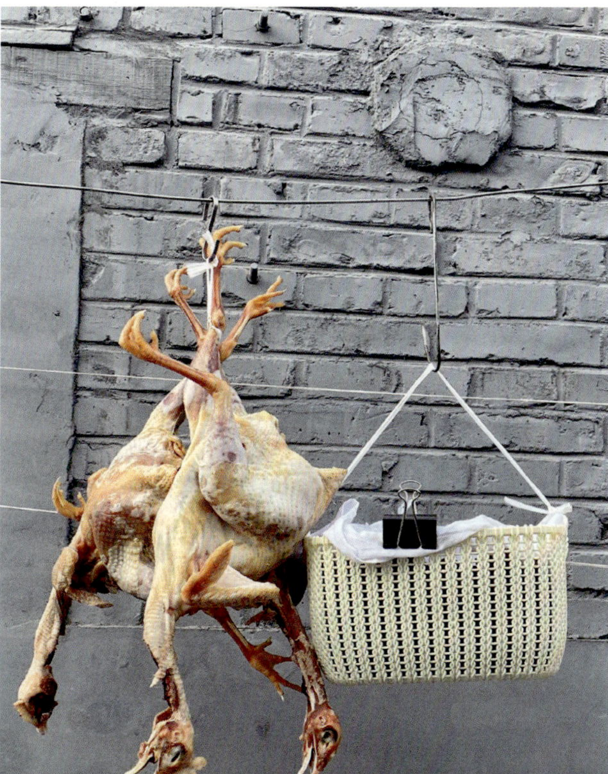

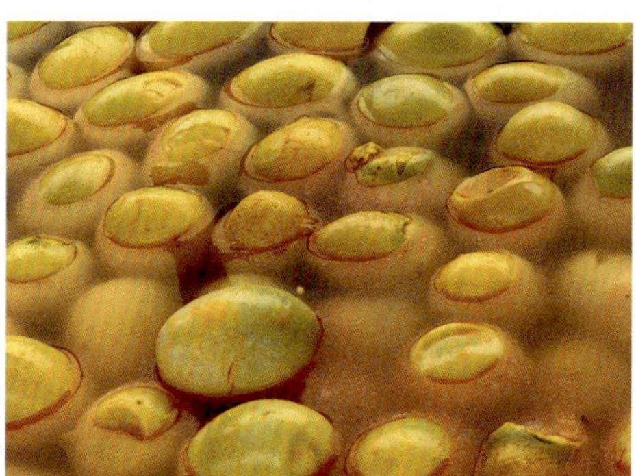

Grey-colourful China in the 21st century

Grau-buntes China im 21. Jahrhundert

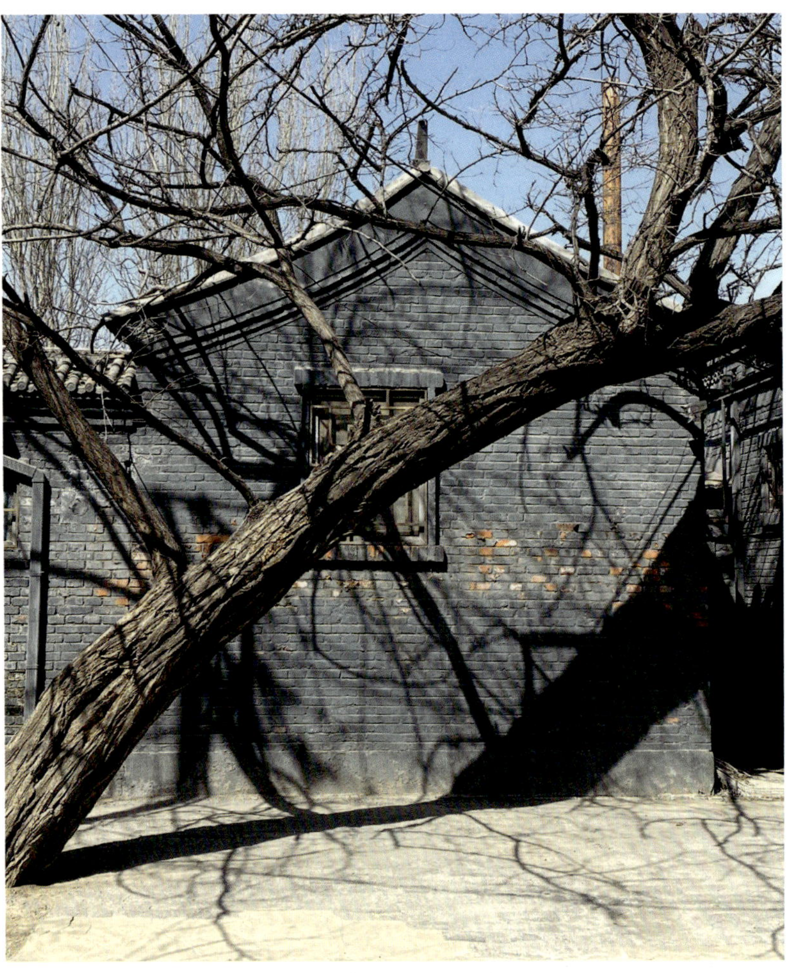

Ein architektonisches Erbe dieser nach innen gekehrten Sichtweise sind die mausgrauen *Siheyuan*, traditionelle Vierseithöfe, die in ganz China und besonders häufig in und um Peking anzutreffen sind. Diese Innenhofresidenzen stellen ein wichtiges kulturelles Element der Stadt Peking dar. Mauer an Mauer streng nach Feng-Shui-Regeln gebaut, lag der Hauseingang idealerweise Richtung Süden. So ergaben sich lange, schmale Ost-West-Gassen, die man *Hutong* nannte. Das Wort „Hutong" ist mongolischen Ursprungs und bedeutet „Quelle" oder „Wasserbrunnen". Stadtteile wurden gebildet, indem man einen *Hutong* mit einem anderen verband. Die diversen Namen wurden dann je nach Standort, lokalem Wahrzeichen oder Geschäft vergeben. Der *Yangshi-Hutong* heißt auch heute noch Schafmarkt-*Hutong*, und der Name *Yizi-Hutong*, verrät, dass in dieser Gasse die Seifenmacher lebten und arbeiteten. Bereits seit der Yuan-Dynastie (1279–1368) gibt es *Hutongs* in Peking.

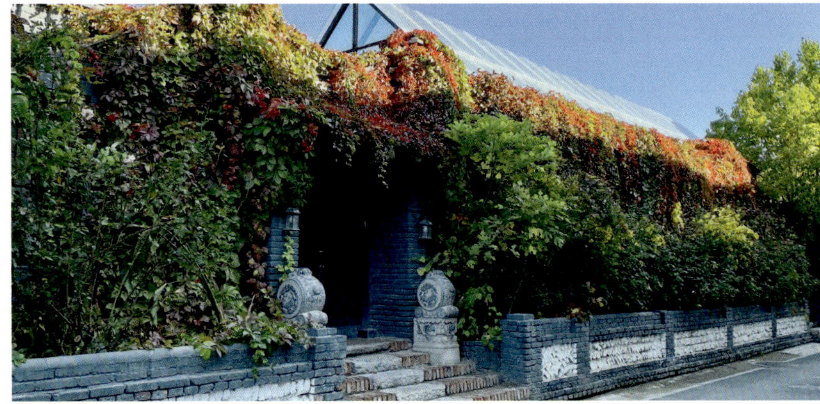

One architectural legacy of this inward-looking view is the mouse-grey *siheyuan*, traditional four-sided courtyards found throughout China and especially common in and around Beijing. These courtyard residences represent an important cultural element of Beijing. Built wall to wall and strictly according to the rules of feng shui, the house entrances ideally faced south. This resulted in long, narrow east-west alleys called *hutongs*. The *hutongs* are the roots of traditional Chinese life. The word is of Mongolian origin and means "spring" or "water well".

Districts were formed by connecting one *hutong* to another. The various names were then given depending on the location, local landmark or business. The *Yangshi Hutong* is still called Sheep Market *Hutong*, and the name *Yizi Hutong* reveals that soap makers lived and worked in this alley. There have been *hutongs* in Beijing as early as the Yuan Dynasty (1279–1368).

Above:
The two stones to the right and left of the house entrance, which are designed either as circular military drums or rectangular stone blocks in the form of books, reveal whether the former resident was in military service or as an official for the imperial court.

Oben:
Die beiden Steine rechts und links vom Hauseingang, die entweder als kreisrunde Militärtrommeln oder rechteckige Steinquader in Form von Büchern ausgeführt sind, verraten, ob der ehemalige Bewohner im Militärdienst oder als Beamter für den Kaiserhof tätig war.

Right page:
The red ribbons with writing are traditionally used on Chinese New Year and are mostly blessings for the residents. However, they are also used for party propaganda slogans.

Rechte Seite:
Die roten Schriftbänder werden traditionell am chinesischen Neujahrfest angebracht und sind meistens Segenswünsche für die Bewohner. Sie werden aber auch für Propagandasprüche der Partei gebraucht.

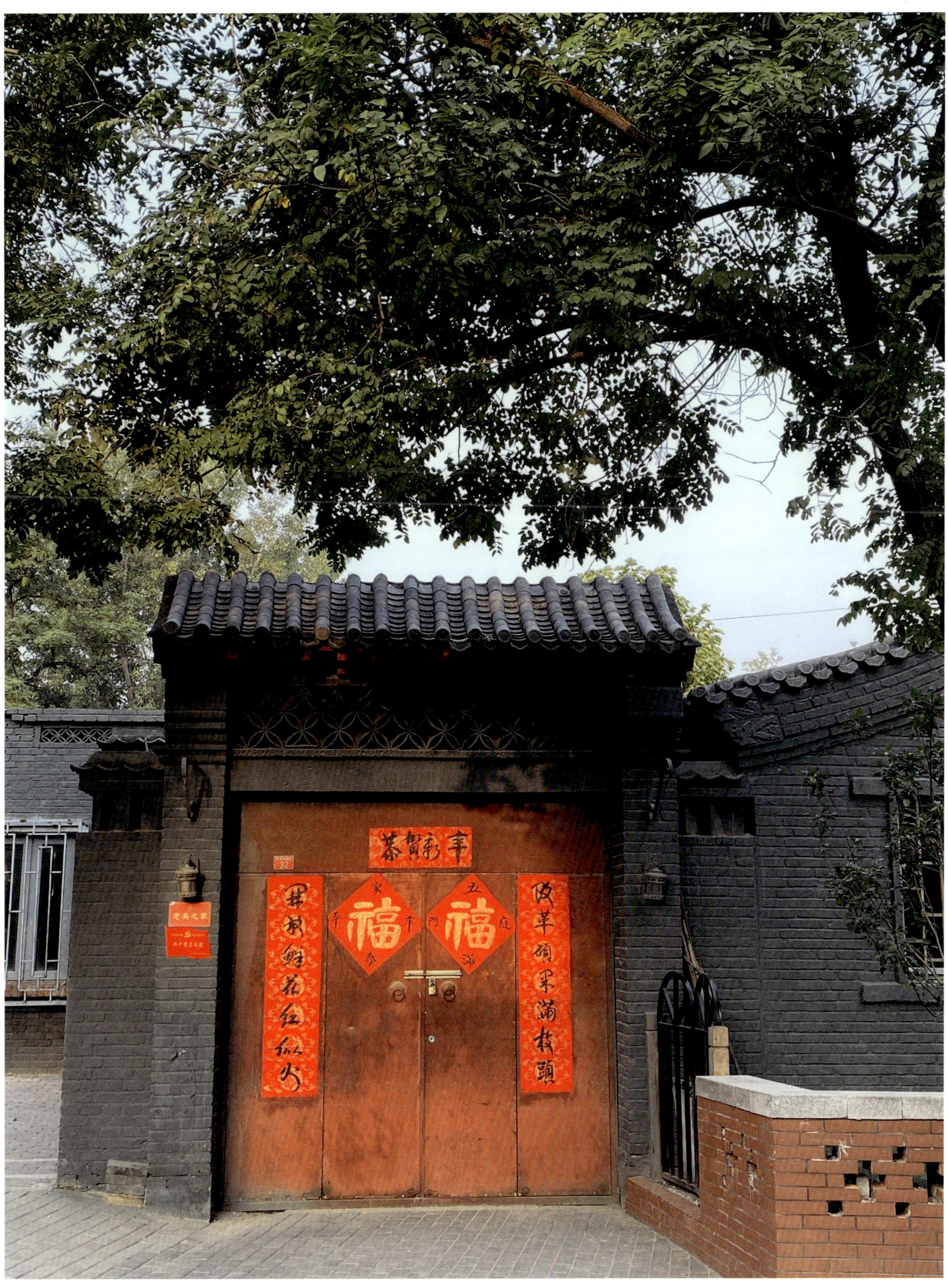
32
福
福
改革碩果滿枝頭

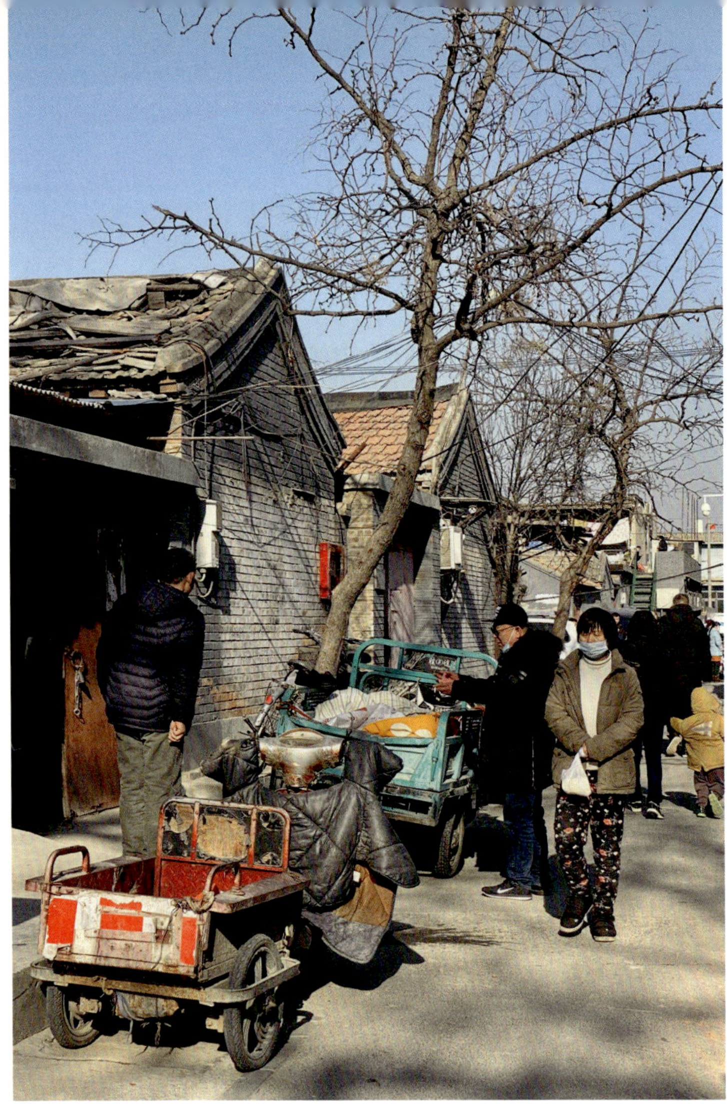

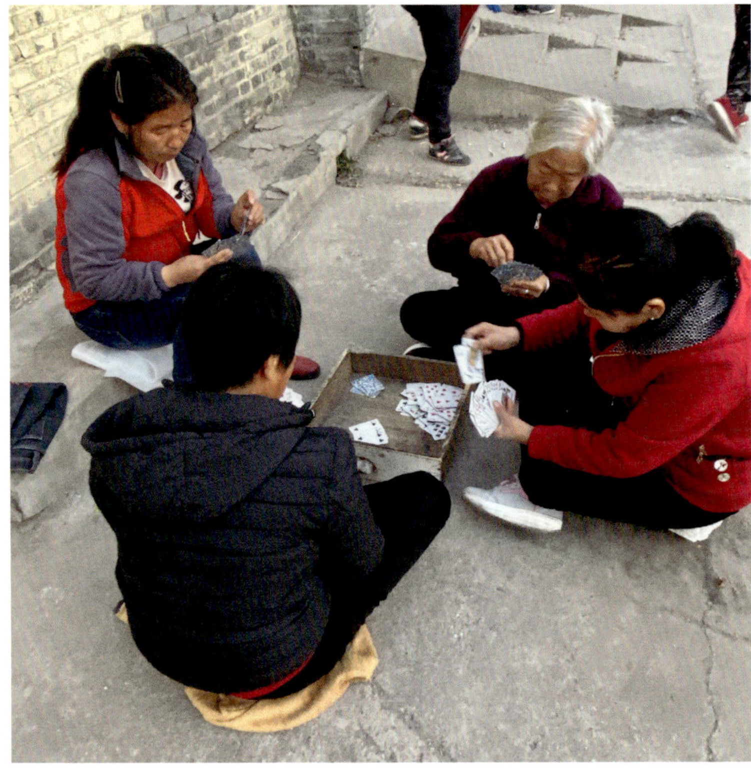

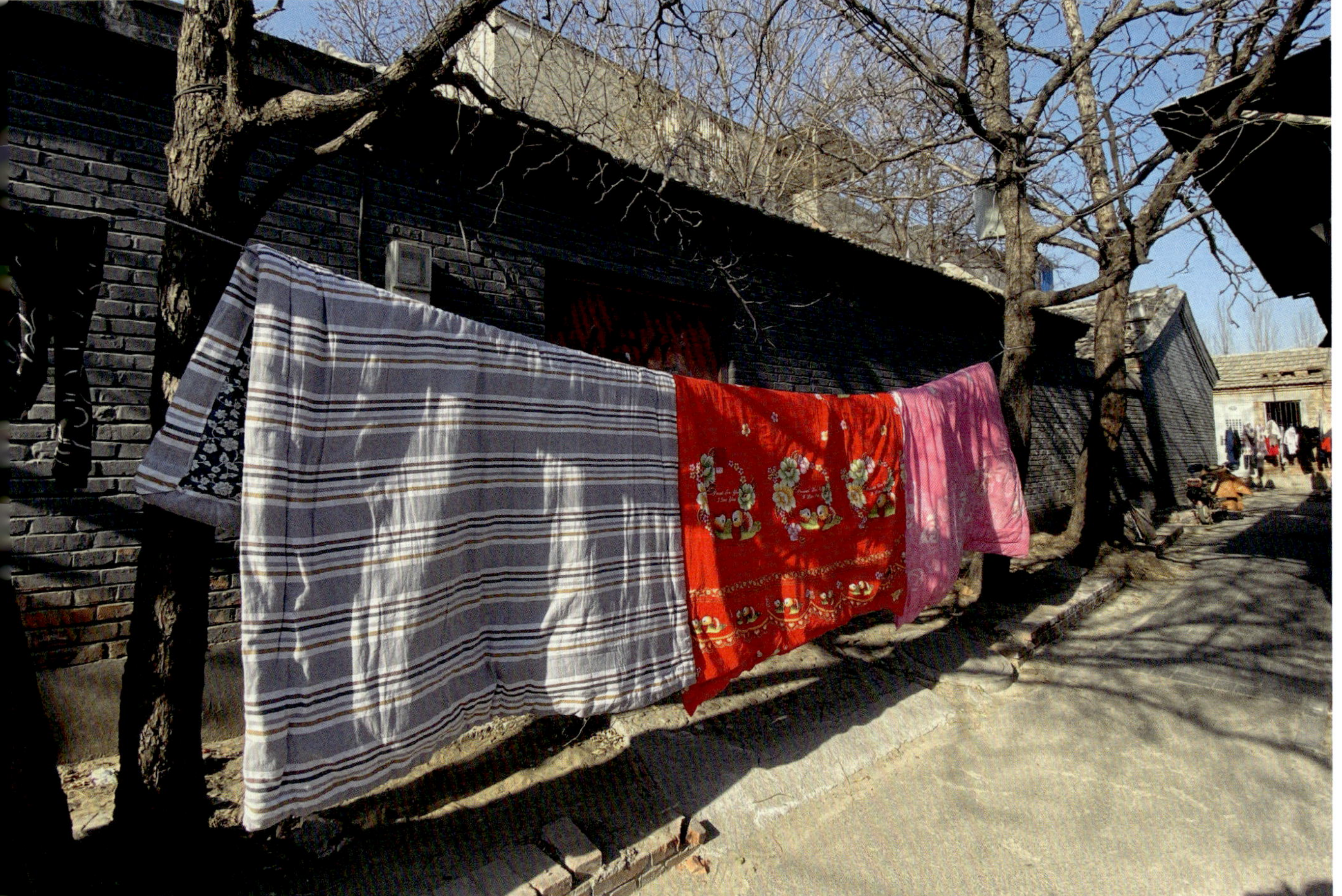

Everyday situations in China: Playing cards after a midday nap is a popular pastime among women, as is playing mah-jongg among men.

Alltagsituationen in China: Ein Kartenspiel nach dem Mittagsschläfchen für die Damen oder eine Runde Mah-Jongg für die Herren

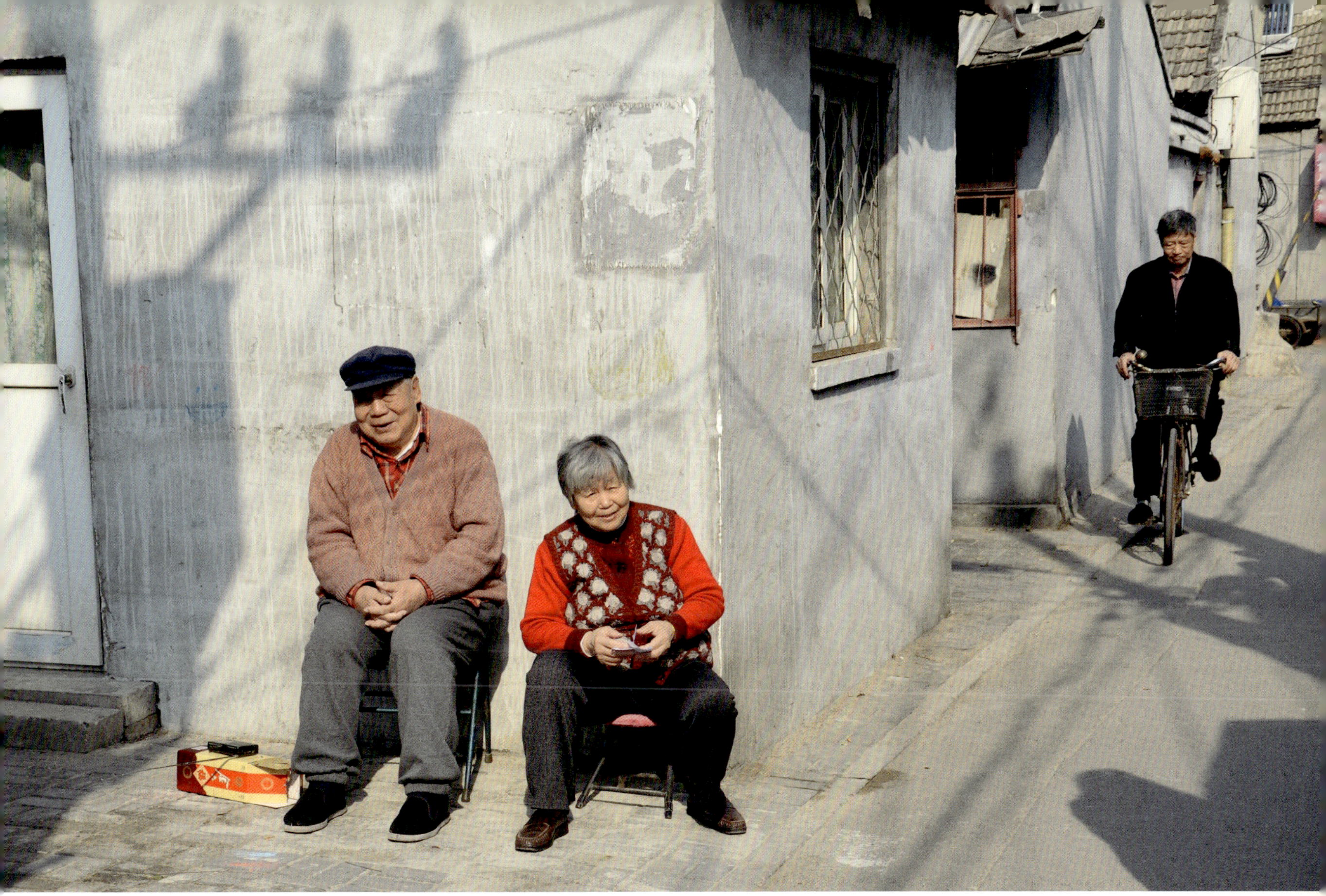

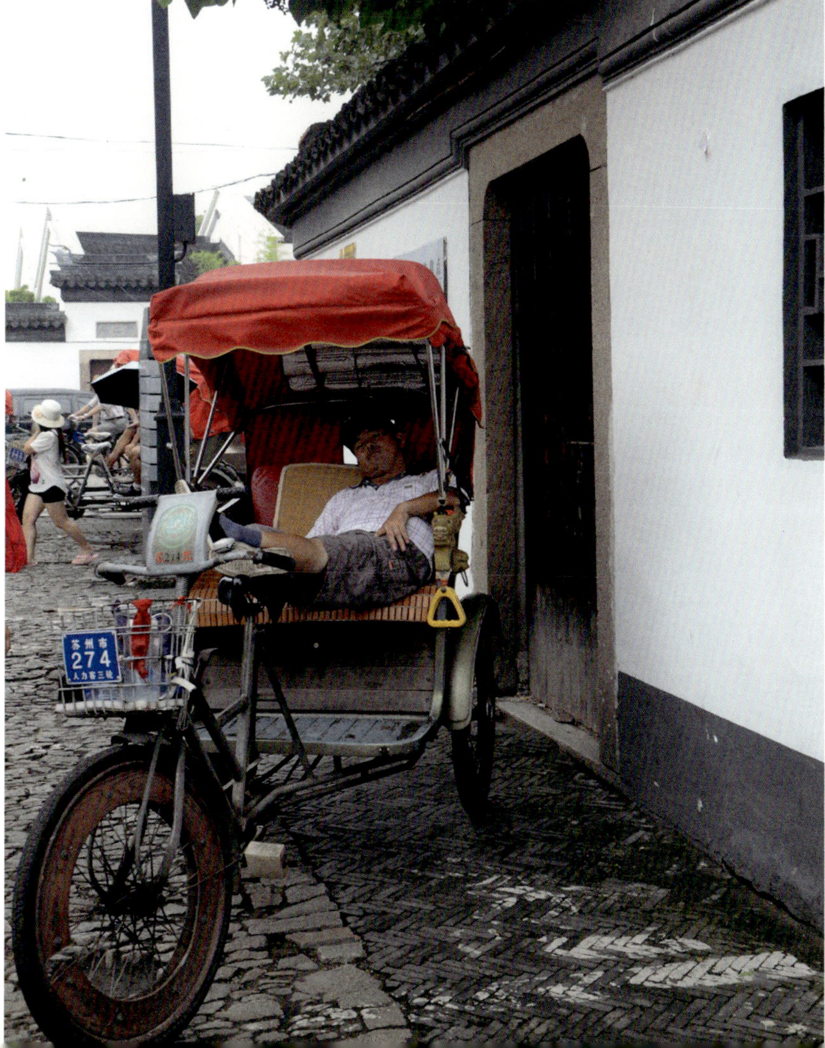
苏州市
274
人力客三轮

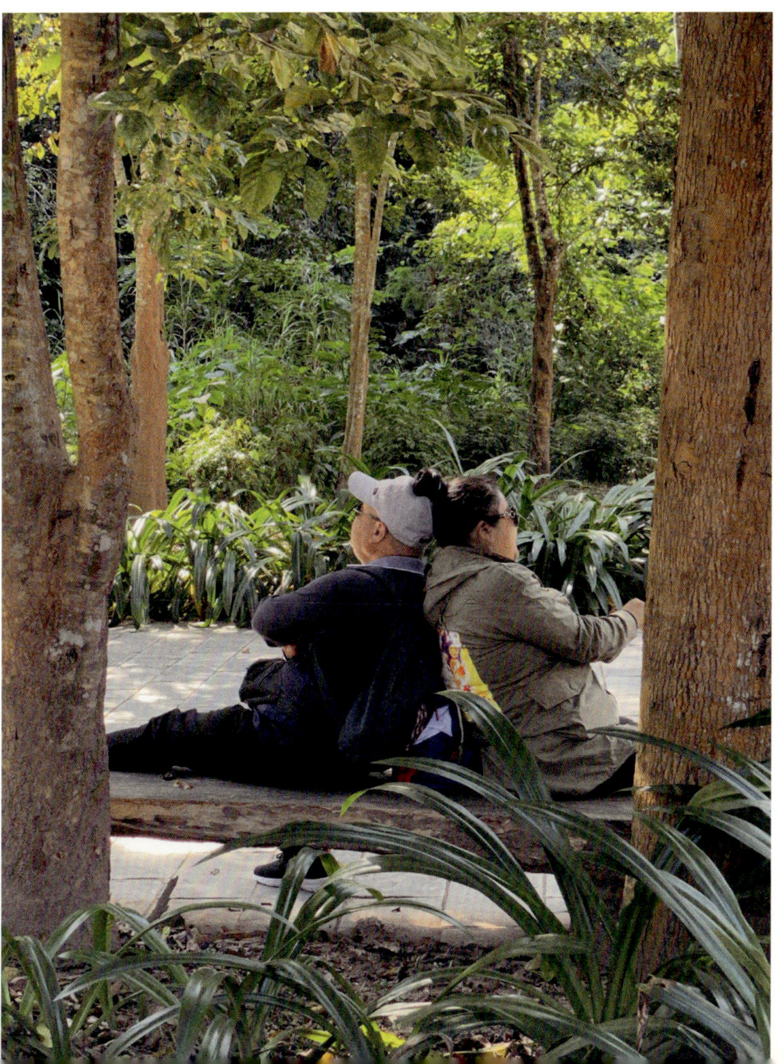

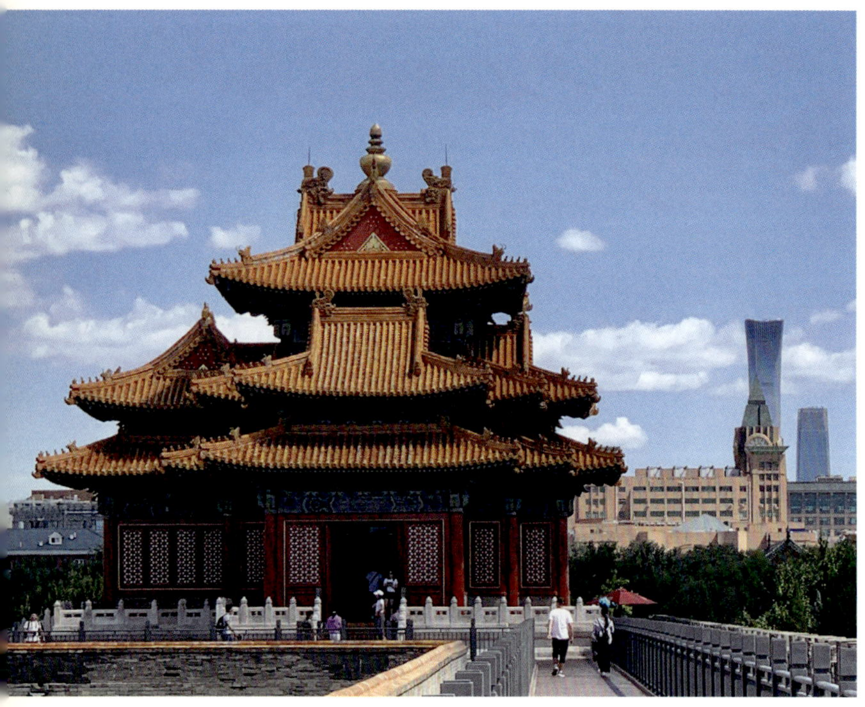

A *zun*, a historic Chinese bronze vessel type used in religious ceremonies to drink or heat wine, is said to have been the inspiration for Kohn Pedersen Fox's architects for client CITIC Heye Investment in designing Beijing's tallest skyscraper at 528 metres. The skyscraper in the Central Business District, with its unusual "waisted" shape, is currently the ninth tallest in the world and is also still affectionately known as the "Flower Vase". The iconic new landmark changes width in height from 78 metres at the base to 54 at the waist and 69 metres at the top. Because Beijing is located in an earthquake zone, extensive safety measures and stability had to be taken into account during planning and construction.

An einem *Zun*, einem historischen, chinesischen Gefäßtyp aus Bronze, der bei religiösen Zeremonien zum Trinken oder Erwärmen von Wein gebraucht wurde, inspirierten sich angeblich die Architekten von Kohn Pedersen Fox für den Auftraggeber CITIC Heye Investment beim Design des mit 528 Metern höchsten Wolkenkratzers von Peking. Das Hochhaus im Central Business District mit der außergewöhnlichen, „taillierten" Form ist derzeit das neunthöchste der Welt und wird auch liebevoll „Blumenvase" genannt. Das ikonische neue Wahrzeichen ändert seine Breite im Höhenverlauf von 78 Metern an der Basis zu 54 an der „Taille" und 69 Metern an der Spitze. Weil Peking in einer Erdbebenzone liegt, musste bei Planung und Errichtung auf umfassende Sicherheitsmaßnahmen und Stabilität geachtet werden.

The higher their social status, the closer citizens were allowed to live to the imperial palace. Aristocrats lived directly east and west of the palace walls. The large *siheyuan* of high-ranking officials and wealthy merchants were decorated with beautifully carved and painted roof beams. They usually had a brightly painted walkway around the carefully landscaped courtyard garden. Further away from the palace to the north and south, citizens, merchants, craftsmen and workers lived in much smaller and simpler *siheyuan*. The structure of these farms followed the same rules as in the villages in the countryside. The *hutongs* are the roots of traditional Chinese life.

Nowhere in Beijing is it quieter and shadier in high summer than in the narrow alleys of the *hutongs*. In the morning, older people from Beijing meet in the small squares for dancing, singing or shadow boxing. Others walk their bird in a cage or their dog without a leash. Shortly before noon, people pick up fresh noodles, tofu, vegetables and meat from one of the numerous vendors lining the narrow streets. Here also the hairdresser has put out his chair, and at 12 noon sharp aromatic smells waft from the many small food stalls. The short nap is essential for young and old from the Chinese point of view for a healthy life. It is not dispensed with either in the ultra-modern office building or outside on the go: There is always a place for naps.

Desto höher der soziale Status war, desto näher durften die Bürger am Kaiserpalast wohnen. Aristokraten lebten direkt östlich und westlich der Palastmauern. Die großen *Siheyuan* der hochrangigen Beamten und wohlhabenden Kaufleute wurden mit wunderschön geschnitzten und bemalten Dachbalken verziert. Meist hatten sie einen bunt bemalten Wandelgang um den sorgfältig angelegten Innenhofgarten. Weiter vom Palast entfernt im Norden und Süden lebten Bürger, Kaufleute, Handwerker und Arbeiter in wesentlich kleineren und einfacheren *Siheyuan*. Der Aufbau der *Siheyuan* folgt den gleichen Regeln in den Dörfern auf dem Land. Die *Hutongs* sind die Wurzeln des traditionellen chinesischen Lebens.

Nirgendwo ist es ruhiger und schattiger im Pekinger Hochsommer als in den schmalen Gassen der *Hutongs*. Am Vormittag treffen sich die älteren Pekinger auf den kleinen Plätzen zum Tanzen, Singen oder Schattenboxen. Andere wiederum führen ihren Vogel im Käfig oder den Hund ohne Leine spazieren. Kurz vor Mittag holt man sich frische Nudeln, Tofu, Gemüse und Fleisch bei einem der zahlreichen die engen Gassen säumenden Händler. Hier hat auch der Frisör seinen Stuhl rausgestellt, und um Punkt 12 Uhr riecht es köstlich aus den vielen kleinen Essensstuben. Der kurze Mittagsschlaf ist wesentlich für Jung und Alt aus der chinesischen Sicht des gesunden Lebens. Auf ihn wird weder im hochmodernen Bürogebäude noch unterwegs verzichtet. Ein Plätzchen findet sich dafür immer.

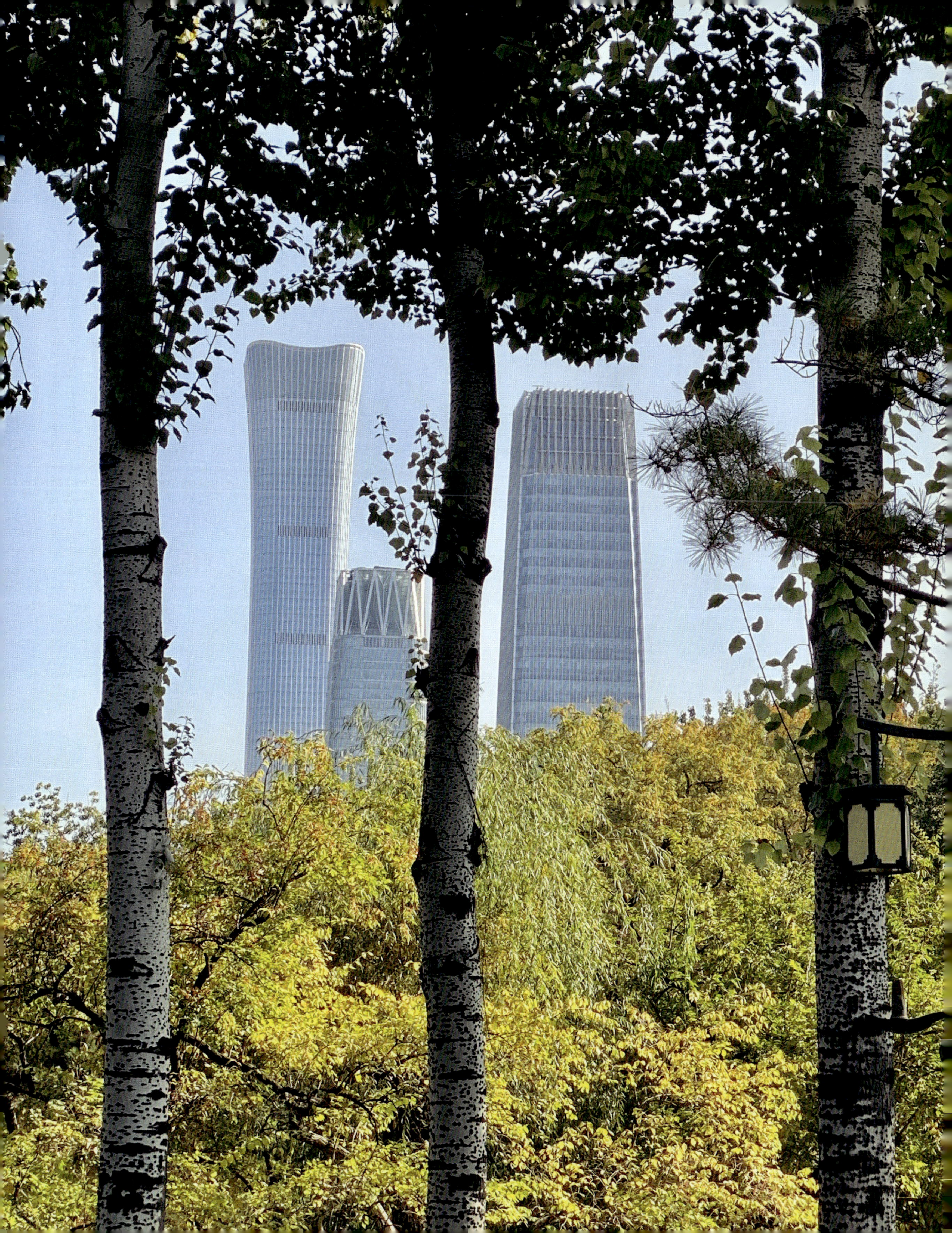

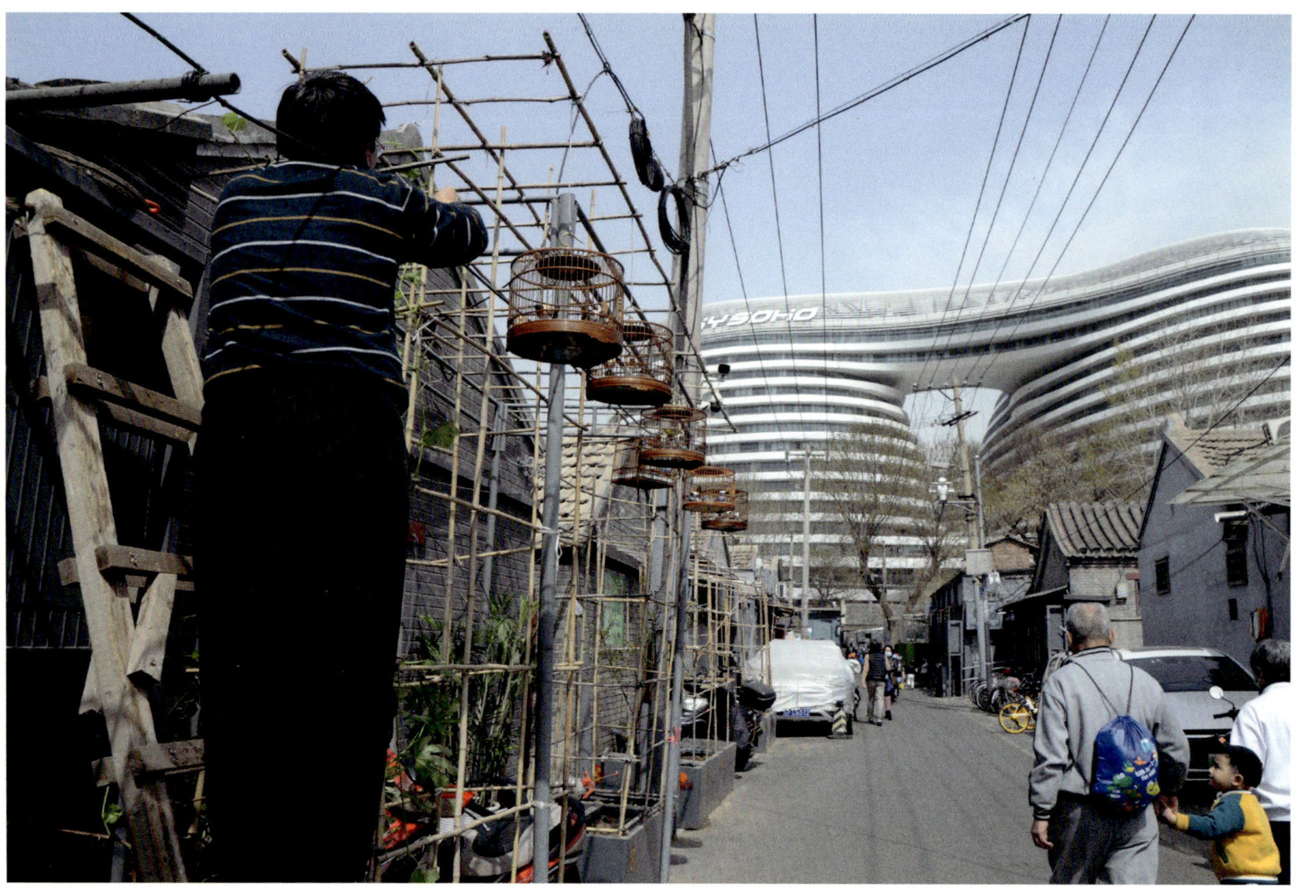

Futuristic modernity and resonant history come close in the *hutong* alleys around the historically significant Zihua, the music temple built in 1443 by Ming Dynasty eunuch Wang Zhen, and the Galaxy Soho shopping and office temple, opened in 2012, by famed British-Iraqi architect Zaha Hadid.

Futuristische Moderne und klangvolle Geschichte rücken zusammen in den *Hutong*-Gassen rund um den historisch bedeutenden Zihua-Musiktempel von 1443, erbaut von dem Eunuchen Wang Zhen in der Ming-Dynastie und dem 2012 eröffneten Einkaufs- und Bürotempel Galaxy Soho der berühmten britisch-irakischen Architektin Zaha Hadid.

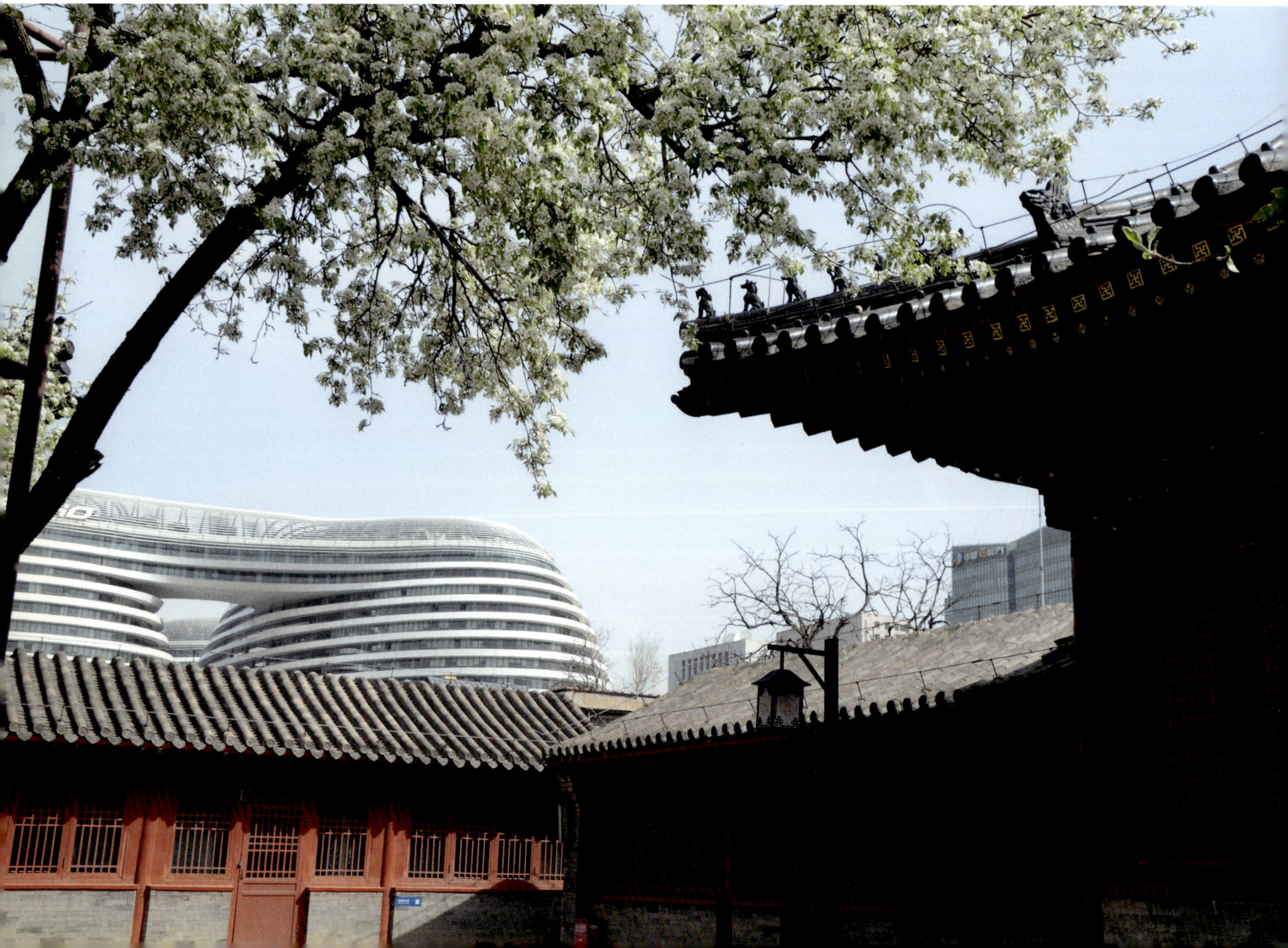

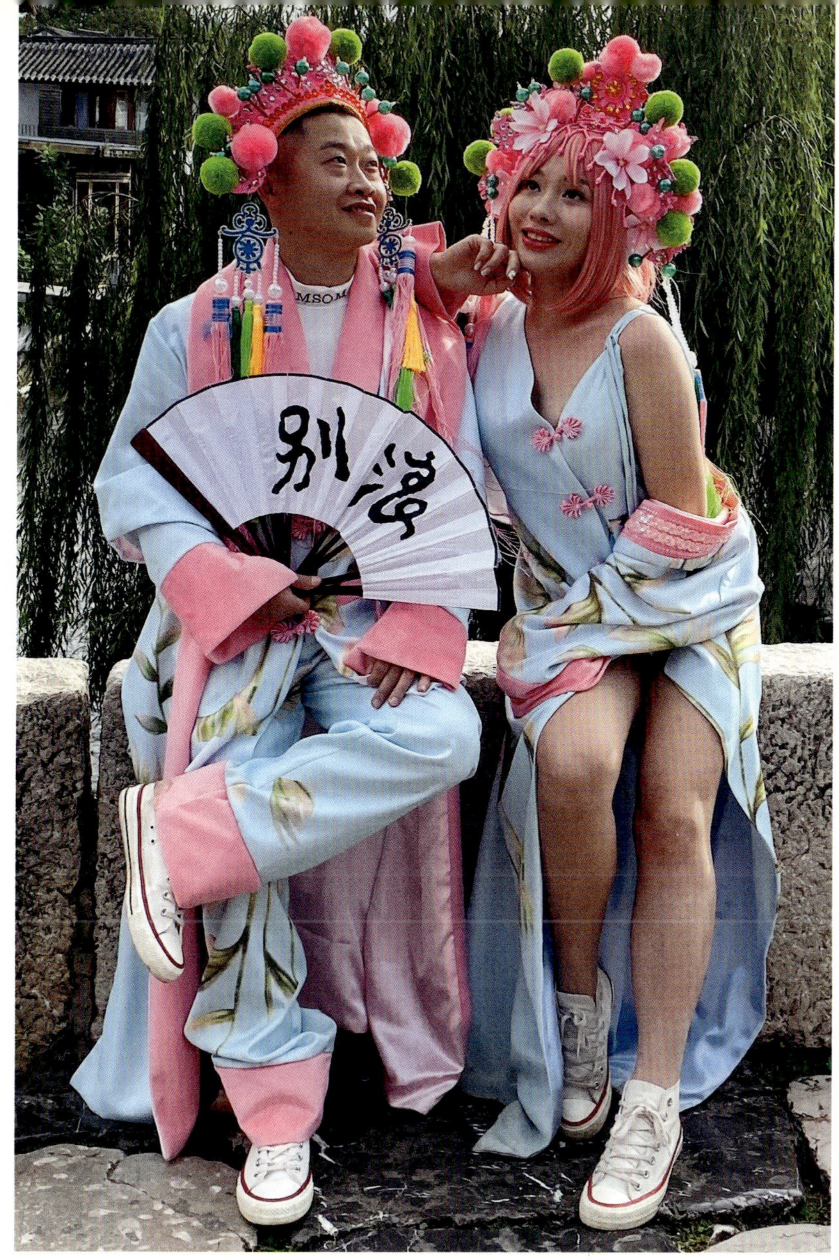

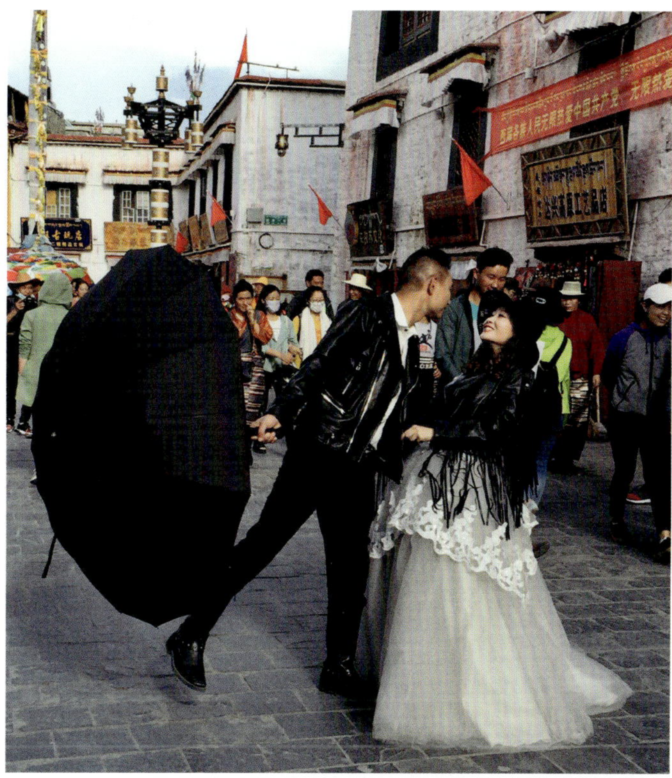

The photos before the wedding are very important in China and are often staged with a lot of creativity and masquerade. The celebration itself is then accompanied by loud fireworks, similar to New Year's Eve, to keep bad vibes away from the upcoming marriage.

Die Fotos vor der Hochzeit sind in China sehr wichtig und werden oft mit viel Kreativität und Maskerade inszeniert. Das Fest selbst wird dann, ähnlich wie Silvester, von lautem Feuerwerk begleitet, um schlechte Schwingungen von der bevorstehenden Ehe fernzuhalten.

Regrettably, these cultural symbols are disappearing from the cityscape faster and faster to make way for new streets and buildings. And in other *hutongs*, excessive renovations are contributing to gentrification. Local natives are increasingly disappearing from downtown, and with them, Beijing's endearing, real-life old culture. Nowhere is a better place to learn mah-jongg or observe what Traditional Chinese Medicine means by healthy living: Kite flying for the old man, prescribed by the doctor as therapy because it is supposed to loosen his tense neck muscles, or walking backwards for the elderly lady to strengthen her sense of balance.

Beijing's urban setting is an unmistakable example of the continual interaction between tradition and modernity: dizzyingly high, glass skyscrapers in the Central Business District, in between hidden isolated old temples with purple borders.

Bedauerlicherweise schwinden diese Kultursymbole immer schneller aus dem Stadtbild, um Platz für neue Straßen und Gebäude zu machen. Übermäßige Renovierungen tragen in wieder anderen *Hutongs* zur Gentrifizierung bei. Die lokalen Einheimischen verschwinden zunehmend aus der Innenstadt und damit die liebenswerte, gelebte alte Kultur Pekings. Nirgendwo kann man besser Mah-Jongg spielen lernen und beobachten, was die traditionelle chinesische Medizin unter gesunder Lebensführung versteht: Das Drachensteigenlassen wird dem alten Mann als Therapie vom Arzt verschrieben, weil es angeblich seine verspannten Nackenmuskeln lockert oder das Rückwärtsgehen der älteren Dame, die ihren Gleichgewichtssinn stärken soll.

Pekings urbanes Bild ist ein unverkennbares Beispiel der ständigen Interaktion zwischen Tradition und Moderne. Schwindelerregend hohe gläserne Wolkenkratzer im Central Business District und vereinzelt dazwischen versteckt ein alter purpurrot umrandeter Tempel.

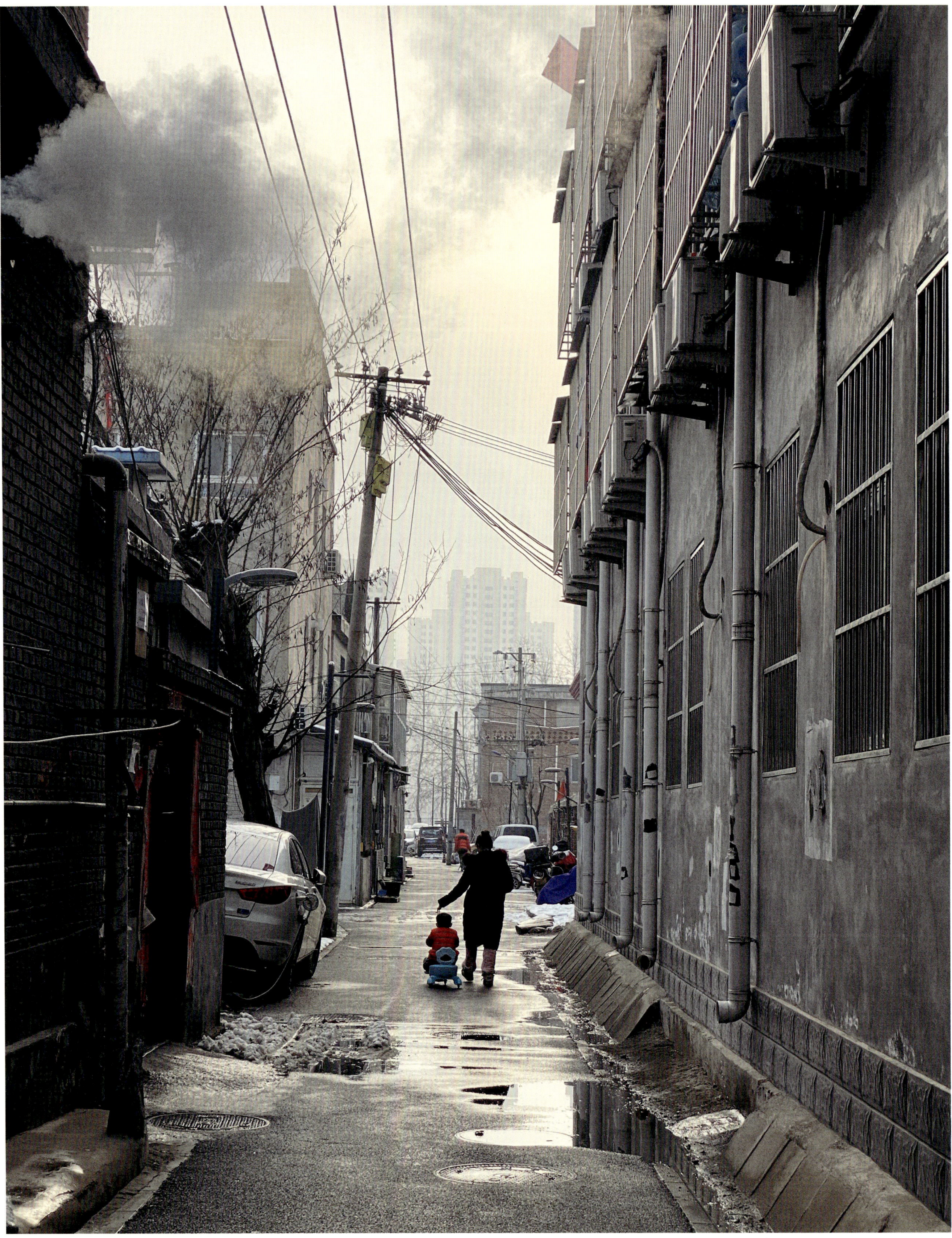

Left page:
In the extremely cold Beijing winter, the alleys seem to be giving off steam.

Linke Seite:
Im extrem kalten Pekinger Winter scheinen die Gassen zu dampfen.

On the frozen lakes of the capital, here at the Summer Palace, ice skating is practiced in winter, but also the practice only popular in Beijing of "ice chair driving" on skates with two pointed metal rods to push.

Auf den zugefrorenen Seen der Hauptstadt, hier am Sommerpalast, wird im Winter Schlittschuh gelaufen, aber auch das nur in Peking übliche und beliebte „Eisstuhlfahren" auf Kufen mit zwei spitzen Metallstangen zum Anschieben praktiziert.

The colourful passenger ferries transport people in Hong Kong since 1888 across the Victoria Harbour between Hong Kong Island and the Kowloon Peninsula. The crossing is worth it just for the unforgettable view over the harbour and the Hong Kong skyline.

Die bunten Personenfähren transportieren in Hongkong seit 1888 die Menschen durch den Victoria Harbour zwischen Hongkong Island und der Halbinsel Kowloon. Die Überfahrt lohnt allein wegen des unvergesslichen Blicks über den Hafen und die Skyline von Hongkong.

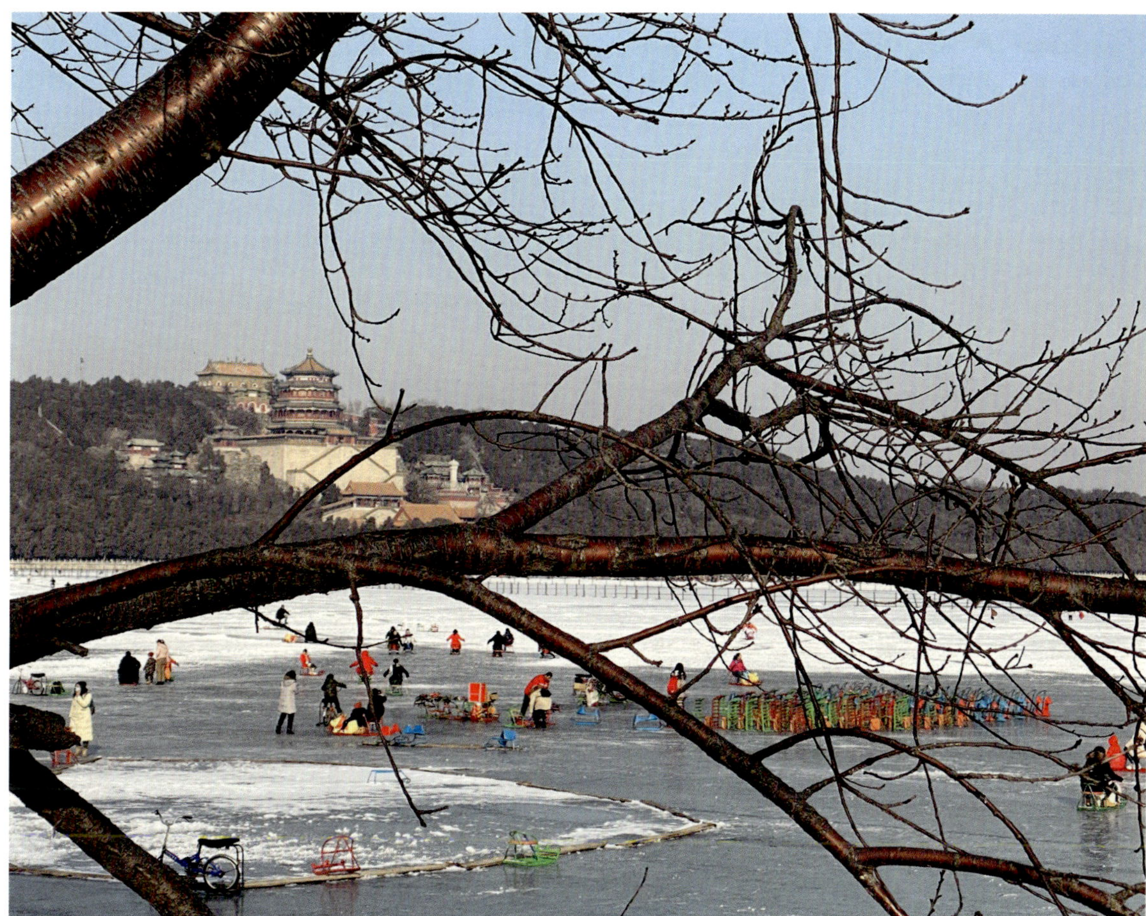

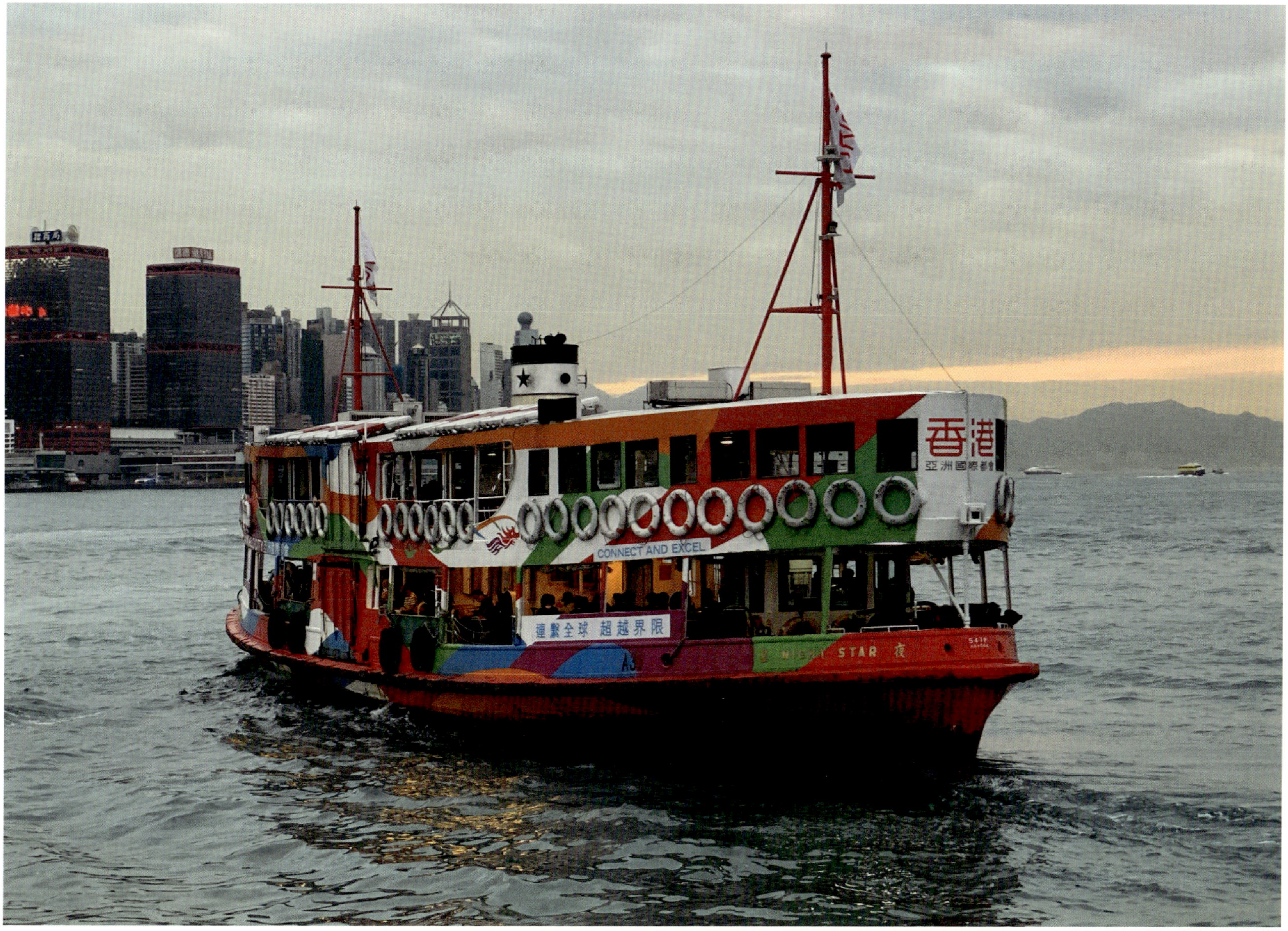

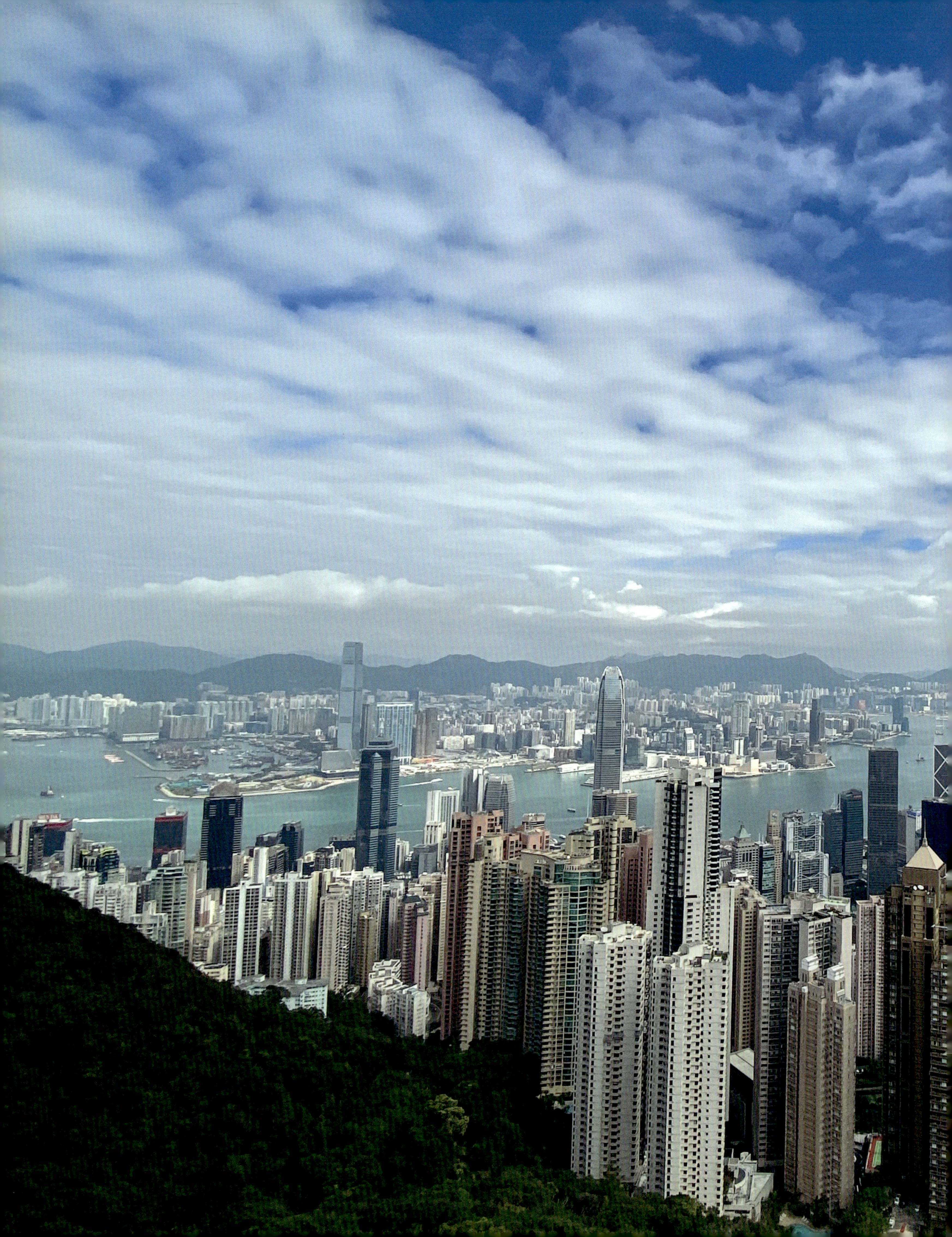

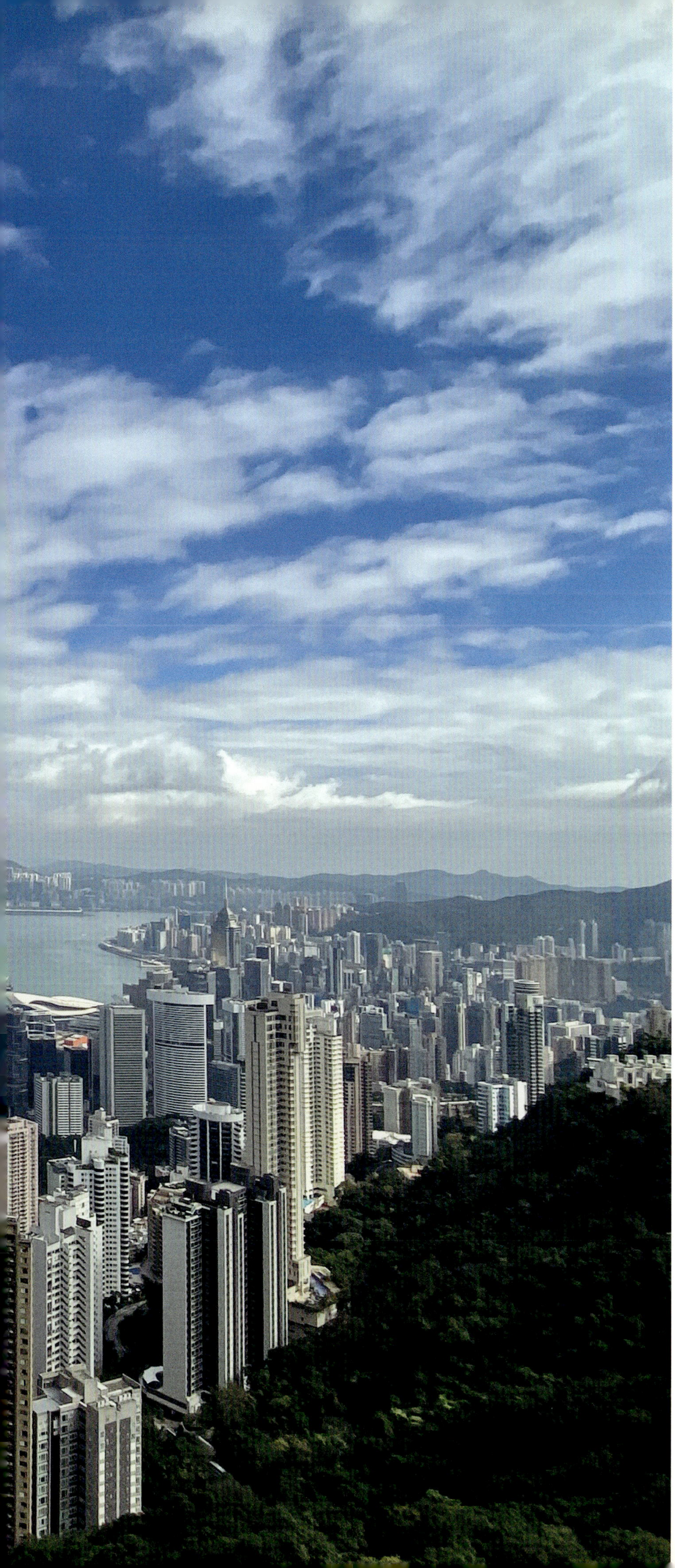

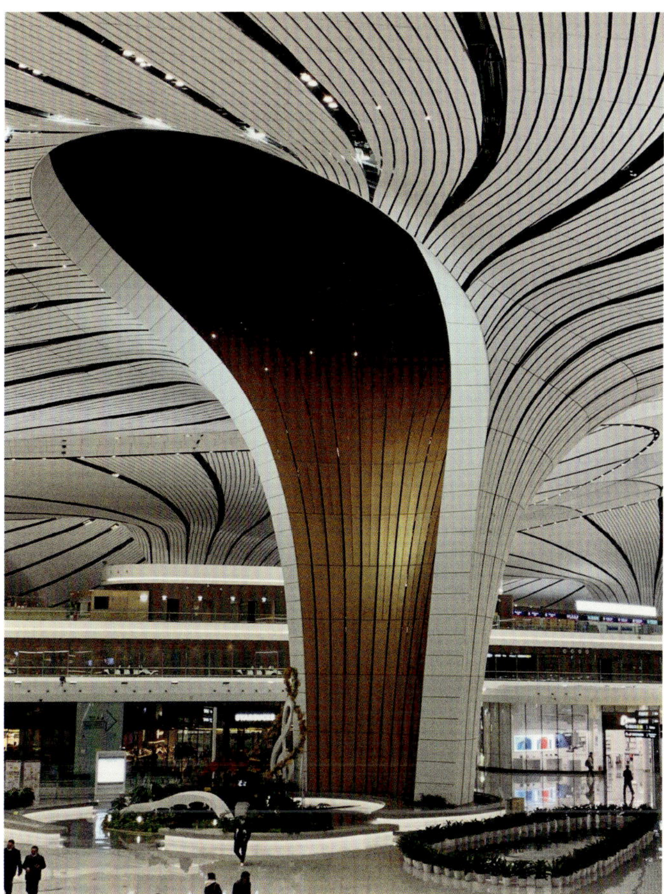

The new futuristic Beijing mega airport Daxing Airport, which is also the world's largest airport, was planned by Lord Norman Foster. The 700,000-square-metre terminal was designed by Zaha Hadid Architects and the French firm ADP Ingénierie. Much too beautiful to take off! The plan was for a capacity of 45 million passengers in 2021 and, in a second expansion phase, a capacity of 72 million passengers by 2025.

Der neue futuristische Pekinger Mega-Flughafen Daxing Airport, zugleich der größte der Welt, wurde von Lord Norman Foster geplant. Die Gestaltung des 700 000 Quadratmeter großen Terminals übernahmen Zaha Hadid Architects und die französische Firma ADP Ingénierie. Viel zu schön zum Abfliegen. Geplant war eine Auslastung von 45 Millionen Passagieren im Jahr 2021 und in einer zweiten Ausbaustufe bis 2025 eine Kapazität von 72 Millionen Fluggästen.

Only the richest of the rich can live at the very top of Hong Kong's local mountain, Victoria Peak (552 metres). Everyone else is best off taking the Swiss funicular, which opened in 1888, to the breathtaking viewing platform at 379 metres.

Nur die Reichtsen der Reichen können ganz oben am Hongkonger Hausberg, dem Victoria Peak (552 Meter) wohnen. Alle anderen fahren am besten mit der 1888 eröffneten Schweizer Standseilbahn zur atemberaubenden Aussichtsplattform auf 379 Metern Höhe.

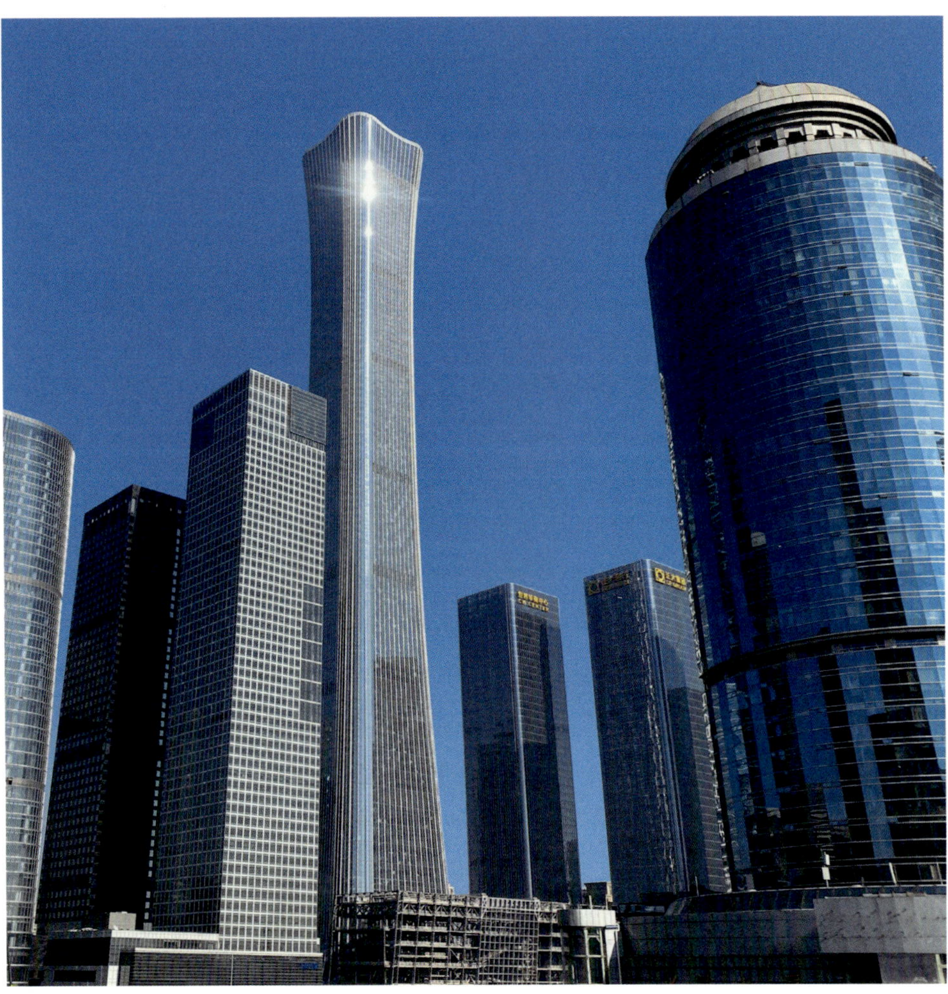

Beijing's modern business district (Beijing CBD) in the Chaoyang District, characterised by avant-garde buildings, is the main area for finance, media and business services.

Das moderne Geschäftsviertel von Peking (Beijing CBD) im Chaoyang-Distrikt, gekennzeichnet von avantgardistischen Bauwerken, ist das Zentrum für Finanzen, Medien und Unternehmensdienstleistungen.

Right page:
Particularly striking is the 224-metre-high, 54-story CCTV building, popularly known as "Underpants", which houses the broadcasting headquarters of the state-owned China Central Television. If you were to unfold the square loop, it would be over 800 metre long. The OMA (Office for Metropolitan Architecture) of the Dutch architect Rem Koolhaas designed the building, which was completed in 2012.

Rechte Seite:
Besonders auffällig das 224 Meter hohe und 54 Stockwerke umfassende CCTV-Gebäude, im Volksmund „Unterhose“ genannt, in welchem die Sendezentrale des staatlichen Fernsehens China Central Television untergebracht ist. Würde man die eckige Schleife „auffalten“, wäre diese über 800 Meter lang. Das Büro OMA (Office for Metropolitan Architecture) des niederländischen Architekten Rem Koolhaas entwarf das Gebäude, das 2012 fertiggestellt wurde.

In the stone-grey villages around Beijing, the race to catch up with modernity is progressing somewhat more slowly, and one can still observe the customs that follow the seasons. In autumn, for example, this is expressed in the storing of green and white Chinese cabbage and the laying out of yellow corn kernels on the village street afterwards. After the first frost then follow the fish, chicken and home-made sausages hung up to dry. And when the whole family celebrates the spring festival in the red-decorated farmhouse, serving up everything the kitchen has to offer. *Jiaozi*, stuffed dumplings, are prepared together, and tea or rice wine is drunk. A balanced diet with at least five different colours is important to the Chinese. Thus, the Yellow Emperor wrote over 3,000 years ago in his book about internal medicine, that people who strive for good health and a long life should always eat dishes with five colours, five tastes and five smells. With this knowledge, it is no wonder that after we ordered our Beijing duck, the waitress encouraged us to choose something green and something black as well. As a dessert we had delicious white *tang yua*, little balls made of rice flour, filled with sesame paste.

In den steingrauen Dörfern um Peking schreitet die Aufholjagd in die Moderne etwas langsamer voran und man kann noch das den Jahreszeiten folgende Brauchtum beobachten. Im Herbst das Einlagern des grün-weißen Chinakohls und danach das Auslegen der gelben Maiskerne auf der Dorfstraße. Nach dem ersten Frost dann die zum Trocknen aufgehängten Fische, Hühnchen und selbstgemachte Würste. Wenn zum Frühlingsfest die ganze Familie im rot geschmückten Hofhaus feiert, wird kulinarisch alles aufgefahren, was die Küche hergibt. Gemeinsam werden *Jiaozi*, gefüllte Teigtaschen, gefaltet und Tee oder Reiswein getrunken. Für die Chinesen ist eine ausgeglichene Ernährungsweise mit mindestens fünf verschiedenen Farben wichtig. So schrieb der Gelbe Kaiser bereits vor über 3000 Jahren in seinem Buch über Innere Medizin, dass Menschen, die nach Gesundheit und einem langen Leben streben, Speisen mit fünf Farben, fünf Geschmacksrichtungen und fünf Duftstoffen zu sich nehmen sollten. So verwundert es nicht, dass die Kellnerin uns nach der bestellten Peking-Ente auffordert, noch etwas Grünes und Schwarzes auszuwählen. Zur Nachspeise gab

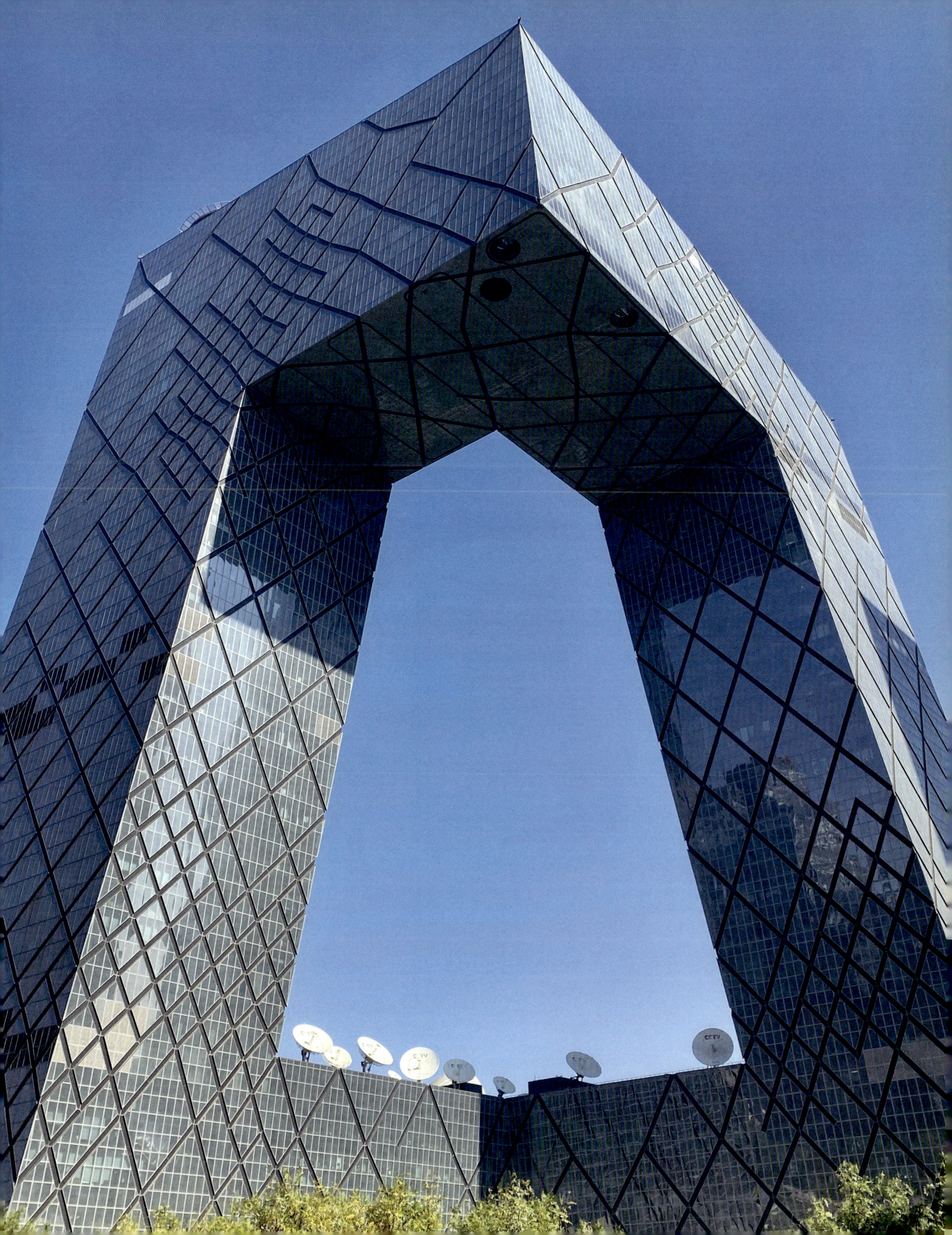
CCTV

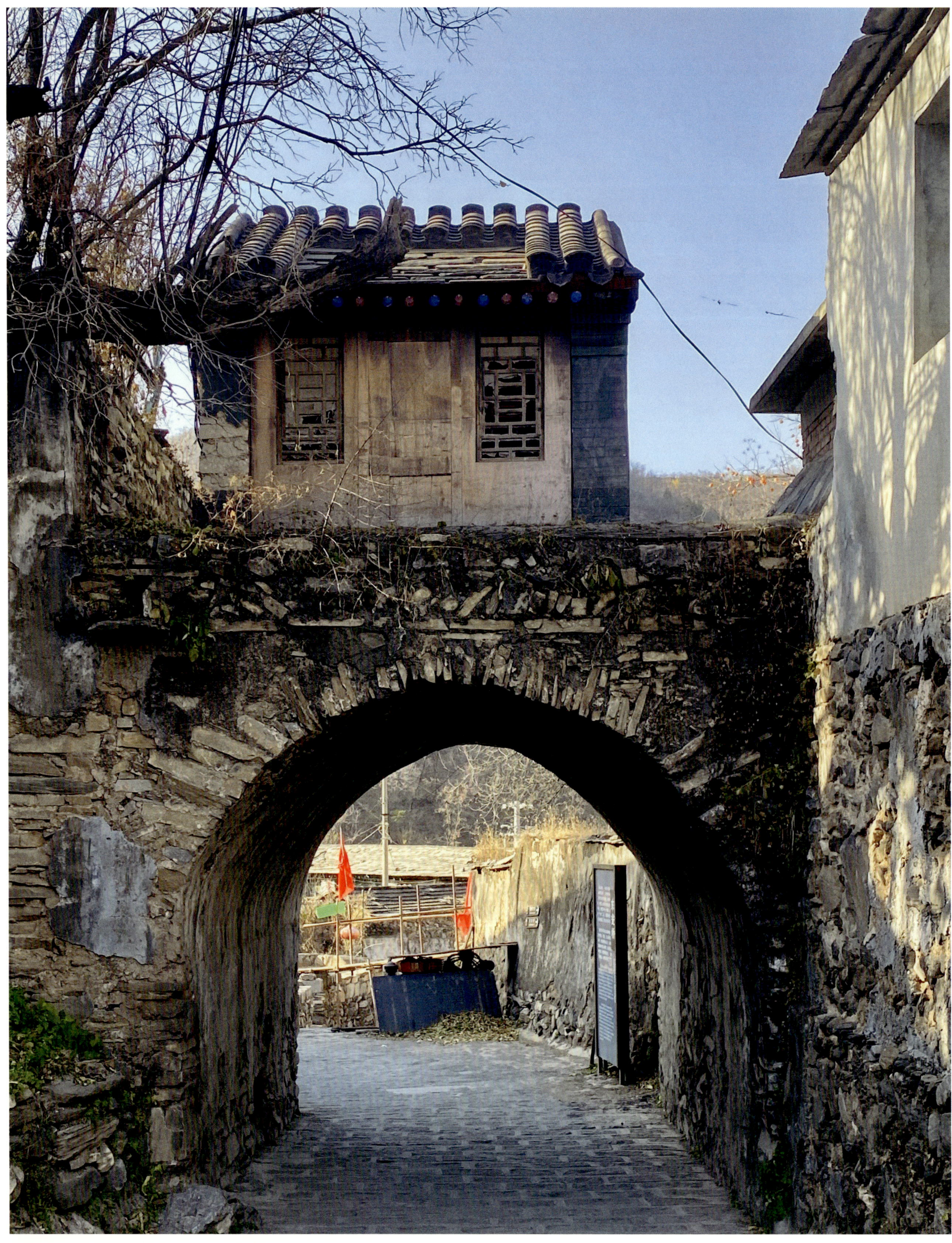

Left page:
In rural villages, time seems to stand still and old buildings still tell of traditional customs. Here is the guard's house above the archway to the village entrance.

Linke Seite:
In den Dörfern auf dem Land scheint die Zeit stehen geblieben und alte Bauwerke erzählen noch von traditionellen Bräuchen. Hier das Wächterhäuschen über dem Torbogen zum Dorfeingang.

The ducks, bacon and sausages hang to dry on clotheslines or high up in the trees in the cold late autumn. This in the middle of Beijing in one of the old *hutong* districts.

Die Enten, der Speck und die Würste hängen im kalten Spätherbst zum Trocknen an Wäscheleinen oder hoch oben in den Bäumen. Dies mitten in Peking in einem der alten *Hutong*-Viertel.

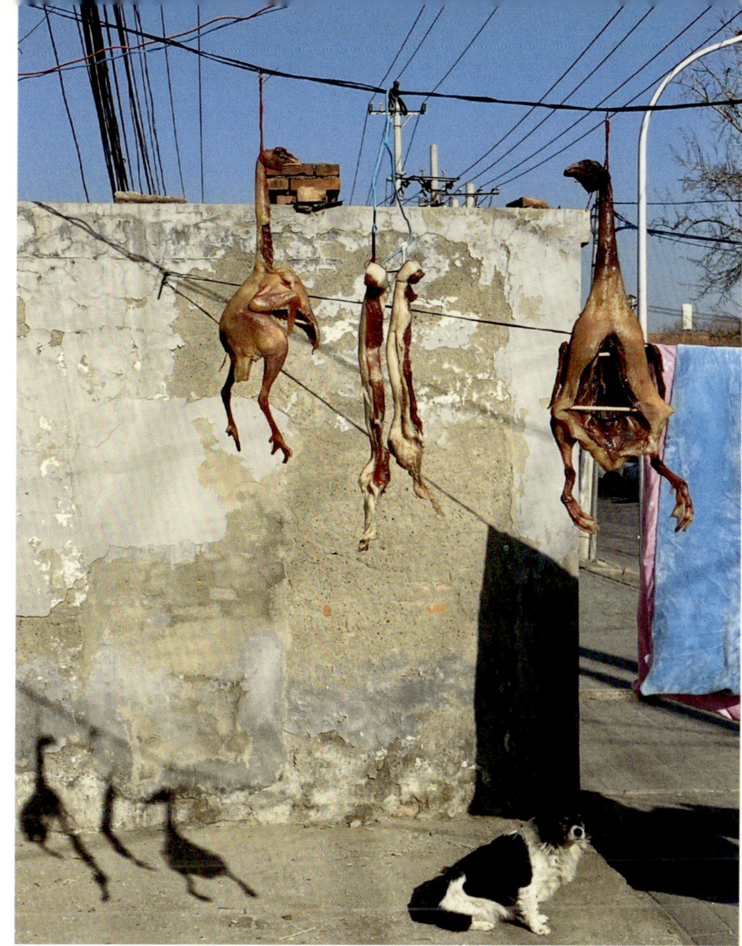

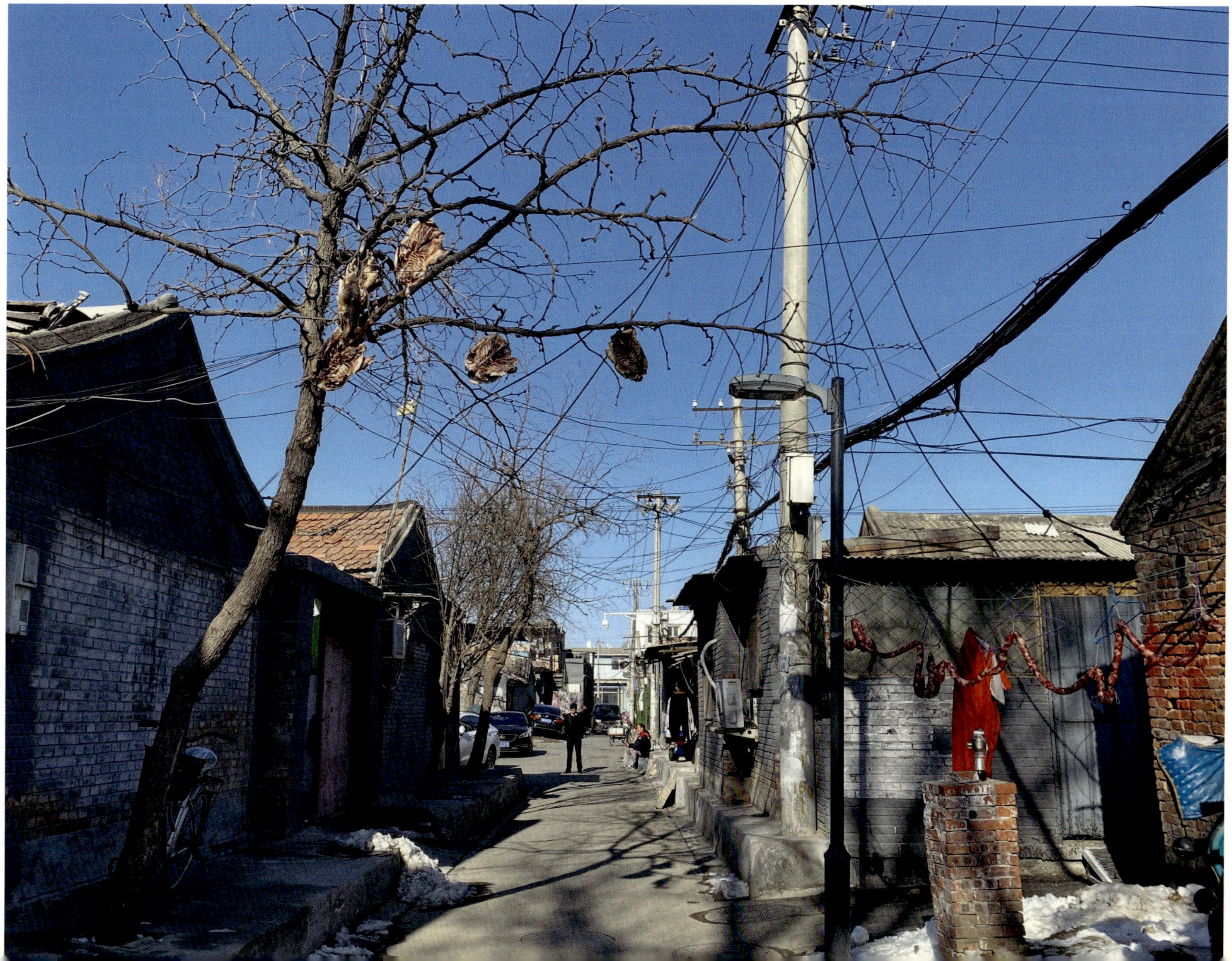

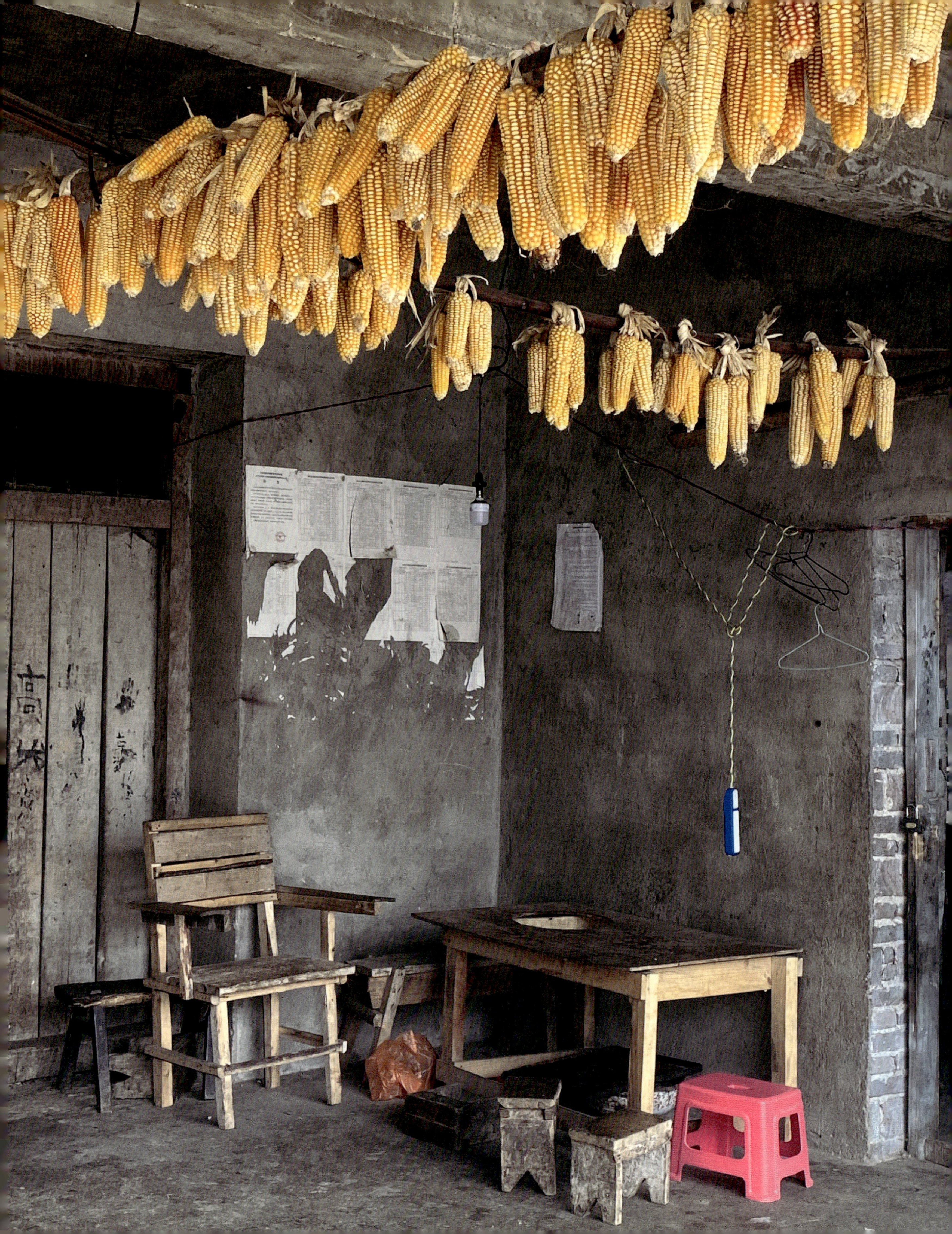

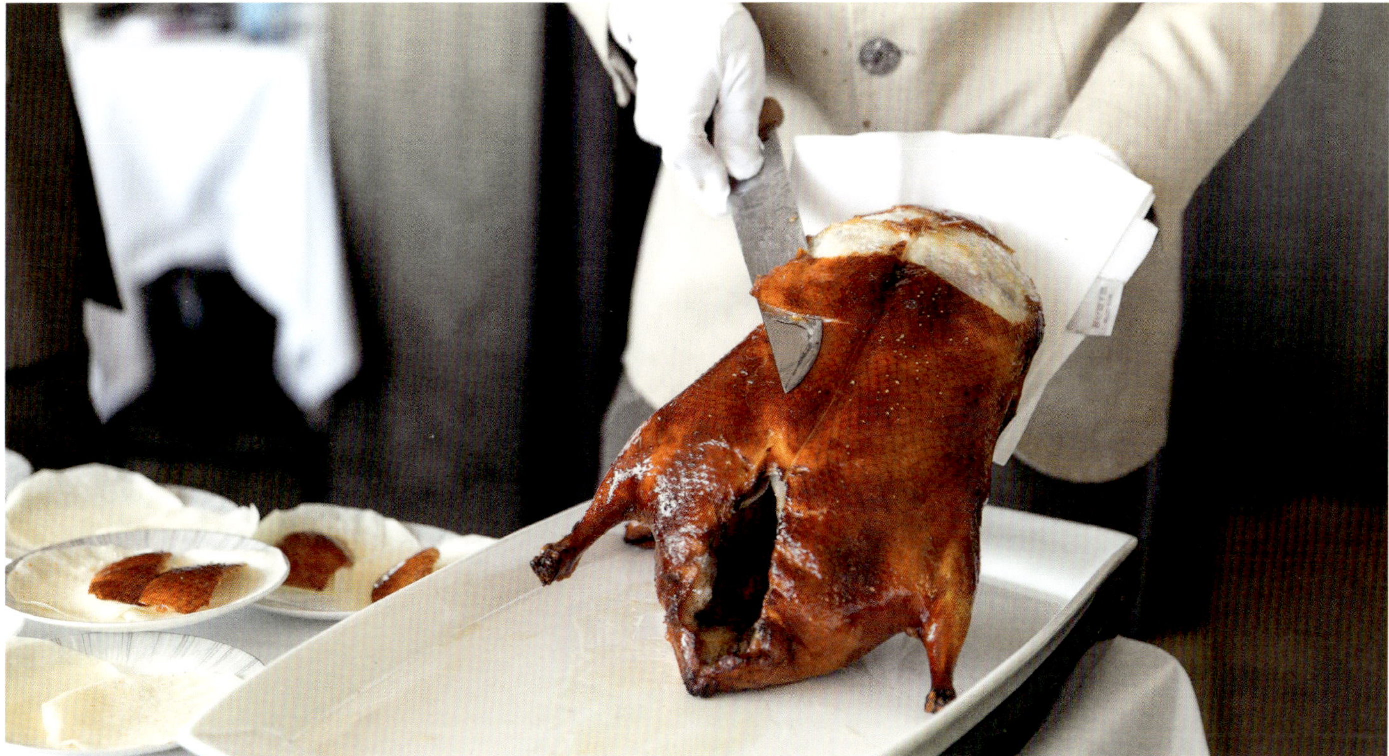

The classic Peking duck, especially popular for its crispy skin, is carved in front of guests at the gourmet restaurant. The very elaborate original recipe is said to date back to the Ming Dynasty.

Die besonders wegen ihrer krossen Haut beliebte klassische Peking-Ente wird im Feinschmeckerrestaurant vor den Augen der Gäste zerlegt. Das sehr aufwendige Originalrezept soll angeblich aus der Ming-Dynastie stammen.

This multi-coloured diet is based on the belief that the colours – red, yellow, green, white, black – correspond with important organs – heart/small intestine, spleen/stomach, liver/gall bladder, lungs/large intestine, kidneys/bladder. If the spleen is weak, more yellow foods should be eaten. Black foods strengthen kidney and bladder because black is associated with the element of water. Thus, black mushrooms, dark rice or black sesame seeds are especially good for people who have lower back pain or suffer from infertility or potency problems.

"When there is light in the soul, there is beauty in the person", according to a Chinese proverb. So emotional balance is also significant for a healthy person. Keeping *chi*, the life force or vital energy, in a naturally balanced, flowing state is the basic principle of the traditional Chinese way of life. Through proper nutrition, a sound sleep and balancing sports such as t'ai chi chuan or qigong, the *chi* is strengthened on a daily basis. Massages, acupuncture or herbal teas are often used to boost health.

Left page:
Corn kernels hang from the ceiling to dry. Mostly they are used to feed the pigs in winter.

Linke Seite:
Maiskörner hängen zum Trocknen an der Decke. Meist werden sie zum Füttern der Schweine im Winter verwendet.

es leckere weiße *Tang Yuan*, kleine Bällchen aus Reismehl mit Sesampaste gefüllt. Diese mehrfarbige Ernährungsweise beinhaltet, dass die Farben – rot, gelb, grün, weiß, schwarz – mit wichtigen Organen – Herz/Dünndarm, Milz/Magen, Leber/Gallenblase, Lunge/Dickdarm, Nieren/Blase – in Zusammenhang stehen.

Ist die Milz schwach, sollten mehr gelbe Lebensmittel gegessen werden. Schwarze Lebensmittel stärken Niere und Blase, Schwarz ist dem Element Wasser zugeordnet. So sind schwarze Pilze, dunkler Reis oder schwarze Sesamkörner besonders gut für Menschen, die Schmerzen im unteren Rücken habe oder an Infertilität oder Potenzproblemen leiden.

„Wenn Licht in der Seele ist, ist Schönheit im Menschen", sagt ein chinesisches Sprichwort. Auch emotionale Ausgeglichenheit ist bedeutsam für einen gesunden Menschen. Das *Qi*, die Lebenskraft, Lebensenergie in einem natürlich ausgeglichenen fließenden Zustand zu halten, ist das Grundprinzip der traditionellen chinesischen Lebensweise. Durch die richtige Nahrung, einen gesunden Schlaf und ausgleichenden Sport wie Tai-Chi-Chuan oder Qigong wird das *Qi* täglich gestärkt. Massagen, Akupunktur oder Kräutertees werden gerne unterstützend eingesetzt.

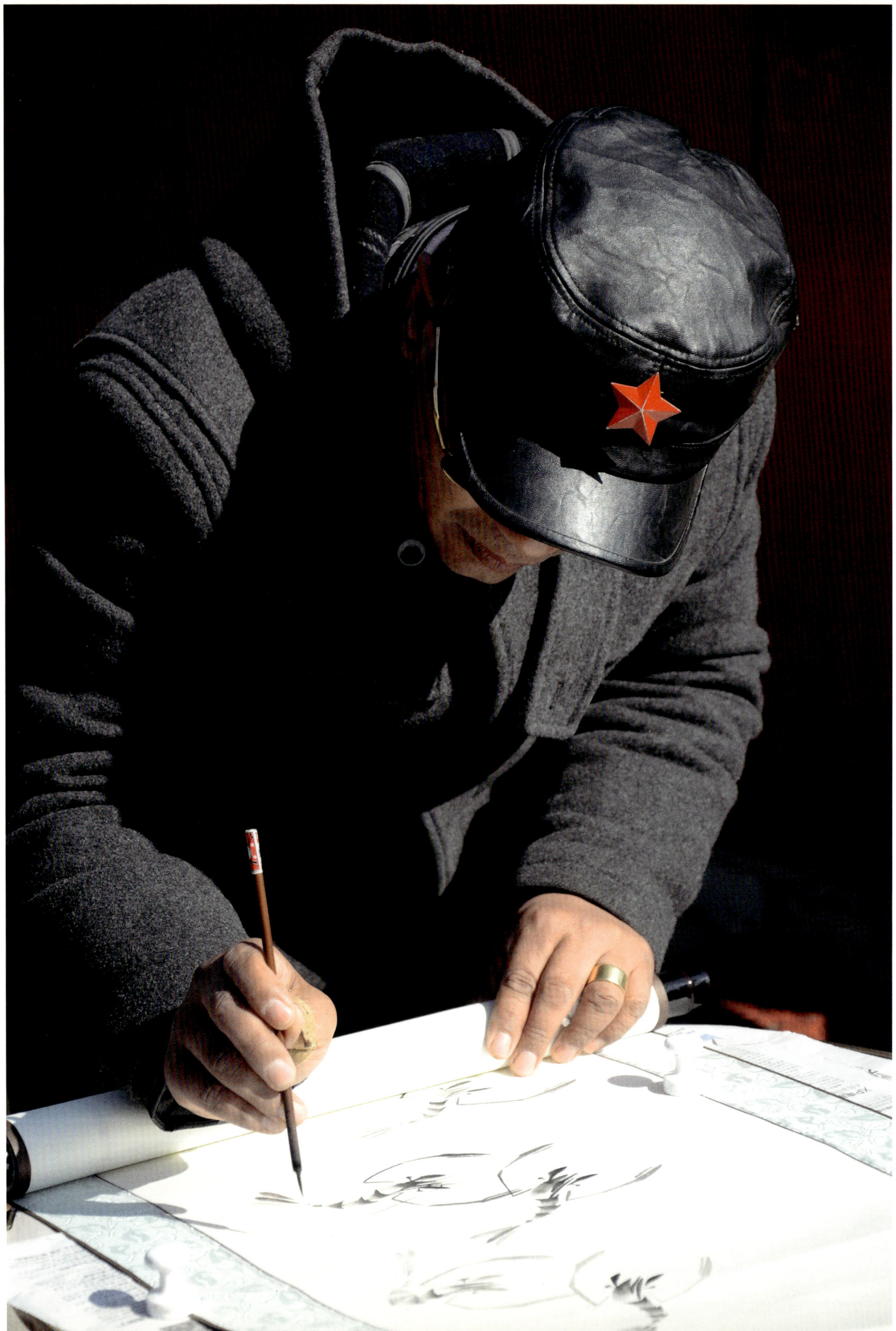

The gentle colour progression of language
Der sanfte Farbverlauf der Sprache

The grey-white area leaves lots of room for interpretation.

With their language, Chinese people often remain vague. They like to leave things vague, are ambiguous. A popular and frequently used expression is *chabuduo*, which translates as "roughly". One avoids clear answers and direct contradiction, because this way one can protect oneself and the other person from losing face. There is no translation for the word "no". It is better to say nothing than "no". But a "yes" can also mean "maybe". The language illustrates a basic attitude. Harmony trumps conflict. In this way, one also retains several options for action.

"In everything, the noble man tries to slowly approach what is right", Confucius says.

Unlike in Western languages, Chinese is a very vivid language. The word for "landscape" is composed of the words "mountain" and "water"; for "careful" you say "small heart", and the traffic light is the "red-green light". In China, people like to speak in metaphors.

If you are lucky, you can occasionally watch elderly Chinese practising the art of calligraphy.

Mit etwas Glück kann man ab und an älteren Chinesen beim Üben der Kalligraphie-Kunst zuschauen.

Der Grau-Weiß-Bereich bietet viel Spielraum für Interpretation.

Mit ihrer Sprache bleiben Chinesen häufig im Unklaren. Sie lassen Dinge gerne im Ungefähren, sind vieldeutig. Ein beliebter und häufig gebrauchter Ausdruck ist *Chabuduo*, das heißt übersetzt „in ungefähr". Man vermeidet klare Antworten und direkten Widerspruch, denn so kann man sich selbst und das Gegenüber vor Gesichtsverlust schützen. Eine Übersetzung für das Wort „Nein" gibt es nicht. Man sagt lieber nichts als „Nein". Aber auch ein „Ja" kann „vielleicht" bedeuten. Die Sprache verdeutlich eine Grundhaltung. Harmonie geht über Konflikt. Man bewahrt sich so außerdem mehrere Handlungsoptionen.

„In allem versucht der Edle, sich dem Richtigen langsam anzunähern", heißt es schon bei Konfuzius.

Im Unterschied zu westlichen Sprachen ist Chinesisch eine sehr bildhafte Sprache. Das Wort für „Landschaft" setzt sich aus „Berg" und „Wasser" zusammen, für „Vorsicht" sagt man „kleines Herz" und die Straßenverkehrsampel ist das „Rot-Grün-Licht". In China drückt man sich gerne in Metaphern aus.

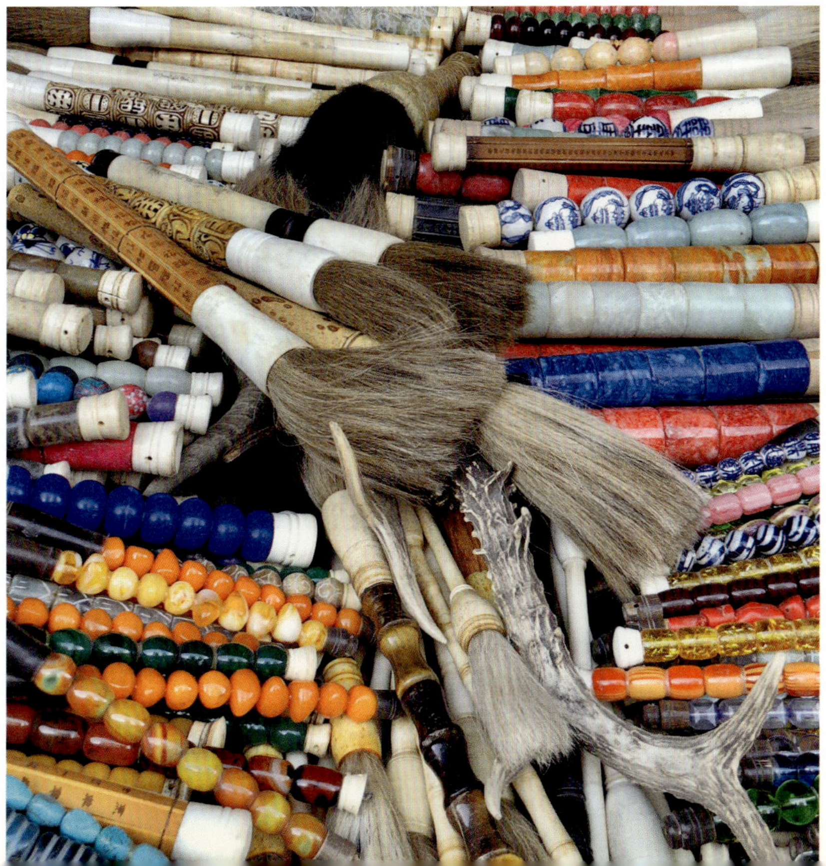

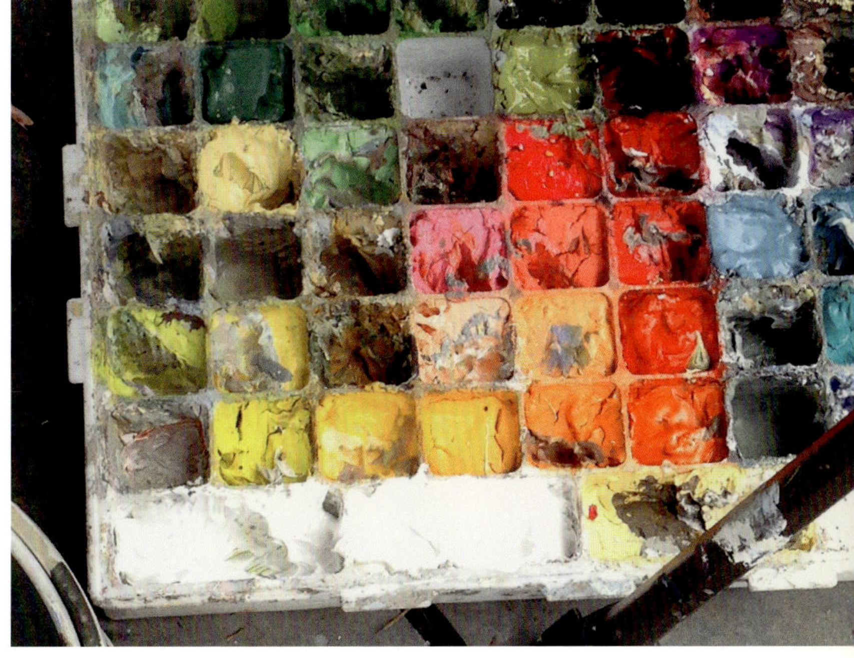

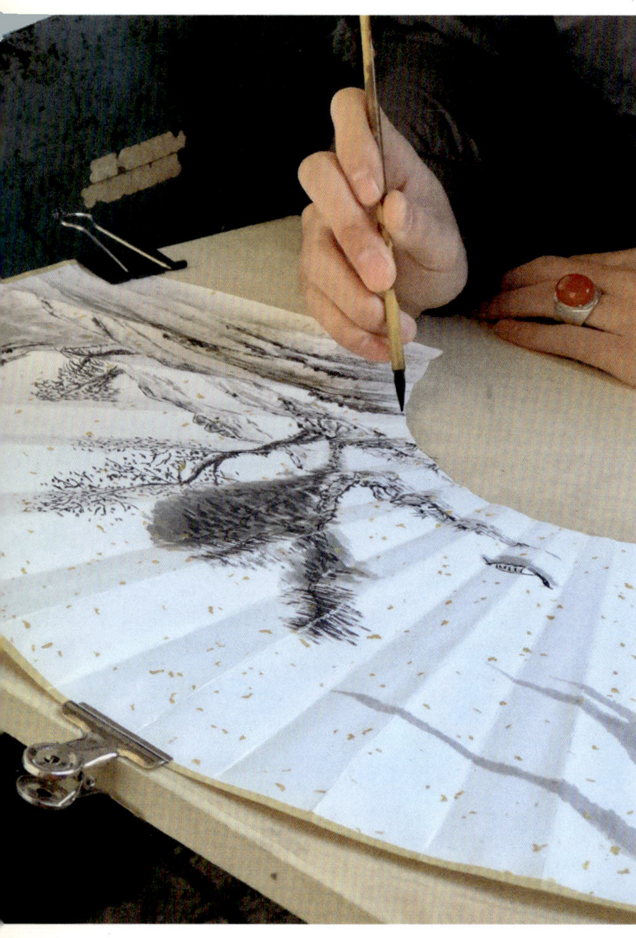

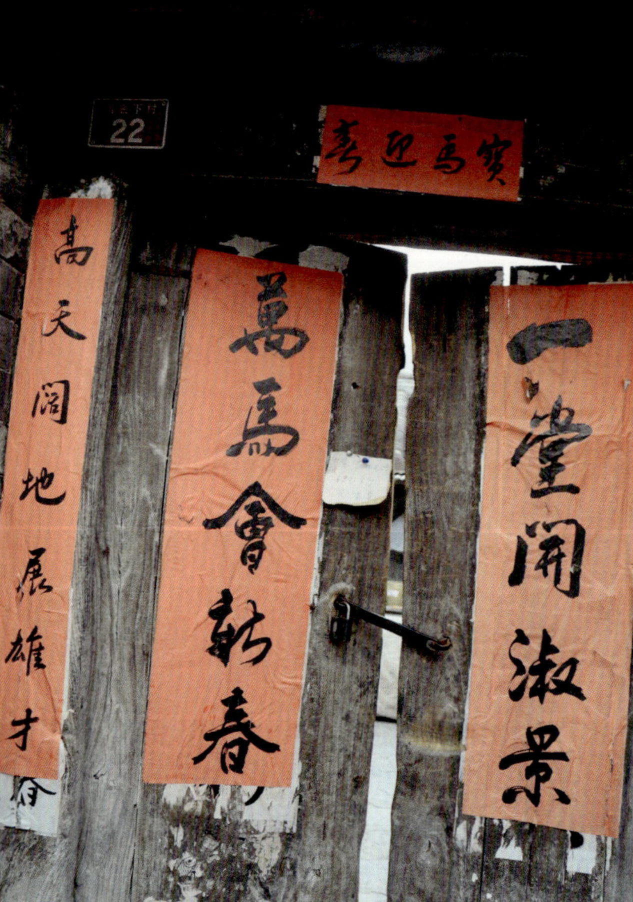

The "Four Treasures of the Scholar's Room" was the name given in the traditional empire to the items a scholar needed in order to write and paint: writing brush, ink stick, rubbing stone and paper.

Die „Vier Schätze des Gelehrtenzimmers" nannte man im traditionellen Kaiserreich die Gegenstände, die ein Gelehrter zum Schreiben und Malen brauchte: Schreibpinsel, Stangentusche, Reibstein und Papier.

Right page, right:
Calligraphy, the art of beautiful writing, distinguished Chinese scholars. Even the Emperor highly valued distinguishing himself with this skill.

Rechte Seite, rechts:
Die Kalligrafie, die Kunst des schönen Schreibens, kennzeichnete chinesische Gelehrte. Sogar die Kaiser legten großen Wert darauf, sich darin auszuzeichnen.

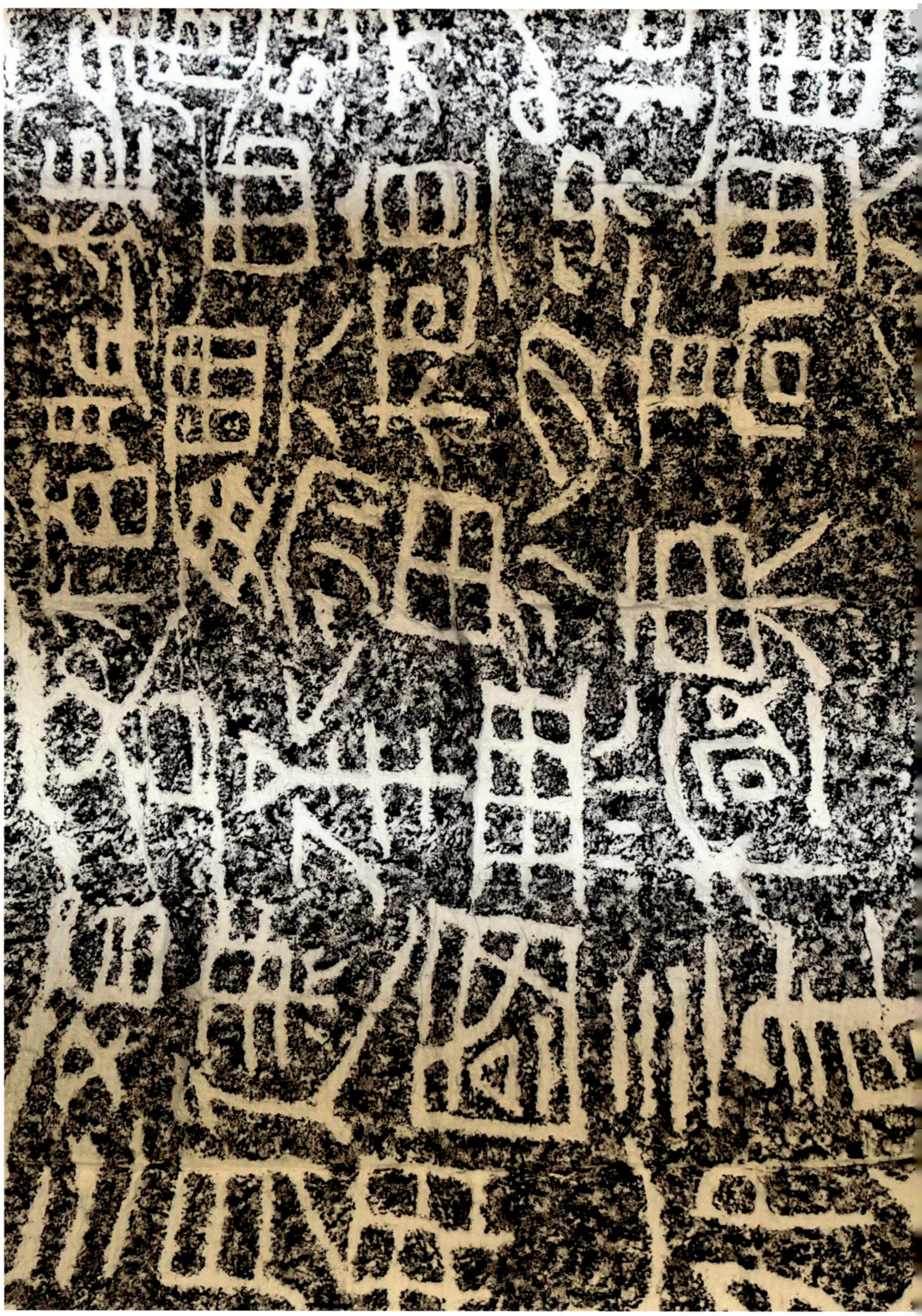

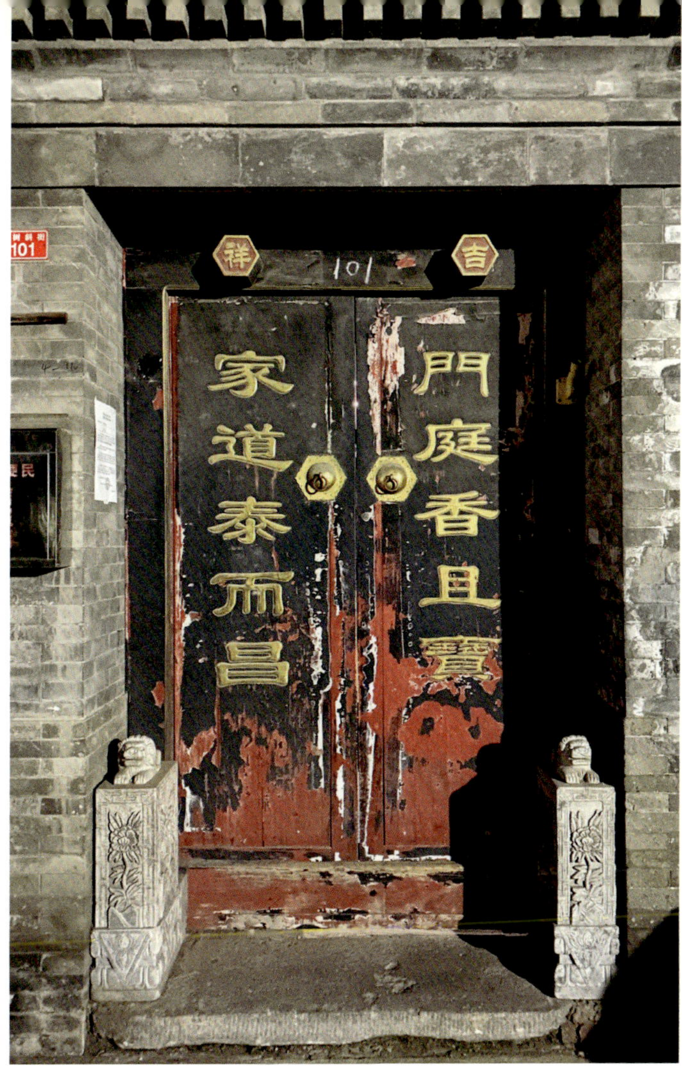

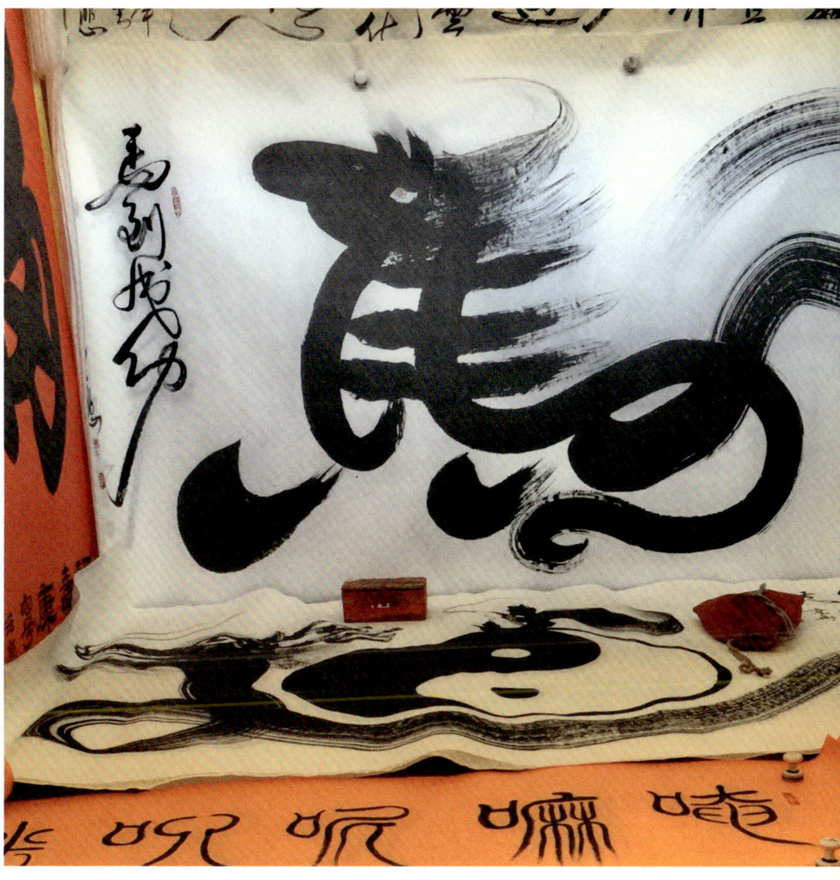

It is important to read between the lines and feel out the other person. Only in the modern protection of the anonymous Internet is this fine, sensitive way of conducting a conversation disappearing more and more. But at the Chinese conference table or at a business dinner, it is an advantage if the participants have mastered these imaginative rules of grey-white painting. It becomes particularly exciting when translation is required. Knowing what someone has said does not mean that you have understood what they mean. Interpreters or translators can only ever convey their personal interpretation. Basically, when speaking or writing, a great deal is omitted that would seem essential in Western languages; instead, a large number of words are added to make a sentence "complete". Knowing that words can deceive or provide room for interpretation, Chinese are generally more taciturn with outsiders. Talking too much is considered foolish, while keeping silent and listening is considered wise.

The best way to paint your own grey-white or colourful picture of China is by taking a nature- and people-oriented journey through the yesterday and tomorrow of this mysterious and exciting country.

Es gilt, den Gesprächspartner zu erspüren, zwischen den Zeilen zu lesen. Einzig im modernen Schutz des anonymen Internet verschwindet diese feine, gefühlvolle Art der Gesprächsführung mehr und mehr. Doch am chinesischen Konferenztisch oder beim Geschäftsessen ist es von Vorteil, wenn die Teilnehmer diese fantasievollen Regeln der Grau-Weiß-Malerei beherrschen. Besonders spannend wird es dann, wenn übersetzt werden muss. Zu wissen, was jemand gesagt hat, bedeutet noch lange nicht, verstanden zu haben, was er meint. Dolmetscher oder Übersetzer können immer nur ihre persönliche Interpretation vermitteln. Im Grunde genommen wird beim Sprechen oder Schreiben sehr viel weggelassen, was in westlichen Sprachen als wesentlich erscheint; dafür wird eine große Anzahl Wörter hinzugefügt, um einen Satz „rund" zu machen. Da Chinesen wissen, dass Worte täuschen können oder Spielraum für Auslegung bieten, sind sie im Allgemeinen schweigsamer gegenüber Außenstehenden. Zuviel Reden gilt ihnen als dumm, zu schweigen und zuzuhören dagegen als klug.

Am besten malt man sich sein eigenes grau-weißes oder buntes Bild bei einer natur- und menschennahen Reise durch das Gestern und Morgen dieses geheimnisvollen und spannungsgeladenen Landes.

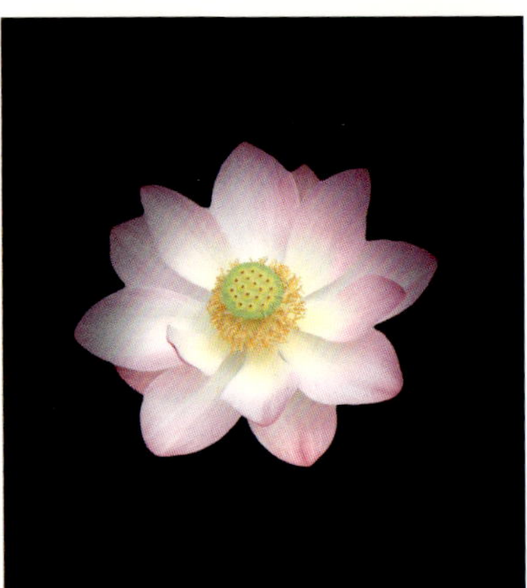

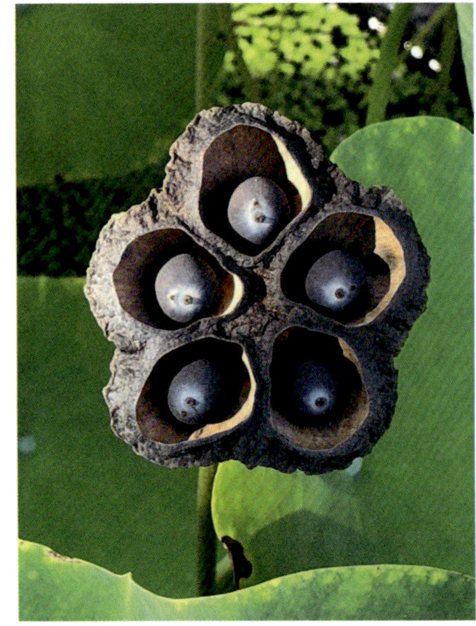

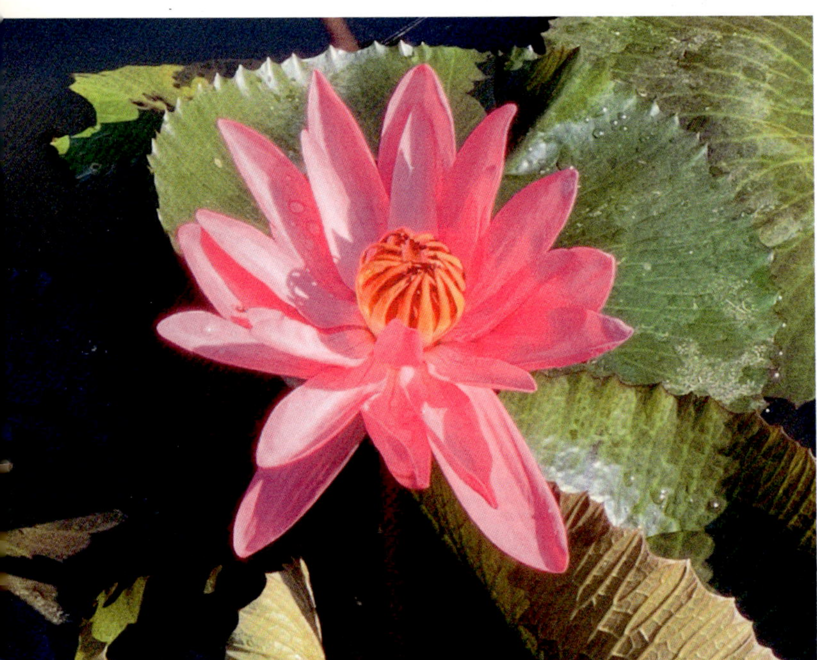

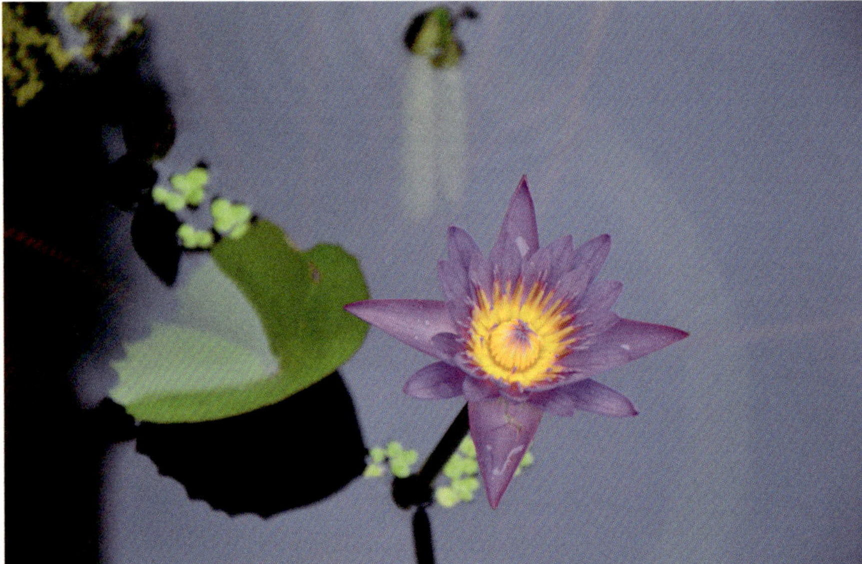

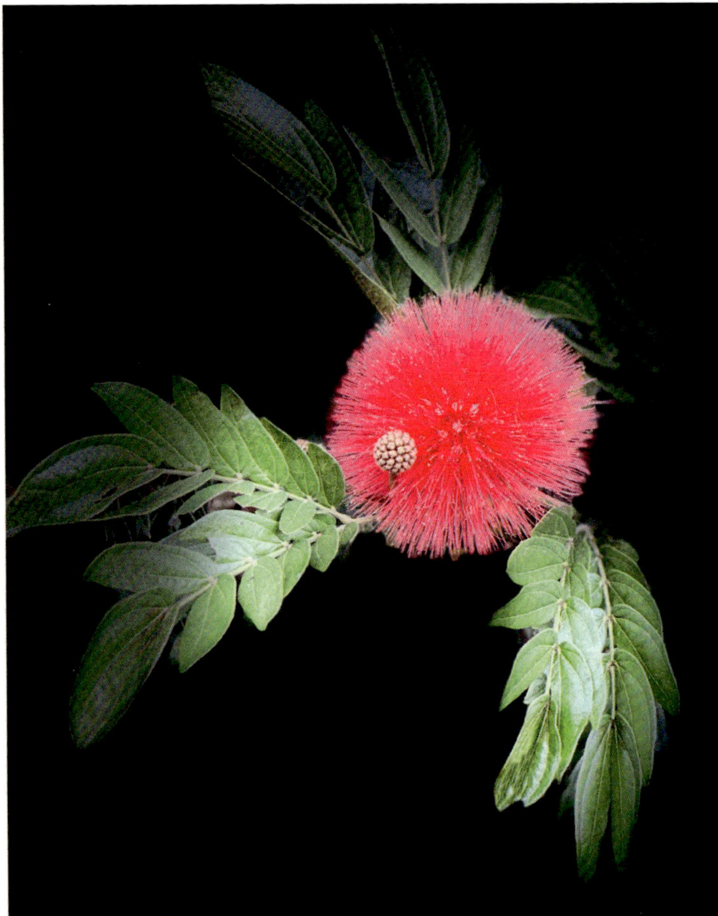

The lotus flower is strikingly beautiful and present throughout China in symbolic and real form. In Buddhist religion, it embodies purity, wisdom and enlightenment, transformation, new beginnings and love. The white lotus flower is a symbol of spiritual purity, knowledge and innocence. The purple lotus flower is the symbol of the divine, but is also associated with mystical powers, as well as the ability of self-knowledge. The blue lotus blossom represents control over the senses and stands for steadfastness, strength and endurance, as well as wisdom and knowledge. The red lotus flower is associated with sensations and feelings of the heart: passion, love and kindness. The pink lotus flower is the highest form of enlightenment and represents the Buddha.

Auffallend schön und in ganz China in symbolischer und realer Form präsent ist die Lotusblume. In der buddhistischen Religion verkörpert sie Reinheit, Weisheit und Erleuchtung, Transformation, Neubeginn und Liebe. Die weiße Lotusblume ist ein Symbol für geistige Reinheit, Wissen und Unschuld. Die violette Lotusblume ist das Sinnbild für das Göttliche, wird aber auch mit mystischen Kräften in Verbindung gebracht sowie mit der Fähigkeit zur Selbsterkenntnis. Die blaue Lotusblüte repräsentiert die Kontrolle über die Sinne und steht für Beständigkeit, Kraft und Ausdauer sowie Weisheit und Wissen. Die rote Lotusblume ist verbunden mit Empfindungen und Gefühlen des Herzens: Leidenschaft, Liebe und Freundlichkeit. Die pinkfarbene Lotusblume ist die höchste Form der Erleuchtung und repräsentiert Buddha.

Thanks to the proximity to Myanmar this strikingly beautiful plant called powder puff shrub or *Calliandra* can be found in Xishuangbanna. It belongs to the mimosa family.

Seiner Nähe zu Myanmar verdankt Xishuangbanna diese auffallend schönen Pflanze, Puderquastenstrauch oder *Calliandra* genannt, die zur Familie der Mimosen gehört.

Literature included

Eingeflossene Literatur

Detailed academic citation has been deliberately omitted, as this book draws in large part on experiences and countless conversations with many different residents of China.

Auf eine detaillierte akademische Zitierweise wurde bewusst verzichtet, da dieses Buch in großen Teilen auf das Erleben, Erfahren und auf unzählige Gespräche mit vielen verschiedenen Bewohnern Chinas zurückgreift.

Farbsymbolik in China – Goethe Institut China, Yang Chunyu, Januar 2013

Colours: A Natural History of the Palette – Victoria Finlay, Random House 2003
Das Geheimnis der Farben – Victoria Finlay, Ullstein 2019

Die Chinesen – Stefan Baron, Guangyan Yin-Baron, Econ 2018

The Art of War – Sun-Tzu, Penguin 2014
Die Kunst des Krieges – Sun Tsu, Anaconda 2016

Geschichte Chinas – Kai Vogelsang, Reclam 2012

56 Ethnic Groups in China – Reader's Digest, Shanghai Press & Publishing Development Company 2010

https://www.iging.com/laotse/LaotseD.htm

http://www.guenter-wohlfart.de/Docs/Der%20Philosophische%20Daoismus.pdf

https://www.wasser-kooperation.de/wasser-in-der-kulturgeschichte/honghe-hani-reisterrassen/

https://www.nomos-elibrary.de/10.5771/9783956506093-133/richard-wilhelm-als-kulturvermittler-und-sein-einfluss-auf-hermann-hesse?l=de

https://spchina.de/chinesische-gedichte-der-tangzeit

https://austria-forum.org/af/Wissenssammlungen/Essays/Weltreisen/Das_chinesische_Dach

https://www.mandalingua.com/de/china-guide/leben-in-china/peking/sightseeing/himmelstempel/

https://nl.mozaweb.com/de/Extra-3D_Modelle-Chinesischer_Wohnhof_Siheyuan-421383

https://www.geo.de/geo-tv/3827-rtkl-china-im-reich-der-mosuo-frauen

https://www.liportal.de/china/ueberblick/

http://www.gesundheitspsychologin.net/joomla/index.php/blog/gesundheit/38-grundbegriffe-der-tcm-lebensenergie-qi

https://de.wikipedia.org/wiki/Huangdi_neijing

https://de.wikipedia.org/wiki/Buch_der_Riten

https://www.wikinger-reisen.de/blog/buddha-im-himalaya-gebetsfahnen-und-ihre-bedeutung/

Imprint | Impressum

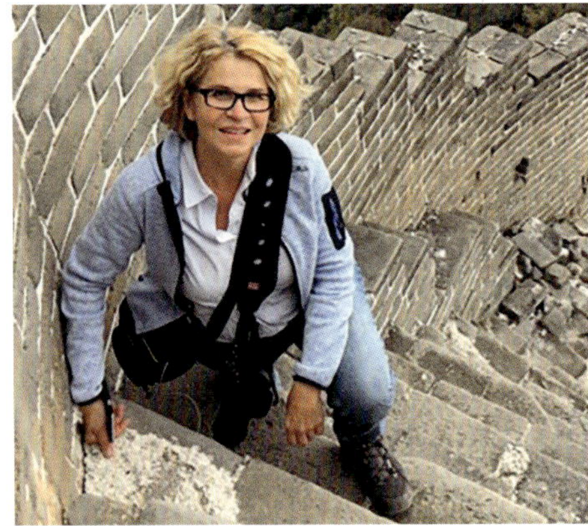

Author

Luxembourg-born photojournalist Annette Morheng has been living and working in Beijing for nine years. She travels to the most remote provinces and to where the most diverse ethnicities live, capturing moods and smiles with her camera and being in continuous cultural dialogue. In 2019, some of her images could be seen at the photo exhibition *The Altai Mountains* at Green T. House in Beijing. As the founder and curator of Beijing Floor Art Gallery, she enjoys supporting the creative potential of the Chinese and international artists. With this book, the author paints a refreshingly colourful picture of China, its rich culture and smiling people.

Autorin

Die Luxemburger Fotojournalistin Annette Morheng lebt und arbeitet seit neun Jahren in Peking, China. Sie reist in die abgelegensten Provinzen und zu den unterschiedlichsten Ethnien, fängt mit ihrer Kamera Stimmungen und Lächeln ein und ist im kontinuierlichen kulturellen Dialog. 2019 konnte man einige ihre Bilder bei der Fotoausstellung *The Altai Mountains* im Green T. House in Peking sehen. Als Gründerin und Kuratorin der Beijing Floor Art Gallery unterstützt sie mit Freude das kreative Potenzial der chinesischen und internationalen Künstler. Mit diesem Buch zeichnet die Autorin ein erfrischend farbenfrohes Bild von China, seiner reichen Kultur und den lächelnden Menschen.

Texts and Photographs © Annette Morheng except Wikimedia Commons: p. 115, 116 (below) by Chlukoe, p. 122 by Chensiyuan, p. 124 by JialiangGao/peace-on-earth.org, p. 169 by City Foodsters
Project Management and Creative Direction by Peter Feierabend
Copyediting by Stephanie Iber
Typesetting and Design by Frank Behrendt
Translations by Joy Hawley
Production by Nele Jansen
Colour Seperation by Jens Grundei

ISBN 978-3-96171-305-9
(English version)

Library of Congress Number: 2020935926

ISBN 978-3-96171-306-6
(German version)

Printed in Slovakia by Neografia a.s.

Published by teNeues Publishing Group

teNeues Verlag GmbH
Werner-von-Siemens-Straße 1
86159 Augsburg, Germany

Düsseldorf Office
Waldenburger Straße 13
41564 Kaarst, Germany
e-mail: books@teneues.com

Augsburg/München Office
Werner-von-Siemens-Straße 1
86159 Augsburg, Germany
e-mail: books@teneues.com

Berlin Office
Lietzenburger Straße 53
10719 Berlin, Germany
e-mail: books@teneues.com

Press department Stefan Becht
Phone: +49-152-2874-9508
+49-6321-97067-97
e-mail: sbecht@teneues.com

teNeues Publishing Company
350 7th Avenue, Suite 301
New York, NY 10001, USA
Phone: +1-212-627-9090
Fax: +1-212-627-9511

www.teneues.com

Bibliographic information published by the Deutsche Nationalbibliothek
The Deutsche Nationalbibliothek lists this publication in the Deutsche Nationalbibliografie; detailed bibliographic data are available on the Internet at dnb.dnb.de.

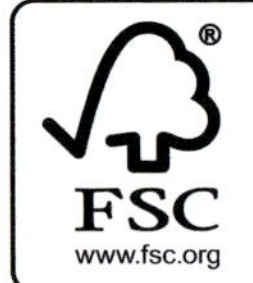

MIX
Paper from responsible sources
FSC® C020353

teNeues Publishing Group
Augsburg / München
Berlin
Düsseldorf
London
New York

teNeues